HOW THE WEST CAME TO

How the West Came to Rule

The Geopolitical Origins of Capitalism

Alexander Anievas and

Kerem Nişancıoğlu

PlutoPress
www.plutobooks.com

First published 2015 by Pluto Press
345 Archway Road, London N6 5AA

www.plutobooks.com

British Library Cataloguing in Publication Data
A catalogue record for this book is available from the British Library

ISBN 978 0 7453 3521 6 Hardback
ISBN 978 0 7453 3615 2 Paperback
ISBN 978 1 7837 1323 3 PDF eBook
ISBN 978 1 7837 1325 7 Kindle eBook
ISBN 978 1 7837 1324 0 EPUB eBook

This book is printed on paper suitable for recycling and made from fully managed and sustained forest sources. Logging, pulping and manufacturing processes are expected to conform to the environmental standards of the country of origin.

10 9 8 7 6 5 4 3 2 1

Typeset by Curran Publishing Services, Norwich, England
Text design by Melanie Patrick
Simultaneously printed by CPI Antony Rowe, Chippenham, UK
and
Edwards Bros in the United States of America

Contents

Figures

* please note that the maps are not precisely to scale.

Acknowledgements

This book has been almost three years in the making. Its origins lie in a collaborative article written for *Millennium – Journal of International Studies* in 2012–13 entitled 'What's at stake in the transition debate? Rethinking the origins of capitalism and the "rise of the West"'. It was here that we first explored the possibility of rewriting the history of capitalism's genesis by drawing on the framework of uneven and combined development. As this led us to a radical departure from histories centred on European developments, it became evident that there was a considerably more extensive and complex story to tell about the origins of capitalism. Our initially brief engagement with the global history of the 13th–17th centuries rendered evident a palpable dissatisfaction with the Eurocentrism of dominant accounts of this period. It appeared not only that vast swathes of key historical events, actors and processes had been left hidden behind the veil of Eurocentrism, but that the theorisations constructed from this narrow geohistorical vantage point had left the field of historical sociology with only a partial understanding of capitalist modernity. Moreover, it appeared that our very engagement with the historical record would demand some reconsideration of the theoretical conclusions we drew back in 2013. We were thus driven back to the drawing board – back to history, back to theory and into an enormously stimulating collaborative project of research, debate and writing. *How the West Came to Rule* is the result.

We see this book as an outcome of a collective endeavour in three respects. First, although much of the research and drafting process for the book was done individually, the end product was built on constant dialogue and various moments of creative agreement and disagreement. Indeed, the chapters we are most proud of are those where our collaboration – in terms of research, discussion and drafting – were most intensive.

Second, this book covers a roughly 600-year time span, and stretches geographically from Indonesia, along the Indian Ocean littoral, through the Middle East to Europe, West Africa, and across the Atlantic to the Americas. Such is the sweeping nature of the project that we have, out of necessity, deferred to and critically engaged with specialists in numerous areas of expertise beyond our own. We have also, out of necessity, selected and bracketed certain historical events, actors and processes from our narrative – gaps that we hope will be the source of further scholarship and critique for future researchers to follow up. As such, we appreciatively recognise that this book would not have been possible were it not for the extensive and important work carried out by the scholars we draw on. We hope that in writing this book, we will have done justice to these specialists, and hope to have made a humble yet critical contribution to the fields they work in.

Third, we are indebted to the wider network of personal, moral and scholarly support that has undergirded this entire project. We are grateful to the many colleagues and scholars who provided helpful comments on or discussed particular aspects of earlier chapter drafts, including Jamie Allinson, Josef Ansorge, Tarak Barkawi, Duncan Bell, Gurminder Bhambra, Pepijn Brandon, Gareth Dale, Neil Davidson, Kyle Geraghty, Henry Heller, John Hobson, Joseph Kay, Rob Knox, Tor Krever, Nivi Manchanda, David Ormrod, Charlie Post, Gonzalo Pozo-Martin, Justin Rosenberg, Andrés Sáenz de Sicilia and Ben Selwyn. Special gratitude is owed to Luke Cooper, Kamran Matin and Cemal Burak Tansel who were all kind enough to read over multiple drafts of chapters. We'd also like to thank David Castle at Pluto Press for his continuing enthusiasm for the project and patience in waiting for its completion. We are also grateful to Susan Curran who did a fantastic job with the copy-editing.

Kerem would like to thank his parents, Şule and Murat, and brother Deniz for their unflinching and unconditional love and support. Kerem is especially grateful to Hollie Hutton – without her encouragement and compassion this project would have never been started, let alone completed. Alex would like to thank his family (Arturo, Pam, Erik, Cathy, and Uncle Ralph), and friends, particularly Luke, Vin, Andy, Dominic, Craig, and the dearly missed Matt Gibney and Lisa Smirl – to the latter of whom this book is dedicated. He would also like to thank his wife, Linda Szilas, who not only gave a fair amount of her own time in designing the map illustrations in this book, but also provided her wholehearted and unwavering love and support throughout the writing and researching of this project. Finally, Alex would like to acknowledge the generous funding and support provided by the Leverhulme Trust.

In addition to the above-noted *Millennium* article from which this project originated, we published two further articles based upon the research for this book: 'The Ottoman origins of capitalism: uneven and combined development and Eurocentrism', *Review of International Studies*, Vol. 40, No. 2 (2014): 325–47; and, 'Revolutions and international relations: rediscovering the classical bourgeois revolutions', *European Journal of International Relations*, forthcoming . Some of the materials originally published in these articles are reproduced in the following pages, and we are grateful to the journal publishers for their permission to use those materials.

Alexander Anievas
Kerem Nişancıoğlu
April 2015

Dedicated to the loving memory of Lisa Smirl

Introduction

History is the Nightmare from which I am trying to awake.

James Joyce, 1922[1]

The writing of historical sociologies is inescapably wedded to the contexts in which they emerge; we write history but do not do so in conditions of our choosing. For decades, these conditions have been marked by 'End of History' triumphalism and claims that 'there is no alternative' to liberal capitalism. In turn, capitalism as a transient, historically specific and contradictory unit of study has been bracketed out of – if not completely wiped off – the scholarly and political agenda. Yet, after stock markets came crashing down in 2008, the force of history reasserted itself in a series of revolutions, occupations of public places, anti-austerity protests, strikes, riots and anti-state movements taking place from London to Ferguson (Missouri), Athens, Cairo, Istanbul, Rojava, Santiago and beyond. Such movements have torn at the hubristic certainties of 'capitalist realism' and started to sporadically – if inconsistently – challenge such long-held 'common sense' truisms and the power structures that undergird them.

Consequently, capitalism and critiques of it have reentered the public discourse in ways previously unimaginable. From mainstream media outlets to traditional academic publishing media, the tide has seemingly turned against the concept's long banishment to the margins of radical Left critique and returned as a 'respectable' object of analysis. Indeed, a number of the most celebrated publications of recent years have in different ways oriented themselves around reinvestigating and understanding (both theoretically and historically) the meaning of capitalism, be they social democratic, Marxist, Keynesian or neoconservative.[2] In universities across the world, students and scholars are now collaborating in ways that seek to challenge ruling class orthodoxies.[3] As a recent *New York Times* article put it, 'A specter is haunting university history departments: the specter of capitalism'.[4]

This renewed attention to the study of capitalism is a welcome development, particularly as capitalism's return to the limelight as the *dramatis persona* of modern history has come fit with a certain renaissance in Karl Marx's critique of it. 'Marx is Back', lamented the *Economist*,[5] and with it so too are an array of novel avenues for renewed Marxist-inspired understandings and critiques of capitalism, and particularly its formation as a historical mode of production. Why was capitalism successful in supplanting other modes of production? What propelled it to global dominance? And finally, what are its historical limits?

This book cannot hope to offer complete answers to all of these questions.

1

Rather, our aim is to provide new theoretical and historical perspectives in which these questions can be re-examined and answered anew, hopefully better than previous attempts. Simply stated, we argue that the origins and history of capitalism can only be properly understood in international or geopolitical terms, and that this very 'internationality' is constitutive of capitalism as a historical mode of production. Although this may seem intuitively obvious to many readers, in what follows we show that existing conceptions of capitalism have hitherto failed to take this internationality seriously. This has led to problematic theorisations of its origins and development that limit not only our histories, but also our critiques of the present.

This distinctly geopolitical character of the origins of capitalism is brilliantly anticipated in German Renaissance painter Hans Holbein's 1532 masterpiece *The Ambassadors* (Figure 0.1), which illustrates a meeting between French envoys Jean de Dinteville and George de Selve in London. The painting astounds because these two aristocratic subjects are placed at the periphery, and the only explicitly religious symbol, a cross, is veiled by a curtain. While these two pillars of medieval power – the church and aristocracy – are symbolically pushed to the side, an anamorphic skull and a table littered with objects – with commodities – occupy the focal point of the painting. Was this a prophetic, if unwitting, forecast of feudalism's imminent decline? Did it anticipate a capitalist future where social relations would come to be 'mediated by things'?[6]

Notwithstanding such speculation, these objects constitute a vivid record of the geopolitical milieu that defined European[7] international relations in the early 16th century.[8] The morbidity portrayed by the skull reminds us that death was at the forefront of European consciousness in this period – indeed, Holbein's own life would be taken by plague in the autumn of 1543 in England just ten years after the painting was completed.[9] In the immediate time of the painting, peasant revolts were sweeping through Christendom, leaving the ashes of serfdom in their wake. In preceding centuries, Europe had been ravaged by disease, precipitating a demographic crisis that had reduced Europe's population by between 30 and 60 per cent by the 15th century.

On the bottom right-hand side of the table in the painting, a book of Lutheran hymns sits by a broken lute, signifying the discord in Christendom between Protestants and the Catholic Church. To the left of these items rests Martin Benhaim's terrestrial globe, made under the commission of Nuremberg merchants seeking to break the Portuguese hold on the spice trade. The globe is tilted so that after European towns, 'Affrica' and 'Brisilici R'. (Brazil) are the most legible markers. We can also see the *Linea Divisionis Castellanorum et Portugallenum* ('Line of division between Spain and Portugal') demarcating the division of the New World between Habsburg Spain (west of the line) and Portugal (east of the line), here signifying the importance of these discoveries and the subsequent competition between European states over commercially profitable territories.

Figure 0.1 Hans Holbein, *The Ambassadors*, 1533

In front of the globe is Peter Apian's *A New and Well Grounded Instruction in All Merchant's Arithmetic*, an early textbook of commercial scholarship that covered profit–loss calculation, trading customs, navigation and route mapping. Placed alongside Benhaim's globe, it demonstrates the inseparability of commercial interests from maritime exploration, as well as the increasingly global – and competitive – character of trade. Above these items, on the top of the table, numerous scientific instruments highlight the rapid development of techniques in seafaring. Continuing the theme of Christendom's decline, these also indicate a mounting shift away from the divinity of religion as the predominant *episteme* and towards the rationality of scientific inquiry and humanism. Finally, linking the resting arms of the two ambassadors, and tying the objects together, is a Turkic rug, indicating the rivalry between the Ottoman and Habsburg empires. The presence of this 'Eastern' commodity indicates that the numerous changes taking place in Europe in this period were often undergirded by processes emanating from non-European sources, by social formations and actors that were unambiguously more powerful than anything seen in Europe at the time.

Let us run through these themes once more: a demographic crisis brought about by the Black Death; the Ottoman–Habsburg rivalry; the discovery of the New World and its division along linearly demarcated spaces of sovereignty; the festering atmosphere of revolt and rebellion; the economic significance of colonisation. Each in their own way either captures or anticipates the central dynamics and historical processes behind the collapse of feudalism and the emergence of capitalist modernity. Moreover, running throughout the themes of the painting is a resolute awareness of the *geopolitics* behind these processes. The emphasis on the New World and the Ottoman Empire reminds us that the making of capitalism in Europe was not simply an intra-European phenomenon, but a decidedly *international* (or intersocietal) one: one in which non-European agency relentlessly impinged upon and (re)directed the trajectory and nature of European development. Tracing this international dimension in the origins of capitalism and the so-called 'rise of the West' is what concerns us in this book.

Our primary motivation in making this argument is to subvert, and we hope displace, the dominant wisdom in the historiography and theoretical analyses of the period. For despite the latent centrality of 'the international' implied by Holbein's painting, dominant theorisations of early modern Europe have been constructed with non-European societies *in absentia*. Whether in the sphere of politics, economy, culture or ideology, the emergence of capitalist modernity is generally understood as a *sui generis* development unique to Europe. Where non-European societies do figure, they are typically relegated to the status of a passive bystander, at the receiving end of Europe's colonial whip, or a comparative foil – an Other – against which the specificity and superiority of Europe is defined. In short, the history of capitalism's origins is an unmistakably *Eurocentric* history.

The Problem of Eurocentrism

So what exactly is Eurocentrism? At its core, it represents a distinctive mode of inquiry constituted by three interrelated assumptions about the form and nature of modern development.[10] First, it conceives of the origins and sources of capitalist modernity as a product of developments primarily *internal* to Europe. Based on the assumption that any given trajectory of development is the product of a society's own immanent dynamics, Eurocentrism locates the emergence of modernity exclusively within the hermetically sealed and socio-culturally coherent geographical confines of Europe. Thus we find in cultural history that the flowering of the Renaissance was a solely intra-European phenomenon.[11] Analyses of absolutism and the origins of the modern state form are similarly conducted entirely on the terrain of Europe, with non-European cases appearing (if at all) comparatively.[12] Dominant accounts of the rise of capitalism as either an economic form[13] or a social system[14] similarly place its origins squarely in Western Europe, while non-Europe is relegated to an exploited and passive periphery.[15]

This internalist story of an autonomous and endogenous 'rise of the West' constitutes the founding myth of Eurocentrism.[16] By positing a strong 'inside-out' model of social causality (or *methodological internalism*) – whereby European development is conceptualised as endogenous and self-propelling – Europe is conceived as the permanent 'core' and 'prime mover' of history. In its worst forms, this can lend itself to an interpretation of European society and culture as somehow superior to the rest of the world. This second normative assumption of Eurocentrism can be termed *historical priority*, which articulates the historical distinction between tradition and modernity through a spatial separation of 'West' and 'East'. Through this method, non-European societies have been opposed to Europe as an ideological Other against which the specificity and distinctiveness of Western modernity has been and continues to be defined.[17] Through numerous sociological trends, the 'East' has in turn been (re)constructed as an intransigent and threatening foe representing a fundamental and irreconcilable challenge to the values of the 'West'.[18]

In establishing this 'Iron Curtain'[19] of mutual obstinacy, both Eurocentric internalism and notions of historical priority have been reinforced, not only ideologically but also materially. Expressed through either the comparative approach[20] or 'methodological nationalism',[21] Eurocentrism tends to overlook the multiple and interactive character of social development. In doing so, it sets up an epistemological distinction between Europe and 'the Rest' as theoretically incommensurable objects of study, turning the study of the origins of capitalism into an exclusionary process in which the agency of non-European societies is erased or overlooked.

From these two assumptions emerges a third predictive proposition: that the European experience of modernity is a universal stage of development through which all societies must pass. This stadial assumption posits a *linear developmentalism* in which endogenous processes of social change – from tradition to modernity, feudalism to capitalism and so on – are conceived as universal stages which encompass all societies of the world, at different times and different places. These three propositions (methodological internalism, historical priority and linear developmentalism) make up the core of Eurocentric accounts.

Confronting the Problematic of Sociohistorical Difference

How the West Came to Rule challenges these assumptions by examining the 'extra-European' geopolitical conditions and forms of agency conducive to capitalism's emergence as a distinctive mode of production over the *longue durée*. We do so by tracing the processes of societal transformation through an analysis of the various internationally determined historical dynamics, structures and agencies that emerged and unfolded over the late Medieval and early modern epochs. In this respect, we hope to contribute to what has proven in recent years to be a veritable historiographical revolution in the study of the early modern epoch. This has come from a disparate group of scholars challenging what they see as the fundamentally Eurocentric nature of extant theoretical and historical approaches to the genesis of capitalist modernity.[22] Debates over the origins of capitalism have subsequently taken on new dimensions as scholars have forcefully problematised notions of a self-propelling 'rise of the West' while relativising the uniqueness of Western modernity.[23] Once sidelined to the margins of historical and sociological investigation, the non-European sources, dynamics and experiences of capitalist modernity have thus been at the forefront of these literatures, acting as a much needed corrective to the essentialising, self-aggrandising narratives of an internally generated 'European miracle'.

Perhaps the most significant contribution of this body of literature has been the resolute focus on the relations of interconnection and co-constitution between 'the West' and 'the Rest' in their joint, if uneven, making of the modern world. This attention to 'the international' as a thick space of social interaction and mutual constitution should put International Relations (IR) scholars in a unique position to make important contributions to these debates. Yet thus far, post-colonial and world history critiques[24] have made little impact on the mainstream of the discipline, even after the historical sociological 'turn' in IR.[25] Instead, historical sociological approaches to IR have been criticised for reproducing Euro-centric assumptions, as they predominately conduct their analysis on the basis of European history.[26] Many of the foundational engagements with history in IR have been – and continue to be – primarily carried out on the terrain of European history and intra-European dynamics.[27] Where they do exist, substantive engage-ments with non-European societies tend to emphasise the 'Iron Curtain' of ideological-cultural difference.[28]

Calls for a genuinely 'international historical sociology'[29] have thus remained locked within this Eurocentric cage, as they have yet to fully provincialise Europe, treating it instead as the privileged locale and organic birthplace of capi-talist modernity (see Chapter 1). To change this perspective is the central aim of *How the West Came to Rule*. Widening the spatial optic of capitalism's emer-gence beyond Europe over the *longue durée*, we offer a fundamental rethinking of the origins of capitalism and the emergence of Western domination that puts non-Western sources (both structural and agential) at the forefront of analysis. In doing so, we elucidate the manifold ways that 'the West' itself, as both an ideo-political and a socioeconomic entity, was only formed in and through its interactive relations with the extra-European world. These international dimensions are explored in the substantive historical chapters (Chapters 3 to 8). In each, we shift or decentre the sites of analysis on which most theoretical attention to the origins of capitalism and the 'rise of the West' has focused. Some of these sites are relatively unfamiliar or overlooked in the existing debates, as exemplified by the Mongolian and Ottoman Empires' 'contributions' to the development of capitalism (see Chapters 3 and 4 respectively). However, we also revisit more familiar sites common to contemporary debates – for example, the role of the American 'discoveries' in the making of global capitalism (Chapter 5), the 'classical' bourgeois revolutions in European history (Chapter 6), and the colonisation of Asia (Chapter 7 and 8) – precisely in order to make them *unfamiliar* through a more 'international', non-Eurocentric framework.

In so doing, we also seek to go beyond extant contributions in world history and postcolonial literatures. That is, *How the West Came to Rule* does not aim simply to add new, non-European perspectives that might expand the empirical scope of the study of capitalism's origins. Rather, it offers an alternative framework through which our theorisation of capitalism might be significantly revised. We do so by drawing on and further refining Leon Trotsky's theory of uneven and combined development which, we argue, uniquely incorporates a distinctly international dimension of causality into its very conception of development (see Chapter 2).[30]

The debate on the transition to capitalism is a particularly apposite body of literature for assessing uneven and combined development's efficacy in theorising social change as positions within it well demonstrate the very methodological problems the theory seeks to overcome: specifically, the hardened division between 'internalist' and 'externalist' modes of explanation. In particular, the debates within (neo-)Marxist approaches have largely split between these two 'internalist' and 'externalist' poles. On the one side, scholars such as Maurice Dobb,[31] Robert Brenner[32] and Ellen Meiksins Wood[33] locate the generative sources of capitalist social relations in the internal contradictions of feudal European societies, and particularly England. On the other, Paul Sweezy[34] and Immanuel Wallerstein[35] view capitalism as having developed from the growth of markets, commerce and trade in Europe over the Long Sixteenth Century (1450–1650). The main issue between these different positions revolves around whether the intensification of exchange relations (trade) or class conflict was the prime mover in the transition to capitalism. More recently, anti-Eurocentric scholars have broadened the debate in considering the emergence of antecedent forms of capitalism (or 'proto-capitalism') in the non-West, while further emphasising the contingent, or accidental, factors explaining the rise of a globally dominant Western European capitalism.[36] Yet, for the most part, the anti-Eurocentrics have moved within the main methodological parameters set out by the original debate, accepting an essentially externalist explanation of the genesis of capitalism. By highlighting the spread of commerce and markets as the prime movers, they equate 'antediluvian forms' of capital[37] with capitalism.[38]

What is Capitalism?

The stark disagreements over precisely what factors were central in the making of capitalism beg the question: what is capitalism? In some respects this is a trick question, in that it conceals from view more than it opens to enquiry, since the content of capitalism is of a complexity that resists any single-line definition. Treating capitalism as 'generalized commodity production'[39] or 'competitive accumulation of capital through the exploitation of wage-labour'[40] or 'market dependence'[41] captures, in some respects, a 'hard core' around which it functions. However, the argument we advance in this book is that there is a wider complex web of social relations that stretch our understanding of capitalism far beyond what is captured in any of these phrases. We explicate further what these social relations are over the course of the book, progressively introducing more determinations and categories that we consider crucial to the origins and reproduction of capitalism. For the time being, then, we restrict ourselves to identifying a basic heuristic framework through which we may theorise capitalism.

To say what capitalism 'is' runs the risk of reducing capitalism to a thing, which tends to obscure the multivalent connections in society that facilitate, structure and ultimately limit its reproduction. More specifically, it carries the implication that any given social factor contains an essence that is logically independent of other factors to which it is related. Capital 'as a thing' is often understood simply as 'profit', or an accumulated pool of money, or perhaps machinery, whose existence is independent of wider social relations. Treating capital solely as a 'thing' therefore tends to naturalise and eternalise capitalism.

In contrast, we follow Marx in conceiving capitalism as encompassing historically specific configurations of social relations and processes. Such a relational-processual approach helps us move away from 'abstract one-sided' self-representations of capitalism and toward uncovering the 'concrete living aggregate' of 'definite social relationships'.[42] For example, Marx's observation that some categories (such as capital) necessarily presuppose others (such as wage-labour) allowed him to uncover, analyse and criticise an array of structural conditions of exploitation and power that reproduce the capitalist mode of production. This reminds us that just as social relations are historically specific and constructed, they can be transformed, abolished and reconstructed. Similarly, the emphasis on process further begs a historicisation of the development of capitalism not as a fixed entity, but as one that morphs and reconfigures social relations according to certain historical problems, challenges, struggles, contradictions, limits and opportunities.

We hope this emphasis on process will assist us in moving away from any sociological or political position that posits a certain phase (or place) in capitalism's history or geography as 'pure', 'ideal-typical', 'unchanging' or its 'highest stage'. From such a perspective, we seek to subvert any attempts to read the history of capitalism as a linear progression of clearly discernible stages. Finally, 'process' should help us capture one of the defining characteristics of capital as social relation, the necessity of its movement and motion – in production, circulation and realisation.

In both senses, then – as social relations and as process – it might appear to make more sense to talk about *capitalisms* rather than capitalism. Indeed, a central thesis of this book is that the history of capitalism is a multiple, polyvalent one, irreducible to any singular process or social relation. Nonetheless, we argue that there is a certain unity to its functioning that renders necessary the study of the capitalist mode of production as an intelligible (albeit contradictory) object of analysis.

Treating capitalism in such terms – as a contradictory social totality – helps us trace the ways in which multiple relations of domination, subordination and exploitation intersect with and reproduce each other. From this perspective, we argue that capitalism is best understood as a set of configurations, assemblages, or bundles of social relations and processes oriented around the *systematic reproduction of the capital relation*, but not reducible – either historically or logically – to that relation alone. By placing an emphasis on such configurations and assemblages, we also seek to highlight how the reproduction and competitive accumulation of capital through the exploitation of wage-labour presupposes a wide assortment of differentiated social relations that make this reproduction and accumulation possible. These relations may take numerous forms, such as coercive state apparatuses, ideologies and cultures of consent, or forms of power and exploitation that are not immediately given in or derivative of the simple capital–wage-labour relation, such as racism and patriarchy.

To take one example, one of the great achievements of feminist scholarship has been to show how the existence of wage-labour presupposes a vast 'reproductive sphere' that sits outside (albeit related to) the immediate production process. Here, non-waged forms of production – cooking, house-keeping, child-bearing and so on – are fundamental to the reproduction of wage-labour, and capitalism as such. As we demonstrate throughout the book, such relations (and others) were absolutely crucial to both making the accumulation and reproduction of capital possible, and producing forms of subordination, exploitation and social stratification that were at the heart of alienating workers from their labour and from each other. We argue that an analysis of the making of capitalism should thus be one that seeks to disclose ever more complex webs, assemblages and bundles of social relations that feed into the origins and reproduction of capitalism as a mode of production.

In this book we argue that uneven and combined development provides a way into disclosing and analysing the historical emergence and development of such assemblages, which were and still are constitutive of capitalism. By constitutive, we mean *historically* constitutive: that is, those historical processes that fed into the emergence and development of capitalism. But we also use 'constitutive' to designate those relations and processes that continued to function (albeit in different forms) over the course of subsequent centuries, and persist today: that is, social relations that capitalism cannot do without. As we shall argue, what we consider 'constitutive' is considerably broader than many existing theorisations of capitalism. We argue that this necessitates a broader historical and geographical scope for the proper study of the origins of capitalism, and a theoretical framework capable of making this wider scope intelligible.

Nonetheless, it must be stressed that what follows is not intended to be a 'total' account of the origins of capitalism and the 'rise of the West'. Indeed, our historical account cannot help but be partial, emphasising certain processes and leaving out others. Similarly, we must recognise that this is not a total history but one that privileges those processes that were central to the making of capitalism in Europe. This carries within itself its own dangers of Eurocentrism, in that non-European societies are studied only insofar as they are relevant to European development. We acknowledge the potential concerns that arise from this, but insist that something unique did happen in Europe that propelled it to global dominance at the expense of non-European societies. Uncovering the histories of subjugation and exploitation that lay behind this 'rise' is therefore crucial to critiquing the mythologising of European (or Western) exceptionalism. Taking Europe as an object of study in the telling of this history is both essential and unavoidable. Yet, insofar as gaps exist, we hope that the framework we offer nonetheless provides scope and avenues for future research, and the incorporation of further historical processes that may complement our analysis. In this respect, we seek to provide a more inclusive account of the origins of capitalism that highlights hitherto significantly neglected aspects of the story: particularly, regarding the role of 'the international', 'intersocietal' and 'geopolitics'. Of course, this then begs the question: what are 'the international' and 'geopolitics'?

What Is Geopolitics?

Most broadly defined, geopolitics and 'the geopolitical' can be conceived as encompassing both: first, the variegated processes and practices of communities, societies and states occupying, controlling, socialising, organising, protecting, and competing over territorial spaces and their inhabitant peoples and resources; and second, the multivalent forms of knowledge, discourses, representations, ideologies and strategies, along with the articulations, modes and relations of power generated from such processes. From this perspective, we may then examine how the (re)production, structuring and organisation of space and the construction of human 'territoriality' itself are inherently social processes rooted in, conditioned by, and articulated through historically specific and changing power relations. This allows for the conceptualisation of territorial spaces and the exchanges that take place within, across and between them as pivotal sites of social contestation, change and transformation.[43]

Under capitalism, for example, specific forms of territoriality and other socially constructed spaces are being persistently constituted and reconstituted, borders continually drawn and redrawn, human geographies constantly fashioned and refashioned in and through the uneven development, production, accumulation and circulation of capital across time and space, as well as by the resulting differentiated relations of power, domination, exploitation and conflict accompanying the global reproduction of capitalism as a social whole. Our focus on these geopolitical dimensions of development and reproduction is, then, not intended to reproduce the well-worn problems of geographical or geopolitical determinism. Rather, it aims to spatially broaden our analytical optic to the multiplicity of different 'geo-social' processes and determinations through which capitalism emerged. We would argue that such a spatial widening of our analytical imaginary is in fact a necessary methodological first step in any endeavour to furnish a genuinely non-Eurocentric theorisation of capitalism's genesis and development.

In order to avoid (neo)realist (mis)conceptions of 'the international' as an absolutely autonomous, suprasocial sphere of geopolitical interactions,[44] our uses of the concepts of 'the international' and 'international system' do not denote a permanent state of anarchy, or necessarily imply competition between discretely constituted political units in which the autonomous logic of this competition dictates their strategies. To make the realist move of deriving intersocietal competition from political multiplicity is to unproblematically accept the anthropologically dubious assumption that societies necessarily threaten each other.[45]

We must call out all such ahistorical reificatory and essentialist perspectives for what they really are: thinly veiled rationalisation (intentional or not) of power politics in attaining states' putative 'national interests'. In short, they are particular representations and articulations of the hegemonic ideologies of modern world politics masquerading as social 'scientific' theories[46] – traditional IR as 'the Discipline of Western Supremacy', as Kees van der Pijl aptly terms it.[47] In direct contrast to such approaches, geopolitics, human territoriality and intersocietal/international conflict, along with the very demarcation of the geopolitical as such, must be conceptualised as emergent properties of a wider, interactive and uneven process of development.[48]

11

But with these definitions of 'geopolitics and 'the geopolitical' at hand, honesty compels us to admit that the subtitle of this book (*The Geopolitical Origins of Capitalism*) is something of a misnomer. While we do indeed examine a wide range of sociohistorical processes that are, strictly speaking, geopolitical (such as great power rivalries, colonialism and war), many other developments we investigate are more properly captured under the rubric of 'intersocietal' or 'international' relations, as exemplified by cross-cultural diffusions of trade, commerce, ideas, technologies and disease. We nonetheless settled on this subtitle not simply because it was catchier than, say, *The Intersocietal Origins of Capitalism*, but rather because it captures a fundamental point we are at pains to make throughout this book: that capitalism could only emerge, take root and reproduce itself – both domestically and internationally – through a violent, coercive, and often war-assisted process subjugating, dominating, and often annihilating many of those social forces that stood in its way – processes that continue to this day.

In this sense, our book seeks to offer a 'counter-history' to the many liberal-inspired narratives emphasising the fundamentally pacifying and 'civilising' nature of capitalist development. They present a world where the spread of free trade and markets is equated with the promotion of a more cooperative and peaceful international order; one in which 'globalisation' is viewed as transforming contemporary international politics into a series of 'positive-sum' games whereby states can realise absolute gains; where increasingly integrated transnational circuits of capital and global market relations are in turn identified as advancing more liberal-democratic civic cultures, identities and norms.[49] As we demonstrate through the pages that follow, this is a conception of capitalist development that is fundamentally at odds with the historical record, both past and present.

CHAPTER 1

The Transition Debate: Theories and Critique

In order to examine the object of our investigation in its integrity, free from all disturbing subsidiary circumstances, we must treat the whole world as one nation, and assume that capitalist production is everywhere established and has possessed itself of every branch of industry.

Karl Marx, 1867[1]

... events strikingly analogous but taking place in different historic surroundings led to totally different results. By studying each of these forms of evolution separately and then comparing them one can easily find the clue to this phenomenon, but one will never arrive there by the universal passport of a general historico-philosophical theory, the supreme virtue of which consists in being super-historical.

Karl Marx, 1877[2]

Introduction

In this chapter, we critically assess a number of influential Marxist-inspired theorisations of the transition to capitalism. We focus on such Marxist-inspired perspectives not because they exhaust the range of possible approaches to theorising the transition or because we think other perspectives have nothing to offer. Rather, we centre our attention on them because the Marxist tradition has arguably examined and debated the subject of capitalism's genesis more than any other social theoretical tradition. For these reasons, our critical examination of other important perspectives to capitalism's origins is in later chapters – Smithian approaches in Chapter 5, new institutionalism in Chapter 7, and neo-Weberian historical sociology and the California School in Chapter 8.

The chapter is divided into three sections. The first section examines World-Systems approaches to the origins of capitalism, particularly through an engagement with the works of its most influential representative and 'founder', Immanuel Wallerstein. While highlighting the important contributions that World-System Theory (WST) has made to the study of capitalism's genesis over the *longue durée*, we nonetheless argue that this approach – especially Wallerstein's rendition of it – remains hamstrung by two particularly debilitating problems: the unwitting reproduction of Eurocentrism that erases non-European agency; and the inability to provide a sufficiently historicised conception of capitalism.

The next section investigates the 'Brenner thesis' and the theoretical apparatus (Political Marxism) that Robert Brenner's works on the transition to capitalism have engendered. We focus on three particularly problematic and interconnected issues in their theorisation of capitalism's inception: first, their commitment to a methodologically internalist and concomitant Eurocentric (or Anglo-centric) analysis of the origins of capitalism; second, the resulting deficiencies in their examination of the relationship between the making of capitalism and geopolitics; and third, their highly abstract and minimalist conception of capitalism.

In the third section, we consider the merits and problems of post-colonialism. The inclusion of postcolonial studies in our overview of the different approaches within the transition debate might seem unusual given that postcolonial scholars have predominantly focused on the experiences of moder-nity outside – and subsequent to – the emergence of capitalism in Europe. The existence of capitalism is then something largely taken for granted by post-colonial studies – a point that we argue limits their ability to fully 'provincialise' Europe. We nonetheless also draw out the important methodological and theo-retical contributions postcolonialism offers in the study of capitalism's origins – contributions that we seek to take up and further develop in the chapters that follow.

The 'Commercialisation Model' Revisited: World-Systems Analysis and the Transition to Capitalism

The Making of the Modern World-System: The Wallerstein Thesis

The most systematic exposition of WST can be found in the works of Immanuel Wallerstein, who sought to bring together *longue durée* history writing with the anti-hegemonic politics of the 1960s Third World movements. From dependency theorists Wallerstein took the importance of colonisation in order to explain unequal regional differentiation between the capitalist core and periphery. From Sweezy and Braudel came the emphasis on the 'world-system' as the unit of analysis, and relatedly the importance of trade and exchange.[3] Finally, Wallerstein emphasised the historical specificity of the crisis of feudalism and the collapse of world empires as a precondition for the emergence of the capi-talist world-system. This was because Wallerstein was additionally concerned with how to denaturalise capitalism, and so explore the possibility of its eventual demise.[4] At the heart of this project was then establishing the historical specificity of capitalism by:

> reopen[ing] the question of how and when the capitalist world-economy was created in the first place; why the transition took place in feudal Europe and not elsewhere; why it took place when it did and not earlier or later [and]; why earlier attempts of transition failed.[5]

The specificity of the capitalist world-system is explained through a negative comparison with the social form that preceded it, world empires. The latter were integrated systems of political rule which controlled and exploited differentiated communities on a regional and sometimes inter-regional basis. According to Wallerstein, world empires restricted economic development because large state bureaucracies would absorb surpluses appropriated from agrarian production, hindering or precluding the accumulation of capital and (re)investment in production.[6] The collapse of world empires was a precondition for the emergence of capitalism, for it released profit-seeking commercial activities from the fetters of overarching imperial states. Now unrestrained, production would be 'constantly expanded as long as further production is profitable', and capitalists would 'constantly innovate new ways of producing things that expand their profit margin'.[7] Consequently, trade tended towards constant expansion and subsumption – 'an expansion of the geographical size of the world in question'[8] – which created a capitalist world economy by progressively 'incorporating' greater proportions of economic activity into its own 'logic'. This subsumption of 'non-capitalist zones' into the capitalist world-system took place 'through colonization, conquest, or economic and political domination'.[9]

At the heart of this expansion was an ever-increasing regional specialisation and a world division of labour.[10] From this perspective, Wallerstein distinguished the emergence of the world-system via overseas expansion from the freeing of labour, deriving the latter from the former.[11] That is, the world-system is capitalist not because it involves the systematic exploitation of formally free wage-labour throughout its regions, but rather because it is characterised by different societies' integration into a transnational network of market exchanges and trade.[12] Wallerstein effectively denies the necessity of the wage-labour side of the capital relation for his definition of capitalism itself, writing for example that:

> The point is that the 'relations of production' that define a system are the 'relations of production' of the whole system, and the system at this point in time is the European world-economy. Free labor is indeed a defining feature of capitalism, but not free labor throughout the productive enterprises. Free labor is the form of labor control used for skilled work in core countries whereas coerced labor is used for less skilled work in peripheral areas. The combination thereof is the essence of capitalism.[13]

It is only with the capitalist world-system that we find different localities integrated into a single but differentiated world-system – a unified division of labour distinguished along the hierarchical axes of core, semi-periphery and periphery.[14] This unequal relationship is the *sine qua non* of capitalism for Wallerstein, in which differences between core (Western) and peripheral (non-Western) states determine the transfer of surplus from the latter to the former. This allowed for the observation that just as the core was experiencing an extensive freeing of labour, it was also siphoning off, via unequal exchange, huge amounts of surplus from unfree, coerced labour in the periphery, leaving the periphery in a permanent condition of developmental 'backwardness'.

Hence, part of the value of WST is to situate capitalist exploitation in this broader – international – grid of power and economic relations, beyond the singular act of an individual wage-labourer being exploited within the unit of production.[15] As such, the importance of international hierarchy, exploitation, and more broadly unequal power relations, is revealed. And by distinguishing this world-system from preceding world empires, Wallerstein's approach usefully emphasises the historical specificity and transience of such a hierarchical, exploitative system. These two elements – historical specificity and global hierarchies – can most certainly be considered the *potential* primary strengths of WST. However, on both counts WST ultimately fails to deliver. As we shall see, its identification of historical specificity is ill defined, to the point of missing it, and core–periphery relations are circumscribed by a problematic Eurocentrism that elides 'peripheral agency'. We now turn to these criticisms in further detail.

The Problem of Eurocentrism

One of the benefits of Wallerstein's emphasis on the world-system as the appropriate unit of analysis is that it has necessitated the study of societies outside of Europe. WST is prolific in this regard, with applications as diverse as the Ottoman Empire[16] and Turkey,[17] Africa,[18] South Asia,[19] East Asia[20] and Latin America.[21] But, for all of Wallerstein's emphasis on the world-system as the unit of analysis, we find within his version of WST a pervasive *internalism* which underpins some unfortunate – if not intentional[22] – Eurocentric assumptions.

First and foremost, the operative concepts in WST such as 'division of labour' and 'specialization' are derived from an internalist classical social theory *par excellence*, Adam Smith's *The Wealth of Nations*.[23] These are then extrapolated in an unmediated fashion onto the international scale without considering how it might refashion such concepts. Falling prey to the 'fallacy of the domestic analogy',[24] WST leaves the distinct determinations arising from the coexistence and interaction of a multiplicity of differentiated societies ('the international') untheorised as their own unique domain of social interactions.[25] Instead, these intersocietal determinations are functionally subsumed under the overriding operative logic of a singularly conceived world-system.[26]

This inside-out method is replicated in WST's study of history. Despite the high degree of emphasis on exogenous, global factors, WST cannot get away from an ontologically singular Eurocentric 'logic of immanence'.[27] Consequently, Wallerstein reproduces the typically Eurocentric view that the transition from feudalism to capitalism took place uniquely and autonomously within the clearly demarcated spatial confines of Europe.[28] Although Asian empires displayed signs of potential development towards capitalism,[29] it was the crisis of feudalism in Europe between 1300 and 1450 'whose resolution was the historic emergence of a capitalist world-economy located in that particular geographical arena'.[30]

World history subsequently became about how this European creation spread outwards and 'eventually expanded to cover the entire globe, eliminating in the process all remaining redistributive world-economies and reciprocal mini-systems'.[31] In short, social transformations from the 16th century onwards are understood in the Eurocentric terms of linear developmentalism, in which European social forms are transmitted to 'the East'. In this approach, we find a typically Eurocentric distinction between an atavistic and despotic East and a capitalist West, now recast as periphery and core respectively. In this schema, 'the West' is once again presented 'as the pioneering creator of modernity', and 'the East' as 'a regressive and unexceptional entity that is incapable of capitalist self-generation';[32] an undifferentiated, passive transmitter of surplus to the core. This leads to a double 'elision of Eastern agency'.[33] 'Eastern' elites are seen to voluntarily follow 'Western dictates in order to better secure their own material reproduction within the capitalist world-system'.[34] Meanwhile, non-Western forms of resistance are either overlooked or seen to unintentionally and passively reproduce the capitalist world-system.[35]

This latter issue is especially striking given Marx's theorisation of the distinct processes of subsumption through which capitalism could expand. For Marx, subsumption involved the possession, subordination and subsequent transformation of the labour process into a form compatible with capital's tendency to self-valorisation. The two chief moments of this process – formal and real subsumption – refer specifically to instances of confrontation with extant labour processes. Formal subsumption denotes capital taking hold of pre-existing forms of production, leaving them intact, and extracting surplus from the labour process as it is given. Real subsumption, in contrast, refers to instances where pre-existing labour processes are either transformed, or destroyed and created anew in the image of capital.[36]

In both cases, the character of subsumption and the relation between labour and capital are determined *in* and *through* class conflicts, through which direct producers attempt to resist, restrict, or perversely enable 'the form and extent of ruling-class access to surplus labour'.[37] That is, the 'world division of labour' – the differentiated and multiple forms in which production is oriented to capital – is not simply a function of capital, wherein different forms of exploitation emerge due to the technical requirements of profit-maximisation. It is, rather, the result of the multiple and variegated outcomes of the struggles of capital with whatever methods of production it encounters. The failure of WST to confront the multiple nonlinear histories through which capitalism has been configured and reconfigured in the course of such struggles consequently involves writing the history of the 'periphery' out of the history of the 'core'.

This points to a more substantive issue in Wallerstein's analysis: the strict binary distinction between non-capitalist and capitalist modes of production excludes the possibility of their coexistence and hence combination.[38] This is a debilitating problem, since it leaves any theorisation of the transition to capitalism largely indeterminate. As Eric Mielants suggests:

> The concept of an 'age of transition' can be interpreted as requiring the operation of at least two coexisting modes of production, and the eventual domination of one over the other. If we want to analyse the rise of one mode of production and the demise of another, at some point we have to acknowledge them as working together. If not, one is left with the argument that feudalism simply disappeared within Europe during the 16th century.[39]

Similarly, for C. P. Terlouw:

> During this long transitional phase, feudalism was slowly transformed into, and superseded by capitalism. This can only mean that during at least two centuries feudalism and capitalism coexisted in one world-system. So what Wallerstein explicitly denies (the coexistence of two modes of production in one world-system) he implicitly assumes for the period between 1450 and 1650. If one accepts that during a very long period, several modes of production coexisted in one single system, it is a small, and completely logical step to admit that at any moment in the history of the world-system several modes production could exist simultaneously.[40]

This inability to theorise the coexistence and interaction of multiple modes of production is at the heart of Wallerstein's Eurocentrism. Since social relations that existed prior to capitalist incorporation are rendered irrelevant to our understanding of developments 'post-incorporation', we are left with a picture of the world-system devoid of differentiation in terms of either agency or outcomes. In Ernesto Laclau's words, Wallerstein's world-system is a 'vacant and homogenous totality' that is both historically and theoretically 'created by eliminating differences rather than articulating them'.[41] By denying the coexistence of multiple, differentiated modes of production, WST negates societal difference and multiplicity, and the interactions that stem from them. The very mechanism through which the history of the 'non-West' could be brought into the history of 'the West' is theoretically and historically occluded from the outset.

The Problem of Historical Specificity

The binary opposition of world empires and world-system forms the basis of Wallerstein's historicisation of capitalism, his account of the transition between the two, and ultimately his Eurocentrism. In a sympathetic critique, Mielants suggests that this strict opposition overlooks many key factors of capitalist development that were already well in place in the pre-capitalist era of world empires. He argues that it is possible to identify periods of commercial 'transition', 'acceleration' or 'revolution' in the long durational period between 1100 and 1500.[42] This period witnessed not only substantial changes in the agrarian structure of society, but also developments in urban production and trade that were crucial to the later consolidation and domination of capitalism.[43]

For example, 12th-century Florence[44] was dominated by commercial and financial interests that developed a sophisticated weaving and spinning industry, while Flanders developed a robust textile export industry based on 'a far reaching division of labour, employing both semi-skilled and unskilled workers in large numbers'.[45] Moreover, the mining industry in 12th-century Tuscany was led by private partnerships using wage-labour and capitalist property rights.[46] Land reclamation – the use of 'land as a commodity that one could acquire, improve and profit from' – constituted an important aspect of 14th-century capital formation in both the Low Countries and Northern Italy.[47] Such was the depth of these developments in land, textiles and mining that Mielants describes Flanders and Northern Italy as 'a genuinely capitalist mode of production' based on wage-labour.[48] What is more, Jairus Banaji has shown how these developments toward capitalism in the Mediterranean were in fact 'preceded by (and built on) an earlier tradition of capitalist activity', including partnerships and advance payments, that had developed in the Arab world over the 9th and 14th centuries.[49]

These prototypical developments in capitalism were not exclusively local. Mielants claims that the capitalist subsumption of non-capitalist regions through 'through colonization, conquest, or economic and political domination' can also be observed in the Italian city states' 14th and 15th century activities in the Mediterranean and Black Sea. He also suggests that the Iberian Reconquista[50] used practices that were identical to the more 'global' form of Atlantic colonialism, albeit on a much smaller scale.[51] Similarly, in the 15th century, the Portuguese monarchy, according to Banaji, was a '"driving force of a capitalist revolution" of far-flung trading establishments [feitorias, factories] buttressed by military fortresses'. Imperial Portugal became the '"pioneers of the modern colonial system", harnessing the Crusader tradition of a marginalised aristocracy within the peculiar fusion of Crown and commercial capitalism'.[52] It is also possible to detect instances of world 'divisions of labour' that existed prior to the emergence of the world capitalist system. Noting unequal divisions between the Italian city states and the Baltic, Mielants argues that nascent core–periphery relations were present in Medieval Europe, with the Baltic supplying raw materials in exchange for finished goods from the Italian states. The emergence of Eastern Europe as 'the granary of Western Europe' was itself rooted in a longer evolution that started with the Italian city states in the 13th and 14th centuries (for a further discussion of antediluvian instances of capital see Chapter 7).[53]

Taking all of these 'antediluvian' examples of capital together, Mielants asks, 'when discussing the emergence of capitalism, why not use such world-systems terminology before the 16th century?'[54] Mielants' argument poses an interesting problem for WST: how far is it possible to combine a *longue durée* analysis of capitalism with one that clearly demarcates the specificity and hence transience of capitalism? Many authors working in the WST tradition circumvent this issue altogether by simply doing away with any notion of historical specificity.

Fernand Braudel's use of concepts such as 'capitalism' and 'core–periphery' prior to the 16th century is well known.[55] Kasja Ekholm and Jonathan Friedman argue that systems characterised by capital accumulation and centre–periphery structures based on such accumulation have existed from ancient systems onwards.[56] Similarly, Andre Gunder Frank and Barry Gills suggest that some kind of world-system has been ever-present in the history of human societies, and openly dismiss the possibility of any sharp modal breaks. They argue that 'the same world-system in which we live stretches back at least 5,000 years', in which 'capital accumulation has played a ... central role'.[57] Historical development is subsequently theorised in terms of shifts between different institutional forms through which accumulation takes place, and in terms of hegemons that dominate an otherwise qualitatively similar world-system.[58] Since such changes are only formal, historical change is articulated as the 'cumulation of accumulation'.[59]

One of the benefits of such a move has been to make WST more amenable to non-Eurocentric modes of history writing. Indeed, a variety of authors have developed in-depth historical analyses of flourishing world economies throughout Eurasia and Africa, based on sophisticated commercial links, divisions of labour and core–periphery relations.[60] Janet Abu-Lughod therefore argues that 'it would be wrong to view the "Rise of the West" as ... an event whose outcome was attributable exclusively to the internal characteristics of European society'.[61] Similarly, for Mielants, 'the emergence of capitalism can hardly be explained by focusing exclusively on certain transformations within Europe'.[62]

Nonetheless, in these accounts, Eurocentrism is overcome at the expense of historical and theoretical specificity. By assuming the transhistorical presence of capitalism and not explaining its historically specific origins, this strand of WST fails to develop any kind of historical theorisation of the transition itself. Capitalism, according to this view, has always existed, and has if anything been extended gradually over time. In such a view, an explanation for why 'the West' was able to eventually subordinate and peripheralise 'the Rest', at a particular (if long durational) historical period, is left undeveloped. Although Mielants describes this as an 'extreme'[63] version of WST, his line of reasoning shows that this transhistorical turn appears to be inscribed in the conceptual apparatus and theoretical assumptions of WST. For once Wallerstein's conceptual claims are taken to their logical – or rather historical – conclusion it is possible to see 'commercialisation', 'divisions of labour', 'incorporation', and 'core and periphery' throughout all of human history.

This is precisely the charge of Robert Brenner's searching critique of Wallerstein. According to Brenner, Wallerstein's primary mistake is not historical, but rather theoretical. By placing an overemphasis on the profit motive and the expansion of trade, Wallerstein provides a 'neo-Smithian' model of capitalism.[64] In the pursuit of profit, regions are separated in a world division of labour by specialisation, in which the forms of exploitation tend to correspond to the technical requirements of the world economy.[65] This functional division of the globe into different regions or 'zones' in turn assures the 'flow of surplus' from periphery to core, which enables 'the capitalist system to come into existence'.[66] In short, for Wallerstein, 'the growth of the world division of labour *is* the development of capitalism',[67] wherein *qualitative* transformations in the class structure of societies are seen as the result of the *quantitative* expansion of exchange. The basis of capitalism, the class system of free wage-labour, is understood simply as a 'techno-economic adaptation' undertaken by individual capitalists in order to 'maximize surplus and compete on the market'. Yet this model assumes precisely what needs to be explained: the 'conditions required for the prevalence of these tendencies'[68] – that is, the origins of capitalism as a mode of production.[69] The crux of the issue for Brenner is that by omitting any analysis of class struggle, Wallerstein's theorisation of capitalism is indeterminate.

While the intensification of urban growth, trade and markets throughout Europe in the early modern era could act as 'preconditions' for the eventual development of capitalism, such developments, taken on their own, were incapable of engendering the transition to capitalism, as cities and markets were not by 'nature or even tendentially capitalist'. For Brenner, the compulsion to maximise surpluses, reinvest in production, and develop labour-saving innovations is given in the relation of competition between capitalists and the nature of exploitation through increasing relative surplus. Yet both these conditions crucially depend on the separation of direct producers from the means of production – the freeing of labour – and the subsequent employment of wage-labour as the primary form of exploitation.[70] These conditions themselves presuppose a historical process through which labour, otherwise bonded by serfdom, becomes free – that is, a historical process of class struggle between lords and serfs (see the next section of the chapter).

In contrast, Wallerstein simply 'takes it for granted' that the subjective rationale for profit maximisation will lead to innovation, a world division of labour, and thus capitalism. In doing so, he does not consider the objective, historically specific conditions which give rise to, and necessitate, such capitalistic behaviour.[71] This theoretical indeterminacy in turn leads to a lack of historical specificity. Since 'flowerings of commercial relations cum divisions of labour have been a more or less regular feature of human history for thousands of years', Wallerstein is unable to explain 'why the rise of trade/division of labour should have set off the transition to capitalism in the case of Europe'.[72]

Therefore, the sort of 'historical continuity' in the analysis of capitalism that Mielants, Abu-Lughod, Frank and Gills call for is in fact an unfortunate byproduct of Wallerstein's theorisation of historical development.[73] Once Wallerstein's neo-Smithian assumptions are laid bare, it appears that the sharp historical divide between world empires and world economies effectively dissolves into a transhistorical model of quantitative economic development.[74] With it, the very notion of a mode of production becomes indeterminate, and the historical specificity and transience of capitalism disappears.

Whether Brenner's alternative theoretical analysis of the transition to capitalism marks an advance over Wallerstein's is examined below. A significant point worth recalling, however, is the very important contribution that Wallerstein's concept of the 'world-system' – a contribution all too often overlooked or forgotten after the 'non-debates' of the late 1970s[75] – made in rescaling the primary ontological unit of analysis from the nation-state to the world-systemic perspective. This opened a potential – if largely unfulfilled – means of integrating the causal impact of intersocietal relations into our conceptions of development.

The Spatiotemporal Limits of Political Marxism

The Brenner Thesis: Explanation and Critique

In what has become one of the most influential theorisations of capitalism's emergence, Robert Brenner mobilised Marx's emphasis on changing relations of production (for Brenner, reconceptualised as 'social property relations'[76]) in order to historicise the origins of capitalism in terms of class struggles specific to feudalism.[77] These struggles were determined by relations based on the appropriation of surplus from the peasantry by lords through extra-economic means: lords would habitually 'squeeze' agricultural productivity by imposing fines, extending work hours and extracting higher proportions of surpluses. In the 15th century, this sparked class conflicts in the English countryside, where serfs rebelled against their worsening conditions and won formal enfranchisement. The liberation of serfs from ties and obligations to the lord's demesne in turn initiated a rise in tenant farming and led to increased market dependence, as peasants were turned away from their land and forced into wage-labour as an alternative means of subsistence. Although peasant expulsions were met with significant resistance, the strength and unity of the English state ensured victory for the landed ruling class.[78] This concentrated land in the private possession of landlords, who leased it to free peasants, unintentionally giving rise to 'the classical landlord–capitalist tenant–wage labour structure'.[79]

By contrast, in France, the freeing of the peasants and their ability to retain the land was bound up with the development of a centralised monarchical state that came to take on a 'class-like' character as an independent extractor of surpluses through the taxing of land. The French absolutist state consequently had an interest in securing and protecting peasant landowning as a source of revenue against the re-encroachments of the lordly classes. The ability of the peasants to hold on to the land in turn prevented the systematic emergence of wage-labour in France, hampering the transition to capitalism.[80]

For Brenner, the differential outcomes of the class struggles in England and France are explained by the divergent evolution of the English and French states. Curiously, in explaining these divergent state trajectories Brenner explicitly evokes 'international' factors: the Normandy invasions for England, and the political-military pressures of the English state on the French. The 'precocious English feudal centralization ... owed its strength in large part to the level of feudal "political" organization already achieved by the Normans in Normandy before the Conquest, which was probably unparalleled elsewhere in Europe'.[81] As Brenner notes:

> the English feudal class self-government appears to have been 'ahead' of the French in the twelfth and thirteenth centuries, not only because its starting point was different, but because it was built upon advances in this sphere already achieved on the Continent, especially in Normandy. In turn, when French centralization accelerated somewhat later it was influenced by English development, and was indeed, in part, a response to direct English politico-military pressure. Thus the development of the mechanisms of feudal accumulation tended to be not only 'uneven' but also 'combined', in the sense that later developers could build on previous advances made elsewhere in feudal class organizations.[82]

Although evoking the concept of 'uneven and combined development' here, Brenner's analysis proceeds within the confines of a comparative historical analysis whereby 'the international' remains an ad-hoc addendum to an essentially 'internalist' analysis of the changing balance of class forces and state formation. Nowhere does 'the international' enter into Brenner's theoretical presuppositions centred, as they are, around his concept of 'social property relations'. Yet, as Neil Davidson argues, '[b]y focusing almost exclusively on what [Political Marxists] call social property relations, they "have no terms" to explain events that lie outside these relationships'.[83] This is particularly problematic for Brenner and his followers, who explicitly reject any conception of the origins of capitalism as *immanently* developing from the contradictions of feudal society.[84] Rather, feudalism is conceived as a 'self-enclosed, self-perpetuating system that cannot be undermined by its own internal contradictions'.[85]

Hence, in spite of an extensive and informative historical explanation, Brenner's conception of the origins of capitalism based on shifting social property relations is conceptually too narrow and too simple; Brenner ultimately tries to explain too much with too little. In Brenner's schema, Marx's master concept, the 'mode of production' – conceived as the composite totality of relations encapsulating the economic, legal, ideological, cultural and political spheres – is reduced to the much thinner 'social properly relations' concept, which is itself reduced to a form of exploitation. Brenner's error is to take the singular relation of exploitation between lord and peasant as the most fundamental and axiomatic component of the mode of production, which in turn constitutes the foundational ontology and analytical building block upon which ensuing theoretical and historical investigation is constructed. Yet, as Ricardo Duchesne argues, this stretches the concept of the 'relations of production' too far, as it seeks to incorporate under the logic of 'class struggle' *all* military, political and economic factors, while reducing military, political and legal relations – conceptualised as 'political accumulation' by Brenner – to functions of this singular relation.[86]

The result of this ontological singularity is a dual tunnelling – both temporal and spatial – of our empirical field of enquiry. *Temporally*, the history of capitalism's origins is reduced to the historical manifestation of one conceptual moment – the freeing of labour – and in turn explained by it. *Spatially*, the genesis of capitalism is confined to a single geographical region – the English countryside – immune from wider intersocietal developments. Such tunnelling cannot explain why the extensive presence of formally free wage-labour prior to the 16th century (both inside and outside England) did not give rise to capitalism.[87] Nor can it explain subsequent social developments; by obliterating the histories of colonialism, slavery and imperialism, Brenner 'freezes' capitalism's history.[88]

This substantially narrows Marx's more robust conception of the process of 'primitive accumulation' to which Brenner and his students give so much analytical weight in explaining capitalism's origins. In a famous passage, Marx wrote:

> The discovery of gold and silver in America, the expiration, enslavement and entombment in mines of the indigenous population of that continent, the beginnings of the conquest and plunder of India, and the conversion of Africa into a preserve for the commercial hunting of blackskins, are all things which characterize the dawn of the era of capitalist production. These idyllic proceedings are the chief moments of primitive accumulation .... The different moments of primitive accumulation can be assigned in particular to Spain, Portugal, Holland, France, and England, in more or less chronological order. These moments are systematically combined together at the end of the seventeenth century in England; the combination embraces the colonies, the national debt, the modern tax system, and the system of protection.[89]

In Marx's temporally and spatially more expansive view, capitalism's genesis was not a national phenomenon, but rather an *intersocietal* one. It therefore makes sense to follow Perry Anderson in viewing the origins of capitalism 'as a value-added process gaining in complexity as it moved along a chain of interrelated sites'.[90]

In contrast, Brenner spatially reduces capitalism's origins to processes that occurred solely in the English countryside; towns and cities are omitted, Europe-wide dynamics are analytically active only as comparative cases, and the world outside Europe does not figure at all. Similarly excluded are the numerous technological, cultural, institutional and social-relational discoveries and developments originating outside Europe that were appropriated by Europe in the course of its capitalist development.[91] In short, Brenner neglects the determinations and conditions that arose from the social interactions *between* societies, since 'political community', in his conception, is subordinated to 'class', while classes themselves are conceptualised within the spatial limits of the political community in question.[92] This leads to the various moments of Eurocentrism outlined in the Introduction. Temporal tunnelling gives rise to the notion of *historical priority*; spatial tunnelling gives rise to a *methodologically internalist* analysis. For Brenner's followers these problems are only compounded, as the possibility of the development of early capitalisms outside of the English countryside that Brenner allows for is rejected.[93] The notion of the origins of 'capitalism in one country'[94] is thus taken literally.

This Eurocentrism of Political Marxist analyses is further reinforced by their conception of pre-capitalist societies as generally incapable of significant technological innovations by either the direct producers or exploiters. For in the absence of the market compulsions that are unique to capitalist property relations, Political Marxists claim that there was no equivalent systemic 'imperative' to increase labour productivity and generalise technical improvements across different economic sectors.[95] Under feudalism, the consequence of this systemic inability was that 'real [economic] growth' could only be achieved 'by opening up new land for cultivation'.[96] Moreover, the 'cross-cultural' diffusions of technologies and organisational forms which could facilitate modal transformations in recipient societies is explicitly rejected by Brenner since, as he writes, 'new forces of production were readily assimilable by already existing social classes'.[97]

In short, Political Marxists deny the development of the productive forces any causal role in explaining the transition from feudalism to capitalism, since doing otherwise would inevitably run the risk of 'technological determinism', emptying human agency in the process.[98] To counter this common charge of 'techno-determinism', it is important to note that the concept of 'productive forces' not only took on different meanings relating to different historical contexts in Marx's writings (at one point it was identified with early social communities),[99] but, moreover, should not be conflated with mere 'technologies'. Rather, the forces of production refer to both the *means of production* – including 'nature itself, the capacity to labour, the skills brought to the process, the tools used, and the techniques with which these tools are set to work' – and the *labour process* – 'the way in which the different means of production are combined in the act of production itself'.[100]

As this definition indicates, the forces of production (or 'productive powers') cannot be subsumed under any 'techno-determinist' interpretation. They are simultaneously *material* and *social*: for example, the ways in which tools are used involve both accumulated collective knowledge and a particular socio-historical context in which they operate. To say that there is a tendency for the forces of production to develop over time is simply to say that humans have been motivated to change them, and have done so in ways that have increased the social productivity of labour. Human agency is thus crucial to the process.[101]

What is more, the Political Marxist conception of pre-capitalist societies as relatively stagnant social formations, incapable of either endogenous or exogenously driven technological advances, has been challenged by a wealth of more recent studies of economic growth in pre-capitalist epochs.[102] Indeed, sustained technological and organisational innovations, and thus agrarian productivity, were important features of late Medieval and early modern 'European' societies (see Chapters 3 to 6). Denying productive forces any explanatory significance prior to capitalism also generates a pervasive Eurocentrism, since it situates their development exclusively in modern Europe, as the harbinger of capitalist property relations. This obscures from view the extensive development of productive forces in non-European contexts, such as with the early modern tributary empires of the Ottomans and Mughals (see Chapters 4 and 8) and the dynamic colonial plantation systems in the Americas over the 16th to 18th centuries. In so doing, it occludes from the outset the possibility that productive forces transmitted from these extra-European sources to Europe contributed to the formation of capitalism in Europe itself (see Chapters 3, 4, 5 and 8).

So the Political Marxist conception of pre-capitalist societies as essentially developmental dead-ends is an historical claim that is both Eurocentric and difficult to sustain empirically. This should force us to reconsider the significance of productive forces historically, and re-evaluate the possibility of reincorporating their study into our theoretical explanations of the transition to capitalism.

The Geopolitical in the Making of Capitalism

The ontological singularity of the Political Marxist approach gives rise to a series of historico-theoretical exclusions from their account of the origins of capitalism: namely, intersocietal interaction and the concomitant geopolitical relations of political-military competition and war-making. This might at first seem like a strange omission given Brenner's emphasis on the role of 'political accumulation' and state-building, which he and his followers see as immanent to feudal property relations. That war was endemic to the feudal era is generally recognised. But rather than conceiving this as an eternal 'will to power' or a consequence of a transhistorical anarchic condition of the states system, as mainstream International Relations scholars and neo-Weberians do, Brenner's approach firmly roots the tendency to war in the nature of the prevailing social property relations. 'In view of the difficulty, in the presence of pre-capitalist property relations, of raising returns from investment in the means of production (via increases in productive efficiency)', Brenner writes, 'lords found that if they wished to increase their income, they had little choice but to do so by *redistributing* wealth and income away from their peasants or from other members of the exploiting class'.[103] Dependent as they were on political forms of surplus appropriation, feudal lords would therefore seek to expand the political means – land and military – through which their reproduction would be guaranteed. Insofar as this expansion put them into competition with other lords seeking to do the same, intra-lordly conflicts – feuds and wars – were structural outcomes of feudal property relations. Hence, 'the drive to *political accumulation*, to *state-building*, is the *precapitalist analogue* to the drive to *accumulate capital*'.[104]

Drawing on Brenner's analysis of the drive to 'political accumulation' under feudal property relations, Benno Teschke and Hannes Lacher make a sharp theoretical distinction between the historical emergence of capitalism and an antecedent system of territorialised states.[105] Accordingly, they argue, the 'interstate-ness of capitalism' cannot be derived from the nature of the capital relation itself, but must be 'regarded as a "historical legacy" of pre-capitalist development'.[106] They thereby claim that capitalism retains a wholly *contingent* relation to the multistate system, in which both the contemporary system of sovereign states and uneven development are understood as 'historical legacies' of a distant feudal-absolutist past.[107]

This leads Political Marxists to discard formations such as the English East India Company as 'essentially non-capitalist in its logic'. For Ellen Meiksins Wood this was because the English East India Company relied on 'surpluses extracted directly from producers in the age-old manner of non-capitalist extra-economic exploitation in the form of tax and tribute', making it 'an unambiguously non-capitalist institution' – a verdict Wood similarly shares regarding the Dutch East India Company (see Chapter 7).[108] For various Political Marxists, then, geopolitical rivalries and territorialised ('extra-economic') forms of accumulation are part of the undying feudal-absolutist legacy bequeathed to capitalism – war is the nightmare from which capital has yet to awaken.

From such a perspective, how can we begin to understand, let alone respond politically, to the many 'war-assisted' processes of capital accumulation, geopolitical coercion, competition, rivalry and the like littering the history of capitalism's development? More specifically, could not the war-making activities among feudal lords or absolutist states make for capitalist states? In other words, might not an *unintended consequence* of 'political accumulation' be to generate or spur the development of capitalist production relations? This is what Political Marxists appear to reject.[109]

For example, Erica Schoenberger has examined how markets developed out of the state-building tasks of territorial conquest and control during the Medieval period, while being tied to specific modes of war-making. In this connection, markets emerged out of, or were created to respond to, the myriad logistical problems faced by states in 'the mobilization of resources and their management across space and time'.[110] Commodity markets in material resources, property and labour were all crucial to the movement of wealth and goods that was necessary for Medieval war-making. This is not to say that the development of markets in itself led to the emergence of capitalist social relations. However, it would suggest that the effects of war – territorial integration – provided a more amenable environment for the extensive development of markets, while certain modes of war could actually spur commercialisation and the intensive development of productive forces.

The reliance of state managers on private entrepreneurs in the financing and making of war also involved the widening and deepening of market relations. The symbiotic relationship between advances in war-making activities and the rise of capitalism has been perhaps most systematically explored by William H. McNeil, who writes that 'by the sixteenth century even the mightiest European command structures became dependent on an international money and credit market for organizing military and other major undertakings'. As a consequence, market relations continued to expand, gradually penetrating ever wider spheres of European society. Although it is important to avoid the pitfalls of McNeil's subscription to the 'commercialisation model', it is clear that these changes were important to understanding 'the emergence of the bourgeoisie as a ruling class'.[111]

But perhaps even more important for explaining the rise of capitalist relations were the shifts in the forms of production associated with the changing
nature of warfare. Marx was aware of the revolutionising effects of military
activities on the relations of production, noting that dependence on wage-labour
first developed in armies rather than in the 'interior of bourgeois society'.[112] As
with Marx's conception of primitive accumulation, the role of state intervention, violence and war was therefore conceived as 'functionally promiscuous', as
Michael Mann put it in critiquing Marx's putative economism.[113] In particular,
the expansion of naval capacities contributed to the development of capitalist
relations, since land reclamation, felling trees, building harbours, dry-docks and
ships all required a steady and large supply of wage-labourers.[114]

As early as the first half of the 16th century, some 16,000 workers employed
at the state-run Venetian Arsenal[115] were 'becoming disciplined to the demands
of integrated wage labor'.[116] Constructing standardised galleys using assembly
line production methods, the *Arsenale Nuovo* (established in 1320) may rightly
lay claim to being one of 'Europe's first modern industrial factories', preceding
the Industrial Revolution by four centuries.[117] The Arsenal also employed
sophisticated managerial and accounting discourses, and practices exemplary
of modern forms of 'management through accounting'. For these reasons,
some historians have referred to the Venetian Arsenal as a 'hybrid organisation' which fused capitalist and pre-capitalist forms of labour organisation,[118] a
kind of micro-example of a combined development. Similarly, in Amsterdam,
the extensive application of economies of scale made Dutch naval shipyards
'pioneers' of distinctly 'capitalist forms of production'. Using 'free' wage-
labour, hierarchised and strictly managed labour processes, and the systematic
employment of science to develop labour-saving technologies, shipyards played
a 'prominent role ... in advancing capitalist methods of production'.[119]

It was not simply the building of ships that employed and promoted forms of
wage-labour, but also the organisation of the maritime workforce itself. Between
1700 and 1750, the concentration of capital in merchant shipping required the
amassing of large groups of formally 'free' waged-labourers, numbering anywhere
from 25,000 to 40,000 at any one time. As Marcus Rediker writes, this exceptionally large and concentrated workforce 'represented a capital–labor relation
quite distinct from landlord-tenant, master–servant, or master–apprentice relationships'.[120] War-making and the industries it spawned were therefore crucial
factors in the long transition to capitalism.

The Political Marxist Conception of Capitalism

The narrow focus on the English countryside and the exclusion of international determinations derives in part from Political Marxism's near Platonic

conception of capitalism as a theoretical abstraction to which empirical reality must conform or remain external. If the concept of capitalism used by Wallerstein and WST scholars is too broad, that of Political Marxists is too narrow. For Political Marxists, capitalism can be said to have emerged only when the direct producers and appropriators have lost nonmarket access to their means of subsistence and production, and become entirely dependent on the market for their self-reproduction.[121] Market dependency and the concomitant separation of the 'economic' and 'political' are thereby taken as the *sine qua non* of capitalism. As Wood puts it, the 'special character' of the capitalist state rests on the fact that 'the coercive power supporting capitalist exploitation is not wielded directly by the appropriator and is not based on the producer's political or juridical subordination to an appropriating master'; rather, the 'the two moments of capitalist exploitation – appropriation and coercion – are allocated separately to a "private" appropriating class and a specialized "public" coercive institution, the state'.[122]

Political Marxists therefore draw a sharp distinction between (non-capitalist) extra-economic forms of surplus extraction and (capitalist) noncoercive forms of surplus extraction mediated by the market. Any mode of surplus extraction that does not conform to the latter market-dependent form, and any social formation characterised by extra-economic forms of surplus extraction, is therefore conceived as non-capitalist. This not only leads to the exclusion of geopolitical forms of accumulation and capital formation, but also justifies the narrow focus on England (and then Europe) as the historically privileged site in which this separation of the political and economic first took place.

Yet to reduce a mode of production to its immediate form of exploitation runs the risk of conceptualising capitalism as an 'ideal-type' abstraction, erasing 'the many shades and connections between free and coerced labour that characterize actually existing capitalist social relations and labour regimes'.[123] For example, Marx conceived of 'extra-economic' forms of exploitation in North American and Caribbean slavery as at least partially capitalist, because of their place in a wider set of international economic relations dominated by capitalism.[124] The expansion of slavery in the colonies and free wage-labour in the imperial metropole were two sides of the same coin (see also Chapters 5 and 7). While wage-labour is certainly an integral feature of capitalism – in part defining it – to claim that capitalism can only exist where the majority of direct producers are 'free' is unnecessary, if not unhelpful. Rather, wage-labour should be conceived as a norm in capitalist societies, 'beyond which there are many gradations of formal freedom',[125] and wherein 'the "sale" of labour-power for wages is mediated and possibly disguised in more complex arrangements'.[126] What the Political Marxist conception of capitalism thus erases are the various transitional or mediated forms of labour relations and regimes, involving different combinations of modes of production. Indeed, the idea of 'combined development' – as an amalgamation of differentiated modes of production within a social formation – is absent from the Political Marxist discourse,[127] which unduly abstracts from the messy and contradictory reality of 'really existing' capitalisms.

Politically, there is much at stake in this. The externalisation of 'extra-economic' forms of exploitation and oppression from capitalism ultimately leads Political Marxists to exclude the histories of colonialism and slavery from the inner workings of the capitalist production mode. They argue instead that such practices were rooted in the feudal logic of geopolitical accumulation.[128] While we would not go as far as to claim that Political Marxists ignore colonialism and slavery per se,[129] they do nonetheless absolve capitalism of any responsibility for these histories. However, as will be shown throughout this book, these phenomena were very much integral to the formation of capitalism as the globally dominant mode of production (see especially Chapters 5, 7 and 8). Equally, it is possible to point to the continuing prevalence of racial, gender and sexual hierarchies, often reproduced via nonmarket (as well as market) mechanisms, and ask how far these forms of oppression can be included in the Political Marxist critique of capitalism. The answer, it would seem, is that they cannot. In a critique of 'diversity, "difference", and pluralism', Wood argues, for example, 'that gender and racial equality are not in principle incompatible with capitalism … although class exploitation is constitutive of capitalism … gender or race inequality are not'.[130]

These are difficult claims to sustain empirically. A variety of authors from traditions as diverse as Marxism,[131] feminism[132] and Subaltern Studies[133] have convincingly demonstrated that the origins of capitalism were heavily circumscribed – and in fact often constituted – by such coercive, nonmarket forms of exploitation and oppression. Others have shown how inequalities based on gender[134] and 'race'[135] continue to be inscribed in the very 'logic' of capital accumulation. But constrained as they are by disavowing the 'extra-economic' side of capitalism's history, it is somewhat inevitable that Political Marxists might consider their historical status secondary. Such claims strike an especially discordant note when considered in light of recent debates on the Left about getting gender politics 'right' as well as the general disdain about postcolonial studies found in some quarters.[136] Narrow conceptions of capitalism typical of Political Marxism risk descending into a politics of myopia, in which the manifold, complex and 'intersectional' forms of oppression (re)produced by capitalism are obscured, disavowed and externalised, rather than exposed, criticised and dismantled.

These points all derive from the central problem with Political Marxism: that conceptual abstractions and empirical realities do not correspond to each other, or are misrecognised. As Teschke put it (in a critique levelled at the theory of uneven and combined development, but actually much more appropriate to Political Marxism), 'significant degrees of violence have to be done to the richness of history to orchestrate a "fit" between theory and history. Ultimately, however, theory and history drift apart, inhabiting two different forms of reality'.[137] History is, of course, a messy, complex affair, full of accidents, contingencies and the untheorisable. A grand theory of everything is unlikely. Problems emerge, however, when the central objects of our theories (the origins of capitalism, the modern states system, intersocietal relations and so on) are considered pure contingencies in relation to the abstractions we seek to explain them with. Wood once criticised the Althusserians as viewing the relationship between the state and modes of production in actually existing social formations as having 'little to do' with capitalism's structural logic, thereby appearing 'almost accidental'.[138] Might not the same be said of Political Marxists' conceptualisation of the relationship between 'the international' and capitalism? Or, for that matter, their theorisations of the origins of capitalism itself?

Ultimately, despite its rigour and its many insights into the origins of capitalism, Political Marxism must be judged as sorely lacking. Its pristinely abstract and consequently Eurocentric theorisation of capitalism and its origins is, we argue, historically untenable as it excises such huge swathes of capitalism's history (including colonialism, slavery and war) that it becomes historically (and theoretically) unrecognisable. This abstraction from violence – from these geopolitical conditions in the making of capitalism – results in a violence of abstraction. Consequently, non-European agents who were most affected and made abject by these processes are written out of the making of capitalism. It is this theoretical and historical exclusion of non-Europeans that postcolonial theorists have so resolutely sought to correct. We now turn to consider their position.

The Problematic of Sociohistorical Difference: Postcolonial Studies Engaging Capital

Correcting the Eurocentric bias of extant social theory is at the heart of what has been broadly termed postcolonialism. Yet at first glance, its inclusion might seem incongruous in a study of capitalism's origins, since the specific focus of postcolonialism has been the examination of an already existing and presupposed capitalist modernity in non-European contexts.[139] We shall come back to this issue, and find it problematic. But before we do, it is necessary to highlight the immense methodological and theoretical contributions postcolonialism offers for the study of the origins of capitalism. Two central elements of postcolonialism are especially worth highlighting in this regard.

First, postcolonial scholars have sought to 'provincialise' Europe by decentring the Eurocentric claim that Western social forms and accompanying discourses are homogenously universal.[140] By emphasising how European modernity has always been constituted against – and through the subordination of – a non-Western 'Other',[141] these authors have stressed how colonial practices are deeply embedded in the structures of European power and identity.[142] Postcolonialism therefore places the particularity of alternative representations of modernity in non-Western cases at the heart of its research programme.[143] By 'giving a voice to the Other', postcolonialism shows how subaltern experiences have disrupted Eurocentric visions of history, reasserting the significance of non-Western agency in world history.[144]

Second, postcolonialism emphasises the heterogeneity of social development and its irreducibility to exclusively European forms. Accordingly, history is neither universal nor homogenous, but marked by difference, hybridity and ambivalence – in short, multiplicity. As such, postcolonialism also seeks to dislodge the linearity of historical time, and rejects any possibility of stadial conceptions of development.[145] These two pointers – a non-Eurocentric and multilinear history – are the primary strengths of the postcolonial approach. It is here that its promise for the study of the origins of capitalism lies. We examine each in turn, with a particular – but not exclusive – focus on Dipesh Chakrabarty's *Provincializing Europe*. In this way, we hope to avoid some of the pitfalls of attempting a general overview of a highly heterogeneous research programme. Nonetheless, we also consider Chakrabarty's work to be, in the words of Vasant Kaiwar, 'undoubtedly the most important work to emerge out of the postcolonial phase of Subaltern Studies',[146] and thus deserving of special attention.

The Eurocentrism of Historicism

Postcolonialism is, first and foremost, a specific reaction against attempts in Western thought to subsume all sociohistorical experiences under the universal rubric of capitalist modernity. These universalist accounts suffer, because they tend to misread, or worse, overlook difference. Chakrabarty calls this 'historicism' – a way of writing history that both 'both recognizes and neutralizes difference', in which 'differences among histories' are 'overcome by capital in the long run'.[147] Historicism tends to portray capitalism 'as a force that encounters historical difference' externally, struggles with this difference, and eventually negates, or more precisely, subsumes it 'into historically diverse vehicles for the spread of its own logic'.[148]

Such an approach carries with it a specific kind of politicised prescription. By positing Europe 'as the site of the first occurrence of capitalism, modernity, or Enlightenment', non-Europeans were assigned a place 'elsewhere'.[149] Historical developments subsequently came to be judged almost exclusively against a

European norm, and those histories that did not fit or comply with that norm were dismissed as 'incomplete' or 'aberrations'. Differences are thereby articulated through – and abolished by – essentialised binaries such as 'precapitalism' and 'capitalism', 'modern' and 'premodern', 'archaic' and 'contemporary', 'world empires' and 'world-system', and so on.

The very notion of incompleteness carries within it the sort of hierarchies that were present in colonialism (such as notions of 'barbarism', 'uncivility', 'backwardness', 'inadequacy' and the like). Consequently historicism posits 'a measure of the cultural distance ... that was assumed to exist between the West and the non-West',[150] and acts as a way of saying to non-Europeans, 'not yet!' in their calls for autonomy and recognition.[151] This becomes most evident when examining the 'peasant' or 'subaltern'. For example, Eric Hobsbawm's characterisation of the (Indian) peasant in history as 'pre-political' and 'archaic' is rooted in an understanding of non-European development as 'incomplete'.[152] These agents are then seen as a survival or remnant of pre-capitalist relations. More recent iterations of this same strategy can be found, according to Chakrabarty, in notions of 'uneven development', which ascribes 'at least an underlying structural unity (if not expressive totality) to historical process and time that makes it possible to identify certain elements in the present as "anachronistic" or "outmoded"'.[153]

Historicism becomes especially problematic when we consider the centrality of the peasant in the making of modernity. Peasant agency – although distinctly nonbourgeois, nonsecular, and historically connected to practices that existed prior to colonialism – was still unequivocally both political and modern.[154] As David Washbrook has argued, the very prevalence of a 'backward' or 'traditional' stratum of society (in contrast to the 'modern') was itself a construction of colonialism in South Asia.[155] The act of subsuming the peasant under the rubric of the 'premodern', 'pre-capitalist' or 'precapital' therefore reflects nothing other than the violent attempt to fit subalterns 'into the rationalist grid of elite consciousness', in a way that makes them intelligible to colonialists and bourgeois nationalists.[156] The upshot is that an otherwise politically significant peasantry becomes silenced, misrepresented or marginalised by history writing.

For this reason, Partha Chatterjee seeks to recast the historical question of non-European modernity in different terms by explaining 'the limits to the historical actualisation of Capital as a universal economic category'.[157] One of the primary concerns of Chakrabarty is therefore to 'Provincialize Europe' by showing 'how universalistic thought was always and already modified by particular histories'.[158] Put differently, this approach seeks to demonstrate that concepts and categories that purport to be universal always contain within them traces of the *not-universal*.

This is evident in two respects. First, Chakrabarty seeks to show how seemingly 'universal' concepts of political modernity 'encounter pre-existing concepts, categories, institutions and practices through which they get translated and configured differently'.[159] Second, he demonstrates how ostensibly universal categories are in fact themselves particular and provincial, in that they were the product of a specifically European experience.[160] Similarly, Chatterjee highlights that the supposed universalism of European social forms in fact masks a particular historical experience, which only became universal due to the specific history of capitalism:

> If there is one great moment that turns the provincial thought of Europe to universal philosophy, the parochial history of Europe to universal history, it is the moment of capital – capital that is global in its territorial reach and universal in its conceptual domain. It is the narrative of capital that can turn the violence of mercantile trade, war, genocide, conquest and colonialism into a story of universal progress, development, modernization, and freedom.[161]

It should be clear from the outset then, and in contrast to Vivek Chibber's recent broadside against Subaltern Studies,[162] that the likes of Chatterjee, Chakrabarty and Ranajit Guha do not deny capital's universalising tendency. Indeed nowhere do each of the Subaltern Studies scholars castigated by Chibber deny that capital demonstrates a *real* tendency toward universalisation. Rather, their claim is an altogether different one: that capital's universalising tendency is necessarily limited, *always* and *everywhere* partial – all points made by Chibber himself. For example, Chakrabarty highlights the '"resistance to capital"' that Marx speaks of as 'something internal to capital itself'. Hence, 'the self-reproduction of capital', as Chakrabarty notes, going on to evoke another quote from Marx:

> 'moves in contradictions *which are constantly overcome but just as constantly posited*'. Just because, he [Marx] adds, capital gets ideally beyond every limit posed to it by 'national barriers and prejudices', 'it does not by any means follow that it has *really* overcome it'.[163]

Interestingly, this passage taken from Marx's *Grundrisse* is also quoted in full by Guha, after which he writes that 'Nothing could be more explicit and indeed more devastating than this critique of the universalist pretensions of capital'.[164] Moreover, Guha views this contradictory unity of universalising and counter-universalising tendencies as operating within both 'the East' and 'West' (specifically Europe). As Guha puts it, for Marx:

> the discrepancy between the universalizing tendency of capital as an ideal and the frustration of that tendency in reality was, for him, a measure of *the contradictions of Western bourgeois societies of his time* and the differences which gave each of them its specificity.[165]

The 'structural fault in the historic project of the bourgeoisie' Guha highlights[166] was then not between 'the Indian bourgeoisie and its predecessors' in Europe.[167] It was instead a broader spatiotemporal fault line traversing the entire world: one between the 'early' bourgeois revolutions in England and France, on the one hand, and the later bourgeois revolutions running east of the Elbe in Europe to those beyond Europe (as with India), on the other.

The Violence of Abstraction

The postcolonial project of provincialising Europe is then not about rejecting the universality of capitalist modernity out of hand, or in Chakrabarty's terms, it is not a project of cultural relativism.[168] These authors accept that capitalism has a universal reach, only too brutally demonstrated by the histories of colonialism and imperialism. What they reject is using this universal conception of capital as the 'sole' or 'sovereign' author of historical processes, in a way that turns all other particular histories into differentiated expressions of European history.[169] The aim is to 'displace a hyperreal Europe from the center toward which all historical imagination currently gravitates',[170] by (re)writing these non-universal, particular and local histories 'back in'. In doing so, these scholars seek to highlight the liminality of universal categories in capturing the broad range of sociohistorical processes operating in the 'extra-European' world while examining the myriad hybrid sociopolitical forms produced by capital's differentiated but interactive universalisation.

This aim of identifying parts of social life not subsumed by the universality of capital leads Chakrabarty to a highly stimulating reading of Marx's category of 'abstract labour' in capturing the homogenising tendency of capital.[171] According to Marx, the practice or performance of abstraction becomes apparent in workplace discipline, wherein the 'life' or 'living labour' of the worker is abstracted from and subsumed by 'dead labour' – the machine. Such an abstraction enables the homogenisation and equalisation of various, particular or concrete instances of labour, thus establishing labour (labour-time) as the measure of wealth under capitalism. It is also through this abstraction that wealth itself is created. In order to extend relative surplus labour, labour-saving technologies are introduced, which reduce to a minimum the amount of living labour necessary for production. In this respect, the abstraction of labour also acts as the mechanism through which labour is 'emancipated'.[172] This tendency to simultaneously exploit and emancipate labour constitutes what Marx calls the 'moving contradiction' of capital.[173]

For Chakrabarty, this is significant because inscribed in the very universality of abstract labour is its opposite – the element of 'life' or 'living' for the worker, and the attempt of workers to reappropriate their 'life' – which forms the basis of resistance to capital. Given in the very universality of abstract labour is a particularity – the life of individual workers – that remains never quite conquered by capital. It is on the basis of this distinction that Chakrabarty introduces the concepts of 'History 1' and 'History 2'. History 1 refers to that past presupposed by capital, 'a past posited by capital itself as its precondition' and 'its invariable result'.[174] Although Chakrabarty leaves this largely unspecified, it is clear from his preceding discussion that this refers to abstract labour. History 1s abstract from specific instances in order to 'make all places [histories] exchangeable [comparable] with one another',[175] designating what Alfred Sohn-Rethel called 'real abstractions'.[176] These are more than just 'abstract descriptions' or 'abstract delineations' – that is, concepts – but concrete relations and processes that affect the functioning of capitalism as a mode of production. The very act of abstracting – as both Marx and Chakrabarty argue – from the individual concrete labour of each worker is the precondition for their exchangeability on the market, and hence the precondition for capitalism as such.

By contrast, History 2 refers to those histories that are encountered by capital 'not as antecedents' established by itself, nor 'as forms of its own life-process'.[177] History 2s are not 'outside' of capital or History 1. Instead, they exist 'in proximate relationship to it',[178] while 'interrupt[ing] and punctuat[ing] the run of capital's own logic',[179] providing 'affective narratives of human belonging where life forms, although porous to one another, do not seem exchangeable through a third term of equivalence such as abstract labour'.[180]

Although Chakrabarty is clear in his definition, he is somewhat elusive when it comes to the exact content of History 2. Nonetheless, with his discussion of abstract labour in mind, he appears to be talking about those elements involved in the reproduction of labour-power that are not subsumed by abstract labour itself. Others, most notably feminist authors, have theorised this as the 'reproductive' or 'unwaged' sphere.[181] History 2 also draws affinities with biopolitics, those elements of politics and society found 'in the person's bodily habits, in unselfconscious collective practices, in his or her reflexes about what it means to relate to objects in the world as a human being and together with other human beings in his given environment'.[182]

History 2s may well include non-capitalist, pre-capitalist or local social relations and processes, but the concept is not exhausted by these, and can refer to universal and global categories, social relations and process. Indeed, following Marx, two of the examples Chakrabarty gives of History 2s are commodities and money – two universal categories central to the reproduction of capitalism.[183] Therefore, Chibber's criticism that Chakrabarty uses History 2 to refer to merely local ('Eastern') manifestations of abstract and universal (or 'Western') processes[184] is wholly inaccurate. History 1 is not simply 'an abstract definition', the 'universal' or 'the West'; nor is History 2, by contrast, seen as a concrete manifestation, local and/or Eastern, as Chibber reads it.[185] Notably, Chakrabarty himself nowhere defines History 1 and History 2 as any of these.[186]

Most revealingly, the category through which Chakrabarty seeks to elucidate such 'difference', 'modifications' and 'interruptions' is Marx's (universal)
category of *real labour*, the category that alongside – and in tension with –
abstract labour inheres in all commodities in the capitalist mode of production.
It is clear, then, that when Chakrabarty is talking about History 2s – about real
labour, about difference – he is doing so in a way that both depends upon and
reveals a dialectical relation with History 1s, with abstract labour, and with
universality as such. That is, 'just as real labor cannot be thought of outside
of the problematic of abstract labor, subaltern history cannot be thought of
outside of the global narrative of capital'.[187] Hence, it is important to reject from
the outset Chibber's denunciation that Chakrabarty is providing '*a license for
exoticisim*'.[188] In fact, Chakrabarty is unequivocal in his description of History 2;
these are 'histories that capital everywhere – *even in the West* – encounters as its
antecedent, which do not belong to its life process'.[189]

In this respect, History 2s are not simply differentiated functional moments
in the development of capitalism, nor are they concrete – local – instantiations
of an otherwise universal process. Rather, they designate 'institutional forms,
regimes of value and alternative temporalities that have their lineage in other
histories and modes of being'.[190] History 2s are spheres of social being that are
inhabited and remade by capital, but also processes that remake capital itself.
As Marcus Taylor argues, 'while capital may indeed seek to rewrite social life
to further the cause of "endless accumulation", it does not do so – to twist a
famous maxim – in conditions of its own choosing'.[191]

Indeed, Chakrabarty's critique of Marx*ism*'s 'blind spot'[192] is focused on its
inability (or unwillingness) to take History 2 'seriously'.[193] The Marxist analysis
of the capitalist mode of production tends to create – and methodologically
situate itself within – 'abstract space', which erases 'the local' and 'evacuates
all lived sense of place'.[194] Although History 1 may seek to negate, destroy or
sublate History 2, there is no guarantee that 'this could ever be complete'.[195]
Therefore, the correct method, according to Chakrabarty, is to write history in
a way that combines History 1s and History 2s, wherein the 'universal history
of capital and the politics of human belonging are allowed to interrupt each
other's narrative'; and wherein capitals' 'histories are History 1s constitutively
but unevenly modified by more and less powerful History 2s'.[196]

There is, then, much at stake in retaining some of the insights gleaned from
Chakrabarty's interpretation of Marx. For his emphasis on the tensions between
History 1s and History 2s appears crucial to mitigating against the potentially
ahistorical, essentialising and (economically) homogenous reading of capi-
tal(ism) found in so much of the traditional literatures on its origins. For this
reason, Chakrabarty's method strikes us as an altogether positive advance for
scholars going about writing the history of capitalism. In Chapters 5 and 7 we
attempt to construct a history of the making of capitalism in which the sorts

of history targeted by 'History 2' – those found in the 'unwaged' or 'reproductive' sphere – are understood as constitutive of 'History 1' – the formation of 'abstract labour' and an industrial proletariat. Taking a multiple and differentiated agency as a starting point, and subsequently exploring encounters and interactions within this multiplicity is, moreover, precisely the sort of method that we ourselves outline in the following chapter. It is therefore worth briefly noting some of the affinities between Chakrabarty's approach (and postcolonialism more broadly) and the theory of uneven and combined development as articulated in this work.

The Lacuna of Postcolonial Theory

Positing a 'not-yet' to 'backward' peoples was a prevalent and distinctly 'Historicist' sentiment in Russia precisely at the time Trotsky was developing the theory of uneven and combined development. Pointedly, Trotsky rejected the Menshevik idea of 'waiting' for a bourgeois stage before a proletarian revolution could occur, and insisted on the 'now'. The Bolshevik Revolution and strategy of permanent revolution are direct outcomes of this, while uneven and combined development was its methodological and theoretical foundation. This is especially revealing given the centrality of the peasant – the supposedly nonmodern agent *par excellence* – in Russian social life generally, and the Bolshevik Revolution specifically. In the *History of the Russian Revolution*, Trotsky's explicitly characterises Russia's revolutionary conditions in terms of the imbalance between town and country, and revolutionary agency in terms of the combination of a newly formed proletariat and pre-existing peasantry. We can trace this back even further to Marx, who himself saw the potential for a communist revolution in Russia ahead of the capitalist heartlands due to the very prevalence and dominance of the peasant commune.[197]

The reason both Marx and Trotsky identified forms of divergence and differences similar to those found in the postcolonial literature was because both were sensitive – with some important limitations[198] – to the intersection of History 1s and History 2s. As we shall see, it is through the idea of 'combination' that Trotsky's theory provides a nonstadial, multilinear understanding of development that explicitly denies essentialised and externally related dichotomies of pre-capitalist and capitalist. Similarly, we find in Marx an outright rejection of any 'supra-historical' application of his categories in *Capital*. This was because 'events strikingly analogous but taking place in different historic surroundings led to totally different results'. They could not, therefore, be explained 'by the universal passport of a general historico-philosophical theory'.[199] The explicit disavowal of historicism in the writings of Trotsky and Marx should alert us to the possibility that postcolonialism and Marxism need not be seen as mutually exclusive endeavours.

With this in mind, we suggest that uneven and combined development provides a theoretical approach that may strengthen the broader aims of the postcolonial research programme. We make this suggestion because there remains a tension within postcolonialism that ultimately undermines its efforts in both fully subverting Eurocentrism and reasserting non-European agency into the history of capitalism. The tension is rooted in the parochial – dare we say 'provincial'? – scope of its critique. That is, the subject rarely extends beyond the particular experience of modernity in specific localities, and particularly those experiences in the colonial modernities of the Global South. Chakrabarty notes that '*Provincializing Europe* is not a book about the region of the world we call "Europe"',[200] but is instead concerned with the generalisation of its forms and categories. Similarly, Chatterjee claims that '[t]he universality of Western modernity ... is a product of its local conditions', which is then subsequently 'transported to other place and times'.[201] And although Guha's classic *Dominance Without Hegemony* provides a sharp critique of the liberal historiographies of bourgeois rule, it never provides an alternative substantive historical sociology of the European experience.

Consequently, each of these authors uncritically presupposes a discrete and hermetically sealed European history in which modernity was created before being subsequently expanded globally.[202] As we have seen, and will see further, such an idealised view is an integral part of the myth of Europe as an exceptional, pristine and autonomous entity that happened to be especially well suited to the endogenous transition to, and subsequent spread of, capitalism.[203] Insofar as 'the West is constituted as an imperial fetish, the imagined home of history's victors' and 'the embodiment of their power',[204] many of the processes of developmental differentiation that created hierarchical imbalances between colonisers and colonised are occluded.[205] The lack of any substantive engagement with the question of how capitalism emerged and developed in Europe is therefore a – perhaps *the* – critical lacuna of postcolonial theory, continually frustrating its abilities to offer a satisfactory non-Eurocentric theory and history of the modern epoch.

To modify Frederick Cooper's call to arms: in order to truly 'provincialise' Europe we must dissect European history itself, and there is no more central myth to be dissected than that of narrating European history around the history of capitalism.[206] As Kamran Matin argues, such a task ultimately requires 'a general social theory, and not just a theory of modernity', one 'that goes beyond a mere phenomenology of capital's expansion and comprehends capital itself as a product of the interactive multiplicity of the social'.[207] In short, the foregoing analysis demands an 'internationalist historiography'[208] and theorisation of capitalism's emergence and reproduction. This would, in turn, require that we 'distinguish between the inflated, utopian self-presentation of capital as abstract and homogenous and the contradictions internal to historical capitalism that produce a global, differentiated, and hierarchical space-time'.[209] These are some of the main tasks taken up in the pages that follow.

Conclusion

As examined in this chapter, existing theoretical approaches to the transition from feudalism to capitalism have suffered from two particularly debilitating and interconnected problems. The first concerns their general inability to substantively *theorise* the coexistence and interaction of a multiplicity of societies as a distinct domain of 'geo-social' developmental pressures, behavioural patterns and causal dynamics ('the problematic of the international'). The second relates to these extant approaches' predominant, if not exclusive, focus on Europe as the 'prime mover' of sociohistorical change and transformation ('the problematic of sociohistorical difference'). The two problems are interrelated in that the *methodological internalism* or 'domestic analogy' fallacy that the first predicament gives rise to – implicitly or explicitly – lends itself to theoretical analyses that conceive the genesis and sources of capitalism as an exclusively European affair (*historical priority*), and/or extrapolate from the distinct developmental paths and modalities of European societies and project them onto the 'extra-European' world in a unidirectional manner (*linear developmentalism*). The European experience of capitalist modernity is thereby elevated to a universal stage of development through which all societies must pass in one form or another (*universal stagism*). The false sense of universality that such forms of analysis have given rise to has been the bane of social theory's existence since its inception.[210]

Whether the approach in question conceptualises the primary 'unit of analysis' as operating at the domestic or world level – as exemplified by Political Marxism and WST, respectively – the dilemma remains the same. By working outwards from a conception of a specific social structure (be it slavery, feudalism, capitalism or whatever), the theorisation of 'the international' takes the form of a reimagining of domestic society *writ large*: an extrapolation from analytical categories derived from a society conceived in the *ontologically singular* form. This then erases what is arguably unique to any intersocietal system: a superordinating 'anarchical' structure irreducible to the historically variegated forms of societies constituting any given system.

This is a particularly debilitating problem for Marxist theories of sociohistorical change, as one of the hallmarks of such theories is a claim to a holistic conception of social relations and systems, in which 'social totality' is conceived as being composed of interactive and co-constitutive parts; that is, one that theoretically interiorises the interdependency of each element within it 'so that the *conditions of its existence* are taken to be part of what it is'.[211] If such a claim is to be taken seriously, then the theoretical standing of 'the international' for a historical materialist approach to the origins of capitalism requires a direct engagement with the question of what 'the international' is, understood and theorised in its own substantive historical and sociological terms.

One theoretical answer to this question, we argue, is offered by a reconstruction of the concept of uneven and combined development. In contrast to WST and Political Marxism, uneven and combined development offers a way of theorising 'the international' without jettisoning a historically sensitive sociology. Not only might this provide a way of uniting the externalist and internalist accounts offered here, it would also be able to capture and articulate the manifold excess of (intersocietally produced) determinations overlooked by both WST and Political Marxism. In its appreciation for the intersocietal and geopolitical, uneven and combined development also provides a way of capturing the multilinearity of development that is so central to displacing Eurocentric accounts. As such, it shares many affinities with postcolonial approaches. In particular, uneven and combined development provides a particularly fertile framework through which the sort of interconnections between History 1s and History 2s emphasised by Chakrabarty might be identified, explored and explained. However, beyond Chakrabarty, the advantage of uneven and combined development lies precisely in its broader temporal scope. This uniquely positions it as a framework through which we might reconstitute the master categories of Eurocentrism – such as capitalism – on the very terrain they were purportedly generated – that of Europe. We explore further the potential of uneven and combined development – theoretically and historically – in the pages that follow.

CHAPTER 2

Rethinking the Origins of Capitalism: The Theory of Uneven and Combined Development

Sociological problems would certainly be simpler if social phenomena had always a finished character. There is nothing more dangerous, however, than to throw out of reality, for the sake of logical completeness, elements which today violate your scheme and tomorrow may wholly overturn it.

Leon Trotsky, 1936[1]

Introduction

To better account for the biography of capitalism's development, we need an approach that captures the geopolitically interconnected and sociologically co-constitutive nature of its emergence. The very absence of 'the international' in theorising sociohistorical development has been identified by various scholars as a fundamental lacuna of not only Marxist theory but, more radically still, the classical sociology tradition as a whole.[2] According to this line of critique, both traditions work with the ontologically singular[3] assumption that the growth and change of a society 'should be explained with reference to its internal constitution'. While the interactions between societies may not be viewed as entirely 'inconsequential', they are 'in principle insignificant for sociology, since its effects on the essential process [are] seen as negligible'.[4]

While numerous historical sociologists have forcefully recognised the problem of abstracting the development and reproduction of societies from their intersocietal contexts, arguably none of them have ever found a substantive theoretical solution to the problem.[5] For despite their attention to pointing out the inadequacies of 'societal-based theories',[6] they too have continually introduced this international dimension of development as an *externality* to their analyses in ways that actually reinforce the theoretical disconnect between the 'geopolitical' and the 'social'. This problem cuts across the theoretical and methodological divides, as attested by Martin Hall's critical survey of the different theoretical contributions of historical sociological approaches to International

43

Relations (IR). 'There is a danger', Hall warns, that historical sociology 'serves to strengthen the dichotomization of "the international" and "the domestic". Although ... international and domestic forces interact or combine to produce a certain outcome, *analytically they are still distinct*'.[7]

It is this lacuna that requires the formulation of a unified theory of how societies interact, of how they change, and the relationship between these historically dynamic processes. Such a theory would have to capture how the historical reality of 'the international' is itself part and parcel of wider socio-historical developmental processes. As argued below, the theory of uneven and combined development provides one such answer to this problematic, for it uniquely interpolates an international dimension of causality as an intrinsic aspect of sociohistorical development itself. This then allows for the organic – rather than contingent or external – integration of 'geopolitical' and 'socio-logical' determinations into a single, unified theory of sociohistorical change, sublating 'internalist' and 'externalist' theories of modal transitions. In other words, 'the international' – 'that dimension of social reality which arises specifically from the coexistence within it of more than one society' – is theo-retically internalised in a way that 'formulates this dimension as an object of social theory – organically contained ... within a conception of social develop-ment itself'.[8] For this reason, the theory has enjoyed an unprecedented revival over the last two decades in the disciplines of IR, development studies and historical sociology,[9] where a number of scholars have sought to tease out and further refine the theoretical implications of Trotsky's concept in fashioning the possibility for an entirely 'new understanding of human history'.[10]

In what follows, we begin by offering a schematic exposition of the theory's main concepts – unevenness and combination – from which the 'whip of external necessity', 'privilege of historic backwardness', 'advantages' and 'penalties of priority', 'contradictions of sociological amalgamation', and 'substitutionism' necessarily follow. In this section, we explain how the conditions of unevenness and combination produce these component mechanisms, before proceeding in the next section to consider the concept's precise spatiotemporal generalisability: that is, whether it can be fruitfully employed beyond the capitalist epoch.

The Theory of Uneven and Combined Development: Exposition and Critiques

Unevenness

Unevenness posits developmental variations both within and between societies, along with the attendant spatial differentiations between them. The starting point for Trotsky was an empirical observation about the basic ontology of human development: that a multiplicity of societies varying in size, culture, political organisation, material and non-material productivity, is a transhistorical feature of human history – its 'most general law'.[11] From this empirical observation, Trotsky was able to infer both the quantitative (multiple societies) and qualitative (different societies) character of social development[12] – what he termed *uneven development*. But rather than simply describing two static conditions or dimensions of such development (multiplicity – difference), Trotsky instead sought to capture how their dialectical interaction (social multiplicity ➔ intersocietal interaction ➔ societal difference) formed the basic onto-relational texture of the historical process as a whole, wherein the shifting identity of any particular society accumulated and crystallised.[13]

Emphasising the specificities of any given society's development within this wider interactive intersocietal milieu, Trotsky showed how they were irreducible to any unilinear path of development. Hence, for Trotsky, 'Russia stood not only geographically, but also socially and historically, between Europe and Asia'.[14] As both cause and effect of this international differentiation, unevenness also denoted the peculiar, local sociological forms of internal differentiation in institutional, cultural and class relations.[15] Differential tempos and forms of change over time were matched by variations in space. This was true not only of the uneven (interactive) relations between societies, but also of the uneven relations within societies. The 'force of uneven development', Trotsky wrote, 'operates not only in the relations of countries to each other, but also in the mutual relationships of the various processes within one and the same country'.[16] For example, Trotsky noted the imbalances between town and countryside[17] and state and society,[18] along with the differential pace of social stratification and differentiation among the peasantry[19] in Russia, in contrast to other European forms.

Traversing the multiple, intersecting spatial fields of social constitution and organisation, breaking with any discretely conceived notions of the national and international,[20] Trotsky's conception of unevenness prefigured later conceptions of social relations as networks or webs,[21] without losing sight of their territorialisation and statisation in the modern epoch.[22] Crucially, such relations of unevenness created structural competitive conditions between societies themselves – 'the whip of external necessity', which in Trotsky's case referred to the competitive pressures of the European absolutist-cum-capitalist states on the 'less-developed' Russian social formation.[23] As Russian development did not occur endogenously, but always under the influences, pressures and lessons of these more 'advanced' societies, this in turn permitted – indeed compelled – Russia to reap a certain 'privilege of historic backwardness', adopting and potentially innovating on the most cutting-edge technologies, institutions and materials practices 'pioneered' by the leading states of the international system. The assimilation and adaptation of such capitalist methods and organisational forms to Russian society as 'finished products[s]' also meant that the Tsarist state did not need to repeat the developmental steps or 'stages' originally required to get there. As Trotsky put it, '[s]avages throw away their bows and arrows for rifles all at once, without travelling the road which lay between those two weapons in the past'.[24]

Yet while Trotsky emphasised the transformational effects of the more 'advanced' European societies on the more 'backward' Tsarist state, the 'whip of external necessity' should be conceived not as a unidirectional structural imperative, but as one that operates in a co-constitutive and multilateral fashion: meaning that the 'less-developed' societies also influence the 'more' developed ones in their mutually interactive processes of social and geopolitical reproduction. This was dramatically exemplified by the Mongolian Empire's transformative effects on 'European' development over the Long 13th Century (see Chapter 3).[25] Hence, developmentally differentiated societies constantly impact upon one another's geosocial development and reproduction, which in turn instigates various forms of combined development. From this perspective, social development is conceived as ineluctably *multilinear, causally polycentric,* and *co-constitutive* by virtue of its very interconnectedness.

In the premodern world, unevenness was expressed and articulated across the various dimensions and planes of internal differentiation within the ontological whole of world-societal development. The natural bases of unevenness thus lie in the ecologically given conditions that originally confronted the human species. Here we find one side of the 'double relationship' examined by Marx and Engels in *The German Ideology*.[26]

In the first instance, humans must produce and reproduce the means of their material subsistence to survive,[27] entering into an interactively transformational relationship with their natural and social surroundings, shaping and reconstituting these conditions in the process. In early history, the ecologically given conditions confronting the human species formed the starting point of their development. 'The way in which men [sic] produce their means of subsistence', Marx and Engels wrote, 'depends first of all on the nature of the means of subsistence they actually find in existence and have to reproduce'. Thus, '[a]ll historical writing must set out from these natural bases and their modification in the course of history through the action of men'.[28] Commenting on this passage, Justin Rosenberg notes how this 'natural world is not only the physical foundation of human life; it is also ... the largest single source of uneven development'. As he goes on:

> Climatic, topographic and ecological differentiation across geographical space offered an enormous variety of habitats to which human groups adapted as they spread outwards from their East African home .... Temporally too, the earth was (and is) a dynamic phenomenon, uneven across time. ... Thus the process of

peopling the earth, largely accomplished by HGBs [hunter-gatherer bands], was necessarily uneven in both space and time. This unevenness was expressed in (and further compounded by) an 'enormous variation' in human socio-ecological adaptation. And that ...was heavily consequential for the course of development both locally and globally.[29]

The starting point of human development was then constituted by this nature-generated uneven, spatial topography from which all specific 'societies' subsequently developed. What is more, the ecological variations across geographical space worked to promote further processes of internal differentiation. In the case of Russia – or more precisely, the networks of social relations forming what is now called Russia – the 'natural-historical conditions' (above all, Russia's 'less than favourable geographical situation' standing between Europe and Asia) were the initial causes for the 'comparative primitiveness and slowness' of its social development, stunting class formation processes and their relations with the state.[30]

But human development, even in its earliest stages, was not simply uneven but also combined, as it continually contained a multiplicity of differentially developing communities that came to interact with one another in causally significant ways in their own collective reproduction. Take the example of HGBs during the Palaeolithic period. Inter-band relations were crucial to each band's survival. HGBs could not survive 'as isolated units'[31] as they 'depended for their biological reproduction on exogamous interaction with other bands, extending networks of consanguinity which provided the basis for periodic gatherings, shared language and security against environmental stress'.[32] It was only through the uneven and interactive nature of social multiplicity entailed in such reproductive relations that political multiplicity – that is, proto-state formations – emerged in the first place.[33] Hence, Marx and Engels's 'double relationship' was, from the very start, circumscribed by social relations that were both uneven and combined. Reframed from such a perspective, this universal characteristic of human development (the double relationship) may be reconceptualised as ontologically plural and interactive: that is, as a *triple relationship* spanning from: (1) nature to (2) the social to (3) the intersocietal.[34]

As societies became more complex in their development, geographical factors would become progressively less fundamental in shaping the course of their co-evolution. '[H]uman development', as Robert W. Cox put it, 'loosens the determining influence of geography'.[35] There were, in other words, emergent layers and axes of the unevenness of human development that would be articulated through a multiplicity of state forms, social relations, and ideological and cultural institutions. We examine the specificities of these forms in the chapters that follow – nomadic, tributary, feudal and so on. One of the central claims of *How the West Came to Rule* is that capitalism emerged from within and through these antecedent processes of unevenness. From its inception, capitalism's expansion thereby took a 'combined' character, fusing with the plurality of existing sociological forms through its internationally mediated emergence. In so doing, distinctly capitalist processes would come to progressively gain control over this extant unevenness, reconstituting its fundamental quality as it unified the various instances and forms of uneven development into a single, causally integrated, world-historical totality.[36]

Combination

Combination, conceived at the most abstract level, refers to the ways in which the internal relations of any given society are determined by their interactive relations with other developmentally differentiated societies, while the very interactivity of these relations produces amalgamated sociopolitical institutions, socio-economic systems, ideologies and material practices melding the native and foreign, the 'advanced' and 'backward', within any given social formation. Bringing out the relational character of these developmental differentiations in societies, Trotsky argued that 'from the universal law of unevenness thus derives another law ... the law of *combined development*'.[37] As with unevenness, combination has a strong empirical referent: multiple societies do not simply exist hermetically side by side, but interactively coexist, which by necessity (and to varying degrees) determines their collective social and geopolitical development and reproduction.[38]

Trotsky's sociological explanations are consequently imbued with processes in which societies draw 'together different stages of the journey', combining the spatiotemporally variegated experiences of societies into unstable amalgams of the new and old.[39] In Trotsky's *History of the Russian Revolution*, we find numerous examples in which the more 'backward' Russia attempted to developmentally catch up with a more advanced Europe by making use of Europe's existing developmental achievements. The 'privilege' of Russia's backwardness entailed a 'skipping over intermediate steps' of development, ensuring attempts at catch-up did not follow the same paths of antecedent developments.[40] Hence, 'historical backwardness does not imply a simple reproduction of the development of advanced countries, England or France, with a delay of one, two, or three centuries', Trotsky wrote, but 'engenders an entirely new "combined" social formation in which the latest conquests of capitalist technique and structure root themselves into relations of feudal or pre-feudal barbarism, transforming and subjecting them and creating peculiar relations of classes'.[41]

The outcome of this geopolitically interactive process was the creation of entirely new forms and modalities of development, producing 'amalgam[s] of archaic with more contemporary forms'.[42] Such combinations served to 'smash the limited boundaries of classification', thus 'revealing the real connections and consecutiveness of a living process'.[43] In this respect, combination belies any stagist model of development, as the effects of the amalgamation of different modes of production within social formations are sociologically transformed into more than the sum of their parts. It would therefore be a mistake to conceive of any form of combined development as a kind of ideal-type with which others can be compared and contrasted. Rather, there is no uniform type of combined development, but only a multiplicity of differentiated forms and trajectories.

Trotsky's concept of combined development thus dispenses with all notions of 'deviant' or 'aberrational' forms of societies and their development. Here, however, it is important to note that while they are usually rooted in the interlacing and overcharged fusion of different modes of production (feudal, tributary, nomadic, capitalist and so on), the effects of combined development suffuse every aspect of society. It is much more than an economic phenomenon, but captures the totality of relations constitutive of a social order as a whole. As Neil Davidson puts it, 'The archaic and modern, the settled and disruptive, overlap, fuse, and merge in all aspects of the social formations concerned … in entirely new and unstable ways'.[44] By deploying the concept of combined development, Trotsky was able to uncover the contradictory and complex 'concentration of many determinations'[45] which ultimately led to a trajectory of development in which proletarian revolution first took place in Russia – economically the most 'backward' and ideologically most reactionary state in Europe at the time.

Part and parcel to these forms of sociological amalgamation are processes and methods of substitutionism. In the first instance, Trotsky employed the term 'substitutionism' to critique Lenin's proposed reforms to party organisation in 1904: 'the organisation of the party substitutes itself for the party as a whole; then the Central Committee substitutes itself for the organisation; and finally the "dictator" substitutes himself for the Central Committee'.[46] Trotsky's prescient remarks well captured the bureaucratic processes ultimately leading to the degeneration of the Bolshevik Revolution as it slowly devolved into the personal dictatorship of Josef Stalin.[47] After 1905, however, Trotsky appears to have broadened the scope of the term (albeit implicitly) in coming to identify it with various forms of 'replacement' agents and institutions involved in spearheading capitalist processes of development in late-industrialising societies.

Examining the meagre ways by which the Tsarist regime sought to solve Russia's agrarian problem, for example, Trotsky wrote of how the 'solution of the problems of one class by another is one of those combined methods natural to backward countries'.[48] In other words, the attempts to solve the agrarian problem were not pursued by an indigenous capitalist class or even by the natural operation of the capitalist mode of production, for both these conditions were lacking in half-feudal Russia. So the Tsarist regime had to 'substitute' itself for the putative tasks of a capitalist class corresponding to earlier processes of capitalist modernization. Referring to this extended remit of the concept which sought to capture 'a much wider and multifaceted phenomenon, intrinsic to combined development' operating in 'the political, intellectual, ideological, economic and bureaucratic spheres', Kamran Matin writes of how:

> substitution involves the mobilization of various replacements, native and foreign, in backward polities, for the agency, institutions, instruments, materials or methods of earlier processes of capitalist modernization in West European ountries, a process in which the 'threatening western foe becomes a teacher'.

Hence, substitutionism 'necessarily involves and generated amalgamated forms that are dynamically *tension-prone*'.[49]

It is precisely these 'dynamically tension-prone' elements integral to any combined development that we conceive as 'contradictions of sociological amalgamation': the inorganic melding of native and foreign agencies, institutions, practices, ideologies and socio-economic systems, resulting in time-compressed, accelerated developmental transformations 'assum[ing] the form of terrible convulsions and drastic changes of former conceptions'.[50]

In the capitalist epoch, the overlapping and fusion of different temporalities – of different modes of productions – characteristic of such sociological amalgamations finds some affinities with Ernest Bloch's concept of 'nonsynchronism' (*Ungleichzeitigkeit*): the 'simultaneity of the non-simultaneous' (*Gleichzeitigkeit des Ungleichzeitigen*). 'The objectively nonsynchronous is that which is far from and alien to the present', as Bloch writes. This may in turn involve some forms and degrees of agency in which capital employs:

> that which is nonsynchronously contrary, if not indeed disparate, as a distraction from its own strictly present-day contradictions; it uses the antagonism of a still living past as a means of separation and struggle against the future that is dialectically giving birth to itself in the capitalist antagonism.[51]

While imbued with all kinds of problematic 'historicist' assumptions (in Chakrabarty's sense of the term), the focus on these agential features of a combined development that Bloch discusses in terms of 'nonsynchronism' are significant. For whether the 'whip of external necessity' translates into a privilege or disadvantage of backwardness – and relatedly, the degrees by which the political and ideological effects are progressive or reactionary – is dependent on the outcome of social conflicts both within the ruling class and between the ruling and subordinate classes. Thus, as Ben Selwyn highlights, it is of 'great importance' to examine 'how contending social classes shape and respond to development processes through struggles', as the 'outcomes of these struggles impact significantly upon process and outcomes of late development. And, because the outcomes of these struggles cannot be predicted in advance, neither can the process of uneven and combined development'.[52] To this extent, the sociopolitical and economic effects of uneven and combined development are partly and necessarily *indeterminate*: we cannot say in advance exactly how the developmental pressures of intersocietal relations will impact on any given society without an analysis of the changing balance and struggle of class forces (in other words, human agency), among other factors. And that changing balance is itself shaped and partly determined by the wider intersocietal milieu.

This point regarding the necessity of an agential analysis as a required component of any satisfactory employment of uneven and combined development is an important one, as it directly challenges a common criticism of the theory as overly structuralist, and thus deterministic, with little or no room for political agency.[53] While the role and direction of agency is always a partly indeterminate, political process, it is nevertheless not a 'structure-less' one: that is to say, it can be explained retrodictively by invoking structural properties. One of the great benefits of the theory of uneven and combined development is how it explains sociologically differentiated forms of agency, contradicting any predetermined unilinear readings of sociohistorical development: an explanation of why and how '[t]he tasks of one class are shouldered off upon another'.[54] Hence, in challenging such charges of 'structuralism', Michael Burawoy draws attention to the intrinsically agential aspects of Trotsky's theory, which captures the 'accumulation of micro-processes' in explaining molecular forms of social change and transformation. In this sense, it is carrying 'forward Marx's project of establishing the micro-foundations of a macro-sociology, of understanding how individuals make history but not necessarily in ways of their own choosing'.[55]

More generally, at the heart of such criticisms there seems to be a worry that casting uneven and combined development as a 'general abstraction' evacuates concrete human praxis, rendering it an 'overly abstract and contentless register'[56] devoid of any substantive theoretical explanatory capacity. And, indeed, if left at the level of a 'general abstraction', this would surely pose a problem: decontextualised from any conception of historically distinct social structures, the precise scales, mechanisms and qualitative forms of unevenness and combination – to say nothing of the historically specific dynamics of political agency they give rise to – could hardly be illuminated. Yet, as detailed below, this is certainly not the intention of the theory, which proceeds through a series of descending levels of abstraction, further approximating, and reconstituting in thought, empirical reality along each step of the way.

The emphasis placed in this work on the structural constraints and enabling properties of uneven and combined development, therefore, in no way seeks to erase the critical role of agents and human praxis in processes of large-scale social transformation and change. Quite the contrary: as later chapters will demonstrate, our purpose is to re-excavate the 'lost history' of the multitude of agential processes that – whether intentionally, but more often than not unintentionally – led to and conditioned the rise of distinctly capitalist production relations over the early modern period.

In particular, we aim to explore the – at times – decisive role of non-European agency in directly engaging with and subverting Eurocentric conceptions of development. From the hugely significant agency of the Mongolians over the Long 13th Century (Chapter 3) to that of the Ottomans during the Long 16th Century (Chapter 4) to the multiplicity of societies making up Southeast Asia in the 17th century (Chapter 7) – through all these examples, among others, we seek to offer an analysis of the rise of capitalism that pays resolute attention to the plurality of ways in which the structural determinations emanating from both within and outside societies interactively developing alongside one another, came to be interpreted, shaped, and often reconstituted through concrete political agency and praxis. We aim to systematically disclose the socially 'thick' relations of interconnection and co-constitution between the 'West' and 'the Rest' in their joint, if uneven, making of the modern capitalist world.

These points regarding the need for a non-Eurocentric, agent-sensitive approach to the study of capitalism's origins are further borne out in considering how we might reconceptualise the role of the forces of production in the transition to capitalism from the perspective of uneven and combined development. For the diffusion of more 'advanced' scientific ideas, organisational forms and technologies from 'East' to 'West' was an important factor in European societies' ability to reap a 'privilege of backwardness', constituting a key precondition for the eventual emergence of capitalist social relations within them (see Chapters 3 and 4). Yet it is necessary to emphasise that such processes of diffusion did not take place in a linear or even cumulative manner. Innovations in certain locales are not replicated (to borrow Trotsky's term) 'slavishly' in all contexts, but can be appropriated, adapted, reconfigured and repurposed by different people, classes and organisations, in variegated ways. This is not to argue that productive forces are neutral, but simply to emphasise that the specific outcomes of their development are not essential or preordained. They are determining, but not deterministic, 'biased but ambivalent'.[57] Productive forces that push forward certain developments or benefit certain groups in particular contexts can have very different consequences in other contexts, for other groups. The innovations of the Industrial Revolution that solidified ruling class power in Britain led to social revolution in Russia. What matters then is not the primacy of productive forces, but how their adoption and adaptation is plugged into and related to other aspects of a social assemblage.

In this respect, the development of productive forces cannot be understood as uniform or equalising, but multilinear and uneven. The emphasis on multilinearity suggests we should avoid any ontologically singular conception of productive forces as pertaining to a single enterprise or a single society, hermetically sealed off from others. The variegated nature of productive forces (including labour processes, organisations of production, tools and technologies) should alert us to the possibility that this multiplicity can be 'combined' – they can be integrated with and interrelated to each other – across a wider intersocietal plane. This, we believe, better captures the spirit of what 'productive forces' denote: 'the way in which the different means of production are combined in the act of production itself'. In turn, it opens the possibility of theorising historical developments via the heuristic of uneven and combined productive forces.

For example, we demonstrate in Chapters 3 and 4 how the tributary practice of 'caging' allowed for the absorption of the techniques, capacities and organisational forms of various societies into an integrated system of ruling class reproduction. In Chapters 5 and 7, we further analyse how capitalism was built on the combination of a multiplicity of labour processes in various locales stretching from Barbados to Banda, and back to London and Amsterdam. In short, productive forces should be conceived as uneven and combined, wherein the intersocietal – rather than the nation-state – forms the proper unit of analysis.

In these different ways, uneven and combined development offers a cogent means of theoretically explaining the differentiated social forms and historically distinct agencies emerging from a single, unified process of sociohistorical development, as well the geosocial effects of their interactive differences. Moreover, it is important to note that while the dynamics of combined development were revealed to Trotsky most sharply and violently in later-developing societies, he nonetheless also viewed these phenomena as applicable to even the most economically 'advanced' capitalist state of his time, the United States. In an instance of what we might call a 'perpetuated' form of combined development, Trotsky wrote:

> In America we have another kind of combined development. We have the most advanced industrial development together with the most backward – for all classes – ideology. The internal colonization … was the basis on which the retarded consciousness of the workers existed.[58]

On this basis, it was possible for Trotsky to advocate the strategy of 'permanent revolution' for the Black Nationalist movement for self-determination in the United States.[59] Trotsky's identification of these combined paths of development in some of the most advanced capitalist societies of his time (the United States and also Germany) is particularly significant given the tendency of contemporary scholars to portray Trotsky's theory as solely confined to explaining late capitalist developers (more on this below).[60]

Seeing Through a Prism Darkly? Uneven and Combined Development beyond the Eurocentric Gaze

The theory of uneven and combined development offers a potentially useful perspective in overcoming the many problems and pitfalls of the Eurocentric analyses characterising so many extant theoretical approaches to the origins of capitalism. As our employment of 'unevenness' and 'combination' suggests, we must go beyond any 'historicist mode of thinking', as Dipesh Chakrabarty terms it, that conceives of development as the 'secular, empty, and homogenous time of history'.[61] Hence, against Gurminder Bhambra's criticism that uneven and combined development theoretically reproduces the strong stagism of Enlightenment thinking,[62] it rather presupposes stagism in order to scramble, subvert and transcend it.[63] The notion of 'stages' is deployed precisely to counter stagist thinking, as Trotsky continually emphasised in his diatribes against the Menshevik position that the socialist revolution in Tsarist Russia had to wait for the bourgeois stage to complete itself. More radically still, Trotsky's political strategy of 'permanent revolution' represented 'a fundamental *rejection* of the notion of stages as such in the definition of a qualitatively new type of revolution'.[64]

Underlying Bhambra's critique, however, is a more fundamental point about the concept of 'development' itself. This might be reformulated in terms of the following question: Can any conceptualisation of human change and transformation from the perspective of development (uneven, combined or whatever) escape certain historicist assumptions? This point is brought out in Meera Sabaratnam's searching critique of various historical sociological approaches to IR,[65] including the theory of uneven and combined development as formulated by Justin Rosenberg.[66] Although she claims that the theory makes a 'critical contribution to wrestling the notion of "development" away from a methodologically nationalist' foundation, it nonetheless remains an 'unsatisfactory solution to the issues created by using the idea of "development" as a natural benchmark for understanding human societies and their relationships'.[67] As the 'central problematic of capitalist modernity' and the 'founding question of historical sociology as a project', the concept of development comes packed with a number of normative assumptions about what is meaningful and (causally) significant in understanding human societies.[68] The problematic of 'development' thus tends to conceptualise the polities of the Global South as 'subordinate articulation[s] of a normalised capitalist modernity that finds its full expression in the contemporary West'. This reproduces a 'developmentalised framing of human history' and 'a politics of "developmentality" in the space of former empires'.[69]

However, we consider Trotsky's notion of 'combined development' useful precisely because it subverts many of the normative and historicist assumptions that Sabaratnam argues are inherent to the category of development. Indeed, the concept of combination denotes that there has never existed any pure or 'normal' model of development; each and every society's development has always been 'overdetermined'[70] by its interactions with others, creating a plurality of variegated sociological amalgamations. The very unevenness and combination of historical development thus resists any kind of 'stylised and abstracted' conceptions of European history – or any history, for that matter – that can be used as the privileged 'benchmark' to normatively judge or comparatively contrast with others.

What is more, the course that European development took throughout the historical periods we examine below was continually conditioned by non-European structural determinations and agents. The multiple histories of non-European societies and the 'causal' processes emerging from them were, from the very outset, inscribed in the generative grammar of modern European development. In this sense, any notion of a 'normalised capitalist modernity that finds its full expression in the contemporary West' is a pure myth. Each and every instantiation of capitalist modernity – from England to Germany, to Japan, to Bolivia, to Senegal – was, so to speak, a 'bastard birth'.[71] Indeed, if we are to take Marx's 'absolute historicism' (in Gramsci's sense of the term)[72] seriously, 'pure' developmental forms do not exist. This destabilises normative claims about any singular developmental model – whether it be England's economic development or France's political development, to take just two oft-cited examples in comparative studies – as the benchmark or standard by which other developmental trajectories are to be judged.[73]

This in turn has radical implications for how comparative historical sociological analyses can be pursued fruitfully. It requires a methodological shift to something akin to Philip McMichael's notion of 'incorporated comparison', in which specific instances of sociohistorical development are dialectically related to one another as constitutive moments of a broader world-historical process.[74] The 'whole' thereby crystallises via a comparative analysis of its 'parts' as moments of a differentially developing, interactive 'self-forming' totality.[75] Hence, 'variations in the actual process whereby the same historical development manifests itself in different countries', Antonio Gramsci wrote, 'have to be related not only to the differing combinations of internal relations with the different countries, but also to the differing international relations'.[76]

Following the above analysis, one might find a potential contradiction in our employment and juxtaposition of such concepts as 'advanced' and 'backward', 'modern' and 'archaic', so central to Trotsky's works. Such terms are indeed intrinsically problematic as conventionally used and understood in popular and scholarly discourses. According to Baruch Knei-Paz, Trotsky's own use of the term 'backwardness' was not intended as a 'moral judgement', but instead sought to demarcate a 'clear social and historical uniqueness' which the terms 'less developed' or 'under-developed' do not convey.[77] Of course, this is easier said than done.

Irrespective of how Trotsky employed the terms, our own use of such categories as 'advanced' and 'backward' is of a rather specific kind. They denote asymmetrical relations or imbalances of power ((geo)political, economic, ideological), within and between societies, in the ways and forms by which ruling classes reproduce themselves. For example, a social formation such as the Habsburg or Ottoman Empire during the 16th century might be considered more 'advanced' than, say, the emerging capitalist societies of the United Provinces or England, since the modalities of ruling class reproduction in the former were relatively more powerful, strong and stable. This was not only because of the geopolitical and military power differentials between these two sets of feudal-tributary and nascent capitalist societies, but also possibly due to the 'staying power' of their dominant ideologies and political institutions. Our conception of these terms thus rests on the standards set by the dominant mode of production of the epoch.

By analogy, the concept of 'class' also refers to power differentials (ruling and ruled, exploiter and exploited), expressed as a sociopolitical or economic – and not a normative or developmental – hierarchy. In the capitalist mode of production, for example, the capitalist class is not temporally or normatively more 'advanced' than the working class. But it is more 'advanced' in terms of its possession of power; if it were otherwise, the capitalist class would be incapable of oppressing and exploiting subaltern classes. Thus, we employ the categories of 'advanced/backward' in this sense (unless otherwise stated) to capture the various asymmetrical and uneven power relations.[78] As such, our reconceptualisation of the terms shares some affinities with Sabaratnam's proposed alternative concepts 'rich' and 'poor' or 'possessing/dispossessed'. Whichever categories one prefers, they all allow for, as Sabaratnam puts it, 'a relational understanding of material conditions in the world without labelling them as deviant from the model of modernity'.[79]

Where we see an advantage in the use of uneven and combined development, however, is in its potential to extend the historical scope of analysis beyond the capitalist mode of production (in which categories of rich-possessing/poor-dispossessed are markers of power hierarchies), to non-capitalist contexts, and the very making of capitalism itself. For while the categories of 'advanced' and 'backward' only take on their full force under specifically capitalist conditions, their empirical referents (asymmetrical and uneven power relations) undoubtedly held in preceding epochs. This was illustrated in the widespread awe and fear that the more 'advanced' Ottoman Empire conjured in the minds of so many 16th-century Europeans (see Chapter 4). Hence, in order to truly subvert the 'pristine' and 'pure' self-image of European capitalism that Sabaratnam identifies as so problematic, we need a conceptual framework that is not beholden to the capitalist epoch.

Such a historical extension of uneven and combined development would appear crucial to claiming its non-Eurocentric credentials. For, as John M. Hobson suggests, the concept of uneven and combined development, insofar as it is exclusively identified with capitalism, is no less guilty of conflating 'the international' with exclusively 'intra-European relations', falling prey to the typical Eurocentric assumptions of 'Western priority and Eastern passivity'.[80] Similarly, Bhambra suggests that for all of theory's focus on societal difference, its very origins remains wedded to a Eurocentric conception of capitalism derived from the Enlightenment conception of stadial development.[81] For Burak Tansel, so long as uneven and combined development is considered specific to capitalist modernity, and this capitalist modernity is attributed to European origins, then the theory appears no different to the diffusionist claims of modernisation theory and WST.[82] In short, without problematising the origins of capitalism in Europe, the non-West remains excluded as an empirically significant yet theoretically secondary entity.[83] For uneven and combined development to simply invoke intersocietal processes is therefore not enough. It must also be capable of establishing an alternative conception of the making of capitalism, one that includes the historical (and theoretical) significance of non-European societies as active agents in the process. We turn to this question of the historical generalisability of uneven and combined development next.

Trotsky beyond Trotsky? Uneven and Combined Development before Capitalism

Thus far we have proceeded in using uneven and combined development as (unproblematically) operating across time and space. However, in doing so, we must be careful not to fall into the kind of 'tempocentric ahistoricism' so common to mainstream IR theories, such as realism, in which a reified nation-statist ontology of contemporary world politics is projected back in time as the suprahistorical essence of 'the international' in general.[84] There is indeed a similar danger in using uneven and combined development as a 'transhistorical' general abstraction[85] that projects back in time what may in fact be the historically specific characteristics of the capitalist mode of production.

This has been a criticism explicitly raised by various scholars, who have argued that Trotsky only used the concept in this more temporally delimited sense (that is, within capitalism).[86] More importantly, they claim that to extend uneven and combined development beyond capitalism would end up providing mere descriptive claims rather than explanatory ones.[87] As Sam Ashman puts it critiquing Rosenberg's work in particular:

To state that societies exist in the plural is mere description that neither helps explain the dynamic (or 'actual modalities') of combination between these societies... nor offers any explanation of unevenness or of the differences between societies. This is precisely because general (transhistoric) abstractions do not have explanatory power (Marx 1973 [1953]). To the extent that something akin to U&CD [uneven and combined development] can be discerned in pre-capitalist modes of production, we can only illuminate such a phenomenon with a theory of the particular mode of production in question.[88]

To help us address the important issues raised by Ashman, we pick through three different ways uneven and combined development can be used. First, it can be seen as an ontology of human development – that is, as a general, abstract set of determinants highlighting a general condition confronted by all societies irrespective of historical context. Second, it can act as a methodology or set of epistemological coordinates, derived from the preceding basic ontological claim, that informs what historical material may be deemed ('causally') significant, and how that material relates to each other. However, these general ontological and epistemological assumptions taken on their own do not constitute a theory as such – at least not in the specifically Marxist sense. That is, theory is only possible at the more historically specific level at which the ontological and epistemological coordinates of study are connected to more determinate, concrete categories.

For example, Marx did not provide a general theory of production or a theory of modes of production in general, but rather a theory of the capitalist mode of production. In this respect, we do not consider theory and history to be distinct; they are mutually intertwined and reinforcing. In this theoretical respect, third, uneven and combined development also refers to and theorises concrete historical processes, be they epochal or conjunctural. In other words, we may speak of a theory (or theories) of uneven and combined development in this more historically delimited sense: that is, in terms corresponding to specific epochs or conjunctures characterised by different modes of production that animate the broader dynamics of such historical temporalities. Moreover, it would also comprise the surplus of determinations deriving from the interactively generated (that is, intersocietally produced) combinations of modes of production and social formations. We consider it viable and indeed useful to deploy uneven and combined development in these related, but distinct, ways and encourage readers to keep in mind these distinctions and the different contexts in which they are used.

More Questions than Answers: Method, Abstraction and Historicity in Marx's Thought

As Frederic Jameson once exclaimed, 'Always historicize!' is 'the one absolute and we can even say "transhistorical" imperative of all dialectical thought'.[89]

Does Jameson's injunction necessarily translate into a denial of the use of 'tran-shistoricals' in Marx's own methodology? We believe not, as a number of studies have well demonstrated that transhistorical abstractions did in fact play quite an important role in Marx's work.[90] As Robert Wess notes in a discussion of Marx's method outlined in the *Grundrisse*, Marx 'insists, at the very outset, that to avoid the bourgeois misconception of capitalism as "natural", one must para-doxically begin on the transhistorical level, with production in general...[as] *the transhistorical renders visible the concrete historicity of capitalism*'.[91] Explaining his method of abstraction, which begins with the 'general, abstract determinants which obtain in more or less all forms of societies', Marx wrote that:

> although the simpler category may have existed historically before the more concrete, it can achieve its full (intensive and extensive) development precisely in a combined form of society, while the more concrete category was more fully developed in a less developed form of society.[92]

In keeping with this method of abstraction, Marx worked with a number of trans-historical categories: 'use-value', 'concrete labour' and 'production in general'. Marx's use of these transhistorical categories was, however, strikingly different from their employment within much contemporary mainstream political economy and IR. In realist theories of IR, for example, a theoretical abstrac-tion such as 'anarchy' takes the form of the primary *explanans* of the argument, from which all other relevant concepts (such as the 'balance of power', 'national interest' and 'security dilemma') are deduced. From this perspective, *the abstraction forms the theory itself.*

In contrast, for Marx, a general abstraction functions as an inbuilt assump-tion: the existence of a concrete general condition whose historically specific form has to be accounted for by still further *explanans*. General abstractions are, in other words, *question-begging*. They serve the purpose of isolating particular objects of study, which in turn raise analytical questions that can only be answered through their connection to other abstracted moments and concretised through their historical contextualisation and analysis.

Marx's explanations took place not by the reduction of social reality into a simplified and elegant abstraction, but by the expansion and complexification of the object under study. Hence, again in contrast to the 'bourgeois' method which seeks to identify a unitary essence in the object(s) of study (the abstraction), for Marx an abstraction cannot be judged heuristically useful by what elements of concrete reality it successfully excludes, but by what elements of concrete reality are opened up for further exploration. In short, rather than positing abstrac-tions (such as anarchy) as the *explanans* of theory, general abstractions need to be conceived as *explananda*: things that require further explanation. Used in this way, general abstractions are best understood as 'a guiding thread, an orientation for empirical and historical research, not a theoretical substitute for it'.[93]

As such, Marx's abstractions do not provide, on their own, the concepts required for theory.[94] Nor do they act as axioms from which secondary and tertiary concepts are derived, where concretisation takes place in a unilinear fashion from the abstract to concrete. Instead, they provide the basic ontological presuppositions needed for more determinant, historically specific categories to be brought to light.

In *Capital Volume I*, for example, the commodity is understood as a bearer of both the general, transhistorical need to produce 'use-values' and the historically specific conditions under which such production occurs – the production of 'exchange-values'. Similarly, 'labour' is at once conceptualised as 'concrete labour' (the general feature of all human labour) and 'abstract labour' (the historically specific condition under which concrete labour takes place in capitalism). Marx thus claims that the general abstraction of 'concrete labour' 'expresses an immeasurably ancient relation valid in all forms of society, [which] nevertheless achieves practical truth as an abstraction only as a category of the most modern society'.[95]

Here again we see how Marx employs 'transhistorical' abstractions to bring out the very historicity of their more concrete and specific forms in different epochs. Marx was not seeking to build a transhistorical theory of labour or use-value, for example, but instead sought to introduce these concepts as question-begging presuppositions in his construction of a historically specific theory of the capitalist mode of production. As such, the contents of categories are not rigidly fixed, but 'developed in their historical or logical process of formation'.[96]

The method required to do this involves viewing the object of study through different historically specific contextual prisms, different analytical vantage points or 'windows'. The view from any singular vantage point will tend to be 'flat and lack perspective'. Therefore, it is necessary to analyse the concrete from a multiplicity of different abstractions; that is, to deploy *multiple vantage points* in order to disclose the complexity of social relations and determinations in any given historical context. By moving across different vantage points in this way, those elements formerly hidden by any one-sided abstraction will come into view, thus reconstituting the object of study by adding 'greater depth and perspective'.[97]

In short, Marx 'explained' by carving open analytical and theoretical spaces that would necessitate the introduction of – and relation to – additional explanatory determinations, derived from alternative vantage points. Hence, across *Capital* as a whole, Marx repeatedly changed register and (re)analysed social relations through different conceptual prisms, moving from the singular capitalist enterprise,[98] to circulation,[99] to many capitals.[100] In *Capital*, each analytical shift of this kind served to 'destroy the simplicity' of anterior vantage points and 'complicate their phenomenology' by bringing them into interrelation with other abstracted moments.[101]

Through the disclosure of the relations between these expanding sets of abstracted moments, the multiplicity of concrete conditions and determinations pertaining to the capitalist mode was unearthed and reconstituted in thought. In like fashion, we argue that uneven and combined development can be utilised in a similar (though not identical) way in filling out a distinctively historical materialist theory of 'the international'. Used in this way, uneven and combined development is not a theory in itself. It is, rather, a methodological fix – or more precisely, a 'progressive problem-shift' – within the broader research programme of historical materialism.[102] The why, how and in what forms development is uneven and combined in different historical periods can only be explicated by more concrete categories and determinations accompanying a mode of production-centred analysis.

As our exposition demonstrates, the *ontology* of uneven and combined development postulates that historical processes are always the outcome of a *multiplicity of spatially diverse nonlinear causal chains* that combine in any given conjuncture. What this compels historians and sociologists to do methodologically is to analyse history from a multiplicity of different spatiotemporal vantage points – or overlapping spatiotemporal 'vectors' of uneven and combined development[103] – in order to uncover these causal chains. In this schema, an emphasis on the origins of capitalism in Europe, or the English countryside à la Brenner, would constitute one of many spatiotemporal vectors of uneven and combined development – one that must be complemented and combined with other determinations analysed from alternative vantage points.[104] It would be one that is, in turn, related to a number of extra-European determinations bound up in the histories of colonialism, slavery and the Asian merchant trades, to name but a few of the processes examined in the following pages. In short, uneven and combined development stresses, indeed necessitates, a genuinely 'internationalist historiography'[105] of the origins of capitalism. We now explicate how these ontological and methodological pointers would be generative of a *theory* – or more precisely *theories* – of uneven and combined development.

Modes of Production Versus Uneven and Combined Development? A False Antithesis

Ashman's injunction to contextualise any historically determinant form of uneven and combined development through a 'theory of the particular mode of production in question and its relations and dynamics' is exactly how we seek to employ the concept in the pages that follow.[106] Indeed, as Rosenberg explicitly states regarding the use of uneven and combined development as a 'general abstraction', the concept 'cannot furnish the particularities of any given mode of production, which ... are necessary for the general abstraction to be "cashed in"'.[107] We are in complete agreement with this type of approach.[108]

While uneven and combined development can indeed be conceived as a transhistorical phenomenon – or more precisely, a *transmodal* one – it must remain sensitive to the massive qualitative differences between its various iterations in any given mode of production. We have come to prefer the term 'transmodal', as the 'transhistorical' can be – and has been – interpreted as conceiving of uneven and combined development as a kind of 'suprasocial', ahistorical phenomenon that replaces, rather than complements, a mode of production-centred theory of development.[109] To say uneven and combined development functions in a transmodal sense therefore highlights the ways in which it only operates *in* and *through* historically distinct modes of production, which provide the explanations for the specific dynamics, scales and qualitative forms of unevenness and combination. The incorporation of uneven and combined development as a 'general abstraction' into such a mode of production-based framework in turn offers a sensitivity to and theoretical internalisation of those intersocietal dimensions of causality which so often fall out of mode of production-based analyses or remain external to their theoretical premises. This method of analysis consequently demands the reconstruction of historical materialism's basic theoretical premises in a way that incorporates these interactive, differentiated and multilinear – that is, intersocietal – aspects of human development as a whole.[110]

In this book, we examine the historically distinct dynamics, scales and forms of uneven and combined development in no less than five modes of production: the nomadic, tributary, feudal, slave-based and capitalist. As we demonstrate, each of these modes generated very different forms of unevenness and combination, belying any kind of suprahistorical theorisation. Moreover, the various interactions between these modally differentiated societies produced a multiplicity of variegated sociological amalgamations, representing entirely new modalities of development whose 'laws of motion' were more than the sum of their parts, defying any neat modal classificatory schemas. Such sociological combinations were not either/or but both and more.

Following this perspective, uneven and combined development's distinct causal determinations, articulated and expressed through intersocietal relations, are in every instance historically specific to and variable across any given mode of production. In other words, a theory of any given mode of production must be incorporated into an understanding of the particular form of unevenness and combination, as the specific articulations, scales and dynamics of such a phenomenon will, without it, remain entirely inexplicable. At the same time, what the 'general abstraction' of uneven and combined development provides is a methodological sensitivity to those intersocietal dimensions of development that are either entirely ignored or only externally related to the emergence and reproductive dynamics of any given mode of production. The specific theorisations we offer – nomadic, tributary, feudal, slave, and capitalist – will be provided in the substantive historical engagements that follow, not least because the theoretical articulation of uneven and combined development can only take place, we argue, in and through historical study.

Conclusion: Towards an 'Internationalist Historiography' of Capitalism

As shown in Chapter 1, the debate on the transition to capitalism has been marked by the dual intersecting problems of abstracting capitalism's development from the intersocietal conditions in which it is inherently embedded (the coexistence and interaction of a multiplicity of differentiated societies) and the concomitant focus on Europe as the prime mover of sociohistorical change and transformation. This led to the universalisation of Europe as the 'originary and privileged space of modernity'.[111] Directly engaging these two problems in the proper study of capitalism's emergence, this chapter has offered the theory of uneven and combined development in furnishing a more 'internationalist', non-Eurocentric framework.

We have argued that uneven and combined development is best understood in three related yet distinct ways. First, it operates as an ontology that fundamentally reconstitutes a materialist conception of history by incorporating non-identity and multiplicity – unevenness – into its premises. From this first feature arises the second – a methodology which emphasises the need to study historical sociology from a multiplicity of spatiotemporally diverse vectors of uneven and combined development. We argued that these first two features do not, on their own, constitute theory. The latter can only be generated by linking more abstract categories to more concrete, determinant, historically specific ones. That is, it is only at the level of any given mode of production that we can speak of theory. But we have also argued that uneven and combined development goes beyond mode of production analysis by capturing the surplus of determinations created by the interaction of different modes of production or social formations. Finally, we argued that due to the inseparability of theory and history, uneven and combined development also refers to concrete historical processes.

From these ontological and methodological pointers we now seek to 'cash in' our hitherto abstract discussion on the terrain of history. The next chapter proceeds with our historical investigation into the 'extra-European', intersocietal origins of capitalism over the *longue durée*. It begins with an analysis of the transformative impact of the Mongol Empire's expansion and the resulting westward spread of the Black Death on the rise of capitalism in Northwestern Europe over the Long 13th Century.

CHAPTER 3

The Long Thirteenth Century: Structural Crisis, Conjunctural Catastrophe

History is always written from the sedentary point of view and in the name of a unitary State apparatus, at least a possible one, even when the topic is nomads. What is lacking is a Nomadology, the opposite of a history.

Gilles Deleuze and Félix Guattari, 1980[1]

Introduction

The study of nomadic societies has typically been framed by a dichotomy between the state and nonstate, and a complementary stadial or evolutionist model of development. Positing a unidirectional historical movement from nomadic to sedentary societies, from tribal communities to modern states, this model has informed a broader historicist prioritisation of state over nonstate agents. In this evolutionist model, nomadic societies have functioned as the equivalent to 'primitive communities' in classical social theory – a comparative ideal-type against which modern forms of state and society can be defined.[2] Similarly, models of the 'segmentary tribe' that were developed as part of a wider ideology of 19th-century colonialism have often been superimposed onto the study of Eurasian nomads.[3] In the colonial period, the dominant image of the nomad was that of a 'simple people, fierce and free', living an 'exotic' life of 'barbaric lawlessness'.[4] In later historiography, nomadic empires were presented as 'arrested'[5] and 'static'[6] social forms that acted as 'brakes'[7] on development, and were therefore susceptible to 'degeneration'.[8] These images have subsequently been juxtaposed against the dynamism, civilisation, rationality, and social stratification that supposedly characterises the modern state.

With these rigid distinctions between 'civilised' and 'barbaric', the study of nomadism has shared (and continues to share) significant similarities with other forms of Orientalism and Eurocentrism. As such, it is worth remembering that the ideological construction of the 'primitive nomad' tallied with a history of violent subordination, annihilation and sedentarisation of nomadic communities. Through modern state formation and colonialism, nomads were subdued and subsumed into the codified and territorialised ambit of the modern state – a process that continues to this day.[9] For example, the supposed 'failure' of Native American nomads to enclose and replenish their land led many Europeans to conclude that their colonisation of the New World was legitimate (see Chapter 5).[10] Subsequently, the remnants of nomadic life in North America were systematically eradicated through state-led sedetarisation in the 19th century.[11] Similarly, the modernisation of the Ottoman state in the 19th century was accompanied by a policy of forced settlement of nomads, along with a legitimating ideology of 'Ottoman Orientalism' which painted nomads under its jurisdiction as 'savages' who required 'civilising'.[12] In the same period, the Russian Empire forced its nomadic population to settle as part of its attempts to modernise the creaking Tsarist state. This too was complemented by an ideological construction of the nomad as 'uncivilised'.[13]

The legacy of this subjection has reverberated through the social sciences, which have subsequently been relatively dismissive of the role played by nomadic people in the shaping of modern states and societies, both histori-cally and contemporaneously.[14] As Iver Neuman and Einar Wigen argue, the very assumption of nomadic 'backwardness' precluded the possibility of more 'advanced' sedentary states being positively influenced by nomads. Conse-quently 'even the most sophisticated contributions to the literature on state building do not touch base with the Eurasian steppe'.[15] In short, the historiog-raphy of nomads is marked by a persistent and, we argue, problematic *erasure of nomads* from the history of capitalist modernity.

This chapter aims to demonstrate that this exclusion is no longer sustain-able, and that an appreciation of the influence of the nomadic Mongol Empire is central to any analysis of how the modern capitalist world came into being. In this respect, we follow the lead of a number of scholars who have highlighted the pervasive influence on world history of nomadic communities operating on the Eurasian steppe, from the formation of Asian empires to the commercial prefiguration of the modern world system.[16] We acknowledge and take up some of these arguments, but with two important modifications.

First, accounts that have emphasised the influence of nomadic empires in the making of Asian history[17] have not extended their geographical scope to address how this history impacted the origins of capitalism in Europe. Second, those authors who do focus on their influences on Europe[18] have typically concentrated on *quantitative* increases in trade and transfers of knowledge and artefacts that took place in the Medieval period.[19] However, what they have yet to capture is how such commerce-induced transfers impacted on the *qualitative* transformation from feudal to capitalist social relations. In contrast to both tendencies, we argue that the expansion of the Mongolian Empire was a crucial 'vector' of uneven and combined development which contributed to the making of capitalist modernity over the *longue durée*.

Considering the task at hand, it is worth noting two ways in which we consider uneven and combined development especially useful in redeeming the agency of the Mongolian Empire. First, uneven and combined development calls for a radically anti-stadial model of development and a nonlinear conception of history. This provides an important corrective to evolutionist assumptions that underpin the study of nomadic societies, for any ideal-typical understanding of nomadism would in every instance have to be reconceptualised in a way that incorporates the sorts of 'combination' that arise from intersocietal relations. To paraphrase Peter Jackson, there are no 'pure' nomadic polities, but only 'hybrids'.[20] The subversion of the evolutionist approach also undermines the assumption that, on the historicist hierarchy of sedentary versus nomadic societies or state versus nonstate, nomadic communities lack historical agency.

So second, the idea of uneven and combined development does away with intersocietal relations conceived in realist terms as externally related but occasionally colliding states, and instead allows us to grasp more itinerant and nonstate forms of territoriality as an active part of international relations, state formations and world history more broadly. An awareness of this itinerant territoriality is precisely why uneven and combined development can offer a way of theorising the significance of nomadism in general, and the Mongolian Empire in particular, for world history. In doing so, uneven and combined development also provides theoretically and empirically generative ways of reintroducing the importance of nomadism into historical narratives of the origins of capitalism.

We take up this task in the sections that follow. In the first section, we examine the impact of the Mongolian Empire on the socio-economic and political development of Europe, demonstrating how it facilitated cross-cultural flows of commerce, trade, technologies, ideas and more, while also spurring significant technological innovations. The second section goes on to examine the unintended destructive yet regenerative consequences of the Mongol Empire's 'unification of the world by disease' – an often overlooked and undertheorised form of intersocietal interaction. The spread of the Black Death to Europe engendered significant institutional and socio-economic developments and a transformation of the balance of class forces, which directly led to the transition from feudalism to capitalism in the English countryside. The conclusion then teases out the historical analysis's broader implications for the study of world history and historical sociology more generally.

Pax Mongolica as a Vector of Uneven and Combined Development

It is worth recalling that in the late Medieval and early modern epochs, Europe was in no sense destined to rise to the position of global prominence it currently holds. Up until at least the mid-13th century, the social formations making up 'Europe' were in fact the least developed region of a 'world system' of increasing economic integration and cultural contacts between 'East' and 'West'.[21] Arising late on the periphery of this world system, European development had the most to gain from the new intersocietal links being forged, particularly through the diffusion of new technologies and 'resource portfolios' spreading from East to West.[22]

The principles of mathematics, navigational inventions, arts of war and significant military technologies all originated in the more scientifically and militarily advanced Asian societies, only to then eventually pass to the more 'backward' European societies.[23] This then enabled European (proto)states to acquire the means to revolutionise their own societies in much more intensive concentrations of time than had the original purveyors. Such 'late-developing' societies did not need to start from scratch, but could instead acquire and refine the most advanced technologies and organisational forms pioneered by earlier developers. In these ways, the societies that came to form Europe benefited from a certain 'privilege of historic backwardness',[24] a key precondition for the eventual emergence of capitalism in them.

Crucial to this process of worldwide interconnection was the 'globalising' dynamic of the robustly expansionist Mongol Empire, which over the course of the Long 13th Century (1210–1350) unified much of the Eurasian landmass, putting 'the termini of Europe and China in direct contact with one another for the first time in a thousand years'.[25] The emergence of the Mongol Empire and its effects on other societies' development were of world-historical significance, as this section demonstrates. We must first, however, examine the dynamics of the nomadic mode of production in explaining the precise forms, scales and articulations of uneven and combined development during this epoch.

The Nomadic Mode of Production and Uneven and Combined Development

The sources of the expansionist tendencies of the Mongolian steppe clans can be found in their distinctive form of production: nomadic pastoralism. Unlike sedentary agricultural societies, the means of production for nomads were herds rather than soil.[26] Since herds were themselves dependent on land not occupied

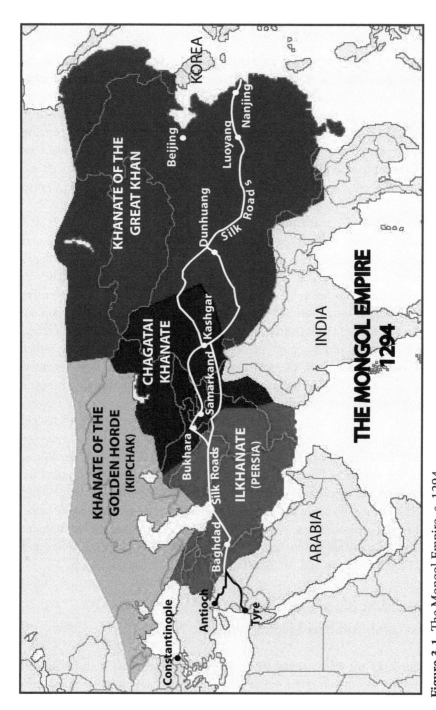

Figure 3.1 The Mongol Empire, c. 1294
Source: www.thestudentroom.co.uk (accessed 12 January 2015).

by nomads, any systematic development of productive forces was limited, as was the quantity of surplus produced. In order to generate new surpluses, nomads had to therefore integrate – by conquest or consent – more and more productive units from which they could extract tribute.[27]

Consequently, the nomadic mode of production had a tripartite mechanism for the reproduction of social life. First, there was the necessity of locating grazing land for animals in the herd. Constrained by the 'spotty and archipelagic'[28] distribution of cultivable land in the steppe, migrations tended to be semi-annual between high pastures in the summer and lower steppes in the winter, imbuing nomadism with a continuous and far-reaching mobility. This mobility, and the social structure it entailed, endowed nomadic life with militaristic traits: war and conquest developed from being necessities in the (re)productive process to forming a part of the polity and identity of the community's members.[29] Second, there was the necessity of raiding sedentary communities for grains, manufactures and luxury goods.[30] Here the mobility, discipline and hardiness of the nomadic mounted archer proved an irresistible military force which contributed to innovations both technical and strategic.[31] Third, in their interactions with sedentary societies, nomads also made use of their mobility to develop extensive trade relations with widely disparate sedentary communities. This in turn facilitated the communication and transfer of technologies and information over long distances, as further examined below.[32] Nomadic empire building was consequently invariably conducted along caravan routes that facilitated the appropriation of surpluses through the mechanisms of trade and tribute.[33] Economic 'openness' in the conquered lands was therefore crucial to the reproduction of nomadic empires. These lands acted as logistical mechanisms for the supply of food, strategic resources, luxury goods, tributes and taxes.[34]

Such a mode of production tended towards a proto-state or 'headless'[35] state form which could manage these three elements – coordinating migrations around new pastures, leading conquering missions, and mediating between a multiplicity of nomadic and sedentary societies. The mobility of migrations also meant that the nomadic relationship to land was not one of ownership, and the limited nature of extensive pastoral farming meant that the accumulation of surpluses was restricted by climactic unreliability.[36] Thus, nomadism was adverse to the centralisation of power and resources – an essential basis for any private ownership of land and form of sovereign authority – and was instead marked by horizontal and disaggregated social relationships between society members.[37] This was complemented by an ideology of inclusiveness and quasi-equality, where social relations between members of the community were articulated in terms of companionship and comradeship.[38]

In particular, this horizontality and flexibility of nomadic groups facilitated collective collaboration in raiding better protected sedentary communities. Because intratribal or supratribal organisations were so heavily predicated on warfare,[39] unification tended to occur through the appointment of a supreme chief, or khan, who would represent the 'higher unity' of these horizontal structures.[40] Hence, political authority tended to be concentrated according to the personal qualities of the most skilled warrior in the position of chief, who was best suited to leading the 'joint ventures' of migration and raiding.[41]

With intersocietal interactions between uneven polities at the heart of social reproduction, the nomadic mode of production begot combined development. This was most clearly expressed in the transformation of both nomadic and sedentary societies through their interactions. Because nomadism required the material products of sedentary societies, many sedentary cultures became a 'source' and 'model' for 'comparison, borrowing, imitation, or rejection'.[42] Moreover, combination worked reciprocally: nomadic technologies, cultures and traditions were also imitated by sedentary societies.[43] The qualities of mobility and war-readiness made nomads especially attuned to extorting surpluses from sedentary societies through raids, and under certain conditions conquest.[44] This external nomadic 'whip' necessitated a response from sedentary societies toward more ordered politics and better equipped military organisations, something that was only possible with greater accumulation and centralisation of resources. As a result, sedentary societies required the creation of surpluses, and their appropriation, and so social stratification and the concentration of political powers were needed in personified arbitrary authorities or states. In these ways, sedentary societies tended to unwittingly replicate political features of nomadic societies.[45]

At the same time, interactions with sedentary states led to the consolidation of larger and stronger administrative and military institutions among nomads, in order to better conduct wars and raids, or to control trade routes. Such expansions precipitated the emergence of centralised standing armies and the Supreme Khan's personal bodyguards, often to unprecedented scales.[46] Such a growth of centralised military functions was maintained primarily through the semi-institutionalisation of the raid, through tribute and eventually by the direct taxation of sedentary subjects.[47] And as the importance of tribute and taxation to the modalities of ruling class reproduction grew, nomadic empires tended to incorporate bureaucrats from conquered sedentary territories in order to administer these functions of surplus extraction.[48] Finally, nomadic ideology was rearticulated in order to legitimise this shift in social relations 'from horizontal to vertical and from semi-egalitarian to hierarchical'.[49]

In short, the uneven relations between nomadic and sedentary societies tended towards the complexification of nomadic political structures as a result of the confrontation and consequent amalgamation,[50] synthesis[51] or 'caging'[52] of these multiple and varied social forms.[53] And it was through such processes of combined development that nomadism could tend towards semi-tributary modes of production – either through processes of nomadic empire building (Mongol, Ottoman), or through the nomadic pressures on sedentary states to consolidate, as exemplified by the Mughal, Chinese, Byzantine and Muscovite empires. When we see nomadism as developing combined social formations, it is therefore possible to move away from an essentialised understanding of nomadism as 'static', 'simple' or 'primitive' to an understanding that recognises the often unprecedented levels of sophistication in the organisation of state and society achieved by polities such as the Mongolian Empire, along with their impact on other more 'advanced' sedentary societies.

Moreover, these combined characteristics help to clarify the central contradiction in the nomadic mode of production between tendencies towards a hierarchical, stratified sedentarisation, on the one hand, against the horizontal flexibility of nomadism, on the other. Because this contradiction was so deeply imbued with intersocietal determinations, it tended to be expressed first and foremost geopolitically.[54] The ebb and flow of nomadisation and sedetarisation, created by intranomadic and nomad–sedentary internecine conflicts over access to land or spoils of raids, meant that communities were constantly uprooted and moved to more secure areas for grazing and/or agriculture.[55]

Waves of nomadic empire building therefore tended to create chain reactions of displacement, migration and resettlement that transmitted the peoples and traditions of nomadism throughout Inner Asia to its hinterlands. Such was the reach of Inner Asian nomadic empires that their legacy could be found to the north in the Muscovy Empire, to the south in the Mughal Empire, to the West in the Saffavid and Seljuk Empires, and to the East in the Yuan and Manchu Dynasties.[56] In short, the contradictions at the heart of nomadic form of uneven and combined development meant that nomadic empire building could be simultaneously generative and destructive. The varied developmental experiences implied in this contradiction are explored below.

The World-Historical Significance of the Mongol Empire

The impact of the Mongol conquests on the subsequent trajectory of world history was profound. Once relatively isolated entities, the different sedentary and nomadic societies making up the whole of the Eurasian landmass were now 'interactive components of a unified system'[57] of geopolitical relations. What we then find in the world of the 13th and 14th centuries is a plurality of differentiated societies, based on different modes of production (tributary in Asia, nomadic in the steppes, feudal in Europe), constituting a single interactive geopolitical whole. Within this ontological whole, each society's conditions of existence necessarily impinged on and entered into its logics of reproduction, creating an 'interdependence ... of the structures of social, material and cultural life'.[58] Nomadic expansionism thus represented an early form or vector of uneven and combined development.

The effects of the Mongol raids and conquests on 'West' and 'East' were, however, gravely different. The pressure of nomadic expansionism was one of the main reasons for the differentiated development of Eastern and Western Europe, as the former's internal evolution was continually impeded by successive nomadic invasions. 'The pattern and frequency of these invasions', Perry Anderson writes, 'made them one of the basic coordinates of the formation of Eastern Europe'.[59] The invasions hindered both the development of the productive forces and the states system in Eastern Europe, marking it off from Western Europe as its own distinct geopolitical and socio-economic unit.[60]

For China too, the Mongol invasions profoundly arrested economic development. E. L. Jones claims that the human destruction wrought by the Mongol conquest of Sung China 'was so large that it must have obliterated economic life over wide areas'.[61] Similarly, according to Alan Smith, 'after the overthrow of the Sung dynasty by the invading Mongols in 1276, China never regained the dynamism of its past'.[62] For this reason, Eric Mielants cites the Mongol conquest as an 'important variable' in explaining why China, despite its high levels of economic growth, was unable to make the transition to capitalism.[63] As Europe would come to expand economically as a result of the transcontinental trading system established by the *Pax Mongolica*, many of the pre-Mongolian commercial networks and trading states of Central Asia were negatively affected, if not entirely destroyed, by the Golden Horde.[64] While the hitherto more powerful states that made up China, the Middle East and Russian territories were persistently 'burdened' by the 'Tartar yoke', Western Europe benefited.[65] This was a key reason for the divergent, variegated paths of socio-economic development in different regions.[66] It can be said, then, that the uneven and combined development of the *Pax Mongolica* exacerbated the developmental unevenness between 'East' and 'West', as well as within Europe itself.

Although by 1350 the Mongol Empire had disintegrated into a number of rivalling khanates, the continuing nomadic threat to China's inner Asian land frontier persisted. The strategic dilemma posed by the nomads is often cited as a key reason for the Ming dynasty's retreat from the sea, represented by their famous decision not to follow up Admiral Zheng He's naval expeditions in the Indian Ocean. The inward turn of the Ming Empire, though often exaggerated, nonetheless did signal the abandonment of seaborne expansion, and as an indirect result, the eventual weakening of the Empire vis-à-vis its soon to be Western competitors.[67] The very withdrawal of powerful Chinese fleets from commercially and strategically important nodes of the Indian Ocean littoral meant that the Portuguese and Dutch had a considerably freer rein during their later, 16th-century penetration into the region, assisting their success in capturing 'vital emporia and crucial strategic locations' throughout the Ocean. 'In this sense, "Chinese abdication was Europe's gain"'.[68] Had it not been for

China's central strategic problem, the nomadic threat, we could speculate that it might well have reached the Americas first.[69]

By contrast, for Western Europe, the effects of the Mongol invasions and the formation of the *Pax Mongolica* were primarily beneficial for economic development.[70] In addition to lowering commercial protection and the transaction costs of overland trade, in many cases the Mongols actively guaranteed the safety of merchants travelling in the regions they controlled, while offering lucrative commercial and territorial privileges to European states on the basis of treaties or concessions. An example of these concessions is the agreement negotiated by the Venetian ambassadors Giovanni Quirino and Pietro Giustiniano with Khan Ozbeg for the founding of a *comptoir* in Tana, which included a 'territorial concession, favourable taxation, protection for the merchants, and provisions in case of legal disputes'.[71]

The Mongol Empire also facilitated the diffusion of such key military technologies as navigational techniques and gunpowder[72] from East Asia to Europe – all of which were crucial to Europe's subsequent rise to global prominence. As new military technologies were critical tools of conquest and administration, the Mongols would acquire such technologies in one society and then deploy them in another to better enable imperial expansion and control, resulting in their continual spread.[73] 'Without the Mongol peace, it is hard to imagine any of the rest of Western history working out quite as it did', Felipe Fernandez-Armesto writes, 'for these were the roads that carried Chinese ideas and transmitted technology westward and opened up European minds to the vastness of the world'.[74]

While the Mongol threat to China represented a whip of external necessity structuring and redirecting Chinese development, the structural geopolitical space created by the *Pax Mongolica* and its effects on Western European societies was something more akin to what we might term a 'gift of external opportunity'. But crucially, these 'gifts' were determined by the agency of the Mongolians themselves, 'by what the Mongols liked, needed and were interested in'. Consequently, the sorts of cross-cultural exchange that took place in the *Pax Mongolica* were functions of – and adaptations to – the requirements of Mongolian imperial reproduction.[75] Hence, as further examined below, Mongolian agency played a significant role in the creation of some of the crucial preconditions that launched Europe onto the path of capitalist development and, much later, global supremacy.

Trade, Commerce, and Socio-Economic Development under the *Pax Mongolica*

The Mongol rulers formed a symbiotic relationship with merchants from all over Eurasia as the booty from their conquests became increasingly insufficient to

Figure 3.2 Master of Busico, *Kublai Khan giving support to the Venetians*, 1412

Source: http://en.wikipedia.org/wiki/File:Kublai_giving_support_to_the_Venetians.jpg (accessed 27 October 2014).

finance the Empire's administration. To supplement their finances, the Mongols sought to derive profit from trade across their domains. They were, Ronald Findlay tells us, the 'natural supporters of "free trade" as the Mongols materially benefitted from the free flow of goods and factors across their domains since this increased the wealth they could extract for themselves'.[76] Merchants thereby became the 'foundation of the state'.[77] In search of a steady stream of income, the Mongol rulers therefore actually sought to promote trade, making them a key agent in the rise of the virtual 'world market' of the 13th and 14th centuries. 'No effort was spared to encourage all kinds of commercial activity', Virgil Ciocîltan writes, as:

> they allowed unhindered access for foreigners in the lands which they governed, guaranteed safety for travellers, and ensured the proper conditions for transport of goods, which of course also included setting custom duties at an attractive level. Any measure which would increase trade was considered good.[78]

The Mongols were 'exceptional' in their willingness and capacity to provide the infrastructural foundations for intersocietal trade even when the formal backing of European states was lacking or absent.[79]

The establishment of the *Pax Mongolica* was then a major boon for overland trade connecting East to West, which notably benefited Northwestern Europe. It created a transcontinental trading system in which commerce, trade, technologies and ideas travelled along the Silk Road like never before.[80] This has led some scholars to go so far as to attribute the origins of 'globalisation' to the unification of the Eurasian land mass accomplished by the Mongols.[81] Having connected the disparate regions of Eurasia under a single authority for 'the first and indeed only time in history',[82] the Mongols contributed to the emergence of a nascent 'world economy' by facilitating 'land transit with less risk and lower protective rent'. Merchants and goods were now able to travel more safely over 'these vast distances', thereby establishing a trade route which briefly 'broke the monopoly of the more southerly routes'.[83]

This was particularly beneficial for the 'proto-capitalist' merchants of the Italian city-states Venice and Genoa, for whom Mongolian protection in Central Asia was central to their preponderance and growth in the Black Sea region.[84] The activities of Italian merchants crucially depended on the Mongols' willingness and capacity to create and maintain favourable trading conditions.[85] While a number of historians have emphasised the importance of the Treaty of Nymphaeus (1261) in establishing Genoa's commercial monopoly east of the Bosporus, less noted is the fact it was the Mongols that allowed its merchants to 'set up shop' in the Crimea in the first place.[86]

What is more, the decreased transaction and protection costs across the overland trade routes resulted in an 'unprecedented expansion of the market for Western European cities', in turn promoting growing and complexified divisions of labour in most European urban industries.[87] In particular, the expanded international demand for cloth stimulated the textile industry in the Low Countries,[88] which proved critical to the 'urban-agrarian' symbiosis that characterised the rise of capitalist social relations in parts of the Late Medieval Netherlands (see Chapter 6).[89] The widened market for wool in Flemish towns would in turn encourage English landowners in the Stuart period to convert to commercial agriculture.[90] For these reasons, Mielants concludes, it would be 'Eurocentric to claim that "medieval development" in Europe was nothing but "auto-development"'.[91]

In all these ways, the Mongol Empire provided the propitious geopolitical conditions for the extensive development of market relations, trade, urban growth, and perhaps most importantly an increasingly complex division of labour in Western Europe – the latter constituting an integral aspect of the development of the productive forces. To be clear, this did *not* automatically entail the advent of capitalist relations of production, but it did provide the preconditions for their subsequent emergence.[92] For growing urban centres provided not only the gravitational pull on peasants seeking to escape serfdom, but also a growing demand for agricultural products, which were increasingly produced for the market. As Terence Byres explains, 'The sizeable market for agricultural products was the outcome of considerable urban development, and the consequent existence of considerable urban demand, and the emergence of an enormous network of smaller markets and craft centres'.[93] The development of complex commercial networks of interconnected city sites was, then, an important aspect of the story of capitalism's emergence – one significantly enhanced by the intensification and securing of long-distance trade relations under the *Pax Mongolica.*

Although trade between 'West' and 'East' would significantly decrease with the disintegration of the Mongol Empire, European interest in trade with the Far East never died. Memories of the commerce carried on by European merchants, and especially Marco Polo's stories, maintained knowledge of the Far East, and the desire for renewed access to it. Moreover, by unifying hitherto isolated 'civilisations' as interactive components of a single geopolitical system, the Mongol conquests significantly altered the conceptual and ideological horizons of the Europeans as they came to view the world as a unified whole. This widened conception of the world would eventually prove a further motivation for long-distance voyages among Europeans in the age of expansion, instigating Genoan-Portuguese ventures around the Cape of Good Hope, as well as the accidental discovery of the Americas.[94] Consequently, as S. A. M. Adshead puts it, '[i]f Europe came to dominate the world, it was possibly because Europe first perceived there was a world to dominate. There is a straight line from Marco Polo to Christopher Columbus, the eastward-looking Venetian to the westward-looking Genoese'.[95]

Finally, we must note the important benefits afforded to Europe in the wake of the Mongol Empire's collapse. For after *Pax Mongolica* had established the trade links and intersocietal exchanges facilitating the first 'world system', its fall provided critical advantages for Europe's subsequent rise to global domination. First, it was precisely the disintegration of the Mongol Empire that provided the propitious *geopolitical space* through which the societies of Europe could make strident developmental gains. This was because the increase in protection and transportation costs on the overland route, and the concomitant shift to maritime trade in the Indian Ocean littoral, precipitated a political crisis in numerous Inner Asian states.[96] In this sense, as Janet Abu-Lughod notes, it was the 'Fall of the East' that set the conditions for the later 'Rise of the West', as the 'devolution of this pre-existing system' established by the *Pax Mongolica* 'facilitated Europe's easy conquest'.[97]

In yet another instance of the 'gift of external opportunity', Europe conquered or subsumed commercial routes and networks that had been previously developed by the *Pax Mongolica* over the Long 13th Century. The Europeans 'did not need to *invent* the system, since the basic groundwork was in place by the thirteenth century when Europe was still only a recent and peripheral participant'.[98] But, moreover, the commercial shift to the Indian Ocean intersected with Europe's own entry into these maritime routes, forming a crucial economic and strategic platform from which particular European powers (especially Britain) would later launch their drive to global domination (see Chapter 8). The rise and fall of the *Pax Mongolica* were thus crucial moments in kick-starting the developmental trajectory that eventually led to the rise of capitalism in Europe, while providing the critical intersocietal conditions from which Europe would begin its ascent to global supremacy.

Apocalypse Then: The Black Death and the Crisis of Feudalism

The Black Death is often cited as a major conjunctural factor in explaining both the terminal crisis of the feudal mode of production in Europe and the crucial shifts in the balance of class forces leading to the eventual rise of capitalist social relations.[99] Some scholars have gone so far as to cite the Black Death as *the* main reason for the development of capitalism in Western Europe.[100] Whatever emphasis is placed on the precise significance of the Black Death, it is generally agreed among historians that the already existing crisis within the feudal mode of production was supercharged by the 'pandemic shock caused by the Black Death', heralding 'a watershed in the transition to capitalism'.[101] By stimulating state formation processes throughout Western Europe while spurring on urbanisation and commercialisation, the late Medieval crisis 'may have marked the most decisive step in the continent's long trajectory to capitalism and world hegemony'.[102] Yet rarely, if ever, does this contingent factor enter into the theorisation of the process of systemic dissolution and reconstruction itself. And, we might ask, why should it? How could any historical sociology theorise such a phenomenon?

The reason is that in both origin and effect the Black Death was a social phenomenon, or more precisely an intersocietal one. It is 'indicative', Neil Davidson writes, 'of a rather oversocialized notion of human existence if our struggle with ... non-human aspects of nature is treated as an exogenous factor'. Davidson goes on to give the example of the Black Death which, he correctly notes, plays a critical role in Robert Brenner's explication of the changing balance of class forces at the end of the 14th century. Against conceptions of the Black Death as a pure contingency, however, Davidson notes how 'the extent of its [the Black Death's] impact was a function of the weakened resistance to disease of a population who were already suffering from reduced caloric intake as a result of the feudal economic crisis'.[103]

Indeed, by the middle of the 14th century, feudalism in Europe was losing steam. Population had stopped rising, food costs were higher and famines became more frequent, as was exemplified by the Great Famine of 1315–17. Feudal Europe's long period of expansion had apparently come to an end, which explains why the impact of the Black Death was so severe;[104] the plague's effects were conditioned by this socio-economic environment. What is more, it was only through the Mongolian unification of the Eurasian landmass, and

Figure 3.3 Albrecht Dürer, *Die Offenbarung des Johannes: 4. Die vier apokalyptischen* [*The Revelation of St. John: 4. The Four Horsemen of the Apocalypse*], 1497–98

Source: http://commons.wikimedia.org/wiki/File:Durer_Revelation_Four_Riders.jpg (accessed 27 October 2014).

the increasing intersocietal interactions that this facilitated, that allowed the plague to spread to Europe in the first place.[105] What Le Roy Ladurie called 'the unification of the globe by disease'[106] should therefore be seen as an unintended consequence of the uneven and combined development of the Mongolian Empire.

The transformative effects of the Black Death on Europe were both causative and indicative of a wider social crisis in feudalism. For many contemporaries, the Black Death appeared as an apocalyptic event, heralding the 'End Times' that would sweep away all vestiges of the extant structures of society. The ideas of catastrophe and salvation generated by the eschatology of the time were thus indicative of a 'historical context in which one mode of production and life was being supplanted by another'.[107]

Such themes are stunningly captured in Albrecht Dürer's 1498 *The Four Horsemen of the Apocalypse,* in which the four harbingers of reckoning furiously rout all before them. Straddling the horses of 'pestilence', 'war', 'famine', and 'death', each signified the chokepoints of feudalism: the bubonic plague, internecine military competition, the vicissitudes of agrarian production, and demographic fluctuations. Meanwhile, a diabolical monster drags members of the ruling class into hell, representing and demonising the widespread rebellions that would attack the institutions of serfdom, empire and papacy from below. The extensive reproduction of Dürer's *Apocalypse with Pictures* (there were 750 editions and commentaries from 1498 to 1650)[108] suggests that his vision resonated through the 16th century among the ruling and ruled classes alike, capturing the disorders of a mode of production nearing its final end.

The Black Death was 'an event of great historical importance', for it not only expedited the breakdown of feudalism, but also impelled 'economic, technological, social and administrative modernization'.[109] We examine these in turn through: first, an analysis of the breakdown of feudal class structures; second, an examination of the increasing socio-economic stratification of the peasantry; and third, a focus on the significant developments to the productive forces.

Class Struggle and the Changing Balance of Class Forces in Europe

One of the single most important effects of the demographic collapse resulting from the plague was how it temporarily functioned to tip the balance of class forces in favour of the peasantry throughout much of Western Europe, but most notably in the English countryside.[110] In particular, the high demand for land that had hitherto upheld the manorial lords' positions was severely undermined by the population decline resulting from the plague. Where lords could previously use the threat of expulsion to discipline peasants, now abundant land allowed the peasantry opportunities to flee and cultivate new lands.[111] One immediate consequence of the Black Death was rent strikes – the 'refusal to pay' – among peasants, reinforced by the threat of flight from manorial lands to unoccupied territories or cities.[112]

As the peasantry became less docile, the potency of extra-economic means of surplus extraction – coercive, legal, religious and so on – was curbed.[113] As a consequence, many direct producers across the West European countryside either experienced an upturn in their living conditions, or were altogether emancipated by the dissolution of serfdom.[114] Wages doubled and trebled across Western Europe, and work obligations for peasants were considerably reduced. With the greater availability of work and increasing wages, landless peasants also experienced a notable upturn in their conditions.[115] Wage differentials between men and women were also greatly reduced following the Black Death.[116] For a brief period, the peasantry held historically 'unprecedented power' in what proved 'a golden age of the European proletariat'.[117]

The unprecedented demographic downturn resulting from the plague in turn exacerbated a declining rate of seigniorial revenues, generalising and deepening the systemic crisis of feudalism that had begun in the early 15th century.[118] For in 'a system where the social reproduction of the ruling class hinged upon a growing population in order to sustain seigneurial revenues', Jason Moore writes, 'the Black Death quickly transformed the agrarian depression of the early fourteenth century into a terminal crisis of the feudal system'.[119] In these respects, the Black Death was 'not simply one episode among the many dramatic conflicts that punctuate[d] the history of feudalism', Guy Bois notes, but represented *the* 'watershed' event signalling the beginning of the end: an organic crisis besetting the totality of power structures making up feudal production as a whole.[120]

Further avenues for feudal survival came to be predominantly oriented around three main axes of ruling class reproductive strategies: first, a forcible redistribution of already occupied lands represented by war-assisted processes of (geo)political accumulation (that is, intra-lordly conflict); second, a redirection of expansionist strategies away from land accumulation on the continent to the capturing of commercially lucrative overseas markets and trade routes; and/or third, a clamping down and intensification of the rate of exploitation of the direct producers (known as the 'seigniorial reaction'). Such ruling class strategies aimed at recuperating lost surpluses could be found throughout Europe. In the face of labour shortages caused by the plague and the consequent upturn in wages, the ruling class sought to reimpose strictures on the peasants that had until then been gradually diminishing, by attempting to strengthen serfdom, and hold down wages in both town and country.[121] This was exemplified by the Statues of Labourers decreed in England in 1349–51, immediately following the Black Death, and the French Ordonnance of 1351, which partly followed provisions laid out in the English statues, along with similar decrees controlling labour wages by the Cortes of Castile in 1351, the German princes in Bavaria in 1352 and the Portuguese monarchy some two decades later in 1375.[122]

Attempts to reinforce servile conditions and pass the costs of the feudal crisis onto the labouring class were met by fierce and often violent resistance. Peasant revolts broke out across most European countries, along with workers' uprisings in the more urbanised Low Countries.[123] In 1358, northern France was set aflame by the Grande Jacquerie, one of the largest peasants' revolts recorded in Western European history since the Bacaudae of the 3rd century. France erupted again in 1379 and 1382 in what Prosper Boissonnade described as a 'whirlwind of revolution'.[124] The more developed urban regions in Flanders and Northern Italy also experienced autonomous communal revolts, while in 1378 a more radical peasant revolt in Florence led to the brief dictatorship of the Ciompi wool combers, made up primarily of wage-labourers. Then in England, the Peasants' Revolt of 1381 sought nothing less than the total abolition of serfdom and the existing legal system.[125] Political and economic struggles prompted by the Black Death continued into the 15th century, often escalating into civil wars. In Catalonia, peasants demanded land, the freedom of movement, an end to enclosures, and the abolition of rents, in a series of struggles that culminated in the Remensa Wars of 1462–86.[126] The peasant revolts in Germany, beginning in 1476, inaugurated and prefigured a long series of rebellions that reached its apogee with the great Peasant Wars of 1522–25.[127]

Peasant Differentiation in the Age of the Black Death

By transforming the agrarian depression of the 14th century into the terminal crisis of feudalism, the Black Death ushered in a new era of profound social dislocations and economic change. In this context, many peasants increasingly turned to the market in order to escape the machinations of serfdom. This is a particularly significant point given the tendency among Political Marxists to stress that market dependency must be imposed upon economic agents; under no circumstances, they argue, would peasants willingly *choose* to be capitalists or subject themselves to the systematic imperatives of the market. While this position has the great merit of denaturalising the emergence of capitalism, the historical evidence does nonetheless indicate that, under certain circumstances, peasants sought to use the market to escape from serfdom. Over time this often had the unintended consequence of making them market-dependent.[128]

In the immediate aftermath of the Black Death, many English peasant producers were able to use their improved conditions to accumulate land,[129] produce surpluses[130] and participate in the market as a means to secure their material reproduction.[131] The ongoing process of peasant differentiation was greatly accelerated by the impact of the plague on England's feudal agrarian economy. This was above all the result of the demographic shifts resulting from the plague's diffusion from the Mongol Empire to Europe. 'There can be little doubt as to the importance of the Black Death', Michael J. Bennett notes, 'to both the progressive amelioration and differentiation of peasant fortunes'.[132] For in numerous regions of England, high mortality rates left unbreachable gaps in the ranks of the peasantry. The consequent shortage of labour was bound in the long run to work to the advantage of most sections of the peasant class, and the large number of vacant holdings inevitably enabled the more enterprising survivors to add to their tenancies on a scale hitherto unimaginable.

Similarly, as Jane Whittles writes specifically in regards to the situation in the county of Norfolk, England:

> Manorial lords had retained their hold on the economy in the century before the Black Death because of the high demand for land. Once this factor was removed by population decline, the diversified economy undermined the manorial lords' position. Land was still an important element in the economy, but it was not the only element, and it was now not difficult to acquire…. Peasants, or rather wealthy peasants, had capitalized on the fifteenth-century situation, building up their land holdings, and orientating themselves increasingly towards market production.[133]

Such statements generally confirm the picture painted by Rodney Hilton of the dramatic changes to Europe's agrarian economy in the wake of the Black Death. The plague's effects in transforming the 'land : labour ratio' in Europe had, according to Hilton, two major long-term consequences for the European peasantry: first, it increased the availability of suitable land to farm; and second, it diminished the rent burden on property holdings.[134] In the century following the Black Death, rent revenue fell at rates ranging between 40 per cent in the Tuscan *contado* and 70 per cent, as witnessed in Normandy and some regions in Flanders. Moreover, rents paid per crop shares dropped from a half to a seventh or an eighth, while at the same time real wages rose. In England, wages doubled over the same period, placing a much greater strain on the seigneurial economy than the peasant economy, which remained largely dependent on family labour. The diminishing of the rent burden was in turn 'partly due to peasant pressure, and partly (especially in war-devastated areas) to the anxiety of landowners to attract tenants to keep land in cultivation'. Increases in money wages for peasant labourers were 'no doubt the immediate consequence of their scarcity (though the demand must also have fallen) but could not have been sustained at the high level without a considerable increase in the productivity of labour'. Such increases in labour productivity were, in turn, the 'consequence of the abandonment of marginal soils, the increased availability of pasture and the increased number of animals'. The effects this had on increasing the process of internal differentiation and stratification within the peasant class were hugely significant, as the 'number of smallholders was considerably reduced', the 'middle stratum' appreciably strengthened, and the richer peasantry also 'improved their position', though not as 'consistently as did the middle peasants'.[135]

The reduction in the proportion of smallholders was perhaps the most important development in the changing landscape of the feudal agrarian economy. As 'the families of smallholders were more likely to die out than those of the better-off peasants' and since the latter held larger holdings and had generally smaller families, 'the heads of richer households could endow their sons without depressing them into the smallholding class'.[136] This decline in the number of smallholdings was most markedly demonstrated in the English case.

The Cistercian Abbey of Stoneleigh in the Forest of Arden saw the proportion of tenants holding under 8 acres (across all its land that was leased by the peasantry) drop from 61 per cent in 1280 to 46 per cent in 1392. In a less extreme but more representative case, in five Midland counties in 1280 the average proportion of smallholders was 46 per cent, but by the late 14th and 15th centuries the percentage had dropped in a number of Midlands manors to somewhere between 11 and 28 per cent. It is difficult to overstate the significance of these reductions in the proportion of smallholding peasants for the functioning of the agrarian economy as a whole, since the smallholders predominantly made up the 'hired labour reserve for the lords' demesnes and the rich peasant holdings'. Moreover, these were the very labourers 'who pushed up wages and were generally regarded as an insolent and demanding group' among the feudal ruling classes; that is, they were those at the forefront of the class struggle against the lords. Further, because of the commutation of labour rents resulting from intensifying peasant struggles and changing lordly practices over the years, 'lords had to rely largely on the labour of these independent workers for the cultivation of the demesnes, as had the richer peasants for their holdings'.[137] Thus, Hilton argues:

> [i]t is likely that the cost of labour was largely responsible for the abandonment of demesne cultivation and it is possible that, at any rate before the latter part of the fifteenth century, high labour costs restricted the expansion of the economy of the large holding.[138]

The particular significance of these plague-induced processes in England during the period between 1350 and 1450 is not that we find merely a 'relative abundance of land', since this abundance could already be found in the early Medieval epoch, which had witnessed 'the strengthening of the power of the landed aristocracy and of considerable pressure for rent, service and jurisdictional profit'. Instead, we find in the years between 1350 and 1450 that the 'relative land abundance was combined...with a *relaxation of seigneurial domination* and a notable lightening of the economic burden on the peasant economy'. Hence, English peasant society, 'in spite of still existing within (in broad terms) a feudal framework', Hilton concludes, began to develop 'according to laws of motion internal to itself'.[139]

The importance of Hilton's account, as Byres tells us, is his identification and tracing of 'some of the processes of class formation critical to [the emergence of] a later agrarian capitalism'. For while the middle peasantry prospered during this period, 'a class of "quasi-capitalists"' was also being formed in the graziers. At the same time, the rich peasantry, though still constrained, were beginning to acquire the means of production (that is, land) 'that would be a critical part of their transformation into capitalist farmers in the sixteenth century'. By this time, 'it was not only the nature of the leases upon which they held the land' that was significant but 'their ability to acquire larger holdings'. And, crucially, by the end of this period, there emerged the possibility 'that the constraint associated with high labour costs was coming to an end, and that a true potential rural proletariat existed'.[140]

Each of these developments contributed to a long drawn-out process of class differentiation within the peasantry. On the one side, there emerged a class of wealthy peasants, possessing capital and larger plots of land,[141] who were consequently imbued with 'the desire, the means and the capacity to accumulate and expand, if the opportunity presented itself'.[142] It was these wealthier peasant tenants who would also come to contribute to the engrossment of land and the formation of capitalist farms,[143] which were not, contrary to what Brenner claims, solely the preserve of the lordly class.[144]

On the other side of this process of peasant differentiation was the emergence of a stratum of peasant wage-labourers compelled to work the land as tenant farmers. As Colin Mooers, a sympathetic critic of Brenner, writes, 'The ability of the English lords to carry through an assault on the peasant rights in the seventeenth century can only be explained by the prior weakening of the peasant community as a result of economic differentiation'. The breakthrough of the yeomanry that emerged through the process of 'petty capitalist accumulation', Mooers notes, 'was a crucial intervening stage in the later development of large-scale capitalist farming. How else is it possible to explain the unique triadic pattern of English agrarian capitalism?' For the tenant peasants who would later work as wage-labourers on the large-scale capitalist farms of the 18th century 'had to have come from somewhere'.[145] In short, the long drawn-out process of socio-economic stratification among the peasantry was an integral aspect of the story of how capitalist relations of production first emerged in Europe, and in particular in the English countryside. And it is this story that really took off and matured in the age of the Black Death.

The crucial upshot of all these interrelated developments for understanding the transition from feudalism to capitalism is well summarised by Byres, who discusses the transformations in the English agrarian economy in relation to the sharpening of class conflicts as the 1350–1450 era progressed and the '"well-to-do peasant farmers" were able to take on the new leases'. Without the presence of this stratum of wealthier peasants that had emerged from the preceding period of peasant differentiation under feudalism, the possibility of taking extended leases would not have existed, or at the very least would have taken much longer to develop. Those richer peasants wishing to further expand their holdings would have then needed to take on additional hired labour (both seasonal and permanent). As a consequence, 'their relationship with such labour would change, and the likelihood of conflict would increase'.[146]

Whether or not we agree with Byres that this process of peasant differentiation was the 'primum mobile' behind the transition, the point should nonetheless be clear: the Black Death's effects on the feudal agrarian economy and its class configurations, particularly in England, spread wide and deep in hastening the myriad developments heralding the demise of the old – the feudal system – and the awakening of the new capitalist dawn. The Mongol vector of uneven and combined development through which the plague was first transmitted to Europe thereby acted to further exacerbate processes of internal unevenness (peasant differentiation) and class conflict, substantially weakening extant feudal power relations while simultaneously hastening the development of new (capitalist) productive relations and social forces. We now turn to examine one final significant factor in the transition to capitalism resulting from the Black Death: that is, its effects on the development of the productive forces.

Development of the Productive Forces

Given the massive loss of working-aged people[147] resulting from the plague, land became more abundant vis-à-vis labour. This pushed the prices of agricultural products down relative to manufactures, particularly those with high labour ratios. Both land rents and interest rates also declined relative to wages. Consequently, the income of the feudal landowning classes began to decline as labour and peasant incomes rose. Out of necessity, agriculture and manufactures began to develop along more capital-intensive lines, spurring new improvements in the productive forces.[148] Likewise, the dramatic collapse of the working-age population also functioned to free resources, such as land, and put them to use in new and – more often than not – more productive applications. Freed lands could now be employed in ways other than cultivating grain, while mills that had traditionally been used to grind grain could now be adapted to full cloth, saw wood, operate bellows and so on.[149]

In these ways, the redeployment of material resources could act to release and develop new productive forces. For as wages rose sharply relative to rents and the price of capital,[150] producers and landowners across the continent began to systematically replace labour with land and capital.[151] David Herlihy has examined how this systematisation of factor substitution – the substitution of cheap land and capital for increasingly expensive labour – led to various processes which directly or indirectly stimulated labour productivity and the development of the productive forces more generally.

For example, in the agricultural sector, the purchasing of oxen to assist peasants in ploughing became more common, as did the use of fertiliser. Both material inputs enabled peasants to work more efficiently, which increased the overall productivity of labour. Likewise, in the urban sector, factor substitution allowed for the purchase of improved tools or machinery, again assisting the overall productivity of urban labour. These processes not only involved replacing labour with existing tools and machines, they also led to quite widespread instances of technological innovation. This period saw the development of entirely new tools and machines, as high labour costs systematically incentivised the use of labour-saving inventions. 'Chiefly for this reason', Herlihy notes, 'the late Middle Ages was a period of impressive technological achievement',[152] as 'a number of more capital-intensive industries emerged'.[153] This is exemplified in the maritime revolution and dramatic innovations in the use of firearms.[154]

Consequently, the epidemic-driven crisis of the 14th century led to the emergence of a number of novel rural and urban textile industries in Holland, England, Southern Germany and some sections of Italy.[155] Yet during this period of general economic contraction, most 'national' markets were far too limited to sustain such industries. 'Hence this industry had to look for markets abroad', which 'it did not fail to do in England and Holland from the second half of the fourteenth century on'.[156] The Baltic countries were to make up the bulk of this export expansionism. And as the Portuguese and Spanish embarked upon their overseas expansion, the English, and particularly the Dutch, became crucial intermediaries in the commercial exchanges between the Baltic states and the Iberian peninsula. 'Thus, the countries of north-western Europe, and especially Holland and England, had from the fifteenth century onwards great chances of development through their trading connexions, both with the Baltic countries and Spain and Portugal'.[157] Taken together, the 14th-century crisis, driven in part by the demographic devastation accompanying the epidemics, resulted in new industrial activities and trading opportunities for the Northwestern European states. As such, the age of the Black Death witnessed the structural reconstruction of intra-European economic relations, as 'industries in the Low Countries and England began to outstrip Mediterranean producers in woollen textiles'.[158]

In line with such changes in Northwestern Europe, the Black Death also significantly stimulated processes of urbanisation, a key indicator of rising productivity and economic development in the pre-modern epoch.[159] In the aftermath of the plague, urbanisation was particularly rapid in the Netherlands during the 15th and 16th centuries and in England during the 16th century. What is more, the longer-term effects of the Black Death marked the very beginning of a *structural shift* in Northwestern Europe spanning nearly six centuries, from a labour force primarily based in agriculture to one increasingly based in services and industry.[160]

There were also important changes in the agricultural economy. With the mass exodus of peasants from the land, the competition between lords and tenant struggles resulted in much lower rents, fewer obligations and longer leases. As population growth did not fully recover from the plague for several generations in Western Europe, such arrangements subsequently led to the dissolution of the manorial economy, as money rent payments came to eventually replace labour services by the 16th century. A major upshot of all this was that such extensive institutional changes to the agricultural economy paved the way for its increasing commercialisation, specifically in Northwestern Europe. Consequently, peasant producers in the region became more and more capable of responding to new opportunities such as producing for markets and raising productivity. Again, all these developments occurred in the Northwest of Europe rather than the South.[161]

These processes also had a distinctly political aspect to them, for the shortages in labour magnified the bargaining powers of both the wealthier peasant classes and the urban elites, who stood to gain from weaker feudal rights and levies. In attempting to counter such tendencies, aspiring political rulers sought to increase the jurisdictional integration of their territories. This in turn led to the creation of more competitive markets, with the added effect of further stimulating commercialisation, thereby 'setting the stage for the long sixteenth-century boom'.[162] We can then partially conclude with Stephen Epstein that the Black Death significantly 'contributed to the feudal economy's transition from a low-level "equilibrium trap" to a higher growth path by sharply intensifying pressures that had been building up over centuries'.[163]

While Epstein continually refers to the Black Death as an untheorisable 'exogenous event', widening this perspective to the level of the *intersocietal*, and its concomitant dynamics of uneven and combined development, offers a theoretical optic through which the plague's causes and consequences can be internalised into a broader conception of sociohistorical development. Hence, the Black Death and its socio-economic and political consequences marked a key moment in the epochal transformations of the Late Medieval era. It did so not only by spurring developments that eventually led to capitalist breakthroughs in Northwestern Europe in the early modern epoch (specifically, in Holland and England), but also by creating the socio-economic conditions under which these rising capitalist societies came to developmentally catch up with and overtake the hitherto leading economies of Southern Europe.[164]

Conclusion

In this chapter we have argued that the multilinear perspective offered by uneven and combined development provides a way of subverting and indeed dismantling the evolutionist approaches that have long relegated nomadic communities to the margins of history. By asserting uneven and combined development's sensitivity to itinerant forms of territoriality, we have provided a theoretical framework through which nonstate agency can be captured and reinserted into world historical narratives. In these ways, we hope to have offered a way of redeeming the historical agency of the Mongolian Empire in the making of capitalism. On the one hand, we have shown that the unification of the Eurasian landmass under its imperial authority provided propitious conditions for commercial growth in Europe. The *Pax Mongolica* thus prefigured the commercial relations that would later become a dominant feature of the modern capitalist world system. On the other hand, we have also shown that the impact of Mongolian expansion reached beyond the commercial relations that are typically emphasised by World-Systems theories and world historians alike, as the integration of different regions in and through the Mongol Empire had the unintended consequence of 'unifying the globe by disease'. As we argued, the subsequent spread of the Black Death had catastrophic consequences for the feudal mode of production in Europe.

In these two ways – the creative integration of commercial networks, and the destructive effects of the Black Death – the Mongolian Empire proved decisive to the emergence of capitalism. Specifically, the long-term agrarian revolts precipitated by the Black Death spurred variegated forms of revolution and counter-revolution around seigniorial rule, reordering feudal social relations in ways that the feudal system would eventually prove unable to recover from. Whether the seigniorial reaction was successful depended on the balance of class forces and antecedent processes of internal differentiation. As Findlay and O'Rourke note:

> In each region the impact effect of the plague was to raise wages, lower land rents, and hence increase the demand on the part of landowners for serfdom.... Trade and population recovery favoured urban interests in the west and rural interests in the east.[165]

The central reason for these different outcomes lay in the varied relations between land and labour in Eastern and Western Europe. Although the demographic collapse in Eastern Europe was actually less in absolute terms than that in Western Europe, the strain was greater given the already endemic shortages of labour characterising the region. 'Given the vast underpopulated spaces of Eastern Europe', Anderson remarks, 'peasant flight was an acute danger to lords everywhere, while land remained potentially very abundant .... The land/labour ratio thus in itself solicited the noble class towards forcible restriction of peasant mobility and the constitution of larger manorial estates'.[166]

According to Robert Brenner, the key factors in explaining the different effects of the demographic collapse lay in the dynamics of the class struggle including: first, the differential levels of peasant organisation, class consciousness and internal solidarity in each society; and second, the differential levels of ruling class unity and their relationship to the state.[167] In other words, the key variables explaining the variegated effects of the Black Death were the *unevenness* in the social forms of internal differentiation – particularly between the peasant and lordly classes in agrarian production, on the one hand, and between the lords and the state, on the other. It seems then that 'unevenness' and 'combination' played a central role in the ending of serfdom in Western Europe, paving the way for the subsequent emergence of capitalist production relations.

Crucially, for Brenner, these variables explain the divergent developmental paths taken by England (towards agrarian capitalism) and France (toward the strengthening of feudalism) in the aftermath of the Black Death. In France, the monarchical state developed a 'class-like' character, emerging as a competitor to the lords for the peasants' surplus. This meant that when peasant revolts occurred, the state would habitually support them against landlords, by protecting their freehold and fixing dues. The consolidation of peasant freedom precluded market forces of compulsion emerging in agrarian relations, leaving France a fundamentally feudal state. In contrast, England developed significant unity among the landed class vis-à-vis each other and with the state, so that when the peasant revolts took place, the state acted on behalf of landed interests. This allowed English landlords to maintain landholdings by 'engrossing, consolidating and enclosing' peasant freeholds, leading to the development of market forces in production and the emergence of symbiotic relations with tenant capitalists; in short, presaging the sustained economic development of agrarian capitalism.[168]

Remarkably, Brenner cites a distinctly international determination – the Norman conquests of the 11th century – as the central causal factor behind England's uniquely intralordly cohesion.[169] Similarly, as Anderson notes, '[t]he early administrative centralization of Norman feudalism, dictated by both the original military conquest and the modest size of the country had generated ... an unusually small and regionally unified noble class'.[170] The appearance of the Normans in this manner is however problematic, for nowhere does Brenner's treatment of this external determination enter into his theorisation of the development of agrarian capitalism. Instead it appears as an ad-hoc international addendum.[171]

Without theorising 'the international', Brenner finds no trouble tracing English nobility–state relations in the 16th century to an 11th-century cause. Spatial tunnelling in theory leads to temporal tunnelling of history, where historical conjunctures are explained by phenomena half a millennia apart. This leaves numerous questions over how far this picture of intralordly unity going back to the 11th century stands up when tested against the evidence of the intervening years. What, for example, explains the fits of English intralordly struggle during the Hundred Years' War and the War of the Roses?

The next chapter seeks to address this deficiency by looking at how England's internal ruling class unity was in fact predicated on its relative seclusion from the geopolitical tumult that gripped Europe in the aftermath of the Black Death. Although this insulation from geopolitical factors could seemingly lend itself to kind of the internalist method practised by Brenner, on closer inspection we shall find that England's isolation had distinctly international roots, bound up in the geopolitical conflicts taking place on the continent. In particular, this shifts the scope of our international explanation of the origins of capitalism to yet another non-European actor, the Ottoman Empire. We examine the impact of the Ottomans on the making of capitalism in the next chapter.

CHAPTER 4

The Ottoman–Habsburg Rivalry over the Long Sixteenth Century

Modern History begins under stress of the Ottoman Conquest.

Lord Acton, 1899[1]

Introduction

European 16th-century history occupies a peculiar place in historical socio-logical narratives. Compared with the preceding Medieval age, it was a period of striking social alteration and development. Both in its encounter with unchar-tered territories and in its own self-definition, this was very much Europe's 'Age of Discovery'. And yet the 16th century occupies only a marginal place in the 'Age of Revolution'[2] that followed, in the 17th, 18th and 19th centuries. Such a duality is represented in the period's very characterisation as 'early modern'. The term 'modern' anticipates the developments of the next 300 years, whereas the prefix 'early' suggests an epochal budding that has not quite blossomed, or the embryonic shaping of a society that is yet to come. Just as the culture of the Renaissance was defined by a Janus-faced view of the past and future, its geopolitics was characterised by new inventions in diplomacy and warfare that were nonetheless bound by the social relations of the old. And while filling the womb of a bloated aristocracy, trade, commerce and production displayed the first signs of tearing open this archaic order with the deep breath of primitive accumulation that preceded capitalism's screeching birth.

In examining this early modern period, this chapter takes as its starting point the clue of the Turkic rug in Holbein's *Ambassadors*, in order to trace the historical significance of the Ottoman Empire in the making of capitalism. If we recall, this rug alerts us to the fact that in the context of the New World discoveries, primitive accumulation, religious revolt and Habsburg ascendency, the Ottoman Empire was a persistent and prominent presence, lying behind and in many ways underpinning these manifold European developments.[3] In this period, the Ottomans constituted the most prevalent non-Christian 'Other' that confronted Europe,[4] 'persistently capturing the headlines and profoundly transforming the geopolitics of (and beyond) the Mediterranean world'.[5] In the words of Daniel Goffman, 'this was an Ottoman Europe almost as much as it was a Venetian or Habsburg one'.[6] Yet despite the latent centrality implied by Holbein's painting, dominant theorisations of early modern Europe have been constructed with the Ottomans *in absentia*. Whether in the sphere of politics, economy, culture or ideology, the emergence of capitalist modernity is generally understood as a *sui generis* development specific to Europe. In short, the history of capitalism's origins is an unmistakably Eurocentric history (see Chapter 1).

There are two moments to the Eurocentric approach that will be the subject of scrutiny and criticism in this chapter. The first is *historical priority*. Based on the assumption that any given trajectory of development is the product of a society's own immanent dynamics, Eurocentrism 'posits the endogenous and autonomous emergence of modernity in Europe'.[7] Thus we find in cultural history that the flowering of the Renaissance was a solely *intra-European* phenomenon.[8] Analyses of the rise of absolutism and modern state systems are similarly conducted exclusively on the terrain of Europe, with non-European cases appearing (if at all) comparatively.[9] Dominant accounts of the origins of capitalism as either an economic form[10] or a social system[11] place its origins squarely in Western Europe, while the world outside Europe is relegated to an exploited and passive periphery.[12] As such, a prevailing problem of Eurocentric analyses in the extant historiography of the period is rooted not only in deficient theorisations of the Ottoman Empire, but in an equally problematic and one-sided view of European modernity.

A consequence of the epistemological separation (or *epistemological exteriority*) of 'Eastern' from 'Western' societies, Eurocentrism articulates and situates the developmental (and in some cases normative) distinction between tradition and modernity through a spatial separation of 'West' and 'East'. As such, the study of the origins of capitalism has been an exclusionary process in which the agency of the Ottomans has been erased or overlooked. This is not to say that in studies of the 16th century the Ottoman Empire have been heedlessly avoided.[13] But where its imperial apogee has been studied, it has been largely considered a 'social formation apart … largely a stranger to European culture, as an Islamic intrusion on Christendom', or as a comparative case study, against which the specificity and distinctiveness of Western modernity has been defined.[14]

The epistemological distinction between the Ottomans and Europe depends on an *ontologically singular* narrative of the emergence of modernity within the spatially delimited and hermetically sealed boundaries of Europe. Here the second moment of Eurocentrism becomes evident: an *internalist methodology*. Conceptions of the 'East' have subsequently focused on its essential(ist) characteristics – typically Islam, Oriental despotism, or the Asiatic mode of production. Simultaneously, the distinctiveness of the 'West' is presented in terms of its own endogenous and autonomous history. This ontological claim gives rise to the assumption that any given trajectory of development is the product of a society's own *immanent* dynamics, and hence sociological theorisations can only be derived solely from within the domestic confines of a single society.

Recent scholarship in the fields of World History and postcolonial studies has attempted to 'ReOrient'[15] historiography in order to both destabilise and potentially escape the Eurocentric trap. However, despite providing extensive additional empirical frameworks that have decentred the historical priority of Europe, these works have also largely overlooked the role of the Ottomans in the construction of capitalist modernity, while eschewing any concomitant theorisation of capitalism's origins in light of their empirical findings. Even Ottomanists working within the anti-Eurocentric research programme have tended to stand outside of debates concerning the origins of capitalism.[16] Hence, the gnawing separation between 'East' and 'West', Europe and the Ottomans, tends to be replicated even in anti-Eurocentric accounts.

To return to and extend our critique of postcolonialism in Chapter 1, a truly non-Eurocentric interpretation of history must pose an alternative theoretical framework to these traditional conceptions in which to conduct historical and sociological study. That such an alternative has not yet been forthcoming has left the study of modernity at a peculiar impasse that we might term *Eurocentric realism* – the claim that owing to the historical record, there simply is no alternative to Eurocentric accounts of the origins of capitalism. Indeed, for those who subscribe to this realism, Eurocentrism is straightforwardly unproblematic.[17]

In this chapter, we 'return to Holbein' via uneven and combined development to recapture the significance of the Ottomans in the geopolitics of the Long 16th Century. In particular, we seek to bring out the causal impact of the Ottoman Empire on the primary historical themes in *The Ambassadors* – the political fragmentation of feudal Europe in resistance to Habsburg attempts at empire building, the structural shift away from the geopolitical and commercial centrality of the Mediterranean towards the Atlantic, and the primitive accumulation of capital. We argue that these developments – each crucial to the emergence of capitalism – were causally inseparable from Ottoman geopolitical pressures on Europe. In developing this argument, we seek to challenge and criticise Eurocentrism through the theory of uneven and combined development, and in the process further demonstrate its non-Eurocentric credentials. We argue that uneven and combined development can make a positive and illuminating contribution to these debates because it speaks directly to each of the two moments of Eurocentrism identified above. By positing the multilinear character of development as its 'most general law', uneven development provides a necessary corrective to the ontological singularity and attendant unilinear conception of history that underpins assumptions of historical priority. By positing the inherently interactive character of this multiplicity, combined development in turn challenges the methodological internalism of Eurocentric approaches (see Chapter 2).

In this chapter, we further develop the argument that the question 'why Europe?' can only be properly addressed by situating its peculiar development within the context of the international relations of the Long 16th Century. Consequently, a theorisation of the dimension typically elided by Eurocentric analysis – 'the international' – is required for us to break out of the Eurocentric spatiotemporal limits of the hegemonic perspectives provided by the likes of World-System Theorists and Political Marxists. As argued in Chapter 2, uneven and combined development provides precisely such a theorisation, by positing that historical processes are always the outcome of a multiplicity of spatially diverse nonlinear causal chains that combine in any given conjuncture.

In what follows, we show that geopolitical relations between the Ottoman Empire and European states over the Long 16th Century provided one of these vectors of uneven and combined development that fed into the emergence of capitalism. In the first section, we explicate the social relations that underpinned a relation of *unevenness* between the tributary Ottoman Empire and the feudal European states. This Euro–Ottoman relation of unevenness gave rise to numerous political, military, economic and territorial advantages held by the Ottoman Empire over Europe. These forms of unevenness entailed both an Ottoman 'whip of external necessity' and a European 'privilege of historic backwardness' which we argue were crucial preconditions for the eventual emergence of capitalism in Europe. In the second section, we demonstrate how these moments of Euro–Ottoman interactivity entailed various instances of combined development, in which European 'backwardness' compelled the adaptation to and adoption of the developmental advantages possessed by the Ottomans. In particular, we argue that Ottoman attempts at empire building curtailed the imperial threat of the Habsburgs, giving Northwestern European states the structural geopolitical space in which modern state-building practices and the formation of capitalism could take place. In so doing, the Ottomans unwittingly facilitated the primitive accumulation of capital and brought about a *structural shift* to Atlantic trade and Northwestern European dominance, leading to processes of developmental 'catch up' and overtake in Europe that would give rise to capitalism.

Unevenness: A Clash of Social Reproduction

Ottoman–European Relations

Ottoman relations with the outside world have primarily been understood by scholars through an idealised and uncritical notion of diplomatic precepts rooted in Sharia law.[18] Here, the supposed self-regarded superiority of the Ottomans constituted the basis of a unilateral policy on international affairs, and a religious commitment to permanent war with Europe. This mystified conception of Euro–Ottoman relations – articulated as a continuation of the eternal clash between Christianity and Islam – was captured in the literature, philosophy and art of early modern Europe. In the work of artist Leonardo Dati, Sultan Mehmet II was portrayed as a minion of the devil,[19] while Martin Luther argued that the Ottomans were a punishment from God for the degeneration of Christianity.[20]

Yet alongside this widespread belligerence there were also significant levels of European appreciation for Ottoman achievements. For example, reflecting the resistance to the Habsburg alliance, German pamphleteers downplayed the need to intervene militarily against the Ottomans, with some pointing to the Turks' efficiency as a model for German reform.[21] Similarly, the legal code established by Süleyman II was studied by a legal mission sent from England by Henry VIII.[22] The efficient and merit-based character of the Ottoman administrative system was also widely appreciated by European diplomats and visitors to the region. '[A]mong the Turks, dignities, offices, and administrative posts are the rewards of ability and merit', the ambassador to the Ottoman Empire in Constantinople for the Holy Roman Emperor Ferdinand I (1556–64), Ogier Ghiselin de Busbecq, wrote. 'This is why the Turks succeed in all that they attempt and are a dominating race and daily extend the bound of their rule'. This was in stark contrast to the European 'method', de Busbecq went on, where 'there is no room for merit, but everything depends on birth; considerations of which alone open the way to high official position'.[23] Likewise, in their examinations of European state forms, Machiavelli, Bodin, Bacon and Montaigne all heralded Ottoman military discipline and administrative efficiency.[24] To quote Busbecq again:

> I tremble when I think of what the future must bring when I compare the Turkish system with our own .... On their side are the resources of a mighty empire, strength unimpaired, experience and practice in fighting, a veteran soldiery, habituation to victory, endurance of toil, unity, order, discipline, frugality, watchfulness. On our side is public poverty, private luxury, impaird strength, broken spirit, lack of endurance and training; the soldiers are insubordinate, the officers avaricious; there is contempt for discipline; licence, recklessness, drunkenness, and debauchery are rife; and, worst of all, the enemy is accustomed to victory, and we to defeat.[25]

This mixture of fear, awe, belligerence and admiration reflected a material relation of unevenness in which the Ottomans held numerous advantages over their European allies and foes.[26] Perry Anderson goes as far as to suggest that under Süleyman I's reign the Ottomans were 'the most powerful Empire in the world. Overshadowing his nearest European rival, Suleiman enjoyed a revenue twice that of Charles V'.[27] This relation of unevenness was neatly captured by Aeneas Sylvius (the future Pope Pius II) who, after the fall of Constantinople, reflected on the existential threat the Ottomans posed to a disunited Christendom:

> [Christendom] is a body without a head, a republic without laws or magistrates … every state has a separate prince, and every prince has a separate interest …. Who will make the English love the French? Who will unite the Genoese and the Aragonese? Who will reconcile the Germans with the Hungarians and Bohemians? … If you lead a small army against the Turks you will easily be overcome; if a large one, it will soon fall into confusion.[28]

Almost a century later in 1554, Cardinal Pole – an envoy sent by Pope Julius III to negotiate an accord between the French and English – berated Francis I, Henry II and Emperor Charles V for their 'dissensions and wars', which were supposedly to blame for the Ottoman conquest of Belgrade and Rhodes.[29] While Europe struggled with divisions, the Ottomans faced them as a unified, resourceful and disciplined force,[30] one that was able to expand consistently into Europe and beyond. The phenomenon of Christian renegades 'turning Turk' and converting to the 'Ottoman way' appeared to be a pertinent danger, especially since, in certain regions of conquest, the Ottomans had been welcomed as 'liberators' owing to their less onerous taxation systems and respect for local customs.[31] '[H]ow it comes to pass', a contemporary R. Carr lamented, 'that so many of our men should continually revolt, and abjuring all Christian rites, become affectors of that impious Mahumetane sect, whilst on the other part we finde none or very few of those repaying unto us'.[32] Such was the awesome ideological and material force that the Ottoman Empire brought to bear upon the less developed feudal Europeans. But what were the sources of this uneven set of relations between the Ottomans and Europeans?

The Tributary and Feudal Modes of Production: Unevenness Combined

The unevenness between the Ottomans and Europe was underpinned by the divergence in forms of social (re)production associated with the tributary and feudal modes of production. This was expressed in three ways. The first was in the relations that pertained among social classes based on predominantly agrarian production: between exploiter and exploited (and therefore also in the forms and character of surplus appropriation by the ruling class in these societies); second, in the contradictory relations between different sections of the ruling class (and hence political relations as such); third, in relationship between merchants and states to which these forms of social reproduction gave rise. In order to better understand these forms of unevenness, we must first explicate the modal differences between the Ottoman tributary and European feudal modes.

A number of scholars have explicitly denied that there ever existed a historically specific 'tributary mode of production', instead viewing tributary formations as a distinct subvariant of feudalism. This 'universal feudalism' thesis has been most coherently and systematically developed by Halil Berktay and John Haldon.[33] Their central methodological claim is that a distinction should be drawn between a 'mode of production' as an abstract ideal-type and a 'social formation' as a concrete 'really existing' society.[34] This allows them to develop Marx's argument that the mode of production – 'the same economic basis' – can, 'due to innumerable different empirical circumstances', exhibit 'infinite variations and gradations in appearance' at the level of a social formation.[35] For both authors, the economic basis of feudalism therefore resided in the *form of exploitation*,[36] and more specifically in the juxtaposition of a ruling aristocracy exploiting a class of peasant direct producers through extra-economic means.[37] Consequently, for Haldon, 'both sides of the couplet tax/rent are, in fact, expressions of the politico-juridical forms that surplus appropriation takes, not distinctions between different modes'.[38] For Berktay, 'political decentralisation … is a superstructural feature. Thus no clear cut *economic* differences of a primary nature can be pinpointed between Western feudalism and Ottoman society – both were based on peasant production'.[39] Accordingly, the precise natures of these extra-economic means – whether tax or rent – constitute superstructural variations of the same mode of surplus appropriation. Such variations are therefore only ascertainable through the more historically specific analytical level of the social formation.

However, Haldon's and Berktay's insistence on the distinction between modes of production and social formations (and equivalently, between economic bases and political superstructures) generates an array of disconcerting separations between history and theory. By defining a mode of production in terms of an economic basis distinct from a political superstructure, and then conceptually conflating this economic basis with a form of exploitation, they exclude the very social relations that make such exploitation an historical possibility, as conjunctural and contingent specificities that lie outside of the 'mode of production' conceived as an ideal-type theoretical construct. Hence, Haldon argues that:

> the actual conditions in which coercion occurs, and which makes possible its continuation, are fundamental to the ways in which the claims to the appropriation of wealth are enforced and validated. But these can take a multiplicity of different forms and, while they are fundamental to the process of the reproduction of the social relations of production in a specific historical context, *they are still not a part of the economic relations of appropriation*.[40]

This tendency to keep history at an arm's length from theory is a striking position for a historical materialist to take, for it omits any theorisation of three crucial conditions under which any form of surplus appropriation takes place. First, there is a tension between Berktay and Haldon's claim that extra-economic exploitation was a defining characteristic of the feudal mode of surplus appropriation, and their dismissal of the specificity of these extra-economic means – that is, whether they are tax or rent – as entirely political or super-structural. Both Derek Sayer and Perry Anderson have convincingly argued that the very 'fusion' of political and economic functions of coercion and consent that underpin surplus extraction in a pre-capitalist context makes any such separation of economic basis from political superstructure inherently problematic.[41]

Second, in Haldon's and Berktay's accounts, the concept of mode of production becomes detached from history, wherein the specificity of a social formation is rendered independent from the dynamics or 'laws of motion' of any given mode of production. Haldon quite explicitly states that 'a mode of production is not a concrete social reality', that it does 'not exist in any real form' and does 'not develop'.[42] Hence, analysis into the processes of state formation and class conflict becomes entirely a question engaged with at the level of the 'social formation', leaving us with a static 'ideal-type' conception of a production mode.[43]

Taking these two exclusions together, Haldon and Berktay's explanation for the 'variations and gradations' in a mode of production comes to rest entirely on historical chance and accidents. So, third, historical variation – unevenness, multiplicity – appears only as a contingent fact of social reality which sits outside the explanatory purview of a mode of production-centred analysis. Theoreti-cally, this involves a conflation of universality with homogeneity, whereby sociological differences are obscured rather than articulated. In turn, the very dimension of socio-spatial multiplicity – 'the international' – also becomes obscured or overlooked. We are instead left with a pervasive commitment to an ontological singular conception of society. Indeed, Berktay argues that 'it is permissible to investigate the Ottoman Empire in the 15th–16th centuries as *an autonomous pre-capitalist social formation, without referring it to any significant external economic dynamics*'.[44] As demonstrated below, such a methodologically internalist perspective is not only unsustainable empirically, but also does violence to any theoretical understanding of the developmental dynamics of the Ottoman Empire.

In what follows, we seek to reframe the Ottoman mode of production debate by confronting this question of 'the international' overlooked by Berktay and Haldon. In doing so, we argue that a 'mode of production' should be seen not as a simple economic relation, or merely a form of exploitation, but as a composite totality of social relations that encapsulate certain conditions of production – be they political, cultural or intersocietal – and the 'laws of motion' that arise out of those conditions (see further Chapter 7).

From such a perspective, the Ottoman Empire can be fruitfully conceptualised as a tributary mode of production, distinct from – rather than a subvariant of – feudalism. Following Jairus Banaji, we may define the tributary mode as constituted along two class-relational axes: first, the vertical opposition of a ruling, tax-collecting class in a contradictory relationship with a class of peasants exploited for the appropriation of productive surpluses; and second, the horizontal differentiation between a 'landed nobility' and 'patrimonial authority' within the tax-collecting class, in which the state controlled the nobility as well as the means of production.[45] Hence, the relations of production of the tributary mode 'involved both the control of peasant-labour by the state … and the drive to forge a unified imperial service based on the subordination of the ruling class to the will of the ruler'.[46]

The emphases on these social relations help to identify some of the essential elements of the Ottoman form of the tributary mode. The first – ruling class–peasant – division was articulated through the appropriation of peasant production surpluses through taxation. The most common tax was the *öşür* tithe, which took one-tenth of agricultural produce, followed by the *cizye* head tax for non-Muslims. In addition, the *orfi* 'sovereign prerogative' could be levied on decree, and included the *adat* customary and *avârız* household taxes. While it was initially levied to meet extraordinary expenses – in particular for war-making – this became a regular tax on villages and towns.[47]

The preponderance of taxation as a mechanism for surplus appropriation was distinct from the European lord–peasant rent nexus of exploitation because taxation was regulated by regional and central agents of the Ottoman state.[48] This meant that peasants had greater access to their surplus than in Europe because of the preservation of subsistence plots, as well as state-fixed limitations on taxation by intermediaries at local (*beys*) and regional (*beylerbeys*) levels.[49] Peasants also had inalienable rights to land,[50] were better protected from market fluctuations,[51] had the option – albeit limited – to legal recourse should their conditions worsen,[52] and were legally considered free.[53] Without overlooking the fact that peasants were subject to highly exploitative conditions and abuses of power, such differences suggest that Ottoman subjects' experiences diverged from those of their European counterparts.[54]

The second division – between a landed nobility and patrimonial authority – was distinct from intra-ruling class relations in Europe because almost all land was formally owned by the Sultan, while military fiefs – *timars* – were predominantly nonhereditary, changeable and regularly rotated among individuals in the ruling class.[55] This created a contradictory distribution of political power and surplus, forming a centre–periphery sociopolitical structure.[56] Located primarily in Constantinople, the Ottoman centre consisted of the sultan, his household and the imperial council, comprising the army judge (*kadi-asker*), Grand Vizier, treasurers and slave elites (the *devşirme* or *kapıkullar*).[57] The latter, despite their slave status, occupied the highest administrative and military positions in the Empire, comprising a large and unified bureaucratic administration and the Janissary (*yeniceri*) military.[58] Together they provided the state with well-trained standing troops and administrative officers capable of overseeing the complexity of the Ottoman tax system.[59] Because the *kapıkullar* were recruited through levies (*kul*) on children from conquered territories and then transferred to and assimilated into the Ottoman centre, they were entirely dependent on (and therefore loyal to) the Sultan.[60] By the 14th century these centralised institutions acted as a crucial counterbalance to provincial power, and by the time of Mehmed II's conquest of Constantinople in 1453, they came to predominate over other sections of the Empire.

Although the state established control over provincial notables and land, central authority was relatively dispersed. The Ottoman state was able to regulate both production and exploitation by devolving power to its agents in the rural provinces through the *tımar* system.[61] A *tımar* was the predominant form of land division,[62] an allocation of land from which the holder could extract revenue. *Tımars* provided the basic income for the *sipahi* cavalrymen and imperial officers (*sancak beys*) in return for their performing state services. *Tımar* holders were also responsible for the collection of land taxes and the periodic redistribution of peasant holdings, as well as the maintenance of civil order.[63] Some larger *tımars* were assigned to more powerful and entrenched sections of the Ottoman ruling class, such as the *devşirme* and those close to the house of the Sultan.[64] In these cases, the holding was often passed onto the *tımar* holder's son, establishing a degree of hereditary ownership in some sections of the ruling class.[65] For example, in the early period of Ottoman expansion, a number of the old Turkish clan elite – *ghazis* – were able to retain ancestral lands as *tımar* grants, enabling them to maintain an economically dominant position. As such, the *tımar* system was partly designed to placate through compensation the *ghazi* leaders and local notables of newly conquered lands by admitting them into the ruling *askeri* class.[66]

Nonetheless, *tımar* holders were fundamentally dependent on and constrained by the Ottoman central state functions for their social reproduction. *Tımar* holdings were assigned by the Sultan, and possession was granted through the acquisition of a Sultanic diploma.[67] Scrupulously maintained tax registers kept a strict record of the size of *tımars* and their contents, in turn setting the level of taxes that could be levied by the *tımar* holder from the peasantry.[68] Moreover, the rotation of *tımar* allocations were used to remove potentially discontented *ghazis* from their local environment.[69] By resettling *ghazis* in Ottoman-controlled Europe, the administration could prevent the growth of provincial centres of power while filling the Empire's frontiers with a powerful military force.[70] Through these mechanisms the Ottomans were able to institutionalise the social reproduction of *tımar* holders into a relationship of dependence to the Sultan.[71] Consequently, the *timar*, despite providing a basis of provincial power, was a function of a form of social stratification that was crucial to the reproduction of the tributary state. In this sense, the *timar* embodied the distinction in tributary ruling class relations between the patrimonial authority of the sultan and his household, and the local nobility, in which the former controlled the latter.

The devices of ruling class reproduction under the tributary mode proved remarkably efficient and stable, so much so that theorists have often mistaken its very dynamism in ruling class reproduction for a static and unchanging social form.[72] Due to the nature of Ottoman power sharing and the alienability of notable land, there was limited potential for unified class interests acting outside the purview – or counter to the interests – of the Ottoman state.[73] Instead, discontented sections of the ruling class sought to articulate disaffection within the confines of the extant political system,[74] while the state was able to maintain the internal integrity of the Empire by co-opting local elites,[75] or coercively centralising power.[76] Furthermore, the relatively lenient form of surplus extraction levied on Ottoman peasants, as well as tolerance for local religions and identities, meant that rebellion in the countryside was a less marked feature of the Ottoman tributary mode than it was of European feudalism.[77] Hence, there was little impulse or necessity for reform of the tributary system from above, or revolutionary pressure from below.[78] Consequently, through their contradictory relations to production, the state, provincial ruling classes and the peasants, as well as more marginal groups such as merchants and religious foundations, were overwhelmingly geared towards the reproduction and expansion of the state and its functions. This was the defining feature of the tributary mode and its 'laws of motion'.

The primary contradiction of the tributary mode therefore lay in the structure of the ruling class itself, which could potentially come into conflict over the distribution of surplus between its central and provincial sections. The prevention of this conflict, and hence the continued reproduction of the tributary mode, was possible so long as the Ottoman ruling class could maintain its material well-being and ideological unity.[79] Haldon suggests that such unity was achievable only through a policy of military and economic expansion.[80] Provincial notables and would-be members of the Ottoman ruling class could best be guaranteed expanded access to surplus only through the accumulation of more land that would in turn be redistributed to them in the form of *timars*.[81] Similarly, the burgeoning central state required greater access to taxes, tributes and a population from which to recruit slave elites. Both objectives were possible only through continual territorial accumulation. These specific historical configurations of the tributary mode of production were therefore inextricably bound up with not simply an internal temporal dynamic of a society – its 'laws of motion' – but also its interactive relations with other societies. Put differently, the laws of motion of the tributary mode had an inherently uneven and combined component to them, and this uneven and combined feature explains sociological differences between tributary societies.

As detailed above, tributary laws of motion consisted in the reproduction of the imperial state through the appropriation of surpluses derived from the centre's control of the ruling class and means of production. The social reproduction of the tributary state thus took place not only through 'internal' relations of surplus appropriation, but also through the 'external' means of geopolitical accumulation. By conquering land, the tributary state was able to extend and widen its control of the means of production – land – enabling it to extract greater tribute from its population. In the Ottoman case, this involved not only the appropriation of productive surpluses but also the power of workers (in particular, slaves) for the expansion of state functions. Territorial conquest also enabled the Ottoman state to control the ruling class through the triple means of consent, coercion and competition.

First, subservient members of the ruling class could be co-opted by being offered access to more land, building relations of dependence and consent between centre and province in the process. Second, discontented or rebellious sections could be relocated to the frontiers of expansion and away from the imperial centre. In some cases, by incorporating pre-existing notables in conquered territories, troublesome members of the ruling class could be expropriated and replaced. For although Ottoman expansion was predicated on conquest, 'outsiders' would also willingly seek to become part of the ruling class, with the knowledge that subordination to the state would confer privilege and security: that is, it would guarantee social reproduction. So third, such incorporation could foster competition between different sections of the ruling class with differential relations of dependence on – and autonomy from – the imperial system.

Imperial geopolitical accumulation was therefore crucial to maintaining state power over sections of the ruling class. This made tributary societies particularly sensitive to external conditions – either through conquest, assimilation, diplomacy, secession or conflict – as a fundamental component of their social reproduction. That is, geopolitical accumulation was not just an externalisation of internal contradictions, arising from logics of reproduction 'within' societies.[82] Nor was it – in contrast to Marx's 'Asiatic' model – simply a process in which the tributary form was unidirectionally superimposed onto pre-existing communities.[83] It was rather a mechanism through which relations with other societies would feed back upon and reconfigure the internal class composition and laws of motion of the tributary mode itself.

In reference to nomadic empires, but equally applicable to the tributary mode, Kees van der Pijl calls this relational form of social reproduction 'caging'.[84] On the one hand, conquered territories would assimilate tributary social relations into their own pre-existing forms.[85] On the other hand, the tributary state would habitually absorb the local customs, laws, forms of social organisation, and individuals of conquered territories.[86] Such 'caging' through geopolitical accumulation was a central part of tributary laws of motion and a concrete practice of combined development, in which the developmental experiences of differentiated societies were syncretically merged in an 'amalgamated state' form.[87] As van der Pijl puts it:

> the principles of sovereignty and bureaucratised authority of empire, heralding the territorial state, here mix with the notion of shared space reminiscent of tribal foreign relations. Different ways of life are pressed together, and the density and intensity of social interaction works to accelerate development.[88]

Consequently, the reproduction of tributary rule was fundamentally dependent on agrarian production in support of geopolitical accumulation and vice versa – what Burak Tansel aptly calls the Ottoman 'military-agricultural complex'.[89] Provincially, this involved the maintenance of *sipahi* cavalry troops who reproduced themselves and their retainers by appropriating peasant surpluses on their *tımar* land allocations. In return, they provided arms, horses, food and other supplies for themselves and their retainers in military campaigns.[90] Through the institution of *devşirme*, the Ottoman centre was able to fill its ranks with the most able boys in the Empire, training them into a well drilled military force, the Janissaries. This section of the military was supported by the extensive accumulation of agrarian surpluses, redistributed to them through the treasury in the form of wages. Janissary pay constituted the single largest item of treasury expenditure, costing 44 per cent of the treasury's budget in 1527.[91]

Through these mechanisms of social reproduction, the Ottomans were able to raise seasoned, disciplined and steadfast armies on an unprecedented scale. The *kapıkullar* army – which included the Janissaries, as well as a cavalry and artillery – comprised the best trained and most loyal section of the Ottoman army, numbering an estimated 30,000 by the reign of Suleiman I.[92] In the provinces, the *tımar* system could raise up to 80,000 men between the *sipahis* and their retainers. These were supplemented by auxiliary troops and *akıncıs* drawn from peasant and nomadic populations within the Empire.[93] For example, relations of tribute with the Tatar Khan of Crimea could supply up to an estimated 100,000 additional *akıncıs* to the Ottoman army.[94] Similarly, North African corsairs under Ottoman vassalage provided a large and skilled naval force in the Mediterranean.[95] Taken together, in the 16th century the Sultan could potentially deploy over 200,000 men without putting the Ottoman treasury or peasantry under any exceptional strain.[96]

The Ottomans' ability to raise vast and loyal armies for military campaigns was matched by the development of 'centralized modes for resource extraction and allocation for use in war' that provided the administrative basis of military support.[97] The state's regulation of production though records of land tenure enabled them to encourage grain production that would feed this vast army, as well as raise oxen and buffalo in Rumelia and horses from the Danube for transporting supplies.[98] Routinised levying of military provisions in the form of *avârız* taxes was an established procedure by the 16th century.[99] Armies were supplied with basic foodstuffs from the state treasury or locally from state-owned lands, rather than resorting to forced contributions from peasant populations.[100] Integrating agrarian production with war-making in this way left agrarian and civilian life relatively undisturbed by war-making, imbuing the military-agricultural complex with a continuous stability unmatched in feudal Europe.[101] In the fields of transport, logistics and food supply, the unity of the tributary mode made the Ottomans 'trend-setters and models of perfection whom the others strove to emulate'.[102]

Ottoman 'Penalties of Progressiveness' – European 'Privileges of Backwardness'

The unity and stability of the Ottoman Empire examined above contrasted significantly with European forms of social reproduction. These too were predominantly based on agrarian production, where peasants had direct access to the means of production and subsistence. And like the Ottoman Empire, this condition meant that an aristocratic ruling class required political, ideological and military means in order to exploit the peasantry and extract a surplus for the purpose of lordly consumption. However, unlike in the Ottoman Empire, these means were not controlled by – or concentrated in – a centralised and unified state, but were dispersed across the nobility.[103] As a consequence, peasants were more susceptible to coercive squeezes on their productivity, while having no recourse to outside legal protection from their lords. This regularly led to declining living conditions and, in turn, rural rebellions.[104] At the same time, the dispersion of coercive capabilities meant that political authority in Europe was unusually fragmented, parcellised and therefore also highly competitive, with heightened intralordly struggles taking place over territories both within and outside of feudal 'states'.[105] In short, both war and rebellion was more pronounced within Europe than in Ottoman territories.

Because of the fragmented and parcellised character of political power, Europeans who wanted to make war required extraordinary financing outside the day-to-day mechanisms of ruling class reproduction. In order to raise armies, European rulers borrowed from international banking houses[106] or asked wealthy and powerful sections of society for contributions, in terms of either military support or taxes.[107] This was often conducted via 'local estates and assemblies or city-leagues in which the merchant-entrepreneurial class wielded significant – even military – power'.[108] Hence, a byproduct of European feudal war-making was an attendant rise in the political autonomy, power and influence of merchants, with increasing degrees of representation in the decision-making structures of states;[109] for 'behind every successful dynasty stood an array of opulent banking families'.[110]

By contrast, the Ottoman Empire had little requirement for monetary financing outside of the customary levies already imposed on agrarian production.[111] Consequently, there was scarce potential for autonomous merchant activity outside of the functional requirements of the tributary state. The relations between merchants and the Ottoman ruling class were balanced considerably in favour of the latter, who exercised significant control over merchant activities through the guild system.[112] Moreover, conflicts or tensions between merchants and guilds tended to curtail merchant autonomy and power,[113] while merchant access to state apparatuses and decision making was limited.[114] The accumulation of wealth was discouraged and restricted by controlling coin circulation, production and prices, and anti-luxury laws were deployed to confiscate merchant fortunes.[115] Inter-regional trade was heavily regulated, and provisions for towns came almost exclusively from their own hinterlands, narrowing the geographical remit of production and distribution to local regions.[116] Caravan endpoints geographically coincided with seats of government authority, ensuring close supervision of prices and commodities traded. Taxes on trade also enabled state extraction of surpluses from mercantile activities.[117]

The subordination of merchants to the tributary state was also evident geopolitically. For a ruling class fundamentally dependent on agriculture and tribute for their reproduction, the capturing and control of trade routes was considered essential to tributary power in order to bring those outside of its imperial purview within its tributary regime.[118] So while the state could at times show signs of 'economic intentionality',[119] merchants were not considered important enough for state protection or support. Rather, agriculture remained the priority. Following the capture of the Mamluk Empire in 1517, for example, the Ottomans were placed in a position of direct competition with the Portuguese over access to the spice trade in the Indian Ocean, and gold and slaves in Africa.[120] But instead, imperial policy reverted to territorial expansion into the agriculturally more fertile and populous territories of Southeast Europe. That the Ottomans did not pursue the Indian course was primarily due to the reproductive requirements of a ruling class based primarily on agrarian production,[121] reflecting the swelling claims made by provincial notables on access to booty, land, and power as such.[122]

By contrast, European powers were explicitly focused on bringing commercially valuable territories under direct conquest and political control for specifically (though not exclusively) economic purposes. The reason was the relative 'backwardness' of European structures of ruling class reproduction, which were dependent on the wealth drawn from merchants and financiers to either fund (geo)political accumulation (in the case of Habsburg Spain and Austria) or for the direct reproduction of the ruling class itself (in the case of city-states such as Genoa and Venice). Consequently, the state was sensitive to – or at the behest of – merchant interests, and state resources, especially military, were deployed in order to obtain commercial advantages.[123] Such was the extent of merchant power that no European ruler could have withdrawn or demanded the return of ships in the Indian Ocean as the Ottomans had done.[124]

These uneven internal relations – between ruling and ruled class in agrarian production, on the one hand, and between state and merchant, on the other – formed the basis of an international relation of Euro-Ottoman unevenness: the relative backwardness of the European ruling classes, and the comparative weakness in its form of social reproduction when opposed to the Ottoman Empire. These European 'privileges of backwardness' encouraged and compelled its people – both ruling and ruled classes – to develop and adopt new ways of securing their social reproduction, which we elucidate in the next section. At the same time, the relative strength of the Ottoman social form entailed 'penalties of progressiveness': the stability of their structures of social reproduction provided the Ottoman ruling class with various mechanisms through which their power could be sustained, even in the face of social upheaval.[125]

This relation of unevenness goes some way to explaining why the so-called 'miracle' of capitalism would occur in Europe, and why it would not be repeated in Ottoman territories. That this divergence was a product of Ottoman 'progressiveness' and European 'backwardness' suggests that Eurocentric assumptions of historical priority need to be reconsidered. Moreover, these two elements – Ottoman strength, and European 'privilege of backwardness' – were ultimately *interrelated* and *co-constitutive* phenomena. As a consequence of its comparative strength, the geopolitical pressure of the Ottomans (the 'whip of external necessity') constantly affected and redirected European development, in turn compelling changes in its forms of social reproduction. This meant that while the Ottomans were faced as a significant existential threat, they were also an opportunity for the most 'backward' part of Europe – the Northwest – to outflank the more advanced Habsburg Empire and Italian city-states.

Combination: *Pax Ottomana* and European Trade

Coupled with the unevenness in forms of social reproduction, the Euro–Ottoman relation entailed a curious form of combined development. The development of European culture over the course of the Renaissance cannot be separated from such interrelations. In certain cases, such as that of Constanzo da Ferrara, European artists spent time in the Ottoman court and worked under the Sultan's commission.[126] Ottoman imagery was widely featured by Italian Renaissance painters seeking to elicit support for crusades by representing the Ottomans as the embodiment of the Islamic threat.[127] Humanist literature would similarly deploy the Ottomans as a comparative allegorical vehicle through which medieval forms of European statecraft could be analysed and criticised.[128] In both Shakespeare's *Othello* and Thomas More's *Dialogue*, Ottoman military supremacy revealed the underlying divisions in Christendom.[129]

These comparisons with the Ottoman Empire therefore reflected a period of European self-examination and criticism in the context of Christendom's breakdown as a unifying principle.[130] It was in the context of the Ottoman threat that propagandists, politicians and thinkers began talking about Europe as a normative as well as geographical concept. The aforementioned Aeneas Sylvius invented the very adjective 'European' following the fall of Constantinople to the Ottomans.[131] Habsburg and Polish publicists began appealing to secular 'European values' in order to defend Hungarian territories from Ottoman incursions.[132]

In terms of diplomacy, culture and religion, the Ottoman presence was inseparable from the breakdown of the old and the emergence of increasingly modern ways of thinking. Considering the extensive ideological effect of Euro–Ottoman relations, we might wonder why the historiography of capitalism's origins has been constructed with the Ottomans absent. For the remainder of this chapter, we explore this as an additional and underappreciated trajectory of combined development between the Ottomans and Europe in the 16th century and argue that this constituted a fundamental and necessary (but not sufficient) condition for the emergence of capitalism in Western Europe.

The Ottoman 'Whip of External Necessity'

Prior to the definitive establishment of the Ottoman Empire in the 14th century, Europe existed in an interdependent commercial relationship with the rest of the world in which it was relatively peripheral to global trade.[133] European traders of this period greatly benefited from pre-existing networks, relations and cultures of exchange,[134] as well as the exposure to extensive sources of technology and knowledge (see also Chapter 3).[135] Because of this condition of 'backwardness', the recovery of European feudalism, the flourishing of commerce and the cultural Renaissance that accompanied it were directly connected to the re-establishment of peaceful lines of communication and trade between 'East' and 'West' that followed the expansion and consolidation of the Ottoman Empire.[136]

Through the institutional support of the Ottoman state, the *Pax Ottomana* lowered commercial protection and transaction costs, established relatively

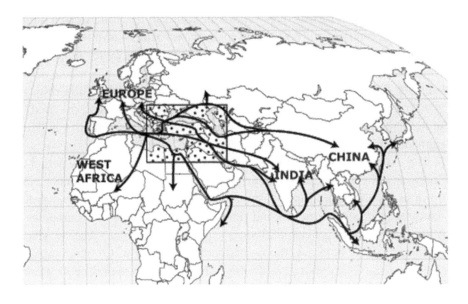

Figure 4.1 Eurasian trade routes during the *Pax Ottmana*

uniform trading practices and hastened the alacrity of trade. On land and sea, Ottoman rule was crucial to safeguarding traders from banditry or piracy, while building roads and canal routes that would facilitate inter-regional trade.[137] The emergence of the *Pax Ottomana* also brought together highways of commerce linking Russia and Central Asia with Europe via the Black Sea, and the Levant and North Africa to the Indian Ocean where the bulk of Euro-Asian trade was conducted.[138] Geographically and economically, 'the Ottoman Empire was the hinge that connected the rapidly growing economies of Europe with those of the East'.[139]

The safe passages into the Indian Ocean and along the Silk Route were crucial to the transmission of commodities that gave rise to the European demand for Eastern goods, which aided the further development of commerce in Europe.[140] The 'engines of the economic boom of the late fifteenth century [such] as Venice, Marseilles, and Ragusa depended on the Ottoman Empire' for both luxury and bulk goods,[141] and in the course of the 16th century less established states such as France, England and the Low Countries became increasingly reliant on Ottoman raw materials.[142] The spice trade that would become a cornerstone of colonial capitalism was primarily conducted between the Indian Ocean and the Middle East, with European markets only receiving surpluses left over from Middle Eastern consumption; by the late 1500s, 80 per cent of the pepper trade was being conducted through the Levant.[143] Supplies of Iranian silk were transmitted to the West via Aleppo, significant amounts of wheat came from Crimea and Greece, rice from Egypt, cattle from Hungary, Wallachia and Moldova, and timber, wool, mohair, cotton and hides from the Balkans and Anatolia.[144]

Trade and communication between the Ottomans and Europe also assisted the transmission of social and technological knowledge, leading to a spurt of developments in European manufacturing, particularly those sectors imitating 'Eastern' products.[145] The boost in French economic activity following a trade agreement with the Ottomans led to the 'proto-industrialisation' of towns such as Marseilles.[146] The competition in silk markets between the Levant and Venice inspired the creation of the hydraulic mill in Bologna which would later be adapted to construct Lombe's Mill in Derby in the early 18th century[147] – arguably the world's first fully mechanised factory.[148] Because Ottoman merchants themselves were active agents in bolstering trade within the Empire and beyond, their own credit system and methods of accumulation such as the *simsar* monopoly association and *mudaraba* advance system[149] became woven into the fabric of European commercial relations, prefiguring the 'complete control of a commodity from production to sale'[150] that would become the hallmark of 'company capitalism'.

However, despite the commercially regenerative effects of *Pax Ottomana*, for Europe the Ottoman incursions seemed like a semi-apocalyptic event. With a standing army the size of which no alliance of European rulers could match, the Ottomans constituted a formidable military danger that threatened the very existence of Christendom. This Euro–Ottoman confrontation was rooted in a relation of unevenness: the Ottoman tributary system allowed for the raising of armies on a stable and unified basis, while the feudal system in Europe required extraordinary financing for armies, which weakened intra-ruling class unity and rural stability. The very efficacy of the Ottoman military meant that from the mid-15th century and '[u]p to 1596 there was no question of international politics which did not somehow involve the Ottomans'.[151]

This involvement was permanent and regularly hostile. In 1453, the Ottomans conquered Constantinople, subsequently using it as a base to conduct further excursions into Greece, Bosnia and Albania. Europe's Eastern preoccupation was soon justified, as Ottoman armies surged onward to Budapest and Vienna in the 1520s, putting them in direct conflict with the Habsburgs. The ensuing wars between these two 'superpowers' were conducted primarily on the southeastern terrain of Europe, with an especially long drawn-out war over Hungary and Mediterranean possessions. Having conquered Egypt and Syria in 1517, and thus obtaining access to this crucial hinge in the Eurasian trade routes, the Ottomans became, perhaps briefly, the most impressive seaborne power in the Mediterranean.[152] Access to this crucial artery of seaborne trade, teeming with Ottoman-sponsored corsairs, became conditional on the outcomes of the Ottoman–Habsburg rivalry.

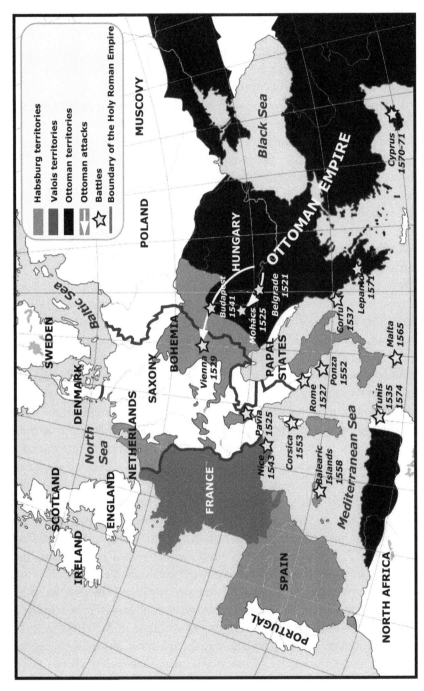

Figure 4.2 The Ottoman–Habsburg rivalry during the 16th century

The Breakdown of Christendom

Such was the concern over 'the Infidel' that 'the papacy put more of its resources into fighting the Ottomans than it did into combatting Protestantism'.[153] The very purpose of a united Christendom was repeatedly emphasised in functional terms to launch a new wave of crusades against the Ottoman Empire. After Francis I was captured by the Hapsburgs in the Italian Wars (1521–26), his release was negotiated on the condition that wars with the Ottomans would become his 'principal intention'.[154] Similarly, the Peace of Cambrai (1529) called on its signatories to stop the Turkish invasions, as did the Peace of Crepy (1544), which required Francis I to provide soldiers to fight in Hungary against the Ottomans.[155] Legitimacy for that other bulwark of Christendom, the Habsburg Empire, was similarly constructed in the Ottoman mirror. By 1519, concern for the 'Terrible Turk' loomed so large that the election of Charles V as the Emperor of the Holy Roman Empire was in part based on his ability to unite Christendom in wars against the Ottomans.[156] The pre-eminence of Charles's son, Philip II, was also legitimised through appeals to his ability to repel the Ottoman threat.[157] In such respects, it could be argued that Ottoman belligerence, despite tearing into Christian lands, served as a common enemy around which the disparate factions of Christendom could unite.

Calls for harmony, however, generally fell on deaf ears. One exception was the Holy League formed in 1571, which brought together the Papal States, Spain, Venice, Genoa, Tuscany, Savoy, Parma, Urbino and Malta. Deploying 290 ships carrying 44,000 sailors and oarsmen, 28,000 soldiers and 1,800 guns, the Holy League established 'the largest naval force mounted by Christendom, and the largest ever deployed against Islam'.[158] Confronting an Ottoman naval force of a similar size, the ensuing victory for the Holy League at the Battle of Lepanto in 1571 came to be regarded as one of the greatest victories for the forces of Christendom. Subsequently mythologised, it long remained a central plank in the 'clash of civilizations' narrative, distinguishing the 'liberated West' from a 'despotic East'.[159] In this respect, the battle was central to the formation of a European identity that was distinctly 'non-Ottoman'.

But revealingly, Lepanto had little actual impact on the sort of crusading missions that the Holy League was created for. For starters, such was the strength of the Ottomans that they suffered no further territorial losses and had the resources to immediately replace the armies lost in 1571. In fact, when the Ottomans conquered Tunis in 1574, they did so with a naval force larger than the one that fought at Lepanto: 'The Ottomans thus reminded Christendom that they could still bring war to Europe's heartlands'.[160] At the same time, the Holy League betrayed the divisions within Christendom by disbanding in 1573. Here again, the Ottomans played a determining role. Venice, seeking to defend

Figure 4.3 Battle of Lepanto, 7 October 1571, depicted by an unknown artist

Source: http://commons.wikimedia.org/wiki/File:Battle_of_Lepanto_1571.jpg (accessed 22 November 2014).

its commercial interests in the Mediterranean, approached the Ottomans for a peaceful resolution to ongoing conflicts in the region. In doing so, the Venetians effectively abandoned the continuing Habsburg military campaign in North Africa.[161]

In short, the very notion of the crusade as a unifying ideology, with its implication of an offensive on the Infidel, proved impracticable and unsustainable. The reality was, as we have seen, the opposite; the 16th century was one of near-permanent victory for the Ottomans and defeat for Christendom. With the unifying principle of the crusade in tatters, the legitimacy of Christendom, already divided, came more and more into question.

Here again, the Ottomans were active participants. Aside from direct instances of military pressure, the Ottomans also deployed alliances and connections with dissident groups in Europe as a means of undermining Habsburg and Papal hegemony.[162] Francis I, king of Valois France, recognised the significance of the Ottoman Empire as a 'power-balancer', candidly admitting:

> I keenly desire the Turk powerful and ready for war, not for himself, because he is an infidel and we are Christians, but to undermine the emperor's power to force heavy expenses upon him and to reassure all other governments against so powerful an enemy.[163]

But the 'unholy alliance' between the French and Ottomans went beyond mere power balancing, and instead constituted – for both sides – a useful strategic union against the Habsburgs and Papal alliances.

After Charles V attacked Provence in 1536, Francis I was able to call upon Barbarossa, a corsair commander under Ottoman suzerainty, to attack the Genoese.[164] The following year, an Ottoman attack on Corfu in 1537 called on the assistance of 13 French galleys. Even more remarkably, in 1543, Barbarossa's fleet participated in a French invasion of Nice (then under the duchy of Savoy), eventually occupying the town. Unable to provision their troops in Nice, the Ottomans were given permission by Francis I to station troops in nearby Toulon for eight months. Francis cleared the town of its French population, effectively turning it into an Ottoman colony including a slave market and Mosque.[165] Even after Francis's reign, Ottoman-French strategic relations continued to thrive. Henry II signed a treaty with Süleyman I, leading to the 1551 siege of Tripoli by Ottoman ships. Triggering the Italian War of 1551–59, the French and Ottomans conducted joint operations against Charles V, with the Ottomans committing up to 100 galleys. The Franco-Ottoman alliance captured Reggio in 1552 and invaded Corsica in 1553.[166] A decade later, the Capitulation agreement given to the French in 1569 was deployed as an attempt by the Ottomans to 'divide its European neighbours on the eve of its assault upon Cyprus'.[167]

The Ottoman-French alliance grabbed the headlines, but the Ottomans also established more clandestine links with dissident groups in Christendom. For example, Sultan Süleyman I contacted the Schmalkaldic League of German Protestant princes, urging them to cooperate with France against the Habsburgs, and offering them amnesty should Ottoman armies conquer Europe.[168] Moreover, the military pressure of the Ottoman Empire proved a crucial contributing factor in the origins and expansion of the Reformation. Lutheran revolts swept through Germany during a period in which the Habsburgs were especially dependent on German military support and financial aid in wars against the Ottomans.[169] This proved to be forthcoming only on the condition that Charles V agreed to religious reforms. In this context, Lutherans sought to carve out greater religious freedoms whenever conflict between the Ottomans and Habsburgs surfaced, using the Ottoman threat as a bargaining chip in negotiations with Charles V.[170]

The ensuing spread of the Reformation often occurred in territories that bore the mark of the Ottomans, most notably in Hungary. The Ottomans encouraged religious heterodoxy in Hungarian lands as a check on Roman Catholic (and by extension Habsburg) claims to power and authority in the region.[171] Under the rule of John Sigismund Zápolya – elected king of Hungary twice (1540–51 and 1556–71), very much due to Ottoman protection – Hungary became 'a haven for Reformed Protestants'[172] which recognised or at the very least tolerated Latin-rite Christians, Calvinists, Lutherans, Unitarians and Orthodox Christians. The Ottomans went so far as to provide direct military assistance to the Hungarian Protestant revolt against Habsburg-Catholic rule (1604), and awarded its leader Stephen Bocskay an *ahitname* (treaty) which confirmed him Prince of Transylvania and King of Hungary.[173]

The '*Calvino-turcismus*' would reach as far as the French Calvinist party, who called for the use of an Ottoman alliance against Spain in the second half of the 16th century.[174] The Ottomans also developed links with the Moriscoes, committing on occasion infantries of 200–400 men to assist in rebellions against the Spanish.[175] By 1580, Sultan Murad III had established connections with Queen Elizabeth I, leading to a 1580 commercial treaty and a capitulation in 1583. By the 1590s, Anglo-Ottoman relations were considered a key strategic alliance against the shared enemy of Habsburg Spain, although the hoped-for assistance by Barbary corsairs in the English naval wars against Spain never materialised.[176]

With slightly greater success the Ottomans also established links with Protestants in the Low Countries[177] in order to internally destabilise Habsburg Spain. William of Orange sent ambassadors to the Ottoman Empire in 1566 to assist with the Dutch Revolt, stating, 'the Turks are very threatening, which will mean, we believe, that the king will not come to the Netherlands this year'.[178] Later, in the 1570s, Dutch rebels were known to use the slogan '*Liever Turks dan Paaps*' ('Rather Turkish than Papist').[179] However, the conflict between the Ottomans and Christendom was not restricted to the geographical confines of Europe. The Ottomans built alliances with Islamic sultanates in South Asia and East Africa – such as Calicut, Ajuran and Adal – as part of a concerted effort to undermine Portuguese attempts to infiltrate these regions.[180]

Various authors have noted that it was the accumulation of such 'cross-pressures generated by the heterogeneity and scale'[181] of the Habsburg domain that hindered attempts at the establishment of a unified imperial hegemony in Europe.[182] And in numerous ways it was the Ottoman threat that so persistently redirected both Habsburg and Papal resources away from the internal divisions that were stretching the Empire in the northwest, contributing in turn to the perpetuation of 'multiple polities within the cultural unity of Christian Europe' that 'time and again frustrated universal imperial ambitions'.[183] Both Charles V's and Philip II's prioritisation of the Ottoman front came at an extremely high cost. The former could not maintain either religious or Austro-Castilian unity, and the latter oversaw the eventual breakaway of the Dutch Provinces that would mark the beginning of the end for the Spanish Habsburg epoch. It was only after the Ottoman threat was dispelled from the Mediterranean that Philip II could concentrate Spanish efforts on consolidating rule in the Netherlands and invading England in the late 16th century, by which time it was arguably all too late.[184]

It could be said, then, that the uneven and combined development of relations between the Ottomans and Europe created further vectors of unevenness throughout Europe. Consequently, 'combination' was itself felt unevenly, with its specific causal effects varying across different European states. The more 'advanced' European states constituted the primary focus of Ottoman military operations, while alliances with more 'backward' European states were utilised to balance against the Habsburgs. As such, while the Habsburgs, Genoese, Venetians, Spanish and Portuguese were antagonistically engaged with the Ottomans, Northwestern European states such as France, the Low Countries and particularly England were afforded the geopolitical space to conduct modern state-building practices. This 'privilege of backwardness' became manifest along two causal vectors of combination: first, by bringing about a structural shift away from the dominance of the Mediterranean to the Atlantic; and, second, by isolating England from Habsburg geopolitical pressures. These will be discussed in turn.

The Ottoman Blockade and the Emergence of the Atlantic

In accordance with Ottoman geopolitical interests, the commercial effects of the *Pax Ottomana* were felt unevenly across Europe. Following Ottoman conquests of the Black Sea, Red Sea and much of the Mediterranean, European traders were only allowed conditional admittance to these areas.[185] Once the Ottomans had obtained these territories, commercial activity became subject to state regulations and supervision thus limiting the export of key commodities such as timber, horses, grain and alum.[186] At the same time, the Ottoman–Habsburg military conflict exacerbated Mediterranean volatility, 'cutting the arteries of Venetian seaborne trade'.[187] The Spanish and Portuguese fared little better, failing to push into a Mediterranean rife with Ottoman-sponsored corsair attacks on merchant ships.[188] Therefore, besides facilitating trade, the *Pax Ottomana* broke the commercial monopoly previously held by leading traders (primarily Venetian and Genoese) in the Mediterranean and Black Sea,[189] while exposing such trade to competition from Northwestern European traders, as well as Ragusan, Armenian and Jewish merchants under Ottoman suzerainty.[190]

By blocking the most dominant European powers from their customary conduits to Asian markets, the Ottomans directly compelled them to pursue alternative routes. Having lost its Black Sea monopoly, Genoa sought to circumvent the Ottoman passage to Indian and Far Eastern markets,[191] while turning to private business and financial operations in Western Europe and the Atlantic.[192] With the Ottoman-dominated Mediterranean inaccessible to Genoese capital, the Atlantic became a considerably more promising avenue for commercial activity.[193] In both Spain and Portugal, the relationship between Genoese merchant-financiers and New World colonialists grew as Genoa's position in the Eastern Mediterranean declined. The Atlantic ventures that this alliance gave rise to were ultimately made possible through the investments of Genoese capital that had been forced out of the Mediterranean by the Ottomans.

In the course of the Ottoman blockade, capitulations also came to play a major role, mediating between European commercial and Ottoman geopolitical interests through alliance building and blockading rivals. The Genoese, Habsburgs, Spanish and Portuguese were all excluded, while the French (1536), English (1583) and Dutch (1612) benefited from capitulations. Political in scope for the Ottomans, capitulations proved an economic boon for the merchants of Northwestern Europe. These states that had been otherwise peripheral to the Mediterranean (and thus Eurasian) commerce were now able to trade under significantly more advantageous terms than their competitors. Plugged into the security afforded by the Ottoman state along its trade routes, Northwestern European connections with Asian commodity markets were significantly expedited.

With the conquests of the eastern Mediterranean and its subsequent blockade, the Ottomans reconfigured the entire European balance of power, bringing with it a 'structural shift'[194] from the commercial dominance of Adriatic city-states such as Genoa and Venice to the Northwestern European states positioned on the Atlantic coast. As Michael Mann notes, '[t]he trade of the central Mediterranean powers declined at the same time as their military commitments grew. The Atlantic powers seized their opportunity, and the West became dominant'.[195]

The competition over markets that arose from this shift gave a major impulse to the development of 'company capitalism' and anticipated the increasing unity of merchant and state interests that became a hallmark of English and Dutch politics in the 17th and 18th centuries.[196] These developments would lead to efforts to build permanent circuits of capital through the advance system, in turn escalating merchant intervention and control over international production.[197] An additional unforeseen consequence of the incessant competition among the city-states 'for access to Eastern markets and the threat of the expanding Ottoman Empire' was that it would eventually lead the Europeans to the discovery of the Americas.[198] For '[w]ith the Eastern frontiers blocked by the powerful Ottoman Empire after the fall of Constantinople in 1453 the brighter horizon was in the West, into and eventually across the Atlantic'.[199] The line connecting the 1492 Discoveries with Europe's subsequent 'global destiny' ran through Constantinople in 1453.

The Ottoman Buffer and English Primitive Accumulation

The states best placed to take advantage of this structural shift were those where the Ottoman geopolitical buffer was most keenly felt. As we have seen, the protagonists most intensely involved in the continental conflicts of the 15th and 16th centuries were concerned with the Ottoman presence in the Mediterranean and Southeast Europe. The Habsburg–Ottoman rivalry thereby formed a geopolitical centre of gravity that often redirected imperial concerns away from England and the Low Countries. The Dutch made use of the divisions in Christendom to make a long-desired break away from Habsburg domination.[200] The English were perpetually buffered from European geopolitical pressures precisely at a time when the continent was experiencing a demographic and commercial revival. And typical of Ottoman manoeuvres, both states were offered diplomatic agreements – capitulations[201] – that weaved political alliances with commercial privileges in Ottoman territories. This was a major contributing factor to the integration of Levant and Atlantic trade in the 17th century and the ensuing rise of these Atlantic commercial powers. The Dutch became dependent on the Ottomans for supplies of the raw materials for which they had the heaviest demand – silk, cotton, mohair and wool – and equally dependent on the Ottoman market for their principal exports, textiles and precious metals.[202] England became similarly attached to both the import of wool and silk from, and export of manufactured cloths to, the Ottoman Empire.[203] In both cases, the attempts of merchants and financiers to monopolise and control such trade led to the establishment of strong trading companies.[204]

At the same time, raw materials from Ottoman territories acted as a stimulus for the development of European manufacturing, in particular textiles.[205] As the Levant trade fed Northwestern Europe with staple commodities produced through extensive land use, the need for self-sufficient production at home was removed. And by 'freeing' agricultural land from extensive production, land around European towns and ports became geared toward more capital-intensive and labour-intensive forms of use, such as (proto)industrial manufacturing.[206] The concomitant increase in land value – especially among those plugged into inter-regional and international trade networks – increased the profitability and hence frequency of short-term land lets, sales of land and land transfers. This contributed to 16th-century population increases, pressures on land, rises in rents and short-term tenures, depression in rural wages and growing demand for staples.[207] In short, the upsurge in Euro–Ottoman trade contributed to the preconditions of rural revolt and the primitive accumulation of capital in Northwestern Europe.

Aside from these new commercial privileges, the effects of the Ottoman geopolitical buffer were especially pronounced in English intra-lord class relations and the peculiar development of the English state. A variety of authors have stressed the significance of England's lack of involvement in the continental geopolitical conflicts from 1450 onwards as a fundamental factor in its 'precocious' development of capitalism.[208] Theda Skocpol suggests that 'England could remain somewhat aloof from the continental military system' which made it 'uniquely responsive to commercial-capitalist interests'.[209] For

Fernand Braudel, this isolation abetted a highly beneficial protectionism, helping England 'remain independent and to fend off interference from foreign capitalists ... more successfully than any other European country'.[210] For Derek Sayer, England's privilege of isolation meant it was not 'squandering productive resources on Continental empire building, nor obliged, to the same degree or in the same ways as Continental powers, to defend itself against others' expansionist predilections'[211] during the period when agrarian capitalism was set to take hold.

One of the more peculiar features of Tudor 'absolutism' flowed directly from this isolation – a regression in the military resources held by the state and aristocracy. For example, in the 1470s, the Spanish and English military numbered 20,000 and 25,000 men respectively. By the 1550s, Spain's military forces had risen to 150,000 while England's manpower had fallen by 5,000 to 20,000.[212] Disarmament among the English aristocracy was even more pronounced: 'in 1500, every English peer bore arms; by Elizabeth's time ... only half the aristocracy had any fighting experience'.[213] This demilitarisation meant that England effectively 'skipped over' the development of the strong, tax-appropriating bureaucratic state structures characteristic of French and Spanish absolutism from the 16th century onwards.[214]

This exceptional historical trajectory proved especially conducive to capitalist development in 16th-century England. First, demilitarisation among the nobility meant limited access to the means of coercion required to raise feudal rates of exploitation. This inability to 'squeeze'[215] peasant surpluses meant that the option of dispossessing peasants and exploiting them through market mechanisms became an increasingly preferable means for ruling class reproduction.[216] Second, the English state did not possess the coercive or administrative strength to protect the peasantry from attempts by the nobility to 'engross, consolidate and enclose' land.[217] This contrasted with the French state, which competed with the nobility over agrarian surpluses by habitually protecting the peasantry from attempts at dispossession.[218] Third, geopolitical isolation meant that the English ruling class was unusually homogenous,[219] with a relative absence of social stratification across the state, the pre-existing landed aristocracy and an emergent commercial class. Under conditions of demilitarisation, the English landowning class became disassociated from 'patented peerage'.[220] Influence and office became a more important source of power for the 'untitled gentry' who would come to dominate English political and economic life.[221] As such, the English landowning class was 'unusually civilian in background, commercial in occupation and commoner in rank'.[222] The lack of social stratification in turn engendered an intersection between the landed classes, would-be capitalists and state officers that became a central plank of the landlord–capitalist tenant–wage-labourer triad.

These three factors help to explain one of the fundamental propositions of

Robert Brenner's argument on the origins of capitalism: that it was in England alone that agrarian revolts were met with a unified and successful attempt by the state and landed class to remove the peasantry from their land through enclosures.[223] As peasants were dispossessed, they turned to an alternative means to secure their means of subsistence and social reproduction: selling their labour to landlords and capitalist tenants in return for a wage.[224] The persistent success of the state–nobility alliance in dispossessing the peasantry of the means of production led to the emergence of a 'free' class of wage-labourers. The social property relations through which surplus were appropriated was thus transformed, from the extra-economic means of feudalism to the 'economic' or 'market' mechanisms of agrarian capitalism.

Considering that English isolation was such a crucial condition for the processes outlined in the 'Brenner thesis', a fuller exposition of capitalism's origins requires that this geopolitical isolation be satisfactorily accounted for. We argue that this condition of geopolitical isolation, rather than signalling an absence of international determinations, is inexplicable if it is separated from the broader processes of uneven and combined development within which it took place. As the preceding analysis has shown, this isolation should be understood as the outcome of a distinctly intersocietal condition arising from the European continent's preoccupation with the Ottoman Empire. The peculiar social form to which this isolation gave rise proved especially conducive to the symbiotic unity of state and landed class interests that underpinned the exceptional growth of agrarian capitalism in England. When considered in this specifically international context, English development in the 16th century can be best understood as a particular outcome of 'combined development': the developmental outcomes of an intersocietal condition rooted in the uneven relation of England to the Euro-Ottoman geopolitical milieu. Ottoman geopolitical pressures must therefore be seen as a necessary but not sufficient condition for the emergence of agrarian capitalism in England.

Conclusion: The Ottoman Empire as a Vector of Uneven and Combined Development

It must be re-emphasised that none of these developments were sufficient conditions for the emergence of capitalism; there were numerous other causal chains – vectors of uneven and combined development – both European and extra-European that must be incorporated into a full understanding of capitalism's origins. It is nonetheless difficult to establish a proper appreciation of the key developments in 16th-century history and the (Northwestern) European trajectory towards capitalism without looking at the Euro–Ottoman relation as a fundamental determinant.

The duality of Euro–Ottoman relations – both belligerent and collaborative – was a crucial driver in the development of capitalism. By establishing a node of international trade, the Ottomans contributed to the internationalisation of merchant activity and a cultural revival in Europe. More significantly, through their military conflict with the Habsburgs the Ottomans abetted the Reformation and the break-up of Habsburg geopolitical hegemony. The breakdown of Christendom as the unifying principle of the feudal age must therefore be understood as a product of the multiplicity of geopolitical interactions with the Ottoman Empire that converged over the course of the 16th century.

We have, moreover, argued that the very breakdown of Christendom, and the Habsburg concern for the Ottomans in particular, gave Northwestern Europe the geopolitical space to conduct modern state-building practices. The isolation of England was a direct product of a continent occupied with the Ottoman threat in Southeast Europe and the Mediterranean. This 'buffer' – and the isolation it permitted – gave rise to the peculiar fusion of interests among the landed nobility, capitalist tenants and the state in England, which proved crucial to the success of the English ruling class in enclosing land. We can therefore see how Ottoman geopolitical pressure on Europe inadvertently contributed to the process of primitive accumulation in the English countryside.

We have also seen how, through their geopolitical policies, the Ottomans actively and directly brought about a *structural shift* away from Mediterranean trade and the concomitant ascendancy of Italian city-states, toward the Atlantic powers that would eventually come to dominate the world through colonialism. In this respect, many of the developments that emerged out of Euro–Ottoman interactions prefigured the integration of every corner of the globe into a unified world system. Before Europe could 'batter down all Chinese walls' and 'create a world in its own image',[225] the Ottoman Empire had to first shatter the citadel of Christendom. Paradoxically, once it had done so, a 'New World' began to supplant the Ottomans as the primary preoccupation of Europeans. This novel geopolitical concern – the Atlantic and the Americas – is the subject of the next chapter.

CHAPTER 5

The Atlantic Sources of European Capitalism, Territorial Sovereignty and the Modern Self

> ... the veiled slavery of the wage-labourers in Europe needed the unqualified slavery of the New World as its pedestal.
>
> Karl Marx, 1867[1]

> There is no document of civilization which is not at the same time a document of barbarism.
>
> Walter Benjamin, 1940[2]

Introduction

The New World 'discoveries' of 1492 were a decisive moment in the formation of modern European societies, constituting a fundamental vector of uneven and combined development through which the modern world order was born. For the discoveries and the socio-economic and geopolitical relations they produced would come to profoundly affect the differential developmental trajectories not only between the European and Western hemispheres, but also within Europe itself, laying the foundations for Northwestern Europe's subsequent global ascendancy. The discoveries would arrest Spain's socio-economic development and accelerate its geopolitical decline as a great power, while simultaneously affording numerous benefits to Europe's two latecomers, Holland and England. They also provided the structural geopolitical space in which the latter could rapidly develop in a capitalist direction. Moreover, it was through the colonial encounter on the American continent and its attendant colonial rivalries that the institutional and legal structures of modern territorial sovereignty were first formed.

In the spheres of European ideology and culture, the discoveries were no less consequential, as the Americas would come to constitute the principal crucible through which modern European political thinking and identity relations were forged. The web of commercial and financial relationships engendered by the Atlantic slave trade would also subsequently prove a critical factor in Britain's capitalist industrialisation, further assisting its rise to global supremacy. It was these myriad patterns of developmental differentiation that, as Robbie Shilliam claims, 'constitute[s] the *deepest structural unevenness* upon and through which the modern world order developed'.[3] The importance of this point for understanding the origins of capitalism, its differentiated developmental trajectories and the subsequent 'rise of the West', cannot be overstated. For if it is recognised 'that non-capitalist social forms and political organizations are not simply sublated under the movement of capitalism', but are instead 'co-constitutive of the movement itself, then ... we cannot adequately explain modern world development through a narrative that starts with the rise of capitalism, nation and class within England or Europe'.[4]

Recognising the decisive importance of the transformative interactions between Europe and the Americas further problematises the rigid epistemological separation between 'West' and 'East' or Global North and South, while going beyond the assumption of ontological singularity that frames traditional theoretical explanations of the 'rise of the West'. Only by drawing attention to the interaction of a multiplicity of unevenly developing polities can we begin to theoretically explain their subsequent developmental trajectories in ways that eschew both Eurocentric notions of an internally generated 'European miracle' and the linear developmentalism supposedly marking each and every society's transition to capitalist modernity.

This chapter is divided into four sections. In the first section, we provide an overview of how the Spanish jurists of the 16th century sought to reconcile the increasing gap between Christendom as an all-encompassing universal ideology and the encounter with non-Christian peoples in the Americas. We show that the jurists' response invited a reconceptualisation of universality based on an ontological distinction between Europeans and 'Indians'. This in turn provided the basis for the ideological emergence of Eurocentrism, and the development of the modern legal principle of sovereignty. In turn, we argue that each innovation was bound up in, and provided legitimacy for, broader processes of subjugation, exploitation and plunder accompanying the colonial encounter.

In the next section, we demonstrate how the Americas came to affect the differential developmental trajectories between the European and Western hemispheres and within Europe. Specifically, we examine how the plunder of precious metals from the Americas exacerbated the contradictions of feudalism and facilitated the commercial expansion of Northwestern European states into Asian markets. In the third section, we go beyond this Smithian appreciation of commerce and trade by highlighting the wider processes of primitive accumulation outlined by Marx. Here, we argue that the limits of 17th-century English agrarian capitalism were only overcome because its ruling class was able to exploit the widened sphere of economic activity offered by the Atlantic. In particular, in the fourth section of the chapter, we show how the combination of English capital, American 'virgin' land and the labour of enslaved Africans created, in the plantation system, a key input for the reproduction of wage-labour and capital in England, and later the Industrial Revolution.

Imagining Europe in the Atlantic Mirror: Rethinking the Territorialised Sovereign, Self and Other

The discovery of the New World was in many respects 'astonishing'.[5] The scope of humanity was now framed by a universality that was not merely imagined,[6] but based on an unprecedented geographical combination of all the world's inhabited continents. The colonial encounter that took place in the Americas was marked by an exceptionally 'intense' and 'radical'[7] recognition of differences between its protagonists, in which the sharp divergences of sociological unevenness were to be revealed. It is no exaggeration to say that the challenges presented by the disorienting experiences of the colonial encounter were one of the most formative and constitutive of modern European developments, destroying and creating in equal measure.

On both sides of the Atlantic, 'the old' was being systematically and violently dismantled, subsequently clearing the path for the emergence of 'the new', the modern, capitalist mode of production. While colonialists were conducting the 'greatest genocide in human history'[8] in the Americas, ideologues in Europe were busying themselves with tearing down an authority – Christendom – that was proving incapable of articulating New World experiences. It was out of the resultant debris that the twin conceptions of the European Self and the non-European Other would emerge, paving the way for an ideological apparatus – Eurocentrism, racism, patriarchy – that would serve to both legitimise the horrors of colonialism and spur the development of capitalism.

Tearing Down the Ideological Walls of Christendom: From Sacred to Secular Universalism in the Construction of the European Self and Non-European Other

The colonial encounter posed two significant challenges to the universalist claims of Christendom. First, the presence of different European states with competing claims to colonial preponderance meant that both expansion into and rule over New World territories were 'contested and open to rival interpretations'.[9] Second, the confrontation with American populations called into question why the application of universal, natural laws diverged so sharply between the Europeans and Amerindians. There was a pervasive and intractable contradiction between notions of Christian universality and the absence of any Christianity in the Americas. In this context, 'claims to universal authority upon the old foundations of Christendom were, when looked at in this global perspective, as Hugo Grotius bluntly said in 1625, daft (*stultum*)'.[10] Reconciling the facticity of unevenness in the context of the increasingly global scope of European activity required a rejection of imperial and papal conceptions of legality based on universal divine law. Through this rejection, a new conception of universality was constructed which would prove central to the justification of colonial expansion.

The self-reflection this involved was made possible through a comparison between the Spanish and the populations of the Americas, and the attempt to reconcile the two under a universal framework applicable to both. The Spanish jurist Francisco de Vitoria – a forerunner in modern international law[11] – based his legal thought on a characterisation of Amerindians which emphasised their supposedly 'natural' commonalities with Christians. Both peoples, Vitoria argued, were capable of 'reason'. Like the Spanish, Amerindians displayed 'orderly arranged' polities in which rules pertaining to 'marriage and magistrates, overlords, laws and workshops, and a system of exchange' were observable.[12] A shared possession of 'reason' consequently formed the basis of equivalence between Europeans and non-Europeans, binding both under the same – universal – legal framework.[13] Vitoria therefore began reconstructing papal universalism on the *secular* basis of natural laws and the principle of *jus gentium* (law of nations) which, rather than being dictated by the papacy or emperor, would be administered by sovereigns.[14]

By treating the Spanish and Amerindians as 'equal' participants in the colonial system, Vitoria's approach provided a system of law which legitimised the Spanish presence in the New World in terms of commerce and expansion.[15] However, the specificities of Vitoria's argument reveal a considerably more insidious underbelly, as his innovations in jurisprudence not only legitimised the unfettered penetration of the Spanish into the Americas but, moreover, provided a legal basis on which the coercion of local populations could be justified.[16] For despite the idealised conformity between Amerindians and universal principles of natural law, Spanish colonialists were all too aware that the colonial relationship between the two was marked by *nonconformity* and *difference* – an opposition among the local population to the Spanish 'way of life'. As Beate Jahn argues, this eventually forced Spanish jurists to 'grapple with an ontological rather than just a political or legal question: what was the nature of these Amerindians; were they human beings at all?'[17]

In the mid-16th century debates among Spanish jurists, a popular idea took hold that although Amerindians were indeed human, they were hamstrung by a developmental 'backwardness' – a 'primitivism' – caused by their own cultural peculiarities. Vitoria's sociology of local populations in the Americas thus served to identify those universal (read Spanish) qualities that the 'Indian' lacked. Hence, the *absence* of certain qualitative characteristics became *constitutive* of their very being as 'Others'.[18]

Both Vitoria and the influential theologian Juan Ginés de Sepúlveda were instrumental in identifying markers of 'barbarian', 'evil' and 'savage' characteristics among Amerindians.[19] While sodomy and cannibalism were indicative of a heathen, diabolical, even bestial character ('little different from brute animals' as Vitoria put it),[20] the physical nudity of the Amerindians exposed, in the minds of the Spanish, a more pervasive spiritual and cultural nudity, 'an absence of customs, rites, religion'.[21] Amerindians were also considered economically naïve, excessively generous and possessing no conception of private property, while appearing unable to properly extract precious metals or cultivate land. The difference in systems of production, property and exchange observed by the likes of Columbus and Cortes served as markers of an absence of social system altogether, from which a view of the Amerindians as 'backward' was extrapolated.[22] The upshot of such 'observations' was that the Amerindians were by nature and divine sanction destined to be slaves.[23] As Sepúlveda put it:

> those who are dim-witted and mentally lazy ... are by nature slaves. It is just and useful this way. We even see it sanctioned in divine law itself, for it is written in the Book of Proverbs: 'He who is stupid will serve the wise man'. And so it is with the barbarous and inhuman people [the Indians] who have no civil life and peaceful customs.[24]

Both Vitoria and Sepúlveda saw in the Amerindian character a series of defects, each a product of years of socialisation in 'evil' customs and practices, which prevented the Amerindians' salvation.[25] A long process of counter-education and supervision by the Spanish designed to 'undo' such 'barbarity' subsequently became a necessity, no less a duty.[26] Moreover, because such 'barbarity' was so deeply ingrained, force, coercion, discipline and punishment became necessary to compel local populations to abandon their beliefs and customs.[27] If 'they refuse our rule', as Sepúlveda wrote, 'they may be compelled by force of arms to accept it'.[28]

The brutality of Spanish colonialism led another Spanish thinker, Bartolomé de Las Casas, to produce a 'counter-history'[29] of the Amerindians.[30] He emphasised their 'gentle and peace-loving'[31] characteristics, upon which he articulated a principle of Christian equality and 'the natural laws and rules and rights of men'.[32] Las Casas contrasted this image with that of the Spanish conquistadors as 'devils',[33] thus criticising Spanish practices in the Americas. However, despite his more 'benevolent' starting point, Las Casas also saw Amerindian culture as something to be negated and replaced by Spanish practices, albeit 'peacefully'.[34] In justifying this position, Las Casas argued that since Amerindians were 'docile' and 'less resistant', they were particularly primed for conversion to Christianity.[35]

Here, Las Casas invoked a paternalistic conception of Amerindian developmental immaturity – these people were 'borne late' and were hence 'rustic' in character. The 'cultural vacuum'[36] that characterised Amerindians would therefore have to be filled through tutelage from the more advanced Spanish.[37] Hence, in both belligerent and benevolent sides of the debate, the conclusion was the same: both Spanish and Amerindians were subject to the same universal, natural laws, but because of a deeply ingrained cultural 'backwardness', Amerindians were incapable of adhering to such laws. Since Amerindians were incapable of governing themselves, the Spanish were required to govern on their behalf. Spanish rule and tutelage was therefore necessary in order for Amerindians to conform to the 'universal' principles of natural law and 'achieve salvation'.[38]

Associating 'universality' with 'the adoption or the imposition of the universally applicable practices of the Spanish'[39] meant that colonisation and the aggressive transformation of the 'New World' were subsequently presented as moral and legal obligations. Should indigenous communities deny colonialists the 'right of communication'[40] through which the indigenous people would be transformed, the colonialists would be entitled to conduct a 'just war' against them.[41] With this move, war became justified 'under the cover of an international law of reciprocity'[42] and took centre stage in the ideology of colonialism. It became the 'means by which Indians and their territory [were] converted into Spaniards and Spanish territory, the agency by which the Indians thus [achieved] their full human potential'.[43] In short, the destruction of indigenous communities, customs and modes of production became reframed as the 'humanitarian obligation of the Spaniards'.[44] These ideas advanced by the ideologues of the Spanish Empire prefigure – if in incomplete form – the basic components of Eurocentrism to which we now turn.

Legitimising Colonialism: The Historical Sociological Foundations of Eurocentrism

As was demonstrated above, the making of both the European Self and Atlantic Other were fundamentally interactive processes based on extant and changing forms of sociological unevenness. Likewise, the ideology of Eurocentrism cannot be historicised within the cultural or geographical borders of Europe alone, but only as an essentially *intersocietal* development.[45] For it is in the colonial encounter that we find the emergent tendencies to read cultural differences between societies not simply as differences, but as *absences*: the Amerindians *lacked* those features the Spanish possessed. Absence in turn served as a marker of 'backwardness' in the Amerindian Other, and enabled the hierarchical demarcation of the European Self as 'advanced' and 'superior'. Through this practice of demarcation, Europeans were able to imagine themselves as a culturally homogenous entity – civilised, advanced, distinct and separate from the 'savage' world outside. In this way the basic premises of Eurocentrism were prototypically established. A *methodological internalism* (in which European development is conceptualised as endogenous and self-propelling) and assumptions of *historical priority* (which 'posits the endogenous and autonomous emergence of modernity in Europe'[46]), first began to take shape in the Atlantic encounter.

Setting up this hierarchy established a 'standard of civilization', and with it, the moral obligation for the 'the civilized to take control of the uncivilized'.[47] As such, the practice of comparison established difference as something to be negated and overcome – an absence to be filled with the content of Spanish practices. 'Indians' had to be civilised, their peculiarities annihilated. Sepúlveda chillingly captured the affinities between 'civilising' activities and societal annihilation when he argued that 'the loss of a single soul dead without baptism exceeds in gravity the death of countless victims, even were they innocent'.[48] Sepúlveda's imperative – a 'moral' and 'humanitarian' one, no less – implied 'a projection of the subject speaking about the universe, an identification of *my* values with *the* values',[49] the projection of Spanish practices as universal.

This projection and the possibility of civilisation through annihilation would in turn invoke the third marker of Eurocentrism – *linear developmentalism* based on a homogenous conception of time, or what Dipesh Chakrabarty calls 'historicism'.[50] By setting up sociocultural distinctions in terms of linear history, non-Europeans were seen to present an image of Europe's past, and in turn Europe posited itself as the image of non-Europeans' future. Amerindians, on this view, 'served as a paradigm for an original state [of nature] before property became individuated and secure: "In the beginning all the world was America" as John Locke put it'.[51] Or, as Adam Ferguson would later write:

> It is in their [the American savages] present condition, that we are to behold, as in a mirror, the features of our own progenitors; and from thence we are to draw our conclusions with respect to the influence of situations, in which, we have reason to believe, our fathers were placed.[52]

Such conceptions of linear developmentalism (re)constructed sociological relations of unevenness (that is, difference) through temporal conceptions of distance or separation.[53] They also functioned as a framework to legitimise the annihilation of substantive sociological differences between the Spanish and Amerindians by naturalising the 'culturally peculiar path of Western development based on private property and state-formation'.[54]

By the time of the Enlightenment, conceptions of linear developmentalism would find their fullest expression in Eurocentric stadial thinking.[55] With an emphasis on clearly distinguishable stages of development (what the French Physiocrats and Scottish Enlightenment thinkers conceived in terms of successive 'modes of subsistence')[56] on the continuum of unilinear time, stagism would establish one of the key intellectual foundations for the emergence of 'scientific' conceptions of racism.[57] In keeping with these unilinear stagist models, the employment of scientific and technological criteria in proving the superiority (and thus domination) of Europeans over non-European peoples would become the norm over the course of the 17th and 18th centuries. As material disparities between a rising capitalist core and non-capitalist periphery developed, broader philosophical, societal, religious and cultural distinctions were superseded by those 'based on things'.[58] This was one instance of a more generalised technological fetishism emerging from the rapid, but uneven, development of the productive forces under capitalism in its world-wide expansion. The level of technological development was perceived as determining the moral worth of a particular 'race' and/or society.[59] In these ways, modern racism organically arose with the *systematisation of unevenness* constitutive of the capitalist mode of production and its interactions with other societies.[60]

The dispossession of the Amerindians, along with the many later European 'humanitarian' interventions abroad, thereby became justified on the basis of a stadial conception of development through which non-European societies were deemed materially (and thus normatively) 'backward' in comparison with the 'West'. Hence, as with the formation of the United States, 'Native Americans, like other less-powerful groups who possessed territory coveted by White Americans, were declared racially inferior and incapable of productive use of the land'.[61] Those communities or 'races' that did not 'adequately' develop the productive forces were judged unfit to exist, or in need of instructive rule from the morally and culturally superior 'Western' societies. Tellingly, the so-called 'father' of modern liberalism, John Locke, evoked similar justifications for the dispossession of the Amerindians in the English-held Atlantic colonies. For Locke, the dispossession of the Amerindians was both necessary and legitimate since the 'Indians had no right, or very tenuous right, to the land, because they had not "mixed their labour" with it sufficiently'.[62] As E. P. Thompson notes, since Locke saw Amerindians as 'poor "for want of improving" the land by labour', and since such 'labour (and improvement) constituted the right to property, this made it the more easy for the Europeans to dispossess the Indians of their hunting grounds'.[63] In these ways, Europe's colonisation of the Americas and the ideological apparatuses it spawned marked the embryonic origins of the 'global colour line'[64] that would subsequently evolve with capitalism's development into a world system of imperialist domination.

Culture Wars in the Americas

However, political and legal questions were not the primary challenge posed by subjugating the Amerindians. Instead, it was the more existential questions regarding the ontology of the Other – with, of course, determinant (geo)political and legal effects – that proved most problematic, destroying and creating in roughly equal measure. This was a problem that touched on all aspects of Native American being, including fundamentally their 'cultures'. The various challenges that this presented to the European colonialists are the subject of this section.

To better understand the ontological separation of Europe as a discrete sociocultural entity, we must trace a specific challenge found in the colonial confrontation against which these ideologies were created: the resistance of indigenous communities in the Americas. As Silvia Federici argues, the debates among Spanish jurists that took place in the mid-16th century over the ontological status of Amerindians (and therefore also 'Europeans') 'would have been unthinkable without an ideological campaign representing the latter as animals and demons'.[65] Travel literature was embellished with bestial, diabolical and nonhuman imagery (cyclops, troglodytes, pygmies, people with tails, giants) as a way of sharpening the differences of local populations from Europeans.[66] In this period, cannibalism, polygamy, devil worship, sodomy and bestiality became European obsessions, since they 'seemed a perversion of the law of nature'.[67] The ontological separation of Europeans from Amerindians at the heart of the ideological innovations of sovereignty (more on this below), European identity and Eurocentrism was therefore based on a prior attempt to demonise the local populations of the Americas.

The spur for this demonisation was the conditions of crisis that emerged within the pre-1550 structure of the colonial plunder economy.[68] Up until then, appropriation was based on the *encomienda* – a legal framework which enabled colonialists to siphon off surpluses via tribute systems that were already in place among the local ruling class (albeit at higher rates of exploitation). The *encomienda* was a unique – indeed, perhaps historically singular – hybrid mode of organising and controlling the production process which combined features of feudal, tributary, Amerindian, slave and (in a later period) capitalist forms of exploitation, labour and property relations.[69] In the first instance, the feudal institutions that the Spaniards brought with them were superimposed and grafted onto existing indigenous social relations of production, leading to a combination of feudal and Amerindian modes of production.[70] Indeed, significant features of indigenous social structures 'remained substantially intact for at least the first several decades of Spanish rule and persisted in modified form for the duration of the colonial period'.[71]

Production in the lands of the Aztec Empire of later Mexico, for example, was characterised by the tributary mode, in which the direct producers retained access to the means of production and formal vestiges of kin-based, 'communal' social relations persisted, while indigenous elites extracted surpluses from these producers through 'extra-economic' means. The Spanish Crown saw no reason to fundamentally disturb these indigenous relations of production, as they served the monarchy's aim 'to prevent the unruly conquers of Mexico from enhancing their own power by gaining direct control over land and other key resources'. Nor could the Crown 'completely ignore the wishes of those who had risked their lives in a military campaign that had so spectacularly extended Spanish sovereignty'.[72]

So while the Spaniard monarchy initially intended to import their own feudal institutions to the American colonies, they ended up making use of extant indigenous productive relations, social institutions and power structures, while limiting the autonomy of the Spanish colonial 'warrior-merchants'. A new overseas feudal nobility could not be tolerated by the growing royal absolutism of the Spanish state because, 'left to themselves', Spanish merchants would have given 'verbal homage but little else to the Crown'.[73] Indeed, as Eric Wolf notes, it had been the 'initial intention of the Crown to deny the incoming conquerors any direct control of land and of Indian hands to work it'. This was because it wanted to 'inhibit the development of an independent class of tributary overlords in the Indies, and thus insisted at first on granting the services of native Americans only on its own terms'.[74]

The compromise forged out of these competing interests between Crown and conquistadors was the *encomienda*. To prevent the development of any independent class of feudal aristocrats or 'tributary overlords' in the colonies, the Crown issued temporary grants of trusteeship: the *encomienda*. This was a form of *señorío* (or manor) comprised of towns, villages and other populated areas held in the royal domain that the Crown granted to deserving persons or corporations for a specified period of time.[75] The recipient of an *encomienda* was allowed to extract a stipulated amount of tribute – whether in the form of goods, money or personal services – from the Amerindian labouring inhabitants who, after 1542, were proclaimed legally 'free'.[76] In return, *encomienderos* were required to protect, 'civilise' and Christianise those Amerindians working their lands. Crucially, however, the Crown's granting of an *encomienda* did not 'bestow on the *encomiendero* (trustee) rights over Indian land or unlimited rights to Indian services', as these 'rights the Crown reserved to itself'.[77] In other words, the commendation of an *encomienda* did not convey a property title to its temporary trustee.[78]

In these ways, the Spanish monarchy sought to separate *encomienderos* as much as possible from both claims to the land and, through the interposition of royal officials, their subject Amerindian workers – a goal further achieved through the abolition of Amerindian slavery in 1542.[79] To these ends, the monarchy also permitted – and in many ways sought to cultivate – the existence of an indigenous noble class of elites (the *caciques*), who continued to exercise considerable power at the local level. *Caciques* concurrently borrowed from established customs, and exploited their 'new sanctioned positions as intermediaries in colonial government' by organising production, extracting tributes and transferring surpluses to the *encomiendero*.[80] In some colonial regions, such as Rio de la Plata, conquering Spaniards formed marriage alliances with the existing Guarani elite while making use of 'Guarani modes of labour control in the mini-state organization of the region'. When the *encomienda* was finally introduced there in 1556, the 'system simply accepted the existing arrangements using an *encomiendero* class of mixed Spanish-Guarani origin'.[81] While indigenous peasants formally retained direct control over the land they tilled, the *encomienda* system combined existing practices of surplus-appropriation with the introduction of new forms of coerced labour and semi-servile productive relations.

In separating *encomienderos* from direct control and ownership over their allotted land and labourers, the Spanish Crown established what some scholars have described as a 'post-feudal' mode of production,[82] which not only retained some of the pre-colonial Amerindian tributary structures but created entirely new quasi-tributary relations of production (see also Chapters 4 and 8). However, with the rapid decimation of the indigenous populations through war, disease, illness, over-exploitation, and peasant flight and resistance, the Spanish monarchy turned to replacing their dwindling labour supplies with the importation of slave labourers from West Africa.[83] The result was a dizzying array of different labour regimes, relations of exploitation, property relations, and productive organisational forms all operating along increasingly racialised lines: African slaves, Amerindian serfs, quasi-tributary Spanish overlords, indigenous noble elites, and mestizos and white masters who owned lands and mines. Such peculiar combinations of non-capitalist productive relations were further distinguished by their (later) market-driven imperatives as they increasingly became oriented towards and integrated into international trading markets and circuits of capital, while nonetheless remaining governed by pre-capitalist 'laws of motion'.[84]

The persistently crisis-prone nature of the *encomienda* system, with its continual exhaustion of labour-power and resulting labour shortages, proved particularly problematic for the reproduction of Spanish colonial rule. Within the limits of this extant system of surplus extraction, the Spanish found they were unable to meet an array of economic requirements – not least, the growing indebtedness of both the Spanish Crown and individual colonisers.[85] The Spanish monarchy thus sought to obtain greater control over land and people. People were considered especially crucial, since the *obrajes* (manufactures for the international market) and the silver and gold mines which stuffed the

Spanish Crown's coffers with American precious metal required steady supplies of labour.

Establishing control over production and strengthening the grip of colonial rule was primarily enacted by 'declaring war' on Amerindian cultures.[86] This included mass executions, tortures and displacement of the existing population under the charges of diabolism, which were enforced through the destruction of indigenous worship practices. Temples and idols of old deities were destroyed.[87] Previous rites and rituals including songs, dances, painting, sculpture, astrology, and writing were banned. Any Amerindians found continuing such practices were hunted, imprisoned, tortured and killed by colonial authorities under charges of devil worship.[88]

These strategies served not only to attack indigenous cultures in the name of Christianity and colonial tutelage, but also to remove people from land, subjugate them, destroy their autonomy and tear apart their communal relations. It was, in short, a *'strategy of enclosure ... of land, bodies or social relations'*[89] resulting in greater subordination and exploitation of the local population by the Spanish colonists. Quotas of labour were increased, and regulation of surplus extraction was taken from local chiefs and placed under the watch of Crown representatives.[90] New labour regulations were supplemented by a resettlement programme (*reducciones*) intended to move rural populations into villages where they could be better controlled.[91] Women were most negatively affected by these changes, as they were denied access to land and water rights that had previously been communal. New regulations banned them from freedom of movement independent of men, and demanded that women either become wives or be classified as maids, thus redefining them as the property of men, while denying mechanisms through which they could assert their autonomy.[92]

Such ravages to the local population's existing mode of life meant Spanish attempts at subjugation were met with resistance. Indigenous anticolonial movements rejected the sort of communication and collaboration demanded by the Spanish, seeking instead to reassert their own local cultures.[93] In some areas, such as the Sierra Zapoteca, rebellions were led by *caciques* who revived the culture of 'old gods' in order to encourage the youth to take up arms in a violent struggle for their liberation.[94] People of the Taki-Onqoy movement claimed bodily possession of Huachi gods as a way of cleansing themselves of Christian conversions, and prophesised a millenarian upheaval that would destroy the Spanish in a wave of pestilence and floods.[95] They rejected Spanish customs – clothing, religion, tributes and labour services – and sought to resurrect local gods. The eschatological emphasis on the sources of communal rights such as land and water suggests that the Taki-Onquy expressed much more than other-worldly aspirations. The resonance of the Taki-Onqoy message throughout Amerindian communities, and the waves of direct and passive resistance, threatened Spanish control over their rural and urban possessions.[96]

In other cases, migrations escaping the widespread human desolation produced by colonialism drew on precolonial millenarian discourses as their source of legitimation. Many groups resisted by taking flight to the hills, where colonial rule was more difficult to impose, in order to continue the practice of precolonial traditions.[97] The Tupi-Guarani in Amazonia, for example, described their journey as a migration to a 'Land without Evil'.[98] In many cases, resistance was articulated not by already exiting elites among the local population, but by *carais* or *caraibas*: spiritual leaders who operated on the margins of existing social structures. In a context where local elites often exploited pre-existing hierarchies to conspire with colonialists against their populations, many resistance movements therefore also challenged existing local elites and hierarchies.[99]

In this respect, women often became the chief protagonists of resistance against Spanish rule, having been disproportionately affected by colonisation. Female resistance was articulated culturally by refusing to submit to colonial rules governing marriage and the baptism of children. In instances of collective flight, women sought to reorganise communities along the lines of precolonial customs, taking on the mantle of spiritual leadership – previously the preserve of men. Pan-Andean movements based on the revival of indigenous culture were often led by women.[100] Because women constituted both representatives of the old cultures, and the backbone of resistance to colonial rule, the Spanish again turned to a culturally motivated form of subjugation based on accusations of diabolism. Charges of witchcraft were used to subjugate women and redefine their position in society, establishing a new system of patriarchy that undergirded colonial rule and exploitation.[101]

It becomes apparent that the push and pull of colonial subjugation – and indigenous resistance to it – was articulated primarily through *cultural difference*. In the first instance, it provided the moral and legal basis through which colonialism could be justified: the Spanish were rational, moral, universal, advanced and thus sovereign; the Amerindians were irrational, backward, and so exempted from sovereign agency. For these reasons, Amerindians were obliged to adopt universal – that is, Spanish – ways of life. But, moreover, the definition of Amerindians in 'state of nature' terms was driven by the compulsion among the Spanish ruling class to exert greater control over indigenous communities, especially since Amerindian attempts to reassert their own culture constituted a fundamental attack on the reproduction of Spanish colonialism. Cultural difference became a threat, something to be violently negated by colonial rule. Where colonialists could not make indigenous communities conform to the 'universal' standards set by the Spanish, they were defined as diabolical or irrational. Colonialists were thus able to exclude 'women and men in the colonies from the social contract implicit in the wage and "free labour"' economy,[102] and in the process naturalise the exploitation of colonial labour based on 'unfree' methods.

The exclusion of indigenous populations from this 'social contract' – an exclusion that went right to the heart of colonial rule – helps us understand the compulsion felt among Spanish jurists to make a cultural distinction between themselves and the Amerindians based on the 'state of nature'. The culture wars waged in the Americas were therefore constitutive of altogether new and unique relations of patriarchy, class, and later white supremacy, that would be formative of capitalist social relations in both the 'periphery' and 'core'. In this context, the associated 'state of nature' discourse was not an empirical observation, or an innocent thought experiment. It was rather a colonial(ist) construct born out of the culture wars waged – and ultimately won – by Spanish colonialists against the Amerindians in the name of colonial exploitation.

A line of continuity can thus be drawn from the comparative work of Spanish colonialists, through Enlightenment and imperial conceptions of stadial development, to current practices of imperialism. In each, cultural, political and economic differences in so-called 'backward' countries have been presented as 'absences', with a particular emphasis on lacking or 'failed' structures of political and economic governance. The concomitant exclusion of indigenous people from the 'social contract' and the perceived inability of 'backward' countries to govern has in turn been central to legitimising external rule over them – a practice that continues to this day.[103] In its more belligerent manifestations, the perceived absence of proper governance structures has served to validate military interventions under the rubric of 'just wars'.

Hence, the capacity for and battle over sociopolitical organisation and self-government – that is, statehood and sovereignty – constitutes a key component of the 'standard of civilization'.[104] The ideological, institutional and legal structures of territorialised state sovereignty that would come to be seen as a hallmark of capitalist modernity in Europe were in fact forged in the (racialised and gendered) crucible of the colonial Atlantic.[105] Only after these institutional and ideological innovations came to prove their efficacy as a particular form of (bio)political rule and control did such organisational 'advances' then radiate back to the European imperial metropole.[106] We now turn to examine the theoretical debates and historical processes involved in this often overlooked colonial dimension in the making of the territorialised sovereign states system in Europe.

The Colonial Origins of the Modern Territorialised States Systems

Debates surrounding modern state formation and the origins of territorial sovereignty have been overwhelmingly characterised by endogenous (internalist) and exogenous (externalist) logics of explanation primarily – if not exclusively – operating in the European theatre. On one side, Weberian and Hintzian-influenced approaches to the origins of modern states have emphasised the effects of war-making and geopolitical rivalries in increasing state institutional and material capacities. In this model, geopolitical and military competition among the great powers in Europe is seen as the prime catalyst and driver in the making of modern, territorially bounded states.[107] Focusing on *intra*-European developments, the constitutive role of the colonial encounter and empire building is accorded, if recognised at all, a secondary place in the explanatory schema. Consequently, the agency of the Amerindians is given little to no attention.

On the other side, (neo-)Marxist approaches have focused on transformations in the social relations of production (or social property relations) within societies as the 'prime mover' in the origins and development of the modern territorialised states system in Europe.[108] While some of these perspectives take the endogenous development of capitalism in England as their point of departure, they nonetheless recognise the subsequent role of geopolitical competition in spreading the modern nation-state form, as continental European states sought to confront the systemic pressures posed by the modernising challenge emanating from Britain.[109] The primary focus is again centred on intra-European dynamics as the primary site of capitalism's inception and the modern sovereign states system. While broadening this perspective to include the economically functional role of the 'periphery' to the rise of capitalism in the imperial 'core', World-Systems Theory pays little, if any, attention to the mutually transformative nature of the colonial encounter in producing (and reproducing) the modern state form.[110] Hence, even where intersocietal determinations are invoked by (neo-)Marxist approaches in explaining processes of social change, they fall short of offering a genuinely 'international' non-Eurocentric perspective.[111]

The overwhelming attention to solely European or Western agents is similarly reproduced in constructivist accounts of the rise of the modern states system.[112] What all these accounts miss is the fundamentally co-constitutive nature of the colonial encounter in the making of the modern territorial state. Indeed, the transformative effects of Europe's interactions with non-European societies were evident in the earliest forms of European colonisation.

Returning to the writings of the Spanish jurist Vitoria is again instructive. In his work, we see a pervasive attentiveness to 'the international', taking in European geopolitics, but also those of the Americas and Asia. In Vitoria's writings we see how the colonial encounter was not only generative of Eurocentrism as an ideology of colonial legitimation, but also instrumental in mobilising the assumptions of Eurocentrism to develop what would become modern conceptions of territorial sovereignty. Emphasising the absence of proper governance structures among the indigenous populations of the Americas, Vitoria writes, for example, that:

they have no proper laws nor magistrates, and are not even capable of controlling their family affairs ... they lack many other conveniences, yea necessaries, of human life .... It might, therefore, be maintained that in their own interests the sovereigns of Spain might undertake the administration of their country, providing them with prefects and governors for their own towns, and might even give them new lords.[113]

He then goes on to further substantiate the permissibility of Spanish rule, by articulating the absence of Amerindian governance structures in terms of their historical 'backwardness':

for if they are all wanting in intelligence, there is no doubt that this would not only be permissible, but also a highly proper, course to take; nay, our sovereigns would be bound to take it, just as if the natives were infants. The same principle seems to apply here to them as to people of defective intelligence; and indeed they are no whit or little better than such so far as self-government is concerned, or even the wild beasts, for their food is not more pleasant and hardly better than that of beasts. Therefore their governance should in the same way be entrusted to people of intelligence.[114]

For Vitoria, the 'justness' of war could not be founded on a subjective belief that those conducting war were inherently just, since this opened the possibility that 'even Turks and Saracens might wage just wars against Christians, for they think they are thus rendering God service'.[115] Vitoria's paradoxically subjective solution to the problem was to demonstrate that Saracens, due to the absence of any conformity to natural law, were incapable of waging a just war. In this way, Vitoria was able to exclude Saracens – and by extension Amerindians – from admittance to the legal rights of sovereignty. Finally, Vitoria incorporates into his legal framework a way of distinguishing who is and who is not sovereign, to justify rule over the Amerindians and the exclusivity of this rule to the Spanish:

if there was to be an indiscriminate inrush of Christians from other parts to the part in question, they might easily hinder one another and develop quarrels, to the banishment of tranquillity and the disturbance of the concerns of the faith and of the conversion of the natives.[116]

Taken together, Vitoria's statements demonstrate that the perceived absence of recognisable sovereign authority in the Americas not only legitimised 'just wars', but also necessitated original ways of dividing, claiming and asserting power over newly conquered territories against other European competitors.[117] 'Almost any seventeenth- or eighteenth-century map of America', Samuel Edgerton notes, 'reveals the absolute faith Europeans of all religious persuasions had in the authority of the cartographic grid'. For as colonial powers 'laid claim to lands solely on the basis of abstract latitudes and longitudes ... [t]roops were sent to fight and die for boundaries that had no visible landmarks, only abstract mathematical existence'.[118]

Indeed, Francis I of France voiced a celebrated protest to these types of argument, claiming that '[t]he sun shines for me as for others. I should very much like to see the clause in Adam's will that excludes me from a share of the world'. The king of Denmark in turn refused to accept the Pope's ruling for the East Indies. Sir William Cecil, the famous Elizabethan statesman, also denied the Pope's right 'to give and take kingdoms to whomsoever he pleased'. In 1580, the English government thus countered with the principle of effective occupation as the determinant of sovereignty.[119]

In these ways, newly formulated notions of linear time came to be complemented by novel conceptions of *linear geographical space* and a concomitant modern form of territorialised state sovereignty. 'The ostensibly empty spaces of the Americas could be comprehended, negotiated over, and competed for *only* by using an abstract conception of space built on mathematical cartography', as Jordan Branch writes. 'The novel requirements of making extra-European political claims demanded new authoritative practices by colonial powers, practices that were made manifest immediately in linear territorial divisions between spatial expanses'.[120] Such novel articulations of linearly demarcated forms of territorial sovereignty in the Americas also had major repercussions for their development in Europe. For the principles of cartography, based on abstract space and linear territorial divisions, were first generated in the colonial encounter in the Americas and then subsequently transported back to Europe.[121]

The originality of colonial conceptions of linear territoriality can be found most clearly in the treaties of the period. In the Old World, treaties concluding wars typically emphasised nonlinear or noncontiguous territoriality, and the spoils of conquests were divided according to places rather than territories. This was evident as late as the Treaty of Westphalia of 1648, which despite its purportedly modern credentials, still listed every noncontiguous 'place, jurisdiction, and right to be granted to one party by the other'.[122] In contrast, treaties pertaining to the New World used cartographic or geographic language in order to delineate territorial claims based on linear demarcations and supposedly 'natural' frontiers. Territories could be claimed in this way precisely because the known political authorities – that is, the Amerindians – were not recognised, were denied their right to sovereignty and were therefore excluded from any such treaties.[123]

The first examples of linearly defined claims to political authority can be found in the 1493 Papal Bulls and the 1494 Treaty of Tordesillas between Spain and Portugal. These treaties apportioned to Spain all newly discovered territories west of a line drawn in the Atlantic Ocean, with Portugal receiving those territories to the east (see Figure 5.1). The significance of such treaties was

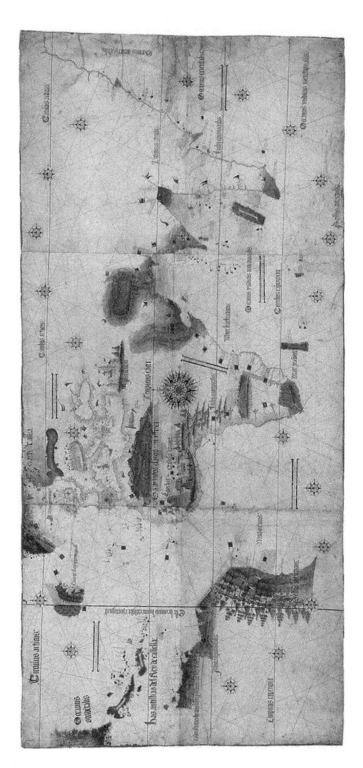

Figure 5.1 'Catino Planisphere' (1502) by an unknown Portuguese cartographer, showing the Tordesillas line (left-hand side of map)

Source: http://commons.wikimedia.org/wiki/File:Cantino_planisphere_(1502).jpg (accessed 21 November 2014).

'not in the details of the lines', Branch notes, 'but instead in the very idea of using a linear division to assign political authority: "For the first time in history an abstract geometric system had been used to define a vast – global – area of control".'[124]

These linear territorial divisions apportioning political authority to European powers over specific locales in the Americas were only partly directed at local 'sovereigns'. Rather, their novel utility lay in dealing with existing and future European rivals. For while such claims to sovereignty initially served to posit non-European spaces as *terra nullius*, thereby opening them to European acquisition, the primary aim was in regulating the relative claims of competing European powers.[125] Thus, 'such treaties were not concluded with the local "sovereigns" in mind at all, but functioned rather as a means of demonstrating a relationship of authority or control to other European powers'.[126]

The origins of the modern form of territorialised sovereignty were therefore an outcome of an *aleatory encounter* with societies that Europeans considered 'empty' – stuck in a 'state of nature' and not under or capable of any sovereign authority – and the competing claims to occupy such 'empty' spaces by various colonial powers. Rather than being derived from some internal impulse, they represented a response to the particular challenges of jurisdiction in these territories produced by historically specific intersocietal interactions. Such state practices and modalities of territoriality then radiated back to the imperial core in Europe, forming a crucial step in the formation of the modern territorially defined state, but only 'after the usefulness and legitimacy of linearly bounded authority claims were made clear by centuries of colonial practice'.[127] Such legal and political innovations must therefore be understood as various forms of combined development – constructions specifically based on 'attempts to resolve the unique legal problems arising from the discovery of the Indians'.[128]

The significance of our spatially decentred, non-Eurocentric conception of the origins of sovereign state territoriality for understanding the rise of capitalism in Europe and its later ascendency to global domination is threefold. First, it gives the lie to the dominant myth that the European states system was a product of geopolitical and socio-economic processes *internal* to Europe, while further problematising those accounts that conceive of the European state-formation process as an exclusively elite-driven affair. Rather, it was the very struggle to dominate and subjugate the indigenous populations of the Americas that laid the ideological and material foundations for novel conceptions of linearly demarcated, territorialised spaces of sovereignty. These conceptions further functioned to defend territory against the claims of other rival colonial powers. The territorialising process of state formation was then fundamentally Janus-faced: it gazed inward or vertically at the domination of newly claimed 'empty spaces' and subject populations, while also looking outward or laterally toward fending off other competing imperial states.

Second, the development and consolidation of territorialised state sovereignty and capitalist social relations in Europe was an intimately intertwined and co-constitutive process, as the following sections and chapters demonstrate. Hence, in contrast to influential neo-Weberian and Marxist accounts,[129] the formation of the European system of territorialised sovereign states did not *precede* the rise of capitalism. Instead, the early modern epoch witnessed the co-evolution and transformation of capitalism and the states system in Europe that was 'overdetermined' by interactions with the extra-European world. Capitalism did not only emerge as a consequence of developments internal to England or Europe during the Long 16th Century. It did not later suddenly 'burst on the international [read: European – AA/KN] scene in the nineteenth century'[130] and subsequently radiate outwards in a unidirectional process of European-driven change. Similarly, the territorially bounded states system did not first emerge in Europe during the absolutist era, and it was not exclusively the consequence of the military and geopolitical rivalries operating on the European continent. The upshot of all this is that capitalism and the modern territorialised system of sovereign states retain not only a theoretically internal relationship as conceived from the perspective of uneven and combined development, but a historically organic one as well. And as we have been at pains to emphasise, this was a relationship that was fundamentally rooted in and constituted by historical processes emanating from outside Europe.

Third, the development of territorially bounded state sovereignty was crucial to the subsequent bundle of processes that eventually led to Europe's ascendency to global domination. The modern territorial state, particularly in its later post-absolutist incarnation, proved a militarily and fiscally efficient vehicle of class rule at home and imperial dominance abroad. The two were in fact inextricably bound together, as the development and consolidation of capitalism at home was fundamentally secured and buttressed by imperial expansion abroad (see the next section and Chapters 7 and 8). Moreover, the territorialisation of state and military power was a powerful (geo)political vehicle for the 'endless' accumulation of capital which, over a relatively short period of time, outpaced non-capitalist rivals (see Chapters 6, 7 and 8). In other words, the co-development and co-evolution of the territorialised state and capitalism was a necessary, but not sufficient, condition for the subsequent 'rise of the West'. Their co-constitutive and reinforcing developmental tendencies formed a kind of cumulatively building virtuous circle,[131] setting Europe – or more precisely, Northwestern Europe – on the path to global supremacy.

To be clear, this is not to argue that such institutional and socio-economic innovations directly translated into victories on the battlefield or even in war, as the long history of 'Western' defeats in colonial 'small wars' has demonstrated all too well. War is perhaps the ultimate realm of radical contingency. Like a boxing match, no one can know with certainty who will emerge victorious, however imbalanced the power relations.[132] Nonetheless, the kinds of radical power imbalances that emerged in Europe with the co-formation of territorialised states and capitalist social relations did give these states significant advantages in imposing 'their' will – either directly by coercive-intensive forms and/or structurally via the abstract mechanisms of the world market – over other states and societies (see Chapters 7 and 8).

1492 in the History of Uneven and Combined Development

As the preceding section has shown, the Atlantic vector of uneven and combined development proved a formative moment in the unmaking of European Christendom, reconstituting 'universalism' on secularised conceptions of linear time and space. Relatedly, the Atlantic was also key to the development of novel ideological articulations of a European 'Self' and non-European 'Other' in the legitimation of European claims to govern in the colonies. Such articulations were central to the formation of new forms of racialised and gendered rule over the indigenous peoples of the American continents. At the same time, 'the old' was destroyed and 'the new' forged, in bringing the Americas under Europe's heel in a history of unprecedented violence and brutality.

The next section further analyses this history of domination and exploitation by demonstrating the impact the 'discoveries' had on the making and hastening of capitalism. It begins by examining this impact in the sphere of circulation before moving on to an analysis of the effects of the colonies on the sphere of production. The section therefore aims to dialectically sublate these Smithian and Marxian moments of analysis into a higher synthesis via 'the international' – an approach sketched out, but not substantively developed, by Marx in his famous quote:

The discovery of gold and silver in America, the expiration, enslavement and entombment in mines of the indigenous population of that continent, the beginnings of the conquest and plunder of India, and the conversion of Africa into a preserve for the commercial hunting of blackskins, are all things which characterize the dawn of the era of capitalist production. These idyllic proceedings are the chief moments of primitive accumulation. Hard on their heels follows the commercial war of the European nations which has the world as its battlefield. It begins with the revolt of the Netherlands from Spain, assumes giant dimensions in England's Anti-Jacobin War, and is still going on in the opium wars against China. The different moments of primitive accumulation can be assigned in particular to Spain, Portugal, Holland, France, and England, in more or less chronological order. These moments are systematically combined together at the end of the seventeenth century in England; the combination embraces the colonies, the national debt, the modern tax system, and the system of protection.[133]

Here we see, in rough form, the significance of the colonies and 'the international' in the making of capitalism as a world system interconnecting the myriad differentiated societies constituting it. To these issues we now turn.

The Smithian Moment: American Treasures and So-Called Primitive Accumulation

There is a long tradition of Marxist thinking emphasising the profound impact the 1492 'discoveries' had on the development and consolidation of capitalism as a world system.[134] Yet today, the hegemonic Brennerite approach to the origins of capitalism emphasising the internal, agrarian sources of its genesis explicitly sidelines the contribution of the 'periphery'. Noting some Marxists' emphasis on the importance of the wealth amassed from the New World, Ellen Meiksins Wood writes that 'we cannot go very far in explaining the rise of capitalism by invoking the contribution of imperialism to "primitive accumulation" or, indeed, by attributing to it any decisive role in the *origin* of capitalism'.[135] As reasons, she cites the relatively late start of British colonisation and Spain's failure to develop in a capitalist direction.

The immediate effects of the New World colonies on the Spanish Habsburg Empire were indeed to further entrench the feudal monarchy while arresting economic development in the region.[136] Yet there were also significant knock-on effects that worked to hasten the rise of Dutch capitalism. While colonial surpluses were able to (partly) finance the Habsburg military expeditions across Europe,[137] 'the influx of bullion from the New World also produced a parasitism that increasingly sapped and halted domestic manufacturers'.[138] This led to a virtual deindustrialisation of the Castilian economy as the home market collapsed, with American silver raising production costs and an ascendant Dutch manufacturing sector penetrating the Castilian textile market.[139] This meant Philip II's imperial projects could only be sustained through 'reckless borrowing'.[140] Despite – or perhaps because of – the vast imports of New World silver, fiscal-military pressures bankrupted the Spanish monarchy eight times by the end of the 17th century.[141] And as Genoese bankers held Spain's public debt, they came to 'reorient their "surplus capital" from the American trade towards the bond market, thereby opening the door for Dutch capital. The rise of the United Provinces and the decline of Spain were therefore intimately connected'.[142] What is more, the inflow of silver may have accelerated the decline of Spanish military power by encouraging attempts to conduct what proved to be an unsustainable two-front war against the Ottomans in the Mediterranean and the Dutch to the north. For as William McNeil notes, 'it was the swelling flow of New World silver after the 1550s that made Philip [II] think he could conduct war both in the Mediterranean against the Turks and in the north against the Dutch'.[143]

From the perspective of the *longue durée*, these 'penalties of priority' beset-ting Spain's development in the early modern age go some way in explaining the country's relative 'backwardness' in the later modern epoch.[144] Here again we see how the socio-economic and strategic benefits afforded to earlier devel-opers would at a later point in their development turn into strategic liabilities, as less-developed societies came to reap the 'privileges of backwardness'. In particular, the plundering of the Americas functioned as a means of 'primi-tive accumulation' on a Europe-wide basis which overwhelmingly benefited two latecomers, Holland and England, at the expense of the more (feudally) advanced colonising powers, Spain and Portugal.

Indeed, throughout the 16th and 17th centuries, Spain and Portugal acted as conduits for the transfer of much of the American bullion into the coffers of financiers in Antwerp, Amsterdam, London, Paris and Genoa. New World silver thereby further aided the structural geopolitical space opened to Northwestern Europe (again, notably the Dutch and English), and its capitalist development (see Chapters 3 and 4). Thus, the overall material benefits to Europe from the overseas discoveries, P. K. O'Brien writes, 'accrued disproportionately to two latecomers and free riders – the Netherlands and Britain'.[145] Further, as Roland Findlay notes, 'the two East India Companies used the American treasure to balance their imports of Indonesian pepper, clove and nutmeg, Indian cotton textiles and Chinese silk and porcelain for profitable re-export to consumers in Europe'.[146] This was a particularly important development aiding the multi-lateral trade flows that would come to interconnect Western Europe with the highly lucrative East Asian trades through the enforced plundering of the Americas (see Figure 5.2).

Why the Dutch, rather than English, became the first leading force in the subsequent development of the world market during the Long 16th Century is also explained by the country's close ties to the Spanish-American trading system. This afforded Holland greater access to Spanish wealth than England, and this wealth was subsequently redeployed to drive its own commercial and financial operations.[147] It is perhaps no coincidence that almost half of the gold and silver acquired by Spain ended up in Holland,[148] Marx's 'model capitalist nation of the seventeenth century', and the first state to experience a bourgeois revolution (see Chapter 6).[149] Indeed, for a time the Netherlands acted as a 'distribution center from which American silver passed to Germany, Northern Europe, and the British Isles', which 'was crucial to European economic activity'.[150] And even after the Netherlands' break with the Habsburg monarchy, the Spanish still allowed Amsterdam considerable access to American silver.[151] Thus the Netherlands' economic ascendancy was built, at least in part, on American bullion.[152]

The immense quantities of bullion from Spanish America were also crucial in kick-starting the Netherlands' Europe–Asia trade.[153] This point was noted in

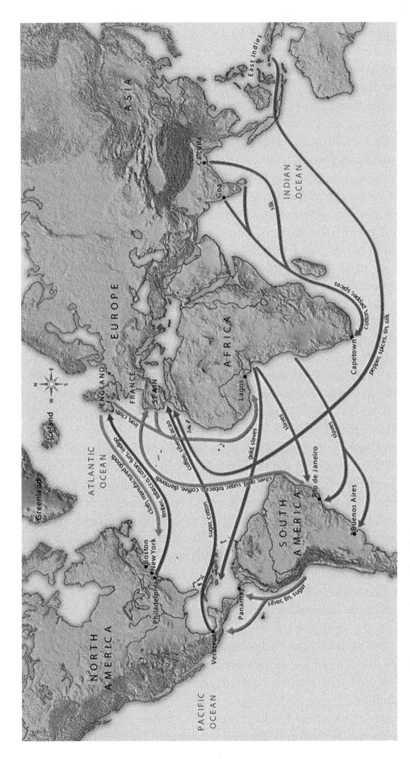

Figure 5.2 The 'triangular trade' of the 1600–1700s

the often quoted description of Dutch trade in 1619 by then VOC director Jan Pieterszoon Coen:

> Piece goods from Gujarat we can barter for pepper and gold on the coast of Sumatra; rials [silver currency] and cottons from the coast [of Coromandel] for pepper in Bantam; sandalwood, pepper and rials we can barter for Chinese goods and Chinese gold; we can extract silver from Japan with Chinese goods; piece goods from the Coromandel coast in exchange for spices, other goods and gold from China; piece goods from Surat for spices; other goods and rials from Arabia for spices and various other trifles – one thing leads to another. And all of it can be done without any money from the Netherlands and with ships alone. We have the most important spices already. What is missing then? Nothing else but ships and a little water to prime the pump. (By this I mean sufficient means [money] so that the rich Asian trade may be established.) Hence, gentlemen and good administrators, there is nothing to prevent the Company from acquiring the richest trade in the world.[154]

In the first instance, the bullion confiscated in the Americas lubricated the circuits of capital accumulation in Europe as a whole, providing the liquid specie for Europe's vibrant trade with 'the East'. By 1650, the estimated flow of precious metals from the Americas reaching Europe amounted to at least 180 tons of gold and 17,000 tons of silver. Between 1561 and 1580, about 85 per cent of the entire world's production of silver came from the Americas. This provided the capital for European merchants' profitable trade with Asia and East Africa in textiles and spices.[155] It also assisted European states in obtaining raw materials and primary products from areas (particularly China and India) which would otherwise have had little incentive to trade with the Europeans on such a scale.[156] Indeed, it was the enormous demand for silver coming from China that allowed the mines in t he New World to operate so profitably.[157]

There was, then, a clear connection between American treasure and the expansion of the extremely lucrative East India trade. Holland, England, Portugal and France were only able to finance their trade with Asia because of the vast streams of precious metals coming from Mexico and Peru.[158] This enabled the relatively 'backward' European merchants to tap into Asian markets and eventually monopolise them, creating conditions under which 'the West' would displace, subordinate and subsequently dominate 'the East' in their own trading arena (see Chapter 7).[159] The re-export of Asian colonial goods in turn contributed to developing markets in Europe, the Americas and Africa. Hence, a world market directed in the interests of the European ruling classes was ultimately funded by plundered 'New World' precious metals.[160] One recent study has gone so far as to conclude that 'the differential growth of Western Europe' over the 16th to early 19th centuries 'is almost entirely accounted for by the growth of nations with access to the Atlantic Ocean', including, notably, those 'nations most directly involved in trade and colonialism in the New World and Asia'.[161]

In fine, the socio-economic effects of the Atlantic vector of uneven and combined development on European geopolitics spread vast and wide. Locking Spanish development in place, the American colonies monetarily facilitated Madrid's engagement in a classic bout of imperial overstretch, precipitating the monarchy's decline as a great power. In turn, the fiscal adjustments of the Spanish state created the geopolitical and economic space for Europe's two latecomers, England and Holland, to reap the 'privileges of backwardness' assisting their 'rise' to global supremacy. The only way to explain the variegated developmental trajectories of the Spanish vis-à-vis the Dutch and later English is by recognising the various means through which the New World specie and plundered resources from the Americas fed into and gave a much needed boost to emergent processes of capitalist development in the Netherlands and England, while locking in an already existing feudalism in Spain. The uneven and combined development of the Western and European hemispheres therefore conditioned and reconstituted patterns of differentiated development within Europe itself, enabling the incipient rise of Northwestern Europe as the 'organic heartland' of capitalist development. This intersocietal, 'extra-European' context through which European capitalism developed was its critical precondition.

Sublating the Smithian Moment: From Smith to Marx via 'the International'

As is well known, Adam Smith recognised the significance of American silver in 'West–East' trade relations, noting how East Asia was a major market for the silver being pumped out of the American mines. This was a 'market which, from the time of the discovery of those mines, has been continually taking off a greater and greater quantity of silver'. The precious metals flowing out of the Americas were a commodity that was 'extremely advantageous to carry from Europe to India' as there was scarcely any other commodity which brought a 'better price there', and it was in fact 'even more advantageous to carry silver to China'.[162] The silver extracted from the American continent would provide the basis for commercial relations between the 'two extremities' of the Old World, and the means by which 'those distant parts of the world are connected with one another'. Smith also noted how the European commodity trade to the East Indies, along with the gold and silver purchased for those commodities, necessarily created increases in European productivity. As such, Europe went from being a regionally limited economic system of manufacturers and carriers to being one covering 'almost all the different nations of Asia, Africa, and America'.[163]

For Smith, it was the widening of markets brought about by the acquisition of American wealth that would bring about divisions of labour and technological developments. In this respect, the Atlantic also acted as a 'vent-for-surplus', in which the international trade it instigated absorbed commodities 'for which there was no domestic demand'.[164] Such Smithian arguments have been widely invoked by political economists seeking to (re)insert the Atlantic into our understanding of European capitalist development. For Eric Williams, the international division of labour across the Atlantic triangular trade helped to generate profits by effectively buying cheap and selling dear between its three nodes. The Northwestern European states provided manufactures, which were shipped to Africa in exchange for slaves. Slaves were then shipped to American plantations, which subsequently provided raw materials that were sold back in Northwestern Europe (see the next section). Subsequently, the accumulated wealth generated from these activities was reinvested into the 'core', financing the technological developments that resulted in the Industrial Revolution.[165]

Max Weber also recognised the great significance of the Atlantic discoveries in hastening the development of capitalism in Europe, writing:

> The acquisition of colonies by the European states led to a gigantic acquisition of wealth in Europe for all of them. The means of this accumulation was the monopolizing of colonial products, and also of the markets of the colonies, that is the right to take goods into them, and, finally, the profits of transportation between mother land and colony.[166]

Even Marx, for all his criticism of Smith and other bourgeois economists, was keen to emphasise the 'acquisition of wealth' as a crucial moment in the process of primitive accumulation. As he put it:

> There can be no doubt ... that the great revolutions that took place in trade in the sixteenth and seventeen centuries, along with the geographical discoveries of that epoch, and which rapidly advanced the development of commercial capital, were a *major moment in promoting the transition from the feudal to capitalist mode of production*. The sudden expansion of the world-market, the multiplication of commodities in circulation, the competition among the European nations for the seizure of Asiatic products and American treasures, the colonial system, all made a fundamental contribution towards shattering the feudal barriers to production.[167]

Elsewhere, Marx also wrote of how:

> [t]he colonial system ripened trade and navigation as in a hothouse .... [colonial companies] were powerful levers for the concentration of capital. The colonies provided a market for the budding manufactures, and a vast increase in accumulation which was guaranteed by the mother country's monopoly of the market. The treasures captured outside Europe by undisguised looting, enslavement and

murder flowed back to the mother-country and were turned into capital there. Holland, which first brought the colonial system to its full development, already stood at the zenith of its commercial greatness in 1648.[168]

However, it is important to remember that although Marx incorporated this 'Smithian moment' into his understanding of the origins of capitalism, his own explication of primitive accumulation was based on considerably wider processes. Hence, immediately after noting 'the discovery of gold and silver in America', Marx goes on to argue that the:

> expiration, enslavement and entombment in mines of the indigenous population of that continent, the beginnings of the conquest and plunder of India, and the conversion of Africa into a preserve for the commercial hunting of blackskins, are all things which characterize the dawn of the era of capitalist production.[169]

What Marx points to is an *intersocietal* process in which the labour of different societies was subordinated to and subsumed by the requirements of capital. However, beyond a few brief passages, he offers little substance to the historical significance of the processes of subordination on this international scale. This has led an array of Marxists and non-Marxists alike to bracket the international scope of his analysis and limit Marxian notions of primitive accumulation to exclusively domestic processes.[170] In what follows, we argue that this internalist perspective limits our understanding of the history of capitalism, and its continued reproduction, and that it is therefore necessary to redeem – and indeed expand upon – Marx's original emphasis on 'the international' in order to overcome these limits.

Primitive Accumulation Proper: From 'Simple' to 'Expanded' Reproduction

In Chapter 1, we saw how Ellen Wood, following Brenner, argued that primitive accumulation was an entirely domestic process, taking place through the dispossession of the peasantry in the English countryside and the creation of an internal market which could satisfy and reproduce market dependence.[171] On the one hand, the reproduction of now dispossessed direct producers became based on obtaining a wage through which their means of subsistence could be purchased, establishing their market dependence as such. On the other hand, capitalist production in agriculture made the market a viable medium through which the means of subsistence could be secured. Technological improvements led to increases in productivity and the expansion of outputs per unit, lowering prices on goods that would have otherwise been affordable only to the wealthy or would require nonmarket access (through subsistence farming, for example).

Wood thus succeeds in tracing the historical origins of what Marx would come to term 'simple reproduction' (although Wood does not explicitly make this claim). As Marx put it:

> [Capital's reproduction] takes good care to prevent the workers, those instruments of production who are possessed of consciousness, from running away, by constantly removing their product from one pole [labour] to the other, to the opposite pole of capital. Individual consumption provides, on the one hand, the means for the workers' maintenance and reproduction: on the other hand, by the constant annihilation of the means of subsistence, it provides for their continued re-appearance on the labour market.[172]

Marx's argument here perhaps explains Wood's own emphasis on dispossession and the creation of an internal market,[173] for these appear to constitute the basic preconditions for the 'simple reproduction' of the capital–wage-labour relation. However, Wood's explanation remains wedded to a decidedly one-sided view of the capital–wage-labour relation. For not only is there a basic necessity for the means of subsistence to be produced, there is also a necessity for those products to be consumed. That is, the market can function as a medium for reproduction only insofar as the proletariat have the sufficient means to purchase the goods required for their reproduction. Capitalist crises occur, Marx argued, because that very means – (access to) a wage – is constantly undermined by capitalist accumulation, and more specifically by 'expanded reproduction'.[174]

Marx's argument about 'expanded reproduction' demonstrates that capital, because of inter-capitalist competition, must always return to the market and reinvest its surpluses into expanding its productive capacities. By introducing labour-saving techniques into production, individual capitals can reduce costs and reap super-profits, or reduce prices to obtain a greater market share. As innovations reduce costs, more and more products are transformed into consumer goods, thus spurring the expansion of markets and lines of production beyond already existing market capacity. While this creates the sort of 'internal market' envisaged by Wood, it also causes prices to fall more slowly than costs, creating conditions for high profitability; 'capital then rushes to line, pulling labour with it'.[175] However, as more and more capital is mobilised in expanding production, the market becomes saturated, and innovations cause productive capacity to rise beyond what the market is capable of absorbing. Hence, prices fall quicker than costs, and overall profitability tumbles. As a consequence, vast swathes of both capital and the working population are shed by productive lines seeking to drive down costs, and re-establish the conditions of profitability and continued accumulation.

This is exactly what happened to agrarian production in England over the course of the 17th century. The enclosures, and later the agricultural revolution, introduced various labour-economising techniques such as the reclamation and engrossment of land, the reduction of fallow, and four-field crop rotation.[176] This allowed for the expansion of food production to an unprecedented level, driving down costs and creating a domestic market for labourers to secure their means of subsistence.[177] But once this expanded capacity reached the limits of what could be profitably absorbed by the domestic market, both labour and capital were systematically shed from agrarian production and pushed into urban areas.[178] The rapid urbanisation of England and the expansion of London into the largest city in Europe were the consequence of an emergent 'surplus' population created by the limits of agrarian capitalism. In England, the emergence of this vast surplus population constituted a fundamental problem for the continued reproduction of capitalism. The 17th century was rife not only with the emergence of rural social movements such as the Diggers and Levellers that would challenge the status quo,[179] but also with various ruling class lamentations over what to do with the 'multitudes' or 'swarmes' of 'vagrants' and 'idlers'[180] that had been shed by agrarian production in the course of the enclosures, and later the agricultural revolution.

And yet the capitalist dynamic of 'expanded reproduction' indicates that this surplus population shed by agrarian capitalism will eventually be reabsorbed into new productive lines elsewhere. Wood makes a similar argument, showing that the dispossession of the peasantry and their absorption into waged labour in urban areas further contributed to the expansion of the domestic market. What Wood does not account for convincingly is precisely how and where this surplus population was absorbed:

> the English city, London in particular, was disproportionately enlarged by the poor dispossessed by agrarian capitalism. In any case, what made the English market for basic goods distinctive was not simply the demographic distribution between town and country but also the growing proportion of the population, whether urban or rural, that was dispossessed and reliant on wages for survival, together with the more direct relation of production to consumption of this kind.[181]

However, the reliance on a wage does not guarantee access to it; in fact, one of the primary results of expanded reproduction is the increasing *superfluity* of labour, and a growing surplus population with no direct access to a wage. So a proper understanding of why English capitalism was able to survive the agrarian limits suffered by prior protocapitalist social formations would necessitate some historical account of what made England exceptionally attuned to absorbing populations rendered superfluous by this prior round of capitalist transformation. Wood's omission of any such account is undoubtedly not intentional, but it is a crucial one. For it was specifically those sectors attached to the Atlantic that eventually provided the outlet for capitalists to absorb the surplus population created by the expulsion of peasants from agrarian production.

First, a large mass of proletarians were integrated into forms of work that presupposed colonies – shipbuilding, harbour building, and later sugar refineries and textile production. For example, huge quantities of labour were required to clear forests and transport timber, which would subsequently be used to build the ships that formed the backbone of English colonial expansion.[182] Similarly, colonial enterprises were the precondition for the extensive construction of ports for long-distance trade. Pre-existing towns and cities such as Bristol and London expanded significantly in the 17th century, while entirely new conurbations – Liverpool most notably, but also Glasgow and Derry – later sprang up as nodes in the growing network of international shipping spurred on by the Atlantic trading system.[183] The construction of ports and harbours was based on the labour-intensive activities of reclaiming marshy coastal lands, felling and transporting timber and rubble, and constructing seawalls, breakwaters, piers, quays and jetties. As Adam Ferguson noted in 1767:

> The pestilent marsh is drained with great labour, and the sea is fenced off with mighty barriers .... Harbours are opened, and crowded with shipping, where vessels of burden, if they are not constructed with a view to the situation, have not water to float. Elegant and magnificent edifices are raised on foundations of slime.[184]

Second, where the internal market could not absorb them, the dispossessed were exported *en masse* to the colonies as settlers or indentured servants. In particular, those considered indebted, poor, dispossessed, criminal, vagrant or rebellious were targeted – what propagandists of the time described as the 'rank multitude', those 'who cannot live at home'. Richard Hakluyt, a propagandist for English colonialism, noted the concurrence of the emergent surplus population with England's 'late entry into the European scramble for New World colonies .... England, unlike Portugal, Spain, the Netherlands, or France, had a huge and desperate population that could be redeployed overseas'.[185] In 1606, Francis Bacon advised James I that in exporting such 'surplus' populations, England would gain 'a double commodity, in the avoidance of people here, and in making use of them there'.[186] Similarly, in 1609 the Virginia Company argued that its colonisation project would serve 'to ease the city and suburbs of a swarme of unnecessary inmates, as a contynual cause of death and famine, and the very originall cause of all the plagues that happen in this kingdome'.[187] These claims were reflected in state legislation. The Beggars Act in 1597 and 1598 authorised the transportation of vagrants and criminals to work in penal servitude in the colonies.[188] By 1652, another legislative act was passed that enabled magistrates to ship vagrants and beggars to the colonies. Over the course of the 17th century, some 200,000 people were moved to the Americas, thus 'removing out of the city' the 'matter of sedition'.[189]

The absorption of the surplus population, and the expanded reproduction of capital as such, was therefore dependent – as its precondition – on the exploitation of a widened sphere of activity beyond the boundaries of the domestic market. That is, if it were not for the specifically international conditions created by Europe's expansion into the Atlantic, it is likely that capitalism would have been choked off by the limits of English agrarian capitalism. In this respect, we might be able to construct an 'inside-out' argument that attributes the growth of English (and later British) colonialism to the ways in which it overcame the limits of domestic capitalist production. But it is also possible to go beyond this orthodoxy, and demonstrate how intersocietal determinations arising from the Atlantic fed back into and decisively reordered the configuration of a capitalism based on agrarian production, and prefigured the industrial capitalism that drove Britain to global dominance. In particular, the combination of the sociologically uneven sources of English capital, African (slave) labour and American land – concentrated in the institution of plantation slavery – would provide both the international conditions and the spur to British domestic development. We now explicate these international determinations in turn: first, by tracing the combination of American land with African slave labour; and second, by examining how plantation slavery fed back into and determined the course of British development.

The Uneven and Combined Development of Plantation Slavery

> Lions have no historians, and therefore lion hunts are thrilling and satisfactory human reading. Negroes had no bards, and therefore it has been widely told how American philanthropy freed the slave.
>
> W. B. du Bois, 1920[190]

The reason why 17th-century colonialists were so enamoured by the promise of the Americas was that unlike Europe, the land appeared 'virgin'. It was considered empty, vacant, and as such presented an exceptional opportunity for a ruling class seeking to dump a surplus population that was not needed at home. Despite the purity implied by the notion of 'virgin lands', the sparseness of the continent was in part a product of European colonialism itself. Specifically, the mass slaughter of indigenous communities through murder, overwork or disease had left a pre-conquest continent of 90 million inhabitants with only 10 million people by 1650.[191] Among those who survived, many existing territories were abandoned, as communities fled to the highlands to escape the reach of colonial authority (see above).

Therefore, in contrast to England, where a vast surplus population was causing the ruling class widespread consternation, the New World posed very different challenges. In England, a unified ruling class concentrated in the state was able to legislate for and coercively impose private property rights and anti-vagrancy laws. The iron discipline of the English state was one of the fundamental levers through which the dispossessed class of peasants could be terrorised into a new work discipline based on the capitalist mode. Such institutions and practices had little efficacy in the Americas, where 'property rights [existed] legally, but because of the extent of land, they [were] valueless'.[192] In the context of 'unoccupied' lands and the weakness of the wholesale absence of any recognised authority, the idea of production based on the combination of private property and 'free labour' proved initially unworkable.[193] In particular, colonialists found worker resistance to be a persistent dilemma that proved difficult to solve because of the sociological characteristics of the Americas.

The Sociological Unevenness of the Atlantic

First, the sociological unevenness between colonial and Native American communities provided an impulse for rebellion. Many among those who had been sent to work on the colonies saw in native communities alternative modes of production and ways of life that offered a better guarantee of food and freedom. When confronted with strict and onerous work regimes in the colonies, in which subsistence was barely guaranteed, migrant workers found flight and defection to indigenous communities to be a way to resist and reassert the communality and autonomy that they had been dispossessed of in England. Thus, 'a steady stream of English settlers' fled colonial settlements and became 'Anglo-Powhatans', joining a Native American confederation 'of small-scale societies without ownership of land, without classes, without a state'.[194] In other cases, the sheer abundance of land offered the opportunity to escape and create altogether new settlements, although this often meant the active dispossession of indigenous populations.[195] Other servants and slaves fleeing from colonial authorities would form more itinerant communities in the shape of bands of pirates and buccaneers.[196]

Second, the combination of people from sociologically different backgrounds served as the basis for resistance. Colonial transport and work presented new collaborative opportunities for the 'rank multitude', wherein dispossessed Irish peasants, veterans of the English Revolution, enslaved indigenous Americans and African slaves could collectively rebel against authorities. Strategies of resistance included refusal to work, sabotage of production, flight from the colonies and outright revolt. In fact, such was the collaboration among Irish and Africans in resistance movements that the '"Black Irish" were considered an ethnic group in Montserrat and Jamaica'.[197]

In short, the problem of the idle, vagrant, rebellious worker reasserted itself in the colonies, where the persistent resistance and flight of workers made the new American communities periodically unsustainable. The combination of a resistant European workforce, the decimation of the indigenous population, large tracts of vacant land, and the concomitant absence of effective state coercion meant the colonial economy soon suffered from a crisis in the supply of labour. The peculiarity of this colonial arrangement in the New World meant that the possibility of capitalist development based on a 'free' and waged workforce was effectively closed off.[198] In fact, many initial experiments in colonial plantations failed because of the prohibitive costs of accruing 'free' labour.[199] However, once the colonisation of the Americas had been instigated – and with it a section of the ruling class invested in developing the colonial economy – a new dynamic took hold. The making of Atlantic colonies became less about dumping surplus populations, and more about obtaining a viable supply of workers that was otherwise not forthcoming from England.[200]

By the 18th century, with the onset of industrialisation, population control thereby became a central concern of English economists. Whereas in the first period of colonisation, the ruling class were trying to rid themselves of the 'rank multitude', in the age of the factory, surplus populations became central to profitability. It was in this context that the likes of Malachy Postlethwayt, a mercantilist and propagandist for the Royal African Company, argued that 'the provision of black labor for the colonies had distinct advantages over that of white labor. Specifically, the use of African slaves on the plantation would not depopulate Britain'.[201] The turn to slavery was therefore a historically specific response to the challenges noted above that confronted the ruling class – in both Europe and America – in the 17th/18th centuries. But why African slavery? Robin Blackburn suggests that African slaves were 'better suited, stronger, more resilient' than either European or Native American workers.[202] On the 'supply' side, World-Systems approaches have often reinforced an essentially conservative view of African societies as passive, and the slaves extracted from them as docile and submissive.[203] For Walter Rodney, because Africa was at a 'lower level' of economic development than Europe, it was forced into a colonial relation in which African rulers gave up slaves in exchange for manufactured goods.[204]

However, such approaches mistakenly project the 'modern' colonial relation retrospectively back to a time in which the power balance between Europe and Africa was much less clear cut. In doing so, Africa's 'backwardness' (and Europe's 'privilege') is presupposed but not explained, thus reifying an otherwise historically constructed (and contested) social relation. Although the eventual long-term effects of the relations between European and African societies would prove constitutive of a colonial relation and white supremacy, the colonial relation itself was not the starting point. Such explanations, whether benign or not, therefore tend to reinforce the naturalisation of black slavery, by reproducing the idea that Africans were naturally prone to colonial subjugation and exceptionally suited to plantation work.

Consequently, it must be remembered that in the 16th century when Europeans first began to develop the transatlantic slave trade, West African states held numerous geopolitical and economic advantages over Europeans. Much has been made of the superior military might of Europeans, but this again tends to read a later era of colonial domination back into a historical period in which domination was not the norm. Although European states would eventually subjugate the continent from the 18th century onwards, prior to that period African states proved very effective in repelling European territorial encroachments.[205] Moreover, in terms of trade, Europe offered very little to Africa that it did not already produce or obtain from elsewhere.[206]

The clearest indication of European weakness in relation to African states was their abortive attempts to establish plantations in West Africa. Such attempts failed because the Europeans were unable to subjugate and transform the communal subsistence bases of agrarian production into a privatised market-based system.[207] This was largely because, unlike in the Americas, Europeans were unable to conduct extensive territorial conquests and raiding missions on the African continent until well into the 18th century. Despite holding naval advantages at sea, Europeans were unable to transfer this superiority onto the African mainland, where indigenous naval techniques proved considerably better suited to manoeuvring in, and hence protecting, riverways.[208] A curious stand-off characterised the geopolitical relations between Atlantic African and European states in the 16th and 17th centuries, where the Europeans were unable to fully conquer Africans on the mainland, and the Africans failed to expel the Europeans from the coast

More in common with the Indian Ocean littoral (see Chapter 7), the experiences of European colonialists on the Atlantic African coast were governed by commercial activities conducted on the terms set by the African ruling classes. European merchants had to fulfil a number of local obligations to gain market entry, dealing with an array of actors including kings, state intermediaries, merchants, brokers, notables and producers. Their obligations included obtaining licences, or providing gifts, taxes, rent and charges. Moreover, rulers of African states often compelled Europeans to trade below fixed prices, withdraw from trade, and opened and closed markets at will.[209] In some cases they actively coerced the Europeans into submission, by seizing European ships that engaged in unsanctioned trade.[210] These advantages held by Atlantic African states over Europeans meant that the 'human capacity' of slavery had to be bought, and then employed elsewhere – in the Americas – where land was easier to obtain and the 'local population easy to coerce'.[211]

When seen in this context, the slave trade should not be conceived as an external shock, designed or compelled by Europeans, but instead as a pre-existing part of ruling class strategies for reproduction in certain African societies. The specificity of the slave trade was rooted in the very unevenness that existed between European and (Atlantic) African modes of production. To be clear, slavery was widespread not because Atlantic Africa was more 'backward' than feudal Europe, but rather because the character of ruling class reproduction differed. While in Europe land ownership constituted the basis of private property and ruling class wealth and power as such, in Atlantic Africa quasi-communal ownership of land predominated. Therefore, ruling class reproduction was guaranteed by mechanisms based on the ownership and accumulation of people rather than land: head taxes, military dues and labour services, of which slavery was the most common. Indeed, slaves constituted the primary form of private property in West African law. Hence, European contemporaries observed that local rulers and notables were predominantly wealthy in slaves rather than land, cash or goods.[212]

One consequence of Atlantic African slaving was that slaves occupied a social position and standard of life that was little different from European peasants or workers.[213] In fact, and similar to the Ottoman state structure (see Chapter 4), slaves could often take up positions that were functionally part of the ruling class. In the case of Songhay, Kongo and Ndongo, slaves were crucial to the centralisation of the ruler's authority, acting as 'administrators, soldiers, and even royal advisors, enjoying a great freedom of movement and elite life-styles'.[214]

In short, ruling class power could be reproduced and increased by accumulating slaves. Hence the centrality of slaves to the reproduction of the Atlantic African ruling class contained, as its precondition, an intersocietal component. Due to the predominance of quasi-communal forms of land, there was a lack of compulsion for – and outright resistance towards – the acquisition of large tracts of territory through geopolitical accumulation. Instead, West African geopolitics was governed by what might be termed *biopolitical accumulation*:[215] wars aimed at acquiring slaves were 'the exact equivalent of Eurasian wars aimed at acquiring land'.[216] The accumulation of humans as a rule of reproduction in Atlantic African societies was thus central to the conflicts and raids enacted between the Kongo and Ndongo, the imperial expansion of the Songhay, and the reproduction of the Senegambian states.[217] Taken together, the various factors that placed slave and slaving at the heart of ruling class reproduction made the Atlantic African ruling classes exceptionally capable of providing and sustaining a steady supply of slave labour to European colonialists.

Nonetheless, once Europeans entered the slave trade, and especially once slavery became a crucial component of ruling class reproduction in the Americas, the (geo)political composition of Atlantic Africa was radically transformed. In certain areas, such as the Gold Coast, the processes of state formation that took place in the 16th and 17th centuries were made possible by the encounter of Atlantic African societies with each other, and with Europeans. Such interactions generated increasing migration, settlement and centralisation in a region where nomadic and village communities were the norm. Following the introduction of maize, the increased caloric capacity helped spur rapid population growth throughout regions plugged into the Atlantic trade. The Atlantic coast thus shifted from a 'periphery' of the 'Sudanese center' into 'a center in its own right: a magnet that drew people and trade from all sides to its burgeoning "central places"'.[218]

But the importance of biopolitical accumulation as a rule of reproduction, and the relatively advanced position of Atlantic African societies in other trades, meant that the import of military commodities took precedence. Europeans, who were producing firearms on an unprecedented scale, were exceptionally well placed and only too willing to take advantage. The extensive influx of European weapons into Atlantic Africa substantially reconfigured the geopolitics of the region, and in particular the dynamic of biopolitical accumulation, changing the nature and scope of warfare. Prior to the arrival of European guns, the politically fragmented character of Atlantic Africa was relatively balanced, whereby 'no single state was militarily stronger than its neighbors'. Warfare was instead primarily defensive, short lived and limited to 'small-scale' operations, 'embracing tens rather than hundreds of square miles'.[219]

From the mid-17th century, with African states now plugged into dense networks of commercial-cum-military relations with Europeans, this dynamic fundamentally changed. Wars became more extensive, giving rise to a series of expansionist state formations along the Atlantic African littoral, with states such as the Denkyira, Akwamu and Asante springing up, expanding, and widening the geographical scope of slave acquisition.[220] At the same time, states outside the slave trade were deprived of access to weaponry and increasingly 'found themselves on the losing side of an arms race. Their dilemma: without firearms defence was precarious. To get muskets, there must be something to export. The only item in great demand was slaves'.[221] As the capacities of states for obtaining slaves increased, societies previously outside of the transatlantic slave trade were pulled irrevocably into it, either as sources of slaves, or as slave traders themselves.[222] Overall, the slave trade came to serve a dual purpose. It was the medium through which the firearms crucial to war-making could be imported, and it was also the medium through which states could shed the surplus slaves accrued from their now enhanced war-making capabilities.

The Europeans' insatiable thirst for slave labour in the Americas, on the one side, and the subsequent reordering of African geopolitics, on the other, help explain why, from the mid-17th century onwards, there was a radical increase in the transatlantic slave trade. In the first half-century of the transatlantic slave trade, 700,000 Africans boarded boats destined for the Americas.[223] The export of slaves from West Africa as a whole doubled; in some cases, as in Angola, it tripled.[224] Slaving in and around Allada – which would eventually take the title of the 'Slave Coast' – grew from no exports in 1500 to over 19,000 slaves per year by 1700. Parts of the Gold Coast, such as Lower Guinea, experienced a similar expansion, switching from a net importer of slaves to a net exporter in the 17th century. The expansion proved exponential, especially once the English entered the trade.[225] In 1670, an average of 888 slaves were exported from the Gold Coast each year. By 1720, the average had risen to 4,708 per annum.[226]

By the mid-18th century this had resulted in the increasing militarisation of West African states, geopolitically destabilising the region as a whole. The expansion of slaving for export, combined with the ravages of conflict, produced a concomitant demographic exhaustion of West Africa and its tributaries. In a region where people were considered the primary source of wealth, population decline had a negative impact on agrarian productivity, which in turn increased exposure to famine and disease.[227] Plundered of its source of power, wealth and international 'comparative advantage' – human labour – Africa was left prone to an emergent relation of subjugation and dependence vis-à-vis Europe, which would come to characterise the later ravages of colonialism on the continent.

Sociological Combination in the Plantation System

The plantation brought these disparate, unevenly generated forces of production together: English capital, American land and African slavery. This combination was historically unprecedented and distinct from prior forms of either slave labour or plantation production – a productive unit geared specifically towards capitalistic production. Plantations thus functioned as sites of significant capitalistic experimentations in agro-industrial combinations of productive forces,[228] and are best characterised as 'transitional forms' of social relations combining complex amalgams of capitalist and non-capitalist relations, production techniques and practices – 'dependent and hybrid socio-economic enterprises'.[229] They were distinct from the form of agrarian and later industrial production based on wage-labour that predominated in England, and also different from European serfdom and the modes of slavery in Africa. From top to bottom, these were societies where the 'archaic' and 'modern', the most 'backward' and 'advanced', were juxtaposed, overlapped, and fused in multiple and contradictory ways. The myriad constitutive contrasts making up this colonial mode of combined development are well illuminated by Robin Blackburn:

> The social relations of colonial slavery borrowed from an ancient stock of legal formulas, used contemporary techniques of violence, developed manufacture and maritime transport on a grand scale, and anticipated modern modes of co-ordination and consumption. Slavery in the New World was above all a hybrid

mixing ancient and modern, European business and African husbandry, American and Eastern plants and processes, elements of traditional patrimonialism with up-to-date bookkeeping and individual ownership .... These borrowings necessarily involved innovation and adaptation, as new social institutions and practices, as well as new crops and techniques of cultivation, were arranged in new ensembles.[230]

These bundles of sociopolitical, economic and ideocultural processes and relations are perhaps best captured under the conceptual rubric of *créolisation* – a distinct and novel articulation of an uneven and combined development in the historically specific conditions of the New World. The term is particularly helpful in understanding the conditions of hybridity and combination forged through the New World experience, as the concept of *créolisation* is 'organically linked to Atlantic slavery'. Though it was 'initially designed to denote African slaves brought up in a master's house', the term was subsequently generalised 'to refer to anything that, first introduced into the New World from elsewhere, managed to reproduce itself in its new setting'.[231] From the African coastal depots to the reprovisioning points in the Atlantic islands to the American ports to the plantations, colonial marketplaces and backlands – from all these 'new spaces' came 'new languages, new musics, new religions and new laws', giving 'birth to the creole, to mixtures of European, African and Amerindian elements'.[232] Such processes of *créolisation* on the plantation economy and the concomitant hybrid social relations, identities and 'new syntaxes of racial hierarchy'[233] that were fashioned in the colonial crucible would come to cohere and develop in ways that escaped all extant European developmental models and forms. Such was the 'melting pot' of the Americas, founded on the some of the most vicious forms of exploitation, oppression and racism the modern world has known.

Insofar as European, Amerindian and African workers shared relatively equivalent experiences of the disciplinary work regime in the Americas, new potentialities for collective collaboration and resistance emerged. In addition to the forms of escape and resistance outlined above, the late 17th century saw uprisings against the ruling class in centres of the nascent plantation system, as exemplified by the Chesapeake rebellions in 1676.[234] The sorts of solidarity fashioned in the early colonial system would eventually be dismantled through the differentiation and stratification of certain groups within the workforce. Less onerous labour functions and greater privileges were assigned to white European workers, while African slaves were redefined as a legally abject section of the workforce.[235] Subsequently, ruling class fears of revolt were directed less at 'multiracial rebellions', and more at exclusively slave revolts. 'Negro insurrections' became an object of fear among colonialists, reflected in two acts legislating against such revolts in 1680 and 1682. According to Peter Linebaugh and Marcus Rediker, the transition to a racially hierarchised mode of production 'was completed with "An Act Concerning Servants and Slaves" (1705), which guaranteed the rights of servants and defined slaves as a form of property that would constitute the basis of production in Virginia'.[236]

With the defeat of these rebellions in the late 17th century came the recomposition of the plantation proletariat by the formation of class divisions between white and black workers through the ideology of scientific racism.[237] As the cartographer and physician William Petty put it in 'The Scale of Creatures' (1676), 'There seem to be several species even of human beings' in the colonies and 'the Europeans do not only differ from the aforementioned Africans in colour ... but also ... in natural manners and in the internal qualities of their minds'.[238] Here we find in Petty's works, which followed those of Francis Bacon, the development of 'a new discourse, an ideological racism different in tone and methods from the racial prejudice of the overseer with a whip or the bully on the deck'.[239] Such spurious biological arguments for 'white supremacy' were later redefined by the two titans of modern English philosophy, John Locke and David Hume, along with various English biologists. Similarly, the Church of England clergyman and missionary Morgan Godwyn explained the 'inherent inferiority' of black slaves – and black people as such – by their refusal to work, writing, 'Surely Sloth and Avarice have been no unhandy Instruments and Assistants to midwife it into the World, and to Foster and Nurse it up'.[240] Of course, as noted, such refusals to work were quite often part of slave strategies to resist colonial rule, rather than symptomatic of putative essential(ist) racial attributes.

The construction of racism as a class relation, and as an ideology legitimating divide and rule, was therefore central to the formation and reproduction of the colonial economy in the Americas.[241] But its effects would prove considerably more wide-ranging, eventually constituting the broader development and reproduction of capitalism as a totality of socio-economic, political, legal and ideocultural relations. For at the core of the sociological amalgamations within the colonial plantations was the interlacing and systemic fusion of different relations of production. Slaves themselves were not directly subject to capitalist rules of reproduction and were often dependent on the 'natural economy' for subsistence. Rather than the market dependence of the wage-labourer, 'slaves grew much of their own food and built shelter for themselves'. In fact, this allowed plantations a degree of self-sufficiency outside of the vagaries of the market, enabling them to better 'survive times of war, revolution or commercial depression'.[242] Due to this element of self-sufficiency, slavers themselves could temporarily withdraw from the market in ways that merchants and industrialists could not.

Nonetheless, plantations also mobilised modern techniques in crop specialisation, cultivation, book-keeping, packaging and shipping, signalling various developments in the productive forces. Such developments in the labour process made slavers considerably more responsive to market pressures than most non-capitalist rulers or merchants.[243] Being plugged into networks of international capital for both the supply of labour and the realisation of commodities produced also meant that slavers (and by extension slaves) could regularly turn to the market for food and manufactured goods traded in plantation products. Consequently, specialised production in the plantation could operate on a permanent basis. To draw a contrast with 17th-century Indian cotton, where producers would often turn to subsistence production in times of famine leading to substantial decreases in cotton output, plantations were receptive and responsive to the market as a basis for reproduction and were thus not subject to the same limitations.[244]

Perhaps most importantly, market competition compelled plantations to operate according to distinctly capitalist rules of reproduction.[245] The maintenance of the plantation was subject to costs and 'market stimuli' that constantly demanded renewed and expanding commodity production, where profit maximisation was the cardinal aim.[246] As assets of fixed capital, slaves were 'put to work' in the name of profit, or else sold off to someone who would do so.[247] Consequently, at least 'nine tenths of American slaves were put to commodity production',[248] in which modern techniques of discipline and violence were deployed to concentrate and mechanise work, as well as accelerate its intensity. Such features meant that the condition of slaves was considerably closer to that of the proletarians of England than that of the self-subsisting peasants of feudal Europe.[249] Moreover, planters often made large investments in slave labour that could 'enhance the productivity of future laborers', as exemplified by South Carolina's tidal rice plantations.[250] Elsewhere slavers introduced labour-saving technologies, as in the case of the ginning machine, which in 1794 mechanised cotton cleaning.[251]

The intensification of cultivation – its increasing commercialisation, mechanisation and industrialisation – brought with it an intensification of exploitation for the slaves who worked the plantations. Notably, slaves working on plantations that were plugged into international networks of trade – for example, cotton – were considerably more exploited than those in other sectors.[252] In short, the plantations showed all those features we would expect from a capitalist enterprise.[253]

What is more, as slave plantations were so thoroughly integrated into the world market, the evidence reveals a sharp convergence of average rates of profits and standardised methods of procedure, as we would expect from enterprises operating on a fully capitalist market.[254] These 'transitional forms of social relations' and 'the trading links connecting them to Europe would form part of a network through which capitalist laws of motion could become operative on a global scale, once the existing states system was overthrown'.[255] Hence, against Charles Post's claim that 'plantation slavery, even when subordinated to a capitalist world-market, cannot be understood as a capitalist form of social labour',[256] the plantations operated according to capitalist laws of motion, even if the slaves themselves were not subject to capitalist rules of reproduction. This was a 'combined' social formation, imbued with entirely novel and distinct (amalgamated) social relations and processes of a complexity and richness that falls out of any neat modal classification as either capitalist or non-capitalist.

Such was the curiosity of the plantation as a combined capitalist enterprise that operations conducted in the American 'periphery' were often far in advance, in terms of production techniques and forms of labour organisation, of those found in the imperial metropole. These were 'the most intensely commercialised farms in the world',[257] something particularly true of the Brazilian sugar plantations of the Portuguese Empire, where:

> [t]he merchants who owned the plantations were involved in the process of production, from cultivation to processing to ultimate transportation to market, to an extent that they were very rarely in the metropolitan centre. And the same process would often happen in reverse with planters becoming merchants in their turn. Plantations, although often smaller than the average area owned by landowners in Europe, occupied labour forces up to ten times as large. These were more akin to later factories than to the actual manufacturing as it existed in most of Europe at the time in the form of the largely unsupervised putting-out process.[258]

The plantation combined extensive land use with a labour force that was self-subsisting in reproduction but proletarianised in production, operating within an international market for the realisation of goods produced. Hence, we can indeed speak of the slave plantations in the Americas and West Indies as entirely novel 'combined' social formations, amalgamating different modes of production (Atlantic African slavery and European merchant capitalism) into new forms and modalities of development entirely distinct from those found previously in Europe, the Americas or Africa. These were, in other words, *sui generis* modes of combined development. And failure to grant explanatory 'agency' to these combined modalities of development born and nurtured in the Atlantic furnace is to externalise the intertwined histories of slavery, patriarchy, racism, colonial subjugation and exploitation so fundamental to the making of capitalist modernity.

New World Slavery and the Rise of Industrial Capitalism

The implications of the plantations for the development of English capitalism, and the capitalist mode of production more generally, are wide-ranging and striking. If we recall, the limits of England's domestic agrarian capitalism had created a surplus population and a concomitant fall in the overall rate of profit. Whether intentional or not, plantation slavery provided an avenue through which an array of countervailing tendencies could: first, put a halt to any fall in the rate of profit; and second, facilitate the 'expanded reproduction' of capitalism through the Industrial Revolution.

For Marx, there were six countervailing tendencies which could prevent the rate of profit from falling: 1) a more intense exploitation of labour; 2) reduction of wages below their value; 3) cheapening the elements of constant capital; 4) absorbing surplus populations by developing new lines of production; 5) foreign trade; and 6) increases in share capital.[259] As William Darity notes, 'in the colonial setting, especially with slave labour in place, all of these counter-effects except the sixth can be operative'.[260] The significance of the plantation was not missed by Marx, who observed:

> As far as *capital invested in the colonies*, etc. is concerned, however, the reason why this can yield higher rates of profit is that the *profit rate is generally higher there on account of the lower degree of development*, and so too is the exploitation of labour, *through the use of slaves and coolies*, etc. Now there is no reason why the higher rates of profit that capital invested in certain branches yields in this way, and brings home to its country of origin, *should not enter into the equalization of the general rate of profit* and hence raise this in due proportion, unless monopolies stand in the way.[261]

It is difficult to overstate the importance of this quote, as it demonstrates that, at least empirically, Marx understood sociological unevenness, intersocietal interactions and hybrid systems of production (combined developments) as constitutive of capitalism's laws of motion.[262]

In what follows, we trace the significance of the plantation to two key factors of capitalist accumulation – two 'spheres' in which the expanded reproduction of the Industrial Revolution was manifest. First, we look at the sphere of circulation, and the contributions the plantations made to the rate of profit and to foreign trade. Second, we look at how the plantation reordered the composition of labour and capital in Britain, with a particular focus on the reproduction of wage-labour and the real subsumption of labour under capital during the Industrial Revolution.

Contributions to the Sphere of Circulation

The peculiar combination of extensive land, capital and slave labour in the plantation entailed both a low organic composition of capital (countervailing tendency 4) and the means through which increases in absolute and relative surplus labour (countervailing tendency 1) were made possible. The very modal 'hybridity' of the slave plantations 'made it a powerful engine of primitive accumulation … cheapening the supply of the means of production or reproduction to the metropolitan regions' (more on the latter below). Hence, the rate of surplus extraction and rate of profit on the plantation were exceptionally high.[263]

In the Jamaican sugar plantations, for example, the rate of return was 10 per cent or more higher than the prevailing rate of interest in England.[264] On Barbara Solow's estimates, the year 1770 saw slave profits forming 0.5 per cent of Britain's national income, nearly 8 per cent of total investment and 39 per cent of commercial and industrial investments, constituting 'enormous' ratios.[265] As Solow puts it, '[s]lavery made more profits for investment, a larger national income for the Empire, and a pattern of trade which strengthened the comparative advantage of the home country in industrial commodities'.[266] In the late 18th century, income from colonial properties in the Americas was equal to approximately 50 per cent of British gross investment.[267] Since much of this would have been reinvested in British industries, it provided a significant input into British industrialisation.[268] An indication of the impact of such developments was the sharp decline in British interest rates. In the early 1690s, the rate of interest in Britain was 12 per cent, declining thereafter to 8 per cent after the establishment of the Bank of England in 1694, and then to 3 per cent in 1752. Rates on British public debt displayed a steady decline, falling from a high of 14 per cent in 1690 to 6 per cent and 7 per cent between 1707 and 1714. Rates subsequently remained low, at around 5 per cent up to the 1730s, falling to 3 per cent by 1750.[269]

These rates indicate that the plantation economy was central to the expansion of foreign trade (countervailing tendency 5). The import of 'luxury items' from the New World (tobacco, sugar, coffee and so on) provided goods in global demand, enabling the colonial powers to engage in a lucrative re-export trade with the rest of Europe.[270] Access to cheap sources of cotton lowered the cost of production in the all-important textile industry, raising the competitiveness of British exports. In particular, the transatlantic trades boosted the manufacture of cottons checks[271] for export either in the form of Indian-piece imitations in West Africa or as 'clothing material for the African slaves in the New World'.[272]

According to one estimate, British exports accounted for approximately 56 per cent of all industrial production between 1700 and 1760, and over 46 per cent between 1760 and 1800. North America, Latin America and the Caribbean were far and away the major markets for these overseas sales.[273] Moreover, it is estimated that this Atlantic trade constituted as much as 55 per cent of Great Britain's 'gross fixed capital formation investment'.[274] By 1772, the Americas consumed 37 per cent of English exports, making them a critical market for the imperial metropole while allowing the West Indies to concentrate exclusively on sugar.[275] If we include all the colonies, the proportion of British manufacturing exports rose from 14 per cent in 1700 to 55 per cent in 1773 to 71 per cent in 1855.[276] For the 1750–1800 period alone, British trade with the colonies accounted for approximately 15 per cent of national income – a 'colossal figure'.[277] Hence, it seems clear that during the critical early stages of Britain's industrialisation, the colonial export markets played a particularly crucial role making up for the demand often lacking in the highly protected home market – Smith's 'vent for surplus'.

Certainly in the 17th century, cotton textiles were central to the widening of Britain's export markets, saving British industry as a whole from a crisis of stagnation. Initial domestic demand was stimulated by the East India Company trade in Indian textiles. In 1613, the Company's first sales amounted to 5,000 pieces. By 1625 this had increased to 221,500 pieces. In 1681 sales peaked at 3,445,000 pieces.[278] The negative effects Indian imports had on domestic woollen manufacturing in turn led to 'noisy agitation' among English producers, who petitioned for protective legislation. Such constraints subsequently stimulated the production of home-made calicoes – using Indian methods – which were then sold as East Indian products in the domestic market.[279] Again woollen and silk producers moved against this market by pressuring Parliament to pass legislation banning the domestic consumption of calicoes. The unintended effect was to provide a boost to cotton manufacturing.[280] 'As the expansion reached the limits of the protected pre-existing domestic market', Joseph Inikori writes, 'stagnation set in'. Not surprisingly, the means to resolve this crisis of stagnation was 'through the exploitation of export opportunities in the transatlantic slave trade from Africa and in the slave-based economy of the Atlantic system'.[281]

Indeed, the larger market offered by the Atlantic increased the number of firms engaged in textile production. Consequently, Solow and Engerman argue that these foreign outlets 'provided Britain with new markets as old ones were drying up' and that 'increased demand for British manufacturing exports played an important role in the expansion of the British industrial sector'.[282] Hence, the 20 years from 1782 to 1802 have a marked originality, owing to their very high growth rate in exports, in which transatlantic commodities and markets played a leading role.[283] The role of the Atlantic colonies for the British economy was particularly important during periods of intense international economic competition. In the period after 1650, for example, the North American colonies had a positive net impact on English demand, 'thereby opening up an exclusive market for English industrial output precisely when intra-European trade was depressed and competition intensifying'.[284]

In sum, the American colonies and slave plantations generated both the markets and needed surpluses that assisted, through reinvestment, in jump-starting the engine of industrial accumulation. In Britain, the growth of an array of sectors – sugar refining, rum production, metallurgical products such as guns, chains and iron bars, wool and cotton textiles – benefited from capital investments derived from the transatlantic trade. Moreover, the profits from such sectors were often realised in this same trade, as all of these goods were transported to Africa, the Americas or both. The development of port cities such as Bristol and Liverpool, and centres of manufacture such as Manchester, was a direct product of slavery.

To take an anecdotal but revealing example, the business activities of the Hibbert family embodied the transatlantic sociological combination of plantation slavery and capitalism. The Hibberts owned 'a 3,000-acre sugar plantation in Jamaica and sugar commission enterprise in London as well as a cotton cloth manufactory in Manchester'.[285] The investments derived from dealings such as these were, moreover, constitutive of British finance. The bulk of exchange bills and company bonds circulating in England 'originated directly and indirectly from the trans-Atlantic slave trade and the trade centred on slave produced American products'.[286] Many banks and insurance firms grew and reproduced themselves on the basis of ownership and/or investment in plantations, and their related trades. Most notably, Barclays and Lloyds developed from slave trade profits, and subsequently became sources of credit for British industry.[287]

Contributions to the Sphere of Production

Nonetheless, the significance of the plantation extended far beyond surpluses realised in export markets. Specifically, in the sphere of production, the plantation had a twofold impact on the development of industry in Britain. First, the production of consumer goods such as sugar, coffee and tobacco on the plantations proved crucial to reducing the costs of labour-power (countervailing tendency number 1) in Britain. In contrast to Europe, where labour and land costs were comparatively prohibitive,[288] the cheaper use of slave labour in the ecologically 'boundless' American colonies facilitated increases in productivity. The result was reduced prices on these so-called 'luxury items', enabling access to and consumption of them on a mass scale. The effect on British workers was significant, since sugar provided 'virtually free calories'[289] that had previously been unobtainable with their wage via the market. The plantation was thus instrumental in widening the scope of market dependence, and reducing the proportion of the working day required for British workers to reproduce themselves. Hitherto luxurious items such as sugar, coffee and tobacco both metaphorically and literally fuelled the British Industrial Revolution, allowing labourers in the factories to work more productively over longer periods of time.[290]

However, it would be a mistake to read this as a triumph for British workers in cahoots with European capitalists at the expense of those toiling on the plantations. For the expanded consumption of the working class brought with it the possibility of reconstituting the labour process in Britain by expanding the 'unpaid part of the waged working-day' as well.[291] While increases in calorific intake meant workers could remain productive for longer, the cheaper cost of the workers' reproduction meant a concomitant reduction in the value of their labour-power. Either by reducing wages or by increasing productivity, capitalists could thus siphon off a larger proportion of workers' labour as profits, without affecting the latter's reproduction. This increase in the rate of exploitation (countervailing tendency 1) was the basic precondition[292] on which the Industrial Revolution was built, for it enabled a shift from 'absolute' to 'relative' surplus: 'from a type of exploitation based upon the lengthening of the working day... to a regime where higher wages and shorter hours would be compensated with an increase in the productivity of work, and the pace of production'.[293] In other words, a shift in the qualitative nature of the labour process brought about a different configuration of how the 'means of production [were] combined in the act of production itself'.[294]

Second, the absorption of labour into industry – and the 'real subsumption' of labour as such – was most pronounced in the production of textiles, wool[295] and later cotton. In 1840, textiles accounted for 75 per cent of industrial employment in England, with cotton textiles accounting for half of this total.[296] By 1850, British cotton production employed 374,000 people, of whom 89 per cent worked in factories where production was almost entirely mechanised.[297] Here too we find the pervasive influence of the plantation economy as a key 'input'. Both the impulse and conditions for mechanisation came from the attempt to lower the costs of inputs in the form of labour and raw materials, and improve the quality of textiles produced.[298]

On the one hand, British attempts to emulate and outdo the quality of Indian textiles explain the long durational process of experimentation with production techniques, of which the Industrial Revolution was the 'final stage'.[299] With factories came altogether new techniques in exploitation, many of which were borrowed directly from American plantations. The increasing complexity and scale of machinery necessitated centralised and concentrated sites of production, capable of employing thousands in small areas. While labour methods were standardised and deskilled, strict regulations were imposed on 'working hours, expected productivity, breaks and conduct'.[300] These were all inventions of the American plantation.[301]

On the other hand, had it not been for the steady stream of cheap raw cotton flowing out of the New World (which supplied nearly three-quarters of Britain's imports of raw cotton), the British cotton industry would have never been able to play such a central role in Britain's industrialisation.[302] As David Washbrook notes, '[c]otton was exceptionally well-placed to lead the move towards mechanization: but favourably placed precisely because its raw material came from abroad'.[303] That the British were able to outsource the production of raw cotton to the Americas – where the costs of production and labour in particular were considerably lower – was central to their industrial take-off in the 18th century. Through the institution of the slave plantation in the colonies, capitalists were able to significantly reduce the costs of constant capital in the form of raw materials (countervailing tendency 3). Without this key input, it is highly unlikely British manufactures could have overcome the formidable competition from Indian cotton textiles, which even in the mid-18th century still held a leading position in world markets.[304] The 'workshop of the world' was thus built on the foundations of plantation slavery.

Conclusion: Colonies, Merchants and the Transition to Capitalism

Emphasising the decisive importance of 1492 on the history of European capitalism is, in some respects, a return to the previous orthodoxies of Smith, Marx, Weber and Braudel. Each in their own way was able to grasp the origins of capitalism not as a single moment of inception, but as a 'value-added' process of increasing systemic consolidation and complexification, unevenly developing in time and space; a cascading and multilayered transformation of states and societies. The uneven and interactive development between the Atlantic and Europe promoted further modalities and relations of unevenness in Europe itself. And it was New World colonialism and slavery that catapulted capitalism into the global industrial system that it subsequently became. As Fernand Braudel put it some years ago, 'Is not America perhaps the true explanation of Europe's greatness?'[305] As the preceding analysis has shown, the answer is an emphatic 'yes'.

Yet to reiterate, this was not simply because of the effects that the American 'discoveries' had on the sphere of circulation (trade and exchange) in Europe, as many WST would have it. More importantly, the 'discoveries' decisively effected changes in the sphere of production, both in the Atlantic colonies and in the metropolitan core, which served to recompose the labour process in ways posited by capital itself – that is, real subsumption. In this respect, the 'arrival of capitalism was not a natural internal process'. Rather, as Irfan Habib writes, the:

> [s]ubjugation of other economies was crucial to the formation of industrial capital within it. In other words, colonialism, in its harshest forms, was not a mere attendant process to the rise of capitalism, it was one of its basic, inescapable premises.[306]

In this chapter, we have examined the various practices of subjugation that took place across three nodes of the Atlantic. In the Americas, colonialists annihilated indigenous populations, communities, modes of life and production. This scorched earth policy was complemented by a legal and ideological apparatus that served to legitimise the violence of and rule by Europeans; Eurocentrism and scientific racism were effectively born in the Americas. In Atlantic Africa, Europeans tapped into – and subsequently reordered around their interests – a slave trade which would serve to populate the 'virgin lands' of the Americas with a mass of labourers capable of working the incipient plantation economy. The combination of African slave labour with the vast expanse of American land created – in the plantation – a sociological amalgamation that proved a boon to a British ruling class struggling to escape the limits of agrarian capitalism at home, and the freedom of labour abroad. In particular, the brutal exploitation of slaves on the plantation provided an array of inputs that contributed to the Industrial Revolution. It was in this respect that the real subsumption of labour under capital in the British factory, and the establishment of 'free' wage labour in Europe, needed as their fundamental precondition 'the unqualified slavery of the New World as its pedestal'.[307]

We thus see how the productive forces – 'the way in which the different means of production are combined in the act of production itself' – cannot be properly examined from an ontologically singular perspective, pertaining to a single enterprise or society. Rather, such combinations transcend single enterprises and take place in an integrated way across multiple sectors, each using different means of production and labour processes. In turn the differentials in the rates and forms of exploitation generated by uneven but combined labour processes can serve to facilitate capitalist accumulation in new and unprecedented ways. The global combination of an assortment of different productive forces between the American plantation and the British factory was a remarkable illustration of this.

Our argument has two major implications for our understanding of the origins of capitalism. First, the Eurocentrism of accounts that focus too narrowly on the development of 'capitalism in one country' will tend to miss how the expanded reproduction of capitalism was only made possible through spheres of activity that presupposed the Atlantic. Second, insofar as internal processes are insufficient for explaining the transition to capitalism in Europe, the agents involved in this process cannot be found exclusively within the confines of any given domestic system. On the one hand, our understanding of labour, and of exploitation under capitalism, requires a more expansive definition than one restricted exclusively to wage-labour. To be clear, none of this is to argue that capitalism could exist or even survive without wage-labour (see Chapter 2). Rather, the point we are making is that capitalism can benefit (and has benefited) enormously from the exploitation of unfree labour in conditions where this is possible, desirable or necessary. As this chapter has shown, the formation of 'free' wage-labour and the real subsumption of labour under capital – that is, the 'maturation' of capitalism as a mode of production – in Britain was driven by and dependent on slave labour in the Americas. This provides, in our view, an important corrective to positions that have attempted to marginalise the nonwaged sphere in analyses of capitalism, since it is precisely in this sphere that those most made abject and marginalised by capitalism (and concomitantly the labour movement) reside – women and people of colour. We further elaborate these points in Chapter 7 and the Conclusion.

On the other hand, an 'internationalist' view of the origins of capitalism requires some scrutiny of those agents that were responsible for tying together the various nodes of the transatlantic triangular system: merchants. As we have seen, merchants involved in transatlantic trade came to *control* and *intervene* in the production process itself, through various attempts to overcome the limits created by declining rates of profits and competition from Indian textiles.[308] In doing so, merchants effectively transformed themselves into capitalists proper, subsuming labour to capital in one form or another. Hence, the self-expansion of merchant capital entailed much more than the simplistic formula of 'buying cheap and selling dear'.[309] Rather, under particular circumstances, merchants could act in ways that altered and eventually transformed the direct production process, thereby reconfiguring their relations of production in a capitalist direction.[310]

This is precisely what took place on the plantations, where merchants were singularly responsible for accumulating slave labour that was then put to work for exclusively commercial purposes. But this was not limited to the plantation alone; as we discuss in Chapter 7, the Dutch VOC also sought to intervene into and control production in the Indonesian spice trades as a means to establish a monopoly of supply and squeeze out its competitors.[311] A similar process can be found at work in the British East India Company's attempts to establish control over the textile producers of the northern Coromandel region in India.[312] In short, merchants could function as 'agents' in the transition to capitalism (see also Chapters 4 and 7).

This point regarding the potential for merchants to become capitalists or for merchant activities to promote capitalist development is of critical import given that one of the most influential schools of Marxist thought on the origins of capitalism – Political Marxism – denies any such possible role for merchants. In an often-cited passage on the different 'paths' to capitalist development in *Capital, Volume III*, Marx wrote:

> The transition from the feudal mode of production takes place in two different ways. The producer may become a merchant and capitalist, in contrast to the agricultural natural economy and the guild-bound handicraft of medieval urban industry. This is the really revolutionary way. Alternatively, however, the merchant may take direct control of production himself. But however frequently this occurs as a historical transition … it cannot bring about the overthrow of the old mode of production by itself, but rather preserves and retains it as its own precondition.[313]

Political Marxists have all too often taken Marx's last sentence on the supposed impossibility of merchants acting as agents of modal transformation and turned it into an article of faith, to which the historical record must either conform, be deemed irrelevant or simply ignored.[314] Yet having outlined these two 'paths' to capitalist development, Marx goes on to outline a third possible path[315] whereby the 'merchant becomes an industrialist directly': 'The transition can thus take three forms'.[316] Or, as Marx put it elsewhere, the activities of merchant capital who 'commissions a number of immediate producers, then collects their produce and sells it, perhaps making them advances in the form of raw materials, etc., or even money' represents the 'form that provides the soil from which modern capitalism has grown and here and there it still forms the transition to capitalism proper'.[317]

It seems clear then that Marx never ruled out the possibility of merchants or merchant activities forming the basis for the subsumption of labour to capital. And why should he have, given the long history of merchants intervening in the organisation of the immediate production process? Robert Brenner himself – the 'founder' of Political Marxism – held a very similar view, specifically regarding English colonial merchant operations in the Atlantic. In one of his earliest articles, published before his famous interventions in the transition debate, Brenner wrote:

> In marked contrast to the established London trades colonial operations required investment in commodity production, not merely in commodity exchange. The growth of American commerce depended in the first instance upon plantation development, and it was difficult to participate in the former without financial involvement in the latter. The nascent *plantation economy* needed constant injections of outside capital to get it started and keep it going. Thus, at least in the early years of development, *merchants interested in trading on a large scale normally could not avoid taking some part in the productive process.* Merchants might purchase and directly operate their own plantations. Otherwise they could enter into partnership with colonial planters, supplying them with land, tools and servants and marketing the final product .... As the number of participants grew, competition became increasingly fierce.[318]

Such observations regarding merchants becoming directly involved in the sphere of production and transforming social relations have been further borne out by more recent research.[319] When this is tied to the wider discussion in this chapter, it is evident that merchant activities could hasten the rise of capitalist relations and not simply act as a solvent on extant feudal relations. Thus, the distinction between production and circulation, capitalist agriculture and merchant capitalism that underpins the whole of Political Marxist thought is, Jairus Banaji writes, a 'false antithesis'.[320]

To be clear, we are not arguing, as do some World-Systems Theorists, that merchants trading on markets or even the intensification of trade and market transactions automatically translated into a capitalist logic of development. Rather, we suggest that the experience of the Atlantic colonies demonstrates how merchants could, in some instances, act on the production process itself and subsume labour to capital. This should alert us to the importance of historical specificity when considering the role of merchants. Against ahistorical conceptions of merchant agency in both World-Systems Theory[321] and Political Marxism,[322] we suggest that the character of merchant activity is only discernible when tied to the wider multiplicity of determinations of the historical conjuncture merchants operate in. It is this transformation within the *sphere of production*, not circulation, that is really decisive.

As we have seen, the tendency among merchants to take control of and reorganise the direct production process was itself intensified by developments in the American colonies. While many merchants pursued 'super-profits' in the American colonies (or Asian trade), others sought to mimic such profitable behaviours by seeking out new areas within Europe that were less resistant to their controlling power than the traditional guild-bound cities. Hence, the 'export of commodity production into the European countryside meant that the growth of the merchants' *hegemony over production*, which perhaps ended in Bengal, Java, and Martinique, began just outside Bristol, Haarlem, and Rouen'.[323]

There is, however, an even more direct way that the transformations in the activities and modalities of production in the merchant colonial plantations of the Atlantic radiated back home to the imperial metropole with hugely significant effects. Indeed, we can trace the specific ways by which the colonial plantations of the 'periphery' were in fact *generative* of precisely those social forces in the 'core' that would end up making a decisive contribution to consolidating England's capitalist transition. Here we reconnect to Brenner's work detailing the role of the merchant community in the making of the English Revolution of 1640–51, which presents 'the metropolitan face of the hybrid economic forms whose development the other side of the Atlantic is traced by Blackburn'.[324] Brenner delineates two distinct factions of mercantile capital in 17th-century England: one dominant faction centred around the City and increasingly tied to the East India Company and merchants importing from the Levant; and a second faction of 'new merchants' predominantly coming from outside the City and connected to the rising colonial trades in the Americas. While the former faction relied heavily on the Crown for politically protected trade routes and monopolies, the latter were much less dependent on the state since – given the merchants' socio-economic backgrounds – they were excluded from government-sanctioned charter companies.

Unlike company merchants that relied on extra-economic privileges, new colonial merchant activities took place independent of politically constituted, state-backed commerce.[325] It was this second faction of colonial mercantile capi-talists – who had begun the process of subsuming labour to capital – that would come to play a leading role in supporting Oliver Cromwell and the Independents during the Revolution. This was then another instance in which 'the merchant becomes an industrialist directly'.[326] The balance of class forces in England was thus directly connected to and constituted by socio-economic developments in the New World, paving the way for England's bourgeois revolution. It is this wider phenomenon of the bourgeois revolutions that we examine in the next chapter.

CHAPTER 6

The 'Classical' Bourgeois Revolutions in the History of Uneven and Combined Development

Sometimes Providence condemns the world with universal and evident calamities, whose causes we cannot know. This seems to be one of the epochs in which every nation is turned upside down, leading some great minds to suspect that we are approaching the end of the world.

Count-Duke of Olivares, 1643[1]

Introduction

In previous chapters, we charted the changing geopolitical conditions conducive to the emergence of capitalist social relations in Northwestern Europe. In doing so, we sought to demonstrate how ostensibly 'internal' processes of social transformation were rooted in broader intersocietal dynamics; that *intra*societal forms of sociality were continually overlain by distinctly *inter*societal determinations. In accounting for this persistently 'overdetermined' nature of social structures by their interactions with one another, we have drawn on the concept of uneven and combined development. This chapter extends our analysis to an examination of the causal role of 'the international' in the making of the 'classical' bourgeois revolutions in Holland, England and France.

In Martin Wight's classic *Power Politics* he estimated that there were '256 years of international revolution to 212 unrevolutionary' years.[2] This was written in 1960. Since that time, the world has experienced a near-perpetual state of revolution, illustrated by the vast array of popular revolts, guerrilla wars and resistance movements emerging time and again over this period. It would then seem that the default setting of modern international relations has been one of revolution: an epoch perhaps best understood as a series of continuing attempts to confront the challenges of social disorder and revolution wrought by the international expansion of capitalist relations. In short, this is an era of *permanent counter-revolution*, out of which the discipline of International Relations (IR) itself crystallised.[3]

In the modern era, revolutions have been central to the structure and dynamics of international affairs. They have always been *international events*: international in origin, ideology, process and effect, supercharging (both ideologically and politically) the rhythms and logics of any given geopolitical system. The interactively co-constitutive nature of revolutions and international relations is well captured by Arno Mayer when he writes of how 'at every point' in a revolution's development, 'international politics impinges on' its course, while the creation and consolidation of revolutionary states 'best dramatizes the centrality of interstate relations and war' to modern social development.[4]

Yet within the discipline of IR, the study of revolutions has remained something of a secondary subject. Not only have there have been relatively few studies theoretically engaging with revolutions and international relations,[5] but the dominant theoretical frameworks in IR – realism, liberalism and constructivism – have largely bracketed out revolutions from their conceptions of international politics. In the extreme case of structural realism, revolutions have been altogether excluded from the study of IR, as they remain outside Kenneth Waltz's discretely conceived international system, which abstracts from the historical sociological terrain (the so-called 'domestic') through which revolutions are formed.[6] Hence revolutions remain at the margins of the discipline, constituting 'the great anomaly' as Fred Halliday put it, as they are continually viewed as 'aberrations' or 'abnormalities' to the anarchic dictates of an international system conceived as a realm of perennial great power struggles over the balance of power.[7] Yet if revolutions are in part both international in cause and effect, transcending the confines of 'second' (domestic) and 'third image' (geopolitical) conceptions of international relations,[8] we require theoretical tools capable of capturing the sociological and geopolitical dimensions of these Janus-faced events without reducing one dimension into the other. We might think that the historical sociological literature on revolutions, which has commonly pointed to 'the international' as a structural cause of revolutions,[9] would show us the way. Yet here too, 'the international' remains 'powerfully acknowledged but analytically unpenetrated', leading to continual charges of 'attaching an essentialized, Realist conception of the international onto historical sociology'.[10]

What we need then is a theory of sociohistorical development that organically fuses both sociological ('internalist') and geopolitical ('externalist') modes of explanation into a single unified theoretical apparatus. And it is perhaps no surprise that the most attuned scholar of revolutions in disciplinary IR, Fred Halliday, came to identify uneven and combined development as one possible theory.[11] Nevertheless, in Halliday's work the concept remained something of an afterthought; Halliday never systematically integrated the concept into his own theoretical understandings of revolutions, thus never realising the potential of uneven and combined development as a unified theory of sociohistorical development as an interactive whole. This task was left to one of Halliday's students, Justin Rosenberg, who has sought to rework Trotsky's concept as a historical sociological theory of 'the international'.[12] For as argued in Chapter 2, what the concept of uneven and combined development uniquely provides is a theoretical internalisation of the distinctly *international* determinants of social development. This then renders 'the international' historically and sociologically intelligible, overcoming both realist reifications of the international system as an absolutely autonomous ('supra-social') sphere and the classical sociological tradition's tendency to falsely subsume its distinctive causal dynamics and behavioural patterns to unisocietal abstractions.

It is surprising that given uneven and combined development's origins as a theoretical tool to explain the Russian Revolution[13] and its recent revival in disciplinary IR, the theory has yet to be deployed in explaining revolutions.[14] This is the aim of this chapter, which seeks to further draw out the theory's implications in explaining three instances of bourgeois revolution: the Dutch, English and French. The chapter is developed in four movements. The first section reconsiders the concept of 'bourgeois revolutions' in terms of the effects of revolutions in creating and consolidating territorially demarcated sovereign centres of capital accumulation, rather than defining them in terms of their primary agents.[15] This 'consequentalist' interpretation of bourgeois revolutions subverts revisionist and Political Marxist critiques of the concept while providing a more apposite framework to understand their effects in their domestic and international dimensions. The next section turns to examine the origins of Dutch capitalism – a highly disputed subject – and the Dutch Revolt against the Habsburg Empire, highlighting the critical importance of the changing geopolitical conditions throughout the course of the Revolution.

The third section analyses the English Civil Wars of 1640–51 and Glorious Revolution of 1688–89, again paying close attention to the often overlooked international origins and effects of the revolutions theoretically captured by the notion of uneven and combined development. The final section then moves to an analysis of the French Revolution of 1789–1815, arguing, against revisionist and Political Marxist accounts, that the revolution was both *capitalist* and *bourgeois* in origin and effect, subsequently transforming the character and dynamics of the European international system over the Long 19th Century. The conclusion then teases out the implications of the preceding theoretically informed empirical analysis for understanding the relationship between revolutions and the modern international system.

The Concept of Bourgeois Revolution

Reconceptualising Bourgeois Revolutions:
A Consequentialist Approach

Before providing our analysis of the classical bourgeois revolutions, we must first define what we mean by 'bourgeois revolution'. For many historians and social scientists, the concept of 'bourgeois revolution' has been shown to be empirically and theoretically untenable. This has been a main finding of the revisionist historiographies of the French and English revolutions currently fashionable in the academy. These were primarily initiated as a critique of the orthodox Marxist model of bourgeois revolution emerging during the interwar years and after. For the revisionists, the revolutions were not heralded by the ascendancy of a distinctly *capitalist* bourgeois class; during the revolutions, the bourgeoisie were not in the lead of the movements and were often found on the opposing sides; after the revolutions, the bourgeoisie did not hold power and were often further removed from state control; and the revolutions did not result in the emergence or consolidation of capitalism.[16] More than anything else, the idea of the bourgeoisie as the primary agent in the making of the revolutions has taken the most sustained beating by revisionist studies.

While the bourgeoisie did in fact play some role in the classical revolutions, as we examine below, this agent-centred conceptualisation of bourgeois revolutions is itself unnecessary, if not unhelpful. Rather than looking at the intentions or composition of the agents involved in the making of revolutions, there is a veritable tradition of thinking (Marxist and non-Marxist) that conceptualises revolutions in terms of their socio-economic and political consequences.[17] The most significant factor for this 'consequentialist' school of thought in classifying a revolution as 'bourgeois' is whether or not it removed the sociopolitical and ideological 'obstacles' (notably, the pre-capitalist state) to the development and consolidation of capitalism thereby establishing the state as an autonomous site of capital accumulation. For '[i]f the definition of a bourgeois revolution is restricted to the successful installation of a legal and political framework in which the free development of capitalist property relations is assured', Gareth Stedman Jones writes, 'there is then no necessary reason why a "bourgeois revolution" need be the direct work of a bourgeoisie'.[18] Bourgeois revolutions are therefore best understood 'not as revolutions consciously made by capitalist agents', but in terms of their developmental outcomes: revolutions that in one form or another promote the further development of capitalism. This then shifts the definitional content of the concept from the class that makes the revolution to the *effects* a revolution has in promoting and/or consolidating a distinctly capitalist form of state, which will in turn benefit the capitalist class irrespective of any role it played in the revolution. Bourgeois or capitalist revolutions there-fore denote a sociopolitical transformation – 'a change in state power, which is the precondition for large scale capital accumulation and the establishment of the bourgeoisie as the dominant class'.[19]

Whether a revolution was the necessary condition to bring about capitalism or whether it worked to facilitate an already existing capitalism[20] varied with each case, France largely being an example of the former and the United Provinces and England more or less a case of the latter. The focus of the theory of bourgeois – or more precisely capitalist – revolution is then not about the origins of capitalism as a socio-economic system, but on the elimination of the sociopolitical 'barriers'[21] to 'its continued existence and the overthrow of restrictions to its further expansion'.[22] Moreover, rather than bourgeois revolutions being seen as a single episode or event, they more often than not entailed much broader processes of long-term sociopolitical transformation and restructuring, sometimes involving extended wars and foreign conquests. While these processes involved 'episode[s] of convulsive political transformation, compressed in time and concentrated in target',[23] it would be a mistake to identify bourgeois revolutions as solely comprised of such instances. While we must be cautious not to overstretch the concept of revolution to cover developmental tendencies more broadly, it does seem that the extended temporalities of the Dutch Revolt and subsequent War of Independence (1566–1648), the English Civil Wars of 1640–51 and Glorious Revolution of 1688–89, and French Revolution of 1787–1815 can, taken in their totalities, all be conceived as forms of bourgeois revolution. They were, in their varied ways, part and parcel of more general systemic crises taking both national and international dimensions.

Moreover, as will be shown, the evolving conditions of the international system, itself transformed by the ensuing revolutions, had a major causal impact on the timing, form and trajectory of the revolutions. Indeed, we might say that revolutions are almost universally international in origin, dynamic and impact. Structural adaptation to geopolitical-military pressures has been a central causal component of modern revolutions, and their resulting effects on the nature of the international system have been profound. Once capitalism emerged and was consolidated in some regions, the international context in which subsequent social developments took place was transformed.[24] Dramatically intensifying the 'coercive comparison'[25] of an interactive multiplicity of differentially developing societies and its attendant 'whip of external necessity', each successive capitalist revolution handed down the geosocial conditions from which the next would emerge. The bourgeois revolutions were, as Perry Anderson notes, 'historically interrelated, and the sequence of their connexions enters into the definition of their differences. *Their order was constitutive of their structure*'.[26]

Reconstructing Consequentialism through Uneven and Combined Development

Rather than discounting different instances of revolution which failed to correspond to some ideal-type notion of bourgeois revolution, this approach opens the possibility for a more historically sensitive perspective, recognising the inherently interconnected, co-constitutive and variegated nature of modern revolutions. Nonetheless, a potential problem with contemporary consequentialist approaches to bourgeois revolutions has been their tendency to emphasise 'developmental identity' over 'developmental difference'.[27] In other words, in the shift to conceptualising revolutions in terms of their socio-systemic effects, some scholars have fallen into a problematic homogenisation of nearly all revolutions in the modern epoch as essentially capitalist, as the societies came to incorporate elements of capitalism into their social structures.[28] From this perspective, the very different developmental outcomes of revolutions in, say, North Vietnam (1945), China (1949), and Cuba (1959) are all conceived as establishing different forms of 'bureaucratic state capitalism'[29] through 'deflected permanent revolutions'[30] – the 'modern version or functional equivalent' of bourgeois revolutions.[31] While such regimes undoubtedly assimilated features of capitalism over time, to conceive of these revolutions as 'bourgeois' is to stretch the concept beyond breaking point.

In providing a more satisfactory, historically attuned consequentialist approach, it is therefore necessary to root this approach in a more robust conception of uneven and combined development which sensitises analyses to the interactively generated qualitative differences between revolutions in the modern epoch.[32] For 'unevenness' incorporates developmental variations both within and between societies, and the attendant spatial differentiations between them; while 'combination' denotes the manifold ways in which the internal relations of societies are determined by their interactive relations with one another, producing sociological amalgamations that meld the 'native' and 'foreign', 'backward' and 'advanced', within their social structures (see Chapter 2). From this perspective, we would expect the consequences of a revolution to combine systemic characteristics of different modes of production, countering their subsumption under any single modal classification, whether this is 'bureaucratic state capitalism', 'state socialism', 'bureaucratic collectivism' or whatever.[33]

Tying a 'consequentalist' approach to the theory of uneven and combined development solves not only the difficulties of revisionist interpretations of bourgeois revolutions, but also the problematic relationship between IR and revolutions more generally. It does so, in particular, by specifying the distinctive causal dynamics and behavioural patterns of the international system affecting capitalist revolutions, while also capturing their different participating agents, methods and outcomes. This helps explain the qualitative differences between revolutions as they co-constitutively interconnect in time and space. Since their sequentiality was constitutive of their structures, historical repetition – and thus the utility of 'ideal-types' – is eliminated. This then provides a theoretical explanation of why each capitalist revolution was a 'bastard birth' – an exception that proved the rule.[34] It further explains the dissonance between agents' intentions and their effects; in other words, how the consequences of a given revolution can turn out to be capitalist – or some combination thereof establishing the conditions under which capitalism becomes the *dominant* mode of production – irrespective of the agents' original intentions, as the systemic pressures and imperatives of 'the international' weigh on the outcomes.[35] From such a perspective we would expect each revolution to diverge (in character, form and agents involved) from previous revolutions: the sole criterion to judge whether they can be considered capitalist is whether they (re)constructed the state as a sovereign territorial site of capital accumulation.

The Origins of Capitalism and the Bourgeois Revolution in the Low Countries

The Rise of Dutch Capitalism: An International Perspective

Although it is generally recognised that capitalism had become the dominant mode of production in England by the time of the 'Glorious Revolution' of 1688 (or at least shortly thereafter), the development of capitalism in the Low Countries – what would later become the United Provinces – is a more contentious case. Some Marxists have been sceptical of the capitalist credentials of the United Provinces in the early modern period. Eric Hobsbawm described the Dutch Republic of the 17th century as a '"feudal business" economy; a Florence, Antwerp or Augsburg on a semi-national scale'.[36] Similarly, for Ellen Meiksins Wood, the Dutch Republic of the Golden Age was the 'last and most highly developed non-capitalist commercial society'.[37] While recognising the 'unprecedented degree of commercialization' of the Dutch economy, and the 'penetration of trade relations into both urban and rural economies', Wood claims the Dutch Republic 'still operated on familiar non-capitalist principles, above all in its dependence on extra-economic powers of appropriation'. And although the 'Dutch pioneered many improvements in labour productivity, not least in agriculture, it is not at all clear that they were driven by the kinds of competitive pressures associated with capitalism'.[38] Yet these claims rest on rather spurious grounds.

In the first place, to compare the Dutch Republic to the Italian city-states of the 13th century, as does Hobsbawm, is to seriously underestimate the unprecedented scope and scale of the Dutch commercial empire. For '[e]xcept for Britain after around 1780', Jonathan Israel notes, 'no one power in history achieved so great a preponderance of over the processes of world trade as did the Dutch'. This was a 'fully fledged world entrepot' that not only interconnected the markets of all the continents, but dominated them, concentrating economic power to a degree found 'never before – or perhaps since'.[39] Not only had the Dutch merchant classes tapped into the lucrative trading markets of the Atlantic, Mediterranean and Baltics by the mid-17th century, they had also through the Dutch East India Company (*Vereenigde Oostindische Compagnie*, VOC) largely succeeded in displacing Portuguese merchants in the Indian Ocean (see further Chapter 7). Dutch primacy in world trade depended, above all, on both this 'East–West' axis of international trade – the 'rich trades' of commodities and luxuries imported from the Spanish Americas, Levant and East Asia[40] – and a 'North–South' commercial axis stretching from the Baltic to the Mediterranean – consisting primarily of European bulk carrying.[41] Here again we encounter the importance of American silver, as it was the principal means by which Dutch merchants effected purchases and bought supplies in Asia.

This was a commercial empire of a magnitude hitherto unknown in human history. One factor that made this achievement possible was the dynamism of the capitalist social relations that had emerged over the course of the late Medieval and early modern eras in the Northern Netherlands. 'The main asset of the upstart republic', Ronald Findlay and Kevin O'Rourke write, 'was its economic system, certainly the most productive and efficient in Europe at the time'.[42] For Robert Brenner, the initial catalyst for this capitalist breakthrough was an ecologically driven process of 'primitive accumulation' in which the peasants were pushed off inutile arable lands (those rendered uncultivable), divorcing them from their means of subsistence and making them market-dependent.[43] But rather than effecting depopulation of the countryside as had occurred elsewhere in Europe, Dutch peasants took a different course: commercialised farming. One of the preconditions for this shift towards commercial farming was the possibility of importing basic foodstuffs. The emergence of commercialised agriculture in the Northern Netherlands was directly connected to the growth of trade with other grain-producing regions of Europe – notably, from the mid-15th century onwards, the Baltics. The various towns of medieval Holland thereby acted as key 'nodal points' linking the developing capitalist agrarian economy 'to those inter-regional networks of trade'.[44]

In this respect, international relations – through foreign trade – played a decisive role in the rise of Dutch capitalism, although the geopolitics of the age would also play their part. In particular, the favourable 'systemic circumstances', as Giovanni Arrighi calls them, established by the particular configuration of the European market at the time were critical to the success of the capitalist relations that took hold throughout the Low Countries by the early modern period. Such systemic conditions were, in the first instance, the interactive 'effect of the actions of a multiplicity of agencies'.[45] For the Dutch, Arrighi writes, 'these systemic circumstances consisted of a fundamental temporal and spatial disequilibrium between the demand for, and the supply of, grain and naval stores in the European world-economy at large'. For throughout most of the 16th century and up until the mid-17th century, demand was 'large and growing rapidly', particularly in Western Europe, due to the inflow of American silver and the intensification of geopolitical conflicts among the states of the Atlantic seaboard.[46]

Supplies of grain were, however, soon limited by the precipitous rise in demand and concomitant exhaustion of Mediterranean provisions. Consequently, supplies came to be concentrated in the Baltic region. These conditions provided the Dutch merchant community with the opportunity, assisted in part by the earlier decline of the Hanseatic League, to dominate the European market. 'By stepping in and establishing tight control over the transfer of Baltic supplies through the Sound', the Netherlands came to occupy what over the course of the 16th century 'turned into the most strategic market niche of the European world-economy'. In turn, they 'became the beneficiaries of a large and steady stream of money surpluses which they further augmented by imposing an inverted fiscal squeeze on Imperial Spain'[47] through their war of independence (examined below).

What is particularly important to note here is how the Netherlands' growing trade relations, both before and after their emergence as a dominant world economic player, interacted with burgeoning capitalist production relations in the countryside. Since as early as the 11th century, the Low Countries had functioned as a central nodal point of European trade.[48] Vital to the precocious development of capitalist social relations there was a particular form of 'urban-agrarian symbiosis'.[49] Indeed, the role of intra-European and colonial trade in the making of Dutch capitalism has been stressed by most scholars in their explanations of the high levels of economic growth and technological advances that set the Dutch economy apart from the rest of Europe during the early modern period.[50] The 'importance of European and colonial trade' in the development of the Dutch economy of the period, Jan Lucassen writes, 'could hardly be overstated'.[51] From the earliest stages, then, the development and reproduction of Dutch capitalism was inextricably bound to international conditions and developments (see further Chapter 7).

Urban industries emerging in Holland and connected to the European-based feudal world market were, moreover, intimately tied to rural development for supplies of raw materials and labour. Much of this agrarian production was oriented around town markets, which acted not only as centres of distribution and consumption but also increasingly as independent centres of production.[52] As early as 1500, Peter Hoppenbrouwers notes, 'the majority of the rural population combined small-scale agriculture with various forms of commercially oriented by-employment linked to urban demand'.[53] Given the high density of urban centres throughout Holland, it was very difficult for any individual town to exert political control over the countryside, as it would provoke reactions from other towns.[54] This had the effect of enabling pockets of agrarian production, uninhibited by the political domination of any single urban centre, to further develop, expand and consolidate in increasingly capitalist directions.

Powerless to control the countryside politically, the bourgeoisie sought to extend their reach by economic means. This led to forms of 'proto-industrial' development, in which urban merchant entrepreneurs invested directly in rural industries as peasant production became increasingly geared toward the world market.[55] Consequently, urban merchants obtained control over the means of peasant production at a relatively early stage, aided by the accessibility of the capital market and low cost of credit.[56] This then 'set the stage for full proletarianisation once these merchant-entrepreneurs started to move large swathes of the production process to the cities. It is this particular urban-agrarian symbiosis that set the stage for the transition to capitalism in Holland'.[57]

By the middle of the 16th century, almost half of all rural labour in central Holland was waged. In the Guelders river area, as much as 60 per cent of work was performed by wage-labourers – a proportion reached in most industrialised areas of Europe only in the 19th century. As a whole, probably more than a third of all labour in the Low Countries during this time was undertaken for wages. This was a high proportion compared with estimates from other parts of Northwestern Europe, England included.[58] In short, by the mid-16th century, more or less market-dependent forms of wage-labour had become a *structural feature*, albeit a geographically uneven one, of the Dutch economy.

Moreover, as Bas van Bavel notes, as early as the 13th century the Low Countries, particularly in their northwestern regions, saw the early commodification of land, with '[o]pen, flexible, competitive, and secure land and lease markets'. These existed alongside other key preconditions for capitalist social relations such as 'buoyant trade, flourishing markets, a money economy, and booming cities'. These were again all more or less established in the 13th century; that is, some three centuries *before* England would experience its capitalist breakthrough.[59] To be clear, these were 'key indicators' for a *later* transition to capitalism, as social relations in the Low Countries at that time were not capitalist, nor were these features characteristic of the development of the Low Countries as a whole.[60] Nonetheless, such developments did provide the crucial 'preparatory conditions' for capitalism's subsequent emergence there (see also Chapter 7). As all of this evidence indicates, claims that the Low Countries was merely a 'highly commercialized feudal' society seem very difficult to sustain.

The dynamism of the Dutch economy of the early modern period was perhaps its most distinguishing feature. In the early 16th century, agricultural labour productivity in the Low Countries was by far the highest in Europe, with some 175 mouths fed by 100 people working in agriculture, compared with from 100 (Poland) to 135 (England, France, Italy) in other parts of Europe.[61] Between 1510 and 1795 the total population of the Netherlands doubled, while between 1510 and 1810 agricultural productivity tripled,[62] with the great bulk of this increase occurring before the mid-17th century.[63] It seems wise to concur with Robert Brenner's conclusion that:

> the Dutch economy as it emerged in the early modern period thus appears to have been quite fully capitalist. It was unburdened by systems of ruling class extraction by extra-economic compulsion … its producers, notably agricultural producers, were entirely dependent on the market and subject to competition in production to survive …. [h]igh levels of investment obtained, which issued in rising capital:labour ratios, rapid productivity growth and, ultimately, high wages and income per person more generally.[64]

Therefore, even in Brenner's restrictive view of capitalism as market dependence, the Low Countries are conceived as having been set on a capitalist path of development by the early to mid-16th century, even if capitalist development there remained 'limited' and constricted until 1580, only after which accumulation fully took hold (see Chapter 7).[65] Much like the English case (see below), capitalist development was pronounced – if still 'incomplete' and restricted – in the Low Countries *preceding* the revolutionary settlement which would establish the sociopolitical conditions for its fuller development and consolidation.

What are crucially missing in Brenner's account, however, are the distinctly international conditions that facilitated the development and systemic consolidation of capitalism in the Low Countries. For it was only through the geopolitical and military struggles raging across Europe that provided the systemically enabling *geopolitical space* from which the Dutch Revolt emerged, and emerged successfully. Moreover, the economic consequences of these rivalries acted to displace the hitherto dominant Genoese high finance that the Dutch came to supplant. As Arrighi writes, '[t]he withering away of Genoese dominance in European high finance, the progressive erosion of the power of Imperial Spain', to which the Genoese financiers were inseparably linked, 'and the break-up of the Genoese–Iberian alliance cannot be understood except in the context of the escalating competitive power struggles that made the fortunes of Dutch capitalism'.[66] This international environment was also crucial to the 'combined' character of Dutch capitalist development, as the Dutch came to fuse earlier forms and methods of protocapitalist organisations and institutions pioneered by the Genoese (the stock market) and Venetians (such as monopolies and the institutional antecedents that came to form the basis of the Dutch's greatest innovative synthesis, the VOC). They also combined Venetians and

Genoese merchant capitalists' different strategies of capital accumulation: the former characterised by regional consolidation based on self-sufficiency in state and war-making: the latter by worldwide expansion based on a relationship of political exchange with foreign governments.[67] All were integral elements to the emergence of the Dutch state as the dominant world economic power over the late 16th and 17th centuries.

The Making of the Dutch Revolt

The 16th century of absolutist state building was a period riven by interdynastic conflict and war. During the century, there were only 25 years without large-scale military operations in Europe. As noted in previous chapters, armed conflict was intrinsic to the feudal mode of production. For in the absence of the kind of economic dynamism afforded by capitalist social relations, 'war was possibly the most rational and rapid single mode of expansion of surplus extraction available for any given ruling class under feudalism'.[68] This was because feudal productive relations gave little incentive for either the peasant or lord to *systematically* introduce labour-saving technologies.[69] Rather, lordly interests lay in extracting more surpluses by coercive means. This could be done by pushing the peasants to the limit of their subsistence or by seizing the demesnes of other lords. The latter course resulted in a process of geopolitical accumulation amongst the lords themselves – a war-driven process of state formation.[70] The lords left standing at the end of this process formed the basis of the absolutist state. Representing a *'redeployed and recharged apparatus of feudal domination'*,[71] the absolutist state system of early modern European remained driven by the systemic imperatives of geopolitical accumulation. This came to interact – and in some cases fuse – with the emerging logic of competitive capital accumulation accompanying those states already making the transition to capitalism, and this in part explains the endemic state of war marking the epoch.[72]

What made this era of permanent war so intense was the generalised crisis of feudal production relations besetting Europe. The persistence of armed conflict throughout the period was not just a result of the normal structural dynamics of the feudal mode – the tendency to geopolitical accumulation – but rather because the process of ruling class reproduction was itself in crisis and under threat. By this time, the feudal system had virtually exhausted all possibilities for further *internal* expansion (within Europe). This in turn precipitated a sharp fall in seigniorial revenues, which was itself further exacerbated by the plague-induced demographic crisis, leading to a dramatic rise in peasant revolts and class struggles more generally (see Chapter 3).[73] This perilous situation was further exacerbated and 'overdetermined' by the persistent geopolitical threat from the Ottoman Empire (see Chapter 4). Under such conditions, a near-continuous state of war – including both intra-ruling class struggles and the incessant efforts to crush peasant rebellions – was a sociological 'necessity'.

The uneven and combined development of feudal-absolutist Europe was thus rooted in this territorially expansionist dynamic of geopolitical accumulation which, more often than not, found its ideological articulation through religious conflicts. Not surprisingly, then, the Dutch Revolt was forged in the crucible of interstate competition and war infused with deeply religious overtones, for overlaying this epoch of war was the religious conflict between Reformation and Counter-Reformation states, 'which never initiated but frequently intensified and exacerbated geopolitical rivalries and provided their contemporary ideological idiom'.[74]

That religion would play such an omnipresent role in the geopolitics of the era is explicable by the structural specificities of pre-capitalist modes of production which, unlike capitalism, operated through *extra-economic* sanctions buttressed by the ideopolitical power of religion. In feudal-absolutist Europe, religion constituted a fundamental foundation of political authority and its legitimation. 'Political legitimacy', Michael Braddick notes, 'was claimed to rest in part on the defense of the true religion'.[75]

As the Catholic Church provided the key ideological underpinning of the feudal system, any attack on the system was necessarily directed against the Church. Since the official Roman Catholic Church was 'part and parcel of existing society', Ivo Schöffer writes, and was 'one of the intermediaries between authority and common man its clergy were blamed for anything which went wrong. Poverty, unemployment, inflation, taxes, corruption, all seemed to have to do … with clergy and church'.[76] The Reformation thus constituted the key ideological context for the emerging Dutch opposition movements of the 1560s. Dutch politics and society were particularly receptive to the international diffusion of Reformation ideologies, given '[t]he relative openness of Dutch society, its urbanisation and its strategic position at a nodal point in the European exchange of both material goods and ideas'.[77] The Dutch Revolt of 1566 was then part and parcel of a broader international religious-political movement sweeping across Europe.[78] It was, moreover, decisively international in origin and impact. Indeed, many historians have viewed the Dutch Revolt as an early example of a national independence struggle against Spanish oppression.[79] Cardinal Granvelle wrote, for example, that:

> people here universally display discontent with any and all Spaniards in these provinces. It would seem that this derives from the suspicion that one might wish to subject them to Spain and reduce them to the same state as the Italian provinces under the Spanish crown.[80]

While irreducible to purely socio-economic considerations, the (geo)politics of the Reformation and Counter-Reformation did find an 'elective affinity' with the emerging struggle between capitalist and feudal social forces. For the Reformation flourished in regions where feudalism was weakest, whereas the ruling classes in the more advanced areas already dominated the Catholic world, and therefore had no need to escape from its control.[81] The flowering of religious diversity in early modern Europe and its attendant (geo)political consequences were thus embedded in a further axis of socio-economic and political unevenness, pitting nascent bourgeois orders against the bastions of feudal reaction.

The divergent paths of socio-economic development between feudal Spain and an incipiently capitalist Netherlands were therefore a structural precondition for the outbreak of the Dutch Revolt. It was no coincidence that the Reformation found its great support in the highly urbanised and less feudal western Netherlands, where it played a disproportionately important role in the outbreak and subsequent course of the Revolt.[82] Here, among other urbanised areas, a long-term process of 'cultural emancipation' of the rising urban middle class took place, in which they began to challenge traditional religious practices. This urban middle class came to play a crucial role in the Revolt.[83] Although the Habsburgs' absorption and unification of the Netherlands was a relatively 'smooth' transition up to the 1540s, in part due to the 'absence of the pressures associated with waging war', the reignition of the Habsburg–Valois–Ottoman wars for hegemony on the European continent in 1551 was critical in intensifying Dutch discontent over Habsburg rule.[84]

The immediate context for the Dutch Revolt against the Habsburg Empire[85] beginning in 1566 was occasioned by the fiscal-military pressures arising from the Habsburgs' protracted struggle against the Franco-Ottoman alliance.[86] Until that time, the Habsburg–Valois rivalry for hegemony in Europe had focused primarily on the Italian peninsula. By the late 1530s, however, France had been effectively shut out of Italy. Seeking to widen the conflict, the king of France, François I, shifted the military theatre to the Netherlands frontier, forcing Charles V of Spain to follow suit. Consequently, the provinces of the Netherlands were subjected to sharply escalating demands for funds, men and supplies from the regime in Brussels, leading to 'an unhealthy financial, logistical, and strategic dependence of the Habsburg Crown on its Netherlands provinces'.[87] The prolongation of the conflict with France and the Ottomans became a major drain on Dutch finances and a source of great resentment against the Habsburgs. As Israel notes:

> the [Habsburg] Emperor was routinely using the Netherlands as his chief strategic bulwark and resource, in pursuit of goals which were vital to him but had little to do with the Netherlands .... With the funded debt overstretched, an unsecured deficit accumulated which, by 1557, had reached seven times the level of 1544.[88]

The high levels of taxation and centralising policies imposed on the Netherlands by the Habsburgs were a major source of grievance among the local elites. Another significant issue in the Revolt involved the contrasting conceptions of state sovereignty represented by the Catholic absolutist state-building project of Philip II, on the one hand, and the more 'communal, federal and constitutional state' held by the Dutch oppositionists, on the other.[89] In these ways, the spatiotemporal unevenness of European development, refracted through its conjunctural geosocial consequences, constituted a key factor in the origins of the Dutch Revolt. For the war-induced escalation in fiscal pressures on the Netherlands had the effect of aggravating deep-seated resentments over the way the Spanish Crown had sought to integrate newly obtained provinces into the rest of the Habsburg Netherlands, and the powers the central government had arrogated to itself.

The eventual result of all this was the emergence of open rebellion among the Dutch population, beginning in April 1566 when 200 members of the lesser nobility marched through Brussels to implore the governess, Margaret of Parma, to moderate the strict anti-heresy laws. Forming the opening act of the revolt, a wave of iconoclasm, known in Dutch as the *Beeldenstorm*, spread throughout the Southern Netherlands. There were spontaneous actions among the poor and 'middling sort' who made up a core constituent of the revolutionaries.[90]

Initially the Dutch nobility subdued the revolt, ensuring its suppression six months before the arrival of the Duke of Alva, who headed a Spanish-backed army of 10,000 to punish the Low Countries. Yet Alva's reign of terror did not spare the Dutch higher nobility. In the midst of Alva's intensified repression and religious persecution of all sections of Dutch society, some of the Dutch nobility came to join in open rebellion against Spanish rule. This phase was exemplified by William of Orange's unsuccessful military campaign to defeat Alva in 1568.[91] A second phase of the revolt was then sparked in April 1572 when 'Sea Beggars', driven from their English base by Queen Elizabeth I, captured the small sea-port town of Brill, setting off a series of uprisings which spread to urban centres in Holland and Zeeland. Over the course of the revolt, many more towns experienced urban uprisings in a complex, uneven pattern of religious radicalisation, military struggle and social clashes within the revolutionary camp. This opened a more militarily intensive phase of the revolt, which took the form of a land war in the Dutch provinces, and later in the 1590s a sea war which took place outside of Europe and was fought largely in the colonies.[92]

The survival of the northern Dutch provinces during this period was in part dependent on the favourable geopolitical conditions produced by Philip II's decision to redirect military resources to campaigns against the English and French, along with the Spanish monarchy's continual preoccupation with the Ottoman challenge in the Mediterranean.[93] At a number of crucial points in the Spanish campaign against the Dutch, Philip II prioritised the Mediterranean struggle against the Ottomans, to the detriment of Spanish operations in the Netherlands. In 1572, in the midst of the steady progress of the Dutch rebels in the north, Alva pleaded with Philip to alter these strategic priorities:

> Everything spent on the League [against the Ottomans] is wasted .... I beat my head against the wall when I hear talk about what we are spending here, since it is not the Turks who are disturbing Christendom but the heretics, and they are already within the gates.[94]

Despite Alva's imploring, Philip refused to change course, and instead continued to pour resources into the Mediterranean theatre.

In the end, the Spanish efforts to divert personnel and resources to other military theatres were critical to the success of the Dutch Revolt.[95] As Immanuel Wallerstein puts it, 'because after 1559, Spain, France, and England balanced each other off, the Netherlanders had the social space to assert their identity and throw off the Spanish yoke'.[96] In this sense, the military balance of power in Europe contributed to tipping the balance of class forces struggling in the Netherlands in favour of the Dutch revolutionaries. This was further borne out by the French Wars of Religion which also had a crucial impact on the course of the Dutch Revolt, especially in 1568 and 1572–73, when the Dutch were able to draw on significant military support from the French Huguenots.[97] With the conclusion of peace in the summer of 1573 in France, the Comte de Montgomery sent a contingent of Huguenots and English troops to the Netherlands to aid the 'sorely pressed' William of Orange. In August, a multinational force of 'English, Scottish, French, and Flemish' companies stormed St Geertruidenberg, defeating the Spanish and making it the first city captured by the rebels. This multinational force then went on to successfully defend Leiden against the Spanish siege of 1573–74 – 'a decisive moment in the history of the Dutch Revolt'.[98]

In short, the geopolitical context of the revolt was of primary importance to both its origins and outcome, as the specific configuration of geopolitical relations of the conjuncture was central to its victory. In turn, the Revolt causally fed back into these geopolitical dynamics, recombining with and reconstituting them in the process. For significantly, the revolt acted as a continual drain on Spanish resources, routing the Habsburg drive to hegemony on the European continent, thereby precipitating Spain's decline as a great power. 'As the imperial center weakened, wars and rebellions proliferated until the Peace of Westphalia institutionalized the emerging European balance of power'.[99]

Lasting nearly 80 years, the conflict only ended with the signing of the Treaty of Westphalia in 1648, which recognised the sovereignty of the seven northern provinces that came to form the Dutch Republic. By that time, the Dutch Republic was firmly dominated by the bourgeoisie, in the form of a merchant oligarchy, establishing the sociopolitical conditions favourable to the optimisation of capitalist development. Although the indigenous bourgeoisie played very little role in leading the Revolt, the *effects* of the Revolution make it an early example of a 'bourgeois revolution' laying the sociopolitical conditions for the dominance of the capitalist mode of production.[100]

The English Revolution in the History of Uneven and Combined Development

The origins of the English Revolution, whether it is taken as comprising the English Civil Wars of 1640–51 or the entire period from 1640 to 1688, have produced an enormously rich and varied body of literature. Yet with few exceptions[101] 'virtually the whole of this literature' has been, as Halliday notes, 'written as if England was not just an island, but was a closed entity, separate from the political, economic and intellectual world of the rest of Europe'.[102] However, the international structure and context of which England formed a part played a critical role in the causal and imaginative coordinates of its revolutionary experience.

That the events of the English Revolution took place in an era of 'general crisis' riven by upheavals, rebellions and wars raging across Europe and beyond has scarcely been taken into account when explaining its main causal sources. Yet this international context of English events was hardly lost on contemporaries.[103] In 1649, Robert Mentet de Salmonet, a Scottish exile living in France, prefaced his account of the English Revolution by noting that Europe was proceeding through an 'Iron Age' marked by a 'Desolation of Countries commonly attending War', an era 'famous for the great and strange revolutions that have happen'd in it' with 'revolts … frequent both in East and West'.[104] Similarly, in January 1643 shortly after the English Civil War had broken out, a protestant preacher, Jeremiah Whitaker, warned the House of Commons, 'These days are a days of shaking … and this shaking is universal: the Palatinate, Bohemia, Germany, Catalonia, Portugal, Ireland, England'.[105]

The crisis that beset the English state was thus European – if not global – in nature and scope. The socio-economic, ideological and political roots of both the long-term (structural) and immediate (conjunctural) causes of the English-cum-British Revolution, through all its phases (1640–42, 1688 and 1745), were decisively international. How are we to understand the interaction of international and domestic conditions leading to the English Revolution?

Rediscovering the English Revolution

The notion that the domestic situation of the Stuart monarchy was reasonably stable – a key tenet of revisionist historiography[106] – seems gravely misplaced, particularly when we take into account the broader European maelstrom of the era, from which the English were hardly immune. Furthermore, over the 16th and 17th centuries, English society underwent rapid socio-economic and demographic change, leading to a prolonged period of economic instability and heightened social tensions. Surveying the state of the English agrarian economy of the 16th and 17th centuries, Peter Bowden concludes that the 1620s to 1640s were times of 'extreme hardship in England ... probably the most terrible years through which the country has ever passed'.[107] This was a period marked by intense social unrest and class conflict (a persistent 'crisis of order', as David Underwood has described the years between 1560 and 1640[108]), escalating to the point where 'contemporaries were conscious of a threat of popular revolt at least from the depression of the 'twenties onwards'.[109]

The immediate events leading to the English Civil War (1640–51) are well known. In 1640, under the military pressure of an advancing Scottish force, King Charles I convened Parliament for the first time since its disbandment 11 years earlier. For much of his reign, Charles had been attempting to strengthen obedience to the Crown by building up a monarchical absolutism styled on the Catholic monarchies of the continent, with comparable Counter-Reformation policies. This was seen as an imperative given the military ineffectuality and weaknesses of the Stuart monarchy displayed in the wars of the 1620s (the Anglo-Spanish war of 1625–30 and the Anglo-French war of 1627–29), which imperilled the domestic legitimacy of the Stuart state. Through these wars, the fierce political and religious conflicts engulfing the European continent were incorporated into the domestic political structures of England. 'The polarization of English politics by 1629–30', J. L. Reeves notes, 'can be seen as one aspect of the polarization of international politics under the pressure of war'.[110]

It had become increasingly clear that on a geopolitical scale, the Stuart state was no match for its Catholic absolutist rivals on the continent. It was in this sense that England's 'failure in war in Europe established the context for rebellion and civil war at home'.[111] The historical unevenness of state-building in Europe, effecting a particular 'whip of external necessity', and its military consequences were therefore crucial to the outbreak of the English Civil Wars. Far from having 'no influence on the English social revolution and relatively little influence on the English political revolution',[112] international military pressures were decisive in the making of the English Revolution. The Thirty Years' War was itself rooted in the unevenness of social development on the European continent: an 'example of two civilizations in ideological conflict'[113] in which the 'political fronts and coalitions of power' in the war reflected deep developmental differences among the states involved.[114]

Generally speaking, the war pitted the least developed (in feudal terms) areas of Europe, which had nonetheless begun to make the first strides towards capitalism – particularly the Netherlands, England and Bohemia – against the regions where feudalism was most entrenched – notably the Spanish and Holy Roman empires.[115] In this sense, the 'general crisis' of 17th-century Europe was rooted in the protracted transition from a feudal to capitalist economy. The 'system-wide attempts at geopolitical accumulation in the form of the Wars of Religion and the Thirty Years' War' were rooted in the intensified but differentiated class conflicts over the distribution of income.[117]

With the exception of the struggle between the Netherlands and the Spanish Habsburgs, this was not a simple case of an aspiring bourgeoisie rising up against the feudal aristocracy, as internal divisions within the bourgeoisie could be found throughout the German lands.[118] Yet it was also no coincidence that the war was triggered by a revolt in the economically dynamic Bohemia region against the German Hapsburgs. Sixteenth-century Bohemia was the site of rapid economic development, containing the richest silver mine in Europe. Socio-economic changes were already taking place in the Bohemian countryside that were beginning to undermine its feudal character and 'liberate production from its fetters'.[119]

Meanwhile, the failed attempts at absolutist state-building during the Tudor period (particularly between 1529 and 1547), and Elizabeth's abandonment of all ambitions to develop a continental-style monarchy, had left the English monarchy painfully dependent on Parliament for raising the revenues required for waging war.[120] In terms of military and fiscal effectiveness, the Stuart state was backward in comparison with its continental competitors. The centralising attempts by the Stuart monarchs, first James I and then Charles I, brought them into direct conflict with England's powerful landed classes who largely dominated Parliament, as the latter had to assent to new taxes or give up some of their control over fiscal policy. This was a landlord class that had, over the preceding century, become increasingly capitalist-oriented, as 'the English greater landed classes gradually gave up the magnate form of politico-military organization, commercialized their relationships with their tenants, rationalized their estates, and made use of – but avoided dependence upon – the court'.[121]

The conflicts between Crown and Parliament over war funding were a major reason for Charles I's initial dismissal of Parliament in 1629. One conclusion from the 1625–29 period was that war was impossible without state reform and that a financially exhausted government required peace in order to reform. The reprise from war was, however, fatefully interrupted by the Scottish rebellion of 1637–40, sparked by Charles I's attempt to impose Anglican services on the Presbyterian Church of Scotland. With the Scottish invasion of 1640, the military conflict in Europe moved back to England. To quote Jonathan Scott:

> A catholicising king, associated with Spain and catholic Ireland, found himself divided from his English and Scots protestant subjects. This was one military outcome of the ideological impact made upon the Stuart kingdoms by the Thirty

Years' War. In the period 1637–40, then, the military struggle between reformation and counter-reformation moved to British soil. That it was not followed
by continental European military intervention was a consequence only of the
exhaustion of the great powers after more than two decades of war.[122]

As with the Ottoman–Hapsburg great power rivalry over the Long 16th
Century (see Chapter 4), the further development and consolidation of capitalism in England was again contingent upon the dynamics and direction of
military conflicts on the European continent, which provided the English with
a certain (albeit temporary) privilege of geopolitical isolation. They offered the
geopolitical space in which modern state-building practices and socio-economic
development could proceed apace. In these ways, the European upheaval of the
Thirty Years' War formed the immediate geopolitical context for the English
Civil War and the eventual collapse of Charles I's monarchy. It was against this
international background that the widespread English fears of 'popery' must be
understood, as Catholic Spain spearheaded the Counter-Reformation across
Europe. Indeed, the majority of parliamentary oppositionists, particularly the
new merchants involved in the American colonial trades, were 'militantly anti-
Spanish' in their foreign policy orientations.[123] The ideological (if not military)
threats of the European Catholic powers were consequently seen as clear and
present dangers.

The reconvening of Parliament unleashed a storm of political controversies, as the Parliamentarians sought to reassert their political power against an
increasingly 'popish' and autocratic Crown, while Charles I sought to defend his
perceived monarchical right to rule without undue parliamentary interference.
The Irish rebellion of October 1641 added further fuel to the fire, as it raised
the question of whether Parliament or the Crown would control the English
armed forces to suppress the rebellion.[124] The eventual outcome of these insol-
uble conflicts between Crown and Parliament, representing two fundamentally
different conceptions of state sovereignty, was the outbreak of civil war in the
summer of 1642.

Social Forces in the Making of the British Revolution

In examining the character of class conflicts in the making of the first 'stage'
in the English Revolution, the 'Great Revolution' of 1640, traditional Marxist
explanations of the Civil War have focused on the role of the rising gentry,
conceived as an emerging bourgeois class.[125] The two sides in the Civil War,
parliamentary forces and royalists, are thus conceived as the agents of two
opposing classes representing antagonistic modes of production: a rising
capitalism and declining feudalism.

This interpretation has not fared well with the more contemporary historiography and has been largely abandoned.[126] A problem with it has been the difficulty in identifying the continuing existence of a distinctly feudal class to which the rising capitalist bourgeoisie was opposed. For by the time of the English Civil War, the ruling landed classes were, according to Robert Brenner, 'by and large – though not of course uniformly – capitalist, in the sense of depending on commercial farmers paying competitive rents, rather than one that was sharply divided into advanced and backward sectors'.[127] For a number of Political Marxists, English society in the run-up to the Civil Wars is conceived as being essentially capitalist, calling into question the classification of the years spanning the Civil Wars to the Glorious Revolution as inaugurating a bourgeois or capitalist revolution.[128] Yet the extent of Brenner's depiction of such a thoroughgoing capitalist transformation of pre-revolutionary England society remains open to much debate.

Henry Heller, for example, has pointed out that the nobility in northwest England remained an outpost of feudal reaction, and that this area was a royalist stronghold throughout the period.[129] Using Brenner's own conception of capitalism as existing with the full commodification of labour-power, Robert Albritton has similarly claimed that English agriculture could not be considered fully capitalist in the early 17th century.[130] Moreover, if we are to take quantitative measures regarding the extent of proletarianisation in England from around the mid to late 16th century, it seems that English society was only slightly more advanced (in capitalist terms) than the European continent. Jane Whittle estimates that in the county of Norfolk around 1525, rural wage-labour constituted approximately 20–35 per cent of the working rural population, and more importantly, that this figure remained more or less constant throughout the 16th century.[131] In other English counties, such as Leicestershire and Lincolnshire, J. P. Cooper has calculated that somewhere between 20 and 33 per cent of the total rural population were employed as wage-labours in the 16th century.[132] In short, England was not very far ahead of the continent in the proletarianisation process,[133] and even lagged behind the Dutch Republic.

Put differently, the feudal remnants of English state–society relations had yet to be fully washed away by the growing capitalist tide in the period prior to the Revolution. It would therefore be more accurate to characterise English society over the 16th to 17th centuries as representing a combined form of development in which feudalism and capitalism coexisted, interacted and fused in various ways, with capitalism progressively coming to predominate. Such a combination gave rise to the sorts of 'contradictions of sociological amalgamation' discussed in Chapter 2, establishing the conditions of possibility for revolution.

These hothouse modalities of combined development and the contradictions of amalgamation they generated during the revolutionary period were perhaps most strikingly illustrated by the colonial merchant ships crossing the

Atlantic. The ship was fundamental in organising 'the exploitation of labor' in ways 'unit[ing] all of the others in the sphere of [capitalist] circulation'.[134] In the ship, we find the bringing together of a vast array of different forms of labour drawn from a wide variety of national and ethnic backgrounds: English, Irish, American, Dutch, and Portuguese sailors engaged in 'press-gang' labour working alongside African slaves under the supervision of English shipmasters and owners, and accompanied by capitalist merchants and 'gentleman adventurers'. As one observer lucidly put it, 'The nails that fasten together the planks of the boat's bow are the rivets of the fellowship of the world'.[135] These floating vessels of combined development functioned as both 'engines of capital accumulation' and, not surprisingly, sites of intense class struggle and resistance – 'a place to which and in which the ideas and practices of revolutionaries defeated and repressed by Cromwell and then by King Charles escaped, re-formed, circulated, and persisted'.[136] The processes of social transformation in England both preceding and during the Revolution were then very much 'a result and part of an international process, involving foreign trade, changes in intra-European relations following on from the discovery of the Americas, and the rivalry of rising mercantile powers in Europe'.[137] Developments across the Atlantic were thus inscribed in the 'generative grammar' of the English Revolution. Indeed, overseas colonial expansion in the Atlantic acted to promote and strengthen merchant capitalist interests advocating political change in their fight against the monarchy.[138]

Here we reconnect with Brenner's analysis of the Civil Wars, and particularly his examination of the role played by the different factions of capital comprising the London merchant community. As discussed in Chapter 5, Brenner identifies the emergence of a distinctly 'aristocratic colonizing opposition' made up of 'new merchants' excluded from the state monopoly privileges and connected to the rising colonial trades in the Americas.[139] Older merchant elites were mostly associated with the East India Company and the Levant trade, whose control of trading routes depended on Crown charters. State-granted monopolies gave them a stake in the monarchy, explaining their general support of the Crown during the Civil War. In contrast, the new merchants, essentially City outsiders, sided with the parliamentary opposition. They 'stood at the head of the City popular movement and played a critical role in connecting that movement to the national parliamentary opposition' of which many individual 'new merchants' formed a crucial part of its leadership.[140]

The majority of parliamentary oppositionists were not, however, seeking a revolution, but sought instead to roll back Charles's drive to absolutism. Yet once war had broken out, the intervention of social forces from below (the 'middling sort' comprised of wage-labouring peasants, craftspeople, artisans and independent small producers) pushed parliamentary leaders in a more radical direction, while driving much of the nobility and gentry into the Royalist camp.[141] While the parliamentary opposition in no way fully embraced the radical demands of the London crowds and other sections of the 'middling sort', they nonetheless utilised the mass movement as a vehicle to victory. This they secured in December 1648 through the conclusive victory of Oliver Cromwell's New Model Army. In a precocious case of substitutionism, the New Model Army came to act as a surrogate for a capitalist class which, although economically dominant, was not yet politically capable of assuming leadership of the new state.[142] Further, at the head of the new state apparatus, the New Model Army functioned as a key agent of capital accumulation, alongside the bourgeois class. After the execution of Charles I, the monarchy was overthrown and a republican Commonwealth of England declared.

Although the war had ended, the mass radicalism it had unleashed did not. The need to restore social order was foremost in the minds of the conservative landowning gentry. Initially fearful of the Republic, the landed classes nonetheless (partly) reconciled themselves to Cromwell's protectorate, as it proved itself an effective bulwark against radicalism and a protector of private property. But when Cromwell's successors proved incapable of providing effective central government the gentry 'panicked, fearing as they had in the early 1650s that a social revolution would occur unless effective central government was restored without delay'.[143] The result was the restoration of the Stuart monarchy, with Charles II taking the crown in 1660. Yet the Restoration was not a return to the status quo of pre-revolutionary England, but rather continued the socio-economic and political reforms of the post-revolutionary period.

Under the 'whip of external necessity' of the Anglo-Dutch wars of 1665–67 and 1672–74, and the later Anglo-French wars of 1689 to 1714, the English-cum-British state underwent a number of dramatic transformations, leading to the emergence of a modern fiscal-military state capable of harnessing vast fiscal and social resources in forging war. English state-building was characterised by the assimilation of the most advanced fiscal, military and administrative practices developed by the Dutch.[144] In this sense, the English state enjoyed a certain 'privilege of backwardness' in comparison with its chief Dutch competitor. Yet for the English monarchy, it was the continental monarchies that remained the chief models of emulation. Indeed, when Charles II's successor James II sought to repeat his father's effort to build an absolutist regime he was overthrown in the Glorious Revolution of 1688 and replaced by the invading forces of William of Orange from the Netherlands.[145] The primary aim of the Dutch invasion was to co-opt England to the Dutch-led war against the French, and in this William was successful. Hence, once again, the geopolitics of the European continent decisively intervened in shaping and reshaping English state–society relations.

The sum result of the socio-economic and political changes taking place over the 1640–88 revolutionary epoch was the establishment of a form of state conducive to the maximisation of capitalist development:

a state in which the administrative organs that most impeded capitalist development had been abolished: Star Chamber, High Commission, Court of Wards, and feudal tenures; in which the executive was subordinated to the men of property, deprived of control over the judiciary, and yet strengthened in external relations by a powerful navy and the Navigation Act; in which local government was safely and cheaply in the hands of the natural ruler, and discipline was imposed on the lowers orders by a Church safely subordinated to Parliament.[146]

In these ways, the English Revolution can indeed be considered a bourgeois revolution.

Nonetheless, the revolutionary process was not yet complete, as the newly capitalist English state still faced both internal and external systemic threats. Abroad, the single greatest counter-revolutionary threat to England was French absolutism. At home, the counter-revolutionary threat lay in Scotland, which in contrast to the maturing capitalist order in England remained an outpost of feudal reaction. After the Union of 1707 combining the kingdoms of England and Scotland into a single nation-state, this systemic unevenness of socio-economic development between the two hitherto separate countries was transformed into a unique pattern of combined development, juxtaposing and fusing the most 'archaic' and 'advanced' social relations in contradictory and explosive ways.

In the British state, a ruling class of feudal lords persisted in the Scottish countryside, drawing their wealth in the form of feudal rents, while in England the landed ruling classes were now mostly capitalist. At the same time, in the wake of the 1707 Union, Scottish industries began to rapidly assimilate the most highly advanced English technologies and organisational methods experiencing, in turn, the contradictions of sociological amalgamation that would come to characterise future forms of combined development. 'By the first quarter of the eighteenth century', Neil Davidson writes, 'Scotland had a coal industry where the most advanced forms of imported English technology were operated by men who were, at least formally, judicially bound to their masters as serfs'.[147] As such, Scotland largely 'skipped the intervening stages' between peasant self-sufficiency and wage labour which England had experienced'.[148] Yet in the Scottish extractive industries, 'transitional' forms of labour persisted, combining feudal and capitalist modes of surplus extraction.

As long as feudalism existed in Scotland, the consolidation of capitalism in England and Britain as a whole remained perilously incomplete and liable to systemic reversal. The Union was correctly perceived by the Scottish Jacobite lords as a threat to their socio-economic status and territorial privileges, and they came to gamble on counter-revolution as a means to preserve themselves as a ruling class. The final episode came in 1745, when nearly the whole of the English army was sent to Belgium to fight France during the War of Austrian

Succession, providing the Jacobites with a propitious opportunity to overthrow the Hanover monarchy. The Jacobite uprising was crushed and led to the enactment of a number of pieces of legislation (notably the Tenures Abolition Act and Disarming Act of 1746, and Heritable Jurisdictions Act of 1747) signalling the end of feudalism in Scotland, and thus the culmination of the British bourgeois revolution.[149]

1789 in the History of Uneven and Combined Development

Peculiarities of the French Revolution?

If the English and Dutch cases of 'bourgeois revolution' represent instances where an already existing capitalist order was consolidated by the overthrow of the sociopolitical conditions obstructing its advancement, the French Revolution signifies a very different case: one where the *dominance* of the capitalist production mode was actually a consequence of the revolutionary settlement. This is not to argue that capitalist social relations were absent from pre-revolutionary France, or that the absolutist state was fundamentally detrimental to capitalist development. Indeed, the putative anti-capitalist nature of French absolutism, conceived as the nonmodern 'Other' to the impeccably pristine capitalist England, has become something of a cardinal tenet in many revisionist and Political Marxist works.[150]

These writings take their cue from Brenner's argument regarding the divergent developmental trajectories between England and France in wake of the feudal crisis of the 14th century. For Brenner, capitalism emerged in England as the outcome of a class struggle in which the lords were too weak to reimpose serfdom, but the peasants not strong enough to maintain their independence from the market. By contrast, in France peasant revolts were largely successful, as the peasants consolidated their control over small and medium-sized farms. This meant that the French peasantry escaped reliance on the market, as they retained direct control over the means of subsistence and production. Consequently, in France the feudal system of lordly surplus extraction through extra-economic means persisted. While it represented 'a transformed version of the old [feudal] system',[151] the development of the French absolutist state retained, in restructured form, the extra-economic feudal character of surplus-value extraction through the 'tax/office state'. As Wood tells us, after the crisis of feudalism, 'the French ruling class gained new extra-economic powers as the absolutist state created a vast apparatus office by means of which a section of the propertied class could appropriate the surplus labour of peasants in the form of tax'.[152] Under such conditions, where the peasants retained direct access to the means of production (land) and the ruling classes continued an extra-economic means of surplus extraction, there was no endogenous impetus toward capitalist development. Instead, as Teschke notes, 'the absolutist state-economy nexus not only failed to progress towards political and economic modernity, but, on the contrary, imposed an economically self-undermining and politically highly divisive logic on early modern France as a whole'.[153] The absolutist state in France, as elsewhere in Europe, is thereby conceived as a fundamental block to capitalist development which could only be transformed from without: that is, through the competitive pressures from the more advanced British capitalist state.[154]

What then of the notion of a 'bourgeois revolution' in France? Positing the 'radically non-capitalist'[155] nature of French absolutism, Political Marxists on the whole have accepted the main findings of the revisionist historiography on the French Revolution; although the leaders of the French Revolution may have been bourgeois, they were emphatically *not* capitalist, and the socio-economic order resulting from the revolutionary settlement 'entrenched rather than removed pre-capitalist forms'.[156] What is more, for Political Marxists, the entire theoretical edifice of Marx and Engels's conception of bourgeois revolutions ushering in capitalist states is questionable, given that Marx and Engels are claimed to have 'uncritically accepted the liberal theory of bourgeois revolution in their early works'.[157] Thus, on both empirical and theoretical grounds, the idea of a bourgeois revolution having occurred in France is refuted, and more generally the concept is relegated to the dustbin of history.[158]

Here we leave aside the exegetical question whether Marx and Engels's conception of bourgeois revolution reflects an uncritically digested liberal theory of sociopolitical change[159] and instead concentrate on the empirical foundations of the Political Marxist arguments against the French bourgeois revolution. This is a particularly significant issue given the widespread claims among Political Marxists and revisionist historians that the French Revolution was neither led by capitalists nor resulted in the establishment of sociopolitical and economic conditions facilitating capitalist development. The latter point is particularly problematic for the 'consequentialist' conception of bourgeois revolutions developed here. So before providing a theorisation of the French Revolution from the perspective of uneven and combined development, we must first engage with these empirical questions head on.

Capitalism and the Absolutist State in France

The standard argument in the revisionist historiography was that the epoch of French absolutism did not see the emergence of capitalist social relations, and that it was in fact antithetical to capitalist development. Yet as we shall demonstrate, this is based on an overly static conception of French development of the pre-revolutionary period.

Thanks in part to a number of more recent works by various historians we now have a much more rounded picture of socio-economic developments in pre-revolutionary France.[160] As Henry Heller has shown, capitalist forces were already making themselves felt in France by the late 16th century. In particular, the Religious Wars, despite the general economic decline in France in this period, acted as a long-term stimulus on technological and economic innovations during the reign of Henry IV. The Wars of Religion hastened the process of primitive accumulation in the French countryside, where poorer peasants were uprooted from the land, resulting in widespread proletarianisation and the revaluation of land as capital. By the 17th century, nearly three-quarters of the peasantry had been deprived of the necessary means of production (land) to support themselves. By the beginning of the 17th century, estimates show that as much as 22 per cent of the rural workforce in France was engaged in industry.[161]

Accompanying this process of primitive accumulation was an increasing differentiation among the peasantry between a mass of producers dependent on wages and a form of nascent rural bourgeoisie.[162] At the same time, feudal rights over the management, sale and acquisition of property were increasingly weakened as peasants became more or less able to dispose of their property.[163] Thus, 'technological innovation and the spread of rural industries stimulated by primitive accumulation', Heller notes, 'held out the possibility that the rural population could expand buoyed by the opportunities provided by a growing capitalist agriculture and industry'.[164]

The process of primitive accumulation continued over the 17th and 18th centuries. Peasant proprietorship steadily declined, particularly in the last decades of the *ancien régime*, as the French countryside emerged as a region of significant capitalist experimentations.[165] According to Gérard Béaur, up to 90 per cent of the rural population in 18th-century France did not have enough land to support themselves, with about 20 per cent of the rural population being completely landless.[166] Hence, by the early 18th century, the 'availability of growing pools of cheap wage-labour became a structural feature of the French economy'.[167] What is more, while feudal relations remained dominant throughout the 18th-century French economy, there were significant counter-vailing forces at work from within the structures of feudalist domination. For example, in their quest for higher feudal incomes, lords often experimented with reorganising economic relations. In some cases this led to the development of (quasi)capitalist relations on their demesne.[168] French economic development after 1720 was also marked by an unprecedented development of global trade, with a concomitant commercialisation of 'vast sectors of production (speculative crops, wine production, grain and transport)'. Moreover, 'industrialization was also progressing, especially on the basis of the proto-industrial model orig-inating in the cities, with the expansion of the linen and hemp textile trade, cotton and small metallurgy'.[169]

Consequently, alongside the increasing weight of wage-labour in the French rural economy, the 18th century witnessed the emergence of a sizeable *capitalist* bourgeoisie primarily made up of merchants, artisans, shopkeepers and the *paysannerie marchande*. On Colin Jones's calculations, the French bourgeoisie grew over the century from approximately 700,000 or 800,000 individuals in 1700 to perhaps 2.3 million in 1789, making up nearly 10 per cent of the popu-lation.[170] Citing the spread of commercialisation and the growth of consumer society in pre-revolutionary France, Jones goes so far as to suggest that France witnessed the 'bourgeoisification' of Old Regime society.[171] The tastes and atti-tudes of the bourgeoisie were permeating French society, 'challenging the former hegemony of the aristocracy'.[172] As even the revisionist historian William Doyle notes, 'the relative weight of the bourgeoisie in society was increasing ever more rapidly than their numbers. Their share of national wealth was enormous. Most industrial and all commercial capital, amounting to almost a fifth of all French private wealth, was bourgeois owned'.[173]

One might criticise the conflation of 'capitalist' and 'bourgeois' here, since the term 'bourgeois' was supposedly used in the 18th century to also refer to non-capitalist town-dwellers or anyone holding non-noble status.[174] This is precisely what many Political Marxists have argued, particularly with regard to the French Revolution.[175] 'We may be utterly convinced that the Revolution was undoubtedly "bourgeois"', Wood writes, 'without coming a flea-hop closer to determining whether it was also capitalist'. As she goes on to clarify, 'As long as we accept that there is no necessary identification of "bourgeois" (or burgher or city) with "capitalist", the "revolutionary bourgeois" can be far from being a fiction, even – or especially – in France, where the model revolutionary bour-geois was not a capitalist or even an old-fashioned merchant but a lawyer or office-holder'.[176]

There are two problems with Wood's (and other Political Marxists') argument here regarding the French bourgeoisie of the late 18th century. First, the Polit-ical Marxist conceptualisation of a distinctly non-capitalist bourgeoisie is both too narrow and ambiguous. It is ambiguous in the sense that it is unclear whether they are referring to the non-capitalist bourgeoisie as a class in its own right or as a social status group. If the former, then what is the precise rela-tionship between a non-capitalist and capitalist bourgeoisie, and why can the former not be considered an 'outer layer' of the latter? If the latter, then what is the relationship between this social status group and other classes? Surely if the bourgeoisie does not constitute an element of the capitalist class, it must be part of some other class.

The Political Marxist conceptualisation of the French bourgeoisie is too narrow in the sense that it identifies social actors as forming part of a partic-ular class in terms of their *direct* relationship to the means of production. Those who are not the direct owners of capital are then not conceived as part of the capitalist class. Yet what of lawyers, administrators, managers, 'organic' intellec-tuals and other more diverse social elements who are not directly involved in the production process, but who nonetheless share similar life conditions of the capitalist class and support them in various ways? Do these social layers belong to another class? It therefore seems more helpful to define the bourgeoisie as a whole as representing 'a social penumbra around the hard core of capitalists proper, shading out into the diverse social elements that function as servitors or hangers-on of capital without themselves owning capital'.[177]

The second point regarding the Political Marxists' denial of the capitalist status of the French bourgeoisie in the 18th century is that, as the evidence above and below demonstrates, there was indeed a growing fraction of the bourgeoisie who derived their incomes from the exploitation of wage-labour. While a non-capitalist bourgeoisie surely existed in France (and elsewhere) before the rise of distinctly capitalist relations of production, this bourgeoisie was decisively transformed over the 17th and 18th centuries as its members became both directly and indirectly involved in the exploitation of workers. For it was during the 18th century that France underwent an era of dramatic socio-economic development, characterised by substantial growth in manufacturing and agriculture, making France arguably the 'strongest economy in continental Europe'.[178] As Peter Mathias notes, '[t]he French record of scientific growth and invention in the eighteenth century was a formidable one'.[179] Statistical indexes confirm the vibrant and dynamic nature of French economic development over this period. French industrial output grew, on an annual basis, by 1.9 per cent between 1701–10 and 1781–90 compared with 1.1 per cent growth in Britain. By the beginning of the 18th century industry accounted for about a quarter of France's total output, compared with a third in Britain. By 1780, however, industry accounted for two-thirds in both countries. Further, by 1789, the iron industry in France was significantly larger than in Britain, producing nearly two and half times the tonnage.[180] Overall, France's manufacturing output was approximately three times as great as Britain's in 1789.[181]

Moreover, the increase in industrial output per head in France during the 18th century was likely faster than that in Britain. From 1715 to 1785, the British economy grew by about 50 per cent, while the French economy expanded by nearly 100 per cent,[182] and the annual average growth of the French economy in 1701–10 and 1781–90 was 1 per cent compared with 0.7 per cent for Britain.[183] In the years between 1716–20 and 1784–88, France's external commerce multiplied by a factor of 3 against a British expansion of 2.4. By the end of the 1780s, France had become the largest trading power in Europe, with a total value of long-distance trade equalling £25 million (sterling), trumping

Britain, whose trade amounted to £20 million.[184] Moreover, in 1715 the value of French trade was less than half of Britain's, but by 1780 it surpassed its rival. In addition, throughout the 18th century, rural 'proto-industry' developed on a massive scale, while the 'introduction of urban patterns of consumption into the countryside further encouraged a growing dependence on the market'.[185] The Lyonnais silk industry was perhaps one of the most advanced centres of industrial production in 18th-century France, and 'stood at the apex of European silk industries'. It encompassed a huge industrial-commercial complex, employing approximately 14,000 adult men and perhaps as many as 20,000 women and children in the 1780s. In a city with a total population of about 150,000, nearly a quarter of the entire population of the city, or about 40 per cent of the active labour force, was employed in the industry.[186]

Nonetheless, capitalist social relations were not yet *dominant* in pre-revolutionary France, as feudal methods of extra-economic domination and exploitation remained salient.[187] Despite impressive growth over the 18th century, and while leading in certain economic sectors over Britain, the French economy as a whole did remain relatively 'backward' vis-à-vis its chief economic and geopolitical competitor. Eighteenth-century France thereby reaped a certain 'privilege of backwardness', adopting numerous technological innovations from its more advanced British competitor.[188]

Although a substantial bourgeoisie emerged, the aristocracy continued to dominate, if not monopolise, political power, with nobles occupying most of the key positions in the French army, navy and judiciary.[189] In 1773, for example, of the 40 state councillors, 30 were nobles of whom 12 were nobles to the fourth degree. Between 1774 and 1776, only one of the provincial intendants in office was not a noble by inheritance.[190] In other words, the growing socio-economic weight of French capitalists had not yet been transformed into the wielding of direct political power. How might we then conceptualise the French social structure?

Many Marxist and non-Marxist historians have conceived of absolutism as a 'transitional' social formation amalgamating features of both the feudal and capitalist modes of production. This view was perhaps most famously developed by Perry Anderson in his magisterial *Lineages of the Absolutist State*. In it, he describes the absolutist states of Western Europe as 'a complex of *feudal and capitalist modes of production*, with a gradually rising urban bourgeois and a growing primitive accumulation of capital, on an international scale'. 'Immensely magnified and reorganized', Anderson writes,

> the feudal state of Absolutism was nevertheless constantly and profoundly over-determined by the growth of capitalism within composite social formations of the early modern period. These formations were, of course, a combination of different modes of production under the – waning – dominance of one of them: feudalism.[191]

Specifically regarding pre-revolutionary French society, Davison similarly speaks of the 'transitional, combined nature of the French economy'.[192]

On this view, absolutism represented a distinct form of combined development, albeit one dominated by its feudal aspects. The absolutist state in France represented a transfigured form of the separation of the political and the economic that characterised the emergence of capitalism in the Low Countries and England. For despite the growing significance of capitalist social relations in town and country, which witnessed the socio-economic abstraction of producers from direct relations of personal domination and dependency characteristic of the feudal mode, the state remained a locus of economic dependency through the sale of venal offices. Hence, the social order produced by the absolutist state in France was marked by what Kamran Matin has described as 'personal independence based upon dependence *mediated by the state*',[193] where differential access to the state apparatus was a key source of conflict. The particular 'contradictions of sociological amalgamation' engendered by this pattern of uneven and combined development in France in turn witnessed 'the precarious compromise between the building of a modern state and the preservation of principles of social organization inherited from feudal times'.[194] In this sense, the capitalist revolution in France represented a 'revolution of backwardness' – a 'condition of developmental agility generated by the belated entanglement of a premodern country in the internationally driven process of capitalist transformation'.[195]

Yet absolutist France was far from the developmental 'dead end' that revisionists and Political Marxists have made it out to be.[196] As we have demonstrated, the pre-revolutionary French economy, particularly during the 18th century, was dynamic and growing, with capitalist social forces playing an increasingly significant role. And after 1750 'the French economy began to reach the limits of merely reproducing the feudal economy'.[197]

In conceptualising the prevailing economic aspects of pre-revolutionary French society, we are thus in agreement with Anatolii Ado that it is not enough simply to claim that feudal and capitalist relations, along with petty peasant production, coexisted in France on the eve of revolution. Rather, such relations were 'inextricably interlaced in the society of the Old Regime forming a *conflictual unity*'.[198] In the run-up to the Revolution, a significant fraction of nobles had become involved, in different ways and degrees, in capitalist or protocapitalist activities, while merchants had already begun to accumulate property and estate incomes based on a combination of feudal and capitalist relations. At the same time, larger farmers, wealthier peasants and the great landowners constituted the primary forces driving capitalist development in the countryside. Hence, as Ado concludes, '[m]ixed forms of property and hybrid social groups played an important role on the eve of the revolution'.[199] This 'imbrication of feudal and capitalist interests' explains the very different reform programmes that developed over the course of the Revolution. The fundamental conflicts driving and developing events over the course of the French Revolution cannot be reduced to either a clear-cut singular struggle between opponents (the rising bourgeoisie) and proponents (the entrenched nobility) of feudalism, or even less plausibly to an 'intra-ruling class struggle' by two sides of the same unreformed feudal class, as George C. Comninel and other Political Marxists argue.[200] Instead, the Revolution was characterised by an 'intricate overlapping of conflicting interests' between and within different classes, along with more 'hybrid social groups', derivative of France's contradictory, sociologically combined form of development. After the overthrow of the monarchy this led to a variety of reform programmes that were often in conflict with one another, but all more or less promising the 'radical destruction of the old order'.[201] To these developments we now turn.

The Origins of the Capitalist Revolution in France

If Political Marxists are mistaken in their characterisations of the French absolutist state as radically non-capitalist, they are on much more solid ground in foregrounding the causal role of international rivalries in precipitating the revolutionary crisis. 'It was through state military competition that the backwardness of French productive relations was initially, and disastrously, demonstrated', Colin Mooers writes. 'The coercive force of England's more advanced system of social relations was experienced by France in a succession of military defeats and the ultimate bankruptcy of the absolutist state'.[202] Indeed, it was the 'whip of external necessity', represented by the internationally mediated modernising challenge of capitalist Britain, that occasioned the revolutionary crisis in France – particularly through the costs of the American War of Independence. In this sense, the British Revolution of the previous century had laid down the geosocial conditions for the French Revolution. Though French absolutism had been formed and strengthened in and through wars and military competition,[203] the international terrain on which France had to compete in the 18th century was radically transformed by the social order inaugurated by the English Civil Wars and the Glorious Revolution of 1688. The differential developmental trajectories of Britain and France (uneven development) and their attendant geopolitical and social consequences (combined development) were therefore critical to the making of the French Revolution.

Throughout the 18th century, British power had been steadily increasing, buoyed by the country's stronghold over American trade and markets. Those states that held colonies or at least had access to the Atlantic system were provided with significant economic-cum-military advantages. In this respect, the European balance of power of the 18th century was built on the pedestal of the Atlantic slave trade. As French Secretary of State between 1761 and 1766, César Gabriel de Choiseul, put it:

> in the present state of Europe it is colonies, trade and in consequence sea power, which must determine the balance of power upon the continent. The House of Austria, Russia, the King of Prussia are only powers of the second rank, as are all those which cannot go to war unless subsidized by the trading powers.[204]

A central aim of French foreign policy was, then, as Foreign Minister Vergennes stated, to 'reduce England to a position of equality ... to take from her a share of her strength, her monopoly of American trade and markets'.[205] It was with this aim in mind that the French regime came to embroil itself in a series of costly colonial wars, particularly the Seven Years' War (1754–63) and the American War of Independence (1778–83), which ultimately led the regime to the brink of bankruptcy.[206] This geopolitically driven bankruptcy was the immediate trigger for the revolutionary crisis of 1787–88. Having borrowed until no more money was forthcoming, the new *contrôleur général*, Charles Alexandre de Calonne, sought to implement a radical programme of reform – taxes on all landowners irrespective of rank and the creation of new provincial assemblies – that provoked the political crisis leading to the monarchy's downfall.[207] The state's fiscal crisis not only came to increasingly loosen the ideological and political cohesion of the French ruling classes, but also translated into an 'unbearable'[208] tax burden on the peasantry, fuelling widespread social discontent and rebellion in the countryside.[209]

The economic crisis affecting France at the time was, however, of a more general nature. Signs of economic troubles had emerged in several key economic sectors as early as the 1760s. According to some historians, 'the economic slowdown marked the exhaustion of further possibilities for accumulation within the system'.[210] This was a structural crisis affecting the totality of the French economy in the second half of the 18th century. Foreign trade had begun to show signs of slowing down between 1760 and 1770, with its most dynamic element, colonial trade, wearing down around 1783. Maritime profits in Nantes and Bordeaux over the second half of the 18th century were in decline, while two large sectors of the manufacturing industry – ordinary textiles and linen and hemp textiles – levelled off after 1760. There was also a slowing-down in total agricultural production between 1781 and 1790 compared with 1770–80, with a slight decrease in agricultural production per inhabitant. Despite these economic troubles, population continued to expand, further exacerbating the socio-economic situation, particularly by forcing food prices upwards.[211]

Moreover, during this period further industrial development was blocked owing to a shortage of capital; stagnation had become apparent in various branches of industries, reflecting insufficient demand at home at a time of growing protectionism; the agricultural economy was affected by severe grain shortages in 1788–89; and the state of French manufacturing was further weakened by the Treaty of Eden of 1786 which lowered tariffs between France and Britain.[212] The second half of the 18th century was also marked by a notable escalation in urban violence and peasant conflict: nearly three-quarters of the 4,400 recorded collective protests in the years 1720–88 occurred after 1765, mostly in the form of food riots and anti-seigneurialism.[213] During this period, the burdens of taxes on common people were increasing because of persistent budget deficits, and rents on the peasantry were raised. The nobility were also further squeezing the peasantry by usurping communal rights and increasing other feudal charges on their tenants.[214] It is safe to say that the Old Regime was in crisis by the 1780s.

Decisive in the immediate conjuncture of revolution, the causal role of the international in the long-term (structural) origins of the Revolution was also significant, as France witnessed a series of geopolitically induced social transformations over the late 17th and 18th centuries. This prepared the sociopolitical conditions for the eventual collapse of the regime. Over this period, the French regime gradually shifted from a relatively defensive foreign policy posture vis-à-vis the Habsburgs to a more expansionist foreign policy on the continent and overseas, partially provoked by the rising power of capitalist England. The domestic effects of this transformation in France's foreign relations were decisive in laying the socio-economic and political conditions for the 1789 Revolution. Bailey Stone lists the key developments emerging from this 'dynamic interplay between international and domestic forces' as including 'the proliferation of venal offices, the deepening divisions within the army, the gradual reduction of social-status-related tax exemptions, and the growing constitutional confrontation between the crown and the tax-resisting parlements of the realm'.[215] These changes, wrought by the attempt to uphold French absolutism in a changing international context, increasingly came into contradiction with the social and ideological basis of the *ancien régime* – upholding noble privilege and the monarchical state.

In order to fund the Bourbon monarchy's belligerent foreign policy, the French state sold off enormous numbers of noble titles, and even more offices conferring nobility or at least enhanced social status. Scholars have estimated that as many as 10,000 people were ennobled over the century. 'Multiplied by five for the families who inherited noble status from their newly ennobled heads, this gives a minimum total of 32,500 or a maximum of 50,000 new nobles during the eighteenth century'.[216] The purchase of ennobling offices acted as a key means of bourgeois infiltration into French society's elite ranks, 'into its central and provincial administration, its financial apparatus, its judiciary, and its armed forces'.[217] The overall effect was to decisively increase the social weight of the bourgeois within France's political order, as the 'French government was driven by geostrategic and derivative fiscal necessity to encourage the assimilation of "new" civilian officeholding (or "robe") nobility to older military (or "sword") noblesse, and of wealthy bourgeoisie to recent "robe" nobility'. 'In this sense', Stone notes, 'the crown was indeed an *agent of social evolution* – more specifically, of the metamorphosis of exclusive nobility into more inclusive notability'.[218]

Yet despite the mass of office sales to replenish the state's ailing finances, by the second half of the 18th century, if not earlier, it was actually becoming more difficult for the bourgeoisie to become nobles, as the increase in offices failed to keep pace with the dramatic expansion of the bourgeoisie over the century.[219] Intensified competition and increased office prices meant that a more aspirant bourgeoisie than ever was failing to purchase its way up the social ladder, fuelling its resentment against the old order.[220] For the emergence of a more numerous and wealthier upper stratum of the bourgeoisie led to a much greater demand for ennoblements. Yet in order to preserve the ideopolitical dominance of the established nobility, while safeguarding its dwindling fiscal resources, the ruling class and state managers refused to respond adequately to these demands. In either ending or relatively reducing access to fiefs, royal offices, and letters of nobility, noble–bourgeois class relations were significantly aggravated.[221]

The traditional means of social promotion for the bourgeoisie was then contracting in the final decades of the Old Regime. In these ways, the absolutist state set clear limits to the extent and character of bourgeois advancement. It was therefore hardly surprising that when the Estates General met in May and June 1789, the bourgeoisie of the Third Estate were overwhelmingly in favour of a single chamber that they would dominate.

The ensuing revolution sparked by the geopolitically induced bankruptcy of the state saw the bourgeoisie acting as a chief leader of the revolutionary movement throughout its phases. Reviewing the social backgrounds of those who held office during the Revolution, Lynn Hunt writes:

> The revolutionary political class can be termed 'bourgeois' both in terms of social position and of class consciousness. The revolutionary officials were the owners of the means of production; they were either merchants with capital, professionals with skills, artisans with their own shops, or more rarely, peasants with land .... The 'consciousness' of the revolutionary elite can be labelled bourgeois in so far as it was distinctly anti-feudal, anti-aristocratic, and anti-absolutist .... The revolutionary elite was made up of new men dedicated to fashioning a new France.[222]

In this sense, the capitalist revolution in France was exceptional for the leadership role that the bourgeois played in it even if, as Hunt goes on to note, factions of the bourgeoisie could be found on both sides of the struggle. Yet the bourgeoisie had not originally sought to overthrow the *ancien régime*, but instead to merely reform the state. It was only under the pressure of counter-revolution from both within and without, and popular pressures from below – especially through the intervention of the peasantry – that drove the bourgeoisie, particularly under the Jacobins, to smash the old order.[223]

The international effects of the French Revolution reverberated far and wide. In Europe, the 1789 revolution and subsequent Napoleonic Wars irrevocably transformed the conditions of the 19th-century international system, and the form subsequent bourgeois revolutions would take. Regarding the former, Metternich's 'Concert of Europe' system inaugurating the so-called 'Hundred Years' Peace' was conceived as a conscious reaction to the revolutionary conditions laid down by the French Revolution, as conservative European state managers sought to balance against other states in the international system and revolutionary social forces at home.[224] The radicalisation of the French Revolution was also viewed by the ruling classes throughout Europe as a warning sign of things to come, inhibiting the bourgeoisie in future revolutions – as witnessed in 1848 – from playing their 'assigned' revolutionary roles lest the 'underclasses' get out of hand.

Subsequent revolutions in Europe and beyond therefore came to take the form of 'revolutions from above', or what Gramsci called 'passive revolutions'. These were largely elite-driven affairs limiting the popular participation of the subaltern classes – as exemplified in the Italian, German and Japanese experiences of the late 19th century – involving 'molecular' processes of transformation, 'progressively modify[ing] the pre-existing composition of forces' in the ruling classes' 'gradual but continuous absorption' of its 'antithesis' (the proletariat).[225] The European ruling classes had learned the lessons of the French bourgeoisie, heeding Bismarck's advice of 1866 that '[i]f revolution there is to be, let us rather undertake it than undergo it'.[226]

In the transformed geosocial milieu handed down by the experience of 1789, passive revolutions became the primary means through which late-developing states achieved their own capitalist revolutions. In these ways, passive revolutions can be conceived as organically emerging from the transfigured world-historical conditions unleashed by the 'Great Transformation'[227] and its political consequences. They heralded a particularly intense form of uneven and combined development generalised through the rise of a distinctly capitalist world economy.[228]

There were also more positive international effects of the French Revolution. For just as the American revolutionaries had first injected the notion of popular sovereignty into contemporary international discourses, which the French revolutionaries drew on and further radicalised, the French Revolution inspired popular and often more radical revolts and revolutions in the 'New World', which eventually came to challenge both the slave system and royal power. In these ways and more, the revolts and popular rebellions of the 'Age of Revolution' – American, French, Haitian and others – must be conceived, as Robin Blackburn suggests, as both interconnected and co-constitutive, with 'each helping to radicalize the next', and in the French and Haitian case, vice versa.[229]

It was in fact only in the midst of the slave revolts in the French Caribbean colonies, and in particular the Haitian Revolution, that the French abolished slavery throughout their colonies, with the Decree of 16 Pluvôse An II (4 February 1794) at the National Convention. This ideologically completed the 'bourgeois revolution' that had begun in 1789. In the United States it was only accomplished through the 'second bourgeois revolution' of the American Civil War of 1861–65.[230] The events of the Haitian Revolution were, Laurent Dubois claims, the:

> most concrete expression of the idea that the rights proclaimed in France's 1789 Declaration of the Rights of Man and Citizen were indeed universal .... The slave insurrection led to the expansion of citizenship beyond racial barriers despite the massive political and economic investment in the slave system at that time.[231]

The interconnected and combined effects of the French and Haitian revolutions represent a fundamental historical rupture from which more (formally) inclusive forms of bourgeois democracy developed, albeit much later.[232] As Dubois puts it, 'If we live in a world in which democracy is meant to exclude no one, it is in no small part because of the actions of the those slaves in Saint-Domingue who insisted that human rights were theirs too'.[233] In these ways, we find yet another striking illustration of the mechanisms through which combined forms of development causally feed back into the very unevenness from which they emerged. For it was only through the interactive relations among a plurality of developmentally differentiated societies that these combinations first arose and then subsequently recombined at the level of the international system, transforming its structural dynamics and logics, while simultaneously generating new forms and instances of combined development which further reconstituted unevenness itself.

Capitalist Consequences of the French Revolution

Thus far, we have examined the driving international and domestic causes of the French Revolution along with the agents involved. The important question to ask now is: was the sociopolitical order established by the Revolution conducive to capitalist development? A main argument against the idea of a bourgeois revolution occurring in France is that the post-revolutionary regime was actually adverse to capitalist modernisation. If bourgeois revolutions are to be understood in terms of their outcomes, an anti-capitalist revolutionary settlement surely poses a problem. According to Comninel, the French Revolution:

did very little in the way of transforming the essential social relations of production ... it did not produce capitalist society. Instead, the Revolution further entrenched small-scale peasant production, and with it the extraction of agrarian surplus through rent, mortgages, etc., by redistributing church lands among the bourgeoisie and peasantry.[234]

Comninel, like Theda Skocpol, further points to the growth of the bureaucratic state as an additional indication of the non-capitalist nature of the Revolution. What are we to make of these arguments?

First, to judge the character of the Revolution we must look at its consequences in its temporal totality (1789–1815). The issue is not whether capitalist conditions were immediately established, but whether the outcome of the Revolution was conducive to capitalist development over this broader conjunctural period and perhaps even slightly beyond it (say, from 1815–48). As noted, revolutions are not simply events, confined to a single moment of their inception, but processes sometimes spanning many decades, as in the case of both the Dutch Revolt and War of Independence (1566–1648) and the English Civil Wars and Glorious Revolution (1640–88). From this more holistic perspective, it does seem that the 1789 Revolution established the amendable sociopolitical conditions for capitalist development. As Albert Soboul notes:

> By wiping the slate clean of all feudal vestiges, by liberating the peasants of seigniorial rights and ecclesiastical tithes, and to a certain degree from community constraints, by destroying the trade monopolies and unifying the national market, the French Revolution marked a decisive stage on the path to capitalism. Suppressing feudal landed property, it even freed small direct producers, making possible the differentiation of the peasant mass and its polarization between capital and wage labor. This led to entirely new relations of production; capital, once under feudal domination, was able to make the value of work mercenary. In this way, the autonomy of capitalist production was finally assured in the agricultural domain as well as the industrial sector.[235]

Furthermore, in an early instance of what can be understood retrospectively as a state capitalist form of substitutionism, the Committee of Public Safety was vested with the control of all foreign commerce, nationalising the existing armouries and building a massive new armaments manufacturer in Paris (employing over 5,000 wage-labourers) and more elsewhere. The majority of furnaces and forges (over a thousand) were confiscated from the ecclesiastics and nobles by the state, and rented out and operated by the so-called *maîtres de forges,* who were bourgeois in origin. Under the Directory and later Napoleon, these industries were then sold off to these same individuals, who came to rapidly centralise ownership and control over the 1789–1815 period. 'The stage was set for a future transformation of this industry – key to the development of nineteenth century industrial capitalism – under the auspices of the *maîtres de forges* who now operated these means of production as their private property'.[236]

Second, the view that the agrarian settlement established by the Revolution entrenched a smallholding peasantry who supposedly retarded agricultural innovation has been forcefully challenged by a number of more recent studies.[237] Comninel's and others' conclusions regarding the detrimental effect of small-scale peasant production on capitalist development essentially assimilate the road taken by French agrarian capitalism to the large-scale capitalist tenant farming of the English model. Yet this merely reproduces the kinds of unilinear conception of sociohistorical development characteristic of Modernisation Theories, in which the '*raison d'etre* of agrarian society should have been to increase productivity along English lines'.[238]

According to the path-breaking work of Anatolii Ado, if the rapid development of agrarian capitalism was inhibited during the 19th century, it was an effect of the *persistence of large property* and the burden of rent, not small peasant property. Thus, according the Ado, 'the popular revolution of the petty producers ought to be seen as an essential element of the capitalist dynamic characteristic of this upheaval'.[239] Hence, as McPhee argues:

> the economic, social, and ultimately political changes in the French countryside in the nineteenth century are best understood as a slow extension of 'simple commodity production', that 'historical premise' of capitalism, whose full capacity as the 'really revolutionising path' was limited by the 'retrograde' effects of large property rented in smallholding.[240]

Although French agriculture lagged behind Britain throughout the 19th century, this does not translate into a denial of its essentially capitalist character. For the outcome of the Revolution's agrarian settlement 'undoubtedly benefitted the "really existing" capitalist class in France as opposed to some ideal construct derived from comparison with England'.[241] Indeed, we would expect the path of French capitalist development taken during the 19th century to diverge from England's previous development, as the international conditions of its emergence had been dramatically transformed. For one of the key reasons why French industrialisation, like much of the European continent, diverged from the British path was the much more serious threat of revolutionary upheavals from below.[242] Although it deviated from the British model, the consensus is that France was indeed relatively successful in its industrial drive, as 'French industry grew relatively rapidly in the period 1815 to 1850 when the era of war ended'.[243]

Estimates of annual industrial growth vary from 2.5 to 3.4 per cent during this period, while agricultural growth was impressive at approximately 1.2 per cent annually between 1820 and 1870. Overall the average annual increase in per capita economic growth between 1815 and the First World War stood at

1.4 per cent, and by 1914 French economic performance was 'broadly comparable' with that of Britain on a per capita basis. Although British per capita income remained higher than France by approximately 20 per cent, the gap between the two countries did not widen even at the height of British industrial dominance during the first half of the 19th century. Thus, Jeff Horn concludes, 'France enjoyed impressive long-term growth, both overall and per capita, particularly in light of its lower population expansion and less lucrative colonial opportunities'.[244] Further, the more advanced nature of the French Revolution, which witnessed the intense mobilisation of peasants and small producers, undeniably set certain limits to the extent of capitalist transformation. In no way, however, did such limits alter the fundamentally capitalist nature of the Revolutionary settlement. In short, myths of a 'failed' industrial revolution in France must be dispelled.

Conclusion

As this chapter has shown, international relations have been causally decisive in the origins, dynamics and outcomes of revolutions. In turn, revolutions have been essential features in the development and reproduction of geopolitical orders, instilling them with distinct social logics and purposes. International relations have not only been concerned with the problems of war and peace, but fundamentally tied to these, they have also 'been very much about the management of change in domestic political orders'.[245] Only by grasping revolutions in these international dimensions can we begin to understand their world-historical meanings.

These basic points fundamentally challenge the persistent theoretical separation of domestic and international politics at the heart of mainstream IR. Capturing the fused linkages between revolutions and 'the international' thus requires a fundamental rethinking of some the core categories of IR theory itself, such as the 'balance of power' and 'security dilemma', as their key empirical referents necessarily cut across and interconnect with both 'second' and 'third'-level images of war and peace, scrambling their hitherto assumed meanings. This not only means dispensing with the 'national-territorial totality'[246] as the primary ontological unit of IR analysis, it also requires the development of theoretical concepts capable of capturing the multiple, interconnecting spatial fields of social constitution and organisation.

The multiple and differentiated forms of 'bourgeois revolution' in the United Provinces, England and France all functioned, in their varied ways, to facilitate the development and/or consolidation of capitalist social relations in their national domains. They did so, in particular, by clearing away or reconstituting the sociopolitical and ideological 'remnants' of the pre-capitalist state apparatus, establishing in its place a state form that operated as a more or less autonomous vehicle of capital accumulation. In further teasing out the differentiated outcomes of these various instances of 'bourgeois revolution' on the reconstruction of capitalist state-forms, it is worth making a similar (though in no way identical) analogy with Marx's discussion of the distinct processes of subsumption through which capitalism can expand.[247]

As you may recall, Marx saw subsumption as involving the possession, subordination and subsequent transformation of the labour process into a form compatible with capital's tendency to self-valorisation. The chief moments of this process – formal, hybrid and real subsumption – refer to specific instances of capital's confrontation with extant labour processes. Formal subsumption denotes capital taking hold of pre-existing forms of production, leaving the material organisation of them essentially intact, and extracting surplus from the labour process as it is given. Hybrid subsumption refers to transitional forms in which the valorisation of capital is achieved without a prior 'freeing' of labour, but is nonetheless not conditioned by relations of direct domination. Real subsumption, by contrast, refers to instances where pre-existing labour processes are either entirely transformed or destroyed, and created anew in the image of capital.

In like fashion, we may conceptualise the differentiated effects of capitalist revolutions in the creation and development of distinctly capitalist states, as different forms and processes of capital subsuming the state. In the case of real state subsumption, the existing pre-capitalist state is entirely transformed or altogether destroyed, and political institutions and the state apparatus are reconstituted in specifically capitalist ways. Under the formal form of state subsumption, some elements of the pre-capitalist state are partially or completely retained but others aspects are transformed in the service of optimised capital accumulation. By contrast, with hybrid state subsumption, the revolution leaves components of the pre-capitalist state intact but nonetheless marshals the state apparatus in the service of capital accumulation.

From this perspective, the consequences of the bourgeois revolutions in the development of capitalist state forms in the United Provinces and England may be considered examples of 'real subsumption'; the case of France, as well as later 'passive revolutions' in late 19th-century Germany and Italy, as forms of 'formal subsumption'; and perhaps the cases of post-1861 Tsarist Russia and Meiji Japan can be considered examples of 'hybrid subsumption'. The benefits of such a conceptualisation are that it offers a historically sensitive and dynamic means of comparing different forms of bourgeois revolution and their resulting capitalist state forms. It dispenses with any kind of unilinear perspective that takes the Dutch or English examples as the normative model or benchmark, from which all other historical instances of capitalist revolution are then inevitably judged to be a 'failure' or 'incomplete'.[248]

CHAPTER 7

Combined Encounters: Dutch Colonisation in Southeast Asia and the Contradictions of 'Free Labour'

I have shewn how Situation hath given [Holland] Shipping, and how Shipping hath given them in effect all other Trade, and how Foreign Traffick must give them as much Manufacture as they can manage themselves, and as for the overplus, make the rest of the World but as Workmen to their Shops.

William Petty, 1751[1]

Introduction

In Chapter 3, we saw that a demographic crisis, precipitated by Mongolian expansion, created a balance of class forces that eventually proved conducive to the 'freeing' of the direct producers from the bonds of serfdom. In Chapter 4, we then demonstrated that the geopolitical pressures of the Ottoman Empire on 'European' development extended this process to enable the separation of the peasantry from their means of subsistence (by methods such as enclosures) and created a structural shift from the Mediterranean to the Atlantic. Each of these chapters indicated steps in the formation of *capital as a social relation* – the making of the capital–wage-labour relation. For many Marxists, this formation exhausts the processes of primitive accumulation, and the origins of the capitalist mode of production as such: the dispossession of the peasantry which, on the one hand, leaves peasants with no access to the means of production other than by the selling of their labour-power and, on the other hand, a ruling class with exclusive ownership of the means of production.

Here we immediately run into a very simple historical problem. As many World-Systems Theorists (WST) insist,[2] it is possible to point to numerous instances in which the capital relation has been dominant prior to the modern epoch. Although these accounts typically emphasise accumulation based on merchant activity, such practices could, at times, make use of wage-labour and the extraction of relative surplus-value through the introduction of labour-saving technologies. In addition to the 'simple' mercantile activity of buying cheap and selling dear, it is possible to find instances of commercial production based on market-dependent wage-labour in what might typically be described as 'pre-capitalist' social formations. For example, 16th-century diamond mines in Kollur, India employed up to 60,000 people, utilising a complex hierarchy of managers and workers to regulate production and distribution. 'Governors' were responsible for providing 'fixed capital' in the form of tools while 'overseers' regulated miners' output.[3] Similarly, in the Sung period (960–1279), mining and metallurgical enterprises in Kiangsu employed up to around 3,000 wage-labourers.[4] Across Italy from the 14th century onwards, serfdom had virtually disappeared and agrarian production was based on a variety of 'modern' employment arrangements including, in some regions, wage-labour (employed either permanently or as day-labourers). In many cases, this was accompanied by the reinvestment of capital in labour-saving techniques such as irrigation and more efficient crops.[5] In short, whether we ascribe to a 'commercialisation' or 'social property relations' perspective, it is possible to locate extensive evidence of *capital before capitalism*.[6]

As we have seen (in Chapter 1), for WST, the identification of earlier forms of capital accumulation led to a theorisation of capitalism that is essentially transhistorical. For Political Marxists, the historical specificity of capitalism is retained, but at the expense of discarding historical evidence that might contradict their theoretical presuppositions. To both we ask: why did these prior instances not entail the wholesale reordering of social relations into a world system based on the capitalist mode of production? Why was it specifically the outbreak of capitalism in the 16th and 17th centuries in the Northwestern European states – England and Holland, to follow both Brenner and Wallerstein – that marked a definitive epochal shift from the 'old' mode of production to the 'new'?

In order to answer this question it is worth taking our cue from Marx, since despite his unrelenting emphasis on the historical specificity of the capitalist mode of production, he was also attuned to the existence of what he called 'antediluvian forms'[7] or 'sporadic traces of capitalist production'[8] in the pre-capitalist epoch. Marx was keen to emphasise that these antediluvian forms were central to understanding the historical dissolution of non-capitalist modes of production, and were therefore crucial to identifying concrete historical processes involved in the emergence of capitalism.[9] It is perhaps for this reason that Marx stated that commercial capital was 'a historical precondition for the development of the capitalist mode of production'.[10] Nonetheless, he also insisted that these forms of capital were unable, on their own, to create a new (that is, capitalist) mode of production – a point not lost on those critical of the commercialisation model.[11] If merchant or interest-bearing capital could not elicit an epochal shift from non-capitalist to capitalist mode of production, what could?[12]

Marx addressed this question by confronting the implied circularity of the capital–wage-labour relation: if each side of this relation presupposed the other, the simple accumulation of one pole was insufficient as an explanation for the emergence of the other.[13] The hoarding of capital, for example, could not alone create the social conditions for the purchase of wage-labour. The possibility of using capital to purchase labour-power was instead premised on the existence of a class with nothing other than their labour-power to sell – that is, the commodification of labour-power itself – which implied a history beyond simply hoarding wealth. For many, primitive accumulation is nothing other than the commodification of labour-power – a bloody and violent history in which the (English) peasantry were torn from their land, leaving them with nothing other than their labour-power to sell.[14]

However, a point often missed among those that emphasise such processes of 'accumulation by dispossession'[15] is that the simple emergence of a class of propertyless workers was also – on its own – not enough to constitute capitalism as a mode of production. Consequently, Marx warned:

> In so far as [primitive accumulation] is not the direct transformation of slaves and serfs into wage-labourers, and therefore a mere change of form, *it only means the expropriation of the immediate producers, i.e. the dissolution of private property based on the labour of its owner.* Private property, as the antithesis to social, collective property exists only where the means of labour and the external conditions of labour belong to private individuals. But according to whether these private individuals are workers or non-workers, private property has a different character.[16]

Just as with merchant and interest-bearing capital, the 'expropriation of the immediate producers' involves 'only' the dissolution of extant social property relations. Once again, Marx insists that expropriation, while identifying perhaps the breakdown of an existing mode of production, does not account for why capital and labour come together and confront each other as a social relation. This suggests that there must be more to primitive accumulation as a historical process beyond the dissolving effects of interest-bearing and merchant capital, or the expropriation of the peasantry. Indeed, the prior existence of this confrontation between capital and wage-labour is, as we have seen, a transmodal (if sporadic and isolated) feature of history. Primitive accumulation is therefore better understood as a broader process that not only separates direct producers from the means of subsistence and production (that is, expropriation), but involves the (often forcible) coming together or encounter of the possessors of capital and those who only have their labour-power to sell.

To understand this process better, we[17] suggest a useful distinction can be made between *capital* as a 'simple' transmodal social relation and the historically specific *capitalist mode of production*. Or put more simply, a distinction must be made between 'capital' and 'capitalism'. While capital – as we have seen – refers to a social relation defined by the relation between capital and wage-labour, capitalism refers to a broader configuration (or totality) of social relations oriented around the systematic reproduction of the capital relation, but irreducible – either historically or logically – to the capital relation itself. This broader configuration may feature social relations that are specific to the modern epoch, but also those that precede it. They would certainly involve the 'accumulation of differences, particularly, race, age, and gender, inequalities, hierarchies, divisions, which have alienated workers from each other and even from themselves',[18] as well as 'institutional' (social) formations such as nation-states, laws, financial and logistical instruments. It would, moreover, include coercive apparatuses such as militaries, police, armaments; but also consensual apparatus such as (specific) culture(s), ideologies, subjectivities, consciousness, psychologies and conducts.

These broader relations of power oriented around the systematic reproduction of the capital relation enable us to distinguish between 'antediluvian forms' of capital from the historically specific epoch of capitalism. In antediluvian forms, the capital relation was reproduced within a broader configuration of relations that pertained to non-capitalist modes of production. As such, antediluvian capital was subordinated to the non-capitalist social relations within which it existed, and could not posit itself as the condition of its own reproduction: that is, as self-valorising capital.

The Northern Italian city-states constitute an archetypal example of this. Between Venice and Genoa, we find formally capitalist institutions and social relations, including the extensive use of wage-labour in agrarian and industrial production, as well as sophisticated financial and commercial operations.[19] Nonetheless, Venice was ultimately at the behest of the war-making tendencies of distinctly feudal or tributary states. Similarly, in terms of trade, Genoese capital was only able to carve out and protect its commercial interests by piggybacking on the coercive capabilities of other feudal states. The Genoese heavily depended on the protection of the Iberian powers, most clearly evidenced in the *Estado da India*, for the facilitation of trade. In this manner, they remained subordinate partners in an alliance with an otherwise pre-capitalist imperial formation.[20] The end of Genoese financial dominance in Europe was very much marked by their inability to control decision making in this 'colonial alliance'.

In short, the extensive subordination of labour-power to capital undertaken by Genoa and Venice and their colonial possessions were undergirded by the most naked forms of feudal power. More significantly, Genoese and Venetian capital was itself instrumental in the reproduction of the feudal ruling class, through the loans and provisionism implied in their financial and commercial power, respectively. We must therefore look at the broader configuration of social relations both *within* and *between* societies along with the modalities through which they (collectively) reproduce themselves in order to gauge the existence (or non-existence) of a distinct mode of production. Both Italian city-states were able to exist as antediluvian social formations based on capital because of their very subordination to the feudal mode of production operating at this *intersocietal* level. Without the transformation of this wider intersocietal environment[21] constituted by the feudal mode of production, any transition to capitalism in the Italian city-states remained necessarily partial and subject to systemic reversal.

This also helps explain why these antediluvian forms of capital ultimately proved at once exemplary, but also localised, fleeting and unsustainable. In both the Genoese and Venetian cases, the immediate problem posed by feudalism was that broader configurations of power subordinated both capital and labour to their own 'internal' requirements. By the same token, there were few incentives within feudal pockets of capital accumulation to transform social relations, as 'they had neither the desire nor the capabilities to undertake such transformative actions', for any attempt to shed or destroy such feudal practices would have constituted an attack on the conditions of their own reproduction.[22] This goes a long way to explaining why their ruling classes showed little interest in revolutionising the mode of production. Consequently, for antediluvian forms of capital, limits based on a reliable and cheap supply of labour-power were a constant source of crisis and decline,[23] since feudal relations on land, being dominant, had the tendency to reassert themselves. On the one hand, workers had opportunities to return to nonwaged forms of subsistence, through either family-oriented labour or subsistence farming. On the other hand, the feudal ruling class could swallow up huge amounts of capital and deploy it to reproduce feudal power rather than directing it toward productive investments.[24]

An implication of this argument is that in order for capital to posit itself – to become self-reproducing – an array of strategies and techniques had to be (and continually have to be) deployed to reproduce the conditions of its own existence. Jason Read is therefore correct to highlight that 'the two essential results of primitive accumulation – workers with only their labour-power to sell, and capital free to invest anywhere – are also effects of the capitalist mode of production's encounter with other modes and economies'.[25] The origins of capitalism is then a history that not only creatively generates a new social relation between capital and labour, but also violently clears away, or appropriates, subsumes and subordinates other modes of power to the requirements of its own reproduction.[26] In *Capital, Volume III*, Marx delineates this inherent multiplicity of capitalism's becoming as a mode of production:

Capital as capital, therefore, appears first of all in the circulation process. In this circulation process, money develops into capital. It is in circulation that the product first develops as an exchange-value, as commodity and money. Capital can be formed in the circulation process, and must be formed there, *before it learns to master its extremes, the various spheres of production between which circulation mediates* .... When the circulation process becomes independent in this way, as a process in which the spheres of production are linked together by a third party, this expresses a double situation. On the one hand, that circulation has still not mastered production, but is related to it simply as its given precondition. On the other hand, that the production process has not yet absorbed circulation into it as a mere moment. In capitalist production, on the contrary, both these things are the case. The production process is completely based on circulation, and circulation is a mere moment and a transition phase of production, simply the realization of a product produced as a commodity and the replacement of its elements of production produced as commodities.[27]

This suggests that there are *two* crucial moments in the transition to capitalism. First, capital via circulation masters 'the extremes' of the 'various spheres of production'; and, second, through this mastering, circulation becomes absorbed into production. Where the commercialisation model emphasises the first moment, the social property relations emphasises the second. As the above quote indicates, however, these processes are not mutually exclusive or even distinct, but can and do form part of the same process. Hence, Marx writes, '[Capitalism] is clearly the result of a past historical development, the product of *many* economic revolutions, of the extinction of a whole series of older formations of social production'.[28]

Elsewhere, Marx's fleeting remarks on subsumption taxonomically identify three different kinds of encounter between capital and labour which may (or may not) be implied in the transition to capitalism: real, formal, and hybrid subsumption.[29] Each depends not only on the confrontation between capitalist and labourer, but also on variations in the control of the production process, subsumption of the means of production, and the character of exploitation and therefore also the character of surplus appropriation (absolute/relative) and level of technological development; that is, an assortment of relations not governed exclusively by the capital–wage-labour relation itself. Finally, and perhaps most revealingly, in Marx's account of primitive accumulation we find a vast array of different 'levers' – themselves irreducible to capital – that bring capital into an exploitative relation with labour: the expropriation of serfs, the freeing of labour, the creation of a global market, the appropriation of New World precious metals, the subjection of indigenous communities, slavery, 'plunder', the public debt, the credit-system, taxation, and so on.[30]

Without wishing to labour the point, we think it is clear that the subsumption of labour under capital reveals 'not the effects of a single strategy or aspects of a single process',[31] but uneven and multiple histories. The multiple vectors of causation that fed into the origins of capitalism as a mode of production are therefore 'entirely disparate'.[32] The unity or 'totality' of capitalism as a mode of production in becoming can only be concretely, historically, traced by identifying these multiple vectors and their points of combination and articulation. An appreciation of this not only helps us to better understand capitalism, but also enables us to properly grasp the historical processes behind the 'coming together' of capital and labour, and so the origins of capitalism as such.

The point of this theoretical digression is this: if we recognise that capitalism is constituted by practices that are non-identical with, subordinate to, and yet constitutive of the capital–wage-labour relation, then an understanding of the origins of capitalism must trace these practices, and how they became related to the capital–wage-labour relation. When we understand the history of capitalism's origins in this broader sense, we are compelled to move away from any singular history (say the freeing of labour in the English countryside) to instead investigate those wider – often international – developments that were coeval with the emergence of capitalism and which may have influenced or determined its very emergence. We argue that once we acknowledge this, we are better able to address the historical puzzle posed at the start of this chapter: why Holland (or England) and not Venice or Genoa?

Our argument in this chapter is that the making of capitalism as a mode of production was inseparable from the coeval processes of violent subordination that took place in Asia at the hands of the Europeans. In particular, we argue that colonisation in Asia was central to the mobilisation of capital and the subsumption of a dispersed mass of labour-power. We argue that this history – a history of the violent coercion of *unwaged* labour – was crucial to embedding and systematically reproducing the wage-labour relation in Europe itself. Put differently, the reproduction of labour-power and capital presupposes for its existence a vast 'unwaged' sphere as one of the many configurations of power that mark capitalism's birth.[33] More specifically, the development of this coerced sphere of unwaged labour was crucial to (re)producing forms of subordination, exploitation and social stratification that were at the heart of alienating workers from their labour and from each other. In Chapter 5, we saw how the origins of plantation slavery as a specifically 'combined' capitalist enterprise, and the creation of social hierarchies of race and gender, emerged as specific functions of capitalist accumulation. In this chapter we examine further processes of subjugation that took place across the Indian Ocean littoral.

In the first section, we show that by the turn of the 17th century, the Dutch ruling class was suffering from a crisis in the relatively low supply of the single most important commodity in the capitalist mode of production: labour-power. In the second section, we then examine how the Dutch ruling class, unlike the Venetians and Genoese who preceded them, were able to solve this crisis through the accumulation, subordination and bringing together of a vast amount of capital and labour-power on a global scale. This involved a combination of New World surpluses with coerced labour in Asia. It took place through the historically specific experience of Dutch colonialism as an encounter – a moment of combination – between the Dutch East India Company (VOC) and various Asian societies in the Indian Ocean littoral. We argue that were it not for this moment of combination, and were it not for the Dutch drawing on an extensive – albeit dispersed – mass of labour-power in Asia, Holland's capitalist development would have been unsustainable in the ways other antediluvian forms were. We then argue in the third section that the emergence of capitalism as a mode of production – as a wider set of practices that enable the reproduction of the capital–wage-labour relation – was necessarily dependent on, and built upon, the exploitation of 'unfree' labour. In fact, the vast quantities of unfree or unwaged labour exploited in Asia were the foundations on which the freedom of waged-labour in the Dutch Republic was built.

The Specificity and Limits of Dutch Capitalism

Dutch Institutional Innovations

Why the Dutch and not the Italian city-states? In his magisterial *The Long Twentieth Century*, Giovanni Arrighi argues that the Dutch represented a break from not only prior instances of capital, but also the feudal structure of power in Europe more broadly. According to Arrighi, the Dutch were the first to 'be presented with, and seize, the opportunity to transform the European system of rule to suit the requirements of the accumulation of capital on a world scale'.[34] As such, they entered into conflict with feudal powers, and simultaneously came to be seen as champions of new dynastic rulers seeking to break from the hold of the Habsburg Empire and Papacy,[35] leading to a broader sociopolitical transformation of the European states system. For Arrighi, this transformation found its clearest expression in the Thirty Years' War and the subsequent conclusion of hostilities with the 1648 Treaty of Westphalia. The concomitant treaties pertaining to the freedom of the seas (and therefore trade) further indicate the reordering of the European states system in line with the requirements of capital accumulation on an expanded scale of operation. In these ways, Dutch policies aimed at transforming the European geopolitical order in the service of extended capital accumulation over the 17th century represented the kind of 'hegemonic agency' (albeit limited and partial) conceived by various neo-Gramscian scholars[36] as the dialectical fusion of coercion and consent.

Arrighi suggests that the Dutch were able to undertake this transformation due to the strong affinities between capital accumulation and state-making, based on an alliance between Dutch merchants and the House of Orange. In contrast to the Venetians, who were 'too capitalist',[37] and the Genoese, who effectively outsourced their territorialism to the Portuguese and Spanish, the Dutch were able to uniquely fuse the 'logics' of territorialism and capitalism better than any preceding state. In particular, Arrighi identifies three activities that proved vital to the establishment of Dutch – and therefore capitalist – hegemony. The first was the emergence and reproduction of Amsterdam as the 'store' or 'warehouse' of Europe, an entrepôt in which global commodity chains were concentrated to an unprecedented level. This enabled the Dutch to centralise 'the storage and exchange of what happened to be the most strategic supplies of European and world commerce at any given time'.[38] The Dutch thus seized on the ability to regulate and exploit price differentials, as well as control the supply of commodities as wide-ranging as 'herrings and spices, English cloth and French wines, saltpetre from Poland or the East Indies, Swedish copper, tobacco from Maryland, cocoa from Venezuela, Russian furs and Spanish wool, hemp from the Baltic and silk from the Levant'.[39]

Second, the establishment of the Bourse as the first stock exchange in permanent session meant Amsterdam was able to act as a 'pivot'[40] that financially tied together the various protagonists engaged in European interstate conflicts.[41] As we have seen, throughout the 16th and 17th centuries, wars were a near-permanent feature of early modern Europe. Alongside growing taxation, lending for war-making was one of the primary levers through which capital was accumulated. However, in contrast to the episodic and localised use of lenders and foreign credit (as with the Genoese and German creditors) that preceded it, sovereign credit practices grew as the Dutch were able to employ long term-credit planning and securities to widen the pool of investors. In these ways, the Bourse was able to act as a vacuum which sucked up capital from around Europe, 'whether idle or not'.[42]

Both the reliability of the Bourse and the scale of Amsterdam's warehousing were tied to the third key development identified by Arrighi: the formation of the joint-stock company, the VOC. The VOC, by 'internalising of protection costs', became the primary institutional hinge through which the logics of territorialism and capitalism were united. According to Niels Steensgaard, the VOC:

> integrated the functions of a sovereign power with the functions of a business partnership. Political decisions and business decisions were made within the same hierarchy of company managers and officials, and failure or success was always in the last instance measured in terms of profit.[43]

With the internalisation of protection costs, the VOC was able to embark on a remarkable, unprecedented period of expansion into and subordination of Asian markets, without experiencing the sorts of monetary drainage that typified the Spanish and Portuguese imperial projects.[44] In the process, the VOC simultaneously acted as a remunerative outlet for capital investment and an agent capable of carving open new sources from which to procure investments. It was an instrument of global expansion and interconnection, 'the medium through which the Dutch capitalist class established *direct* links between the Amsterdam entrepôt on the one side, and producers from all over the world on the other side'.[45]

The value of Arrighi's analysis resides in his emphasis on the distinguishing features between Dutch capital and that of the previously dominant Italian city-states. In doing so, he is able to bring out the importance of territorialism to capitalism, and with it, an appreciation for how the expansion of capitalism's spatial scales and sphere of operations was crucial to its supplanting of feudalism. Nonetheless, in this very emphasis, Arrighi is unable to avoid sliding into the problems typically associated with WST. By not properly distinguishing between capital and capitalism, he anachronistically presupposes but does not explain the operation of a capitalist mode of production before the Dutch 'generalisation' of that mode. As such, the Dutch experience represents not an epochal break from the feudal mode of production and an instantiation of the capitalist production mode, but simply capitalism's generalisation on a continuum of already existing capital. To recall Brenner's critique of WST in Chapter 1, Arrighi's explanation is a *quantitative* one: indeed, he explicitly states the transition that requires explanation 'is not that from feudalism to capitalism but from scattered to concentrated capitalist power'.[46]

As a consequence, his explanation for the emergence and preponderance of the Dutch, and through them capitalism, becomes concerned with an articulation of the institutional innovations that enabled the generalisation of this already existing capitalism.[47] The whole process is largely seen from the perspective of the minimisation of institutional blockages that might hinder capital accumulation. Institutions such as the Bourse lowered 'transaction costs', smoothing the investment opportunities of capital.[48] Similarly, the VOC internalised 'protection costs',[49] enabling the functioning of capital free from the fetters of feudal territorialism. Displaying some uneasy affinities with neoclassical institutionalism, Arrighi therefore presupposes rather than explains the presence and functioning of 'the market'.[50] Equally, the capital–labour relation, in either its formation or its generalisation, is completely sidelined, and exploitation as a source of surplus is removed from the understanding of capitalism.[51]

In contrast, we argue that such institutional levers are significant, but only inasmuch as they enable the initial and then systematic reproduction of the capital relation. That is to say, there is nothing to presuppose that any given institution or logistical arrangement is inherently capitalist by virtue of its very existence. The situation becomes all the more murky – according to

Political Marxists at least – when we consider that the institution at the heart of the process – the VOC – relied so heavily on 'extra-economic', nonmarket, monopoly means for surplus appropriation. As such, the capitalist character of such institutions can only be properly ascribed – if at all – when they are situated within a broader systemic 'logic' of capital accumulation. The key then is to understand how Arrighi's three institutions – and in particular the VOC – functioned as levers for capital accumulation by looking at their connections with the reordering of specific social relations, and in particular the reproduction of capital as a social relation. It might perhaps then seem opportunistic for us to draw on a tradition we have been at pains to criticise, but insofar as these constitute limits in Arrighi's analysis, some understanding of 'social property relations' would appear crucial.

The Limits of Dutch 'Domestic' Capitalism

As we saw Chapter 6, come the 16th century, Holland was experiencing highly urbanised, proto-industrial development, with a concomitant expansion of wage-labour in agrarian production and the widespread orientation of production towards market activities.[53] That is, it bore many of the hallmarks of capitalism, but one riddled with a number of contradictions and limits, which were bound up in its peculiar trajectory out of serfdom. This trajectory was marked by a programme of land reclamation, which opened extensive tracts of land to peasant colonisation.[54] Although driven mainly by the feudal ruling class, land reclamations provided a material basis that tended to favour the Dutch peasantry because of the limited jurisdictional authority of the Dutch nobility, for whom seigniorial rights were decoupled from large landownership. The intersection of colonised land and the absence of large demesnes meant that the Dutch peasantry held exceptionally strong property rights.[55] Consequently, 'even after processes of commercialisation and urbanisation had been sped up in late medieval Holland, small peasant property proved to be very resilient'.[56] In the mid-16th century, peasant ownership of arable land was remarkably high, around 50 per cent on Peter Hoppenbrouwers' estimates.[57] At the same time, the concentration of land into large farms remained 'a slow and protracted process'.[58] Strikingly, of land leases in 1500, 70 per cent were smaller than 4.4 hectares; by 1600, this had *risen* to 79 per cent. This suggests that despite strong indications of capitalist development through the emergence of wage-labour and commercialised land, these on their own did not enable the expropriation of the peasantry and centralisation of capital on a significantly large scale.[59]

As such, capitalist development was marked, but 'rare' in the 15th to early 16th centuries.[60] The strength of the peasantry constituted a block to the ruling class centralising the means of production; and these same restrictions on the ruling classes' ability to engross and enclose land ensured that peasants were not 'freed' from their means of subsistence, which restricted the supply of waged-labour-power. Where peasant freedom was restricted, it was not by a typically feudal class – the landed nobility – but by urban capital, which was able to integrate surrounding rural areas through investments in production and short-term leasing of land on competitive terms.[61] This gave Dutch capital in the 16th century a distinctly 'proto-industrial' character, based primarily on an 'elastic' supply of wage-labour, in which small-scale agriculture was combined with market-oriented waged work.[62]

It was only after 1580 that this 'limited' or 'constrictive' form of capitalist development broke down and 'accumulation got its way':[63] land was concentrated in the hands of the ruling class and rural producers were expropriated and separated from their means of subsistence. Small-scale protocapitalist enterprises based on an elastic labour supply gave way to larger farms worked by hired waged labour.[64] It was in this same period that the United Provinces experienced a large-scale migration of propertyless peasants to urban areas and a subsequent 'enlargement, concentration and proleterianisation in the urban (textile) industries'.[65] Eventually, through this process of primitive accumulation, 'the rural proletariat became an urban "real" proletariat no longer capable of self-reproduction' outside of the sphere of wage-labour (see also Chapter 6).[66]

Crucially, one outcome of this process was an increase in the demand for labour-power concomitant with a reduction in its supply in the 17th century, as population growth could not keep pace with economic growth. This *continual scarcity* of 'flexible and ample' labour-power meant real wages in Holland increased in the first half of the 17th century.[67] This scarcity and the subsequent rise in wages dovetailed with a decline in productivity, as 'proto-industrialisation' in the countryside waned. The rise in wages and decline in productivity pointed to an 'upper limit' of capitalist growth – indeed, precisely such conditions contributed to the decline of antediluvian experiments in Renaissance Italy.[68] And yet these very conditions prefigured, of all things, the Dutch Golden Age. This suggests that the Dutch ruling class not only managed to survive this crisis of scarcity in labour-power, but actually excelled and expanded under such conditions. Their expansion was all the more remarkable considering the general crisis that beset Europe in the 17th century. So how did they do it? For Brenner:

> high wages hardly spelled disaster; quite the contrary. Over the same period exports rose, attesting to the capacity of van Zanden's merchant capitalism to raise productivity in keeping with rising labour costs. Rising wages must indeed have contributed rather significantly to the economy's growth, for so long as they were offset by rising productivity and were prevented from squeezing profits, and so long as the products that were produced could find sufficient demand, rising

wages could provide the sort of dynamic domestic market available in few if any other locations in Europe in this period. In addition, rising wages must have spurred the substitution of capital for labour, the introduction of labour-saving technological changes that, in many instances, must have accelerated the growth of overall productivity.[69]

However, Brenner's suggestion presupposes, but does not demonstrate, increases in Dutch productivity, the 'emergence of a domestic market' and the 'introduction of labour-saving technology'. More specifically, he overlooks the most striking and controversial feature of Dutch capitalism: that it did not bring about the sorts of rapid technological innovation in an industrial revolution that would later mark the experience of British capitalism.[70]

So if the conditions Brenner outlines did not pertain, how were the Dutch able to confront this crisis in the scarcity of labour-power? A clue can be found in *Capital, Volume I*, where Marx describes two ways through which value production is made possible 'by using mechanisms *other* than increasing relative surplus-value'.[71] Marx argued that:

> by incorporating with itself the two primary creators of wealth, *labour-power* and *land*, capital *acquires a power of expansion* that permits it to augment the elements of its accumulation *beyond the limits* apparently fixed by its own magnitude, or by the value and the mass of the means of production, already produced, in which it has its being.[72]

This clue helps us understand how the Dutch were able to overcome the limits of their 'domestic' capitalist development, namely the crisis in the supply of labour-power. In the face of falling productivity and rising production costs, 'workers increasingly *had to be recruited from elsewhere*'.[73] By incorporating labour-power on a global scale, Dutch capital acquired a power of expansion it hitherto did not possess. We argue in the following sections that Dutch colonialism played a fundamental role in this 'recruitment' strategy.[74] As we shall see, it not only offset labour scarcity, enabling the expansion of free wage-labour at home, but was instrumental in the instantiation of capitalism as a mode of production taking an increasingly international form.

The specificity of the Dutch encounter with these Asian states was marked by intersecting levels of unevenness. Advantages derived from the acquisition of New World precious metals and from naval capabilities meant that they were able to successfully integrate themselves into the Indian Ocean trading system. But because of the strength of extant commercial networks and for-market production, undergirded by relatively powerful local ruling classes, the Dutch had to insert themselves into already existing modes of production. This meant that the forms of integration varied depending on the specific society encountered by the Dutch. Therefore, before we go on to explicate these processes in more detail, a brief snapshot of the uneven and combined developmental characteristics of the Indian Ocean littoral is both necessary and revealing. For not only did this uneven and combined character prefigure further uneven and combined relations with the Dutch, it also constituted the very basis on which Dutch dominance in the region – and Dutch capitalism more broadly – was founded.

Unevenness and Combination in the Pre-Colonial Indian Ocean Littoral

The Intersocietal System of the Indian Ocean

Stretching from the South China Sea to East Africa, subsuming the Arabian Sea and the Bay of Bengal, the Indian Ocean littoral was inhabited by an immensely uneven constellation of social formations.[75] Such was the variation of South Asia that some strands in recent historiography have rejected the idea of treating the Indian Ocean (or more broadly still 'South Asia') as a coherent unit of analysis, or reducing these radical differences between different societies to a single taxonomic type.[76] At the same time, the opposite tendency to discuss history in this part of the world in terms of micro-sociologies and/or histories is encumbered with the opposite issue – that these different parts of the Indian Ocean (or again, South Asia) were not disconnected or disarticulated social formations existing hermetically side by side. Rather, they were part of an interactive multiplicity, and as such were fundamentally bound together in terms of their own modalities of social reproduction. Despite the unevenness of the Indian Ocean littoral, it was also a loosely combined intersocietal system, both sophisticated and complex in its integration.[77] Hence, 'the diversity of Southeast Asia and its openness to outside influences were amongst its defining characteristics. Every state in the region was built on cultural trade-offs both internal and external'.[78] These variations, and the interconnections between them, meant the Indian Ocean was a world of dizzying multiplicity, interaction and hybridity, with various overlapping layers of authority, power, culture and social relations.[79]

Melaka (or Malacca, in the English spelling) was a particularly striking instance of this. According to a (perhaps exaggerated) account by Tome Pires, 'in a single day people there were heard speaking 84 different tongues'.[80] Melaka's social norms were, moreover, strikingly 'tolerant' and 'cosmopolitan'. Inter-marriages across different religions and ethnic groupings were allowed, different faiths were taxed equally, and Hindu traditions permeated and coexisted with Muslim ones.[81] There were clear material reasons for this: as the central node of trade linking the South China Sea and Indonesian archipelago to the Bengal coast, it was a flourishing port of trade in which traders from across Eurasia intersected. These combinations were inscribed in the administrative make-up of the port. Resident Asian merchants consisted of four groups: the Gujaratis; other Indian and Burmese merchants; merchants from Southeast Asia; and, merchants from East Asia including Chinese, Japanese and Okinawans. Each of these four groups was allowed to have a *shahbandar*, a harbourmaster who managed the affairs of that particular merchant group autonomously of the local authorities in return for receiving merchants from their own country of origin. *Shahbandar* performed an administrative function for the local rulers, while acting as brokers and intermediaries between their merchant counterparts and the local population.[82]

Such practices were not specific to Melaka alone, but were instead prevalent throughout the region. In various periods, Kelings and Chinese acted as *shahbandar* in Banten. In Ayutthaya, Chinese traders were responsible for captaining trading ships in the mid-17th century.[83] King Narai of Ayutthaya also employed a Persian merchant, Aqa Muhammad, and later a Greek, Constantine Phaulkon, as *okya phrakhlang* – head of the royal guard. In the reign of King Boromakot (1732–58), Phaulkon's grandson became supervisor of Christian merchants and an overseer at the royal storehouses.[84] In Ayutthaya, money changing and accounting was typically assigned to Gujuratis, Sinds and Coromandel. The chief accountant of Ayutthaya was Persian, and his subordinates Chinese.[85] The Chinese also came to prominence in the Ayutthayan state in the 1690s, with a Chinese merchant obtaining the title of *okya yomarat* (chief justice).

Intermarriage between members of different communities often played a crucial role in mediating such ethno-religious 'combinations'. The Teochiu merchant, Cheng Yung, obtained a gambling monopoly in Ayutthaya, subsequently settled there and married a Siamese woman. Their child, Taksin, subsequently became governor and later ruler at the new capital Thonburi (opposite modern Bangkok) after Ayutthaya's fall in 1767.[86] It was also common for VOC officials in Batavia to marry Indonesian women, many of whom became responsible for their private trade. Others would use intermarriage as a way of accessing positions of local power.[87] De Brochebourde, a Frenchman, travelled to Siam with the VOC, and in 1659 he married a local woman there. This enabled him to subsequently enter the service of the King Narai in Ayutthaya as his personal physician. Still under VOC employment, he acted as mediator between the king and the VOC in commercial relations. His son and grandson followed in his footsteps.[88] Similarly, a Portuguese *mestizo*, Jan Domingos de Matto, served King Sanphet VIII as an envoy to the English East India Company in Madras.[89]

South Asia beyond the Eurocentric Gaze

In short, across South Asia, many rulers officially and actively promoted the settlement and intermarriage of foreign individuals, and their incorporation into state administration. Not only was their know-how of markets and political conditions and customs in their own countries valuable, they could also elicit trust among their compatriots. This served an especially significant economic function, since 'operations such as long-distance orders, deferred payments, and *commenda* (entrusting capital) could not be carried out without a basis of mutual confidence and a common code of moral values, if not a common system of law'.[90] Hence, the use of non-indigenous administrators extended beyond technical know-how and commercial benefits to the political reproduction of the local ruling class. As Jeyamalar Kathirithamby-Wells explains, 'as long as they retained their separate identity, foreign merchants posed less of a threat to the ruler than their influential counterparts from among the indigenous elite, who had manpower and factional loyalties at their command'.[91] Equally, the segmentation of different autonomous merchant groups served as a mechanism through which the rulers could effectively check the power of individuals with exceptional access to commercial wealth.[92] We thus find within Ayutthaya and Melaka the juridical and geographical separation[93] and administrative autonomy of different trading communities as a fundamental component of local, indigenous ruling class strategies of reproduction.

A grasp of this particular feature of the Indian Ocean helps us understand the conditions under which the European-Asian encounter of the 16th and 17th centuries took place. As Ulbe Bosma and Remco Raben argue, 'in light of the long history in Asia of ethnic, cultural and legal pluralism, we may conclude that a flexible integration of European immigrants was the norm rather than exception'.[94] Moreover, this alerts us to the specificity of such integration, one rooted in the peculiarity of the uneven relations between Europeans and these Asian societies. In contrast to the prevalent Eurocentric view of Asian commerce as 'mere peddling', precolonial merchants were instead integrated into sophisticated political and economic networks that were often deployed in order to accumulate extraordinary amounts of wealth and power.[95] Precolonial commercial activities involved considerably more than 'buying cheap and selling dear', with Asian merchants using favourable positions within, or relations with, local states to intervene in processes of both production and surplus extraction.[96] At other times, the intersection of merchant and state interests meant state power could be deployed to compete commercially with Europeans should otherwise 'friendly' relations sour. The Portuguese and later Dutch and English found that local rulers were capable of producing and deploying military capabilities that could – on occasion – match them.[97]

Considering the vibrancy, complexity and strength of these networks, it would be a mistake to equate the European arrival in South Asia with a concomitant dominance of the region. Faced by large, powerful and wealthy Asian states, Europeans' ability to act autonomously, let alone dictate terms to Asian rulers, was extremely limited.[98] Unlike the New World, 'these were lands containing large, dense native populations with old and complex military, political, economic, and cultural institutions over which the new European conquerors claimed suzerainty'.[99] The sort of colonialism exercised in the New World was not an option here, which in part helps explain some of the problems faced by Iberian states seeking to settle and develop agrarian forms of surplus extraction in Asia as they had done in the Americas. Unlike the near total control and plunder of American resources, South Asia presented a very different challenge to the early Europeans who entered the region. Where Europeans were able to gain a foothold, it was either through integration into existing networks and social relations of surplus appropriation obtained through careful negotiation with existing power-holders, or failing that, through brute force.[100] As Prakash puts it, 'the Europeans – both the companies as well as the individual traders – had no option but to operate within the given organizational structure of procurement and trade'.[101] Hence, European domination in South Asian was initially marked 'by dispersal through shifting and opportunistically motivated combinations with local power holders'.[102] For, as Janet Abu-Lughod argues, 'the rise of the West was facilitated by the pre-existing world economy that it restructured'.[103] Taking the examples of Dutch activities in the Indonesian archipelago and the subcontinent in turn, we now delineate the manifold techniques used by the Dutch to integrate otherwise disparate arenas of production into an integrated logic of accumulation.

The Dutch Encounter: A Policy of Combination

The Specificities and 'Success' of Dutch Strategies of Integration and Domination in Southeast Asia

The success of the Dutch (and subsequently British) in contrast to the Portuguese should be understood in terms of the strategies of integration delineated above. In particular, the VOC's amalgamation of disparate regions of Asian trade into a self-sustaining and expanding intraregional network helps us understand the success of Dutch colonialism. In contrast, the 'failed hegemony' of the Portuguese was marked by an inability to adapt sufficiently to the local context they entered. Despite achieving some regional integration, centred on the trading networks of Melaka, Portuguese activity was based and dependent on the assistance of Tamil merchants operating in the port city.[104] Eschewing commercial expansion, the activities of the *Estado da Índia Oriental* were primarily directed at the 'unbridled expropriation of late medieval Eurocentric territorialism into judicially alien space'.[105]

Two policies in particular marked out Portuguese activities. First, they concentrated largely on 'redistributive' or 'tributary' activities:

> [The] *cartaza* system of maritime licenses and tolls and the juridically prescribed practice of *qufla* (convoy transport) flowed from the quintessential feudal institution of *mare clausum*; throughout the Indian Ocean economy the Portuguese ruthlessly superimposed closed seas upon the indigenous system of *mare liberum*.[106]

Second, the experience of Iberian success in colonising the 'New World' was combined with an emphasis on coercive extraction, which led the Portuguese to pursue a territorialist form of administration based on the *fortalez-feitoria*[107] fortress system and *foreiro* property rights.[108] The impulse for this territorialist turn was itself geopolitical, circumscribed first by Commander Afonso de Albuquerque's aims of displacing the Venetian spice trade[109] and crusading against Islam, and second by the subsequent conflict with the Ottoman Empire over access to the Indian Ocean (1538–57). Culminating in a series of sieges of the Portuguese-held city of Diu (1538, 1541, 1546, 1549), the Ottoman threat to Christendom now manifested itself in the 'East', thus intersecting with commercial concerns over spice markets.[110]

The Portuguese knew that for expansion to be sustained in this region they would require some form of material support, which was achieved by granting land and privileges to those who participated in military campaigns (a practice originating in colonial Brazil in the 1530s). Crucially, this necessitated a policy of settlement in agricultural areas, which subsequently instigated the tendency for 'land-adventurism' and geopolitical accumulation among the Portuguese in South Asia.[111] Otherwise, the Portuguese sought to obtain from local rulers the rights to revenue collection in the form of customs and taxes.[112]

The territorialist turn had two important consequences. First, the *Estado* became dependent on what proved to be an unsustainable land-based form of surplus extraction via taxation. According to Eric Michael Wilson, this 'ultimately precluded the *fidalgos* from commercially exploiting the ultra-lucrative inter-Asian "country" trade'.[113] Second, surpluses were typically funnelled into maintaining these specifically coercive or redistributive enterprises (as well as seigneurial consumption), rather than productive investments.[114] Hence, the pursuit for monopolies on spices was eventually abandoned in favour of imposing duties and freight charges,[115] and commercial activity did not survive the individual merchant undertaking the enterprise.[116] In short, there was no *permanence* to, or *expansion* in, Portuguese commercial operations.

In contrast, the Dutch took the very different approach of pursing a 'large scale and systematic participation in intra-Asian trade'.[117] This began with the spice-producing islands in the Indonesian archipelago, where the Dutch managed to monopolise nutmeg, mace and cloves. Pepper proved considerably more difficult to monopolise, due to its ubiquity in Asian trade.[118] It was produced in multiple regions and was prevalent in wider networks of Euro-Asian trade that traversed not only the Indian Ocean, but also the Inner Asian land routes. Competition among Europeans over pepper intersected with a variety of Asian merchant communities also dependent on the commodity. For many pepper-producing areas, rice and especially textiles, rather than bullion, were the primary medium of exchange. For this reason, the procurement of Indian textiles became central to the VOC's operations, and it inserted them into networks of trade centred on the subcontinent.

This region, due its own local specificities, presented new challenges to the Dutch. In particular, the trade in textiles depended on capital advances and exchange with precious metals. With limits to how regular bullion could be shipped from European stores bursting with New World silver, the Company was compelled to further integrate Asian commercial networks.[119] Hence, the VOC established a colonial presence in Hirado (Japan) for silver and in Taiwan for silks and gold. With access to these commodities, the Dutch were able to obtain Indian textiles on the Coromandel coast. Similarly, the VOC established trading rights in Persia, accessing silver mines there. Through this process, the Dutch established a network of trade that connected Japan to Persia via the Indian coast and the Indonesian archipelago.

How were the Dutch able to do this? The answer is very much rooted in an appreciation of the uneven and combined interactions between the Dutch and Iberian states. The Dutch were latecomers to the colonial game. While Iberian states had experience of territorialist expansion in the Americas, the Dutch were relatively peripheral to such activity. This meant that the Portuguese were more committed to feudal-territorialist forms of surplus extraction based on *mare clausum*, while, by contrast, the Dutch explored the potential of sustaining and exploiting the already existing South Asian system of *mare liberum*. Moreover, the Dutch saw an aggressive commercial policy in Asia as a mechanism through which they could undermine Iberian power and aid the efforts of liberation from Habsburg Spain back in Europe.[120] This striking passage from Grotius's *De Indis* illustrates these considerations at the heart of the VOC's operations:

> [The Spanish] will be obliged to turn from their attacks upon others in defense of themselves, keeping innumerable ships for their protection in East Indian waters, strengthening their colonies with fortifications, and (most troublesome of all!) maintaining a suspicious vigil over all things at one and the same time. The numerous and heavy expenses thus to be incurred will drain away not only all the

private profits of the Portuguese, but also the whole of the East Indian revenue accruing to their state itself, the unwavering enemy of Dutch liberty... Accordingly, if all the produce and revenue from Philip's East Indian possessions can be encumbered with a burden of expense equal to that already laid upon certain European possessions of his, it must surely follow that the future management of the war will prove much easier for us .... If, then, Spanish revenues fail – and with them, the credit necessary to procure additional funds – what outcome is to be expected other than a military insurrection leading to a great revolution?[121]

In line with their 'privileges of backwardness', the Dutch sought to dismantle the nascent forms of Portuguese colonialism, not by replicating the feudal territorialism of the Portuguese, but by circumventing them altogether and integrating and appropriating Asian practices. Further, the Dutch realised that in order to supplant the Portuguese, they needed to control all the main sources of supply.[122] They reasserted the extant principles of *mare liberum*, leaving existing circulation practices largely intact, and focused more resolutely on *integrating* and *controlling production*.[123]

The resultant intra-Asian network proved central to Dutch domination of the region, for it provided a way to squeeze Spanish Habsburg revenues, facilitating the Dutch rebellion back in Europe. Moreover – and we can only speculate whether this was an unintentional byproduct of an otherwise geopolitical motive – it helped establish what Banaji calls the *permanent* and *expanding* circulation of capital:

> only here, in the early seventeenth century was there a conscious attempt to build a 'permanent circulating capital', that is, generate sufficient reserves for further expansion of the business. By 'permanent circulating capital' Coen meant the permanent and expanded circulation of capital mainly in the form of commodities extracted from one end of Asia to the other and circulating *between* the different Asian markets where the VOC had factories.[124]

Contrary to dominant wisdom, this was not the simple operation of mercantile capital 'buying cheap and selling dear', or even just the establishment of monopoly privileges in the region. Nor was it, as Steensgaard suggests, simply the 'institutional innovation'[125] of the joint-stock company in 'oceanic governance'[126] that placed profit over power in Dutch considerations. Insisting on the exploitation of labour-power as the basis for capital accumulation, we argue that the integration of intra-Asian trade facilitated capital accumulation beyond simply oiling the wheels of commerce. That is, the establishment of permanent circulating capital was instead rooted in *transformations in the social relations of production* across South Asia. Ultimately, Dutch preponderance rested on intervening and eventually establishing control over production and thus also labour-power. The integration of intra-Asian trade, therefore, facilitated for the first time the organisation of 'a hierarchy of capitals connecting a dispersed mass of labour-power'[127] on a 'global' scale.

However, it would be a mistake to suggest that this connection of intra-Asian trade was the product of some inherent entrepreneurial or 'capitalist spirit' in the Dutch.[128] Rather, Om Prakash argues that the impulse to develop these links was specifically devised in Batavia in relation to the 'realities of Asian trade'.[129] By 1612, Hendrik Brouwer, who would later become governor-general of the East Indies, noted, 'The Coromandel Coast is the left arm of the Moluccas, because we have noticed that without the textiles of Coromandel, commerce is dead in the Molucca'.[130]

The compulsion to bring these different sections of Asian trade together did not come from some 'internal' capitalist essence at the heart of the VOC, or an entrepreneurial spirit among Dutch merchants, but was rather the outcome of a series of *aleatory encounters* with the various social formations of South Asia, and the respective 'external' challenges each posed to the viability of VOC operations.[131] It was, in short, an uneven and combined development. In the process, the VOC fostered a form of colonial control over a dispersed mass of largely unfree labour-power,[132] enabling it to accumulate capital despite the absence of a robust market of labour-power domestically. We now trace this sequence of encounters, beginning with the spice trade in the Indonesian archipelago, and then turning to textile production in the subcontinent (Coromandel and Bengal in particular). Finally, we discuss how the integration of these different nodes affected the development of capitalism with specific reference to its relation to free labour in Europe.

The Moluccas

Drawn to the highly profitable spice trade, the VOC initially and predominantly centred its operations around the Indonesian archipelago. It managed to negotiate agreements with the rulers of Ambon (1605) and Ternate (1609) granting exclusive access to clove production. Similar agreements were obtained for mace and nutmeg from the Banda Islands in 1605, and were renewed by conquest in 1621. From Banten, the Dutch conquered Jakarta in 1619, renaming it Batavia, and established the VOC's Asian headquarters there. Batavia subsequently acted as the base for VOC operations in the region, and in particular its campaign to monopolise spice trades in the surrounding islands.[133]

The VOC's attempts were in every instance framed by and refracted through the social formations it encountered in the region. The kingdoms of Melaka, Ternate, Tidore, Bacan and Ayutthaya followed many of the features of a classical tributary structure, building relations with neighbouring

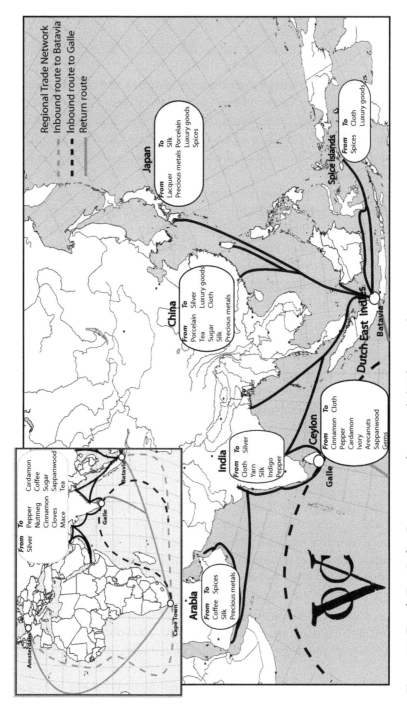

Figure 7.1 Dutch East India Company trade network (17th century)

Source: http://people.hofstra.edu/geotrans/eng/gallery/Map_VOC_Trade_Network.pdf (accessed 25 November 2014).

communities, who would typically pay tribute in kind to the emperor.[134] None-theless, two features separated these kingdoms from archetypal tributary states such as the Ottomans, Mughals and Chinese. First, some, such as Melaka, paid tribute to the Chinese Empire, and were therefore incorporated into wider trib-utary relations as 'peripheral' rather than 'central' agents. Second, the control exercised by these kingdoms over neighbouring communities was never 'complete' or 'total'. Many vied for independence, and acted autonomously through piracy, establishing colonies of foreign merchants, and competing either geopolitically, culturally or commercially with larger kingdoms (such as Siak, Kampar and Pahang).[135] As Anthony Reid argues, 'no state incorporated such dependents fully; they remained a stateless penumbra of the state'.[136] Due to this relative autonomy, the surrounding collection of islands that made up the Indonesian archipelago was marked by further relations of unevenness. Geographically, the region was resistant to large land-based empires, instead consisting of 'a multiplicity of political forms interlinked by the ease of water-borne transport'.[137] The specificity of the spice producing islands thus informed the way in which the VOC sought to integrate into it.

The Middle Moluccas were relatively parcellised, with village communities ruled by a small feudal elite – the *orang kaya*. Local arrangements meant the peasantry were subordinated and ruled via *corvée*-type modalities of surplus extraction,[138] which bound them to the land, imposing labour dues such as cultivating clove trees and other services. In this context, the VOC's acquisition of cloves, or the award of monopoly rights on cloves produced, was mediated not by local brokers, usurers or merchants, but through the *orang kaya*, who were best placed to not only maintain (or increase) peasant cultivation of cloves, but also deliver products to the VOC, for which they received a commission.[139] However, due to local arrangements on the land, the population of the Middle Moluccas were able to reproduce themselves through means outside of the revenue earned from clove production, specifically through fishing, hunting and subsistence farming on common land.[140] In the Middle Moluccas then, 'the reproduction of labour power in subsistence agriculture was completely sepa-rated from the production of cloves; the surplus labour was supplied almost gratuitously to the VOC and the local elite'.[141]

Although the Dutch were able to tap into this gratuitous supply of surplus labour, this also meant that some degree of control over labour-power tended to escape them. The Dutch responded to this challenge by making use of local methods of levying tribute through violence to 'protect their monopoly' and coerce labour. They organised annual *hongi* – naval expeditions mobilised by Moluccan rulers to extract tribute from other Islands. The VOC adopted this practice to extract tribute, but also modified it for the additional purpose of attacking villages with smugglers and destroying clove production in areas outside of its immediate control.[142] By using these extant but modified techniques, the Dutch were able to control production, and in particular prevent over-production, while maintaining monopoly privileges.[143]

Other similar combined geopolitical methods were used elsewhere. In 1605, the VOC conquered the Portuguese fort of Ambon, and subsequently under-took a long-term project to concentrate clove production on the islands around it by eliminating other production areas such as the North Moluccas. They did so, in the first instance, by making arrangements with local rulers in the Northern Moluccan kingdoms to destroy clove trees on their islands, concentrating clove production in the Middle Moluccas.[144] In other cases, they destroyed coconut and sago, two important means of subsistence, to punish any clove-producing peasants who sold spices to smugglers.[145]

Unsurprisingly, such actions were met with local resistance. In 1641 and again in 1646, Hitu elites rebelled against Dutch incursions, and then in 1651 another conflict emerged with the ruler of Ternate. Such rebellions were fiercely and bloodily crushed by the Dutch, which subsequently led to the wholesale destruction of the Hoamol peninsula. On the one hand, this enabled the Dutch to annihilate the production of cloves in the North Moluccas and concen-trate production in the Middle Moluccas in VOC hands. On the other hand, as a result of hostilities between 1653 and 1658, 'the peninsula's population was decimated', while survivors were brought to Ambon to supplement the population, which had declined as a result of the (guerrilla) war.[146] In these ways, the Dutch were able to subsume and control land and labour-power – those two 'primary creators of wealth' that imbues capital with a 'power of expansion' beyond its own limits.

The Banda Islands

Confronted by very different relations of production in the Banda Islands, the VOC had to employ altogether different techniques to obtain the mace and nutmeg produced there. The Banda Islands were more decentralised than the Moluccas, and marked by the absence of any higher tributary or dynastic authority standing above and mediating between them.[147] The *orang kaya*, although still present to some degree, exercised considerably less power and autonomy in the Banda Islands than in the Middle Moluccas. Instead, the small 'city-states' (*negorij*) that composed the Banda Islands were relatively autonomous from each other, and the 'free citizens' in each wielded or influenced political power through the medium of village meetings.[148] Nutmeg and mace produced in this region were central to obtaining rice and textiles from elsewhere, and local producers were unable – largely because of geographical constraints – to rely on subsistence farming. As a result, each village tended to be more dependent on trade for its social reproduction than the communities found in the Middle Moluccas.

This context made it considerably more challenging for the Dutch to impose a monopoly. The forms of 'gratuitous labour' of the Middle Moluccas were unsustainable in the context of a population heavily dependent on the market for their subsistence. In addition, the decentralisation of power and weakness of the *orang kaya* meant there was no autonomous and sufficiently powerful ruling class capable of exercising control over the bulk of the population. Consequently, nascent attempts by the Dutch to assert authority in the region were met with resistance from the local population. This took the form, for example, of guerrilla wars against Dutch attempts to build forts on the islands.[149] In other cases, local workers went on 'strike' by sabotaging production[150] or refusing to pick spices by migrating to the high hills.[151] And although the Dutch set up a monopoly agreement with the local *orang kaya* in return for protection from the Portuguese and English, smugglers were regularly able to circumvent this agreement and the English were able to establish a fort of their own.[152]

Spurred by the resistance of the local population, and competition of other European companies and Asian merchants alike (the 'whip of external necessity'), the VOC resorted to violent means in order to assert its control over nutmeg and mace production.[153] Acting on the pretext that the Banadanese were breaching monopoly agreements, the VOC instigated a remarkably brutal military conflict, killing the majority of the Bandanese population by 1621. Only a few hundred of a population that had numbered around 15,000 survived. Many of those that did survive were set to work on nutmeg production or sent to Batavia as slave labourers.[154]

The genocide of the Bandanese necessitated a 'rebuilding' of the social relations of production in line with VOC interests. The Dutch, confronted with a cultivable but unpopulated land, did not, however, turn to the sort of settler colonialism exercised in other contexts, in particular because of the prohibitively high costs of 'free' labour.[155] Instead, they established 'one of the first modern plantation economies based on slave labour'.[156] Each plantation produced almost exclusively nutmeg and mace, and was divided into 68 parcels called *perken*. *Perkeniers* were recruited from the VOC, and assigned to each *perken* to manage production by purchasing slaves from the VOC at a fixed price, who then worked each parcel of land.[157] Through their contractual agreements with *perkeniers*, the VOC was able to set a low price for the spices and ensure that products were delivered exclusively to its agents.[158]

In the form common to modern plantation slavery, the rate of exploitation was exceptionally high, deaths were common and slaves were unable to reliably reproduce themselves. According to van Zanden, 200 slaves were imported annually to maintain a permanent slave population of around 4,000 on the Island.[159] Although the VOC was plugged into already existing forms of exploitation and production, its appropriation of these techniques created considerably more exploitative practices than what had preceded it. This was not just due to a quantitative increase in the rate of exploitation, but also a qualitative transformation of the role of slavery in the reproduction of the ruling class. Where before, slavery was primarily used by the native ruling class in a 'personalized social hierarchy', the VOC was the first to make slaveholding impersonal and institutionalised, a system in which 'a corporation – not an individual – held persons in perpetuity'.[160] The variant levels of exploitation between the two are evidenced in demographic figures: the percentage of children in the domestic Asian slave population was 8–9 per cent, while for those owned by the VOC, the figure was 20–25 per cent.[161]

Owing to the exceptional rate of exploitation and death in the plantations, the reproduction of labour-power took place outside of the VOC's operations. Slaves were largely obtained as abductees from what Markus Vink calls 'segmented micro-states and stateless societies'[162] in 'peripheral' areas of the region, who were brought to market by local slave traders and bought by the VOC.[163] Among these groups were hunter-gatherer bands, shifting cultivators, pastoral nomads and wet rice farmers.[164] In many instances, 'booms' of slave trade were directly connected to the dispossession of these communities, through famines, revolts or wars in surrounding states.[165] Through this process of combined development, the VOC melded together the hunter-gathering mode of production with plantation slavery via the mechanisms and exigencies of merchant capital. Labour-power that was reproduced in the hunter-gatherer mode of production was deployed and exploited in the plantation. Since the costs of reproducing slaves were far outstripped by the labour performed, the VOC was able to appropriate an exceptionally large quantity of surplus labour. By pushing down the costs of production, the VOC established both the social relations and techniques of exploitation necessary to extract 'super-profits' from the colonies. These were realised through the sale of spices in the European 'core', where gross profits on spices could exceed 1,000 per cent.[166] Beyond this 'quantitative' benefit, this form of exploitation further developed techniques and structures of exploitation and accumulation that would, by the 18th century, be used in the thriving slave trade and plantation production in the New World.[167]

Indian Textiles

An additional mechanism used by the Dutch to ensure monopoly over the spice trade was cornering the Indian textile industry, since textiles were the dominant medium of exchange through which spices were obtained in the region. Rather than pursuing textiles at the point of exchange, the Dutch intervened at the point of production, setting up a permanent presence in the form of factories on the Coromandel Coast from 1606 and in Gujurat from 1618.[168] This put them in contact with the land-based Mughal Empire, which dominated the subcontinent, constituting a pivot around which much of the Indian Ocean trading network was centred. The Empire was, by any standards of the age, highly 'advanced', with a standard of living above that of Europe and a population of over 100 million in 1600, which would expand over the course of the next two centuries.[169] Its mode of production was tributary, with a land-holding patrimonial ruling class – the *zamīndārs* – distributed throughout the Empire and formally subordinated to the emperor (see Chapter 8).

The *zamīndārs* were responsible for extracting land revenue from the peasantry and passing it on to the centre.[170] Although this form dominated, there were some instances, especially in port towns, where merchants or usurers acted as mediators by transferring surpluses to the centre. As we have seen, in many instances merchants, especially foreign ones, played a preponderant political and economic role, sometimes even in an administrative capacity. Equally, the tributary ruling class often used their political privileges to participate in commercial activities, and mediate between rural production and coastal shipping.[171] In this respect, 'mercantile activity and tributary relationships were symbiotic' and at times inseparable.[172]

Production in the Mughal Empire took place primarily in villages[173] by direct producers who had formal control over the production process, means of production and their own labour.[174] In textile production, the individual weaver was the basic 'unit' of production, and typically tended to devote all of their labour-power to production for the market.[175] The weaver manufactured cloths for the market at a set quantity, price and date of delivery agreed with merchants. These agreements were structured around payments advanced by merchants, who offered a large part of the final value of the contract to enable the weaver to pay for raw materials as well as the costs of reproduction for them and their family. The weaver retained formal control over the production process. Nonetheless, this was ultimately an exploitative relation since 'debt obligations often rendered the artisans subject to coercive control by the merchants'.[176]

Such a structure necessitated a significant quantity of readily available capital, which was facilitated by the exigencies of the tributary mode. The reproduction of the Mughal state depended on a reliable system of transferring wealth from periphery to centre, and then from the centre back to the periphery, primarily for the costs of local administration and warfare. The needs of this tributary circulation were often met through a sophisticated network of credit and money markets, organised and administered by *sarrafs* across a complex and broad-reaching network of money clearing houses – often temples flush with religious endowments – throughout the South Asian countryside.[177]

Confronted by the vast strength of the Mughal state in the countryside, and also the competitive wealth and knowledge of local merchants, the VOC (and other European companies) was compelled to integrate into these pre-existing social relations of production. Hence, direct producers were tied to the VOC through a hierarchy of advance payments mediated by an array of local merchants and money lenders. Typically, Asian merchants were responsible for ensuring advances reached weavers at a steady and reliable rate. They did so by employing clerks on a monthly salary who ensured weaver production remained steady.[178] Such was the symbiotic character of these relations that European companies at times made use of *sarrafs* and merchants to obtain capital for advances.[179]

As Banaji argues, when this strategy was situated in the context of South Asia, the self-expansion of capital went well beyond simply buying cheap and selling dear. Under the competitive pressures of Asian merchants and other chartered companies, it required 'some measure of control over production'.[180] By inserting its agents into local practices and social relations, the VOC was able to oversee an increasing subordination of rural producers to production for the market.[181] In fact, such strategies of subordination became especially pronounced when they were met with local resistance. The VOC found that the advance system could be exploited by either intermediaries or direct producers trying to cut costs and keep a greater proportion of the value of the product for themselves. Such 'resistance' became manifest through the dual problem of 'bad debts'[182] and the production of poorer-quality textiles. In response, the VOC felt compelled to intervene more directly in production, and exert greater control over the production process. One of the ways it did so was by setting up factories that dealt with production, storage and distribution in port cities along the Indian Ocean littoral.

One example of this was a centre for silk-reeling installed in the VOC factory at Kasimbazar in Bengal in 1653. It initially employed over 3,000 reelers before being reconstructed in 1715 to accommodate over 4,000 workers. Initially, the VOC recruited 'master-reelers' who were paid in advance against a specified amount of reeled silk, while also providing them with equipment, working space, and raw materials. In 1674, the VOC sought to impose even greater control over the production process by demoting the master reeler and assuming all the 'risks' of capital investment.[183] We then see the VOC going beyond activity in the circulation process and intervening directly in production, assuming both ownership and control of the direct production process. Such factories demonstrated the possibility of forms of hybrid subsumption giving way to something resembling the formal subsumption of labour under capital in the colonies.

Conclusion

If we were to reformulate the above historical overview from the theoretical perspective of uneven and combined development, it would appear that the combination of VOC attempts at monopolisation with pre-existing Asian social relations of production enabled the Dutch to construct an integrated colonial apparatus that established expanding, self-reproducing, permanently circulating capital. Central to this was the integration and subsumption of 'a dispersed mass of labour' through the combination of a multiplicity of uneven forms – advances, debt peonage, *corvées*, plantations and wage-labour– under a single enterprise, the VOC. In these ways, the Dutch 'went beyond the limits of circulation and invaded the arena of production in the process of establishing colonial economies'.[184] This not only 'guaranteed for itself the production of goods in the world market', but formed the basis from which 'super-profits' based on cheap production costs could readily be exploited.[185] In turn, these returns on colonial trade propelled and underwrote the financial preponderance of Dutch financial institutions, and Amsterdam's role as the entrepôt of Europe.[186] As a result, the success of the institutional innovations emphasised by the likes of Steensgaard and Arrighi can only be properly understood when they are situated in an understanding of the 'globalised' subordination of labour-power elucidated in this chapter.

This combined form of primitive accumulation proved central to Dutch economic preponderance, for it effectively overcame the limits of Dutch 'domestic capitalism', in particular the lack of readily available labour-power. This helps us understand why the peculiar form of social relations of production found in the United Provinces proved ultimately sustainable, despite all the odds of success seemingly stacked against it. A scarcity of labour-power and high wages proved no impediment to further capitalist development, for there was a ready store of cheap labour-power available 'elsewhere'. When the European experience is tied to these vectors of colonial exploitation, it becomes apparent that the high wages of European workers proved central to the realisation of super-profits derived from the sale of colonial commodities back in Europe (see Chapter 5). Moreover, the sort of 'internal market' created by high wages only proved sustainable insofar as a ready supply of commodities for the reproduction of wage-labour was made available. Before the Industrial Revolution, this supply could only reliably come from the colonies. Silvia Federici, in comments that focus on capitalist patriarchy and slavery in the New World, but that are equally applicable here, succinctly summarises this interrelation:

> On one side, a global assembly line was created that cut the cost of the commodities necessary to produce labor-power in Europe …. On the other side, the metropolitan wage became the vehicle by which the goods produced by enslaved workers went to the market, and the value of the products of enslaved-labor was realized.[187]

Hence, the simple presence of production based on 'free' wage-labour in the

United Provinces is only one side of the story that enables us to understand its capitalist development. This is not to say that the Dutch embarked on their colonial path in search of a surplus population capable of bringing down wages. What we are after here is not an explanation of how capitalism tends towards colonialism. We argue the reverse: that in part, *colonialism explains the emergence of capitalism* as a mode of production. In this respect, our argument differs from WST. Rather than treating South Asian societies as passive agents in this process, we have demonstrated the ways in which they were actively – both oppositionally and collaboratively – involved in the formation of this process, as constitutive agents in the making of capitalism as a global mode of production. Moreover, we argue that the specificity of this agency, and the Dutch encounter with it, can only be properly explicated – in contrast to WST – by disclosing the multiple vectors of uneven and combined development witnessed in this co-constitutive process.

CHAPTER 8

Origins of the Great Divergence over the Longue Durée: Rethinking the 'Rise of the West'

There are no miracles in nature or history, but every abrupt turn in history... presents such a wealth of content, unfolds such unexpected and specific combinations of forms of struggle and alignment of forces of the contestants, that to the lay mind there is much that must appear miraculous.

V. I. Lenin, 1917[1]

Force is nothing apart from its effect; its being consists entirely in this coming to be and passing away. If the substance of things is force, their mode of existence turns out to be appearance. For, a being exists only as 'vanishing', one that 'is per se straight-away non-being, we call ... a semblance [*Schein*]'.

Herbert Marcuse, 1941[2]

Introduction

How in the space of some 300 years did the leading edge in global economic and military power pass from 'East' to 'West'? What processes led to the breakthrough to capitalism in Western Europe and its subsequent ascendency to global domination? However formulated, questions concerning the origins of the 'rise of the West' have been at the forefront of social scientific debates since their inception: the topic was central to the works of Max Weber and figured prominently (if implicitly) in Marx's studies and within Marxism ever since. Whether focusing on Europe's unique cultural and institutional inheritance (Greek philosophy and science, Roman law, representative forms of governance, citizenship ideals, politically decentralised forms of governance and sovereignty, the rationalising effects of a 'protestant spirit' and so on), its distinctively inherent 'restless rationalism', and/or its advantageous ecological system (temperate climates, deep soils, navigable rivers and large coastlines, abundant and diversified resource endowments), traditional explanations of Europe's rise to global supremacy locate its origins as immanent to Europe itself.[3]

The 'European miracle' is conceived as one of *self-generation* emerging from the unique if not peculiar attributes of a singular culturally and geographically defined sociohistorical experience. 'The "miracle" of massive economic development', Michael Mann writes, 'occurred "spontaneously" in Europe, and nowhere else'.[4] Similarly, Ricardo Duchesne has insisted on the 'uniqueness of the West', emphasising its 'higher intellectual and artistic creativity' and its 'exceptional' development of reason, and freedom.[5] Accordingly, from such perspectives, there was – and perhaps still is – something inherently exceptional about 'the West' that distinguished it from the rest.

Such self-aggrandising narratives of Western exceptionalism have come under heavy criticism from an array of different scholars and disciplinary fields.[6] While diverging in their analyses and conclusions, these critics share a common theme of problematising any notion of a uniquely self-propelling 'rise of the West'. They have instead focused on the purely conjunctural, often 'accidental', and sometimes downright lucky factors that they argue explain Europe's rise. These revisionist or 'decentred' historical perspectives have offered a significant challenge to traditional, Eurocentric historical narratives. We share with these perspectives a concern with the intersocietal conditions and determinations shaping Europe's developmental trajectory to global dominance. As our argument has so far shown, the revisionists are correct in arguing that there was nothing endogenous about Europe's cultural, socio-economic and political development that necessarily led it on the path to global pre-eminence.

We nonetheless take issue with and challenge the revisionists' predominately conjunctural mode of analysis in explaining Europe's late breakthrough, along with their tendency to deny substantive developmental differences between 'West' and 'East' (as well as within Europe itself). In this chapter, we begin by demonstrating the myriad theoretical and methodological difficulties the revisionist historiography runs into when explaining the 'rise of the West'. We then provide an alternative structural and conjunctural explanation by drawing on uneven and combined development. First, however, it is important to note how much of the debate concerning the 'rise of the West' has centred on explaining why it was Europe, and particularly Britain, that industrialised first, and why other non-European states did not follow its lead. While this is certainly a significant part of the puzzle, it nonetheless fails to engage with the earlier history of European colonialism, which was in fact a *key precondition* to Europe's later rise to global pre-eminence. For it was this earlier period of British colonialism that really laid the foundations for its subsequent global primacy, with India in particular providing the material inputs for Britain's industrialisation. The capturing of India also afforded the British Empire crucial strategic advantages.

In addition to occupying a territorialised dominion in the very heart of Asia, Britain obtained a substantial and relatively cheap military force, which it could then use to open up other markets throughout the world.

Therefore, if there is a single conjunctural factor or moment explaining Britain's – and later Europe's – rise to global supremacy, it was Britain's colonisation of India. Before examining this world-historical event in the third section of this chapter, we must first understand why and how Britain was capable of militarily conquering the Mughal Empire in India. We do so in the second section, where we assess one significant structural factor evoked in the neo-Weberian literature on the 'rise' of Europe over the *longue durée*: the unusually competitive and war-prone character of the European feudal states system. But before doing so, we first turn to critically examining the key claims of the revisionist historiography.

Rethinking the 'Rise of the West': Advances and Impasses in the Revisionist Challenge

Points of Agreement: European 'Backwardness' and the Role of the Colonies

Before examining our differences with the revisionist histories of the 'rise of the West', we must first point out our areas of agreement. For when explaining the 'rise of the West' revisionists emphasise a key factor that we too have been highlighting throughout this book: the 'privilege of backwardness' afforded to later-developing European societies and the concomitant 'penalties of progressiveness' eventually encountered by the more advanced tributary empires in Asia. For Andre Gunder Frank, the sorts of commercial expansion experienced from 1400 onwards were initially more keenly felt by Asian powers than other regions, as exemplified by the tributary Ottoman formation (see also Chapter 4). At a certain point, however, these advantages of progressiveness turned into strategic liabilities and 'a growing absolute and relative disadvantage for one Asian region after another in the late eighteenth century'. The very preconditions for growth in Asia led to crisis, 'as growing population and income, and also their economic and social polarization, exerted pressure on resources; constrained effective demand at the bottom, and increased the availability of cheap labor in Asia more than elsewhere in the world'. Less developed societies – Europe (and later North America) – subsequently reaped a 'privilege of backwardness', taking advantage of these crisis conditions in the 19th and 20th centuries, developmentally catching up and overtaking Asia in the international system. This leads Gunder Frank to conclude that:

between 1400 and at least 1700 as well as earlier, there was nothing 'exceptional' about Europe, unless it was Europe's exceptionally marginal, far-off peninsular position on the map and its correspondingly minor role in the world economy. That may have afforded it some 'advantage of backwardness'.[7]

In this sense, the qualitative unevenness of sociohistorical development, exhibited by the asynchronic simultaneity of an interactive multiplicity of different societies, afforded latecomers particular advantages in their development. This was neither an automatic nor a predestined process, but one where both conjunctural and structural factors (specifically, particular constellations of geopolitical relations) and the role of agency were key. It is precisely this 'privilege of backwardness' afforded to European societies that provides one of the clues to how 'the West' ascended to global supremacy over the *longue durée*. However, this factor alone is surely not enough for an explanation of its rise, as the opportunities opened up to later-developing states to adopt the most cutting-edge technologies, organisational forms and state practices from leading states in no way explain how and why they adopted such 'foreign' materials, nor to what uses they were put.

Another factor often identified in the revisionist literature is the colonies, and particularly the American 'discoveries'. Again, to quote Frank:

> So how did the West rise? The answer, literally in a word, is that the Europeans bought themselves a seat, and then even a whole railway car, on the Asian train … how so? … The most important answer is that Europeans obtained the money from the gold and silver mines they found in the Americas.[8]

Putting aside the Smithian trappings of Frank's analysis, it was not so much the rise of bullion flows from the New World in itself that was particularly significant, but the *differential uses* to which they were put. And these different uses of bullion were, in the first instance, influenced by the differential forms of developments already taking place across Europe. Hence, those countries where protocapitalist relations were emerging or had already emerged – Holland and England – made much more productive use of the bullion than did Spain, which was set on a course of empire-expanding geopolitical accumulation congruent with its feudal relations of production (see Chapter 5).

Late and Lucky: Contingences, the Eurasian Homogeneity Thesis, and the Great Divergence

So on these two critical points – the 'privileges of backwardness' and the role of the New World discoveries in explaining the 'rise of the West' – we are in agreement with the revisionists. However, we disagree with the revisionist account insofar as it denies substantive socio-economic and political differences between the 'West' and 'East', as well as in Europe itself prior to the 'rise of the West'. For example, Jack Goldstone argues that the 'conditions in Europe' were no 'different from those in the advanced regions of Asia until ... c. 1800', and that the divergence between the two was the result of 'chance events' rather than 'long standing prior differences'.[9] He suggests, more radically still, that 'the major states of Europe, China, India, and the Ottoman Empire were all experiencing a similar course of advanced organic development'.[10] Similarly, Jack Goody cautions 'against drawing too sharp a contrast between East and West in those features of social organization that could relate to the onset of capitalism, modernization and industrialization'. For, as Goody further notes, 'economically the distinct qualitative difference between East and West came only with industrialization'.[11] Kenneth Pomeranz too writes of the 'variety of early modern core regions' with 'roughly comparable levels and trends of development in their everyday economies'.[12]

In attempting to downplay Eurocentric claims regarding the uniqueness of the European experience, revisionist scholars wash away important differences between the European and non-Western social structures in explaining the advent of capitalism and modernity. As laudable as such attempts are in seeking to displace narratives of European exceptionalism, the methodological and theoretical drawbacks are immense, to say nothing of the empirical difficulties of sustaining such arguments.[13] Ontologically flattening the myriad social structures making up the early modern world makes it very difficult – if not impossible – to explain the striking divergences in their developmental trajectories. As Joseph Bryant puts it, 'The conundrum is inescapable: *a world flattened of determinant social differences makes the local emergence of any historical novelty structurally inexplicable, and restricts explanatory options to conjectures aleatory or incidental*'.[14]

The tendency to deny the forms and sources of differential patterns of development between 'East' and 'West' also leads the revisionists to ignore and often blur the distinctions between industrial and merchant capital, resulting in a precarious engagement with the emergence of capitalism as a historical mode of production.[15] Holding to a neo-Smithian interpretation of capitalism as reducible to 'the market' or levels of commercialisation, such approaches fall into a somewhat different, though no less problematic 'tempocentric ahistoricism' that John M. Hobson criticises realist International Relations theory for – a world where the market 'economy' of the Sung era of the 11th and 12th centuries becomes indistinguishable from that of modern industrial capitalism.[16] Here again we see the significance of differentiating between 'antediluvian' capital and capitalism as a mode of production, as elaborated in Chapter 7: for conflating commerce and markets with capitalism results in a transhistorical extension, and thus a naturalisation of capitalism's existence.

None of this is to argue for a reinstatement of the kind of essentialist understanding of the European experience as somehow 'exceptional', marking it off from 'the rest'. Rather, we call for a recognition of how the *interactively generated* socio-economic and political differences between Europe and other societies played a part in the former's eventual rise to global pre-eminence. For, as noted in Chapter 4 and further examined below, the very 'backwardness' of the European feudal economies – in particular the decentralised and conflictually fragmented nature of their corresponding political structures – facilitated the propitious conditions from which capitalist social relations could emerge. And crucially, this was structurally conditioned by feudal Europe's near-constant interaction with the more 'advanced' tributary Ottoman formation, which persistently acted as a 'whip of external necessity' on European development. This Ottoman whip ultimately offered the structural geopolitical space from which both the Netherlands and England could emerge and consolidate themselves as capitalist states (see Chapters 4 and 6). Here again we see how the asynchronic simultaneity of a plurality of coexisting societies (unevenness) came to interact in ways that generated further substantive sociological differences (geopolitical and sociological combination), in turn leading to sharp divergences in their developmental trajectories. This is in fact a hallmark of any intersocietal system: they are *generatively differentiating* through the very interactive plurality of their units.

Moreover, once the initial breakthroughs in capitalist relations were made in the Netherlands and England, this led to increasing material disparities – a widening of the competitive gulf – between these societies and others. Bryant is thus indeed correct when writing that the:

> protracted and forcible dominion of the West over the Rest ... cannot logically be accounted for on the basis of fundamental similarities between conqueror and conquered, oppressor and oppressed, but must, in the very nature of so inequitable an outcome, register the relational consequences of differences and disparities – political, military, economic, technological, cultural, ecological – as these played out in a coercive contest for land, resources, mastery.[17]

It is precisely through the framework of uneven and combined development that we may seek to comprehend these 'relational consequences of differences and disparities'. For while unevenness incorporates difference into its very premise, 'it involves a conception of difference that is not neutral with respect to the power, and hence the inequality, of its subjects of difference'.[18] The substantive sociopolitical and economic differences emerging between Northwestern Europe and other societies in the early modern epoch also signified differences in material power capabilities which would come to prove crucial in the former's subsequent rise to global domination.

Without recourse to some form of structural explanation of these diverging paths of development over the *longue durée*, the revisionists are left to account for the 'rise of the West' in terms of pure contingencies and world-historical accidents. In the words of Hobson, 'In one sense the rise of the West could indeed be explained almost wholly through contingency'.[19] Similarly, Goldstone describes the conjunctural factors leading to Britain's transformation into a modern, industrialised state as the 'most freakish of accidents'.[20] For Pomeranz, the contingent combination of coal and colonies provided Europe with the necessary resources to launch itself into self-sustaining economic growth, escaping the labour-intensive path of development.[21] Without any substantive conception of interactive, differentiated sociopolitical multiplicity, revisionist accounts can only provide an 'episodic and atomistic view of social change, wherein determinant efficacy is vested not with ongoing trajectories and systemic institutional configurations, but with the autonomous play of variables and the re-routings occasioned by extraneous contingencies'.[22]

This is then a historical sociological approach that erases the 'historical' and 'sociological' from analyses, as sociohistorical developments are conceived in radically discontinuous terms and sharp breaks in which antecedent conditions from which developments usually enfold are entirely displaced. This is not to deny that contingent or fortuitous factors may have aided the process of 'catch-up' and 'overtake' development that occurred in Northwestern Europe during particular conjunctures. Nonetheless, something much deeper – more structural – was also clearly at work in the process, as we examine below.

While marking some important advances over conventional explanations of the 'rise of the West', conceived in wholly endogenous terms of causal factors at play within Europe, the revisionist challenge nonetheless fails in offering a viable alternative. It remains beset by the problems of analytical indeterminacies, empirical shortcomings, and a reliance on a purely conjunctural mode of explanation that forgoes a theorisation of the sociohistorical processes at work for the play of free-floating contingencies. In the absence of any such alternative theorisation, the revisionist approach is unable to fully overturn or dislodge the prevailing 'rise of the West' paradigm. As Bryant concludes: '[w]e need neither a new sociology nor a new history; all that is required is a fully integrative and encompassing historical sociology'.[23] As we hope to demonstrate, this is exactly what the theory of uneven and combined development can provide: a more integrative and encompassing *international* historical sociology.

Structure and Conjuncture in the 'Rise of the West'

The Geopolitical Competition Model and Its Limits

Such an international historical sociology is precisely what neo-Weberians have claimed to offer in their explanations of the genesis of the modern state system and the 'rise of the West'.[24] The basic premise of the neo-Weberian model is that geopolitical competition was the fundamental determination driving processes of state formation and their variations where in the European context it engendered the modern system of territorialised sovereign states. As Mann puts it, '[t]he growth of the modern state, as measured by finances, is explained primarily not in domestic terms but in terms of geopolitical relations of violence'.[25] In some accounts, these systemic pressures of contending European states are also conceived as a fundamental determinant in the rise of capitalism.[26] Benno Teschke schematically explicates the causal sequence at work here: 'international systemic competition → war → cost increases → increased resource extraction → new modes of taxation and fiscality → military-technological innovations → state monopolization of the means of violence → state centralization and rationalization'.[27] The eventual upshot of this causal sequence was the emergence of a more proficient system of territorialised sovereign states which gave Europeans a decisive comparative advantage in the *means of violence* over the rest of the world, laying the foundations for their subsequent rise to global dominance.

However, there are two key shortcomings of the geopolitical competition model as it specifically relates to explaining the 'rise of the West'. The first regards the implicit syllogism underlying the model's causal sequencing: that is, 'political multiplicity – anarchy – competition'. In other words, the significant socio-economic and political effects that the neo-Weberians derive from the 'whip' of geopolitical competition in spawning technological and organisational innovations in European state-building practices takes for granted precisely what needs to be explained: why was the European states system so competitive and war-prone?

Indeed, it is not at all clear why and how political multiplicity itself generates a condition of competitive anarchy, or that it can say anything meaningful about the frequency or changing forms of geopolitical competition and their effects.[28] To move from political multiplicity to competition requires the dubious realist assumption that societies necessarily threaten each other.[29] Yet the syllogism 'political multiplicity – anarchy – competition' only works with the addition of a further intermediary variable: 'existential threat'. This is the surely the insight, albeit divorced from a political economy of interstate competition, provided by social constructivists and the Copenhagen School.[30] Hence, neo-Weberians smuggle in the highly problematic (neo-)realist assumption that any anarchic system of multiple polities will automatically induce geopolitical competition, rivalry and war.[31] Yet 'the mere geographical contiguity of polities cannot in itself explain why late medieval and early modern inter-state relations were bellicose', writes Teschke, 'unless we assume the anthropologically questionable idea of man as a natural power-maximizer or a psychologizing rational-choice model, where risk minimization creates an inherent security dilemma'.[32]

Moreover, in emphasising the undifferentiated effects of military rivalry on European state formation processes, there is a partial convergence between neo-Weberians and neorealists over the role of geopolitical competition as a kind of Darwinian selection mechanism sorting the weak from the strong. According to this approach, the competitive logic of the states system will, by its very nature, reduce the variety of states. Certain kinds of state will (often forcefully) be proven unviable. The military and political rivalries inherent to the Europe states system in the late Medieval and early modern period led to what Charles Tilly calls 'a ruthless competition, in which most contenders lost'.[33] It is in this sense that Kenneth Waltz speaks of geopolitical competition producing 'a tendency towards the sameness of the competitors'.[34] For inscribed in the very logic of the states system is the tendency for political units to become more homogeneous: unfit forms of state are eliminated, while those remaining become more like each other through the process of competition. This 'isomorphic logic of geopolitical survival'[35] is largely accepted by the neo-Weberians.[36] In this respect, the origins of the modern states system, and thus the 'rise of the West', is very much a 'flat' story of how the world became populated with formally equal sovereign states.

The upshot of all this is that the neo-Weberians incorporate a realist conception of 'the international', reproducing the same reified, ahistorical understanding of geopolitical relations as a suprasocial entity detached from any conception of historical social structures. This has in fact been a persistent criticism of the historical sociological literature: that 'the international' remains 'powerfully acknowledged but analytically unpenetrated', leading to the continual charges of 'attaching an essentialized, Realist conception of the international onto historical sociology'.[37] For the neo-Weberian model, the problem is particularly debilitating, as the central factor they posit (geopolitical competition) in accounting for Europe's global ascendency is simply assumed but not explained. Moreover, the different European states' responses to the universal problem of war facing them in the late Medieval and early modern epochs were strikingly different. As Teschke notes:

> different states' responses to military pressures cannot be deduced from geopolitical factors, but have to be explained with reference to specific domestic class constellations and the timing of intensified military exposure. As a rule, the pure logic of international rivalry not only fails to cover the differential development of non-monarchical state forms, it is equally unable to account for developmental variations in the dominant Western monarchies, France, Spain and England.[38]

What we need, in other words, is a theory that organically embraces both sociological and geopolitical factors in a unified conception of sociohistorical development. And again, this is what the theory of uneven and combined development offers, as the historically specific sources, dynamics and scales of unevenness and combination must be continually related back to their foundations in historically distinct social structures. So what then explains the particularly war-prone nature of the European states system, and were its effects beneficial to processes of state modernisation, particularly by affording certain European states a comparative advantage in the means of violence?

Feudalism, Merchants, and the European States System in the Transition to Capitalism

The answer lies in Europe's feudal relations of production. At first sight, this answer might seem like an illicit return to the kind of Eurocentric theorising we have been at pains to avoid. Yet, when widening the analysis beyond Europe, it is important to recognise that while feudal social relations and the geopolitical system emerging with them were unique to Europe, their technological, military and ideological components all bore a distinctly *intersocietal origin*. According to Perry Anderson, the rise of feudalism in Europe was a consequence of the 'catastrophic collision of two dissolving anterior [ancient and primitive] modes of production': namely, the 'decomposing slave mode of production on whose foundations the whole enormous edifice of the Roman Empire had once been constructed, and the distended and deformed primitive modes of production of the Germanic invaders which survived in their new homelands' after the conquests.[39] The developmental trajectory of Europe's Germanic forest 'tribes' thereby converged with the remnants of the ancient Roman Empire, producing an entirely novel, synthesised form of sedentary society hitherto unknown in human history – feudalism. Moreover, the *recombination* of the 'disintegrated elements' of these two anterior modes of production – the 'Romano-Germanic synthesis'[40] – into feudalism proper was 'itself a product of the constant and eventually unbearable pressure of the nomadic Huns on the Germanic world of the Teutonic tribes'.[41]

Hence, the genesis of feudalism in Europe was determined by the systemic syncretism of nomadic-sedentary interactions emanating from within and outside of Europe. We also saw in Chapter 3 how the nomadic-sedentary inter-actions generated by the Mongol Empire's expansion into Europe, and the accompanying spread of the Black Death, fundamentally impinged upon and (re)directed the trajectory and nature of European development over the late Medieval period. However, the 'extra-European', intersocietal dimensions of feudalism's development reached far beyond these initial nomadic-sedentary interactions. For not only was the feudal system the result of new technologies (notably, the stirrup) diffusing from Asia to Europe, but the ideological and normative underpinnings of the system (Christendom) were in constant interac-tion with and continually evolving in response to the geopolitical and ideological 'Islamic threat' emanating from the Ottomans. As Hobson notes, 'Christendom

... was imagined and invented as Catholic Christian in contradistinction to the Islamic Middle East'.[42] What is more, it was only through the combination of the Euro-Ottoman conflict and the Euro-Amerindian colonial encounter that Christendom was destroyed as a defining normative order, clearing the way for an emergent quasi-secular identity of 'Europe' (see Chapters 4 and 5). As a result, it would be fundamentally mistaken to conceive of feudalism and its crisis as solely European developments.[43] But we must now return to the original question we had set out to address: how did feudalism generate such a competitive and war-prone geopolitical system?

In the absence of the kind of unprecedented economic dynamism afforded by capitalist social relations, war was an expedient mode of expanding surpluses available to the ruling classes under feudalism.[44] As explained in Chapter 6, feudal productive relations in Europe gave few incentives to either peasant or lord to *continuously* and *systematically* introduce more productive technological methods, particularly as peasants had direct access to their means of production and subsistence.[45] Consequently the lordly interest lay in extracting more surplus by directly coercive means. This could be done by pushing the peasants to the limit of their subsistence or by seizing the demesnes of other lords. The latter course resulted in a process of geopolitical accumulation amongst the lords themselves – a war-driven process of state formation.[46] This condition meant that the aristocratic ruling class required the political, ideological and military means to exploit the peasantry and extract a surplus for the purpose of lordly consumption.[47] However, unlike in the Ottoman Empire, these means were not controlled by – or concentrated in – a centralised and unified state, but were instead dispersed across the nobility.[48] This dispersion of coercive capabilities meant that political authority in Europe was fragmented, parcellised and therefore also highly competitive, with heightened intra-lordly struggles taking place over territories both within and outside of feudal 'states'.[49] In short, military competition and war were more pronounced in Europe than they were in the tributary societies such as the Ottoman, Mughal and Chinese empires.

Consequently, one of the primary reasons that geopolitical conflict and war in this period was so persistent was not simply due to the structure of feudalism, but also because the process of ruling class reproduction was itself under serious threat. Not only had the feudal system virtually exhausted all possibilities for further internal expansion, but this also precipitated a sharp fall in seigniorial revenues, which was further exacerbated by the plague-induced demographic crisis spread from the Mongol expansion into Europe, leading to a dramatic rise in peasant revolts and processes of class struggle more generally.[50] Moreover, this perilous situation was continually exacerbated and 'overdetermined' by the persistent geopolitical-ideological threat emanating from the Ottoman Empire (see Chapter 4). Under such conditions, a near-continuous state of war – including both intra-ruling class struggles and the incessant efforts to crush peasant rebellions – was a sociological 'necessity'. And since European states 'did not have the resources of an agrarian empire in cheap manpower' they were therefore unable 'to substitute "quantity for quality"'.[51] By the early modern period, this led to an unprecedented dynamism in the military sector in European states, which 'could maintain productivity growth for centuries, a feat virtually unknown elsewhere in pre-industrial economies'.[52]

The lords left standing at the end of the process of geopolitical accumulation formed the basis for the absolutist state. Representing a *redeployed and recharged apparatus of feudal domination*,[53] the absolutism of early modern Europe remained driven by the systemic imperatives of geopolitical accumulation. The uneven and combined development of feudal-absolutist Europe was rooted in this territorially expansionist dynamic of geopolitical accumulation. The resultant endemic state of warfare entailed a deep systemic pressure ('whip of external necessity') for European states to continually innovate upon their means of violence. Over time, this had the unintended effect of generating military and armament industries pioneering distinctly capitalist methods and relations of production (Chapter 1).[54]

The dynamic of geopolitical accumulation in Europe is, however, not enough to explain the forces at work behind states' technological and organisational innovations – particularly in the military sphere – which are so heavily emphasised by the neo-Weberians. For the effects of warfare were extremely uneven within Europe itself, and as examined in Chapter 4, the tributary Ottoman Empire was also driven by the imperatives of geopolitical accumulation. However, as we have argued, the systemic demands of the tributary mode drove the Ottomans towards *territorial expansion* based on an exceptionally robust agro-military complex, which effectively curtailed merchant autonomy and political influence. By contrast, in Mughal India, state managers exhibited an attitude of 'indifferent neutrality' towards merchants' maritime activities.[55] There was very little oppression of merchant activities in India, but neither was there much support.

In Europe, however, states were explicitly focused on bringing under direct conquest and political control lucrative *overseas territories* for specifically commercial purposes. The reason was the relative 'backwardness' of European feudal rules of reproduction, which were dependent on the wealth drawn from merchants and financiers either to fund geopolitical accumulation (in the case of Habsburg Spain and Austria) or for the direct reproduction of the ruling class itself (as with city-states such as Genoa and Venice).[56] A byproduct of European feudal war-making was therefore an attendant rise in the political autonomy, power and influence of merchants, with increasing degrees of representation in the decision-making structures of states.[57] Consequently, feudal-cum-absolutist states were particularly sensitive to – or at the behest of – merchant interests, wherein state resources, especially military, were deployed in order to obtain (and maintain) commercial advantage.[58]

The key difference between the functioning and sociopolitical position of merchants in the feudal-absolutist – and later capitalist – states in Europe, and those within the tributary societies such as the Ottoman Empire, Mughal India and Imperial China, was therefore the *structural dependence* of the former states on merchants for war-financing and social reproduction, which gave the merchants a relatively strong position of social and juridical autonomy. In Europe, governments often provided merchants with considerable resources and state backing. This was most dramatically exemplified in the case of the rising capitalist Dutch Republic, where the VOC represented the institutional fusion of political and mercantile interests,[59] as the often-quoted 1614 letter of VOC Governor-General Jan Pieterszoon Coen to his directors well demonstrates:

> You gentlemen ought to know from experience that trade in Asia should be conducted and maintained under the protection and with the aid of your own weapons, and that those weapons must be wielded with the profits gained by the trade. So trade cannot be maintained without war, nor war without trade.[60]

The overseas orientation of imperial expansionism in the pursuit of commercial advantage among the European states in turn led to a number of significant military innovations, particularly in the naval field. Over time, this would provide them with a decisive competitive edge in the means of naval violence in the Indian Ocean over the primarily land-based tributary empires in the 'East', such as the Mughals and the Ottomans. We may therefore partly agree with Ronald Findlay's assessment that 'it was the long history of naval rivalry in the North Sea and the Atlantic that developed the sailing ship as a floating gun platform, a combination of the two technologies' that later enabled the Portuguese, Dutch, and British to dominate the Indian Ocean and South Pacific.[61] It was these latter two burgeoning Dutch and British merchant *capitalist* empires that would come to attain a critical military advantage on the seas. 'Mediterranean naval techniques and conceptions' – where the Ottomans were dominant – would prove ineffective in competing with the new, Atlantic-based sea powers of Holland and England. 'The consequent transfer of supremacy at sea to northwestern Europe', William H. McNeil w rites:

> had much to do with the general decline of the Mediterranean lands that became manifest in the first decades of the seventeenth century. In effect, the roar of Dutch and English naval guns closed off the last avenue of escape from the economic and ecological impasse confronting the Mediterranean populations.[62]

There was therefore something to Walter Raleigh's often-cited maxim that '[w]hoever commands the sea commands the trade; whoever commands the trade of the world commands the riches of the world and consequently the world itself'.[63]

A further difference between Europe and the tributary empires of Asia was the particular nature of the external enemies facing them, which also dictated that very different military strategies and technologies be developed and used. Hence, in contrast to Hobson's essentialist claims that China's 'inward turn' and abdication of overseas imperialism was a consequence of its 'defensive identity',[64] it seems more likely that the nomadic threat was key to Chinese imperial managers' focus on territorial consolidation. Given this nomadic threat from the northern land frontier, Mann writes:

> China concentrated its resources and its trade there, and not in the sea lanes. Its military posture on its northern frontier was defensive, geared to containing mobile, dispersed enemy forces. It had less incentive than Europeans to intensify aggressive fire-power against concentrated forces, since it did not face them. But this meant that in the long run the Chinese empire would disintegrate in face of the fire-power of European ships and marine.[65]

Unevenness Combined: North–South Interactions in the 'Rise of the West'

These points go some way in turning on its head the typical Eurocentric conceptions of the more 'backward' and 'stagnant' imperial empires of Asia, since it was the less developed nature of European feudal societies – their very reproductive weaknesses – that made them more susceptible to potential capitalist breakthroughs.[66] However, in order to fully subvert Eurocentric accounts of the 'rise of the West', we must move beyond a simple comparative historical sociological analysis of the differences between the feudal and tributary systems, and examine how their interactive developmental dynamics produced the structural and conjunctural conditions enabling European societies' transition to capitalism, and thus their eventual global ascendency. And in so doing, we see again the operation of uneven development, as demonstrated by the 'privilege of backwardness' granted to feudal Europe by the 'penalty of progressiveness' characterising the tributary empires of Asia. In the geopolitical interactions between feudal and tributary societies, it was the latter that presented the 'whip of external necessity' to the former.

In turn, the various state-backed forms of commercial expansion noted above were dependent on the geopolitical conditions generated by Europe's constant interaction with non-European societies. In Chapter 3, we saw how the *Pax Mongolica* lowered commercial protection and transaction costs along

Asian overland trade routes, providing European merchants with an opening to take over the pre-existing trade and exchange links of the 'world system'. In Chapter 4, we then demonstrated how the capitulations given to particular European states by the Ottomans and the concomitant economic blockade they imposed upon Europe resulted in a structural shift away from the geopolitical and commercial centrality of Mediterranean towards the Atlantic. Moreover, the Ottoman 'buffer' provided the propitious geopolitical conditions ('isolation') enabling the modern state-building activities and processes of primitive accumulation in England over the Long 16th Century.

In Chapter 5, we explicated the hugely significant effects of the Atlantic 'discoveries' on trade and production in Europe, and the emergent forms of territorial sovereignty created in the Americas which in turn fed back into the geopolitical structure of Europe. These territorial sovereign states were subsequently taken over and reconstituted by the capitalist revolutions that stretched from the 16th to the 18th centuries, as we saw in Chapter 6. Finally, through the colonial activities of merchant companies, we demonstrated in Chapters 5 and 7 how a globally dispersed mass of labour-power was subsumed under the reproductive requirements of capital. In all these ways, we have seen how Europe's 'unique' developmental trajectory out of feudalism and into capitalism, leading to its subsequent rise to global pre-eminence, was fundamentally rooted in and conditioned by extra-European structural determinations and agents. It was then the combination of these multiple spatiotemporal vectors of uneven development that explains the so-called European 'miracle'.

Moreover, why some states and not others were able to make the kind of socio-economic and institutional innovations leading to a condition of sustained, self-reinforcing military and productive dynamic must be explained by the particular geopolitical conditions facing such states. For some states, notably Imperial Spain, the (geo)political costs of quickly raising taxes and centralising the fiscal system were perhaps too high, as the Habsburg monarchy was simultaneously and continually engaged in a two-front struggle against the more advanced tributary Ottoman Empire and the breakaway Dutch Republic. And this Habsburg–Ottoman struggle in turn meant that other states, specifically the Dutch and English, were afforded the structural geopolitical space from which they could pursue rapid processes of developmental catch-up and overtaking. In these ways, the overall conditions of uneven and combined development emanating from both *within* and *without* Europe created the propitious geosocial environment in which specific countries could emerge and consolidate themselves as capitalist states: territorialised sovereign centres of capital accumulation – a particular form of sovereign territoriality that had first been forged and proven utile in the Atlantic colonial theatre before radiating back to the European imperial metropole (see Chapters 3 to 6).

As we have seen, the methods and means of geosocial reproduction for

Europe and the tributary empires were strikingly different, producing divergent forms and trajectories of geopolitical accumulation which, over the course of Europe's development in the early modern period, came to interact and fuse with the emerging logic of capital accumulation accompanying those states making the transition to capitalism (notably the Netherlands, England and later France). These differential geosocial conditions and rules of reproduction in Europe, and those in the Asia, in turn required varied types of military capabilities. At the same time, the external threat environments prevailing in the two regions were characterised by significant differences lending themselves to different systemic incentives and pressures for developing certain military techniques and technologies over others.

In these ways, both ostensibly 'internal' (sociological) and 'external' (geopolitical) structural factors and conditions interacted and entwined in setting certain European states on the path to acquire what would become a decisive comparative advantage in the means of violence, particularly once these means were buttressed by and harnessed to dynamically capitalist social structures. This, we argue, is what largely explains Europe's eventual ascendency to global preeminence. For, as Geoffrey Parker notes, while the advent of industrialisation 'helps to explain how the Europeans extended their control over the total land area of the globe from 35 percent in 1800 to 84 percent in 1914, it cannot explain how they managed to acquire that initial 35 percent'.[67] What is more, that initial 35 per cent was in fact crucial for conquering much of the other 84 per cent, as exemplified by the Indian case examined below. We may therefore conclude with Philip T. Hoffman that:

> one area in which western Europe possessed an undeniable comparative advantage well before 1800 seems to have been overlooked – namely, violence. The states of western Europe were simply better at making and using artillery, firearms, fortifications, and armed ships than other advanced parts of the world and they had developed the fiscal and organizational systems that armies and navies equipped with this technology required. The Europeans had this advantage long before 1800. By then, they had conquered some 35 per cent of the globe, and they controlled lucrative trade routes as far away as Asia.[68]

To put all of this in more theoretical terms, we can see how 'unevenness', in terms of both the differential development between a feudal-cum-capitalist 'West' and tributary 'East' and the differential forms of their geopolitical systems, and 'combination', operating at the level of geopolitical interactions and competition facilitating military and organisational innovations, were both crucial explanatory factors in the 'rise of the West'. While neo-Weberians are correct to single out geopolitical competition as significant, their inability to root this factor in a strong historical conception of social structures – and thus examine the differential forms and effects that military competition had – leaves them in the well-worn realist cul-de-sac of reification and unit homogenisation. By contrast, the theory of uneven and combined development, continually rooted in a mode of production-centred framework, solves both these problems: it offers a *theoretical explanation* of geopolitical competition and its effects that remains sensitive to substantive differences in historical social structures (in this instance, between the feudal and tributary modes of production), while also incorporating a distinctly geopolitical causal component into its very conception of development thereby eliding any form of reification. But to fully understand how 'the West' would come to rule we must look at the causes of the Mughal Empire's collapse and its colonisation by the British.

The Conjunctural Moment of 'Overtaking': Britain's Colonisation of India

The Significance of India's Colonisation to the 'Rise of the West'

The place of Britain's colonisation of India in the mid-18th century has been generally underappreciated in debates surrounding the 'rise of the West'.[69] As noted, these debates have largely centred around the origins of industrial-isation in Europe, and in particular on the question of why Britain was first to industrialise. Conceived as such, the earlier history of British colonisation is relegated to a secondary status in explaining the 'rise of the West', if it is examined at all. Yet not only was Mughal India the first of the tributary empires in the Asia to fall at the hands of the Europeans, it also arguably provided the greatest material and strategic benefits of all the colonised states. For not only did India offer Britain the material inputs (notably, textiles and cotton) and capital crucial to the start of its industrialisation drive but, after its colo-nisation, it provided the Empire with a relatively cheap and sizeable military force that assisted the British in forcibly opening other markets around the world.

Hence even the more restrictive question of the causes of Britain's industrial-isation have been both *temporally* and *spatially* misplaced within the debates on the 'rise of the West'. They are temporally misplaced in the sense that in order to explain Britain's industrial ascent we must first look at the preceding era of British colonialism in both the Atlantic and India, and this in turn means that our spatial optic must be substantially widened to include an analysis of these extra-European regions' contributions to Britain's subsequent industrialisation. As we saw in Chapter 5, the Atlantic colonies and India provided Britain with the raw materials, mass consumption commodities, capital and external markets crucial to its industrial success. Moreover, the Indian economy was critical to the 'formation and consolidation of a UK-centred system of accumulation', particularly through India's role in providing a continual balance-of-payments surplus for the Empire.[70] It was the huge annual surpluses from the Empire's transactions with India (and through it, China) that allowed Britain to gain 'mastery of world finance' and sustain substantial deficits with the United States, Germany and its white Dominion states.[71]

Since the beginning of the 19th century, the East India Company had relied on opium exports from Bengal to Canton to finance the growing deficits generated by its expensive military operations on the subcontinent and elsewhere. As Mike Davis explains, '[b]y forcibly enlarging the Chinese demand for the narcotic and, thus, the taxes collected on its export, the Opium Wars (1839–42, 1856–8) and the punitive Treaty of Tianjin (1858) revolutionized the revenue base of British India'. The extraordinary trade between India and China – Indian exports made up 35 per cent of Chinese imports, and Chinese exports made up 1 per cent of Indian imports – that Britain orchestrated also subsidised the import of US cottons, which fuelled the industrial revolution in Lancashire. Hence, 'England's systematic exploitation of India depended in large part upon India's commercial exploitation of China'.[72]

In 1750, India produced approximately 25 per cent of the world's manufacturing output. By 1800 India's share had already dropped to less than a fifth, by 1860 to less than a tenth, and by 1880 to under 3 per cent.[73] It is therefore no stretch of the imagination to claim that Britain's industrial ascent was to a large degree predicated on India's forced deindustrialisation.[74] And if so, it is then no mere coincidence that Britain's colonisation of India preceded the start of Britain's industrialisation by some 20 years.

The contribution of the British Indian army to Britain's overall strategic position has also been largely overlooked in the debates on the 'rise of the West'. The British Indian army numbered approximately 160,000 in 1900 and later reached a strength of nearly 2 million persons during the Second World War, making a substantial contribution to Britain's war efforts of the period. Consequently, as Tarak Barkawi notes, 'the British Indian army was not a small part of Britain's overall military power; the "Indian army was the leading British strategic reserve on land"'.[75] Moreover, according to David Washbrook, the British Indian army was of great significance not only to the 'rise of the West', but for the development of capitalism as a global system.[76] The Indian contingent not only opened markets for British manufactures, but subordinated a previously dispersed mass of labourers to the machinations of British capital. The:

> Indian army was in a real sense *the major coercive force behind the internationalization of industrial capitalism*. Paradoxically (or not!), the martialization of north Indian society and, in many ways, the 'feudalization' of its agrarian relations, were

direct corollaries of the development of capitalism on a world scale during the nineteenth century.[77]

Similarly, Geoffrey Parker writes of how:

> the military resources of India, once under European control, were to prove decisive for the further rise of the West. For the Europeans now possessed the means to challenge even their most powerful opponents. The Western armies that invaded China in 1839–42, 1859–60, and 1900 all included important Indian contingents. Immediately after the Boxer Rising, even the traffic of Peking was directed by Sikhs. In the words of the distinguished Sinologist Louis Dermigny: 'It was as if the British had subjugated the Indian peninsula simply in order to use its resources against China'.[78]

For these reasons and more, the causes of the decline of the Mughal Empire and its colonisation are central to the story of how the 'West' managed to ascend to a position of global supremacy. Examining these causes is the primary aim of the following section.

The Mughal Empire and the Tributary Mode of Production

Like the Ottoman Empire, Mughal India was characterised by the tributary mode of production.[79] In contrast to feudal Europe, where lords directly intervened into the production process in order to coercively extract rent surpluses from the peasants,[80] the Mughal tributary formation was defined by a state bureaucracy taxing the peasants. Throughout most of the Mughal Empire, the emperor transferred the rights to land revenue and other taxes within particular territorial limits to specific subjects on a temporary basis (usually between three to four years). These areas were called *jāgīrs*, and the assignees, known as *jāgīrdārs*, were predominantly *mansabdārs* – subjects holding ranks (*mansabs*) bestowed to them by the emperor, making them high-ranking state officials. The primary obligation of the *mansabdārs* was the maintenance of standing armies, and particularly cavalry contingents, which the emperor could call upon for the imperial army in times of war.[81] In their assigned *jāgīrs*, it was the *jāgīrdārs* who then collected land revenues and other taxes from the peasantry, who were nominally free, cultivating the land on behalf of the emperor, who was allotted a set share of such revenues. Over the 16th and 17th centuries, approximately half the agricultural product was extracted from the peasantry in the form of this imperial land revenue.[82]

The *jāgīrdārs* were therefore not equivalent to feudal lords exercising direct personal control over cultivators working and living on the lord's lands. Rather, they approximated more of a 'state class', dispersed throughout the empire by a centralised political apparatus to extract surpluses – as tax or outputs – from a peasantry they did not personally control. In such ways, these two different modalities of surplus extraction (feudal and tributary) entailed very distinct dynamics of social (re)production. A key difference between the ruling classes of these two systems was, then, their proximity to the production process – 'the relative separation of the former and the near-total separation of the latter from the production process'. Hence, the tributary state did 'not need to control the economic and social lives of its subjects', but instead simply required 'the funding that enables it to pursue its chosen objectives'.[83]

So, in the feudal mode, the process of exploitation was much more fragmented and decentralised. Lords sought to uphold and extend the military and juridical powers necessary to control the peasants' lives while safeguarding a steady stream of revenue. At the same time, a comparatively weaker state sought to gain access to income and the means of coercion. By contrast, under the tributary mode, the exploiting class's interest centred on expanding its tax base and tax-extracting apparatus, through the use of the state's coercive functions.[84]

The particularly centralised nature of the tributary state, along with its ability to effectively monopolise the means of violence in comparison with the fragmented and parcellised character of feudal political relations, made for a more cohesive and unified ruling class.[85] Nonetheless, intra-ruling class tensions still remained. In particular, the potential for conflict between local state officials, private landowners and the centralised imperial state was a central contradiction of tributary rules of reproduction. Moreover, in the tributary mode, we can discern a tendency for the state's local agents to develop into feudal-like lords with their own landed estates and armed contingents or for wealthy landowners to emerge with significant independent economic and political powers.[86] Both tendencies could ultimately result in the development of feudalistic power relations emerging from the tributary mode's own 'laws of motion'.

In Mughal India, the imperial state sought to counter the former tendency of state officials to transform themselves into feudal-like lords by divorcing the *jāgīrdārs*, as far as possible, from any permanent rights to the land while constantly transferring them to different territorial assignments after short periods of time, usually between three or four years.[87] While this transfer system generally worked in countering any potential for *jāgīrdārs* to develop into feudal lords, in the long term the system tended to subvert agricultural productivity and growth, as examined further below. In the case of the Mughal Empire, then, it appears that the latter tendency of a landed aristocracy emerging with considerable independent economic and political powers was the most problematic for intra-ruling class relations, as demonstrated by the recurring conflicts between the *zamīndārs* (landowners) and imperial authority.

The *zamīndārs* were a distinct class of potentates with varying claims to the shares in the produce of land and/or part of the land revenue. They shared a number of common attributes: particularly, that their rights to the land did not (with some exceptions) originate from imperial grants; command over armed retainers was usually a complement of this right; and they were frequently leaders of a caste group. The key point of potential conflict between the imperial authorities and the *zamīndārs* was, then, the size of the latter's share in the land revenue or surplus produce. 'The struggle between the imperial administration and the *zamīndārs*, breaking out frequently into armed conflict', Irfan Habib writes, 'was thus an important feature of the political situation'.[88]

The most significant of these armed conflicts between the *zamīndārs* and the imperial authorities was the *zamīndār*-led Maratha Revolt of the late 17th century.[89] As a result of the Maratha Revolt, there emerged a distinct class of feudal-like lords, now separate and autonomous from the Mughals, wielding significant economic and political powers over their subjects in occupied lands. 'Unlike the Mughal *jāgīrdārs*', Hiroshi Fukazawa writes, 'the big assignees in the Deccan Muslim kingdoms exercised wide administrative powers in their assigned territories, which tended to become hereditary, unchecked by the central authority'.[90] This was then a case by which certain features characteristic of one mode of production (feudalism) *emerged from* and *combined with* the existing dominant mode of production (tributary). In this sense, the Mughal Empire of the late 17th and early 18th centuries represented a kind of *organic* mode of sociological combination in which two differentiated modes of production coexisted and causally interacted in contradictory and crisis-prone ways.[91]

The importance of the rise of the Marathas challenging the Mughal Empire cannot be overstated, as it 'constituted the greatest single force responsible for the downfall of the Mughal Empire'.[92] In particular, the Mughal wars in the Deccan (1681–1707) against the Marathas were a major drain on imperial institutions and resources, eventually destabilising Mughal rule throughout its territories.[93] As the imperial demand for revenue increased, so too did the exploitative pressures on the peasantry, as the wars drew key resources out of the agricultural economy while leading to a considerable destruction of existing capital.[94] To understand how this translated into widespread peasant unrest and flight, we must first examine the contradictions of the *jāgīr* system in a little more detail.

The Imperial Revenue System and Agricultural Decline in the Mughal Empire

The land revenue system created by the Mughal Empire was unequalled by any of its contemporaries. It far surpassed any of the revenue structures in Europe in both its scale of operation (in the total land area, population and resources controlled) and its organisational sophistication and cohesion (the

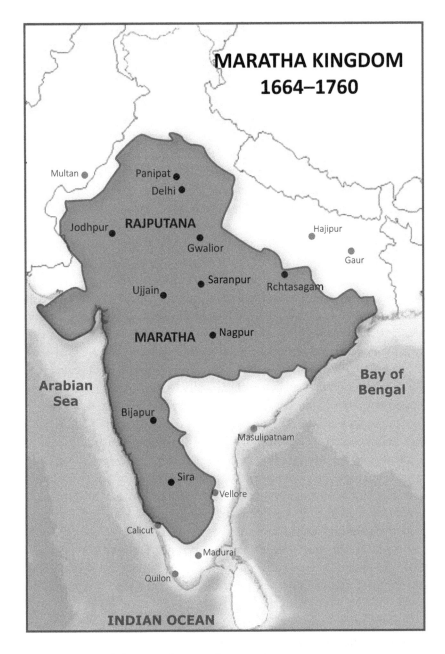

Figure 8.1 Map of the Maratha Kingdom, 1664–1760

use of paid officials and formal administrative mechanisms). In contrast to the French kings of the *ancien régime*, for example, the Mughal imperial authorities did not generally have to resort to private capital, short-term loans and intermediary financiers to fund their war efforts, except in the case of the wars against the Marathas, examined below.[95] Nonetheless, despite its organisational scale and sophistication, the revenue system developed over time a number of problems that came to hinder the overall functioning of the Mughal economy: particularly, the tendency to increasingly over-exploit the peasantry.

As noted, since the time of Akbar (1568), a practice was established in which *jāgīrdārs*, who held no permanent rights to the land, were transferred to new territorial assignments every three to four years. This kept in check any tendency for them to develop into feudal-like lords. However, it also had a number of unintentional negative consequences, increasing over time, for the agrarian economy as a whole. For as the *jāgīrdārs* were being continually transferred to different territorial assignment every few years, their short-term interest was not necessarily in increasing or even maintaining agricultural growth and productivity, but rather in maximising the exploitation of the peasantry in their assigned territorial domain. This subverted the long-term objectives of the imperial authority. As Habib explains:

> The imperial administration, which could contemplate the long-term interests of the empire and ruling class, did, probably, strive to set a limit to the revenue demand .... But there was an element of contradiction between interests of the imperial administration and the individual *jāgīdārs*. A *jāgīdār*, whose assignment was liable to be transferred any moment and who never held the same *jāgīr* for more than three of four years at the most, could have no interest in following a far-sighted policy of agricultural development. On the other hand, his personal interest would sanction any act of oppression that conferred an immediate benefit upon him, even if it ruined the peasantry and so destroyed the revenue-paying capacity of that area for a long time.[96]

Inherent in the Mughal revenue system was therefore a tendency towards the absolute 'maximization of exploitation' to the point of limiting and potentially destabilising the entire agrarian economy.[97] Moreover, as military contingents were maintained by the *mansabdārs* out of the revenues of the *jāgīrs*, the imperial authorities tended to set the revenue demand at a high enough level to secure the greatest amount of military strength for the Empire. However, if the revenue rate was set too high, it would leave peasants without enough subsistence to survive. Consequently, revenue collection could soon fall in absolute terms. Thus, the revenue demand set by the imperial authorities was 'designed ideally to approximate to the surplus produced, leaving the peasant just the barest minimum needed for subsistence'.[98]

Yet, with the costly wars with the Marathas straining imperial revenues in the late 17th and early 18th centuries, increased revenue demands came to press harder still on the lower peasantry. For unlike earlier periods when the Mughal Empire had expanded into wealthy regions, making up the costs of their conquests, the Deccan campaigns were a very different story. There, Mughal military expenditures consistently outpaced revenues and office holders saw their incomes decline. The Mughal state thus sought to step up its 'revenue demands which in turn stirred up resentment in large parts of the empire that, when coupled with religious and political rivalries, manifested itself in the emergence of popular movements such as the Sikhs in the Punjab or the Marathas in Central India'.[99]

State revenue demand had in fact more than doubled between the eras of Akbar (1556–1605) and Aurangzeb (1658–1707).[100] Moreover, as centralised Mughal authority began to crack under the continuing geopolitical pressures from the Marathas, the state increasingly resorted to tax farming, which became ever more widespread in its successor states.[101] This had the effect of raising the effective rent share of the state to 50 per cent or higher, greater than the 40 per cent that the Mughals had previously extracted. 'With revenue assessment geared to 50 per cent or more, in contrast to China's 5 to 6 per cent, the Indian peasant had little incentive to invest labour or capital'.[102] This massive fiscal pressure that the Mughal state brought to bear on the peasantry in turn led to increasing indebtedness in the villages, causing peasant flight and rebellions. 'As oppression increased, the number of absconding peasants grew, cultivation declined and peasants took to arms giving birth to rural uprisings of varying intensity. Consequently the empire fell prey to the wrath of an impoverished peasantry'.[103] Some scholars have located a generalised 'agricultural crisis' manifesting itself throughout the Mughal Empire in the late 17th and early 18th centuries, for which the *jāgīr* system and its associated high taxation, land desertion and peasant unrest, coupled with the increasing costs of war, were primarily to blame.[104] 'The "apparatus of the empire" which was responsible for initiating an endless process of raising revenue demand', writes R. P. Rana, 'was the first to feel the tremor of its diminishing income'. The 'disturbed peasant economy' at the 'root' of the Mughal's 'political crisis' would eventually ruin the Empire.[105]

Indeed, peasant unrest and rebellion were generally increasing over the late 17th and early 18th centuries, politically destabilising many Mughal territories.[106] At the same time, the political fragmentation and warfare accompanying the Marathas Revolt further acted to disrupt India's major internal trade routes, tending to increase transportation costs and insurance rates. As most long-distance transport was by bullock, the scarcity of bullocks resulting from warfare also increased transport costs.[107] In the end, Satish Chandra notes, '[t]he available social surplus [in the Empire] was insufficient to defray the cost of administration, pay for wars of one type or another, and to give the ruling class a standard of living in keeping with its expectations'.[108] Curiously enough, Washbrook has suggested that the very vibrancy and strong economic growth of the Mughal Empire over the 16th and early 17th centuries may well have been a cause of its later troubles, as 'economic growth started to nurture the political ambitions, and the regional and "community" forces, which eventually undermined it'. Here then is another expression of the 'penalties of progressiveness' besetting the Indian economy.[109]

European Trade and Colonial Conquest: Towards 1757

There were, moreover, a number of distinctly international factors further exacerbating the Mughal Empire's economic woes during this period. For over the course of the 17th and early 18th centuries, the world economic and geopolitical environment in which the Mughal Empire was embedded was dramatically transformed, as the Portuguese, Dutch, English and later French made their excursions into the Indian Ocean. First, the Mughal-Maratha Wars (1680–1707) were themselves 'overdetermined' by an array of uneven causal chains generated by a geopolitical environment fundamentally transformed by the entry of the Europeans. Occupying key coastal areas in the commercial shipping lanes of the Indian Ocean, the Marathas experienced extensive geopolitical contacts with Europeans from the 16th century onwards. This was a relation of 'contained warfare', with belligerence and collaboration employed in near-equal measure. On the one hand, the Marathas developed a powerful naval force that was able to repel European ships if and when they so desired.[110] On land, a large and sophisticated network of fortresses formed the backbone of Maratha military might.[111] Both land and sea capabilities were often mobilised in response to European penetration into the region. On the other hand, the Marathas also sought to reap the 'privileges of backwardness' in any areas in which Europeans held a comparative advantage – particularly the use of firearms and modern military strategy.

From the Portuguese and French came the main supplies of firearms – gunpowder, cannonballs and lead were all purchased and entered into use in the Maratha army.[112] Such was the integration of the Euro-Maratha military-commercial complex that the Marathas allowed the French to build a factory at Rajapore in 1679, and 'employed Portuguese agents to purchase artillery from them'.[113] But the integration of Europeans extended beyond exchange in military goods. As early as 1692, the French Governor Martine was providing tactical assistance to the Marathas at the time of their war with the Mughals.[114] A number of European adventurers of Portuguese, French, Dutch and English origin were employed as mercenaries and commanders, responsible for training and organising armies and assisting Maratha chiefs in battles. The expansion of European trained battalions and the purchase of European expertise and weaponry proved costly, incentivising processes of geopolitical accumulation.[115] The Maratha confrontation with the Mughals was arguably a direct – if partial – outcome of the need to finance the hybridisation of Euro-Maratha military operations. This military combination proved remarkably efficient, and up to that point, historically exceptional in challenging the hitherto preponderant Mughal Empire.

Meanwhile, the increasing Dutch and English penetration into Asian markets over the course of the 17th and 18th centuries caused serious disturbances in the Mughal economy, and intensified the financial difficulties of the ruling classes. As the costs of luxury goods consumed by the ruling class increased with their diversion from their traditional markets by the Europeans, this meant that revenue demands had to also be increased. Consequently, the Indian ruling class's 'income previously obtained no longer sufficed. Here was a factor for an attempt at greater agrarian exploitation; and when that failed, or proved counter-productive, for reckless factional activities for individual gain, leading to interminable civil wars'.[116]

The economic difficulties of the Mughal Empire seem to have been quite widespread. K. N. Chaudhuri observes, for example, that 'the 1730s were a bad time for southern India' and that 'the great Anglo-French wars of the mid-eighteenth century further dislocated trade that was already in serious difficulties'.[117] Around the same time, in Jugdia, the most important Bengali cotton-producing region, matters were 'coming to a crisis in the production sphere'. For by the middle of the 18th century there were already 'some signs of deindustrialization' under the impact of strong foreign economic competition and weaker local mercantile organisations.[118]

More generally, Indian merchant groups throughout the Empire suffered from the presence of European traders. 'With the exception of the wealthy, experienced, and tightly organized mercantile houses of Gujerat', J. F. Richards writes, 'most indigenous traders in each exporting region assumed a position subordinate to the servants of the East India companies'.[119] What is more, under the competitive pressures of European trade, the early 18th century witnessed the collapse of one of the Empire's hitherto greatest commercial marines in Gujarat, 'arguably the most important developments in the trade of the Indian Ocean during the period'.[120] Similarly, the substantial commerce of the Coromandel Coast was dramatically hindered by the intrusion of Dutch merchants over the 17th century, which, as Sinnappah Arasaratnam tells us, 'cut deep into the trade that had been traditionally carried out in the region', interrupting the 'the ancient links between Coromandel and Southeast Asia which had been, in many ways, the lifeline of Coromandel's commerce'. As Arasaratnam goes on:

> It was this commercial artery that was punctured violently in the course of the 17th century .... In a series of military and naval actions, these ports and markets were shut off from competitive trading. It meant the denial of a lucrative export trade in spices to Coromandel. And it meant the denial of minerals – gold and tin – which had formed a profitable import to India. It must be emphasized

that all these were achieved by brute force and not by superior commercial expertise.[121]

The last sentence of this quote is particularly important: it was not the 'superior commercial expertise' of the Dutch merchants that made them so competitive and disruptive, but rather their comparative advantage in the means of violence, and particularly their naval superiority.[122]

Indeed, both the Dutch and English had attained a position of relative naval superiority over the Mughal Empire during the 17th century.[123] Given their continuing inability to outcompete Indian merchants on the open market, the Dutch and English continually used or threatened violence to back up their commercial activities. In the end, this superiority in the means of violence would prove crucial in the final fall of the Mughal Empire to the British, dramatised by the Battle of Plassey in Bengal on 23 June 1757. The immediate motivations behind Major-General Robert Clive's coup of 1757 seem to have arisen from Britain's increasing preoccupation with intensified French competition and a desire to protect British trading interests in Bengal against the perceived depredations of local rulers.[124] In these ways, the competitive pressures of European capitalist states, transmitted both economically and geopolitically, 'overdetermined' and redirected the pattern and dynamics of India's development. Again we see how the uneven and combined nature of India's development in relation to the European powers came to play a causally decisive role in the Mughal Empire's eventual collapse. The contemporaneous existence of a multiplicity of societies, all exhibiting varying forms of development (unevenness), thereby came to causally interact (geopolitical combination) in ways that produced further axes and layers of sociologically differentiated patterns of development (sociological combinations), in turn leading to sharp divergences in their developmental trajectories.

It is important to reiterate, however, that the Mughal Empire was already suffering from innumerable economic and political difficulties stemming from the competitive pressures European traders had already brought to bear on the Empire during the preceding century, well before the time of Britain's formal colonisation of the country over the second half of the 18th century.[125] Moreover, the British were critically assisted in the process of conquest by various indigenous merchant and financial groups, whose political and economic power had been steadily growing since the late 17th century as centralised state power began to breakdown.[126] In this rather perverse sense, 'Eastern agency' was then a significant part in how the British succeeded in their colonisation efforts. With the capture of Bengal, arguably the wealthiest province of Mughal India, the East India Company and its servants achieved an enormous advantage in dealing with all other states and economies in the subcontinent, further aiding subsequent British conquests as they came to bring the entirety of the Mughal

Empire under their dominion.[127] And with the colonisation of the entire Indian landmass completed by the early 19th century, the British state came to accrue significant strategic and material advantages in further expanding and buttressing its bourgeoning global empire as it sought to open all the markets of the world to its industrial products. In these ways, the 'decline of the East' and the 'rise of the West' were *mutually conditioning* and *co-constitutive* processes, where one state's gain turned into another's loss.

Conclusion

If we were to choose a single symbolic moment of the *beginning* of the West's systemic 'overtaking' of the 'East' in its rise to global dominance, the years between the British taking of Bengal in 1757 and the signing of the Treaty of Paris in 1763 would likely suffice. For it was during these seven world-transforming years that the first of the great tributary empires in Asia fell at the hands of the Europeans, while the final external systemic threat to the development of British (and thus world) capitalism, the French monarchy, was extinguished in a string of spectacular military victories ending the Seven Years' War. After the defeat of France and Spain in this conflict, Britain acquired dominion over a large portion of three continents under the terms of the Treaty of 1763. This further meant that the white settlers in North America no longer needed protection by British forces.[128] The decisive defeat of the French in 1759 both paved the way for the establishment of the Raj in India, and made the emergence of North America possible. Thus, Frank McLynn is correct to claim that this was the year that marked the beginning of Britain's (and subsequently Europe's) dominance of the world, as the 'entire history of the world would have been different but for the events of 1759. If the French had prevailed in North America, there would have been no United States (at least in the form we know it)' and if 'France had won in India, the global hegemony of the English language could never have happened'.[129] In short, McLynn concludes, '[t]he consequences of 1759 really were momentous; it really was a hinge on which all of world history turned'.[130] The end of the war and signing of the peace treaty in 1763 not only reconfirmed 'British command of the seas', but also, Immanuel Wallerstein writes, 'marked Britain's definitive achievement of superiority in the 100 years struggle with France'.[131] Britain's pivotal defeat of France was also significant as it 'marked a global turning point or moment of irreversibility for the emergence [of the] capitalist system as a whole'.[132]

While anti-capitalist and colonial struggles would continually and forcefully challenge capitalism's global hegemony, the capitalist world system was by this time now firmly entrenched and resting on solid (geo)political foundations (notably, the British Empire). From the second half of the 18th century to the early 20th century, the world witnessed the steady growth and domination of capitalist social relations (spread by force or otherwise). The process of Western domination culminated in the imposition of unequal trade treaties on China and Japan in the mid to late 19th century. By the beginning of the 20th century, the sublime dictatorship of capital over the world had been largely completed.

In the process, the Global South came to be subjugated in a tangled web of economic, (geo)political and racialised hierarchies, with the Europeans and subsequently the United States sitting at the top. The West's dominance continues to this day, even if in a somewhat more hobbled form. We are thus still living in the world made between 1757 and 1763; we have yet to awake from the 'Nightmare' of capitalist history that this dominance was built upon.[133] In an age of impending ecological catastrophe, socio-economic crises and continued imperial wars, it is worth recalling Adorno's admonition that '[n]o universal history leads from savagery to humanitarianism, but there is one that leads from the slingshot to the atom bomb'.[134] We must therefore come face to face with the distinct possibility that no matter how great and wide the collective rage and struggles against the existing order may reach, no matter how grave the situation may get, no matter how barbaric the system may become, the sign on the wall might just one day read in bright blinding red colours: 'THIS IS NOT AN EXIT'.[135] It is for this reason that we conclude in the next chapter with a discussion of the implications of our historical analysis for some possible 'exit strategies' from capitalism.

Conclusion

Once interconnection has been revealed, all theoretical belief in the perpetual necessity of the existing conditions collapses, even before the collapse takes place in practice.

Karl Marx, 1868[1]

There's no need to fear or hope, but only to look for new weapons.

Gilles Deleuze, 1992[2]

Try again. Fail again. Fail better.

Samuel Beckett, 1983[3]

The time has come to 'combine' or 'draw together' the 'separate steps'[4] of the preceding argument. Beginning with the Eurasian steppe in the Long 13th Century, we saw how the Mongolian Empire was fundamental to the formation of a number of geopolitical and economic linkages across the Eurasian landmass. This had the effect of plugging European actors into an interconnected 'world system' of intersocietal relations. The immediate consequence of European engagements in the *Pax Mongolica* was an increased exposure to the technical developments and ideas pioneered in the more scientifically advanced Asia. While these contributed to an array of developments in Europe, the *Pax Mongolica* also proved to be a transmitter not of only social relations and technologies but also disease. The Black Death, and the subsequent demographic reordering which brought feudalism in Europe into crisis, directly stemmed from this widened sphere of intersocietal interaction.

We then demonstrated in Chapter 4 that the subsequent divergences that occurred within Europe in this context were a product of the 'superpower' rivalry between the Ottoman and Habsburg empires. Through military pressure, the Ottomans further undermined existing centres of feudal ruing class power – the papacy, Habsburg Empire and Italian city-states – and supported or encouraged new counter-hegemonic forces – the Protestants, French and Dutch. They acted as a geopolitical centre of gravity, which attracted the Habsburg military to the Mediterranean and Central East Europe. As a result, Northwestern European states were afforded the geopolitical space that proved crucial to their development along capitalist lines. In particular, the Ottomans unintentionally created for the English a condition of geopolitical 'isolation', which directly contributed to the homogeneity of the English ruling class and in turn its success in enclosing and engrossing land. Primitive accumulation and the emergence of capitalist social relations in the English countryside were therefore directly tied to the geopolitical threat of the Ottoman Empire. At the same time, Ottoman territorial dominance of the Mediterranean and land routes to Asia served to push Northwestern European states onto an altogether novel global sphere of activity – the Atlantic.

In Chapter 5, we then focused on this Atlantic theatre, where we examined the manifold impact of the 'New World discoveries' on the development of Europe. We first saw how the intersocietal interactions, conflicts and struggles between Europeans and Amerindians that took place in the Americas were crucial to the emergence of modern conceptions of territorial sovereignty and the development of Eurocentrism, scientific racism and the modern institution of patriarchy. We then demonstrated that the subsequent plunder of American precious metals by Europeans further exacerbated an already nascent divergence between the feudalism of the Iberian states and the incipient capitalisms of Northwest Europeans. Moreover, we argued that the development of capitalism in England was itself dependent on the widened sphere of activity offered by the Atlantic. In particular, we saw that through the sociological combination of American land, African slave labour and English capital, the limits of English agrarian capitalism were overcome. Not only did the widened sphere of circulation implied by the transatlantic triangular trade offer numerous opportunities to British capitalists to expand their domain of activities, but the combination of different labour processes across the Atlantic enabled the recomposition of labour in Britain through the Industrial Revolution. The development of the productive forces – and the real subsumption of labour under capital as such – was thus built on the exploitation of a transatlantic subaltern class made up of Amerindians, African slaves and Europeans.

It was through and out of these crucial preconditions of capitalist development that the foundations were laid for the bourgeois revolutions in Europe. These revolutions had the effect of establishing and consolidating territorially demarcated sovereign centres of capital accumulation first in Holland, then England, and finally France. Moreover, we showed that international determinations, spurred by the sequential character of these revolutions, with each impacting on the next, were crucial to their development.

In Chapter 7, we examined in more detail the 'proto'-development of capitalism in the Low Countries and its attendant limits based on a relatively low supply of labour. This threatened to choke off the United Provinces' incipient form of capitalism, which was only overcome by tapping into a vast well of labour *elsewhere*. In Asia, the VOC was responsible for creating a commercial network that combined uneven labour processes spanning the spice-producing islands in Indonesia, precious metal production in Japan and China, and textile workers in India into a single integrated network of 'global' production. Crucially, this took place in response to the variegated challenges – of resistance and accommodation – posed by Southeast Asian communities in response to Dutch activities in the region. It was in and through these intersocietal interactions with communities across the Indian Ocean littoral – and ultimately through their subordination, subjugation and subsumption – that the Dutch were able to integrate a disparate yet large mass of labour-power into their own operations. The development and ultimate survival of institutional innovations central to the development of Dutch capitalism – the Bourse, Amsterdam entrepôt and VOC – were all based on this subjugated and exploited mass of unfree Asian labour-power.

These multiple determinations emanating from various non-European origins were then combined in order to produce a conjunctural analysis of the so-called 'rise of the West' in Chapter 8. We demonstrated that the multiple geopolitical advantages that thrust Europe to global ascendancy were based on prior influences of more powerful non-European societies. In particular, European 'exceptionalism' – insofar as it existed at all – was rooted in the exceptional accrual and deployment of the means of violence against these non-European societies. The combinations of these 'advantages' were instrumental in the British colonisation of India, which marked the historical conjuncture at which 'the West' came to begin its climb to global rule.

In presenting this history, we have argued that uneven and combined development provides a potent theoretical weapon capable of identifying and articulating these many variegated yet integrated social relations of power and exploitation that make up the capitalist mode of production. Throughout the book, we have shown how uneven and combined development – ontologically, methodologically and theoretically – provides an illuminating framework, through which we can decentre or provincialise Europe as the privileged or sole author of history. This 'Re-Orientation' has highlighted that many of the categories and theories of social development have been built on a problematically singular abstraction of the European experience. In doing so, we have called into question the use of ideal-types derived from or in comparison with this experience – capitalism, modernity, feudalism, nomadism, tributary and so on. Equally we have sought to complicate and overcome any ideal-type conception of Europe or 'the West', and their corollaries – 'the East' or 'the Rest' – as dichotomously opposed essentialisations. We have demonstrated that the study of interactive multiplicity, the intersocietal, unevenness and combination, was central to overcoming the ontological singularity that lies at the heart of these problems of Eurocentrism.

We have further argued that ontologically singular abstractions of this sort are best understood as 'vantage points' or 'windows' that unveil a necessarily partial glimpse into the contradictory and complex 'concentration of many determinations'[5] making up social reality, and subsequently frame our understanding of it. Because the view of this complex historical reality from one limited angle, one viewpoint or window will tend to be one-sided, the use of multiple vantage points, differentiated but brought together, is required in order to gain a fuller picture and grasp of the many determinations that make concrete reality what it is. In this regard, taking a panoramic view of the multiform historical processes from the vantage point of 'the international' is especially instructive, for it reveals the spatial multiplicity of determinations that tend to be missed when focusing on society in the singular. We have argued that this is precisely how uneven and combined development as an analytical framework operates, and what gives it a distinct theoretical depth and breadth in contrast to the more one-sided approaches considered in this book.

Utilising this 'international' vantage point, our approach has identified a multiplicity of interacting 'causal chains' emanating from different uneven spatiotemporal vectors of development that combined in the various conjunctures examined in this book. We then sought to bring out the relations between these determinations, their points of interactivity – their combination – at the heart of this broader and more complex conception of sociohistorical development. In this way, we have endeavoured to demonstrate that uneven and combined development is capable of bringing together – not only theoretically, but concretely – historical processes understood from multiple vantage points into an interactive totality of social relations.

We hope an appreciation for these wider sets of historical processes generates a sustained engagement in the retheorisation of capitalism as a mode of production, for which we have offered some preliminary, if admittedly incomplete, ideas. How might the unevenness and combination of productive forces on an international scale (as discussed in Chapters 2, 5 and 7) alter our understandings of the reproduction of capitalism, not least in the context of 'globalisation'? How do social relations and processes outside of the formal exploitation of wage-labour assist in the reproduction and development of capitalism as a mode of production (as discussed in Chapters 5 and 7)? Can we bring actors – such a tributary states, nomadic empires and peasant populations of non-European lands – previously considered outside of or behind the history of capitalist modernity more resolutely into the history of its formation (as discussed in Chapters 3 and 4)? How might a method that places an emphasis on tracing the multiple vectors of uneven sociological development and their various combinations augment conjunctural analyses of other historical developments, such as wars and revolutions (as discussed in Chapters 6 and 8)?

We have only begun to answer these questions through the relatively limited historical timeframe of 'capitalism's origins'; a more extensive temporal extension of these problematics – one covering the 19th to 21st centuries – is both desirable and necessary. So too is a further spatial extension, incorporating the histories of other (indeed Other) societies and actors – more vectors of uneven and combined development – into the origins of capitalism. To highlight a few notable gaps, not enough attention has been paid to a geopolitical giant of the early modern age, China. Similarly, our inclusion of the African continent is unfortunately marginal, and perhaps falls prey to the typically Eurocentric tendency of studying African history under the rubric of slavery. As such, we recognise that there are numerous histories that have been overlooked or under-explored. We hope, however, that uneven and combined development offers an explanatory framework through which future research can incorporate, and further expand upon, the historical sociological research programme offered here. That is, we hope the gaps made evident in this study will push readers to address, research and fill out such gaps, as there remains a great deal more to say.

Nonetheless, the argument presented in this book necessitates, in our view, a rethinking of what historically and theoretically constitutes capitalism. We have shown that insofar as the spatial scope of capitalism's history is limited to ontologically singular analyses, so too is the theoretical reach of capitalism as an analytical category. An exclusive focus on the English countryside tends to priv-ilege the formation of the capital–wage-labour relation in agrarian capitalism. In contrast, we have argued that although this waged sphere is indeed funda-mental, it is itself dependent on a variety of different social relations that are irreducible to that sphere alone. Vast assemblages of nonwaged labour regimes – from debt peonage to plantation slavery, from Banda to Barbados – formed the foundational basis on which the (re)production of wage-labour and capital in London and Amsterdam was built. And at the heart of these non-European processes were histories of violence, terror, subjugation and coercive exploita-tion meted out by ruling classes to populations across the globe. More often than not, states or state-backed institutions were central to these processes. The very ability of the capitalist mode of production to subsume, exploit and inte-grate (combine) such an array of spatially differentiated production processes (unevenness) is central to its history and logic.

This should alert us to the ways in which capitalism utilises exploitation and oppression – beyond the formally free exchange of labour-power for wages – as (re)sources for its reproduction. The violence that inheres in forms of exploita-tion such as slavery, debt peonage and domestic labour, practices such as state coercion, 'just wars' and territorial divisions, and structures of racism and patri-archy is not external to capitalism as a mode of production, but constitutive of its very ontology. When tied to the critique of Eurocentrism, we should thus be wary of any account of the origins of capitalism that posits Europeans or Westerners as harbingers of a normatively and developmentally privileged 'civilisation' – an exceptionally 'enlightened' group that dragged the world out of 'savagery'. The history of violence upon which the social relations of capitalism were built should lead us to question the idealised self-image of capi-talism as a world of expanding fulfilment and freedom, achieved through the abstract mechanisms of exchange. The invisible hand of the market has always been undergirded by the iron fist of the state, and an array of systemic separations between the subjugated and exploited – patriarchy, 'race', class and so on.

The conquest, ecological ruin, slavery, state terrorism, patriarchal subjugation, racism, mass exploitation and immiseration upon which capitalism was built continue unabated today. The violent past explicated in this book was therefore not merely a historical contingency, external to the 'pure' operation of capital, or a phase of 'incompleteness' out of which capitalism has emerged or will emerge. Rather, these practices and processes are 'constitutive' in the sense that they remain crucial to capitalism's ongoing reproduction as a historical social structure. This should remind us that capitalism is neither natural nor eternal: it has been historically constructed by annihilating or subsuming other – non-capitalist – ways of life. But, moreover, these pointers should alert us to the possibility of ridding ourselves of a mode of production that continually (re)produces such histories of violence, oppression and exploitation.

As such, we believe the arguments presented in this book raise a key issue that must be placed at the heart of any transformative emancipatory politics – the issue of political or societal multiplicity.[6] Far from being a matter of purely scholastic concern, this missing 'international theory' has a number of political implications. We would therefore argue that this issue is anything but an abstract one, since as we have argued, the interjection of the intersocietal is a permanent condition of the way in which states, communities, and individuals shape their lives politically. And indeed, political challenges to capitalism have often identified the 'universality' or 'totality' of capitalism as the basis on which it should be challenged and overcome. This serves as an important warning against any endeavour to build 'socialism in one country'; anticapitalism can only be global in scope.

We agree with this, and an obvious implication of our calls for an internationalist counter-history of capitalism is that an internationalist politics of anticapitalism is a necessity. However, the content of this internationalism is not self-evident, and requires working out – and, of course, not through theory alone but also through struggle. Insofar as 'the international' was central to the emergence and reproduction of capitalism, we should be critical of political positions that treat this internationality – the system of multiple nation-states – as an empty vessel that simply needs to filled with communist or socialist content. Indeed, the very internationality of capitalism might well prove fundamentally antithetical to communist politics under certain circumstances. For if the 'forgotten' history of the social sciences – and, in particular, the discipline of International Relations – has been crucially implicated in confronting the dilemmas of social disorder and revolution wrought by the international spread of capitalist social relations and empire, the subaltern history of 20th-century revolutionary politics has been imbricated with the manifold constraints imposed by the 'inter-stateness' of capitalism on the potentials for emancipatory projects for social transformation.

That capitalism emerged in conjunction with – and in fact perpetuates – a world divided into a multiplicity of interactive, heterogeneous states has held enormous significance for revolutionary politics. For in the process of attempting to build socialism by taking state power and harnessing it to this end, Marxist-inspired revolutions have all too often been transformed into their very negation. Rather than constructing the emancipated society of the future, in which the political state dissolves into a free association of self-governing producers, the trajectories of self-proclaimed 'socialist' societies witnessed the intensive perfection of the oppressive state apparatus they had originally sought to destroy. Hence, the creation and consolidation of revolutionary states 'perhaps best dramatizes the centrality of interstate relations and war' to modern development.[7]

The myriad dilemmas arising from the 'inter-stateness' of capitalism, this international dimension inscribed in all forms of development, confronting any revolution was clearly recognised – if not properly addressed – by Lenin. As he commented to fellow Bolsheviks in March 1919, 'We are living not merely in a state, but *in a system of states*, and it is inconceivable for the Soviet Republic to exist alongside the imperialist states for any length of time. One or the other must triumph in the end'.[8] In the field of IR, the apparent fact that revolutionary states quickly adopted the methods of traditional diplomacy and great power politics has been viewed as a striking vindication of the 'timeless' wisdom of political realism – a conclusion we clearly reject.[9] But while it would be hopelessly naïve, if not intellectually disingenuous, to subsume an explanation of the multitude of forces behind any socialist revolution's 'degeneration', revolutionaries travel at their peril without recognition of the socially transformational power of 'power politics'. And this 'international' dimension of development has much broader implications to revolutionary politics more generally.

Take, for example, our argument that the multiple labour processes in different parts of the world were crucial to the formation and subsequent reproduction of capitalism. In the period of the Industrial Revolution, coerced forms of surplus extraction in the Americas and Asia enabled capitalists in Britain to increase rates of exploitation and subordinate labour to the mechanics of the factory. Here the combination of uneven forms of exploitation was constitutive of capitalism's expanded reproduction, and the real subsumption of labour. In the contemporary period, the divesting machinations of capitalism have continued and expanded into a global system of geopolitical violence and integrated production processes which afford it coercive and disciplinary capabilities with an unprecedented international reach. The fluidities of finance capital, 'just-in-time' production, and logistics have only sharpened this sociological multiplicity – the international – into a machine of tyranny. Today, as always, wage repression, deteriorating work conditions and anti-strike practices are actively determined by variegated labour processes in different societies across the globe. In these ways, unevenness and combination act as disciplining features that maintains the capital relation as the basis of social existence.

So when considering the challenge of political multiplicity, we must not only consider the level of 'many societies', but also many oppressions, many powers, many struggles, many actors and so on. Historically, sociopolitical differences borne of 'many oppressions' or 'many struggles' have been understood as something for the Left – and in particular the Party – to negate and sublate into the unity and singularity of revolutionary thought and practice.[10] In this tradition, the programme has been presented as the higher ideological/strategic unity, and the Party the organisational form, in which political differences are ironed out, unity among disparate parts realised, and a homogenous political perspective pursued. In turn, the perspectives constructed by the leadership of parties and organisations are presented as the historical prime mover – the royal road – which simply needs to replicated everywhere for capitalism to be overthrown. This negation of political difference sought by programmatic organisations generates a form of political autocentrism, and ontological singularity, where any given party or programme is posited as the sole and sovereign author of historical change. In this programmatic approach, difference is something not to be articulated, but destroyed; something to be redirected onto the True Path or – where it cannot be redirected – exiled as a 'bourgeois deviation'.

Drawing on our preceding analysis, we would argue that any politics that takes a singular – historically and geographically specific – experience and generalises beyond its own spatiotemporal conditions and limitations, is inherently limited, problematic and potentially dangerous. It is so precisely because it imposes a false universality on the uneven, multiform social experiences of proletarians.[11] Insofar as capitalism has been built on the subjugation and marginalisation of multiplicity – both historically and historiographically – any anticapitalist politics that reproduces this subjugation and marginalisation is not worthy of the name.

In contrast, the theoretical and historical observations made in this book offer, in our view, a way of integrating into the critique of capitalism an array of social relations that have too often been dismissed as 'externalities' – nonwaged work, forced work, illegal work, state coercion, patriarchy, racism and so on. Any prevailing orthodoxy in the labour movement (broadly conceived) that relegates the multiplicity of these oppressions to a mere ideological or superstructural epiphenomenon that is contingent to the reproduction of capitalism is empirically and theoretically unsustainable. Any attempt to reduce these forms of oppression to the singular relation embodied in wage-labour, or set up a political-normative hierarchy of struggles, with those around wage-labour taking absolute priority, is to attribute a false, homogenous universality onto the many, variegated struggles against oppression.[12]

To be clear, we remain committed to the view that the abolition of wage-labour is central to any anticapitalist politics, and that proletarians are the only class capable of carrying out this abolition. However, we insist that 'proletarian' here does not denote a homogenous category itself derived from the Western experience. Indeed, as our preceding historical narrative has shown, the sources and structural interconnections between different forms of oppression (class, racial, national, gender, sexual, cultural and so on) are not reducible to a singular relation – that is, a historically particular form of exploitation. The forms of oppression mobilised by the capitalist mode of production have been, from capitalism's very origins, 'intersectional'.

We therefore consider uneven and combined development to be a potentially useful framework for uncovering the ways in which the multiple social relations of oppression and exploitation, each originating from a variety of different vectors of sociohistorical development, historically combine and intersect with each other. This would render, for example, an understanding of the historical constitution of racism and patriarchy as tied to, constitutive of, but not reducible to, the emergence of capitalism. In the same way, it would avoid treating struggles that seek to destroy patriarchy and racism as somehow external from – or mere supplements to – the cardinal aim of destroying capitalism. Might it be time to rethink the privileged revolutionary subject (the proletariat) in broader terms than its traditional, singular association with waged-labour? Might this then require a decentring or pluralisation of this revolutionary subject in terms denoting a series of exploitations, oppressions and abjections which subsume individuals in varied, uneven, but intersecting and combined ways?

With this in mind, the very abolition of wage-labour as a category would require that we take the plurality of political experiences seriously; it would consider how unevenness and combination might be effectively weaponised against capitalism. By acknowledging the differentiated and uneven sociologies of different social movements, the politics of revolution must be understood not in terms of a singular strategy. Rather, we must be cognisant of the necessity for *many strategies*, each irreducible to each other and specific to the particular challenges faced in the course of struggle. And in the spirt of combined development, this would also involve considering how such multiple strategies can be learned from, adopted and modified, or if necessary discarded and 'skipped over'. That is to say, insofar as unevenness and combination can be understood as limits and challenges to revolutionary politics, they can also be repurposed, reconfigured, reassembled and ultimately weaponised for political measures geared towards abolishing capitalism. It is perhaps the failure to grasp this possibility that has hitherto constrained communist horizons and revolutionary potentialities in concrete insurrectionary movements. It is this challenge – the search for a multiplicity of new weapons among the oppressed and exploited – that we pose as our immediate task.

Notes

Introduction

1   James Joyce, *Ulysses* (Mineola, N.Y.: Dover, 2002 [1922]), 34.
2   Niall Ferguson, *The Great Degeneration: How Institutions Decay and Economies Die* (London: Penguin, 2012); Joseph E. Stiglitz, *The Price of Inequality* (London: Penguin, 2012); David Harvey, *The Enigma of Capital: And the Crises of Capitalism* (London: Profile, 2011); Owen Jones, *The Establishment: And How They Get Away with It* (London: Penguin, 2014); Naomi Klein, *The Shock Doctrine: The Rise of Disaster Capitalism* (London: Penguin, 2014); Thomas Piketty, *Capital in the Twenty-First Century* (Cambridge, Mass.: Harvard University Press, 2014).
3   See e.g. economics undergraduates forming a 'Post-crash economics' group – www.post-crasheconomics.com/ – and international networks of students seeking to rethink economics –www.rethinkeconomics.org/ and www.isipe.net/ (accessed 15 February 2015)
4   Jennifer Schuessler, 'In history departments, it's up with capitalism', *New York Times*, 6 April 2013, www.nytimes.com/2013/04/07/education/in-history-depart ments-its-up-with-capitalism.html?pagewanted=all&_r=0 (accessed 25 October 2014).
5   'What would Marx say?' *Economist*, 15 October 2008, www.economist.com/blogs/certainideasofeurope/2008/10/what_would_marx_say (accessed 25 October 2014).
6   Karl Marx, *Grundrisse* (Harmondsworth: Penguin, 1973 [1857–58]), 157.
7   Here and throughout this work the terms 'Europe' and 'European' are deployed with the problematic implications of anachronism and intra-European divisions firmly in mind. As such, they are used, unless specified, in a basic geographical sense, predominantly (but not exclusively) denoting the regions that would come to be known as England, France, the Low Countries, Portugal, Hapsburg Spain and Austria, Germanic principalities, Hungary, Russia and the Italian city-states.
8   Our interpretation owes a debt to the brilliant appraisal of *The Ambassadors* by Lisa Jardine in *Worldly Goods* (London: Macmillan, 1996), 425–36.
9   Larry J. Kreitzer, 'Hans Holbein's *The Ambassadors*: biblical reflections on a Renaissance masterpiece', in Martin O'Kane (ed.), *Borders, Boundaries and the Bible* (New York: Sheffield Academic Press, 2002), 217–28, 225.
10 The following draws on Kamran Matin, 'Redeeming the universal: postcolonialism and the inner life of Eurocentrism', *European Journal of International Relations*, Vol. 19, No. 2 (2013), 353–77.
11 Jacob Burckhardt, *The Civilization of the Renaissance in Italy* (London: Penguin, 1990).
12 See e.g. Perry Anderson, *Lineages of the Absolutist State* (London: Verso, 1974); Charles Tilly (ed.), *The Formation of National States in Western Europe* (Princeton, N.J.: Princeton University Press, 1975); Michael Mann, *The Sources of Social Power, Vol. 1: A History of Power from the Beginning to AD 1760* (Cambridge: Cambridge University Press, 1986); Benno Teschke, *The Myth of 1648: Class, Geopolitics, and the Making of Modern International Relations* (London: Verso, 2003).
13 David S. Landes, *The Wealth and Poverty of Nations: Why Some Are So Rich and Some So Poor* (London: W.W. Norton, 1999).
14 Robert Brenner, 'Agrarian class structure and economic development in pre-industrial Europe' and 'The agrarian roots of capitalism', in T. H. Aston and C. H.

E. Philpin (eds), *The Brenner Debate: Agrarian Class Structure and Economic Development in Pre-Industrial Europe* (Cambridge: Cambridge University Press, 1987), 10–63 and 231–328.

15 Immanuel Wallerstein, *The Modern World-System, Vol. I: Capitalist Agriculture and the Origins of the European World Economy in the Sixteenth Century* (London: Academic Press, 1974).

16 Matin, 'Redeeming the universal', 355; cf. John M. Hobson, *The Eastern Origins of Western Civilisation* (Cambridge: Cambridge University Press, 2004).

17 Edward Said, *Orientalism: Western Conceptions of the Orient* (London: Routledge & Kegan Paul, 1978).

18 Samuel P. Huntington, *The Clash of Civilizations and the Remaking of World Order* (New York: Simón & Schuster, 1996).

19 Nancy Bisaha, *Creating East and West: Renaissance Humanists and the Ottoman Turks* (Philadelphia, Pa.: University of Pennsylvania Press, 2004), 12.

20 Gurminder K Bhambra, 'Historical sociology, international relations and connected histories', *Cambridge Review of International Affairs*, Vol. 23, No. 1 (2010), 127–43.

21 Daniel Chernilo, 'Methodological nationalism and the domestic analogy: classical resources for their critique', *Cambridge Review of International Affairs*, Vol. 23, No. 1 (2010), 87–106.

22 The body of anti-Eurocentric literature, which sometimes goes under the label of the 'California School', is now vast. For a sampling of some of the most important contributions, see James Blaut, *The Colonizer's Model of the World: Geographical Diffusionism and Eurocentric History* (Cambridge: Cambridge University Press, 1993); A. G. Frank, *ReOrient: Global Economy in the Asian Age* (Berkeley, Calif.: University of California Press, 1998); Kenneth Pomeranz, *The Great Divergence: China, Europe and the Making of the Modern World Economy* (Princeton, N.J.: Princeton University Press, 2000); Hobson, *Eastern Origins*; Jack Goody, *The Theft of History* (Cambridge: Cambridge University Press, 2006); Jack A. Goldstone, *Why Europe? The Rise of the West in World History, 1500–1850* (New York: McGraw-Hill, 2009).

23 See, among others, Frank, *ReOrient*; Hobson, *Eastern Origins*; Eric H. Mielants, *The Origins of Capitalism and the 'Rise of the West'* (Philadelphia, Pa.: Temple University Press, 2007); Ronald Findlay and Kevin H. O'Rourke, *Power and Plenty: Trade, War, and the World Economy in the Second Millennium* (Princeton, N.J.: Princeton University Press, 2007); Henry Heller, *The Birth of Capitalism: A Twenty-First-Century Perspective* (London: Pluto, 2011).

24 But see the significant contributions by Hobson, *Eastern Origins*; Naeem Inayatullah and David Blaney, *International Relations and the Problem of Difference* (London: Routledge, 2004); Robbie Shilliam, 'What about Marcus Garvey? Race and the transformation of sovereignty debate', *Review of International Studies*, Vol. 32, No. 2 (2006), 379–400; Tarak Barkawi and Mark Laffey, 'The postcolonial moment in security studies', *Review of International Studies*, Vol. 32, No. 2 (2006), 329–52; Robbie Shilliam (ed.), *International Relations and Non-Western Thought: Imperialism, Colonialism and Investigations of Global Modernity* (London: Routledge, 2010); Bhambra, 'Historical sociology'.

25 Stephen Hobden and John M. Hobson (eds), *Historical Sociology of International Relations* (Cambridge: Cambridge University Press, 2002); Stephen Hobden, *International Relations and Historical Sociology: Breaking down Boundaries* (London: Routledge, 1998).

26 For important critiques see Bhambra, 'Historical sociology' and 'Talking among themselves? Weberian and Marxist historical sociologies as dialogues without "others"', *Millennium*, Vol. 39, No. 3 (2011), 667–681; John M. Hobson, *The Eurocentric Conception of World Politics: Western International Theory, 1760–2010* (Cambridge: Cambridge University Press, 2012).

27 See e.g. Garrett Mattingly, *Renaissance Diplomacy* (New York: Dover, 1988 [1955]);

F. H. Hinsley, *Power and the Pursuit of Peace: Theory and Practice in the History of Relations between States* (Cambridge: Cambridge University Press, 1963); John G. Ruggie, 'Continuity and transformation in the world polity: toward a neorealist synthesis', *World Politics*, Vol. 35, No. 2 (1983), 261–85; Justin Rosenberg, *The Empire of Civil Society: A Critique of the Realist Theory of International Relations* (London: Verso, 1994); Hendrik Spruyt, *The Sovereign State and Its Competitors: An Analysis of Systems Change* (Princeton, N.J.: Princeton University Press, 1994); Dale C. Copeland, *The Origins of Major War* (Ithaca, N.Y.: Cornell University Press, 2000); Teschke, *Myth of 1648*; Hannes Lacher, *Beyond Globalization: Capitalism, Territoriality and the International Relations of Modernity* (London: Routledge, 2006); cf. John M. Hobson, 'Provincializing Westphalia: the Eastern origins of sovereignty', *International Politics*, Vol. 46, No. 6 (2009), 671–90; Turan Kayaoglu, 'Westphalian Eurocentrism in international relations theory', *International Studies Review*, Vol. 12, No. 2 (2010), 193–217; Hobson, *Eurocentric Conception*.

28 For example, Hedley Bull and Adam Watson (eds), *The Expansion of the International Society* (Oxford: Clarendon Press, 1984).

29 Justin Rosenberg, 'Why is there no international historical sociology?', *European Journal of International Relations*, Vol. 12, No. 3 (2006), 307–40.

30 The theory of uneven and combined development has, in recent years, witnessed something of a renaissance within the historical sociology and IR literatures as scholars have sought to recast Trotsky's concept into a general theory of 'the international'. For a list of some of the contemporary literature, see www.unevenandcombineddevelopment.wordpress.com/writings/

31 Maurice Dobb, *Studies in the Development of Capitalism* (New York: Taylor & Francis, 1963).

32 Brenner, 'Agrarian class structure'.

33 Ellen Meiksins Wood, *The Origin of Capitalism: A Longer View* (London: Verso, 2002).

34 Paul Sweezy, 'A critique', in Rodney Hilton (ed.), *The Transition from Feudalism to Capitalism* (London: Verso, 1978), 33–56.

35 Wallerstein, *Modern World-System, I*.

36 See e.g. Jack Gladstone, 'The rise of the West or not? A revision to socio-economic history', *Sociological Theory*, Vol. 18, No. 2 (2000), 173–94; Pomeranz, *Great Divergence*; Hobson, *Eastern Origins*, 313–16.

37 Karl Marx, *Capital: Critique of Political Economy*, Vol. III (Harmondsworth: Penguin, 1981 [1894]), 728.

38 Cf. Frank, *ReOrient*; Hobson, *Eastern Origins*.

39 Ernest Mandel, *Late Capitalism* (London: Verso, 1976), 562; Alex Law, *Key Concepts in Classical Social Theory* (London: Sage, 2010), 27.

40 Alex Callinicos, *Imperialism and Global Political Economy* (Cambridge: Polity, 2009), 31.

41 Brenner, 'Agrarian roots', 252; Ellen Meiksins Wood, 'The question of market dependence', *Journal of Agrarian Change*, Vol. 2, No. 1 (2002), 50–87; Vivek Chibber, *Postcolonial Theory and the Specter of Capital* (London: Verso, 2013), 111.

42 Karl Marx, *A Contribution to the Critique of Political Economy* (London: Forgotten Books, 2013 [1859]), 294–5.

43 Alejandro Colás and Gonzalo Pozo, 'The value of territory: towards a Marxist geopolitics', *Geopolitics*, Vol. 16, No. 1 (2011), 211–20, 212. For a groundbreaking work on space, spatiality and built environments in relation to IR theory and, in particular, 'humanitarian aid', see Lisa Smirl, *Spaces of Aid: How Cars, Compounds and Hotels Shape Humanitarianism* (London: Zed, 2015).

44 See e.g. Kenneth Waltz, *Theory of International Politics* (Reading, Mass.: Addison-Wesley, 1979); Robert. Gilpin, *War and Change in World Politics* (Cambridge: Cambridge University Press, 1981); John Mearsheimer, *The Tragedy of Great Power Politics* (New York: W.W. Norton, 2001).

45 For anthropological studies problematising realism's 'multiplicity-anarchy-competition' syllogism, see, among others, Leslie E. Sponsel, 'The natural history of peace: a positive view of human nature and its potential', in *A Natural History of Peace* (Nashville, Tenn.: Vanderbilt University Press, 1996), 95–128; Johan M.G. van der Dennen, *The Origin of War: Evolution of a Male-Coalitional Reproductive Strategy* (San Rafael, Calif.: Origin Press, 1996), esp. 265–9; Raymond C. Kelly, *Warless Societies and the Origin of War* (Ann Arbor, Mich.: University of Michigan Press, 2000).

46 Cf. Robert W. Cox, 'Social forces, states and world orders: beyond international relations theory', *Millennium*, Vol. 10, No. 2 (1981), 126–55; Richard K. Ashley, 'The poverty of neorealism', *International Organization*, Vol. 38, No. 2 (1984), 225–86; Rosenberg, *Empire of Civil Society*, 29–34.

47 Kees van der Pijl, *The Discipline of Western Supremacy: Modes of Foreign Relations and Political Economy, Vol. III* (London: Pluto, 2014).

48 Cf. Justin Rosenberg, 'Basic problems in the theory of uneven and combined development. Part II: unevenness and political multiplicity', *Cambridge Review of International Affairs*, Vol. 23, No. 1 (2010), 165–89.

49 See e.g. Michael W. Doyle, 'Liberalism and world politics', *American Political Science Review*, Vol. 80, No. 4 (1986), 1,151–69; Bruce Russett, *Grasping the Democratic Peace: Principles for a Post-Cold War World* (Princeton, N.J.: Princeton University Press, 1993); John M. Owen, 'How liberalism produces democratic peace', *International Security*, Vol. 19, No. 2 (1994), 87–125; Michael Mandlebaum, *The Ideas That Conquered The World: Peace, Democracy, and Free Markets in the Twenty-first Century* (New York: Public Affairs, 2002); Bruce Russett and John R. Oneal, *Triangulating Peace: Democracy, Interdependence, and International Organizations* (New York: Norton, 2001); Erik Gartzke, 'The capitalist peace', *American Journal of Political Science*, Vol. 51, No. 1 (2007), 166–91.

1 The Transition Debate

1 Karl Marx, *Capital: Critique of Political Economy, Vol. I* (London: Penguin, 1990 [1867]), 727fn2.

2 Karl Marx, 'Letter to the editor of the *Otecestvenniye Zapisky*', November 1877, www.marxists.org/archive/marx/works/1877/11/russia.htm (accessed 29 October 2014).

3 Fernand Braudel, *Afterthoughts on Material Civilization and Capitalism* (London: Johns Hopkins University Press, 1977), *The Mediterranean and the Mediterranean World in the Age of Philip II, Vol. I* (Berkeley, Calif.: University of California Press, 1972), *The Mediterranean and the Mediterranean World in the Age of Philip II, Vol. II* (London: Collins, 1973).

4 Immanuel Wallerstein, 'The rise and future demise of the world capitalist system: concepts for comparative analysis', *Comparative Studies in Society and History*, Vol. 16, No. 4 (1974), 387–415.

5 Wallerstein, *The Capitalist World-Economy* (Cambridge: Cambridge University Press, 1979), 135.

6 Wallerstein, *The Modern World-System, Vol. I: Capitalist Agriculture and the Origins of the European World Economy in the Sixteenth Century* (London: Academic Press, 1974), 15–18.

7 Wallerstein, 'Rise and future demise', 398.

8 Wallerstein, *Modern World-System, I*, 38.

9 Wilma A. Dunaway, 'Incorporation as an interactive process: Cherokee resistance to expansion of the capitalist world-system, 1560–1763', *Sociological Inquiry*, Vol. 66, No. 4 (1996), 454–70, 455.

10 Wallerstein, *Modern World-System, I*, 38.

11 Robert Brenner, 'The origins of capitalist development: a critique of neo-Smithian Marxism', *New Left Review*, Series I, No. 104 (1977), 25–92, 33.

12 Wallerstein, *Modern World-System, I*, 127.

13 Wallerstein, *Modern World-System, I*, 127.

14 Wallerstein, 'World systems versus world-system: a critique', in A. G. Frank and B. Gills (eds), *The World System: Five Hundred Years or Five Thousand?* (London: Routledge, 1993), 294.

15 Wallerstein, 'World systems versus world-system,' 127.

16 Reşat Kasaba, *The Ottoman Empire and the World Economy: The Nineteenth Century* (Albany, N.Y.: SUNY Press, 1988); Huri İslamoğlu-İnan (ed.), *The Ottoman Empire and the World-Economy* (Cambridge: Cambridge University Press, 1987).

17 Çağlar Keyder, *State and Class in Turkey: A Study in Capitalist Development* (London: Verso, 1987).

18 Giovanni Arrighi, 'Peripheralization of southern Africa, I: changes in production processes', *Review*, Vol. 3, No. 2 (1979), 161–191; Immanuel Wallerstein and William G. Martin, 'Peripheralization of southern Africa, II: changes in household structure and labor-force formation', *Review*, Vol. 3, No. 2 (1979), 193–207; William G. Martin, 'Southern Africa and the world-economy: cyclical and structural constraints on transformation', *Review*, Vol. 10, No. 1 (1986), 99–119.

19 Ravi Palat et al., 'The incorporation and peripheralization of South Asia, 1600–1950', *Review*, Vol. 10, No. 1 (1986), 171–208; K. N. Chaudhuri, 'The world-system east of longitude 20°: the European role in Asia 1500–1750', *Review*, Vol. 5, No. 2 (1981), 219–45; Ravi Palat et al., 'Of what world-system was pre-1500 "India" a part?', in Sushil Chaudhury and Michel Morineau (eds), *Merchants, Companies and Trade: Europe and Asia in the Early Modern Era* (Cambridge: Cambridge University Press, 1999).

20 Y. So Alvin, 'The process of incorporation into the capitalist world-system: the case of China in the nineteenth century', *Review*, Vol. 8, No. 1 (1984), 91–116; Satoshi Ikeda, 'The history of the capitalist world-system vs. the history of East-Southeast Asia', *Review*, Vol. 19, No. 1 (1996), 49–77; Stephen K. Sanderson, 'The transition from feudalism to capitalism: the theoretical significance of the Japanese case', *Review*, Vol. 17, No. 1 (1994), 15–55.

21 Ramón Grosfoguel, 'From Cepalismo to neoliberalism: a world-systems approach to conceptual shifts in Latin America', *Review*, Vol. 19, No. 2 (1996), 131–54.

22 Wallerstein in fact highlights the multifaceted character of Eurocentrism, and the issues involved in writing non-Eurocentric history. However, he does not consider the issue of internalism in reference to capitalism's origins. See Wallerstein, 'Eurocentrism and its avatars: the dilemmas of social science', *New Left Review*, Series 1, No. 226 (1997), 93–108.

23 Brenner, 'Origins of capitalist development', 34.

24 Hedley Bull, 'Society and anarchy in international relations', in H. Butterfield and M. Wight (eds), *Diplomatic Investigations* (London: Allen & Unwin, 1966), 35–50.

25 For similar critiques, see Theda Skocpol, 'Wallerstein's world capitalist system: a theoretical and historical critique', *American Journal of Sociology*, Vol. 82, No. 2 (1977), 1075–90; Aristide R. Zolberg, 'Origins of the modern world system: a missing link', *World Politics*, Vol. 33, No. 2 (1981), 253–81.

26 See e.g. Christopher Chase-Dunn, 'Interstate system and capitalist world-economy: one logic or two?' *International Studies Quarterly*, Vol. 25, No. 1 (1981), 19–42.

27 John M. Hobson, *The Eurocentric Conception of World Politics: Western International Theory, 1760–2010* (Cambridge: Cambridge University Press, 2012), 236.

28 Immanuel Wallerstein, *The Politics of the World-Economy: The States, the Movements and the Civilizations* (Cambridge: Cambridge University Press, 1984), 23.

29 Wallerstein, *Modern World-System, I*, 51–63.

30 Wallerstein, *Politics of the World-Economy*, 23.

31 Wallerstein, *Politics of the World-Economy*, 153.

32 Hobson, *Eurocentric Conception*, 236.

33 Hobson, *Eurocentric Conception*, 240.

34 Wallerstein, *Politics of the World-Economy*, 123.

35 Hobson, *Eurocentric Conception*, 240–2.

36 See Marx, *Capital, I*, 975–1059.

37 Brenner, 'Origins of capitalist development', 60.

38 As Wallerstein put the matter: 'To analyze the period from 1450 to 1750 as one long "transition" from feudalism to capitalism risks reifying the concept of transition, for we thus steadily reduce the periods of "pure" capitalism and sooner or later arrive at zero, being left with nothing but transition' (*The Modern World-System, Vol. II: Mercantilism and the Consolidation of the European World-Economy, 1600–1750* (Berkeley, Calif.: University of California Press, 2011 [1980]), 31). In the Prologue to the 2011 revised edition of *The Modern World-System*, Vol. I, Wallerstein goes so far as to dismiss the importance of different societies, characterised by different modes of production, interacting with one another, as not 'adding anything of significance to one's ability to understand social reality' (2011 edn, xxi). This occludes the potential effects emerging from the interactive, differentiated and multilinear forms and trajectories of sociohistorical development.

39 Eric Mielants, *The Origins of Capitalism and the 'Rise of the West'* (Philadelphia, Pa.: Temple University Press, 2008), 22.

40 C. P. Terlouw, *Regional Geography of the World-System* (Utrecht, Neths: State University of Utrecht, 1992), 57–8.

41 Ernesto Laclau, *Politics and Ideology in Marxist Theory* (London: New Left Books, 1977), 45.

42 Mielants, *Origins of Capitalism*, 23.

43 Mielants, *Origins of Capitalism*, 24.

44 Mielants, *Origins of Capitalism*, 24fn48.

45 Mielants, *Origins of Capitalism*, 25fn53.

46 Mielants, *Origins of Capitalism*, 25fn54; Jairus Banaji, 'Islam, the Mediterranean, and the rise of capitalism', *Historical Materialism*, Vol. 15 (2007), 47–74, 55.

47 Mielants, *Origins of Capitalism*, 27. And see our analyses of the Dutch and Italian cases in Chapters 6 and 7.

48 Mielants, *Origins of Capitalism*, 26fn55.

49 Banaji, 'Islam', 57–62.

50 Mielants, *Origins of Capitalism*, 27–9.

51 Mielants, *Origins of Capitalism*, 27.

52 Banaji, 'Islam', 50.

53 Mielants, *Origins of Capitalism*, 18.

54 Mielants, *Origins of Capitalism*, 24.

55 Fernand Braudel, *Civilization and Capitalism, 15th–18th Century, Vol. III: The Perspective of the World* (Berkeley, Calif.: University of California Press, 1992).

56 K. Ekholm and J. Friedman, '"Capital" Imperialism and exploitation in Ancient World Systems', in Frank and Gills, *The World System*, 59–80, 60.

57 Frank and Gills, 'The 5,000 year world system: an interdisciplinary introduction', in *The World System*, 3–55, 3.

58 Frank and Gills, 'The cumulation of accumulation', in *The World System*, 98–105.

59 Frank and Gills, 'The cumulation of accumulation', 105–6. It is worth noting that Giovanni Arrighi, also working within the WST tradition, takes a similar approach when tracing the history of hegemony under capitalism. The sequence of Italian city-state, Dutch, British, and US hegemonies is articulated entirely in terms of a series of cyclical shifts in the institutional apparatus of capitalism. In this account, like many others in WST, the existence of capitalism is already assumed, and no explanation is

given for its origins. We examine the work of Arrighi in greater detail in Chapter 7. See Arrighi, *The Long Twentieth Century: Money, Power, and the Origins of Our Times* (London: Verso, 1994).

60 Frank and Gills, 'World system cycles, crises, and hegemonic shifts, 1700 BC to 1700 AD', in *The World System*, 143–99; Janet L. Abu-Lughod, *Before European Hegemony: The World System A.D. 1250–1350* (Oxford: Oxford University Press, 1989); Mielants, *Origins of Capitalism*; R. J. Barendse, 'Trade and state in the Arabian Seas: a survey from the fifteenth to the eighteenth century', *Journal of World History*, Vol. 11, No. 2 (2000), 173–225.

61 Abu-Lughod, *Before European Hegemony*, 355–61.

62 Mielants, *Origins of Capitalism*, 30.

63 Mielants, *Origins of Capitalism*, 13fn26.

64 Brenner, 'Origins of capitalist development'; cf. Brenner, 'World-system theory and the transition to capitalism: historical and theoretical perspectives', in J. Blaschke (ed.), *Perspektiven des Weltssystems* (Berlin: Campus Verlag, 1983), 80–111.

65 Brenner, 'Origins of capitalist development'.

66 Wallerstein, *Modern World-System, I*, 87.

67 Brenner, 'Origins of capitalist development', 54.

68 Brenner, 'World-system theory', 85.

69 Brenner, 'World-system theory', 85; cf. Sanderson, *Social Transformations*, 178.

70 Ellen Meiksins Wood describing Brenner's position in: 'Capitalism, merchants and bourgeois revolution: reflections on the Brenner debate and its sequel', *International Review of Social History*, Vol. 41, No. 2 (1996), 209–232, 220. For a similar perspective on the relationship of towns and cities to the (non-)transition to capitalism, see John Merrington, 'Town and country in the transition to capitalism', *New Left Review*, Series I, No. 93 (1975), 71–92.

71 Brenner, 'Origins of capitalist development', 55. For Brenner the very possibility of innovation and divisions of labour presupposes the prior historical emergence of free wage-labour as the dominant form of exploitation. We examine this argument in the following section.

72 Brenner, 'Origins of capitalist development', 40.

73 We find in these authors a repetition of the quantitative model of development. For Mielants this takes the form of intensified patterns of capitalist accumulation (see above). For Frank and Gills, this is the 'cumulation of accumulation'.

74 Brenner, 'Origins of capitalist development', 31.

75 See Giovanni Arrighi, 'Capitalism and the modern world-system: rethinking the nondebates of the 1970', *Review*, Vol. 21, No. 1 (1998), 113–29.

76 Brenner's explanation of his preference for the latter term ('social property relations') over Marx's 'social relations of production' rests on two claims. As Brenner puts it:

> First, the term social relations of production is sometimes taken to convey the idea that the social structural framework in which production takes place is somehow determined by production itself, i.e. the form of cooperation or organization of the labour process. This I think is disastrously misleading. Second, I think it is necessary not only to lay bare the structuring or constraining effects of *vertical* class, or surplus extraction, relations between exploiters and direct producers, which is generally what is meant by social relations of production. It is, if anything, even more critical to bring out the structuring or constraining effects of the *horizontal* relationships among the exploiters themselves and the direct producers themselves.
>
> (Brenner, 'Property and progress: where Adam Smith went wrong', in C. Wickham (ed.), *Marxist History-Writing for the Twenty First Century*, Oxford: Oxford University Press, 2007, 49–111, 58).

Brenner's emphasis on both the *vertical* (exploiter–exploited) and *horizontal* (intra-exploiter) dimensions of class relations is certainly a welcome corrective to approaches exclusively focusing on the former at the expense of the latter. Why this entails the conceptual shift from production to property relations is unclear. A number of Marxists – as well as Marx himself (esp. *Capital, Vol. III*) – retaining a production-centred approach have similarly emphasised this dual nature of the relations of production (see e.g. Neil Davidson, 'Many capitals, many states: contingency, logic or mediation?', in A. Anievas (ed.), *Marxism and World Politics: Contesting Global Capitalism* (London: Routledge, 2010), 77–93). Moreover, the concept of 'social property relations' falls short of the kind of 'general abstraction' that Marx's production-centred approach provides, as the concept of 'property' held no discernible meaning – either explicit or implicit – in many early social formations such a hunter-gather bands and many of those characterised by what some have termed the 'lineage' or 'kinship' mode of production.

77 Brenner, 'Agrarian class structure and economic development in pre-industrial Europe' and 'The agrarian roots of capitalism', in T. H. Aston and C .H. E. Philpin (eds), *The Brenner Debate: Agrarian Class Structure and Economic Development in Pre-Industrial Europe* (Cambridge: Cambridge University Press, 1985), 10–63 and 213–328. Brenner draws (albeit critically) on the earlier works of Maurice Dobb: see esp. Brenner, 'Dobb on the transition from feudalism to capitalism', *Cambridge Journal of Economics*, Vol. 2 (1978), 121–40; and Ellen Meiksins Wood, *The Origin of Capitalism: A Longer View* (London: Verso, 2002), 51–2.

78 Brenner, 'Agrarian roots', 252.

79 Brenner, 'Agrarian class structure', 47.

80 For a recent collection countering Brenner's views of the contrast between England and France's agrarian development, see John Broad (ed.), *A Common Agricultural Heritage? Revising French and British Rural Divergence* (Exeter: British Agricultural History Society, 2009). These issues are further explored in our discussion of the pre-revolutionary French economy in Chapter 6.

81 Brenner, 'Agrarian roots', 255, and, more generally, 254–8, 262; see similarly, Wood, *Origin of Capitalism*, 98–9; Benno Teschke, *The Myth of 1648: Class, Geopolitics, and the Making of Modern International Relations* (London: Verso, 2003), 104–7.

82 Brenner, 'Agrarian roots', 254–5.

83 Neil Davidson, *How Revolutionary were the Bourgeois Revolutions?* (Chicago, Ill.: Haymarket, 2012), 408.

84 See e.g. Wood, *Origin of Capitalism*, 42–3; Robert Brenner, 'The social basis of economic development', in J. Roemer (ed.), *Analytical Marxism* (Cambridge: Cambridge University Press, 1986), 23–53, 52–3; Teschke, *Myth of 1648*, 255.

85 Davidson, *How Revolutionary*, 411. For a particularly clear statement of the self-perpetuating nature of pre-capitalist property relations, see Robert Brenner, 'The Low Countries in the transition to capitalism', *Journal of Agrarian Change*, Vol. 1, No. 2 (2001), 169–241, 185–6.

86 Ricardo Duchense, 'Robert Brenner on political accumulation and the transition to capitalism', *Review of Radical Political Economics,* Vol. 33 (2001), 79–98.

87 Subhi Y. Labib, 'Capitalism in Medieval Islam', *Journal of Economic History*, Vol. 29, No. 1 (1969), 79–96; Jairus Banaji, *Theory as History: Essays on Modes of Production and Exploitation* (Leiden, Neths: Brill, 2010).

88 James M. Blaut, 'Robert Brenner in the tunnel of time', *Antipode*, Vol. 26, No. 4 (1991), 351–74.

89 Marx, *Capital, I*, 915.

90 Perry Anderson, *Spectrum: From Left to Right in the World of Ideas* (London: Verso, 2005), 251.

91 See, among others, Cho-yun Hsu, 'Asian influences on the West', in C. Gluck and A. T. Embree (eds), *Asia in Western and World history: A Guide for Teaching* (New York: M.E. Sharp, 1997), 22–31, 27fn2; John M. Hobson, *The Eastern Origins of Western*

Civilisation (Cambridge: Cambridge University Press, 2004), esp. 190–219; Jack Goody, *The East in the West* (Cambridge: Cambridge University Press, 1996).

92 Kamran Matin, 'Democracy without capitalism: retheorizing Iran's constitutional revolution', *Middle East Critique*, Vol. 21, No. 1 (2012), 37–56, 45.

93 Brenner views capitalist property relations as emerging in such regions as Catalonia and the United Provinces in the late 15th and 16th centuries respectively, though he has not reflected on how these developments might problematise his original account of the origins of capitalism, which exclusively focuses on the English countryside. Other Political Marxists have, by contrast, viewed the origins of capitalism as an exclusively English affair. On the Dutch case, see Brenner, 'Low Countries'; and responses from Ellen Meiksins Wood, 'The question of market dependence', *Journal of Agrarian Change*, Vol. 2, No. 1 (2002), 50–87; Charles Post, 'Comments on the Brenner–Wood exchange on the Low Countries', *Journal of Agrarian Change*, Vol. 2, No. 1 (2002), 88–95; cf. Teschke, *Myth of 1648*, 136. On Catalonia, see Brenner, 'Agrarian class structure', 49fn81; and Brenner, 'The rises and declines of serfdom in Medieval and early modern Europe', in M. L. Bush (ed.), *Serfdom and Slavery: Studies in Legal Bondage* (London: Longmans, 1996), 247–76, 264–72. For a critique, see Jaimie Torras, 'Class struggle in Catalonia: a note on Brenner', *Review*, Vol. 4, No. 2 (1980), 253–65.

94 Anderson, *Spectrum*, 251. For some Political Marxists' explicit embrace of the 'capitalism in one country' thesis, see Wood, *Origin of Capitalism*, 48; Teschke, *Myth of 1648*, 255; Lacher, *Beyond Globalization,* 90–2.

95 Wood, *Origin of Capitalism*, 56.

96 Brenner, 'Property relations', 23.

97 Chris Harman and Robert Brenner, 'The origins of capitalism', *International Socialism*, Series II, Vol. 111 (2006), 127–62, 138.

98 See, among others, Brenner, 'Origins of capitalist development', 36–7, 48–9; Brenner, 'Property and progress', 73; Wood, *Origin of Capitalism*, 6–7, 11–12; Lacher, *Beyond Globalization*, 29–30; Vivek Chibber, 'What is living and what is dead in Marx's theory of history', *Historical Materialism*, Vol. 19, No. 2 (2011), 60–91; Spencer Dimmock, *The Origin of Capitalism in England, 1400–1600* (Leiden, Neths: Brill, 2014), esp. 157–232.

99 Derek Sayer, *The Violence of Abstraction: The Analytical Foundations of Historical Materialism* (London: Basil Blackwell, 1987), 28–39. This is a good example of how Marx's general 'transhistorical' concepts only acquire their substantive meanings in and through their particular historical contexts (see further Chapter 2).

100 Davidson, *How Revolutionary*, 128.

101 Davidson, *How Revolutionary*, 522.

102 For an overview of some of this literature, see Chris Wickham, 'Productive forces and the economic logic of the feudal mode of production', *Historical Materialism*, Vol. 16, No. 2 (2008), 3–22.

103 Brenner, 'The social basis', 31–2. See also Brenner, 'Property relations and the growth of agricultural productivity in late Medieval and early modern Europe', in A. Bhaduri and R. Skarstein (eds), *Economic Development and Agricultural Productivity* (Cheltenham: Edward Elgar, 1997), 9–41, 21. It is worth noting that Brenner emphasises that the 'lords turn to political accumulation as a rule of reproduction is *inexplicable* merely in terms of its potential for increasing lordly income. It was *imposed* upon the majority of lords as a consequence of the structure of feudal economy as a whole. Feudal society was constituted by a multiplicity of *separate, initially localized, lordly groups* organized for the purpose of exerting force' ('Property relations', 21, emphasis ours). Again, we see here how the specific determinations arising from the coexistence and interaction of a plurality of political communities ('the international') ends up playing an explanatory role in Brenner's account without itself being

theorised. Brenner assumes without explaining an important condition of feudalism's development and reproduction.

104 Brenner, 'Social basis', 23–53, 32; cf. Brenner, 'Low Countries', 178–9.

105 Teschke and Lacher are returning here to issues first raised by Colin Barker and Claudia von Braunmühl's interventions into the state-derivation debates of the 1970s, but with differing theoretical conclusions: see Barker, 'A note on the theory of capitalist states', *Capital and Class*, Vol. 2, No. 1 (1978), 118–26; Barker, 'State as capital', *International Socialism*, Series II, No. 1 (1978), 16–42; Braunmühl, 'On the analysis of the bourgeois nation state within the world market context: an attempt to develop a methodological and theoretical approach', in J. Holloway and S. Picciotto (eds), *State and Capital: A Marxist Debate* (London: Edward Arnold, 1978), 160–77.

106 Hannes Lacher, 'Making sense of the international system: the promises and pitfalls of contemporary Marxist theories of international relations', in M. Rupert and H. Smith (eds), *Historical Materialism and Globalization* (London: Routledge, 2002), 147–64, 148; Lacher, *Beyond Globalization*, 60; Teschke, *Myth of 1648*, 145–6.

107 Hence, Teschke writes, 'we should expect [capitalism] to bring about the decline of external geopolitical accumulation that defined the war-driven international conduct of the feudal and absolutist ages' (*Myth of 1648*, 267).

108 Ellen Meiksins Wood, *Empire of Capital* (London: Verso, 2003), 110–11.

109 Brenner, 'Low countries', 190–1.

110 Erica Schoenberger, 'The origins of the market economy: state power, territorial control, and modes of war fighting', *Comparative Studies in Society and History*, Vol. 50, No. 3 (2008), 663–91, 663, 686, 689.

111 William H. McNeil, *The Pursuit of Power: Technology, Armed Force, and Society since AD 1000* (Chicago, Ill.: University of Chicago Press, 1982), 115–16.

112 Marx, *Grundrisse* (Harmondsworth: Penguin, 1973 [1857–58]), 109.

113 Michael Mann, *The Sources of Social Power: A History of Power from the Beginning to AD 1760, Vol. I* (Cambridge: Cambridge University Press, 1986), 17.

114 Davidson, *How Revolutionary*, 533.

115 Dante famously compared the Arsenal to the crowded depths of hell in lines 7–15 of *Inferno*, Canto I.

116 Robert C. Davis, *Shipbuilders of the Venetian Arsenal: Workers and Workplace in the Preindustrial City* (Baltimore, Md.: Johns Hopkins University Press, 1991), 5.

117 George Modelski and William R. Thompson, *Leading Sectors and World Powers: The Coevolution of Global Politics and Economics* (Columbia, S.C.: University of South Carolina Press, 1996), 237fn4; Nick T. Thomopoulos, *Assembly Line, Planning and Control* (London: Springer, 2014), 7–8.

118 Luca Zan, 'Accounting and management discourse in proto-industrial settings: the Venice Arsenal in the turn of the 16th century', *Accounting and Business Research*, Vol. 34, No. 2 (2004), 145–75, 146, 149.

119 Pepijn Brandon, 'Masters of war: state, capital, and military enterprise in the Dutch cycle of accumulation (1600–1795)', PhD dissertation, University of Amsterdam, 2013, 314–15.

120 Marcus Rediker, *Between the Devil and the Deep Blue Sea: Merchant Seamen, Pirates and the Anglo-American Maritime World, 1700–1750* (Cambridge: Cambridge University Press, 1987), 114, 78, 114.

121 Ellen Meiksins Wood, 'A reply to my critics', *Historical Materialism*, Vol. 15, No. 3 (2007), 143–70, 145. By contrast, for Brenner, the two key conditions for capitalism's existence are that: (1) economic agents must be separated from their means of subsistence (but not necessarily the means of production); and (2) they must lack the means of coercion which would allow them to reproduce themselves by systematically appropriating by force the required surpluses from the direct producers (Brenner, 'Property and progress', 60).

122 Ellen Meiksins Wood, 'The separation of the economic and the political in capitalism', *New Left Review*, Series I, No. 127 (1981), 66–95, 81–2.

123 Ben Selwyn, 'Beyond firm centrism: re-integrating labour and capitalism into global commodity chain analysis', *Journal of Economic Geography*, Vol. 12, No. 1 (2012), 205–26, 211. On the problems of conflating modes of production to forms of exploitation, see Colin Mooers, *The Making of Bourgeois Europe: Absolutism, Revolution, and the Rise of Capitalism in England, France, and Germany* (London: Verso, 1991), 22–3.

124 Marx, *Grundrisse*, 513. Charles Post has offered a critique of Marxist conceptions of planation slavery as capitalist, emphasising in particular the difference between capitalists purchasing *labour-power* and slave masters purchasing *labourers*, a consequence of the latter being that 'slaves could not be "dismissed at any time" and replaced with more complex tools and machinery' ('Capitalism, laws of motion and social relations of production', *Historical Materialism*, Vol. 21, No. 4, 2013, 71–91, 84). Yet, as examined in Chapter 5, plantation owners could – and often did – expel slaves and introduce labour-saving technologies.

125 Neil Davidson, 'Revolutions between theory and history: a response to Alex Callinicos and Donny Gluckstein', *International Socialism*, Series II, Vol. 142 (2014).

126 Banaji, *Theory as History*, 145.

127 Although Benno Teschke evokes the concept of 'uneven and combined development', combination remains operative only at the level of interstate interactions.

128 Wood, *Empire of Capital*, 44–72; Teschke, *Myth of 1648*, 197–212.

129 See e.g. Charles Post, *American Road to Capitalism: Studies in Class-structure, Economic Development and Political Conflict, 1620–1877* (Leiden, Neths: Brill, 2011), ch. 3.

130 Ellen Meiksins Wood, 'The uses and abuses of "civil society"', in R. Miliband and L. Pantich (eds), *The Retreat of the Intellectuals: Socialist Register 1990* (London: Merlin, 1990), 60–84, 74, 76.

131 Banaji, *Theory as History*.

132 Silvia Federici, *Caliban and the Witch: Women, the Body and Primitive Accumulation* (New York: Autonomedia, 2004).

133 Dipesh Chakrabarty, *Provincializing Europe: Postcolonial Thought and Historical Difference* (Princeton, N.J.: University of Princeton Press, 2nd Ed., 2008).

134 Endnotes Collective, 'The logic of gender', *Endnotes 3: Gender, Race, Class and Other Misfortunes* (2013).

135 Chris Chen, 'The limit point of capitalist equality', *Endnotes 3: Gender, Race, Class and Other Misfortunes* (2013). http://endnotes.org.uk/en/chris-chen-the-limit-point-of-capitalist-equality (accessed 21 February 2014).

136 See esp. Vivek Chibber, *Postcolonial Theory and the Specter of Capital* (London: Verso, 2013).

137 Benno Teschke, 'International relations, historical materialism and the false promise of international historical sociology', *Spectrum*, Vol. 6, No. 1 (2014), 1–66, 35.

138 Ellen Meiksins Wood, *Democracy against Capitalism: Renewing Historical Materialism* (Cambridge: Cambridge University Press, 1995), 55–6.

139 But see the postcolonial-influenced works of A. G. Frank: *ReOrient: Global Economy in the Asian Age* (Berkeley, Calif.: University of California Press, 1998); Hobson, *Eastern Origins*.

140 Chakrabarty, *Provincializing Europe*.

141 Edward Said, *Orientalism: Western Conceptions of the Orient* (London: Routledge & Kegan Paul, 1978).

142 Gurminder K. Bhambra, *Rethinking Modernity: Postcolonialism and the Sociological Imagination* (London: Palgrave Macmillan, 2009).

143 Amitav Acharya, 'Dialogue and discovery: in search of international relations theories beyond the West', *Millennium*, Vol. 39, No. 3 (2011), 619–37.

144 Homi K. Bhabha, *The Location of Culture* (London: Routledge, 2012).

145 See Bhambra, *Rethinking Modernity*, esp. 34–55.

146 Vasant Kaiwar, *The Postcolonial Orient: The Politics of Difference and the Project of Provincialising Europe* (Leiden, Neths: Brill, 2014), 28.

147 Chakrabarty, *Provincializing Europe*, 47–8. This is evident, as we have seen in WST, where the inflation of capitalism into an all-subsuming category gives rise to a particularly problematic and Eurocentric history of non-Western societies.

148 Chakrabarty, *Provincializing Europe*, 48.

149 Chakrabarty, *Provincializing Europe*, 7–8.

150 Chakrabarty, *Provincializing Europe*, 7. Historicism is therefore heavily inscribed within the narrative of historical 'transition'. In the transition narrative, history tends to be hung between 'the two poles of homologous sets of oppositions: despotic/ constitutional, medieval/ modern, feudal/ capitalist'. In colonial histories then 'this transition narrative was an unabashed celebration of the imperialists' capacity for violence and conquest' (ibid., 32).

151 Chakrabarty, *Provincializing Europe*, 8; see also Partha Chatterjee, 'A brief history of Subaltern Studies', in *Empire and Nation: Selected Essays* (New York: Columbia University Press, 2010), 296–7. The clearest example of this is in colonial ideology, of which John Stuart Mill was perhaps the most explicit proponent. But postcolonialists also trace this attitude in more radical thinkers, not least Karl Marx, whose argument that 'the country that is more developed industrially only shows, to the less developed, the image of its own future' has been inscribed into the theoretical presuppositions of WST and Political Marxism.

152 Chakrabarty, *Provincializing Europe*, 11–12.

153 Chakrabarty, *Provincializing Europe*, 112, 47.

154 The peasant is lauded in postcolonialism as the agent that subverts historicism by its very agency, by its very participation in the 'path' of history it has been denied entry to – it is the *non*-rather than *pre*-bourgeois, the *non*- not *pre*-modern (Chakrabarty, *Provincializing Europe*, 10–11).

155 David Washbrook, 'South Asia, the world system, and world capitalism', *Journal of Asian Studies*, Vol. 49, No. 3 (1990), 479–82.

156 Chatterjee, 'Subaltern Studies', 292.

157 Partha Chatterjee, 'Peasants, politics and historiography: a response', *Social Scientist*, Vol. 11, No. 5 (1983), 64–5.

158 Chakrabarty, *Provincializing Europe*, xiv.

159 Chakrabarty, *Provincializing Europe*, xii. Interestingly, Chakrabarty implies that this is itself a universal law of (modern) history, when he suggests that 'if this argument is true of India, then it is true of any other place as well, including Europe'. See also Chatterjee, 'Subaltern Studies', 294.

160 Chakrabarty, *Provincializing Europe*, xii.

161 Partha Chatterjee, *The Nation and Its Fragments: Colonial and Postcolonial Histories* (Oxford: Princeton University Press, 1993), 235.

162 Chibber ultimately overstates his case by arguing that postcolonialists seek to 'defend the specificity of the East' by 'denying the applicability of Western theory's universalizing categories' and 'denying that capital successfully universalizes'. None of these charges are accurate. See Chibber, *Postcolonial Theory*, 212. For important responses to Chibber's ill-handled critique, see Partha Chatterjee, 'Subaltern Studies and capital', *Economic and Political Weekly*, Vol. 48, No. 37 (2013), 69–75; Sanjay Seth, 'Review of Vivek Chibber's *Postcolonial Theory and the Specter of Capital*', *American Historical Review*, Vol. 119, No.4 (2014), 1,218–20; Alexander Anievas and Kerem Nişancıoğlu, 'Chibber's follies: the potentials and pitfalls of *Postcolonial Theory and the Specter of Capital*', unpublished paper, 2015.

163 Chakrabarty, *Provincializing Europe*, 85.

164 Ranajit Guha, *Dominance without Hegemony: History and Power in Colonial India* (Cambridge, Mass.: Harvard University Press, 1997), 16.
165 Guha, *Dominance without Hegemony*, 16, emphasis ours.
166 Guha, *Dominance without Hegemony*, 5.
167 In contrast to Chibber's claims, *Postcolonial Theory*, 39.
168 Chakrabarty, *Provincializing Europe*, 43.
169 Marcus Taylor, 'Histories of world capitalism, methodologies of world labour: rethinking uneven development', paper for ECPR Standing Group on International Relations, Stockholm, Sweden, 15 July 2010.
170 Chakrabarty, *Provincializing Europe*, 45.
171 Chakrabarty, *Provincializing Europe*, 59–68.
172 Marx, *Grundrisse*, 701.
173 Marx, *Grundrisse*, 706.
174 Chakrabarty, *Provincializing Europe*, 63.
175 Chakrabarty, *Provincializing Europe*, 71.
176 Alfred Sohn-Rethel, *Intellectual and Manual Labour: A Critique of Epistemology* (New Jersey: Humanities Press, 1977).
177 Sohn-Rethel, *Intellectual and Manual Labour*, 63; Marx, *Grundrisse*, 105–6.
178 Chakrabarty, *Provincializing Europe*, 66.
179 Chakrabarty, *Provincializing Europe*, 64.
180 Chakrabarty, *Provincializing Europe*, 71.
181 See e.g. Christine Delphy and Diana Leonard, *Close to Home: A Materialist Analysis of Women's Oppression* (London: Hutchinson, 1984); Silvia Federici, *Revolution at Point Zero: Housework, Reproduction, and Feminist Struggle* (Oakland, Calif.: PM Press, 2012).
182 Chakrabarty, *Provincializing Europe*, 66.
183 'Capital originally finds the commodity already in existence, but not as its own product, and likewise finds money circulation, but not as an element in its own reproduction …. But both of them must be destroyed as independent forms and subordinated to industrial capital' (Marx quoted in Chakrabarty, *Provincializing Europe*, 64).
184 Chibber, *Postcolonial Theory*, 227.
185 Chibber, *Postcolonial Theory*, 235, 238.
186 As David Blaney and Naeem Inayatullah put it, Chakrabarty's readings of Marx's narrative in terms of History 1 and 2 'allow two historical stories: one comprising elements that are the logical/historical preconditions of capital (History 1) and another with elements that are not logical/historical preconditions but which capital nevertheless incorporates, internalizes, and transforms (History 2)' (*Savage Economics: Wealth, Poverty, and the Temporal Walls of Capitalism*, New York: Routledge, 2010, 167–8).
187 Chakrabarty, *Provincializing Europe*, 95.
188 Chibber, *Postcolonial Theory*, 238, emphasis original.
189 Chakrabarty, *Provincializing Europe*, 69, emphasis ours. It is worth noting that by invoking the term 'antecedent', Chakrabarty is not making an exclusively diachronic argument, although he does not deny the possibility of it being used diachronically.
190 Taylor, 'Histories of world capitalism', 5; see similarly, Robbie Shilliam, 'The Atlantic as a vector of uneven and combined development', *Cambridge Review of International Affairs*, Vol. 22, No. 1 (2009), 69–88, 72.
191 Taylor, 'Histories of world capitalism', 5.
192 Chakrabarty, *Provincializing Europe*, 67.
193 Chakrabarty, *Provincializing Europe*, 69.
194 Chakrabarty, *Provincializing Europe*, xvii.
195 Chakrabarty, *Provincializing Europe*, 65.
196 Chakrabarty, *Provincializing Europe*, 70.

197 www.marxists.org/archive/marx/works/1881/03/zasulich1.htm (accessed 20 January 2015).

198 It is notable, for example, that neither Marx nor Trotsky integrated the analysis of the nonwaged sphere into their examinations of capitalism in any systematic way. This has led many Marxists since to see relations of patriarchy and white supremacy as mere ideological functions of the otherwise economic logic of capitalism. Such reductionism has been forcefully challenged by an array of authors working from the perspectives (for want of better terms) of critical gender and race theory, who have emphasised that both patriarchy and racism must be viewed as sets of class relations. See Delphy and Leonard, *Close to Home*; Charles W. Mills, *The Racial Contract* (London: Cornell University Press, 1997); Linda Alcoff and Nancy Fraser, *Visible Identities: Race, Gender, and the Self* (Oxford: Oxford University Press, 2005); Federici, *Caliban and the Witch*; Federici, *Revolution at Point Zero*. These components of what might be classified as 'History 2' are looked at in more (although still perhaps not enough) detail in Chapters 5 and 7.

199 www.marxists.org/archive/marx/works/1877/11/russia.htm (accessed 20 January 2015). For good discussions of Marx's break with Eurocentric modes of analysis in his later writings, see Theodore Shanin, *Late Marx and the Russian Road: Marx and 'The Peripheries of Capitalism'* (New York: Monthly Review Press, 1983); August Nimtz, 'The Eurocentric Marx and Engels and other related myths' and Pranav Jani, 'Karl Marx, Eurocentrism, and the 1857 revolt in British India', in C. Bartolovich and N. Lazarus (eds), *Marxism, Modernity, and Postcolonial Studies* (Cambridge: Cambridge University Press, 2002), 65–80 and 81–97 respectively; Gareth Stedman Jones, 'Radicalism and the extra-European world: the case of Marx', in D. Bell (ed.), *Victorian Visions of Global Order: Empire and International Relations in Nineteenth Century Political Thought* (Cambridge: Cambridge University Press, 2007), 186–214; Kevin Anderson, *Marx at the Margins: On Nationalism, Ethnicity, and Non-Western Societies* (Chicago, Ill.: University of Chicago Press, 2010).

200 Chakrabarty, *Provincializing Europe*, 3.

201 Chatterjee, ' Subaltern Studies', 296–7.

202 Frederick Cooper, *Colonialism in Question: Theory, Knowledge, History* (Berkeley, Calif.: University of California Press, 2005), 20.

203 For two notable exceptions, see Bhambra, *Rethinking Modernity* and Shilliam, 'The Atlantic'.

204 Fernando Coronil, 'Beyond Occidentalism: toward nonimperial geohistorical categories', *Cultural Anthropology*, Vol. 11, No. 1 (1996), 51–87, 77–8; see similarly, Neil Lazarus, 'The fetish of "the West" in postcolonial theory', in Bartolovich and Lazarus, *Marxism, Modernity, and Postcolonial Studies*, 43–64.

205 See Arif Dirlik, *The Postcolonial Aura: Third World Criticism in the Age of Global Capitalism* (Oxford: Westview, 1997); Neil Lazarus, *The Postcolonial Unconscious* (Cambridge: Cambridge University Press, 2011).

206 Cooper, *Colonialism in Question*, 22.

207 Kamran Matin, 'Redeeming the universal: postcolonialism and the inner life of Eurocentrism', *European Journal of International Relations*, Vol. 19, No. 2 (2013), 353–77, 364.

208 Banaji, *Theory as History*, 253.

209 Manu Goswami, *Producing India: From Colonial Economy to National Space* (Chicago, Ill.: University of Chicago Press, 2004), 40.

210 See Robert A. Nisbet, *Social Change and History: Aspects of the Western Theory of Development* (Oxford: Oxford University Press, 1969).

211 Bertell Ollman, 'Marxism and political science: prolegomenon to a debate on Marx's method', in *Social and Sexual Revolution: Essays on Marx and Reich* (London: Pluto Press, 1979), 99–156, 105.

2 Rethinking the Origins of Capitalism

1 Leon Trotsky, *The Revolution Betrayed: What is the Soviet Union and Where is it Going?* (Delhi: Aakar, 1937), 240.

2 See, among others, Robert A. Nisbet, *Social Change and History: Aspects of the Western Theory of Development* (Oxford: Oxford University Press, 1969); R. N. Berki, 'On Marxian thought and the problem of international relations', *World Politics*, Vol. 24, No. 1 (1971), 80–105; Theda Skocpol, 'A critical review of Barrington Moore's *Social Origins of Dictatorship and Democracy*', *Politics and Society*, Vol. 4, No. 1 (1973), 1–34; Colin Barker, 'A Note on the Theory of capitalist states', *Capital and Class*, Vol. 2, No. 1 (1978), 118–26; W. B. Gallie, *Philosophers of Peace and War: Kant, Clausewitz, Marx, Engels and Tolstoy* (Cambridge: Cambridge University Press, 1978), 66–99; Charles Tilly, *Big Structures, Large Processes, Huge Comparisons* (New York: Russell Sage Foundation, 1984), esp. 11–12, 20–42; Anthony Giddens, *The Nation-State and Violence: A Contemporary Critique of Historical Materialism, Vol. II* (Cambridge: Polity, 1985), esp. 7–34; Fred Halliday, 'State and society in international relations: a second agenda', *Millennium*, Vol. 16, No. 2 (1987), 215–29; Michael Mann, *States, War, and Capitalism: Studies in Political Sociology* (Oxford: Blackwell, 1988); Andrew Linklater, *Beyond Realism and Marxism: Critical Theory and International Relations* (London: Macmillan, 1990); John M. Hobson, 'The historical sociology of the state and the state of historical sociology in international relations', *Review of International Political Economy*, Vol. 5, No. 2 (1998), 284–320; Friedrich Tenbruck, 'Internal history of society or universal history', *Theory, Culture, and Society*, Vol. 11 (1994), 75–93; Benno Teschke, 'Bourgeois revolution, state formation and the absence of the international', *Historical Materialism*, Vol. 13, No. 2 (2005), 3–26; Justin Rosenberg, 'Why is there no international historical sociology?', *European Journal of International Relations*, Vol. 12, No. 3 (2006), 307–40; Kees van der Pijl, *Nomads, Empires, States: Modes of Foreign Relations and Political Economy, Vol. 1* (London: Pluto, 2007); Andrew Davenport, 'Marxism in IR: condemned to a realist fate?', *European Journal of International Relations*, Vol. 19, No. 1 (2013), 27–48.

3 Rosenberg, 'International historical sociology?'

4 Tenbruck, 'Internal history', 75.

5 But for an alternative to uneven and combined development see Kees van der Pijl's conceptualisation of intersocietal relations as historically distinct 'modes of foreign relations' (in *Nomads, Empires, States*). These two approaches are not mutually exclusive or necessarily incompatible, as long as two significant caveats are taken into account. First, the concept of 'modes of foreign relations' must be extricated from van der Pijl's own particular conceptualisation of them as essentially 'ideal-type' abstractions. Second, van der Pijl's relatively uncritical use of the notion of 'ethnogenesis', drawn from Soviet ethnological studies, needs to be substantially reconstructed or dispensed with altogether, as it reproduces an array of highly problematic essentialist assumptions (see Mark Bassin, 'Nurture is nature: Lev Gumilev and the ecology of ethnicity', *Slavic Review*, Vol. 68, No. 4 (2009), 872–97).

6 Hobson, 'Historical sociology', 288.

7 Martin Hall, 'Review: international relations and historical sociology: taking stock of convergence', *Review of International Political Economy*, Vol. 6, No. 1 (1999), 101–9, 108, emphasis ours.

8 Rosenberg, 'International historical sociology?' 308.

9 For a list of some of these contributions, see www.unevenandcombineddevelopment. wordpress.com/writings

10 Michael Löwy, *The Politics of Combined and Uneven Development: The Theory of Permanent Revolution* (London: Verso, 1981), 87.

11 Leon Trotsky, *History of the Russian Revolution*, 3 vols (Chicago: Haymarket, 2008 [1930]), 5.

12 Justin Rosenberg, 'The "philosophical premises" of uneven and combined development', *Review of International Studies*, Vol. 39, No. 3 (2013), 569–97, 576.

13 Rosenberg, 'International historical sociology?' 324.

14 Trotsky, *History*, 3–4.

15 See Luke Cooper, 'Uneven and combined development in modern world history: Chinese economic reform in the *longue durée* of capitalist modernity', paper for International Studies Association Annual Convention, San Diego, 1–4 April 2012, 6.

16 Leon Trotsky, *The Permanent Revolution and Results and Prospects* (London: Labor, 1962 [1930/1906]), 131.

17 Trotsky, *History*, 335, 474.

18 Trotsky, *History*, 476.

19 Trotsky, *History*, 5–6, 474.

20 Trotsky's original conception of unevenness, registering the multiple and changing socio-spatial fields and scales of historical development, is somewhat at odds with Rosenberg's (at times) more Weberian-influenced conception of states as territorially demarcated sovereign political spaces which could be construed as ontologising and projecting back in time the historically distinct state form that only fully emerged during the capitalist epoch. As Thierry Lapointe and Frédérick Guillaume Dufour point out, 'spatial categories (urban, regional, national, international, global) are historically laden, and the task of Marxist historical sociology, which takes geography seriously, should be to address their historicity' ('Assessing the historical turn in IR: an anatomy of second wave historical sociology', *Cambridge Review of International Affairs*, Vol. 25, No. 1 (2012), 97–121, 117). For a critique of Rosenberg's dehistoricisation of the modern state form, see Benno Teschke, 'IR theory, historical materialism and the false promise of international historical sociology', *Spectrum*, Vol. 6, No. 1 (2014), 1–66, esp. 48–54.

21 See, respectively, Michael Mann, *The Sources of Social Power: A History of Power from the Beginning to AD 1760, Vol. I* (Cambridge: Cambridge University Press, 1986), esp. 9–13; J. R. McNeil and William H. McNeil, *The Human Web* (London: W.W. Norton, 2003).

22 This contradicts Benno Teschke's misguided criticisms of uneven and combined development (rather than Rosenberg's specific conception of it) as *inherently* presupposing the territorialised, modern form of state that is, of course, inapplicable to understanding the overlapping forms of political sovereignty found under feudalism (in 'IR theory', 48–54). Moreover, while Rosenberg has yet to provide an analysis of uneven and combined development under feudalism, his earlier work on hunter-gatherer bands not only demonstrates the dynamics of uneven and combined development operating in non- and pre-state historical contexts, but also that these historically unique forms of unevenness and combination were themselves constitutive of states. See Justin Rosenberg, 'Basic problems in the theory of uneven and combined development. Part II: Unevenness and political multiplicity', *Cambridge Review of International Affairs*, Vol. 23, No. 1 (2010), 165–89.

23 Trotsky, *History*, 4, 477.

24 Trotsky, *History*, 4.

25 See Kamran Matin, 'Uneven and combined development in world history: the international relations of state-formation in pre-modern Iran', *European Journal of International Relations*, Vol. 13, No. 3 (2007), 419–47, 430. However, as examined in Chapter 3, this 'whip of external necessity' sometimes operated more as a 'gift of external opportunity' in the form of trans-spatial flows of technologies, trade, ideas, and disease that enabled, often paradoxically (as the case with the Black Death demonstrates), developmental advances in Europe. We thank John M. Hobson for suggesting this term to us.

26 Karl Marx and Friedrich Engels, *The German Ideology* (Amherst, Mass.: Prometheus,

1998 [1845–6]).

27   See Robert Moore, 'World history', in M. Bentley (ed.), *Companion to Historiography* (London: Routledge, 1993), 941–59, 947.

28   Marx and Engels, *The German Ideology*, 37.

29   Rosenberg, 'Basic problems, II', 180.

30   Trotsky, *Permanent Revolution*, 170, 172–3; Trotsky, *History*, 2–3.

31   Barry Buzan and Richard Little, *International Systems in World History: Remaking the Study of International Relations* (Oxford: Oxford University Press, 2000), 118.

32   Rosenberg, 'Basic problems, II', 180.

33   Whatever the particular faults of Rosenberg's analysis of the emergence of political multiplicity, it does, we believe, have the great benefit of successfully demonstrating that uneven and combined development can offer a coherent historical and sociological theorisation of 'the international' without assuming away the very object of explanation that needs to be explained (that is, political multiplicity), as is so often found in mainstream IR.

34   Karman Matin, *Recasting Iranian Modernity: International Relations and Social Change* (London: Routledge, 2013), 154.

35   Robert W. Cox, 'Thinking about civilizations', *Review of International Studies*, Vol. 26 (2000), 217–34, 220.

36   See Leon Trotsky, *The Third International After Lenin* (New York: Pioneer, 1936), 19–20.

37   Trotsky, *History*, 5.

38   Rosenberg, 'International historical sociology?' 319; see also Eric Wolf, *Europe and the People without History* (Berkeley, Calif.: University of California Press, 2010 [1982]), 18–19.

39   Trotsky, *History*, 5.

40   Trotsky, *History*, 4, 5.

41   Leon Trotsky, 'Introduction to *The Tragedy of the Chinese Revolution*', in Harold Isaacs, *The Tragedy of the Chinese Revolution* (London: Secker & Warburg, 2009 [1938]), xv. In this sense, the concept of combined development cannot be reduced to similar notions of 'articulated modes of production' or the like.

42   Trotsky, *History*, 5.

43   Leon Trotsky, 'Notebook on Hegel', in *Trotsky's Notebooks, 1933–1935: Writings on Lenin, Dialectics, and Evolutionism*, trans., annot. and intro. P. Pomper (New York: Columbia University Press, 1998 [1934–35]), 77.

44   Davidson, *How Revolutionary?* 300.

45   Karl Marx, *Grundrisse* (Harmondsworth: Penguin, 1973 [1857–8]).

46   Quoted in Tony Cliff, 'Trotsky on substitutionism', *International Socialism*, Series I, No. 2 (1960), 14–17, 22–6, www.marxists.org/archive/cliff/works/1960/xx/trotsub. htm (accessed 10 October 2014). See Baruch Knei-Paz, *The Social and Political Thought of Leon Trotsky* (Oxford: Oxford University Press, 1978), 192–8.

47   But for a critical account of Trotsky's own problematic advocacy of substitutionism in 1920, see Luke Cooper, 'Beyond Leninism', *Anticapitalist Initiative* (May 2013) http:// anticapitalists.org/2013/05/23/beyond-leninism/ (accessed 17 November, 2014)

48   Trotsky, *History*, 7.

49   Matin, *Recasting Iranian Modernity*, 19.

50   Leon Trotsky, 'For the internationalist perspective', in *Leon Trotsky Speaks* (New York: Pathfinder, 1972 [1924]), 199.

51   Ernest Bloch, 'Nonsynchronism and the obligation to its dialectics', *New German Critique*, No. 11 (1977 [1932]), 22–38, 31–32.

52   Ben Selwyn, 'Trotsky, Gerschenkron, and the political economy of late capitalist development', *Economy and Society*, Vol. 40, No. 3 (2011), 421–50, 434. The following draws and expands on arguments in Alexander Anievas, *Capital, the State, and War:*

Class Conflict and Geopolitics in the Thirty Years' Crisis, 1914–1945 (Ann Arbor, Mich.: University of Michigan Press, 2014), 48–9.

53 George Lawson, 'Rosenberg's Ode to Bauer, Kinkel, and Willich', *International Politics*, Vol. 43, No. 3 (2005), 381–9; Benno Teschke, 'Marxism', in D. Snidel and C. Reus-Smit (eds), *The Oxford Handbook of International Relations* (Oxford: Oxford University Press, 2008), 163–87, 180; Teschke, 'Advances and impasses in Fred Halliday's international historical sociology: a critical appraisal', *International Affairs*, Vol. 87, No. 5 (2011), 1,087–1,106, 1,102; Teschke, 'IR theory', 35–8.

54 Trotsky, *History*, 54.

55 Michael Burawoy, 'Two methods in search of science: Skocpol versus Trotsky', *Theory and Society*, Vol. 18, No. 6 (1989), 758–805, 784.

56 Teschke, 'Marxism', 180.

57 Daniel McCarthy, 'Technological determinism and "the international", or, how I learned to stop worrying and love determinism', *Millennium*, Vol. 41, No. 3 (2013), 470–90, 477.

58 Leon Trotsky, 'Uneven and combined development and the role of American imperialism: minutes of a discussion', in *Writings of Leon Trotsky (1932–1933)* (New York: Pathfinder Press, 1972 [1933]), 116–20, 117. While Trotsky here only addresses the ideological aspect of this perpetuated form of combination in the United States, this was in fact rooted in the amalgamation of the differential developmental paths of the Northern and Southern halves of the United States right up to the end of the Second World War. Both the United States as a whole and the American South in particular can be thus conceived as combined forms of development (see Brian Kelly, 'Materialism and the persistence of race in the Jim Crow South', *Historical Materialism*, Vol. 12, No. 2 (2004), 3–19, 11). For a reconstruction of Trotsky's thoughts on Nazi Germany as another example of a 'perpetuated combination', see Anievas, *Capital, the State, and War*, 139–84.

59 Leon Trotsky, 'The Negro question in America', in G. Breitman (ed.), *Leon Trotsky on Black Nationalism and Self-Determination* (New York: Pathfinder, 1978 [1933]), 20–31, 25–6.

60 See Sam Ashman, 'Capitalism, uneven and combined development and the transhistoric', *Cambridge Review of International Affairs*, Vol. 22, No. 1 (2009), 29–46; Selwyn, 'Trotsky'.

61 Dipesh Chakrabarty, *Provincializing Europe: Postcolonial Thought and Historical Difference* (Princeton, N.J.: Princeton University Press, 2nd edn, 2008), 23, paraphrasing Walter Benjamin, 'Theses on the philosophy of history', in *Illuminations*, intro. H. Arendt (London: Pimlico, 1999), 245–56, 255.

62 Gurminder K. Bhambra, 'Talking among themselves? Weberian and Marxist historical sociologies as dialogues without others', *Millennium*, Vol. 39, No. 3 (2011), 667–81, 673. In Chapter 5, we offer a historical sociological analysis of the rise of Enlightenment 'stagist' thinking as organically emerging with the colonial encounter between the Europeans and Amerindians.

63 'The modern history of Russia', Trotsky wrote, 'cannot be comprehended unless the Marxist schema of the three stages is known: handicraft, manufacture, factory. But if one knows only this, one still comprehends nothing. For the fact is that the history of Russia … skipped a few stages. The theoretical distinction of the stages, however, is necessary for Russia, too, otherwise one can comprehend neither what this leap amounted to nor what its consequences were …. The quantitative contraction of the two stages was so great that it engendered an *entirely new quality in the whole social structure of the nation*' (*Permanent Revolution*, 240, emphasis ours).

64 Peter Thomas, 'Uneven developments, combined: the First World War and Marxist theories of revolution', in A. Anievas (ed.), *Cataclysm 1914: The First World and the Making of Modern World Politics* (Leiden, Neths: Brill, 2015), 280–301, 287. It is important to note here that although much of the recent scholarly literature on

rethinking uneven and combined development as a theory of 'the international' has proceeded without any attention to its relationship to Trotsky's strategy of permanent revolution, the two are, in our view, connected. Thus, in contrast to both Davidson and Rosenberg's explicit decoupling of the strategy from the theory in contemporary world politics, we will, in this book's conclusion, tease out some of the (geo)political implications of the theory of uneven and combined development for revolutionary politics. In turn, for the strategic importance of uneven and combined development to be brought out, it must be rehistoricised in ways that reflect the very different socio-historical conditions of 'late' capitalism (in ways that may well depart significantly from Trotsky's own politics). On the decoupling of uneven and combined development from permanent revolution, see Justin Rosenberg, 'Anarchy in the mirror of 'uneven and combined development: an open letter to Kenneth Waltz', paper for the British-German IR Conference BISA/DVPW, Arnoldshain, Germany, 2008, 12fn14; Neil Davidson, 'From deflected revolution to the law of uneven and combined development', *International Socialism*, Series II, Vol. 128 (2010); Davidson, *How Revolutionary*, 621–9.

65 Meera Sabaratnam, 'The manacles of (uneven and combined) development: can we be released?' paper for British International Studies Association Annual Conference, Manchester, UK, 27–29 April 2011.

66 Our discussion below of the place of 'development' in the theory of uneven and combined development is not a defence of Rosenberg's use of the concept. As should be clear, our reconstruction of Trotsky's idea, while undoubtedly influenced by Rosenberg, is by no means identical to his approach.

67 Sabaratnam, 'Manacles', 2.

68 Sabaratnam, 'Manacles', 13.

69 Sabaratnam, 'Manacles', 2

70 Althusser's redeployment of the Freudian concept of 'overdetermination' was formulated to capture such processes in which 'a complex process of causality which functions in a contradictory social whole, composed of a multiplicity of distinct, but internally related and mutually constitutive, practices having a tendency – because of their spatiotemporal separation within complex social formations – to drift apart' (Mark Laffey and Kathryn Dean, 'A flexible Marxism for flexible times: historical materialism and globalization', in M. Rupert and H. Smith (eds), *Historical Materialism and Globalization: Essays on Continuity and Change*, London: Routledge, 2002, 90–109, 100). While identifying the problem, Althusser never offered a theoretical solution as the concept remained operative in his works at the conjunctural level, retaining an essentially external relation to theory. Louis Althusser, *For Marx* (London: Verso, 1985).

71 Perry Anderson, 'The notion of bourgeois revolution', in *English Questions* (London: Verso, 1992), 106–18, 116.

72 Antonio Gramsci, *Selections from the Prison Notebooks* (London: Lawrence & Wishart, 1971), 465.

73 See David Blackbourn and Geoff Eley, *The Peculiarities of German History: Bourgeois Society and Politics in Nineteenth-Century Germany* (Oxford: Oxford University Press, 1984).

74 See also Laura Doyle and Sanjay Subrahmanyam. 'Inter-imperiality: dialectics in a postcolonial world history', *Interventions*, Vol. 16, No. 2 (2014), 159–96; Laura Doyle, 'Dialectics in the longer durée: the IIPEC model of inter-imperial economy and culture', *Globalizations*, Vol. 11, No. 5 (2014), 689–709.

75 Philip McMichael, 'Incorporating comparison within a world-historical perspective: an alternative comparative method', *American Sociological Review*, Vol. 55, No. 3 (1990), 385–97, 386. See also Jamie C. Allinson and Alexander Anievas, 'The uneven and combined development of the Meiji Restoration: a passive revolutionary road to capitalist modernity', *Capital and Class*, Vol. 34, No. 3 (2010), 469–90, 480.

76 Gramsci, *Selections*, 84 (Q 19, §24).

77 Knei-Paz, *Social and Political Thought*, 63.

78 With this said we do recognise that the terms 'advanced' and 'backward' conjure a temporal/developmental imaginary with its various normative implications, and would be keen to jettison the terms altogether. However, we have yet to find more suitable alternatives, which is something we and future scholars could attempt to better explicate and conceptualise.

79 Sabaratnam, 'Manacles', 18.

80 John M. Hobson, 'What's at stake in the neo-Trotskyist debate? Towards a non-Eurocentric historical sociology of uneven and combined development', *Millennium,* Vol. 40, No. 1 (2011), 147–66, 153.

81 Bhambra, 'Talking among themselves?' 676.

82 Cemal Burak Tansel, 'Deafening silence? Marxism, international historical sociology and the spectre of Eurocentrism', *European Journal of International Relations,* Vol. 21, No. 1 (2014), 76–100.

83 Bhambra, 'Talking among themselves?' 668, 673.

84 John M. Hobson, 'What's at stake in bringing historical sociology back into international relations? Transcending "chronofetishism" and "tempocentrism" in international relations', in S. Hobden and J. M. Hobson (eds), *Historical Sociology of International Relations* (Cambridge: Cambridge University Press, 2002), 3–41.

85 Rosenberg, 'International historical sociology?'; Matin, *Recasting Iranian Modernity.*

86 Neil Davidson, 'Putting the nation back into "the International"', *Cambridge Review of International Affairs,* Vol. 22, No. 1 (2009), 9–28, 17.

87 See, among others, Neil Smith, 'The geography of uneven development', in B. Dunn and H. Radice (eds), *100 Years of Permanent Revolution: Results and Prospects* (London: Pluto, 2006), 180–95; Ashman, 'Capitalism'; Davidson, 'Putting the nation'; Teschke, 'Advances and impasses'; Selwyn, 'Trotsky'.

88 Ashman, 'Capitalism', 30–1.

89 Fredric Jameson, *The Political Unconscious: Narrative as a Socially Symbolic Act* (Ithaca, N.Y.: Cornell University Press, 1981), 9.

90 See esp. Derek Sayer, *Marx's Method: Ideology, Science, and Critique in 'Capital'* (Atlantic Highlands, N.J.: Humanities Press, 1979), esp. 78–9, 87–8, 91–103, 109–13, 144, 146–7; Derek Sayer, *The Violence of Abstraction: The Analytical Foundations of Historical Materialism* (London: Basil Blackwell, 1987), 21; Allen Oakley, *Marx's Critique of Political Economy, Vol. I: Intellectual Sources and Evolution* (London: Routledge, 2003 [1984]), 139, 152; Joseph Fracchia, 'On transhistorical abstractions and the intersection of historical theory and social critique', *Historical Materialism,* Vol. 12 (2004), 125–46; Alex Callinicos, *Deciphering Capital: Marx's 'Capital' and Its Destiny* (London: Bookmarks, 2014), esp. 152–5.

91 Robert Wess, *Kenneth Burke: Rhetoric, Subjectivity, Postmodernism* (Cambridge: Cambridge University Press, 1996), 16.

92 Marx, *Grundrisse,* 108; and see Marx, 'Economic manuscript of 1861–63 (conclusion)', in *Marx–Engels Collected Works, 1861–63, Vol. 34* (London: Lawrence & Wishart, 1994 [1861–63]), 236.

93 Sayer, *Violence of Abstraction,* 13.

94 Henry Bernstein and Jacques Depelchin, 'The object of African history: a materialist perspective: II', *History in Africa,* Vol. 6, No. 1 (1979), 17–436, 31.

95 Marx, *Grundrisse,* 103, 105.

96 Karl Marx and Friedrich Engels, *Selected Letters* (Foreign Languages Press, 1977), 13–14 as cited in Sayer, *Violence of Abstraction,* 21.

97 David Harvey, *The Limits to Capital* (London: Verso, 2007), 2.

98 Marx, *Capital, Vol. I.*

99 Marx, *Capital, Vol. II* (Harmondsworth: Penguin, 1978 [1885]).

100 Marx, *Capital, Vol. III* (Harmondsworth: Penguin, 1981 [1894]); see also Roman Rosdolsky, *The Making of Marx's 'Capital'* (London: Pluto, 1977 [1968]).

101 Daniel Bensaïd, *Marx for Our Times: Adventures and Misadventures of a Critique* (London: Verso, 2009), 106.

102 Imre Lakatos, *Criticism and the Growth of Knowledge* (Cambridge: Cambridge University Press, 1970), 133–4. See further Anievas, *Capital, the State, and War*, 52–6.

103 Alexander Anievas, '1914 in world-historical perspective: the "uneven" and "combined" origins of the First World War', *European Journal of International Relations*, Vol. 19, No. 4 (2013), 721–46.

104 Bertell Ollman, *Dance of the Dialectic: Steps in Marx's Method* (Chicago, Ill.: University of Illinois Press, 2003), 110.

105 Jairus Banaji, *Theory as History: Essays on Modes of Production and Exploitation* (Leiden, Neths: Brill, 2010), 253.

106 As argued in Alexander Anievas and Kerem Nişancıoğlu, 'What's at stake in the transition debate? Rethinking the origins of capitalism and the "rise of the West"', *Millennium*, Vol. 42, No. 1 (2013), 78–102.

107 Alex Callinicos and Justin Rosenberg, 'Uneven and combined development: the social-relational substratum of "the international"? An exchange of letters', *Cambridge Review of International Affairs*, Vol. 21, No. 1 (2008), 77–112, 88.

108 These points go some way in addressing Benno Teschke's critique of Rosenberg's problematic undifferentiation of uneven and combined development as both a 'law' – meaning, in Marxist terms, a general sociohistorical *tendency* – and a 'theory', thus violating Kenneth Waltz's strict criteria for theory construction that Rosenberg seeks to engage (see Teschke 'IR theory', 28–9).

109 Indeed, a stronger argument could be made that the theoretical potential of uneven and combined development can only be fully realised through a mode of production-centred analysis and that it is incompatible with any (neo-)Weberian forms of theorising as it both rules out the utility of 'ideal-type' analytical constructs and fundamentally rejects any form of multi-causal explanation.

110 We emphasise this point as we hope it will guard against the continual assertions that any extension of uneven and combined development beyond the temporal boundaries of capitalist modernity inherently runs afoul of an overly abstract, ahistorical mode of theorising that offers only 'trivial', descriptive claims rather than substantive explanations. See e.g. John Elster, 'The theory of combined and uneven development: a critique', in J. Roemer (ed.), *Analytical Marxism* (Cambridge: Cambridge University Press, 1986), 54–63, 55–6; Smith, 'Geography of uneven development', 180–3; Ashman, 'Capitalism'; Teschke, 'IR theory', 24–48.

111 Matin, 'Redeeming the universal', 2.

3 The Long Thirteenth Century

1 Gilles Deleuze and Félix Guattari, *A Thousand Plateaus: Capitalism and Schizophrenia* (London: Continuum, 2004 [1980]), 25.

2 Iver B. Neumann and Einar Wigen, 'The importance of the Eurasian steppe to the study of international relations', *Journal of International Relations and Development*, Vol. 16, No. 3 (2013), 311–30, 312–13; David Sneath, *The Headless State: Aristocratic Orders, Kinship Society, and Misrepresentations of Nomadic Inner Asia* (New York: Columbia University Press, 2007), 3–6, 42–3.

3 Sneath, *Headless State*, 53–6.

4 Sneath, *Headless State*, 68–9.

5 Arnold J. Toynbee, *A Study of History: The Geneses of Civilizations, Part 1, Vol. I* (Oxford: Oxford University Press, 1987 [1934]), 164.

6 Toynbee, *A Study of History*, I, 215.

7 Perry Anderson, *Passages from Antiquity to Feudalism* (London: Verso, 1974), 217.

8   Toynbee, *A Study of History, I,* 173.

9   See e.g. Naoki Matsuura, 'Visiting patterns of two sedentarized Central African hunter-gatherers: comparison of the Babongo in Gabon and the Baka in Cameroon', *African Study Monographs,* Vol. 30, No. 3 (2009), 137–59.

10 David J. Silverman, '"We chuse to be bounded": Native American animal husbandry in colonial New England', *William and Mary Quarterly,* Vol. 60, No. 3 (2003), 511–48.

11 Thomas D. Hall, 'Civilizational change: the role of nomads', *Comparative Civilizations Review,* Vol. 24 (1991), 34–57, 46–7.

12 Selim Deringil, '"They live in a state of nomadism and savagery": the Late Ottoman Empire and the post-colonial debate', *Comparative Studies in Society and History,* Vol. 45, No. 2 (2003), 311–42; Ussama Makdisi, 'Ottoman Orientalism', *American Historical Review,* Vol. 107, No. 3 (2002), 768–96; Reşat Kasaba, *A Moveable Empire: Ottoman Nomads, Migrants, and Refugees* (Seattle, Wa.: University of Washington Press, 2009).

13 Sneath, *Headless State,* 71–84; Jeff Sahadeo, 'Conquest, colonialism, and nomadism on the Eurasian Steppe', *Kritika,* Vol. 4, No. 4 (2003), 942–54; Alexander Etkind, *Internal Colonization: Russia's Imperial Experience* (Cambridge: Polity Press, 2013).

14 Hall, 'Civilizational change', 34.

15 Neumann and Wigen, 'Eurasian steppe', 312–13.

16 Janet L. Abu-Lughod, *Before European Hegemony: The World System A.D. 1250–1350* (Oxford: Oxford University Press, 1989); David Christian, 'Inner Eurasia as a unit of world history', *Journal of World History,* Vol. 5, No. 2 (1994), 172–211; Hall, 'Civilizational change'; Neumann and Wigen, 'Eurasian Steppe'.

17 Rudi Paul Lindner, *Nomads and Ottomans in Medieval Anatolia* (Bloomington, Ind.: Indiana University, 1983); Kasaba, *A Moveable Empire*; Hall, 'Civilizational change'; Peter B. Golden, *An Introduction to the History of the Turkic Peoples: Ethnogenesis As State Formation in the Medieval and Early Modern Eurasia and the Middle East* (Weisbaden, Germany: O. Harrassowitz, 1992); Nicola di Cosmo, 'State formation and periodization in Inner Asian history', *Journal of World History,* Vol. 10, No. 1 (1999), 1–40; Thomas Jefferson Barfield, *The Perilous Frontier: Nomadic Empires and China* (London: B. Blackwell, 1989); Owen Lattimore, *Inner Asian Frontiers of China* (New York: Capitol, 1951).

18 Abu-Lughod, *Before European Hegemony*; Eric Mielants, *The Origins of Capitalism and the 'Rise of the West'* (Philadelphia, Pa.: Temple University Press, 2008); John M. Hobson, *The Eastern Origins of Western Civilisation* (Cambridge: Cambridge University Press, 2004), 44; Ronald Findlay and Kevin H. O'Rourke, *Power and Plenty: Trade, War, and the World Economy in the Second Millennium* (Oxford: Princeton University Press, 2007).

19 Peter Jackson has provided arguably the most systematic attempt to incorporate the Mongol Empire into the history of Europe (or rather Christendom). However, his is an exclusively Medieval history, with little attempt to assess its significance in the making of capitalist modernity. See Peter Jackson, *The Mongols and the West, 1221–1410* (Harlow: Pearson Education, 2005).

20 Jackson, *The Mongols and the West,* 5.

21 Abu-Lughod, *Before European Hegemony.*

22 On this general process of 'East to West' diffusion see the indispensable works of Jack Goody and John M. Hobson, especially Jack Goody, *The Theft of History* (Cambridge: Cambridge University Press, 2006); and Hobson, *Eastern Origins.*

23 J. R. McNeil and William H. McNeil, *The Human Web: A Bird-Eye's View of World History* (London: W.W. Norton, 2003), 117–18; Abu-Lughod, *Before European Hegemony,* 112.

24 Chris Harman, *A People's History of the World* (London: Bookmarks, 1999), 141; Hobson, *Eastern Origins,* 192.

25 Abu-Lughod, *Before European Hegemony,* 170.

26 Anderson, *Passages from Antiquity*, 222.

27 Abu-Lughud, *Before European Hegemony*, 183.

28 Eric R. Wolf, *Europe and the People without History* (Berkeley, Calif.: University of California Press, 2010 [1982]), 26.

29 Kamran Matin, 'Uneven and combined development in world history: the international relations of state-formation in pre-modern Iran', *European Journal of International Relations*, Vol. 13, No. 3 (2007), 419–47, 431.

30 Thomas J. Barfield, 'Conclusion', in N. N. Kradin et al. (eds), *Nomadic Pathways in Social Evolution* (Moscow: Russian Academy, 2003), 174; Anatoly Khazanov, 'Nomads of the Eurasian steppes in historical retrospective', in *Nomadic Pathways*, 25–49, 28.

31 Jackson, *The Mongols*, 32. Nomadic inventions such as the bit reins and stirrup were almost universally adopted. The decimal formation became common to all nomads and many sedentarised militaries, including the Ottomans. See Gérard Chaliand, *Nomadic Empires: From Mongolia to the Danube* (London: Transaction, 2006), 11; Reuven Amitai, 'Armies and their economic basis in Iran and the surrounding lands, c. 1000–1500', in D. O. Morgan and A. Reid (eds), *The New Cambridge History of Islam* (Cambridge: Cambridge University Press, 2010), 539–60, 550.

32 Abu-Lughud, *Before European Hegemony*, 154; Hall, 'Civilizational change', 48; di Cosmo, 'State formation', 4.

33 Di Cosmo, 'State formation', 24–5; Isenbike Togan, 'Ottoman history by Inner Asian norms', *Journal of Peasant Studies*, Vol. 18, No. 3–4 (1991), 185–210, 190–2.

34 Nicola di Cosmo, 'Mongols and merchants on the Black Sea frontier in the thirteenth and fourteenth centuries: convergences and conflicts', in R. Amitai and M. Biran (eds), *Mongols, Turks, and Others: Eurasian Nomads and The Sedentary World* (Leiden, Neths: Brill, 2005), 391–424, 391.

35 Sneath, *Headless State*.

36 Di Cosmo, 'State formation', 14–15.

37 Matin, 'Uneven and combined development', 431; see also Togan, 'Ottoman history', 187; Di Cosmo, 'State formation', 15.

38 Togan, 'Ottoman history', 192, 196. It would of course be an exaggeration to argue that nomadic societies were free from hierarchies.

39 Joseph Fletcher, 'Turco-Mongolian monarchic tradition in the Ottoman Empire', *Harvard Ukranian Studies*, Vol. 4, No. 3 (1979–80), 236–51, 237.

40 Matin, 'Uneven and combined development', 431.

41 Hall, 'Civilizational change', 42.

42 Khazanov, 'Nomads of the Eurasian Steppes', 29.

43 Khazanov, 'Nomads of the Eurasian Steppes', 31.

44 Lattimore, *Inner Asian Frontiers*, 519–23; Matin, 'Uneven and combined development', 432.

45 Matin, 'Uneven and combined development', 433.

46 Di Cosmo estimates that at its height, the Chingssid Empire had an army of 100,000, which would constitute almost every male of a fighting age. The personal bodyguard corps numbered around 10,000. Di Cosmo, 'State formation', 17–18.

47 Di Cosmo, 'State formation', 25; Hall, 'Civilizational change', 43.

48 Di Cosmo, 'State formation'.

49 Di Cosmo, 'State formation', 21.

50 Matin, 'Uneven and combined development'.

51 Andrew Linklater, *Beyond Realism and Marxism: Critical Theory and International Relations* (London: Macmillan, 1990), 37.

52 Kees van der Pijl, *Nomads, Empires, States: Modes of Foreign Relations and Political Economy, Vol. I* (London: Pluto, 2007), 63–4.

53 See Dmitri M. Bondarenko et al., 'Introduction: social evolution, alternative, and nomadism', in Kradin et al., *Nomadic Pathways*, 11.

54 Anderson, *Passages from Antiquity,* 222–3.
55 Chaliand, *Nomadic Empires,* 3.
56 Michal Biran, 'The Mongol Empire in world history: the state of the field', *History Compass,* Vol. 11, No. 11 (2013), 1021–33.
57 Findlay and O'Rourke, *Power and Plenty,* 108.
58 Rosenberg, 'Why is there no international historical sociology?', *European Journal of International Relations,* Vol. 12, No. 3 (2006), 307–40, 324.
59 Anderson, *Passages from Antiquity,* 218.
60 Anderson, *Passages from Antiquity,* 218, 227.
61 E. J. Jones, *Growth Reoccurring: Economic Change in World History* (Oxford: Oxford University Press, 1988), 110.
62 Allan K. Smith, *Creating a World Economy: Merchant Capital, Colonialism, and World Trade, 1400–1825* (Oxford: Westview Press, 1991), 27.
63 Mielants, *Origins of Capitalism,* 56.
64 Étienne de la Vaissière, 'Trans-Asian trade, or the Silk Road deconstructed (antiquity, Middle Ages)', in L. Neal and J. G. Williamson (eds), *The Cambridge History of Capitalism, Vol. 1: The Rise of Capitalism: From Ancient Origins to 1848* (Cambridge: Cambridge University Press, 2014), 101–24, 120.
65 Ronald Findlay, 'Globalization and the European economy: Medieval origins to the Industrial Revolution', in H. Kierzkowski (ed.), *Europe and Globalization* (London: Palgrave, 2002), 32–64, 45–6.
66 Findlay, 'Globalization', 45–6.
67 Van der Pijl, *Nomads, Empires, States,* 104–9; John Darwin, *After Tamerlane: The Rise and Fall of Global Empires, 1400–1900* (London: Penguin, 2007), 44–5. On the various strategic dilemmas presented by the nomadic threat, see Arthur Waldron, 'Chinese strategy from the fourteenth to the seventeenth centuries' in W. Murray et al. (eds), *The Makers of Strategy: Rulers, States, and War* (Cambridge: Cambridge University Press, 1994), 85–114.
68 Mielants, *Origins of Capitalism,* 61 quoting in part William H. McNeil, *The Global Condition* (Princeton, N.J.: Princeton University Press, 1992), 113. As di Cosmo writes in regards to the contemporary historiographical literature on the Mongol Empire, '[t]here is therefore agreement, at least in principle, that the role of the Mongols was central to the commercial efflorescence that, in the late thirteenth and fourteenth centuries, allowed Europe and Asia to come closer and know each other better than ever before' ('Mongols and merchants', 392).
69 Speculations aside, although the Chinese certainly had the *capabilities* to make the voyage to the New World, it is unclear whether there was any *incentive* to do so as the Chinese Empire was largely self-sufficient and relied much less on external trade. The methods of collective reproduction for the feudal states of Europe and the tributary empires of the East were therefore strikingly different. See Ronald Findlay, 'The roots of divergence: western economic history in comparative perspective', *American Economic Review,* Vol. 82, No. 2 (1992), 158–61, 159.
70 Mielants, *Origins of Capitalism,* 56 quoting in part Marie Nystazopoulou, 'Venise et la Mer Noire du XIᵉ au XVᵉ siècle', in P. Agostino (ed.), *Venezia e il Levante fino al secolo XV* (Florence, Italy: Parte Seconda, 1973), 541–82, 570.
71 Di Cosmo, 'Mongols and merchants', 409, 411.
72 Mielants, *Origins of Capitalism,* 57.
73 Thomas T. Allsen, *Culture and Conquest in Mongol Eurasia* (Cambridge: Cambridge University Press, 2001), 195.
74 Felipe Fernandez-Armesto, *Civilizations: Culture, Ambition, and the Transformation of Nature* (New York: Free Press, 2001), 113.
75 Di Cosmo, 'Mongols and merchants', 392. Further regarding the role of Mongol agency, see Allsen, *Culture and Conquest,* 193–202.

76 Findlay, 'Globalization', 44.
77 Virgil Ciocîltan, *The Mongols and the Black Sea Trade in the Thirteenth and Fourteenth Centuries* (Leiden, Neths: Brill, 2011), 11.
78 Ciocîltan, *Mongols and the Black Sea Trade*, 11–12. The commercial fees collected by the Golden Horde from Italian merchants were fixed at the low rate of 3 per cent of the value of the merchandise, and later raised for Venice to 5 per cent. Di Cosmo, 'Mongols and merchants', 396.
79 Di Cosmo, 'Mongols and merchants', 418.
80 Bira Shagdar, 'The Mongol Empire in the thirteenth and fourteenth centuries: East–West relations', in V. Elisseeff (ed.), *The Silk Roads: Highways of Culture and Commerce* (Paris: UNESCO, 1998), 127–44, 136. On the broader significance of the Silk Roads as a vector of transcivilisational and ecological exchange in world history, see David Christian, 'Silk roads or steppe roads? The Silk Roads in world history', *Journal of World History*, Vol. 11, No. 1 (2000), 1–26.
81 Notably, Findlay, 'Globalization', 45.
82 Findlay, 'Globalization', 44.
83 Abu-Lughud, *Before European Hegemony*, 154; see also Finlay and O'Rourke, *Power and Plenty*, 106–8.
84 Giovanni Arrighi, *The Long Twentieth Century: Money, Power, and the Origins of Our Times* (London: Verso, 1994), 114; See also Abu-Lughud, *Before European Hegemony*, 128–9, 167–70. As di Cosmo writes, 'long-distance trade between the Mediterranean and China functioned only because it was actively supported by the Mongol states, and this condition was the pre-eminent factor that made the presence of Italian merchants in the Far East possible at all' ('Mongols and merchants', 404).
85 Di Cosmo, 'Mongols and merchants', 406.
86 Di Cosmo, 'Mongols and merchants', 393.
87 Mielants, *Origins of Capitalism*, 81. As Mielants puts it elsewhere: 'It is no coincidence that because of the *Pax Mongolica* over the Eurasian landmass, the market expanded for the western European city-states, and subsequently the division of labor in most of their industries increased c. 1250–1350' ('Perspectives on the origins of merchant capitalism in Europe', *Review*, Vol. 23, No. 2 (2000), 229–92, 271–2fn93).
88 Mielants, *Origins of Capitalism,* 81
89 Pepijn Brandon, 'Marxism and the "Dutch Miracle": the Dutch Republic and the transition-debate', *Historical Materialism*, 19, no. 3 (2011), 106–46, 120–5; see also Bas van Bavel, 'The Medieval origins of capitalism in the Netherlands', *Bijdragen en Mededelingen betreffende de Geschiedenis der Nederlanden*, Vol. 125, No. 2–3 (2010), 45–80.
90 Perry Anderson, *Spectrum: From Right to Left in the World of Ideas* (London: Verso, 2005), 251.
91 Mielants, *Origins of Capitalism*, 81.
92 A point accepted by the strongest critics of the 'commercialisation model' who agree that the 'cities, trade and markets which had evolved throughout Europe were a pre-condition for the development of English capitalism', as Ellen Meiksins Wood writes in describing Robert Brenner's contributions to the transition debate. However, as Wood and other correctly note, these developments in themselves could not act in engendering the emergence of capitalism. Wood, 'Capitalism, merchants and bourgeois revolution: reflections on the Brenner debate and its sequel', *International Review of Social History*, Vol. 41, No. 2 (1996), 209–32, 220. Similarly, in a rich historical study stressing the pre-capitalist nature of commerce and social relations in Europe (and particularly the Low Countries) over the 14th and 16th centuries, Martha Howell notes that 'if it were not for the kinds of changes that took place in these three centuries, the seventeenth and eighteenth century would not have emerged as the turning point in the history of capitalism' (*Commerce*

before Capitalism in Europe, 1300–1600, Cambridge: Cambridge University Press, 2010, 5).

93 Terence J. Byres, 'Differentiation of the peasantry under feudalism and the transition to capitalism: in defence of Rodney Hilton', *Journal of Agrarian Change*, Vol. 6, No. 1 (2006), 17–68, 42.

94 John Masson Smith Jr, 'The Mongols and the Silk Road', *The Silkroad Foundation Newsletter*, www.silkroadfoundation.org/newsletter/volumeonenumberone/mongols.html (accessed 7 February 2013).

95 S. A. M. Adshead, *Central Asia in World History* (London: Macmillan, 1993), 77 as quoted by Findlay, 'Globalization', 45.

96 Eric Mielants, 'The rise of European hegemony: the political economy of South Asia and Europe compared, A.D. 1200–A.D. 1500', in C. Chase-Dunn and E. N. Anderson (eds), *The Historical Evolution of World Systems* (London: Routledge, 2005), 122–54, 146fn14.

97 Abu-Lughod, *Before European Hegemony*, 361.

98 Abu-Lughod, *Before European Hegemony*, 361.

99 See, among others, Maurice Dobb, *Studies in the Development of Capitalism* (London: Routledge & Kegan Paul, 1946), 50–2; Anderson, *Passages from Antiquity*, 201–3; Immanuel Wallerstein, *The Modern World-System, Vol. I: Capitalist Agriculture and the Origins of the European World Economy in the Sixteenth Century* (London: Academic Press, 1974), 35–6; Robert Brenner, 'Agrarian class structure and economic development in pre-industrial Europe', in T. H. Aston and C. H. E. Philpin (eds), *Agrarian Class Structure and Economic Development in Pre-Industrial Europe* (Cambridge: Cambridge University Press, 1985), 10–63, 27, 35–56; Richard Lachmann, *Capitalists in Spite of Themselves: Elite Conflict and Economic Transitions in Early Modern Europe* (Oxford: Oxford University Press, 2000), ch. 2; S. R. Epstein, *Freedom and Growth: The Rise of States and Markets in Europe, 1300–1750* (London: Routledge, 2000), ch. 3.

100 See e.g. B. F. Harvey, 'Introduction: the 'crisis' of the early fourteenth century', in B. M. S. Campbell (ed.), *Before the Black Death: Studies in the 'Crisis' of the Early Fourteenth Century* (Manchester, 1991), 1–24; David Herlihy, *The Black Death and the Transformation of the West* (Cambridge, Mass.: Harvard University Press, 1997).

101 Epstein, *Freedom and Growth*, 54.

102 Epstein, *Freedom and Growth*, 69.

103 Neil Davidson, *How Revolutionary Were the Bourgeois Revolutions?* (Chicago, Ill.: Haymarket, 2012), 409.

104 Sevket Pamuk, 'The Black Death and the origins of the "Great Divergence" across Europe, 1300–1600', *European Review of Economic History*, Vol. 11, No. 3 (2007), 289–317, 293. The massive loss of human life in Europe alone constituted nearly one-third of Europe's entire population within two years of the plague's outbreak. Epstein, *Freedom and Growth*, 39.

105 McNeil and McNeil, *The Human Web*, 120.

106 Emmanuel Le Roy Ladurie, 'A Concept: the unification of the globe by disease (fourteenth to seventeenth centuries)', in *The Mind and Method of the Historian* (Chicago, Ill.: University of Chicago Press, 1981), 28–83.

107 Michael T. Taussig, *The Devil and Commodity Fetishism* (Chapel Hill, N.C.: University of North Carolina Press, 1980), 17.

108 Mark Greengrass, *Christendom Destroyed: Europe 1517–1648* (London: Allen Lane, 2014), 58.

109 Ole Jørgen Benedictow, *The Black Death, 1346–1353: The Complete History* (Woodbridge: Boydell Press, 2004), 393.

110 Brenner, 'Agrarian class structure', 35.

111 Christopher Dyer, 'A redistribution of incomes in fifteenth-century England?' *Past and Present*, No. 39 (1968), 11–33, 26.

112 Silvia Federici, *Caliban and the Witch: Women, the Body and Primitive Accumulation* (New York: Autonomedia, 2004), 44–5.
113 John Hatcher, 'England in the aftermath of the Black Death', *Past and Present*, No. 144 (1994), 3–36, 10.
114 Anderson, *Passages from Antiquity*, 204.
115 Hatcher, 'England in the aftermath', 25.
116 Prosper Boissonade, *Life and Work in Medieval Europe* (New York: Alfred A. Knopf, 1927), 316–20.
117 Federici, *Caliban and the Witch*, 46.
118 Guy Bois, 'Against the neo-Malthusian orthodoxy', in Aston and Philpin, *The Brenner Debate*, 107–18.
119 Jason W. Moore, '"The modern world-system" as environmental history? Ecology and the rise of capitalism', *Theory and Society*, Vol. 32, No. 3 (2003), 307–77, 314.
120 Guy Bois, *The Crisis of Feudalism: Economy and Society in Eastern Normandy, c 1300–1550* (Cambridge: Cambridge University Press, 1984), 405–6.
121 Hatcher, 'England in the aftermath', 11.
122 Anderson, *Passages from Antiquity*, 201–2.
123 Pamuk, 'The Black Death', 293.
124 Boissonade, *Life and Work*, 314.
125 Anderson, *Passages from Antiquity*, 203.
126 Alan Ryder, *The Wreck of Catalonia: Civil War in the Fifteenth Century* (Oxford: Oxford University Press, 2007), 30, 109–18, 254–60.
127 Friedrich Engels, *The Peasant War in Germany* (Moscow: Foreign Languages Publishing, 1956 [1850]).
128 Jane Whittle, *The Development of Agrarian Capitalism: Land and Labour in Norfolk, 1440–1580* (Oxford: Oxford University Press, 2001), 310. Elsewhere, Whittle writes of how as soon as agricultural demand recovered in the15th century 'it was tenants, not lords, who were in a position to exploit' market opportunities as '[t]hey could produce more cheaply than lords by exploiting their own and their family's labour, and by managing their affairs directly' ('Tenure and landholding in England 1440–1580: a crucial period for the development of agrarian capitalism?' in B. van Bavel and P. Hoppenbrouwers (eds), *Landholding and Land Transfer in the North Sea Area (Late Middle Ages – 19th Century)*, Turnhout, Belgium: Brepols, 2004, 237–49). But see the Political Marxist critique of Whittle's work in Spencer Dimmock, *The Origin of Capitalism in England, 1400–1600* (Leiden, Neths: Brill, 2014), esp. 101–3, 119–22.
129 See Whittle, 'Tenure and landholding'; cf. Stephen Hipkin, 'Tenant farming and short-term leasing on Romney Marsh, 1585–1705', *Economic History Review*, Vol. 53, No. 4 (2000), 646–76. Sixteenth-century France saw similar developments as examined in Chapter 6. For further studies demonstrating the empirical inaccuracies of Brenner's key claim that peasants were generally reluctant to relinquish their land holdings (i.e. part of their means of subsistence forming the 'basis of their existence and that of their heirs') unless they were forced to do so (Brenner, 'Agrarian class structure', 29), see Patricia Croot and David Parker, 'Agrarian class structure and the development of capitalism: France and England compared', in Aston and Philpin, *The Brenner Debate*, 79–90, 85–6; Paul Glennie, 'In search of agrarian capitalism: manorial land markets and the acquisition of land in the Lea Valley c. 1450–c.1560', *Continuity and Change*, Vol. 3, No. 1 (1988), 11–40, esp. 14–20; R. W. Hoyle, 'Tenure and the land market in early modern England: or a late contribution to the Brenner debate', *Economic History Review*, Vol. 43, No. 1 (1990), 1–20; Mavis E. Mate, 'The East Sussex land market and agrarian class structure in the Late Middle Ages', *Past and Present*, No. 139 (1993), 46–65; J. A. Raftis, *Peasant Economic Development within the English Manorial System* (Quebec: McGill-Queen's University Press, 1996); R. M. Smith, 'The English peasantry in 1250–1600', in T. Scott (ed.), *The Peasantries of Europe: From the Fourteenth*

to the Eighteenth Centuries (London: Longman, 1998), 366–9; Mark Bailey, *The Decline of Serfdom in Late Medieval England: From Bondage to Freedom* (Woodbridge: Boydell, 2014), esp. 7–8.

130 Byres, 'Differentiation of the peasantry', 55, 57. See also Hoyle, 'Tenure and the land market'.

131 Bruce M. S. Campbell, 'Measuring the commercialisation of seigneurial agriculture circa 1300', in R. H. Britnell and B. M. S. Campbell (eds), *A Commercialising Economy: England, 1086 to circa 1300* (Manchester: Manchester University Press, 1995), 132–93, 133.

132 Michael J. Bennett, *Community, Class and Careerism: Cheshire and Lancashire Society in the Age of Sir Gawain and the Green Knight* (Cambridge: Cambridge University Press, 1983), 103.

133 Whittle, *Development of Agrarian Capitalism*, 310. More broadly, Epstein notes that the 'widespread commutation after 1350 of servile labour dues to market-based tenancy contracts, occurred in response to increased peasant resistance against coerced labour, but it also aligned the tenant's incentives more closely with those of the landlord and increased the quality and intensity of peasant labour. Weaker seigniorial control over peasant labour and land markets made the peasantry more responsive to commercial stimuli' (Epstein, *Freedom and Growth*, 56).

134 Rodney Hilton, 'Reasons for inequality among Medieval peasants', *Journal of Peasant Studies*, Vol. 5, No. 3 (1978), 271–84, 279.

135 Hilton, 'Reasons for inequality', 279.

136 Hilton, 'Reasons for inequality', 280.

137 Hilton, 'Reasons for inequality', 280.

138 Hilton, 'Reasons for inequality', 280.

139 Hilton, 'Reasons for inequality', 280–1, emphasis ours.

140 Byres, 'Differentiation of the peasantry', 51–2.

141 Byres, 'Differentiation of the peasantry', 55, 57; cf. Hoyle, 'Tenure and the land market'.

142 Byres, 'The landlord class, peasant differentiation, class struggle and the transition to capitalism: England, France and Prussia compared', *Journal of Peasant Studies*, Vol. 36, No. 1 (2009), 33–54, 37–8.

143 Hoyle, 'Tenure and the land market', 2.

144 See Whittle, 'Tenure and landholding'.

145 Colin Mooers, *The Making of Bourgeois Europe: Absolutism, Revolution, and the Rise of Capitalism in England, France, and Germany* (London: Verso, 1991), 37. For a historical study demonstrating the significance of the yeoman in the English transition to capitalism, see Robert C. Allen, *Enclosure and the Yeoman: The Agricultural Development of the South Midlands, 1450–1830* (Oxford: Clarendon Press, 1992). We must thank David Ormrod for alerting us to this very important work.

146 Byres, 'Differentiation of the peasantry', 52.

147 It appears this sector was the hardest hit by the plague, resulting in a decline in the labour force greater than the population as a whole. Pamuk, 'The Black Death', 294.

148 Herlihy, *The Black Death*, 48–9; Pamuk, 'The Black Death', 294–5, 310–11.

149 Herlihy, *The Black Death*, 46.

150 According to Epstein, the cost of capital in England declined from a rate of 9.5 to 11 per cent during the 1150–1350 period to 7 per cent in the half-century after the Black Death and to only 4.5 per cent by the late 15th century, with similar gains prevailing elsewhere in Europe (*Freedom and Growth*, 61).

151 Epstein, *Freedom and Growth*, 61–2; Pamuk, 'The Black Death', 294, 310–11.

152 Herlihy, *The Black Death*, 49.

153 Pamuk, 'The Black Death', 294, 311. This article provides a wealth of statistical data on the rise of real wages among different employment sectors of the economy after the Black Death.

154 Regarding the latter, Pamuk notes that as '[s]oldiers had become much more expensive … those with firearms could fight much more effectively than those without' ('The Black Death', 311). More generally, Epstein details the ways by which the plague stimulated and further diffused the development of the productive forces in Europe, noting that:

> Growing regional trade and labour market integration, and particularly the increasing mobility of masters and tramping journeymen, more than compensated for declining population by stimulating technological diffusion. By exposing a larger proportion of the population to new technology, market integration may also have increased the rate of invention. Higher rates of investment spurred by rising demand and declining real interest rates fostered the diffusion and refinement of existing products and the development of new ones.
>
> (Epstein, *Freedom and Growth*, 65).

For a list detailing the various institutional, organisational and technological advances in the aftermath of plague see again Epstein, *Freedom and Growth*, 65–6.

155 According to Epstein, the period immediately following the Black Death saw the emergence of substantial 'industrial and agricultural regions and industrial districts specialising in cheap and medium quality cloth-making, mining and metal-working, glass and timber, silk, olive oil and livestock … across Europe, becoming in many cases the direct precursors of early modern "protoindustries"' (*Freedom and Growth*, 63–4).

156 Marian Malowist, 'The economic and social development of the Baltic countries from the fifteenth to the seventeenth centuries', *Economic History Review*, Vol. 12, No. 2 (1959), 177–89, 178, 179.

157 Malowist, 'Baltic countries', 179.

158 Pamuk, 'The Black Death', 310.

159 The consequences of the plague on the feudal European economy also seemed to have resulted in some of the most wide-ranging attempts 'to overcome coordination problems by integrating money and coinage and standardizing measurements at the regional or national level' (Epstein, *Freedom and Growth*, 58–9).

160 On the rapid urbanisation of the more backward economic regions of Europe see Epstein, *Freedom and Growth*, 62–3; Pamuk, 'The Black Death', 304–6.

161 Pamuk, 'The Black Death', 309.

162 Epstein, *Freedom and Growth*, 55. To be clear, this is not to argue that commercialisation automatically led to the emergence of capitalist social relations. It is, rather, to indicate how this one process – among many – resulting from the Black Death did stimulate developments that would both contribute to altering the *balance of class forces* while creating the material conditions from which both peasants and lords could eventually develop along capitalist lines.

163 Epstein, *Freedom and Growth*, 54.

164 Cf. Pamuk, 'The Black Death'.

165 Findlay and O'Rourke, *Power and Plenty*, 123.

166 Anderson, *Passages from Antiquity*, 252–3.

167 Brenner, 'Agrarian class structure', 36.

168 For a recent study rethinking the divergent trajectories of English and French agrarian developments, highlighting instead their shared common characteristics, see John Broad (ed.), *A Common Agricultural Heritage? Revising French and British Rural Divergence* (Exeter: British Agricultural History Society, 2009).

169 Robert Brenner, 'Agrarian roots of capitalism', in Aston and Philpin, *The Brenner Debate*, 213–328, 254–8; cf. Benno Teschke, *The Myth of 1648: Class, Geopolitics, and the Making of Modern International Relations* (London: Verso, 2003), 104–107.

170 Perry Anderson, *Lineages of the Absolutist State* (London: New Left Books, 1974), 113–14.

171 Cf. Kamran Matin, 'Democracy without capitalism: retheorizing Iran's constitutional revolution', *Middle East Critique*, Vol. 21, No. 1 (2012), 37–56.

4 The Ottoman–Habsburg Rivalry over the Long 16th Century

1   John Emerich Edward Dalberg-Acton, *Lectures on Modern History* (London: Macmillan, 1921 [1899–1901]), 34.
2   Eric J. Hobsbawm, *The Age of Revolution, 1789–1848* (New York: Vintage, 1996).
3   Lisa Jardine and Jerry Brotton, *Global Interests: Renaissance Art between East and West* (Ithaca, N.Y.: Cornell University Press, 2000), 50.
4   Nabil Matar, *Turks, Moors, and Englishmen in the Age of Discovery* (New York: Columbia University Press, 1999), 3.
5   James G. Harper, 'Introduction', in J. G. Harper (ed.), *The Turk and Islam in the Western Eye, 1450–1750* (Farnham: Ashgate, 2011), 3.
6   Daniel Goffman, *The Ottoman Empire and Early Modern Europe* (Cambridge: Cambridge University Press, 2002), 225.
7   Kamran Matin, 'Redeeming the universal: postcolonialism and the inner life of Eurocentrism', *European Journal of International Relations*, Vol. 19, No. 2 (2013), 353–77, 354.
8   Jacob Burckhardt, *The Civilization of the Renaissance in Italy* (London: Penguin, 1990).
9   Cf. Perry Anderson, *Lineages of the Absolutist State* (London: Verso, 1974); Charles Tilly, *The Formation of National States in Western Europe* (Princeton, N.J.: Princeton University Press, 1975); Michael Mann, *The Sources of Social Power: A History of Power from the Beginning to AD 1760, Vol. I* (Cambridge: Cambridge University Press, 1986);
10 David S. Landes, *The Wealth and Poverty of Nations: Why Some Are So Rich and Some So Poor* (London: W.W. Norton, 1999).
11 Robert Brenner, 'Agrarian class structure and economic development in pre-industrial Europe' and 'The agrarian roots of capitalism', in T. H. Aston and C. H. E. Philpin (eds), *The Brenner Debate: Agrarian Class Structure and Economic Development in Pre-Industrial Europe* (Cambridge: Cambridge University Press, 1987), 10–63 and 231–328.
12 Immanuel Wallerstein, *The Modern World-System, Vol. I: Capitalist Agriculture and the Origins of the European World Economy in the Sixteenth Century* (London: Academic Press, 1974).
13 For example, the two giants of European historiography, Fernand Braudel, *The Mediterranean and the Mediterranean World in the Age of Philip, Vol. II*, trans. S. Reynolds (London: Collins, 1973), and Leopold von Ranke, *The Ottoman and the Spanish Empires in the Seventeenth Century* (London: Whittaker, 1843), insisted on the inclusion of the Ottomans within the Europe in the age of Philip II and Charles V respectively.
14 Malcom E. Yapp, 'Europe in the Turkish mirror', *Past and Present*, Vol. 137, No. 1 (1992), 134–55.
15 Andre Gunder Frank, *ReOrient: Global Economy in the Asian Age* (Berkeley, Calif.: University of California Press, 1998), 19.
16 See, for example: Baki Tezcan, *The Second Ottoman Empire: Political and Social Transformation in the Early Modern World* (Cambridge: Cambridge University Press, 2010); Ussama Makdisi, 'Ottoman Orientalism', *American Historical Review*, Vol. 107, No. 3 (2002), 768–96; Selim Deringil, '"They live in a state of nomadism and savagery": the late Ottoman Empire and the post-colonial debate', *Comparative Studies in Society and History*, Vol. 45, No. 2 (2003), 311–42; Selim Deringil, 'The Turks and "Europe": the argument from history', *Middle Eastern Studies*, Vol. 43, No. 5 (2007), 709–23; Rifaat Ali Abou-El-Haj, *Formation of the Modern State: The Ottoman Empire Sixteenth to Eighteenth Centuries* (New York: SUNY Press, 1991).
17 Landes, *Wealth and Poverty of Nations*; John Morris Roberts, *The Triumph of the West* (London: BBC, 1985); Niall Ferguson, *Civilization: The West and the Rest* (London: Penguin, 2012).
18 Anderson, *Lineages of the Absolutist State*, 378; Thomas Naff, 'The Ottoman Empire and European states system', in H. Bull and A. Watson (eds), *The Expansion of the International Society* (Oxford: Clarendon Press, 1984), 143–70, 144.

NOTES

19 Nancy Bisaha, *Creating East and West: Renaissance Humanists and the Ottoman Turks* (Philadelphia, Pa.: University of Pennsylvania Press, 2004), 162.

20 Mustafa Soykut, 'Introduction', in M. Soykut (ed.), *Historical Image of the Turk in Europe: Fifteenth Century to the Present* (Istanbul: Isis Press, 2003), 26.

21 Stephen A. Fischer-Galati, *Ottoman Imperialism and German Protestantism: 1521–1555* (Cambridge, Mass.: Harvard University Press, 1959), 18.

22 Fernand Braudel, *The Mediterranean and the Mediterranean World in the Age of Philip II, Vol. 1* (Berkeley, Calif.: University of California Press, 1972), 682.

23 Ogier Ghiselin de Busbecq, 'Impressions of Turkey (1556–1564)', in D. Englander et al. (eds), *Culture and Belief in Europe 1450–1600: An Anthology of Sources* (Oxford: Basil Blackwell, 1990), 303–4, 304.

24 See Maxime Rodinson, *Europe and the Mystique of Islam* (London: I. B. Tauris, 2002), 37fn82.

25 Ogier Ghiselin de Busbecq, *Turkish Letters* (London: Sickle Moon, 2001 [1554–62]), 76–7.

26 Mehmet Sinan Birdal, *The Holy Roman Empire and the Ottomans: From Global Imperial Power to Absolutist States* (London: I. B. Tauris, 2011), 119–20.

27 Anderson, *Lineages of the Absolutist State*, 365.

28 Quoted in Paul Coles, *The Ottoman Impact on Europe* (New York: Harcourt, Brace & World, 1968), 100.

29 Mark Greengrass, *Christendom Destroyed: Europe 1517–1648* (London: Allen Lane, 2014), 504.

30 Rodinson, *Europe and the Mystique of Islam*, 73. See also Süheyla Artemel, 'The view of the Turks from the perspective of the humanists in Renaissance England', in Soykut, *Historical Image of the Turk*, 161–3; Bisaha, *Creating East and West*, 162; Faroqhi, *Ottoman Empire*, 101; Fischer-Galati, *Ottoman Imperialism*, 18; Rhoads Murphey, *Ottoman Warfare, 1500–1700* (London: Routledge, 2002), 6.

31 Greengrass, *Christendom Destroyed*, 11.

32 Quoted in Matar, *Turks, Moors, and Englishmen*, 9.

33 Halil Berktay, 'The feudalism debate: the Turkish end – is "tax vs. rent" necessarily the product and sign of a modal difference?' *Journal of Peasant Studies*, Vol. 14, No. 3 (1987), 291–333; Berktay, 'The "other" feudalism: a critique of 20th century Turkish historiography and its particularisation of Ottoman society', PhD dissertation, University of Birmingham, 1990; John Haldon, 'The Ottoman state and the question of state autonomy: comparative perspectives', *Journal of Peasant Studies*, Vol. 18, No. 3–4 (1991), 18–108; Haldon, *The State and the Tributary Mode of Production* (London: Verso, 1993); Haldon, 'Theories of practice: Marxist history-writing and complexity', *Historical Materialism*, Vol. 21, No. 4 (2013), 36–70. It is worth noting that Haldon replaced the term 'feudal' (Haldon, 1991) with 'tributary' (Haldon, 1993), but for all intents and purposes, they remain synonymous and interchangeable concepts (Haldon, 1993, 10).

34 Haldon, *The State*, 42–4, 52–7.

35 Karl Marx, *Capital: Critique of Political Economy, Vol. III* (Harmondsworth: Penguin, 1981 [1894]), 927.

36 Haldon, *The State*, 91–3.

37 Berktay, 'The feudalism debate', 311.

38 Haldon, *The State*, 77.

39 Berktay, 'The "other" feudalism', 4

40 Haldon, *The State*, 79, emphasis ours. Similarly: 'Whether these peasants are dependent tenants … whether they are free proprietors … *is therefore not important within the context of the fundamental mode of surplus appropriation here described* … what matters for our point is the processes through which surpluses are actually extracted by the state or by a private landlord' (p. 77, emphasis ours).

313

41   Derek Sayer, *The Violence of Abstraction: The Analytical Foundations of Historical Mate-rialism* (London: Basil Blackwell, 1987), 61; Anderson, *Lineages of the Absolutist State,* 402–3.

42   Haldon, *The State*, 87, 97.

43   Haldon, *The State*, 52.

44   Berktay, 'The "other" feudalism', 16, emphasis ours.

45   Jairus Banaji, *Theory as History: Essays on Modes of Production and Exploitation* (Leiden, Neths: Brill, 2010), 23. A problem for Banaji's conceptualisation, however, is that the questions of how and why the differentiated class configurations of the tributary mode developed in the way that they did are left explicitly unaddressed (Banaji, 23–38). More specifically, there are no explanatory tools in Banaji's approach that help us explain how the tributary mode in the Ottoman Empire became manifested in the social stratification between *askeri* and *reaya*, on the one hand, and between central and provincial elites, on the other. In other words, while Banaji offers a description of these variations he offers no explanation for them, leaving unanswered how these different – uneven – configurations came into being, and how they were reproduced. In short, what is missing in Banaji's account is a theorisation of the tributary mode that is capable of delineating developmental multiplicity. As such, 'the international' as a distinct plane of causality that determines the reproduction of any given society remains outside the theoretical scope of Banaji's mode of production-centred approach. He thus argues that 'the trajectories of the tributary regimes were driven by an internal logic' (Banaji, 38). In the same vein he suggests that Trotsky's depiction of Russia as standing between 'Europe and Asia' was *descriptive* and 'left the issue of theory open' (Banaji, 23). However, as Chapter 2 demonstrated, Trotsky's understanding of Russia in this manner was a *theoretical* expression of uneven and combined development, one that took 'the international' as a composite moment of a mode of production analysis.

46   Banaji, *Theory as History*, 24.

47   Stanford J. Shaw, *History of the Ottoman Empire and Modern Turkey: Vol. 1, Empire of the Gazis: The Rise and Decline of the Ottoman Empire 1280–1808* (Cambridge: Cambridge University Press, 1976), 120.

48   Karen Barkey, *Empire of Difference: The Ottomans in Comparative Perspective* (Cambridge: Cambridge University Press, 2008), 96; Çağlar Keyder, 'The dissolution of the Asiatic mode of production', *Economy and Society*, Vol. 5, No. 2 (1976), 178–96.

49   Halil İnalcık, 'State, land and peasant', in H. İnalcık and D. Quataert (eds), *An Economic and Social History of the Ottoman Empire, 1300–1914* (Cambridge: Cambridge University Press, 1994), 103–78, 115.

50   Huri İslamoğlu-İnan, *State and Peasant in the Ottoman Empire: Agrarian Power Rela-tions and Regional Economic Development in Ottoman Anatolia during the Sixteenth Century* (Leiden, Neths: Brill, 1994), 57.

51   İslamoğlu-İnan, *State and Peasant*, 8.

52   Halil İnalcık, *The Ottoman Empire: The Classical Age, 1300–1600* (London: Phoenix Press, 2000), 112; Islamoğlu-Inan, *State and Peasant*, xiv–xv.

53   Suraiya Faroqhi, 'Rural life', in S. Faroqhi (ed.), *The Cambridge History of Turkey, Vol. III: The Later Ottoman Empire 1603–1839* (Cambridge: Cambridge University Press, 2006), 373–90, 383.

54   Sencer Divitçioğlu, *Asya Üretim Tarzı ve Osmanlı Toplumu [The Asiatic Mode of Produc-tion and Ottoman Society]* (Istanbul: Istanbul University, 1967).

55   Anderson, *Lineages of the Absolutist State*, 370.

56   Şerif Mardin, 'Power, civil society and culture in the Ottoman Empire', *Comparative Studies in Society and History*, Vol. 11, No. 3 (1969), 258–81.

57   Colin Imber, *The Ottoman Empire, 1300–1650: The Structure of Power* (Basingstoke: Palgrave Macmillan, 2009), 144–69; Shaw, *History of the Ottoman Empire*, 118–19.

58   Imber, *Ottoman Empire, 1300–1650*, 130.

59 Shaw, *History of the Ottoman Empire*, 113–14.

60 İnalcık, *Ottoman Empire*, 80.

61 Coles, *Ottoman Impact*, 98–9. How this provincial authority was institutionalised was never fixed and static, but took on a variety of forms throughout the course of the Ottoman Empire. For the purposes of this chapter we simply focus on the centrality of the *tımar* system that predominated in the Ottoman Classical Age (1300–1600).

62 In the classical period, *tımar* constituted about half of all Ottoman land (Perry Anderson, *Passages from Antiquity to Feudalism*, London: New Left Books, 1974, 369). The remaining lands were divided among *miri* state lands for the use of the Sultan and his household, *mülk* private property, mainly in the form of *vaqf* pious foundations, and from the 15th century onwards *iltizam* tax farms. See Reşat Kasaba, 'Incorporation of the Ottoman Empire', *Review*, Vol. 10, Supplement (1987), 805–47, 808.

63 Haldon, *The State*, 179.

64 Halil İnalcık, 'The rise of the Ottoman Empire', in M. A. Cook (ed.), *A History of the Ottoman Empire to 1730* (Cambridge: Cambridge University Press, 1976), 10–53, 28.

65 Haldon, *The State*, 169.

66 Halil İnalcık, 'The emergence of the Ottomans', in P. M. Holt, A. K. S. Lambton and B. Lewis (eds), *The Cambridge History of Islam, Vol. I* (Cambridge: Cambridge University Press, 1977), 263–93, 287, 289.

67 Imber, *Ottoman Empire*, 203–4.

68 Barkey, *Empire of Difference*, 96; Imber, *Ottoman Empire*, 205.

69 Imber, *Ottoman Empire*, 186.

70 William J. Griswold, *The Great Anatolian Rebellion, 1000–1020/1591–1611* (Berlin: K. Schwarz, 1983), 9–10; İnalcık, *Ottoman Empire*, 107–16.

71 Imber, *Ottoman Empire*, 185.

72 Bernard Lewis, *The Emergence of Modern Turkey* (London: Oxford University Press, 2002), 27, 72; Timur Kuran, *The Long Divergence: How Islamic Law Held Back the Middle East* (Princeton. N.J.: Princeton University Press, 2010); Sabri Ülgener, *İktisadi Çözülmenin Ahlak ve Zihniyet Dünyası* [*The Moral and Intellectual World of the Economic Decline*] (Istanbul: Derin Yayınevi, 2006), 30–1, 82–3; Thomas Naff, 'Reform and the conduct of Ottoman diplomacy in the reign of Selim III, 1789–1807', *Journal of the American Oriental Society*, Vol. 83, No. 3 (1963), 295–315, 296.

73 Karen Barkey, *Bandits and Bureaucrats: The Ottoman Route to State Centralization* (London: Cornell University Press, 1994), 58–9.

74 Griswold, *Great Anatolian Rebellion*, 56–7.

75 Barkey, *Bandits and Bureaucrats*, 212.

76 Barkey, *Bandits and Bureaucrats*, 192.

77 Barkey, *Bandits and Bureaucrats*, 91, 241.

78 This is not to say that the tributary mode was not subject to class conflict or to suggest Ottoman society was unchanging.

79 Haldon, *The State*, 173.

80 Haldon, *The State*, 173.

81 Haldon, *The State*, 173.

82 Jamie C. Allinson and Alexander Anievas, 'Approaching "the International": Beyond Political Marxism', in A. Anievas (ed.) *Marxism and World Politics: Contesting Global Capitalism* (London: Routledge, 2010), 197-214, 209.

83 Karl Marx, *Grundrisse* (Harmondsworth: Penguin, 1973 [1857–8]), 473.

84 Kees van der Pijl, *Nomads, Empires, States: Modes of Foreign Relations and Political Economy, Vol. I* (London: Pluto Press, 2007), 63.

85 Van der Pijl, *Nomads, Empires, States*, 63.

86 Van der Pijl, *Nomads, Empires, States*, 67.

87 Kamran Matin, 'Uneven and combined development in world history: the

international relations of state-formation in pre-modern Iran', *European Journal of International Relations*, Vol. 13, No. 3 (2007), 419–47.

88 Van der Pijl, *Nomads, Empires, States*, 76.
89 Cemal Burak Tansel, 'Deafening silence: historical materialism, international relations, and the question of the international', paper for Spectrum Conference on 'Historical Sociology, Historical Materialism and International Relations', Middle East Technical University, Department of International Relations, Ankara, Turkey, 1–3 November 2012, 13.
90 Shaw, *History of the Ottoman Empire*, 126.
91 Murphey, *Ottoman Warfare*, 43–44.
92 Shaw, *History of the Ottoman Empire*, 123.
93 Shaw, *History of the Ottoman Empire*, 127.
94 Virginia Aksan, 'Ottoman war and warfare 1453–1812', in J. Black (ed.), *War in the Early Modern World 1450–1815* (London: Routledge, 2005), 147–76, 151–2.
95 Aksan, 'Ottoman war and warfare', 154.
96 Murphey, *Ottoman Warfare*, 36–7. However, such a number was never fully deployed. Many were held in reserve or required to stay at home in order to perform policing and security functions in Ottoman towns, villages and fortresses. Shaw, *History of the Ottoman Empire*, 117, 123.
97 Murphey, *Ottoman Warfare*, 98.
98 Shaw, *History of the Ottoman Empire*, 130.
99 Murphey, *Ottoman Warfare*, 99.
100 Murphey, *Ottoman Warfare*, 86.
101 Murphey, *Ottoman Warfare*, 86.
102 Murphey, *Ottoman Warfare*, 99. See also pages 95–6 for a nonexhaustive list of contemporary admirers of Ottoman military capabilities.
103 Anderson, *Passages from Antiquity*, 148.
104 Brenner, 'Agrarian class structure', 36.
105 Benno Teschke, *The Myth of 1648: Class, Geopolitics, and the Making of Modern International Relations* (London: Verso, 2003), 43-4.
106 Eric Mielants, *The Origins of Capitalism and the 'Rise of the West'* (Philadelphia, Pa.: Temple University Press, 2008), 70.
107 Tilly, *Formation of National States*, 73–4.
108 Mielants, *Origins of Capitalism*, 70.
109 Daniel Chirot, 'The rise of the West', *American Sociological Review*, Vol. 50, No. 2 (1985), 181–95; Mielants, *Origins of Capitalism*, 79; Thomas A. Brady, 'The rise of merchant empires, 1400–1700: a European counterpoint', in J. D. Tracy (ed.), *The Political Economy of Merchant Empires: State Power and World Trade, 1350–1750* (Cambridge: Cambridge University Press, 1991), 117–61, 149–50.
110 Jan de Vries, *The Economy of Europe in an Age of Crisis, 1600–1750* (Cambridge: Cambridge University Press, 1976), 242. See further William H. McNeil, *The Pursuit of Power: Technology, Armed Force, and Society since A.D. 1000* (Chicago, Ill.: University of Chicago Press, 1982), 102–16.
111 This would change in the 17th and, in particular, the 18th century, when the classical Ottoman *timar* system was reconfigured into one based increasingly on tax farming.
112 Halil İnalcık, 'Capital formation in the Ottoman Empire', *Journal of Economic History*, Vol. 29, No. 1 (1969), 97–140, 104.
113 İnalcık, 'Capital formation', 106.
114 Keyder, 'Asiatic mode of production'.
115 Faroqhi, *Ottoman Empire*, 157; Fatma Müge Göçek, *Rise of Bourgeoisie, Demise of Empire: Ottoman Westernization and Social Change* (Oxford: Oxford University Press, 1996), 92; İnalcık, 'Capital formation', 107.
116 İslamoğlu-İnan, *State and Peasant*, 204.

117 Keyder, 'Asiatic mode of production', 184.
118 Andrew C. Hess, 'The evolution of the Ottoman seaborne empire in the age of the oceanic discoveries, 1453–1525', *American Historical Review*, Vol. 75, No. 7 (1970), 1892–1919, 1916; Hess, 'The Ottoman conquest of Egypt (1517) and the beginning of the sixteenth-century world war', *International Journal of Middle East Studies*, Vol. 4, No. 1 (1973), 55–76, 75. Rhoads Murphey notes that many representatives of key crafts and trades were required to accompany the military on campaigns to establish 'army market places' that would further assist with the provisioning of the army (*Ottoman Warfare*, 91).
119 Palmira Brummett, *Ottoman Seapower and Levantine Diplomacy in the Age of Discovery* (Albany, N.Y.: SUNY Press, 1994), 7.
120 John Alexander, 'Ottoman frontier policies in North-East Africa, 1517–1914', in A. Peacock (ed.), *The Frontiers of the Ottoman World* (Oxford: Oxford University Press, 2009), 225–34, 225–7.
121 Giancarlo Casale, 'Global politics in the 1580s: one canal, twenty thousand cannibals, and an Ottoman plot to rule the world', *Journal of World History*, Vol. 18, No. 3 (2007), 267–96, 291; Hess, 'The Ottoman conquest of Egypt', 69.
122 Faroqhi, *Ottoman Empire*, 12.
123 Philip D. Curtin, *Cross-Cultural Trade in World History* (Cambridge: Cambridge University Press, 1984), 116, 128.
124 Mielants, *Origins of Capitalism*, 81.
125 We emphasise here again that this was by no means an essential feature of the Ottoman Empire but a historically specific one. Come the 19th century, this form of ruling class reproduction did indeed come into crisis, leading to the collapse of the Empire.
126 Jardine and Brotton, *Global Interests*, 42.
127 Soykut, 'Introduction', 74.
128 Artemel, 'View of the Turks', 157.
129 Artemel, 'View of the Turks', 163.
130 Yapp, 'Europe in the Turkish Mirror', 148–9.
131 Yapp, 'Europe in the Turkish Mirror', 141.
132 Coles, *The Ottoman Impact*, 148.
133 Giancarlo Casale, *The Ottoman Age of Exploration* (Oxford: Oxford University Press, 2009), 6.
134 Janet L. Abu-Lughod, *Before European Hegemony: The World System A.D. 1250–1350* (Oxford: Oxford University Press, 1989), 355–61.
135 Cho-yun Hsu, 'Asian influences on the West', in C. Gluck and A. T. Embree (eds), *Asia in Western and World History: A Guide for Teaching* (New York: M.E. Sharp, 1997), 22–31, 27.
136 R. J. Barendse, 'Trade and state in the Arabian Seas: a survey from the fifteenth to the eighteenth century', *Journal of World History*, Vol. 11, No. 2 (2000), 173–225, 192; Kate Fleet, *European and Islamic Trade in the Early Ottoman State: The Merchants of Genoa and Turkey* (Cambridge: Cambridge University Press, 1999), 123.
137 İnalcık, 'Capital formation', 97fn2; James Mather, *Pashas: Traders and Travellers in the Islamic World* (London: Yale University Press, 2009), 26; Niels Steensgaard, *The Asian Trade Revolution of the Seventeenth Century: The East India Companies and the Decline of the Caravan Trade* (London: University of Chicago Press, 1974), 62.
138 Şevket Pamuk, *A Monetary History of the Ottoman Empire* (Cambridge: Cambridge University Press, 2000), 23.
139 Thomas W. Gallant, 'Europe and the Mediterranean: a reassessment', in G. Delanty (ed.), *Europe and Asia beyond East and West* (London: Routledge, 2006), 120–37, 126.
140 Pamuk, *Monetary History*, 11, 18; Morris Rossabi, 'The Mongols and the West', in Gluck and Embree, *Asia in Western and World History*, 55–63.
141 Barendse, 'Trade and state', 190.

142 Bruce McGowan, *Economic Life in Ottoman Europe: Taxation, Trade and the Struggle for the Land, 1600–1800* (Cambridge: Cambridge University Press, 1981), 3–5.

143 Barendse, 'Trade and state', 194; Geoffrey V. Scammell, *The World Encompassed: The First European Maritime Empires c. 800–1650* (Berkeley, Calif.: University of California Press, 1981), 140.

144 McGowan, *Economic Life,* 3.

145 Jack Goody, 'Europe and Islam', in Delanty, *Europe and Asia*, 138–47, 144.

146 De Lamar Jensen, 'The Ottoman Turks in sixteenth century French diplomacy', *Sixteenth Century Journal,* Vol. 16, No. 4 (1985), 451–70, 464.

147 Murat Çizakça, 'Price history and the Bursa silk industry: a study in Ottoman industrial decline, 1550–1650', in İslamoğlu-İnan (ed.), *The Ottoman Empire and the World-Economy* (Cambridge: Cambridge University Press, 1987), 247–61, 253–4; Goody, 'Europe and Islam', 143.

148 Gillian Darling, *Factory* (London: Reaktion, 2003), 104.

149 Goody, 'Europe and Islam', 143; İnalcık, 'Capital formation', 100–1.

150 Scammell, *World Encompassed*, 205.

151 İnalcık, *Ottoman Empire*, 35.

152 Hess, The Ottoman conquest of Egypt'.

153 Greengrass, *Christendom Destroyed*, 10.

154 Greengrass, *Christendom Destroyed*, 300.

155 Greengrass, *Christendom Destroyed*, 300.

156 İnalcık, *Ottoman Empire*, 35.

157 Greengrass, *Christendom Destroyed*, 11.

158 Greengrass, *Christendom Destroyed*, 505.

159 For such contemporary Eurocentric portrayals, see Rodney Stark, *The Victory of Reason: How Christianity Led to Freedom, Capitalism, and Western Success* (London: Random House, 2007); but see also Aslı Çirakman, 'From tyranny to despotism: The Enlightenment's unenlightened image of the Turks', *International Journal of Middle East Studies*, Vol. 33, No. 1 (2001), 49–68; Andrew C. Hess, 'The Battle of Lepanto and its place in Mediterranean history', *Past and Present*, Vol. 57, No. 1 (1972), 53–73. For contemporary uses of the Lepanto myth, see Hans-Georg Betz and Susi Meret, 'Revisiting Lepanto: the political mobilization against Islam in contemporary Western Europe', *Patterns of Prejudice*, Vol. 43, No. 3–4 (2009), 313–34.

160 Greengrass, *Christendom Destroyed,* 506.

161 Greengrass, *Christendom Destroyed,* 506.

162 Gabor Agoston, 'Information, ideology and the limits of imperial policy: Ottoman grand strategy in the context of Ottoman-Habsburg rivalry', in V. Aksan and D. Goffman (eds), *The Early Modern Ottomans: Remapping the Empire* (Cambridge: Cambridge University Press, 2007), 75–103.

163 Quoted in John Elliot, 'Ottoman–Habsburg rivalry: the European perspective', in C. Kafadar and H. İnalcık (eds), *Suleyman the Second (ie the First) and His Time* (Istanbul: Isis Press, 1993), 153–62, 155.

164 Greengrass, *Christendom Destroyed,* 304.

165 Greengrass, *Christendom Destroyed,* 304. Cf. Ina Baghdiantz McCabe, *Orientalism in Early Modern France: Eurasian Trade, Exoticism and the Ancien Regime* (Oxford: Berg, 2008), 40–1.

166 Jeremy Black, *European Warfare, 1494–1660* (London: Routledge, 2002), 177.

167 Greengrass, *Christendom Destroyed,* 514.

168 İnalcık, *Ottoman Empire*, 37.

169 Fischer-Galaţi, *Ottoman Imperialism*, 24.

170 Fischer-Galaţi, *Ottoman Imperialism;* Daniel H. Nexon, *The Struggle for Power in Early Modern Europe: Religious Conflict, Dynastic Empires, and International Change* (Princeton, N.J.: Princeton University Press, 2009), 169.

171 Carl Max Kortepeter, *Ottoman Imperialism during the Reformation: Europe and the Caucasus* (London: University of London Press, 1973), 124–30, 188–9.
172 Greengrass, *Christendom Destroyed*, 498.
173 Kortepeter, *Ottoman Imperialism*, 199.
174 İnalcık, *Ottoman Empire*, 37.
175 Andrew C. Hess, *The Forgotten Frontier: A History of the Sixteenth-Century Ibero-African Frontier* (Chicago, Ill.: University of Chicago Press, 1978), 89–94.
176 Christine Woodhead, 'England, the Ottomans and the Barbary coast in the late sixteenth century', *State Papers Online, 1509–1714* (Reading: Cengage Learning, 2009). See also Nabil Matar, *Britain and Barbary: 1589–1689* (Gainesville, Fla.: University of Florida, 2005).
177 Nexon, *Struggle for Power*, 192.
178 Quoted in Benjamin Schmidt, *Innocence Abroad: The Dutch Imagination and the New World, 1570–1670* (Cambridge: Cambridge University Press, 2001), 103.
179 Schmidt, *Innocence Abroad*, 103–4. This further demonstrates that, aside from material assistance, the image of the Turk was crucial in the ideological mobilisation of anti-Papal sentiment. In 1521, Luther wrote 'how shamefully the pope has this long time baited us with the war against the Turks, gotten our money, destroyed so many Christians and made so much mischief!' (quoted in Reşat Kasaba, *A Moveable Empire: Ottoman Nomads, Migrants, and Refugees*, Seattle, Wa.: University of Washington Press, 2009, 49).
180 Pius Malekandathil, *Maritime India: Trade, Religion and Polity in the Indian Ocean* (Delhi: Primus Books, 2010), 87; Cf. Hess, 'The Ottoman conquest of Egypt'; Hess, *Forgotten Frontier*.
181 Nexon, *Struggle for Power*, 137.
182 Chirot, 'The rise of the West', 183; Fischer-Galaţi, *Ottoman Imperialism*; Paul M. Kennedy, *The Rise and Fall of the Great Powers: Economic Change and Military Conflict from 1500 to 2000* (London: Vintage, 1989), 31–70; Wallerstein, *The Modern World-System, I*, 167.
183 Teschke, *Myth of 1648*, 104.
184 Nexon, *Struggle for Power*, 189.
185 Brummett, *Ottoman Seapower*, 7; Hess, 'The Ottoman conquest of Egypt', 71.
186 Fleet, *European and Islamic Trade*, 132–3.
187 Scammell, *World Encompassed*, 132.
188 Aksan, 'Ottoman war', 154.
189 Hess, 'The Ottoman conquest of Egypt', 59; Scammell, *World Encompassed*, 93–6.
190 Ronald S. Love, *Maritime Exploration in the Age of Discovery: 1415–1800* (London: Greenwood, 2006), 6–7.
191 Scammell, *World Encompassed*, 165.
192 Scammell, *World Encompassed*, 170.
193 Coles, *The Ottoman Impact*, 108; Charles Issawi, 'The Ottoman Empire in the European world economy, 1600–1914', in K. H. Karpat (ed.), *The Ottoman State and Its Place in World History* (Leiden, Neths: Brill, 1974), 107–117, 111.
194 Mather, *Pashas*, 154.
195 Mann, *Sources of Social Power, I*, 508.
196 Mielants, *Origins of Capitalism*, 84.
197 Banaji, *Theory as History*, 270–3. We build on these points in more detail in Chapters 5 and 7.
198 Mielants, *Origins of Capitalism*, 85.
199 Ronald Findlay, 'Globalization and the European economy: Medieval origins to the Industrial Revolution', in H. Kierzkowski (ed.), *Europe and Globalization* (London: Palgrave, 2002), 32–64, 53.
200 Nexon, *Struggle for Power*, 188.

201 For an exploration of the trade benefits accrued from the capitulations, see Edhem Eldem, 'Capitulations and Western trade', in S. N. Faroqhi, *The Cambridge History of Turkey* (Cambridge: Cambridge University Press, 2006), 281–335; A. H. de Groot, *The Ottoman Empire and the Dutch Republic: A History of the Earliest Diplomatic Relations 1610–1630* (Leiden, Neths: Nederlands Historisch-Archaeologisch Instituut, 1978), 114–25.

202 Mehmet Bulut, 'The role of the Ottomans and Dutch in the commercial integration between the Levant and Atlantic in the seventeenth century', *Journal of the Economic and Social History of the Orient*, Vol. 45, No. 2 (2002), 197–230, 209–10, 215–16, 218–23.

203 Mather, *Pashas*, 129–30, 204–5.

204 For Ottoman commercial relations with the Dutch, see Mehmet Bulut, *Ottoman-Dutch Economic Relations: In the Early Modern Period 1571–1699* (Hilversum, Neths: Uitgeverij Verloren, 2001); for the English, see Mather, *Pashas*.

205 Bulut, 'Ottomans and Dutch', 221–2.

206 McGowan, *Economic Life*, 3–5; Mielants, *Origins of Capitalism*, 144.

207 McGowan, *Economic Life*, 4.

208 Interestingly each of the authors subsequently cited place a high degree of explanatory emphasis on England's island geography. Without seeking to discount this geographical factor, the prevalence of naval warfare by the 16th century suggests that England was eminently open to invasion should the will or compulsion have arisen: Susan Rose, *Medieval Naval Warfare, 1000–1500* (London: Routledge, 2002).

209 Theda Skocpol, 'Wallerstein's world capitalist system: a theoretical and historical critique', *American Journal of Sociology*, Vol. 82, No. 5 (1977), 1075–90, 1086.

210 Fernand Braudel, *Afterthoughts on Material Civilization and Capitalism* (London: Johns Hopkins University Press, 1977), 101–2.

211 Derek Sayer, 'A notable administration: English state formation and the rise of capitalism', *American Journal of Sociology*, Vol. 97, No. 5 (1992), 1382–1415, 1391.

212 Kennedy, *Rise and Fall*, 56.

213 Anderson, *Lineages of the Absolutist State*, 125.

214 Skocpol, 'Wallerstein's world capitalist system', 1086.

215 Brenner, 'Agrarian class structure', 61.

216 Ellen Meiksins Wood, *The Origin of Capitalism: A Longer View* (London: Verso, 2002), 53.

217 Skocpol, 'Wallerstein's world capitalist system', 1086.

218 Brenner, 'Agrarian roots', 263.

219 G. E. Aylmer, 'The peculiarities of the English state', *Journal of Historical Sociology*, Vol. 3, No. 2 (1990), 91–108; Brenner, 'Agrarian roots', 256; Wood, *Origin of Capitalism*, 47.

220 Anderson, *Lineages of the Absolutist State*, 127.

221 Sayer, 'A notable administration', 1394.

222 Anderson, *Lineages of the Absolutist State*, 127.

223 Brenner, 'Agrarian roots', 252.

224 Brenner, 'Agrarian class structure', 47.

225 Karl Marx and Friedrich Engels, *The Communist Manifesto* (Moscow: Progress, 1975 [1848]).

5 The Atlantic Sources of European Capitalism, Territorial Sovereignty and the Modern Self

1 Marx, *Capital: Critique of Political Economy, Vol. I* (London: Penguin, 1990 [1867]), 925.

2　Walter Benjamin, 'Theses on the philosophy of history', in *Illuminations* (New York: Harcourt, Brace & World, 1968 [1940]), 253–264, 256.

3　Robbie Shilliam, 'The Atlantic as a vector of uneven and combine development', *Cambridge Review of International Affairs*, Vol. 22, No. 1 (2009), 69–88, 72, emphasis ours.

4　Shilliam, 'The Atlantic', 72.

5　Tzvetan Todorov, *The Conquest of America: The Question of the Other* (Norman, Okla.: University of Oklahoma Press, 1982), 4.

6　Universalism was a pervasive feature of political orders with some attachment to monotheistic religions. Most notably, Christendom and the Ottoman Empire both had universalist aspirations that were nonetheless constrained by the facticity of unevenness – that is, the coexistence of other differentiated societies. In this respect, we could make the argument that theirs was an internalist universalism.

7　Todorov, *Conquest of America*, 4–5.

8　Todorov, *Conquest of America*, 5.

9　Mark Greengrass, *Christendom Destroyed: Europe 1517–1648* (London: Allen Lane, 2014), 152.

10　Greengrass, *Christendom Destroyed*, 152.

11　For the significance of Vitoria to modern international law, see Antony Anghie, *Imperialism, Sovereignty and the Making of International Law* (Cambridge: Cambridge University Press, 2007); Brett Bowden, *The Empire of Civilization: The Evolution of an Imperial Idea* (Chicago, Ill.: University of Chicago Press, 2009); Robert A. Williams, *The American Indian in Western Legal Thought: The Discourses of Conquest* (Oxford: Oxford University Press, 1990); Eric Michael Wilson, *The Savage Republic: De Indis of Hugo Grotius, Republicanism and Dutch Hegemony Within the Early Modern World-System (c.1600–1619)* (Leiden, Neths: Brill, 2008).

12　Francisco de Vitoria, 'Defense of the Indians (1537–1539)', in D. Englander et al. (eds), *Culture and Belief in Europe, 1450–1600: An Anthology of Sources* (Oxford: Basil Blackwell, 1990), 331–7, 336–7.

13　Setting 'universal standards for the assessment of human institutions' would eventually become a hallmark of Enlightenment thinking. In this respect, Vitoria prefigured later attempts to construct 'a critical morality, rationally binding on all human beings, and, as a corollary, the creation of a universal civilization' (John Gray, *Enlightenment's Wake: Politics and Culture at the Close of the Modern Age*, London: Routledge, 1995, 123).

14　Anghie, *Imperialism*, 19–20.

15　Bowden, *Empire of Civilization*, 137–9. Hence, all persons must be permitted free movement, 'to each to go and to travel into all countries he so desires'. In exchange: 'The Indian princes cannot prevent their subjects from engaging in commerce with the Spaniards, and conversely, the Spanish princes cannot forbid commerce with the Indians' (Vitoria quoted in Todorov, *Conquest of America*, 149).

16　Williams, *American Indian*, 96–7.

17　Beate Jahn, 'IR and the state of nature: the cultural origins of a ruling ideology', *Review of International Studies*, Vol. 25, No. 3 (1999), 411–34, 413.

18　This finds some parallels in W. B. du Bois's 'episteme of the veil' which sought to make sense of the inherent relationality of power, hierarchy and divisions within the (global) colour line where 'we are this because you are that and vice versa', as opposed to a 'white episteme' which had the privilege of an assumed (though by no means real) methodological individualism – 'we are this, while you are that'. For a discussion of du Bois's episteme of the veil in the context of International Relations theory, see Alexander Anievas, Nivi Manchanda and Robbie Shilliam, 'Confronting the global colour line: an introduction', in A. Anievas, N. Manchanda and R. Shilliam (eds), *Race and Racism in International Relations: Confronting the Global Colour Line* (London: Routledge, 2015), 1–15, esp. 4–7.

19 Sepúlveda thus argued:

> In wisdom, skill, virtue and humanity, these people are as inferior to the Span-
> iards as children are to adults and women to men; there is as great a difference
> between them as there is between savagery and forbearance, between violence and
> moderation, almost – I am inclined to say – as between monkeys and men.
>
> (*Democrates Alter,* quoted in Todorov, *Conquest of America,* 153).

Notable here is how the opposition to the Other involves an explicit affirmation of the
Self as mature, male, forbearing and moderate.

20 Vitoria, 'Defense of the Indians', 335. Similarly, Sepúlveda wrote that '[t]here is as much
difference between them [the Spanish and Amerindians] as there is ... between ape and
men' ('On the Indians (c. 1547)', in Englander, *Culture and Belief,* 321–3, 322).

21 Todorov, *Conquest of America,* 35.

22 Todorov, *Conquest of America,* 38.

23 During the Valladolid Controversy (1550–51), Sepúlveda based his justifications
for the Spanish colonialists' enslavement of the Amerindians on Aristotle's idea of
'natural slaves' formulated in *Politics, Book I,* chs 3–7. See Alberto Hernández, 'Juan
Ginés de Sepúlveda', in M.A. de la Torre and S. M. Floyd-Thomas (eds), *Beyond the
Pale: Reading Theology from the Margins* (Louisville, Ky.: Westminster John Knox Press,
2011), 79–86.

24 Sepúlveda, 'On the Indians', 321.

25 Vitoria, 'Defense of the Indians', 337.

26 See Sepúlveda, 'On the Indians', 321.

27 Jahn, 'State of nature', 416. See additional Sepúlveda quotes further elaborating how
these supposedly 'barbaric' practices could justify conquest in Todorov, *Conquest of
America,* 156.

28 Sepúlveda, 'On the Indians', 323.

29 Greengrass, *Christendom Destroyed,* 153.

30 Bowden, *Empire of Civilization,* 137fn19–20.

31 Bartolomé de Las Casas, *The Devastation of the Indies: A Brief Account* (Baltimore, Md.:
Johns Hopkins University Press, 1992 [1552]), 53.

32 Quoted in Todorov, *Conquest of America,* 162.

33 Las Casas, *Devastation of the Indies,* 127.

34 Cf. Todorov, *Conquest of America,* 170.

35 'Whatever defects their society may have had can be removed and corrected with the
preaching and spread of the gospel' (Bartolomé de Las Casas, 'On the Indians (1552)',
in Englander, *Culture and Belief,* 324–9, 328).

36 Jahn, 'State of nature', 415.

37 See the Las Casas quote in Jahn, 'State of nature', 415.

38 Anghie, *Imperialism,* 22.

39 Anghie, *Imperialism,* 22.

40 On the significance of communication as a tool of colonialism, see Todorov, *Conquest
of America,* 146–9.

41 Jahn, 'State of nature', 417; Anghie, *Imperialism,* 21–2; Bowden, *Empire of
Civilization,* 140.

42 Todorov, *Conquest of America,* 150

43 Anghie, *Imperialism,* 23.

44 Jahn, 'State of nature', 415. Sepúlveda argued that if the Amerindians 'refuse to
obey this legitimate sovereignty, they can be forced to do so for their own welfare by
recourse to the terrors of war' (quoted in Bowden, *Empire of Civilization,* 136).

45 This relational aspect of Eurocentrism has been most forcefully presented by Edward
Said, *Orientalism: Western Conceptions of the Orient* (London: Routledge & Kegan Paul,
1978).

46 Kamran Matin, 'Redeeming the universal: postcolonialism and the inner life of Euro-

centrism', *European Journal of International Relations*, Vol. 19 No. 2 (2013), 353–77. Refer to the Introduction for a fuller exposition of the assumptions of Eurocentrism.

47   Bowden, *Empire of Civilization*, 115.

48   Quoted in Todorov, *Conquest of America*, 155.

49   Todorov, *Conquest of America*, 154.

50   See Chapter 1 for a discussion of historicism.

51   E. P. Thompson, *Customs in Common* (London: Penguin, 1993), 164.

52   Adam Ferguson, *An Essay on the History of Civil Society* (Basle, Switzerland: J. J. Tourneisen, 1789), 147.

53   Johannes Fabian, *Time and the Other: How Anthropology Makes Its Object* (New York: Columbia University Press, 2002), 16. According to Fabian, linear time existed before capitalist modernity, and so 'decisive steps towards modernity must be sought, not in the invention of a linear conception, but in a succession of attempts to secularize Judeo-Christian Time by generalizing and universalizing it' (2). The pre-Enlightenment Judaeo-Christian conception of time was one based on salvation and was therefore inclusive or incorporative – 'The Others, pagans and infidels (rather than savages and primitives), were viewed as candidates for salvation. Even the *conquista*, certainly a form of spatial expansion, needed to be propped up by an ideology of conversion'. In contrast, the Enlightenment was based on natural, secular, evolutionist notions of historical time and as such – despite very much justifying colonial practice – saw savages and primitives as 'not yet' ready for civilization. In this respect, and in contrast to medieval forms, linear time is conceived in terms of distance and separation (26). The contrast Fabian draws between the two (sacred and secular) requires some nuancing, however. Read against the writings of early colonialists, Fabian misses the contradictory ways in which both distance and inclusion functioned in a contradictory yet mutually constitutive way. Enlightenment constructions of relations between Self and Other were not only marked by distance, since the project of the civilising mission was purportedly directed at closing that distance. In this respect, it was also inclusive. On the opposite side, early colonial conceptions of difference were not wholly inclusive, since in the thought of Vitoria and Sepúlveda, we get a pervasive sense that 'Indians' were 'not yet' ready for salvation – they would require hundreds of years of Spanish 'tutelage' to undo their 'barbaric' culture. Distance and separation were very much a hallmark of earlier thinking, just as much as inclusion and incorporation was pervasive in later Spanish thought. In fact what we see in both is that distance/separation (backwardness, savagery, immaturity) serves to legitimise (even oblige) inclusion/incorporation (salvation/civilising mission). As such, the colonial encounter must be seen as one of the first formative steps in the generalisation and universalisation of linear time and hence also a moment in its transition to its modern, secular form.

54   Jahn, 'State of nature', 412.

55   By the 20th century, modernisation theory would continue this heritage, as would later liberal and neoconservative projects of democratisation and economic restructuring.

56   See Istvan Hont, *Jealousy of Trade: International Competition and the Nation-State in Historical Perspective* (Cambridge, Mass.: Harvard University Press, 2005), 364–70; Neil Davidson, *How Revolutionary were the Bourgeois Revolutions?* (Chicago, Ill.: Haymarket, 2012), 55–71.

57   On the disavowal of Caribbean antislavery movements and the making of scientific racism, see Sibylle Fisher, *Modernity Disavowed* (London: Duke University Press, 2004).

58   Michael Adas, *Machines as the Measure of Men: Science, Technology, and Ideologies of Western Dominance* (Ithaca, N.Y.: Cornell University Press, 1989).

59   It is worth highlighting how modern racism is also indicative of how unevenness was – and continues to be – recast in normative terms under capitalism: that is, sociocultural difference recast as absence or 'backwardness'.

60 We can say that capitalism is defined by a *contradictory fusion* of *universalising* and *differentiating* tendencies, exerting both *equalising* and *fragmenting* pressures on social development. This systemisation of unevenness – so dramatically exemplified by the (re)production of systematic inequalities and power hierarchies within and between societies – is a necessary consequence of the expansionary, competitive logic of capital accumulation.

61 Joseph A. Fry, *Dixie Looks Abroad: The South and U.S. Foreign Relations, 1789–1973* (Baton Rouge, La.: Louisiana State University Press, 2002), 44.

62 Terence J. Byres, *Capitalism from Above and Capitalism from Below: An Essay in Comparative Political Economy* (London: Palgrave Macmillan, 1996), 172.

63 Thompson, *Custom in Common*, 164–5. Further regarding John Locke's views of the Native Americans, see Nagamitsu Miura, *John Locke and the Native Americans: Early English Liberalism and its Colonial Reality* (Newcastle upon Tyne: Cambridge Scholars, 2013).

64 W. E. B. Du Bois, *The Souls of Black Folk* (New York: Crest, 1961 [1903]), 23.

65 Silvia Federici, *Caliban and the Witch: Women, the Body and Primitive Accumulation* (New York: Autonomedia, 2004), 222.

66 Greengrass, *Christendom Destroyed*, 181.

67 Greengrass, *Christendom Destroyed*, 169.

68 Karen Spalding, *Huarochiri: An Andean Society under Inca and Spanish Rule* (Stanford, Calif.: Stanford University Press, 1988), 138–139.

69 The peculiarities of this hybrid formation have led some scholars to classify the *encomienda* system as its own historically distinct mode of production: see e.g. Kalki R. Glauser, 'Origenes del régimen de produccion vigente en Chile', *Cuadernos de la Realidad Nacional*, Vol. 8 (1971), 78–152, esp. 102–48.

70 Jorrge Lorrain, *Theories of Development: Capitalism, Colonialism and Dependency* (Cambridge: Polity, 1989), 187.

71 Cheryl English Martin, 'Modes of production in Colonial Mexico: the case of Morelos', *Estudios de Historia Novohispana*, Vol. 12 (1992), 107–22, 107.

72 Martin, 'Modes of production', 107–8.

73 J. H. Parry, *The Age of Reconnaissance: Discovery, Exploration, and Settlement, 1450–1650* (Berkeley, Calif.: University of California Press, 1982), 222–3.

74 Eric Wolf, *Europe and the People without History* (Berkeley, Calif.: University of California Press, 2010 [1982]), 142.

75 Lyle N. McAlister, *Spain and Portugal in the New World, 1492–1700* (Minneapolis, Minn.: University of Minnesota Press, 1987), 157.

76 McAlister, *Spain and Portugal*, 157; Wolf, *Europe*, 143.

77 Wolf, *Europe*, 142.

78 McAlister, *Spain and Portugal*, 157.

79 Jeremy Smith, *Europe and the Americas: State Formation, Capitalism and Civilizations in Atlantic Modernity* (Leiden, Neths: Brill, 2006), 195–196; Wolf, *Europe*, 142–3.

80 Martin, 'Modes of production', 108.

81 John K. Thornton, *A Cultural History of the Atlantic World, 1250–1820* (Cambridge: Cambridge University Press, 2012), 209.

82 See Nicholas P. Cushner, *Lords of the Land: Sugar, Wine, and Jesuit Estates of Coastal Peru, 1600–1767* (Albany, N.Y.: SUNY Press, 1980), 13–14; Claudio Veliz, *The Centralist Tradition of Latin America* (Princeton, N.J.: Princeton University Press, 1980), 25–6; Smith, *Europe and the Americas*, 195.

83 Jorge Larrain, *Identity and Modernity in Latin America* (Cambridge: Polity, 2000), 46.

84 Larrain, *Identity and Modernity*, 46. By contrast, Wallerstein conceives the *encomienda*, along with the 'coerced cash-crop labor' of the 'second serfdom' in Central Eastern Europe, as unequivocally capitalist since it 'is *not* the case that two forms of social organization, capitalist and feudal, existed side by side, or could ever so exist.

The world-economy has one form or the other. Once it is capitalist, relationships that bear certain formal resemblances to feudal relationships are necessarily redefined in terms of the governing principles of a capitalist system' (*The Modern World-System, Vol. I: Capitalist Agriculture and the Origins of the European World Economy in the Sixteenth Century*, London: Academic Press, 1974, 92, 90–100). Such rigid classificatory dichotomisations obscure and subsume the rich complexities of such sociohistorical processes and relations under an abstract, homogenising 'totality', rather than articulating and illuminating the relationality of their substantive differences (see further Chapter 1).

85   David Graeber, *Debt: The First 5,000 Years* (New York: Melville House, 2011), 316–21.
86   Federici, *Caliban and the Witch*, 225.
87   Spalding, *Huarochiri*, 245.
88   Claude F. Baudez and Sydney Picasso, *Lost Cities of the Maya* (New York: Harry N. Abrams, 1992), 21.
89   Federici, *Caliban and the Witch*, 220.
90   Federici, *Caliban and the Witch*, 226–7.
91   Federici, *Caliban and the Witch*, 227; Ronald Spores, 'Differential responses to colonial control among the Mixtes and Zapotecs of Oaxca', in S. Schroeder (ed.), *Native Resistance and the Pax Colonial in New Spain* (Lincoln, Ne.: University of Nebraska Press, 1998), 30–46, 33.
92   Federici, *Caliban and the Witch*, 230. Further regarding the subjection of women in the colonies and the rise of new forms of patriarchy, see Maria Mies, *Patriarchy and Accumulation on a World Scale: Women in the International Division of Labour* (London: Zed, 1986), 77–111.
93   Spalding, *Huarochiri*, 248–9; Steve J. Stern, *Peru's Indian Peoples and the Challenge of Spanish Conquest: Huamanga to 1640* (Madison, Wisc.: University of Wisconsin Press, 1993), 58.
94   Spores, 'Differential responses', 36.
95   Stern, *Peru's Indian Peoples*, 52.
96   Stern, *Peru's Indian Peoples*, 55.
97   Federici, *Caliban and the Witch*, 231. Such practices of flight can be located prior to and throughout modernity as one of the primary means of resisting and escaping the coercive impact of state formation among nonstate communities. See James C. Scott, *Seeing Like a State: How Certain Schemes to Improve the Human Condition Have Failed* (London: Yale University Press, 1998); James C. Scott, *The Art of Not Being Governed* (London: Yale University Press, 2009). We would like to thank Becka S. Hudson for highlighting this point to us.
98   Hélène Clastres, *The Land-without-Evil: Tupí-Guaraní Prophetism* (Chicago, Ill.: University of Illinois Press, 1995).
99   Stern, *Peru's Indian Peoples*, 59–60; cf. Michael F. Brown, 'Beyond resistance: a comparative study of utopian renewal in Amazonia', *Ethnohistory*, Vol. 38, No. 4 (1991), 388–413, 392.
100 Federici, *Caliban and the Witch*, 230; Stern, *Peru's Indian Peoples*, 55.
101 These methods often fed back into similar practices of subjugating women that were taking place back in Europe in the form of the witch hunt. Possibly the 'whole fury of the witch-hunt', Maria Mies writes, 'was not just a result of the decaying old order in its confrontation with new capitalist forces, or even a manifestation of timeless male sadism, but a reaction of the new male-dominated classes against the *rebellion* of women' (*Patriarchy and Accumulation*, 81). Federici traces the early modern period as one of increasing devaluation of women's labour and social status as a key mechanism through which capitalist primitive accumulation was achieved. According to Federici, the accumulation of human bodies capable of performing labour for the market – that is, the accumulation of labour-power – was central, and here the role of the woman as

the site of the production of labour-power attained a new significance. This required a long durational process of subjugation, discipline and degradation that was quite often fought out on the very terrain of sexuality – the social function of sex and procreation – in a society that increasingly depended on a ready supply of labour-power and a surplus population for its reproduction. This was in short a 'new sexual division of labour', one that 'reshaped male–female relations' and redefined gender relations in the transition to capitalism. Not only did it involve an array of new legal practices restricting female autonomy and access to public space (*Caliban and the Witch*, 100), new cultural norms also emerged which heightened the differences between men and women into binary types that exhibited masculinity and femininity, respectively. Upon this binary, a new hierarchy was erected in which women were classed as naturally inferior to men, a hierarchy which would legitimise the institutional and informal taming and controlling of women by men (101). Where women rebelled against these laws and norms – by living independently of men, by not marrying, by acting promiscuously – this also involved social exclusion, terror and violent subordination in the form of muzzling, whipping, caging, drowning and capital punishment (101). The witch hunts of the 16th to 17th centuries were the most brutal and systematic mechanism through which women who existed outside of or autonomously from these new patriarchal norms were annihilated. The subjugation of women in these ways served to turn 'female sexual activity into work, a service to men, and procreation' (192–4), redefining women as a class through which a limitless supply of the labour-power necessary for capital accumulation could be (re)produced. Federici's excavation of this gendered biopolitical component of primitive accumulation deserves considerably more in-depth treatment and appreciation than can be offered here. We however wish to emphasise in particular the connection she draws between the forms of subjugation, estrangement and 'Othering' suffered by women in Europe with similar practices being meted out to the 'Indian savage' in the time of colonisation. As Federici argues, 'In both cases literary and cultural denigration was at the service of a project of expropriation' and a justification for 'their enslavements and the plunder of their resources' (102).

102 Federici, *Caliban and the Witch*, 200.
103 See Branwen Gruffydd Jones, '"Good governance" and "state failure": the pseudo-science of statesmen in our times', in Anievas et al., *Race and Racism in International Relations*, 61–79; Charles W. Mills, *The Racial Contract* (Ithaca, N.Y.: Cornell University Press, 1997).
104 See Bowden, *Empire of Civilization*, 165.
105 On the racialised origins and reproduction of the modern state, see David Theo Goldberg, *The Racial State* (Oxford: Blackwell, 2002). For feminist perspectives, see V. Spike Peterson (ed.), *Gendered States: Feminist (Re)visions of International Relations Theory* (Boulder, Colo.: Lynne Rienner, 1992).
106 Michel Foucault, *The Birth of Biopolitics: Lectures at the College de France, 1978–79*, ed. M. Senellart (Basingstoke: Palgrave, 2008). As examined below, Foucault's understanding of the rise of biopolitics as a primarily, if not exclusively, European affair is simply untenable – a point made by various postcolonial critiques of Foucault's Eurocentrism. See e.g. Roxanne Lynn Doty, *Imperial Encounters: The Politics of Representation in North–South Relations* (Minneapolis, Minn.: University of Minnesota Press, 1996), 62; Gayatry Chakravorty Spivak, *A Critique of Postcolonial Reason: Toward a History of the Vanishing Present* (Cambridge, Mass.: Harvard University Press, 1999), 279; Paul Gilroy, *After Empire* (London: Routledge, 2004), 47; Vivienne Jabri, 'Michel Foucault's analytics of war: the social, the international, and the racial', *International Political Sociology*, Vol. 1, No. 1 (2007), 67–81, 73–6.
107 See e.g. Charles Tilly, 'Reflections on the history of European state-making', in C. Tilly (ed.), *The Formation of National States in Western Europe* (Princeton, N.J.: Princeton University Press, 1975), 3–83; Aristide R. Zolberg, 'Origins of the modern

world system: a missing link', *World Politics*, Vol. 33, No. 2 (1981), 253–81; Anthony Giddens, *The Nation-State and Violence: A Contemporary Critique of Historical Materialism, Vol. II* (Berkeley, Calif.: University of California Press, 1985); Michael Mann, *States, War, and Capitalism: Studies in Political Sociology* (New York: Blackwell, 1988); Charles Tilly, *Coercion, Capital, and European States: AD 990–1992* (London: Wiley-Blackwell, 1992); Michael Mann, *The Sources of Social Power: Vol. II, The Rise of Classes and Nation States 1760–1914* (Cambridge: Cambridge University Press, 1993); Thomas Ertman, *Birth of the Leviathan: Building States and Regimes in Medieval and Early Modern Europe* (Cambridge: Cambridge University Press, 1997).

108 See, among others, Perry Anderson, *Lineages of the Absolutist State* (London: Verso, 1974); Colin Mooers, *The Making of Bourgeois Europe: Absolutism, Revolution, and the Rise of Capitalism in England, France, and Germany* (London: Verso, 1991); Justin Rosenberg, *The Empire of Civil Society: A Critique of the Realist Theory of International Relations* (London: Verso, 1994); Ellen Meiksins Wood, *The Origin of Capitalism: A Longer View* (London: Verso, 2002); Benno Teschke, *The Myth of 1648: Class, Geopolitics, and the Making of Modern International Relations* (London: Verso, 2003); Adam David Morton, 'The age of absolutism: capitalism, the modern states-system and international relations', *Review of International Studies*, Vol. 31, No. 3 (2005), 495–517; Hannes Lacher, *Beyond Globalization: Capitalism, Territoriality and the International Relations of Modernity* (London: Routledge, 2006); Heide Gerstenberger, *Impersonal Power: History and Theory of the Bourgeois State* (Leiden, Neths: Brill, 2007); Kees van der Pijl, 'Capital and the state system: a class act', *Cambridge Review of International Affairs*, Vol. 20, No. 4 (2007), 619–37; Alex Callinicos, *Imperialism and Global Political Economy* (Cambridge: Polity, 2009), esp. 123–36.

109 See esp. Wood, *Origin of Capitalism*; Teschke, *Myth of 1648*; Lacher, *Beyond Globalization*; van der Pijl, 'Capital and the state system'.

110 Wallerstein, *Modern World-System, I*; Christopher Chase-Dunn, 'Interstate system and capitalist world economy: one logic or two?' *International Studies Quarterly*, Vol. 25, No. 1 (1981), 19–42; Giovanni Arrighi, *The Long Twentieth Century: Money, Power, and the Origins of Our Times* (London: Verso, 1994). But see some of the World-Systems-influenced perspectives in Alfred W. McCoy and Francisco A. Scarano (eds), *Colonial Crucible: Empire in the Making of the Modern American State* (Madison, Wisc.: University of Wisconsin Press, 2009).

111 John H. Hobson, 'What's at stake in the Neo-Trotskyist debate? Towards a non-Eurocentric historical sociology of uneven and combined development', *Millennium*, Vol. 40, No. 1 (2011), 147–66, 153.

112 See e.g. John G. Ruggie, 'Continuity and transformation in the world polity: toward a neorealist synthesis', *World Politics*, Vol. 35, No. 2 (1983), 261–85; Friedrich Kratochwil, 'Of systems, boundaries, and territoriality: an inquiry into the formation of the state system', *World Politics*, Vol. 39, No. 1 (1986), 27–52; John G. Ruggie, 'Territoriality and beyond: problematising modernity in international relations', *International Organization*, Vol. 47, No. 1 (1993),139–74; Hendrik Spruyt, *The Sovereign State and Its Competitors: An Analysis of Systems Change* (Princeton, N.J.: Princeton University Press, 1994); Christian Reus-Smit, *The Moral Purpose of the State: Culture, Social Identity and Institutional Rationality in International Relations* (Princeton, N.J.: Princeton University Press, 1999). But see the notable exception, Daniel H. Nexon, *The Struggle for Power in Early Modern Europe: Religious Conflict, Dynastic Empires, and International Change* (Princeton, N.J.: Princeton University Press, 2009).

113 Quoted in Bowden, *Empire of Civilization*, 115.

114 Quoted in Bowden, *Empire of Civilization*, 116.

115 Quoted in Anghie, *Imperialism*, 26.

116 Quoted in Bowden, *Empire of Civilization*, 139.

117 Jordan Branch, '"Colonial reflection" and territoriality: the peripheral origins of

sovereign statehood', *European Journal of International Relations*, Vol. 18, No. 2 (2012), 277–97, 285.

118 Samuel Y. Edgerton, 'From mental matrix to Mappamundi to Christian empire: the heritage of Ptolemaic cartography in the Renaissance', in D. Woodward (ed.), *Art and Cartography: Six Historical Essays* (Chicago, Ill.: University of Chicago Press, 1987), 10–50, 46.

119 Preceding quotes from Eric Eustace Williams, *Capitalism and Slavery* (Richmond, N.C.: University of North Carolina Press, 1994), 4.

120 Jordan Branch, *The Cartographic State: Maps, Territory and the Origins of Sovereignty* (Cambridge: Cambridge University Press, 2014), 100.

121 Branch, *Cartographic State*, 101.

122 Branch, '"Colonial reflection"', 288.

123 Branch, '"Colonial reflection"', 278–88.

124 Branch, '"Colonial reflection"', 284 quoting in part Robert David Sack, *Human Territoriality: Its Theory and History* (Cambridge: Cambridge University Press, 1986), 132.

125 Robert Knox, 'Race, racialisation and rivalry in the international legal order', in Anievas et al., *Race and Racism in International Relations*, 175–90.

126 Matt Craven, 'Introduction', in M. Craven, M. Fitzmaurice, and M. Vogiatzi (eds), *Time, History and International Law* (Leiden, Neths: Martinus Nijhoff), 1–27, 21.

127 Branch, '"Colonial reflection"', 292; see further, Branch, *Cartographic State*, 100–19.

128 Anghie, *Imperialism*, 14.

129 See e.g. Theda Skocpol, *States and Social Revolutions: A Comparative Analysis of France, Russia, and China* (Cambridge: Cambridge University Press, 1979), 22; Giddens, *Nation-State*, 159–60; Rosenberg, *Empire of Civil Society*, 129–39; Wood, *Origin of Capitalism*; Teschke, *Myth of 1648*, esp. 144–6; Lacher, *Beyond Globalization*, esp. 106–8; Benno Teschke and Hannes Lacher, 'The changing "logics" of capitalist competition', *Cambridge Review of International Affairs*, Vol. 20, No. 4 (2007), 565–80, esp. 569–70.

130 Teschke, *Myth of 1648*, 209.

131 Or a vicious circle depending on which side of the colonial whip you sat.

132 Our thanks to Tarak Barkawi for the boxing match analogy and for an excellent discussion of the theoretical and political implications of small wars and power imbalances in war: see Tarak Barkawi 'On the pedagogy of "small wars"', *International Affairs*, Vol. 80, No. 1 (2004), 19–38; Tarak Barkawi and Mark Laffey, 'The postcolonial moment in security studies', *Review of International Studies*, Vol. 32, No. 4 (2006), 329–52.

133 Marx, *Capital*, 915.

134 Most famously, Williams, *Capitalism and Slavery*.

135 Wood, *Origin of Capitalism*, 148; see also Robert Brenner, 'The origins of capitalist development: a critique of neo-Smithian Marxism', *New Left Review*, Vol. 1, No. 104 (1977), 25–92, 63. For contrasting views, see Earl J. Hamilton, 'American treasure and the rise of capitalism (1500–1700)', *Economica*, Vol. 9 (1929), 338–57, 356; Jairus Banaji, 'Islam, the Mediterranean, and the rise of capitalism', *Historical Materialism*, Vol. 15 (2007), 47–74, 49.

136 If we are to look for the generative effects of New World colonialism in the development of capitalist social relations, they are not to be found in the sheer amassing of wealth. As Neil Davidson correctly notes, 'enforced transfer of wealth in and of themselves will not necessarily lead or even contribute to capitalist development: in some cases it simply acted as a life-support mechanism for the most economically backward absolutist states' (Davidson, *How Revolutionary*, 534). Spain is a case in point.

137 At its peak during the 16th century, American silver accounted for as much as 25 per cent of the Habsburgs' revenue. Allan K. Smith, *Creating a World Economy: Merchant Capital, Colonialism, and World Trade, 1400–1825* (Oxford: Westview Press, 1991), 82–3.

138 Anderson, *Lineages of the Absolutist State*, 73. On Spain's decline, see Wallerstein, *The Modern World-System, I*, 190–6. Interestingly, Trotsky also observed the interactive consequences of the New World discoveries in ushering in a period of geopolitical and economic decline in Spain while affording other later-developing European states (particularly Holland and England) significant advantages: 'The discovery of America, which at first enriched and elevated Spain, was subsequently directed against it. The great routes of commerce were diverted from the Iberian peninsula. Holland, which had grown rich, broke away from Spain. Following Holland, England rose to great heights over Europe, and for a long time' ('The revolution in Spain', in *The Basic Writings of Trotsky* (New York: Random House, 1963 [1931]), 223–33, 224).

139 As Richard Lachman points out, 'American treasure, in the absence of opportunities for the productive investment, stimulated inflation within Spain that further reduced the possibilities for constructing domestic manufacturers that could compete with the cheaper products of established industries in the relatively low-inflation economies of France, the Low Countries, or Britain' (*Capitalists in Spite of Themselves: Elite Conflict and Economic Transitions in Early Modern Europe*, Oxford: Oxford University Press, 2000, 153).

140 James W. Moore, '"Amsterdam is standing on Norway", Part I: the alchemy of capital, empire and nature in the diaspora of silver, 1545–1648', *Journal of Agrarian Change*, Vol. 10, No. 1 (2010), 33–68, 43–6, 45.

141 The Spanish monarchy declared bankruptcy in 1557, 1575, 1596, 1607, 1627, 1647, 1653 and 1680.

142 Moore, '"Amsterdam is standing"', 45–6.

143 William H. McNeil, *The Pursuit of Power: Technology, Armed Force and Society since A.D. 1000* (Chicago, Ill.: University of Chicago Press, 1982), 109.

144 As Trotsky put it, Spain was 'weighed down by the great historic past of the country' ('Revolution in Spain', 224).

145 P. K. O'Brien, 'Metanarratives in global histories of material progress', *International History Review*, Vol. 23, No. 2 (2001), 345–67, 361. As J. H. Elliot put it, [f]rom the 1590s ... the economies of Spain and of its American possessions began to move apart, while Dutch and English interlopers were squeezing themselves into a widening gap' (*Imperial Spain, 1469–1716*, London: Penguin, 2002, 287).

146 Ronald Findlay, 'Globalization and the European economy: Medieval origins to the Industrial Revolution', in H. Kierzkowski (ed.), *Europe and Globalization* (London: Palgrave, 2002), 32–64, 58.

147 Fernand Braudel, *The Mediterranean and the Mediterranean World in the Age of Philip II, Vol. I* (London: Harper & Row, 1972), 635. K. N. Chaudhuri writes, '[t]he Dutch were the unquestioned masters of the European bullion trade' (*The Trading World of Asia and the East Indian Company, 1660–1760*, Cambridge: Cambridge University Press, 1978, 4).

148 Michel Beaud, *A History of Capitalism, 1500–1980* (London: Macmillan, 1984), 26; cf. Herman van der Wee, *The Growth of the Antwerp Market and the European Market (Fourteenth- Sixteenth Centuries), Vol. II* (The Hague: Martinus Nijhoff, 1963), 178.

149 Marx, *Capital*, 916.

150 Braudel, *The Mediterranean, Vol. I*, 481.

151 Fernand Braudel, *Civilization and Capitalism, 15th–18th Century, Vol. III: The Perspective of the World* (Berkeley, Calif.: University of California Press, 1992), 210.

152 As Braudel puts it, 'Holland's fortune was evidently built on *both* Spain and the Baltic. To neglect either of these would be fail to understand a process in which wheat on the one hand and American bullion on the other played indissociable roles' (*Civilization and Capitalism, Vol. III*, 209).

153 Jairus Banaji, *Theory as History: Essays on Modes of Production and Exploitation* (Leiden,

Neths: Brill, 2010), 270–1. Banaji further notes, 'By the late seventeenth century, they [the Dutch] dominated the trade in Spanish silver, so that Amsterdam was the world's leading centre in the trade in precious metals' (271).

154 Quoted in Satish Chandra, *The Indian Ocean: Explorations in History, Commerce, and Politics* (London: Sage, 1992), 139.

155 James Blaut, *The Colonizer's Model of the World: Geographical Diffusionism and Eurocentric History* (Cambridge: Cambridge University Press, 1993), 189, 192; See also Magda von der Heydt-Coca, 'Andean silver and the rise of the Western world', *Critical Sociology*, Vol. 31, No. 4 (2005), 481–513.

156 Kenneth Pomeranz, *The Great Divergence: China, Europe and the Making of the Modern World Economy* (Princeton, N.J.: Princeton University Press, 2000), 70–1.

157 Pomeranz, *Great Divergence*, 190; Cf. Dennis O. Flynn and Arturo Giráldez, 'Arbitrage, China, and world trade in the early modern period', *Journal of the Economic and Social History of the Orient*, Vol. 38, No. 4 (1995), 429–48.

158 S. M. H. Bozorgnia, *The Role of Precious Metals in European Economic Development: From Roman Times to the Eve of the Industrial Revolution* (Westport, Conn.: Greenwood, 1998), 180. Similarly, Richard Drayton writes of how '[t]he luxuries of Calcutta and Canton – silks, calico, spices and tea – depended, in significant part, on the bullions earned in selling Africans in the Americas …. African slaves were thus a currency which … were ultimately enabling the growth of European commerce and empire in Asia' ('The collaboration of labour: slaves, empires and globalization in the Atlantic world, c. 1600–1850', in A. G. Hopkins (ed.), *Globalization in World History*, London: Pimlico, 2002, 98–114, 108).

159 A. G. Frank, *ReOrient: Global Economy in the Asian Age* (Berkeley, Calif.: University of California Press, 1998), 280–1.

160 Findlay, 'Globalization', 58.

161 Daron Acemoglu, Simon Johnson and James Robinson, 'The rise of Europe: Atlantic trade, institutional change, and economic growth', *American Economic Review*, Vol. 95, No. 3 (2005), 546–79, 546.

162 Adam Smith, *An Inquiry into the Nature and Causes of the Wealth of Nations* (New York: Random House, 1937 [1776]), 206–7.

163 Smith, *Wealth of Nations*, 417, 591.

164 Smith, *Wealth of Nations*, 202, 416; Cf. Barbara L. Solow, 'Introduction', in B. L. Solow (ed.), *Slavery and the Rise of the Atlantic System* (Cambridge: Cambridge University Press, 1993), 1–20, 15.

165 Williams, *Capitalism and Slavery*, 51–2.

166 Max Weber, *General Economic History* (New Brunswick: Transaction, 1981 [1924]), 298.

167 Karl Marx, *Capital: Critique of Political Economy, Vol. III* (Harmondsworth: Penguin, 1981 [1894]), 450, emphasis ours.

168 Marx, *Capital, I*, 918.

169 Marx, *Capital, I*, 915.

170 See Wood *Origin of Capitalism*, 148.

171 In this explanation, industrialisation and the real subsumption of labour under capital took place internally, as a progressive and unidirectional expansion of the logic of agrarian capitalism into industrial capitalism. In Wood's schema colonialism is explained as nothing other than the extension of the English form elsewhere, subsuming colonialism and effectively modernising it: that is, making it capitalist. 'The dynamics of the English domestic market expanded outward into international trade' (Wood, *Origin of Capitalism*, 135).

172 Marx, *Capital, I*, 719.

173 Wood, *Origin of Capitalism*, 134.

174 See Marx, *Capital, I*, 781–6.

175 Endnotes Collective, 'Misery and debt', *Endnotes no. 2* (London, 2010), 20–51, 25.

176 Mark Overton, *Agricultural Revolution in England: The Transformation of the Agrarian Economy 1500–1850* (Cambridge: Cambridge University Press, 1996).

177 Wood, *Origin of Capitalism*, 103.

178 Wood, *Origin of Capitalism*, 133–4.

179 See, among others, Christopher Hill, *The World Turned Upside Down: Radical Ideas during the English Revolution* (London: Penguin, 1991 [1972]); Brian Manning, *The Far Left in the English Revolution 1640 to 1660* (London: Bookmarks, 1999); Geoff Kennedy, *Diggers, Levellers, and Agrarian Capitalism: Radical Political Thought in Seventeenth Century England* (Lanham, Md.: Lexington, 2008).

180 Peter Linebaugh and Marcus Rediker, *The Many-Headed Hydra: The Hidden History of the Revolutionary Atlantic* (London: Verso, 2012), 16.

181 Wood, *Origin of Capitalism*, 137.

182 Linebaugh and Rediker, *Many-Headed Hydra*, 43; Williams, *Capitalism and Slavery*, 58–9.

183 Williams, *Capitalism and Slavery*, 60.

184 Ferguson, *History of Civil Society*, 182.

185 Linebaugh and Rediker, *Many-Headed Hydra*, 56.

186 Francis Bacon, 'General considerations touching the plantations', in *The Works of Francis Bacon, Lord Chancellor of England, Vol. 2* (Philadelphia, Pa.: Carley & Hardt, 1841 [1606]), 184.

187 Quoted in Linebaugh and Rediker, *Many-Headed Hydra*, 16.

188 Linebaugh and Rediker, *Many-Headed Hydra*, 20.

189 Linebaugh and Rediker, *Many-Headed Hydra*, 57–8, quotes from 16 and 20.

190 W. E. B. du Bois, 'Darkwater: voices from within the veil', in *The Oxford W. E. B. du Bois Reader*, ed. E. J. Sundquist (New York: Oxford University Press, 1996 [1920]), 483–623, 551.

191 William D Philips Jr, 'The old world background of slavery in the Americas', in Solow, *Slavery and the Rise of the Atlantic System*, 43–61, 45.

192 Barbara L. Solow, 'Slavery and colonization', in Solow, *Slavery and the Rise of the Atlantic System*, 21–42, 35.

193 See Marx's sardonic deconstruction of E. G. Wakefield's lament at the failure of capitalist experiments in the colonies: 'A Mr Peel, [Wakefield] complains, took with him from England to the Swan River district of Western Australia means of subsistence and of production to the amount of £50,000. This Mr Peel even had the foresight to bring besides, 3,000 persons of the working class, men, women and children. Once he arrived at his destination, "Mr Peel was left without a servant to make his bed or fetch him water from the river." Unhappy Mr Peel, who provided for everything except the export of English relations of production to Swan River' (Marx, *Capital, I*, 932–3). We thank Cemal Burak Tansel for reminding us of this passage.

194 Linebaugh and Rediker, *Many-Headed Hydra*, 34. 'They were nourished upon a better all-around diet than the Europeans.... They pursued little economic specialization and attempted little trade; they were self-sufficient. Their society was organized around matrilineal descent, and both men and women enjoyed sexual freedom outside marriage' (34). See also Cedric J. Robinson, *Black Marxism: The Making of the Black Radical Tradition* (Richmond, N.C.: University of North Carolina Press, 2000), 130–1.

195 Robin Blackburn, *The Overthrow of Colonial Slavery, 1776–1848* (London: Verso, 1988), 13.

196 Linebaugh and Rediker, *Many-Headed Hydra*, 143–73.

197 Linebaugh and Rediker, *Many-Headed Hydra*, 126.

198 William Darity Jr, 'British industry and the West Indies plantations', in J. E. Inikori and S. L. Engerman (eds), *The Atlantic Slave Trade: Effects on Economies, Societies, and*

Peoples in Africa, the Americas, and Europe (London: Duke University Press, 1992), 247–82, 259.

199 Sidney W. Mintz, *Sweetness and Power: The Place of Sugar in Modern History* (London: Penguin, 1986), 36.

200 Darity, 'British industry', 259; Williams, *Capitalism and Slavery*, 3; Solow, 'Introduction', 5.

201 Quoted in Darity, 'British industry', 271.

202 Blackburn, *Overthrow of Colonial Slavery*, 10.

203 Stanley M. Elkins, *Slavery: A Problem in American Institutional and Intellectual Life* (Chicago, Ill.: University of Chicago Press, 2013). But see A. Bergesen 'Turning World-System Theory on its head', in M. Featherstone (ed.), *Global Culture: Nationalism, Globalization, Modernity* (London: Sage, 1990). 67–81

204 Walter Rodney, *How Europe Underdeveloped Africa* (Washington DC: Howard University Press, 1981), 69.

205 John Thornton, *Africa and Africans in the Making of the Atlantic World, 1400–1800* (Cambridge: Cambridge University Press, 1998), 36–40.

206 Thornton, *Africa and Africans* 44.

207 Giorgio Riello, *Cotton: The Fabric That Made the Modern World* (Cambridge: Cambridge University Press, 2013), 190.

208 Thornton, *Africa and Africans*, 38–9.

209 Thornton, *Africa and Africans*, 66–8.

210 Thornton, *Africa and Africans*, 39. In fact, many European merchants, frustrated by the restraints of the company or their home state under which they operated, defected and entered the service of African rulers (pp. 60–2).

211 Riello, *Cotton*, 190.

212 Thornton, *Africa and Africans*, 89.

213 Thornton, *Africa and Africans* 87.

214 Thornton, *Africa and Africans* 88. But it is also important to note the unevenness among the various West African communities. Variations would typically exist over levels of state centralisation, and thus also the extent of exploitation. Not only did different West African states deploy different means to procure slaves, and use different ways of trading them (directly or indirectly via intermediaries), slaves were obtained from raids on a vast assortment of distinct communities that populated the fertile zones of West and Central Africa. These were taken to a multiplicity of trading ports, before being moved on to, accumulated and eventually shipped at a few departure ports along the West African coast for the middle passage. Cf. Joseph C. Miller, 'The numbers, origins, and destinations of slaves in the eighteenth-century Angolan slave trade', in Darity, *Atlantic Slave Trade*, 77–115.

215 By this we simply mean the accumulation of human beings, as opposed to land – '(geo)political accumulation' – or capital – 'capital accumulation'.

216 Thornton, *Africa and Africans*, 105.

217 Thornton, *Africa and Africans*, 105.

218 Stephanie E. Smallwood, *Saltwater Slavery: A Middle Passage from Africa to American Diaspora* (Cambridge, Mass.: Harvard University Press, 2009), 15.

219 Ray A. Kea, *Settlements, Trade, and Polities in the Seventeenth-Century Gold Coast* (Baltimore, Md.: Johns Hopkins University Press, 1982), 130.

220 Smallwood, *Saltwater Slavery*, 24–8.

221 Henry A. Gemery and Jan S. Hogendorn, 'The Atlantic slave trade: a tentative economic model', *Journal of African History*, Vol. 15, No. 2 (1974), 223–46, 242.

222 R. A. Kea, 'Firearms and warfare on the Gold and Slave Coasts from the sixteenth to the nineteenth centuries', *Journal of African History*, Vol. 12, No. 2 (1971), 185–213; Martin A. Klein, 'Impact of the Atlantic slave trade on the societies of the Western Sudan', in Darity, *Atlantic Slave Trade*, 25–48, 28.

223 Smallwood, *Saltwater Slavery*, 16.
224 Thornton, *Africa and Africans*, 118.
225 Thornton, *Africa and Africans*, 119.
226 Smallwood, *Saltwater Slavery*, 20.
227 Klein, 'Atlantic slave trade', 26.
228 See the excellent discussions of the modal characteristics of the colonial slave planta-
    tions in Sidney W. Mintz, *Sweetness and Power*, esp. 55–60; Dale W. Tomich, *Through
    the Prism of Slavery: Labor, Capital, and World Economy* (Lanham, Md.: Rowman &
    Littlefield, 2004), esp. ch. 2; Banaji, *Theory as History*, 67–71.
229 Robin Blackburn, *The Making of New World Slavery: From the Baroque to the Modern,
    1492–1800* (London: Verso, 1997), 376.
230 Blackburn, *New World Slavery*, 19.
231 Shilliam, 'The Atlantic', 71.
232 Blackburn, *New World Slavery*, 23.
233 Shilliam, 'The Atlantic', 72.
234 Linebaugh and Rediker, *Many-Headed Hydra*, 135–6.
235 Linebaugh and Rediker, *Many-Headed Hydra*, 137–8.
236 Linebaugh and Rediker, *Many-Headed Hydra*, 138.
237 Linebaugh and Rediker, *Many-Headed Hydra*, 139–40.
238 Petty, 'The Scale of Creatures', quoted in Linebaugh and Rediker, *Many-Headed Hydra*,
    139.
239 Linebaugh and Rediker, *Many-Headed Hydra*, 139.
240 Linebaugh and Rediker, *Many-Headed Hydra*, 139.
241 For a later period in the long history of such divide and rule tactics in the Americas,
    see David R. Roediger and Elizabeth D. Esch, *The Production of Difference: Race and the
    Management of Labor in U.S. History* (Oxford: Oxford University Press, 2012).
242 Blackburn, *Overthrow of Colonial Slavery*, 8.
243 Blackburn, *New World Slavery*, 19; David W. Galenson, *Traders, Planters and Slaves:
    Market Behavior in Early English America* (Cambridge: Cambridge University Press,
    1986), 143.
244 Riello, *Cotton*, 197.
245 For this reason, among others, Marx would describe the plantation slavers as 'capital-
    ists', writing for example that:

> In the second type of colonies – plantations – where commercial speculations figure
> from the start and production is intended for the world market, the capitalist mode
> of production exists, although only in a formal sense, since the slavery of Negroes
> precludes free wage-labour, which is the basis of capitalist production. But the
> business in which slaves are used is conducted by *capitalists*. The method of produc-
> tion which they introduce has not arisen out of slavery but is grafted on to it. In this
> case the same person is capitalist and landowner.
> (Marx, *Theories of Surplus Value, Vol. II*, Moscow: Progress, 1968 [1863], 597).

> Or as he put it elsewhere, the 'fact that we now not only call the plantation owners in
> America capitalist, but that they *are* capitalists, is based on their existence as anoma-
> lies within a world market based on free labour' (Marx, *Grundrisse*, Harmondsworth:
> Penguin, 1973 [1857–58], 513).

246 Galenson, *Traders, Planters and Slaves*, 143.
247 William Dusinberre, *Them Dark Days: Slavery in the American Rice Swamps* (Athens, Ga.:
    Georgia University Press, 2000), 404; Blackburn, *Overthrow of Colonial Slavery*, 8.
248 Blackburn, *Overthrow of Colonial Slavery*, 7.
249 C. L. R. James noted how the slaves 'working and living together in gangs of hundreds
    on the huge sugar-factories … were closer to a modern proletariat than any group of
    works in existence at the time' (*The Black Jacobins: Toussaint L'Ouverture and the San
    Domingo Revolution*, New York: Vintage, 1963 [1938], 85–6).

250 Dusinberre, *Them Dark Days*, 405.

251 Riello, *Cotton*, 205.

252 Riello, *Cotton*, 207–8.

253 See Jairus Banaji, 'Putting theory to work', *Historical Materialism*, Vol. 21, No. 4 (2013), 129–43, 136–7; Banaji, *Theory as History*, 67–71.

254 Blackburn, *New World Slavery*, 10.

255 Davidson, *How Revolutionary*, 537.

256 Charles Post, 'Capitalism, laws of motion and relations of production', *Historical Materialism*, Vol. 21, No. 4 (2013), 71–91, 83.

257 Paul E. Johnson, *The Early American Republic, 1789–1829* (Oxford: Oxford University Press, 2007), 92.

258 Davidson, *How Revolutionary*, 537.

259 Marx, *Capital, III*, 339–48.

260 Darit, 'British industry', 264.

261 Marx, *Capital, III*, 345, emphasis ours; cf. Blackburn, *New World Slavery*, 10.

262 For an excellent discussion of the significance of this quote in demonstrating Marx's acknowledgement of the significance of slavery as an integral aspect of capitalist development, see Banaji, 'Putting theory to work', 138.

263 Blackburn, *New World Slavery*, 558; Blackburn, *Overthrow of Colonial Slavery*, 8.

264 Ronald Findlay and Kevin H. O'Rourke, *Power and Plenty: Trade, War, and the World Economy in the Second Millennium* (Princeton, N.J.: Princeton University Press, 2007), 233.

265 Barbara Solow, 'Caribbean slavery and British growth: the Eric Williams hypothesis', *Journal of Development Economics*, Vol. 17 (1985), 99–115, 105–6.

266 Solow, 'Caribbean slavery', 113.

267 John M. Hobson, *The Eastern Origins of Western Civilisation* (Cambridge: Cambridge University Press, 2004), 267, calculated from Phylliss Deane and W. A. Cole, *British Economic Growth 1688–1959: Trends and Structure* (Cambridge: Cambridge University Press, 2nd edn, 1969), 34.

268 Hobson, *Eastern Origins*, 267.

269 Frank, *ReOrient*, 296, drawing on P. G. M. Dickinson, *The Financial Revolution in England: A Study in the Development of Public Credit 1688–1756* (London: Macmillan, 1967), 470.

270 Joseph Inikori, 'Slavery and the development of industrial capitalism in England', *Journal of Interdisciplinary History*, Vol. 17, No. 4 (1987), 771–93, 786.

271 Joseph E. Inikori, 'Slavery and the revolution in cotton textile production in England', in Darity, *The Atlantic Slave Trade*, 145–82. Cotton checks provided 'a preponderant share of total English cotton textile exports between 1750 to 1774, varying between 48 percent and 86 percent during the period' (157). The advances made in the cotton checks branch would prefigure later shifts to and expansion of European exports in the fustian branch (159–60).

272 Inikori, 'Slavery', 157.

273 Heller, *Birth of Capitalism*, 168.

274 Heller, *Birth of Capitalism*, 168.

275 Smith, *Creating the World Economy*, 174.

276 Hobson, *Eastern Origins*, 271. 'Industrial exports led industrial growth', Solow writes, 'and industrial growth meant structural change and overall growth. American slavery contributed substantially to these exports' (Barbara Solow, 'Capitalism and slavery in the exceedingly long run', in B. Solow and S. Engerman (eds), *British Capitalism and Caribbean Slavery: The Legacy of Eric Williams*, Cambridge: Cambridge University Press, 1987, 51–78, 73).

277 Hobson, *Eastern Origins*, 271.

278 Inikori, 'Slavery', 151–2.

279 Inikori, 'Slavery', 154.

280 Inikori, 'Slavery', 155.

281 Inikori, 'Slavery',146.

282 Barbara Solow and Stanley Engerman, 'British capitalism and Caribbean slavery: the legacy of Eric Williams: an introduction', in *British Capitalism and Caribbean Slavery*, 1–23, 10.

283 Francis Crouzet, 'Towards an export economy: British exports during the Industrial Revolution', *Exploration in Economic History*, Vol. 17 (1980), 48–93, 92. Further, as Drayton notes: 'Atlantic trade, dominated by sugar and slaves, was the most dynamic sphere of Britain's eighteenth-century economy. It was vital to the growth of London and Bristol, Glasgow and Liverpool, to cotton and iron working, shipping, insurance, banking, and to the three million new urban jobs created between 1700 and 1801' ('Collaboration of labour', 104–5). See also Solow and Engerman, 'British capitalism and Caribbean slavery', 11; Heller, *Birth of Capitalism*, 169.

284 Donald Coleman, *The Economy of England, 1450–1750* (Oxford: Oxford University Press, 1977), 197–8.

285 Darity, 'British industry', 257.

286 Quoted in Hobson, *Eastern Origins*, 269.

287 Williams, *Capitalism and Slavery*, 98–104.

288 Especially in a context of existing and increasing land and wood-driven fuel constraints: see Andre Gunder Frank, 'Review of *The Great Divergence*', *Journal of Asian Studies*, Vol. 60, No. 1 (2001), 180–2, 181; cf. Pomeranz, *Great Divergence*, 126–7.

289 Frank, 'Review of *The Great Divergence*', 181.

290 See Mintz, *Sweetness and Power*.

291 Federici, *Caliban and the Witch*, 104–5.

292 The qualitative shift in sugar from a luxury and elite good to one of mass consumption took place *before* the Industrial Revolution: see Ralph Austen and Woodruff Smith, 'Private tooth decay as public economic virtue: the slave–sugar triangle, consumerism, and European industrialization', in Darity, *Atlantic Slave Trade*, 183–203, 186–8; cf. Sheridan, *Sugar and Slavery*, 24–5; Mintz, *Sweetness and Power*.

293 Federici, *Caliban and the Witch,* 99.

294 Davidson, *How Revolutionary*, 128.

295 In particular, a number of scholars have pointed to the significant function of the expansion of the English wool industry as a precursor to Britain's industrial take-off. Here, again, the importance of colonial markets was a vital factor in the industry's expansion. The industrialisation of Yorkshire, in particular, was almost entirely predicated on the expansion of New World trading. As Inikori notes, the 'expansion of the woollen industry was owed entirely to the expansion of the Atlantic system during the period. But for this latter expansion, the English woollen industry, which had been export dependent for many centuries, would have declined absolutely, thereby provoking a nation-wide process of deindustrialization (as occurred in Colyton)' (Inikori, 'Slavery', 789).

296 Blackburn, *New World Slavery*, 554.

297 Inikori, 'Slavery', 146.

298 See Riello, *Cotton*, 223–5.

299 Riello, *Cotton*, 227.

300 Riello, *Cotton*, 229–30.

301 Cf. Edward E. Baptist, *The Half Has Never Been Told: Slavery and the Making of American Capitalism* (New York: Basic Books, 2014).

302 Hobson, *Eastern Origins*, 268.

303 David Washbrook, 'From comparative sociology to global history: Britain and India in the pre-history of modernity', *Journal of the Economic and Social History of the Orient*, Vol. 40, No. 4 (1997), 410–33, 419.

304 Blackburn, *New World Slavery*, 555.

305 Braudel, *Civilization and Capitalism, III*, 414, 387.
306 Irfan Habib, 'Capitalism in history', *Social Scientist*, Vol. 23, Nos 7/9 (1995), 15–31, 23.
307 Marx, *Capital, I*, 925.
308 See Banaji, *Theory as History*, 271, quoting in part Marx, *Capital, III*, 446–7.
309 Banaji, *Theory as History*, 271.
310 It is important to note that this transformative process whereby merchants became capitalists was not peculiar to Europe and their colonial activities in the Atlantic and Southeast Asia. Similar processes can also be found in 19th-century China and Japan – although the former was an outgrowth of European colonial trade: see, respectively, Luke Cooper, 'Explaining the paradox of market reform in communist China: the uneven and combined development of the Chinese Revolution and the search for "national salvation"', PhD dissertation, University of Sussex, 2013, 103–4; David L. Howell, *Capitalism from Within: Economy, Society, and the State in a Japanese Fishery* (Berkeley, Calif.: University of California Press, 1995). Hence, while the feudal mode of production and its fragmented (geo)political system in Europe did prove a more conducive environment for the development of merchant capitalists and capitalism more broadly (see Chapters 4 and 8), as did their colonial possessions, tributary systems such as those found in China and Japan could also engender pockets of capitalist production based on merchant traders intervening in the production process.
311 Peter Musgrave, 'The economics of uncertainty: the structural revolution in the spice trade, 1480–1640', in M. N. Pearson (ed.), *Spices in the Indian Ocean World* (Aldershot: Variorum, 1996), 337–449, 349–50.
312 P. Swarnalatha, *The World of the Weaver in Northern Coromandel c. 1750–1850* (New Delhi: Orient Longman, 2005).
313 Marx, *Capital, III*, 452.
314 For examples of Political Marxists rejecting the notion of 'merchant capitalism' or the potential role of merchants in assisting the transition to capitalism, see Ellen Meiksins Wood, 'Capitalism', in *The Ellen Meiksins Wood Reader*, ed. L. Patriquin (Leiden, Neths: Brill, 2012), 44–6; Teschke, *Myth of 1648*, 197–214; Charlie Post, 'Capitalism', 88–9; and from different Marxist perspectives nonetheless influenced by Brenner and Wood, see Rosenberg, *Empire of Civil Society*, 98–102; John Boyle, 'The mystery of modern wealth: mercantilism, value, and the social foundations of liberal international order', *European Journal of International Relations*, Vol. 14, No. 3 (2008), 405–29; Wolf, *Europe*, 79, 83–86.
315 Alex Callinicos suggests that the apparent contradiction in Marx's thought on the relationship between merchant capital and the rise of capitalism may be due to the unfinished state of the manuscripts that made up the posthumously edited and published second and third volumes of *Capital*. In contrast, we see no contradiction in Marx holding that merchants can revolutionise production in some instances (where other preconditions are present), but not in others. We elaborate on these points in Chapter 7. Regardless, 'there seems no reason in principle to foreclose the possibility that specific forms of merchant capitalism provide conditions under which capitalist rules of reproduction develop' (Callinicos, *Imperialism*, 112). Thus, Julie Adams notes, the 'impact of merchant capital' on the development (or non-development) of capitalism 'cannot be settled in advance' of sustained historical analysis (*The Familial State: Ruling Families and Merchant Capitalism in Early Modern Europe*, Ithaca, N.Y,.: Cornell University Press, 2005, 28).
316 Marx, *Capital, III*, 453; See also Karl Marx and Friedrich Engels, *The German Ideology* (Amherst, Mass.: Prometheus, 1998 [1845–6]), esp. 38–41, 72–80. For a useful discussion of these texts, see Paul Blackledge, *Reflections on the Marxist Theory of History* (Manchester: Manchester University Press, 2006), 42.
317 Marx, *Capital, I*, 1,023.
318 Robert Brenner, 'The social basis of English commercial expansion 1550–1650',

Journal of Economic History, Vol. 32, No. 1 (1972), 361–84, 377, emphasis ours. Brenner's early analysis of the transformation of merchants into capitalists here was taken much further with the publication of *Merchants and Revolution* (1993). As others have pointed out, however, this work sits rather uneasily with Brenner's earlier interventions into the transition debate which emphasised, above all else, changes in the English agrarian economy (class struggle in the countryside as the 'prime mover') heralding the transition to capitalism while seemingly sidelining the potential role of merchants in such transition. Hence, as Perry Anderson notes, it is a 'nice irony' that the 'detractor of the significance of merchant capital in principle has been the first to establish, in spell-binding detail, its role as a demiurge in practice' (*Spectrum: From Right to Left in the World of Ideas*, London: Verso, 2005, 251–2). Callinicos points out the ways in which '*Merchants and Revolution* evokes a more complete picture of capitalist development' than Brenner's earlier works, 'one involving the co-existence of different forms – the classic trinity of landowner, capitalist and labourer in English agriculture, the partnership of merchant and planter in the exploitation of unfree indentured and slave labour in the New World and perhaps other forms' ('England's transition to capitalism', *New Left Review*, Series 1, No. 207 (1994), 124–33, 131–2).

319 See, among others, James A. Brady Jr., 'The rise of merchant empires, 1400–1700: a European counterpoint', in J. D. Tracy (ed.), *The Political Economy of Merchant Empires: State Power and World Trade, 1350–1750* (Cambridge: Cambridge University Press, 1991), 117–60; Jan L. van Zanden, *The Rise and Decline of Holland's Economy: Merchant Capitalism and the Labour Market* (Manchester: Manchester University Press, 1993), esp. ch. 1; Robert S. Duplessis, *Transitions to Capitalism in Early Modern Europe* (Cambridge: Cambridge University Press, 1997), esp. ch. 4; Eric Mielants, 'Perspectives on the origins of merchant capitalism in Europe', *Review*, Vol. 23, No. 2 (2000), 229–92; Banaji, *Theory as History*, esp. ch. 9. For an interesting discussion of merchant capitalism as the 'articulation' of different pre-capitalist modes of production through which it operates, essentially conceiving it as a combined, transitional form of development, see Jan Luiten van Zanden, 'Do we need a theory of merchant capitalism?', *Review*, Vol. 20, No. 2 (1997), 255–67. Relatedly, see the useful analysis of the relationship between mercantilism and the transition to capitalism in China Miéville, *Between Equal Rights: A Marxist Theory of International Law* (Leiden, Neths: Brill, 2005), 214–24.

320 Banaji, 'Putting theory to work', 136, drawing on David Ormrod, *English Grain Exports and the Structure of Agrarian Capitalism 1700–1760* (Hull: Hull University Press, 1985).

321 But see Stephen K. Sanderson, *Social Transformations: A General Theory of Historical Development* (Oxford: Blackwell, 1995).

322 World-Systems Theory and Political Marxism tend to treat the activity of merchants prior to capitalism as a single and unchanging type. World-Systems Theory argues that merchants – whether living in the 19th or 17th century – pursued capitalist forms of accumulation, but were fettered until the birth of capitalism. Political Marxists argue that merchant activity was defined by 'buying cheap and selling dear' – similarly irrespective of time and place – and was therefore incapable of transforming social relations. Both sides of the debate thereby abstract merchant activity from the wider conjunctural conditions they operate in, presenting an ahistorical conception of merchant capital. In contrast, we argue that whether or not a merchant intervenes in the sphere of production, and whether or not this contributes to a modal change, is an altogether historical question.

323 Brady, 'Rise of merchant empires', 157–8, emphasis ours.

324 Callinicos, *Imperialism*, 114.

325 Brenner, *Merchants and Revolution*, 685.

326 Marx, *Capital*, III, 453.

6 The 'Classical' Bourgeois Revolutions in the History of Uneven and Combined Development

1   Quoted in Geoffrey Parker, *Global Crisis: War, Climate Change and Catastrophe in the Seventeenth Century* (New Haven, Conn.: Yale University Press, 2013), xxi.
2   Martin Wight, *Power Politics* (London: Royal Institute of International Affairs, 1966), 92.
3   Cf. Kees van der Pijl, *The Discipline of Western Supremacy: Modes of Foreign Relations and Political Economy, Vol. III* (London: Pluto, 2014).
4   Arno Mayer, *The Furies: Violence and Terror in the French and Russian Revolutions* (Princeton, N.J.: Princeton University Press, 2000), 534, 533.
5   See esp. David Armstrong, *Revolution and World Order: The Revolutionary State in International Society* (Oxford: Oxford University Press, 1993); Stephen M. Walt, *Revolution and War* (Ithaca, N.Y.: Cornell University Press, 1997); Fred Halliday, *Revolution and World Politics: The Rise and Fall of the Sixth Great Power* (Durham, N.C.: Duke University Press, 1999).
6   But see Stephen Walt's attempt to fit revolutions in the system-level framework of neorealism, the result of which is the usual 'external interaction' model in which processes occurring at discretely conceived levels of analysis (revolutions in the 'domestic', wars in the 'international') are theorised as externally interacting in a way that leaves the basic ontological assumptions of the theory intact (Walt, *Revolution and War*).
7   Fred Halliday, 'The great anomaly', *Review of International Studies*, Vol. 27 (2001), 693–9, 693.
8   Kenneth Waltz, *Man, the State, and War: A Theoretical Analysis* (New York: Columbia University Press, 1959).
9   See e.g. Theda Skocpol, *States and Social Revolutions: A Comparative Analysis of France, Russia and China* (Cambridge: Cambridge University Press, 1979); Jack A. Goldstone, *Revolution and Rebellion in the Early Modern World* (Berkeley, Calif.: University of California Press, 1993); John Foran, *Taking Power: On the Origins of Third World Revolutions* (Cambridge: Cambridge University Press, 2005).
10 Justin Rosenberg, 'Why is there no international historical sociology?' *European Journal of International Relations*, Vol. 12 No. 3 (2006), 307–40, 310.
11 See Halliday, *Revolution and World Politics*, 5–6.
12 See esp. Rosenberg, 'International historical sociology?'
13 Leon Trotsky, *History of the Russian Revolution*, 3 vols (Chicago, Ill.: Haymarket, 2008 [1930]).
14 But see Karman Matin, *Recasting Iranian Modernity: International Relations and Social Change* (London: Routledge, 2013).
15 In this sense, the term 'bourgeois' is somewhat of a misnomer as the active role of the bourgeoisie in making revolutions is inconsequential to adjudicating whether or not a revolution can be considered capitalist.
16 Neil Davidson, *How Revolutionary were the Bourgeois Revolutions?* (Chicago, Ill.: Haymarket, 2012), 366.
17 See Davidson, *How Revolutionary*, ch. 14.
18 Gareth Stedman Jones, 'Society and politics at the beginning of the world economy', *Cambridge Journal of Economics*, Vol. 1 (1977), 77–92, 86.
19 Alex Callinicos, 'Bourgeois revolutions and historical materialism', *International Socialism* Series II, Vol. 43 (1989), 113–71, 124.
20 Whether, as Ellen Meiksins Wood inquired, a revolution was a 'cause or effect of capitalism?' (*The Origin of Capitalism: A Longer View*, London: Verso, 2002, 118).
21 This is not imply that capitalism is always somehow 'dormant' in societies, just waiting for the sociopolitical obstacles to be cleared away for it to emerge. Rather, the point

here is to emphasise how once capitalist production relations have *already emerged* in some form, certain sociopolitical institutions can then act as a drag on their further development thus requiring some kind of 'revolutionary' act to un-hinder their fuller development.

22 Davidson, *How Revolutionary*, 420.

23 Perry Anderson, 'Modernity and revolution', *New Left Review*, Series I, 144 (1984), 96–113, 112.

24 This is not to say that as soon as capitalism emerged in one country, say, the United Provinces, this irrevocably transformed the rules of reproduction for all states and societies, since in Holland and later England, significant internal-external systemic threats remained and these could have reversed the ongoing process of capitalist transformation at the international level. The question here might be posed in terms of capitalism's *spatial scale*: that is, at what point in capitalism's emergence, consolidation and expansion at a particular spatial or regional scale, does it irrevocably alter the fundamental nature and 'logic' of interstate relations as a whole? Posed in this way, it makes more sense to view the Dutch Revolt as the first moment in an ongoing process of transforming the rules of reproduction operating at the level of the European states system as a whole. In order to fully consolidate itself on a large enough spatial scale to complete this process, it needed 1688 and the reconstitution of Scotland and France into capitalist societies to systemically secure and embed capitalism as the internationally dominant mode of production. This means that the emergence and consolidation of capitalism presupposes 'the international' as a constitutive moment or dimension in its development and reproduction. We thank Pepijn Brandon for helping us clarify this important point.

25 Colin Barker, 'Beyond Trotsky: extending combined and uneven development', in B. Dunn and H. Radice (eds), *100 Years of Permanent Revolution: Results and Prospects* (London Pluto, 2006), 72–87, 78.

26 Perry Anderson, 'The notion of bourgeois revolution', in *English Questions* (London: Verso, 1992), 106–18, 116.

27 We owe this formulation to Kamran Matin.

28 See e.g. Callinicos, 'Bourgeois revolutions'; Davidson, *How Revolutionary*.

29 Tony Cliff, 'The nature of Stalinist Russia', in *Marxist Theory after Trotsky: Selected Works, Vol. III* (London: Bookmarks, 2003 [1948]), 1–138.

30 Tony Cliff, 'Deflected permanent revolution', in *Marxist Theory after Trotsky, Vol. III*, 187–201.

31 Davidson, *How Revolutionary*, 459.

32 This approach partially complements Kamran Matin's reformulation of bourgeois revolution from the perspective of uneven and combined development while nonetheless maintaining the consequentialist approach he criticises (Matin, *Recasting Iranian Modernity*, 48, ch. 3).

33 For an outstanding navigation through the debates on the nature of 'really existing socialist' states, see Marcel van der Linden, *Western Marxism and the Soviet Union: A Survey of Critical Theories and Debates since 1917* (Leiden, Neths: Brill, 2007).

34 Anderson, 'Bourgeois revolution', 116.

35 Our emphasis on 'original' is necessary as it is vitally important to understand how the consequences of any bourgeois revolution are not only the result of 'systemic pressures' but also a *response* and often *contestation* to such pressures. In other words, what must be explained is how, over the course of these revolutions, pro-capitalist factions ended up attaining a hegemonic position over what may have begun as an amalgam of different social forces with very different aims.

36 Eric Hobsbawm, 'The crisis of the seventeenth century', in T. Ashton (ed.), *Crisis in Europe 1560–1660* (London: Routledge, 1965 [1954]), 5–58, 42.

37 Wood, *Origin of Capitalism*, 94. See also Ellen Meiksins Wood, 'The question of

market dependence', *Journal of Agrarian Change*, Vol. 2, No. 1 (2002), 50–87; Charles Post, 'Comments on the Brenner–Wood exchange on the Low Countries', *Journal of Agrarian Change*, Vol. 2, No. 1 (2002), 88–95; Benno Teschke, *The Myth of 1648: Class, Geopolitics, and the Making of Modern International Relations* (London: Verso, 2003) 136. For a non-Marxist study similarly conceptualising the United Provinces during this period as non-capitalist, see Martha Howell, *Commerce before Capitalism in Europe, 1300–1600* (Cambridge: Cambridge University Press, 2010).

38 Ellen Meiksins Wood, *Empire of Capital* (London: Verso, 2nd edn, 2005), 63. Suffice to note that a social formation's continuing 'dependence on extra-economic powers of appropriation' should not be automatically taken to mean that it is necessarily non-capitalist. The persistence of such 'extra-economic' modalities of social control and surplus extraction are perfectly compatible and often co-constitutively interact with distinctly capitalist forms, as exemplified by the formal and hybrid modes of subsuming labour to capital characteristic of many forms of combined development (see further, Chapters 1, 5 and 7).

39 Jonathan Israel, *Dutch Primacy in World Trade, 1585–1740* (Oxford: Oxford University Press, 1989), 12, 13; cf. David Ormrod, *The Rise of Commercial Empires: England and the Netherlands in the Age of Mercantilism, 1650–1770* (Cambridge: Cambridge University Press, 2003).

40 Israel, *Dutch Primacy*, esp. 3–11, 408–10.

41 While Israel has stressed the significance of the East–West axis of trade, particularly in luxury commodities, as key to Dutch world trade primacy, Fernand Braudel has emphasised trade in bulk-carrying goods as the key determining factor in Dutch trade dominance in the Mediterranean. It seems that Israel's 'revisionist' interpretation may be somewhat overstated, as more recent findings have tended to 'confirm earlier views of the northern [i.e. Baltic] trades as the mainstay of the Dutch commercial system, and place the onset of decline in Europe's trade with the Baltic as coinciding broadly with the slowing down of the [Dutch] Republic's overseas trade in general' (Ormrod, *Rise of Commercial Empires*, 279). Moreover, as Immanuel Wallerstein notes, this 'mother trade' from 'eastern Europe supplied both the grain to feed Dutch cities and the naval supplies essential to Dutch fishing interests and shipbuilding. Shipbuilding in turn was a key to Dutch success elsewhere' (*The Modern World-System, Vol. I: Capitalist Agriculture and the Origins of the European World Economy in the Sixteenth Century*, London: Academic Press, 1974) 211–12). Additionally, bulk trades in Dutch commercial relations were particularly significant as they were, in many ways, more closely connected to local centres of production, at least until the emergence of sugar refining as an important industry connected to Dutch trade with the Americas in the course of the 18th century. For Israel and Braudel's positions, see respectively Israel, *Dutch Primacy*, 3–11, 197–207, 406–11; Israel, *Empires and Entrepots: Dutch, the Spanish Monarchy and the Jews, 1585–1713* (London: Hambledon Press, 1990), esp. 134–9, 158, 190–1; Israel, *The Dutch Republic: Its Rise, Greatness and Fall, 1477–1806* (Oxford: Oxford University Press, 1998), esp. 315–17; and Israel, 'The "new history" versus "traditional history" in interpreting Dutch world trade primacy', *Bijdragen en mededelingen betreffende de Geschiedenis der Nederlanden (BMGN) – Low Countries Historical Review*, Vol. 106, No. 3 (1991), 469–79; compare to Braudel, *Capitalism and Civilization, 15th–18th Century, Vol. III: The Perspective of the World* (London: Collins, 1984), 189–91, 195, 204, 207–9, 251–2, 260–1; Braudel, *The Mediterranean and the Mediterranean World in the Age of Philip II, Vol. 1* (Berkeley, Calif.: University of California Press, 1995 [1966]), esp. 572–4, 630–6. For overviews and assessments of some of the issues at stake, see Mehmet Bulut, *Ottoman–Dutch Economic Relations: In the Early Modern Period 1571–1699* (Hilversum, Neths: Uitgeverij Verloren, 2001), 129–35; Ormrod, *Rise of Commercial Empires*, 278–87; and also the meticulous analysis of the relative importance of different sectors and regions of the Dutch trading

empire in Jan de Vries and Ad van der Woude, *The First Modern Economy: Success, Failure, and Perseverance of the Dutch Economy, 1500–1815* (Cambridge: Cambridge University Press, 1997), chs 9 and 10.

42 Ronald Findlay and Kevin H. O'Rourke, *Power and Plenty: Trade, War, and the World Economy in the Second Millennium* (Oxford: Princeton University Press, 2007), 175–6. Though, as we shall see in Chapter 7, the other 'main asset' for the upstart Republic was its Asian colonies, through which Dutch capitalism reproduced itself. See further de Vries and van der Woude, *First Modern Economy*; Bas van Bavel, *Manors and Markets: Economy and Society in the Low Countries, 500–1600* (Oxford: Oxford University Press, 2010).

43 Brenner, 'Low countries', 207–9; cf. Bas van Bavel, 'The Medieval origins of capitalism in the Netherlands', *BMGN*, Vol. 125, No. 2–3 (2010), 45–79, 54–5.

44 Pepijn Brandon, 'Marxism and the "Dutch miracle": The Dutch Republic and the transition-debate', *Historical Materialism*, Vol. 19, No. 3 (2011), 106–46, 121–2.

45 Giovanni Arrighi, *The Long Twentieth Century: Money, Power, and the Origins of Our Times* (London: Verso, 1994), 137.

46 Arrighi, *Long Twentieth Century*, 137.

47 Arrighi, *Long Twentieth Century*, 133.

48 Wallerstein, *Modern World-System, I*, 201; Peter Wolfgang Klein, 'Dutch capitalism and the European world-economy', in M. Aymard (ed.), *Dutch Capitalism and World Capitalism* (Cambridge: Cambridge University Press, 1982), 75–92, 85.

49 Brandon, '"Dutch Miracle"'.

50 Jan Lucassen, 'Labour and early modern economic development', in K. Davids and J. Lucassen (eds), *A Miracle Mirrored: The Dutch Republic in European Perspective* (Cambridge: University of Cambridge Press, 1995), 367–409, 368.

51 Lucassen, 'Economic development', 368.

52 Brandon, '"Dutch miracle"', 122.

53 Peter C. M. Hoppenbrouwers, 'Town and country in Holland, 1300–1550', in S. R. Epstein (ed.), *Town and Country in Europe, 1300–1800* (Cambridge: Cambridge University Press, 2001), 54–79, 59.

54 See Marjolein t'Hart, 'Town and country in the Dutch Republic, 1550–1800', in Epstein, *Town and Country in Europe*, 80–105, 84–5, 91–2, 104.

55 On the latter point, Marjolein t'Hart notes that 'long-distance trade in grain constituted a regular part of rural activities' ('Town and country in Holland', 89).

56 Van Bavel, *Manors and Markets*, 249–50.

57 Brandon, '"Dutch miracle"', 124.

58 Van Bavel, *Manors and Markets*, 204; Brandon, '"Dutch miracle"', 120.

59 Bas van Bavel, 'Transition in the Low Countries: wage labour as an indicator of the rise of capitalism in the countryside, 1300–1700', *Past and Present*, Vol. 195, S2 (2007), 286–303, 290.

60 De Vries and van der Woude, *First Modern Economy*, 195.

61 Van Bavel, *Manors and Markets*, 333.

62 Though, as examined in the Chapter 7, population growth still lagged behind economic growth up through the mid-17th century, leading to a crisis of scarcity in labour-power that was only ameliorated by gaining control over a dispersed mass of largely unfree labour-power in the Dutch Southeast Asian colonies.

63 De Vries and Woude, *First Modern Economy*, 232.

64 Brenner, 'Low Countries', 231.

65 Peter Hoppenbrouwers, 'Mapping an unexplored field: the Brenner debate and the case of Holland', in P. Hoppenbrouwers and J. Luiten van Zanden (eds), *Peasants into Farmers? The Transformation of Rural Economy and Society in the Low Countries (Middle Ages–19th Century) in Light of the Brenner Debate* (Turnhout, Belgium: Brepols, 2001), 41–66, 49.

66 Arrighi, *Long Twentieth Century*, 129.
67 See Arrighi, *Long Twentieth Century*, 140, 142–3.
68 Perry Anderson, *Lineages of the Absolutist State* (London: New Left Books, 1974), 33, 32; cf. V. G. Kiernan, 'State and nation in Western Europe', *Past and Present*, No. 31 (1965), 20–38, 31.
69 As noted in Chapter 2, this is not to imply that feudalism was wholly inimical to the development of the productive forces. But rather, that the nature of the feudal economy did set certain limits to the extent of socio-economic development and that the relative lack of dynamism vis-à-vis capitalist production relations gave the lords incentives to engage in processes of geopolitical accumulation.
70 Robert Brenner, 'The social basis of economic development', in J. Roemer (ed.), *Analytical Marxism* (Cambridge: Cambridge University Press, 1986), 23–53, 31–2.
71 Anderson, *Lineages of the Absolutist State*, 18. Similarly, Brenner refers to French absolutism as a 'transformed version of the old [feudal] system' ('The agrarian roots of European capitalism', in T. H. Aston and C. H. E. Philpin (eds), *The Brenner Debate: Agrarian Class Structure and Economic Development in Pre-Industrial Europe*, Cambridge: Cambridge University Press, 1985, 213–328, 289) – a position at odds with other Political Marxists' conception of absolutism as a '*sui generis* social formation' distinct from both feudalism and capitalism (Teschke, *Myth of 1648*, 191). For contrasting perspectives on the modal nature of the French absolutist state among Political Marxists, see George Comninel, *Rethinking the French Revolution: Marxism and the Revisionist Challenge* (London: Verso, 1987), 195–6, 204–5; Colin Mooers, *The Making of Bourgeois Europe: Absolutism, Revolution, and the Rise of Capitalism in England, France, and Germany* (London: Verso, 1991), 45–102; Wood, *Origin of Capitalism*, 45; Hannes Lacher, *Beyond Globalization: Capitalism, Territoriality, and the International Relations of Modernity* (London: Routledge, 2005), 73–6; Teschke, *Myth of 1648*, esp. 167–81.
72 See Alex Callinicos, *Imperialism and Global Political Economy* (Cambridge: Polity, 2009), 123–36.
73 Cf. Guy Bois, *The Crisis of Feudalism: Economy and Society in Eastern Normandy, c 1300–1550* (Cambridge: Cambridge University Press, 1984).
74 Anderson, *Lineages of the Absolutist State*, 58.
75 Michael Braddick, *State Formation in Early Modern England, c.1550–1700* (Cambridge: Cambridge University Press, 2000), 287.
76 Ivo Schöffer, 'Protestantism in flux during the revolt of the Netherlands', in J. S. Bromley and E. H. Kossmann (eds), *Britain and the Netherlands, Vol. 2: Papers Delivered to the Anglo-Dutch Historical Conference* (Groningen, Neths: J.B. Wolters, 1962), 67–83, 70.
77 Pepijn Brandon, 'The Dutch Revolt: a social analysis', *International Socialism*, Series II, Vol. 116 (2007), 139–64.
78 'Calvinism, assuming different shapes in different countries', R. H. Tawney wrote, 'became an international movement, which brought, not peace, but a sword, and the path of which was strewn with revolutions'. This was 'an active and radical force ... a creed which sought, not merely to purify the individual, but to reconstruct Church and State, and to renew society by penetrating every department of life, public as well as private, with the influence of religion' (*Religion and the Rise of Capitalism*, New Brunswick: Transaction, 1962, 102). By the late 1560s, with the Dutch Revolt in full swing, Calvinism had become the main ideological force.
79 See Henk van Nierop, 'Alva's throne: making sense of the revolt of the Netherlands', in G. Darby (ed.), *The Origins and Development of the Dutch Revolt* (London: Routledge, 2001), 29–47, 30.
80 Quoted in Geoffrey Parker, *The Dutch Revolt* (Ithaca, N.Y.: Cornell University Press, 1977), 46.
81 Davidson, *How Revolutionary*, 570.

82　Nierop, 'Alva's throne', 41.

83　Guido Marnef, 'The towns and the revolt', in Darby, *Origins and Development of the Dutch Revolt*, 55–106, 88.

84　Israel, *Dutch Republic*, 130.

85　The Habsburg emperor, Charles V, had acquired all 17 provinces of the Netherlands through marriage and conquest by the 1540s, centralising them into a single political unit for the first time in their history.

86　As noted in Chapter 4, Henry II of France had a signed a treaty with Süleyman I, leading to the 1551 siege of Tripoli by Ottoman ships which triggered the Italian War of 1551–59 involving the Habsburgs.

87　Israel, *Dutch Republic*, 130–1.

88　Israel, *Dutch Republic*, 130–1, 133.

89　Nierop, 'Alva's throne', 33.

90　Brandon, 'Dutch Revolt' from which the following paragraph draws. See also Graham Darby, 'Narrative of events', in Darby, *Origins and Development of the Dutch Revolt*, 8–28.

91　On the changing role of the Dutch nobility in the revolt, see Henk van Nierop, 'The nobles and the Revolt', in Darby, *Origins and Development of the Dutch Revolt*, 48–66.

92　Brandon, 'Dutch Revolt'.

93　On the differing strategic priorities and pressures confronting Philip II, see Fernando González de León and Geoffrey Parker, 'The grand strategy of Philip II and the Revolt of the Netherlands', in Darby, *Origins and Development of the Dutch Revolt*, 107–32.

94　Quoted in González de León and Parker, 'Grand strategy', 121.

95　Darby, 'Narrative', 24–5. As Wallerstein notes, 'the constraints on Spain are clearly indicated by the fact that virtually every major political turning point in the Spanish–Netherlands relationship from 1557 to 1648 was immediately preceded by a financial crisis in Spain' (*Modern World-System, I*, 205).

96　Wallerstein, *Modern World-System, I*, 210. As Wallerstein goes on to note, these conflicts among Spain, France and England 'within the world-system, this weakening of Spanish world dominance, made it possible for the bourgeoisie of the United Provinces to maneuver to maximize *its* interests' (210).

97　Thanks again to Pepijn Brandon for stressing this dimension of the conflict to us.

98　D. J. B. Trim, 'Huguenot soldiering c. 1560–1685: the origins of a tradition', in M. Glozier and D. Onnekin (eds), *War, Religion and Service: Huguenot Soldiering, 1685–1713* (Hampshire: Ashgate, 2007), 9–30, 15–16. Further regarding the significance of the siege of Leiden, Netherlands, see Henk van Nierop, *Treason in the Northern Quarter: War, Terror, and the Rule of Law in the Dutch Revolt* (Princeton, N.J.: Princeton University Press, 2009), 76–9.

99　Arrighi, *Long Twentieth Century*, 135.

100　Further regarding the sociopolitical consequences of the Dutch Revolt in solidifying a capitalist state, see Brandon, 'Dutch Revolt'; Marjolein t'Hart, *The Making of a Bourgeois State: War, Politics and Finance during the Dutch Revolt* (Manchester: Manchester University Press, 1993), Part III; Julie Adams, *The Familial State: Ruling Families and Merchant Capitalism in Early Modern Europe* (Ithaca, N.Y.: Cornell University Press, 2005).

101　Most notably, Jonathan Scott, *England's Troubles: Seventeenth-Century English Political Instability in European Context* (Cambridge: Cambridge University Press, 2000).

102　Halliday, *Revolution and World Politics*, 185.

103　See quotes and commentary in Scott, *England's Troubles*, esp. 141–2.

104　Robert Mentet de Salmonet, *The History of the Troubles of Great-Britain* (London: Oliver Payne, 1739), 2. On the depth and breadth of the 'general crisis' of the 17th century, see Geoffrey Parker, 'Crisis and catastrophe: the global crisis of the seventeenth century reconsidered', *American Historical Review*, Vol. 113, No. 4 (2008), 1053–79.

105 Quoted in H. R. Trevor-Roper, 'The general crisis of the seventeenth century', in Ashton, *Crisis in Europe*, 59–97, 59.

106 See e.g. Conrad Russell, *The Causes of the English Civil War* (Oxford: Oxford University Press, 1990).

107 Peter J. Bowden, 'Agricultural prices, farm profits and rents: 1500–1640', in P. J. Bowden (ed.), *Economic Change: Wages, Profits and Rents, 1500–1750* (Cambridge: Cambridge University Press, 1990), 13–115, 41.

108 David Underwood, *A Freeborn People: Politics and the Nation in the Seventeenth Century* (Oxford: Clarendon Press, 1996), 61.

109 Christopher Hill, 'Parliament and people in seventeenth-century England', *Past and Present*, No. 92 (1981), 100–24, 115. See also Brian Manning, *The English people and the English Revolution* (London: Bookmarks, 1991); James Holstun, *Ehud's Dagger: Class Struggle in the English Revolution* (London: Verso, 2000).

110 L. J. Reeve, *Charles I and the Road to Personal Rule* (Cambridge: Cambridge University Press, 2003), 220.

111 Scott, *England's Troubles*, 55, 114.

112 Teschke, *Myth of 1648*, 194fn16. As this quote reveals, despite Teschke's focus on the international, and particularly geopolitical sources of subsequent states transitions to capitalism, he begins with a quintessentially 'internalist' explanation of the origins of capitalism in England, taken from Brenner. He views England as the first capitalist society. This kind of methodological internalist analysis, in which 'the international' is subsequently added onto an otherwise internalist theorisation, is fraught with myriad theoretical and empirical difficulties, as examined in Chapter 1.

113 J. V. Polišenský, *The Thirty Years' War* (London: Batsford, 1971), 9.

114 For a lucid Marxist discussion of the connections between the Protestant Reformation and the origins of capitalism, see Davidson, *How Revolutionary*, 565–74.

115 Davidson, *How Revolutionary*, 570.

116 Eric Hobsbawm, 'The general crisis of the European economy in the seventeenth century', *Past and Present*, Vol. 5 (1954), 33–53.

117 Teschke, *Myth of 1648*, 170.

118 See Sheilagh Ogilvie, 'Germany and the seventeenth century crisis', in G. Parker and L. Smith (eds), *The General Crisis of the Seventeenth Century* (London: Routledge, 2nd edn, 1997), 57–87.

119 Polišenský, *Thirty Years' War*, 47. On the advanced nature of Bohemia's economic development, see Arnost Klima, 'Agrarian class structure and economic development in pre-industrial Bohemia', *Past and Present*, Vol. 85 (1979), 49–67; Klima, 'Industrial development in Bohemia 1648–1781', *Past and Present*, Vol. 11 (1957), 87–99.

120 Lawrence Stone, *The Causes of the English Revolution 1529–1642* (New York: Harper & Row, 1972), 60. On the depleted financial resources and (geo)political weaknesses of the Tudor and subsequent Stuart states, see Stone, 60–4 and Scott, *England's Troubles*, 68–72. During the early Stuart period, the real value of royal income had been devastated by high inflation. Prices increased fivefold between 1540 and 1640.

121 Robert Brenner, 'Bourgeois revolution and the transition to capitalism', in A. L. Beier, D. Cannadine and J. M. Rosenheim (eds), *The First Modern Society* (Cambridge: Cambridge University Press, 1989), 271–304, 302, summarising one of the main conclusions of Lawrence Stone's classic study *The Crisis of the Aristocracy 1558–1641* (Oxford: Clarendon Press, 1965).

122 Scott, *England's Troubles*, 141.

123 Robert Brenner, *Merchants and Revolution: Commercial Change, Political Conflict, and London's Overseas Traders, 1550–1653* (London: Verso, 1993), 245–55.

124 Blair Worden, *The English Civil Wars 1640–1660* (London: Weidenfeld & Nicolson, 2009), 37–8.

125 This 'social' interpretation of the English Revolution is most frequently associated

with R. W. Tawney and Christopher Hill, though the former was not a self-identified Marxist, but a 'Christian socialist'. See R. W. Tawney, 'The rise of the gentry, 1558–1640', *Economic History Review*, Vol. 11 (1941), 1–38; Christopher Hill, 'The English Revolution', in *The English Revolution 1640: Three Essays* (London: Lawrence & Wishart, 1940); and for a later reformulation of Hill's view as a conflict between 'court and country', see Hill, *The Century of Revolution, 1603–1714* (London: Nelson, 1961).

126 For a review of the literature critiquing the traditional social interpretation, see Norah Carlin, *The Causes of the English Civil War* (Oxford: Blackwell, 1999), chs 4 and 5; and Brenner, *Merchants and Revolution*, 638–44.

127 Brenner, *Merchants and Revolution*, 642.

128 See Wood, *Origin of Capitalism*, 63; Teschke, *Myth of 1648*, 165–7; Lacher, *Beyond Globalization*, 77; Vivek Chibber, *Postcolonial Theory and the Specter of Capital* (London: Verso, 2013), 56–62.

129 Henry Heller, *The Birth of Capitalism: A Twenty-First Century Perspective* (London: Pluto, 2011), 120–1. Further regarding the continuing existence of feudal relations of production prior to the English Civil Wars, see Brian Manning, 'The English Revolution and the transition from feudalism to capitalism', *International Socialism*, Series II, Vol. 63 (1994), 75–87.

130 Robert Albritton, 'Did agrarian capitalism exist?' *Journal of Peasant Studies*, Vol. 20, No. 3 (1993), 419–41.

131 Jane Whittle, *The Development of Agrarian Capitalism: Land and Labour in Norfolk, 1440–1580* (Oxford: Oxford University Press, 2001), 227–31.

132 J. P. Cooper, 'In search of agrarian capitalism', in Aston and Philpin, *The Brenner Debate*, 138–91, 167–8.

133 Charles Tilly, 'Demographic Origins of the European Proletariat', in D. Levine (ed.), *Proletarianization and Family History* (Orlando, Fla.: Academic Press, 1984), 1–85, 35–6.

134 Peter Linebaugh and Marcus Rediker, *The Many-Headed Hydra: The Hidden History of the Revolutionary Atlantic* (London: Verso, 2000), 149.

135 Quoted in Linebaugh and Rediker, *The Many-Headed Hydra*, 151.

136 Linebaugh and Rediker, *The Many-Headed Hydra*, 144–5.

137 Halliday, *Revolution and World Politics*, 187.

138 Daron Acemoglu, Simon Johnson and James Robinson, 'The rise of Europe: Atlantic trade, institutional change, and economic growth', *American Economic Review*, Vol. 95, No. 3 (2005), 546–79.

139 See Brenner, *Merchants and Revolution*, 243–69; Geoff Kennedy, 'Radicalism and revisionism in the English Revolution', in M. Haynes and J. Wolfreys (eds), *History and Revolution: Refuting Revisionism* (London: Verso, 2007), 25–49.

140 Brenner, *Merchants and Revolution*, 317, 244.

141 Manning, *English People*, esp. chs 1–5. For a more recent survey of the historiographical literature emphasising the 'importance of the middling sort as a catalyst which polarized the divisions over religions, politics and government in 1640–2', see Carlin, *English Civil War*, 162.

142 Davidson, *How Revolutionary*, 573.

143 Barry Coward, 'The experience of the gentry, 1640–1660', in R. C. Richardson (ed.), *Town and Countryside in the English Revolution* (Manchester: Manchester University Press, 1992), 198–223, 217.

144 Scott, *England's Troubles*, 397–404; cf. John Brewer, *The Sinews of Power: War, Money, and the English State, 1688–1783* (Cambridge, Mass.: Harvard University Press, 1990).

145 See Steve Pincus, *1688: The First Modern Revolution* (New Haven, Conn.: Yale University Press, 2009).

146 Christopher Hill, *The Collected Essays of Christopher Hill: Writing and Revolution in 17th Century England, Vol. 1* (Harvester Press, 1985), 117.

147 Neil Davidson, *Discovering the Scottish Revolution, 1692–1746* (London: Pluto, 2003), 208. Further regarding Scotland's uneven and combined development, see Neil Davidson, *The Origins of Scottish Nationhood* (London: Pluto, 2000), 167–86.

148 Davidson, *Origins of Scottish Nationhood*, 177. A consequence of Scotland's combined development – which took on the supercharged pattern of development characteristic of late-industrialising societies of the 20th century – was a destabilisation and radicalisation of society, particularly among the masses. As 'Scotland entered on the capitalist path later than England', Trotsky wrote, 'a sharper turn in the life of the masses of the people gave rise to a sharper political reaction' ('Where is Britain going?', in *Collected Writings and Speeches On Britain, Vol. 3*, ed. R. Chappell and A. Clinton, London: New Park, 1974 [1925], 37). Consequently, during the early years of the Union, the threat from Scotland had not yet passed.

149 Davidson, *Discovering the Scottish Revolution*, ch. 6.

150 See e.g. Robert Brenner, 'The agrarian origins of capitalism', in Aston and Philpin, *The Brenner Debate*, 213–328; Wood, *Origin of Capitalism*, 79–80, 103–5; Mooers, *The Making of Bourgeois Europe: Absolutism, Revolution, and the Rise of Capitalism in England, France, and Germany* (London, Verso, 1991), 45–102; George C. Comninel, *Rethinking the French Revolution: Marxism and the Revisionist Challenge* (London: Verso, 1987); Teschke, *Myth of 1648*, 167–88; Lacher, *Beyond Globalization*, 73–6.

151 Brenner, 'Agrarian roots', 289.

152 Wood, *Origin of Capitalism*, 104.

153 Teschke, *Myth of 1648*, 167.

154 This view of a nondynamic absolutist social formation perhaps explains the significance that Political Marxists, and Justin Rosenberg in part influenced by them, have accorded 'the international' as a distinct form of social transformation. For without recourse to the systemic pressures of geopolitical-military competition, Political Marxists have no way of explaining the generalisation of capitalism.

155 Lacher, *Beyond Globalization*, 77.

156 Wood, *Origin of Capitalism*, 121. From a very different perspective, Wallerstein has also contested the 'bourgeois' categorisation of the French Revolution, since France was already enmeshed in a capitalist world-system by 1789 and thus, by definition, already capitalist: 'The French Revolution could not have been a "bourgeois revolution" since the capitalist world-economy within which France was located was already one in which the dominant class strata were "capitalists" in their economic behavior' ('The French Revolution as a world-historical event', *Social Research*, Vol. 56, No. 1 (1989), 33–52, 36).

157 Teschke, *Myth of 1648*, 165. Similarly, see Brenner, 'Bourgeois revolution'; Comninel, *Rethinking the French Revolution*, 53–76, 104–78; Wood, *Origin of Capitalism*, 62–3; Lacher, *Beyond Globalization*, 77.

158 As argued by Benno Teschke, 'Bourgeois revolution, state formation and the absence of the international', *Historical Materialism*, Vol. 13, No. 2 (2005), 3–26.

159 For this, see Neil Davidson's works which have, we believe, systematically and decisively refuted this argument: 'How revolutionary were the bourgeois revolutions? – Part I', *Historical Materialism*, Vol. 13, No. 3 (2005), 3–33; 'How revolutionary were the bourgeois revolutions? – Part II', *Historical Materialism*, Vol. 13, No. 4 (2005), 3–54; *How Revolutionary*, 133–80.

160 See, among others, Jonathan Dewald, *Point-St-Pierre 1398–1789: Lordship, Community, and Capitalism in Early Modern France* (Berkeley, Calif.: University of California Press, 1987); Anatolii Ado, 'The role of the French Revolution in the transitions from feudalism to capitalism', *Science and Society*, Vol. 54, No. 3 (1990), 361–6; Guy Lemarchand, 'France on the eve of the revolution: a society in crisis or a crisis of politics?' *Science and Society*, Vol. 54, No. 3 (1990), 266–87; Philip T. Hoffman, *Growth in a Traditional Society: The French Countryside, 1450–1815* (Princeton, N.J.:

Princeton University Press, 1996); Henry Heller, *The Bourgeois Revolution in France* (Oxford: Berghahn, 2009); Jean-Michel Chevet, 'Reconsidering a rural myth: peasant France and capitalist Britain' and Gérard Béaur, 'Alternative agriculture or agricultural specialization in early modern France', in J. Broad (ed.), *A Common Agricultural Heritage? Revising French and British Rural Divergence* (Exeter: British Agricultural History Society, 2009), 37–54 and 121–37.

161 Henry Heller, 'Primitive accumulation and technical innovation in the French Wars of Religion', *History and Technology*, Vol. 16, No. 3 (2000), 243–62, 257; cf. Heller, *Labour, Science, and Technology in France, 1500–1620* (Cambridge: Cambridge University Press, 2002), especially chs 4 and 5. Heller's findings here generally accord with the works of Anatolii Ado and Guy Lemarchand who have well demonstrated the 'de-feudalisation' of the French economy during the 16th century: see Ado, 'French Revolution'; Lemarchand, 'France on the eve'.

162 As Ado notes, France was marked by 'evidence of the social differentiation of the peasantry, the appearance of small-scale peasant production, as well as of capitalist farmers in Northern France; the growth of manufacturing and introduction of textile machines and machine builders – all testify to a fairly mature capitalist economy of the time' ('French Revolution', 363).

163 Henry Heller, 'The *longue durée* of the French bourgeoisie', *Historical Materialism*, Vol. 17, No. 1 (2009), 31–59, 41–2, 44.

164 Heller, 'Primitive accumulation', 257.

165 Liana Vardi, *The Land and the Loom: Peasants and Profit in Northern France, 1680–1800* (Durham, N.C.: Duke University Press, 1993).

166 As cited in Heller, *Bourgeois Revolution*, 47.

167 Heller, '*Longue durée*', 55.

168 Ado, 'French Revolution', 363.

169 Lemarchand, 'France on the eve', 269.

170 Colin Jones, 'Bourgeois revolution revived: 1789 and social change', in G. Kates (ed.), *The French Revolution: Recent Debates and New Controversies* (London: Routledge, 1998), 157–91, 165. Further regarding the exponential rise of the bourgeoisie and their amassing of wealth and cultural influence over the 18th century, see Lemarchand, 'France on the eve', 274–8.

171 Jones, 'Bourgeois revolution revived', 174.

172 Gwynne Lewis, *The French Revolution: Rethinking the Debate* (London: Routledge, 1999), 15.

173 William Doyle, *The Oxford History of the French Revolution* (Oxford: Oxford University Press, 1989), 22–3.

174 Such an interpretation of the category of the bourgeoisie as used in France during the period under discussion is in fact somewhat misleading. It did not simply refer to 'town-dwellers' or any person holding a non-noble status. Rather, it referred to a 'legal category based on wealth which only covers partially the social content' (Lemarchand, 'France on the eve', 274). While Political Marxists are correct to decouple the category of the bourgeoisie from capitalists, it still leaves open the question as to whether the social content – that is, the material bases of their social reproduction – of the French bourgeoisie was becoming more capitalist in the centuries before the revolution.

175 See esp. Comninel, *Rethinking the French Revolution*. The sharp distinction between a 'bourgeois' and 'capitalist' class is a common theme among Political Marxists. As Teschke writes of the English and French revolutions: 'while the English Revolution was not bourgeois, it was capitalist; and while the French Revolution was bourgeois, it was not capitalist' ('Bourgeois revolution', 12); see also Chibber, *Postcolonial Theory*, ch. 3, who essentially reproduces the main findings of the revisionist and Political Marxist accounts.

176 Ellen Meiksins Wood, 'Capitalism, merchants and bourgeois revolution: reflections on the Brenner debate and its sequel', *International Review of Social History*, Vol. 41 (1996), 209–32, 225.

177 Hal Draper, *Karl Marx's Theory of Revolution, Vol. 2: The Politics of Social Classes* (New York: Monthly Review Press, 1978), 289 quoted in Davidson, *How Revolutionary*, 557.

178 Heller, *Bourgeois Revolution*, 14.

179 P. Mathias, 'Who unbound Prometheus? Science and technical change, 1600–1800', in A. E. Musson (ed.), *Science, Technology, and Economic Growth in the Eighteenth Century* (London: Methuen, 1972), 81.

180 Robert Duplessis, *Transitions to Capitalism in Early Modern Europe* (Cambridge: Cambridge University Press, 1997), 242.

181 Jeff Horn, 'Avoiding revolution: the French path to industrialization', in J. Horn, L. N. Rosenband and M. R. Smith (eds), *Reconceptualizing the Industrial Revolutions* (Cambridge, Mass.: MIT Press, 2010), 87–106, 89.

182 A. S. Milward and S. B. Saul, *The Economic Development of Continental Europe, 1780–1870* (London: Routledge, 2013 [1973]), 31.

183 Heller, *Bourgeois Revolution*, 40.

184 Guillaume Daudin, 'Profitability of slave and long-distance trading in context: the case of eighteenth-century France', *Journal of Economic History*, Vol. 64, No. 1 (2004), 144–71, 144.

185 Heller, *Bourgeois Revolution*, 34, 28.

186 William Sewell, 'The empire of fashion and the rise of capitalism in eighteenth century France', *Past and Present*, Vol. 206 (2010), 82–120, 88, 94.

187 For two indispensable studies on French absolutism, which nonetheless underestimate the growing impact of capitalist relations, see David Parker, *Class and State in Ancien Regime France: The Road to Modernity?* (London: Routledge, 1996); and William Beik, *Absolutism and Society in Seventeenth-Century France: State Power and Provincial Aristocracy in Languedoc* (Cambridge: Cambridge University Press, 1985).

188 Heller, *Bourgeois Revolution*, 38–9; Cf. Horn, 'Avoiding revolution', 88–92.

189 Lewis, *French Revolution*, 14; Lemarchand, 'France on the eve', 267–8.

190 Lemarchand, 'France on the eve', 279.

191 Anderson, *Lineages of the Absolutist State*, 428–9, 39.

192 Davidson, *How Revolutionary*, 587.

193 Matin is describing the 'rentier state' of the Pahlavi dynasty in Iran: *Recasting Iranian Modernity: International Relations and Social Change* (London: Routledge, 2013), 204.

194 François Furet, *Interpreting the French Revolution* (Cambridge: Cambridge University Press, 1981), 110.

195 Matin, *Recasting Iranian Modernity*, 55. In the Dutch case, this 'external whip' was not yet capitalist, but nonetheless had similar effects as the incipient Dutch state sought to respond to and counter geopolitical pressures in negotiating their developmental transition while drawing on and appropriating the ready-made developmental achievements of earlier developers such as the Italian city-states.

196 Teschke, *Myth of 1648*, 192.

197 Henry Heller, 'Bankers, finance capital and the French Revolutionary terror (1791–94)', *Historical Materialism*, Vol. 22, No. 3–4 (2014), 172–216, 179.

198 Ado, 'French Revolution', 364.

199 Ado, 'French Revolution', 364.

200 Comninel, *Rethinking the French Revolution*, 201.

201 Ado, 'French Revolution', 364.

202 Mooers, *Making of Bourgeois Europe*, 93–4.

203 As Anderson notes, the key moments in the consolidation of the centralised absolutist state in France were the Hundred Years' War, the Religious Wars, and the Fronde (*Lineages of the Absolutist State*, 89).

204 Quoted in Paul Kennedy, *The Rise and Fall of the Great Powers* (London: Fontana, 1989), 147.
205 Quoted in Bailey Stone, *Reinterpreting the French Revolution: A Global-Historical Perspective* (Cambridge: Cambridge University Press, 2004), 19.
206 On the eve of the Revolution, state finances had become primarily geared towards external security rather than economic innovation and the provision of social services. In 1788, total state expenditure was distributed along the following lines: the Court and civil list made up 6.66 per cent; the army, 16.92 per cent; the navy, 8.18 per cent; foreign affairs, 2.22 per cent; and wages, 5.72 per cent. The maintenance of the state amounted to 42.11 per cent, with debt representing 41.24 per cent and the costs of tax-gathering, 51.57 per cent. There remained a mere 3 per cent for public assistance and economic and social subsidies, and 2.35 per cent for public works. Lemarchand, 'France on the eve', 281.
207 Lewis, *French Revolution*, 21–2.
208 Matin, *Recasting Iranian Modernity*, 51.
209 Lewis, *French Revolution*, 60.
210 Heller, *Bourgeois Revolution*, 67, drawing on the works of Guy Lemarchand and Paul Butel. See also, Lemarchand, 'France on the eve'.
211 Lemarchand, 'France on the eve', 269–70.
212 See Heller, *Bourgeois Revolution*, 67–71.
213 Peter McPhee, *The French Revolution, 1789–1799* (Oxford: Oxford University Press, 2002), 33.
214 Heller, *Bourgeois Revolution*, 69.
215 Stone, *Reinterpreting the French Revolution*, 260.
216 Stone, *Reinterpreting the French Revolution*, 42.
217 Stone, *Reinterpreting the French Revolution*, 42.
218 Stone, *Reinterpreting the French Revolution*, 42.
219 Colin Lucas, 'Nobles, bourgeois and the origins of the French Revolution', *Past and Present*, Vol. 60 (1973), 84–126, 105–7; William Doyle, 'The price of offices in pre-revolutionary France', *Historical Journal*, Vol. 27, No. 4 (1984), 831–60, 857.
220 Doyle, 'Price of offices', 858.
221 Lemarchand, 'France on the eve', 273–4.
222 Lynn Hunt, *Politics, Culture, and Class in the French Revolution* (Berkeley, Calif.: University of California Press, 1984), 117.
223 Albert Soboul, 'The French Revolution in the history of the contemporary world', in Peter McPhee, *The French Revolution*, 23–43, 32; Eric Hobsbawm, *The Age of Revolution, 1789–1848* (New York: Vintage, 1996), 60–2; Callinicos, 'Bourgeois revolutions', 146–7.
224 See Sandra Halperin, *War and Social Change in Europe: The Great Transformation Revisited* (Cambridge: Cambridge University Press, 2004).
225 Antonio Gramsci, *Selections from the Prison Notebooks* (London: Lawrence & Wishart, 1971), 58, 109.
226 Quoted in Lothar Gall, *Bismarck: The White Revolutionary, 1851–1871, Vol. I* (London: Allen & Unwin, 1986), 305.
227 Karl Polanyi, *The Great Transformation* (Boston, Mass.: Beacon, 1957 [1944]).
228 Cf. Jamie C. Allinson and Alexander Anievas, 'The uneven and combined development of the Meiji Restoration: a passive revolutionary road to capitalist modernity', *Capital and Class*, Vol. 34, No. 3 (2010), 469–90.
229 Robin Blackburn, 'Haiti, slavery, and the age of democratic revolutions', *William and Mary Quarterly*, Vol. 63, No. 4 (2006), 643–74, 643.
230 Blackburn, 'Haiti', 646; see also Jeremy D. Popkin, *You Are All Free: The Haitian Revolution and the Abolition of Slavery* (Cambridge: University of Cambridge Press, 2010), esp. 327–75.

231 Laurent Dubois, *Avengers of the New World: The Story of the Haitian Revolution* (Cambridge, Mass.: Harvard University Press, 2009), 3.
232 We say this with caution as it was not until *after* the Second World War that a genuine representative bourgeois democracy took hold in Western Europe. The persistence of the racially segregationist Jim Crow laws in the United State pushed back the emergence of formal democracy for another two decades. On the belated rise of representative democracies in these regions, see Halperin, *War and Social Change*; Halperin, 'War and social revolution: World War I and the "great transformation"', in A. Anievas (ed.), *Cataclysm 1914: The First World War and the Making of Modern World Politics* (Leiden, Neths: Brill, 2015), 174–98.
233 Dubois, *Avengers of the New World*, 3. Further regarding the broader significance of the Haitian Revolution on our conceptions of modernity, development and early modern European geopolitics, see Robbie Shilliam, 'What the Haitian Revolution might tell us about development, security, and the politics of race', *Comparative Studies in Society and History*, Vol. 50, No. 3 (2008), 778–808.
234 Comninel, *Rethinking the French Revolution*, 202; Similarly, see Skocpol, *States and Social Revolution*, 204–5; Chibber, *Postcolonial Theory*, 77.
235 Soboul, 'French Revolution', 32.
236 Davidson, *How Revolutionary*, 532; Heller, *Bourgeois Revolution*, 90, 96, 103.
237 For overviews of this literature, see Peter McPhee, 'The French Revolution, peasants, and capitalism', *American Historical Review*, Vol. 94, No. 5 (1989), 1,265–80; and Heller, *Bourgeois Revolution*, 99–103.
238 McPhee, 'French Revolution', 1,280.
239 Cited in Heller, *Bourgeois Revolution*, 103.
240 McPhee, 'French Revolution', 1,276.
241 Callinicos, 'Bourgeois revolutions', 151.
242 A key point made by Jeff Horn in 'Avoiding revolution'. See also Jeff Horn, *The Path Not Taken: French Industrialization in the Age of Revolution, 1750–1830* (Cambridge, Mass.: MIT Press, 2006).
243 Horn, 'Avoiding revolution', 99.
244 Horn, 'Avoiding revolution', 100.
245 Justin Rosenberg, *The Empire of Civil Society: A Critique of the Realist Theory of International Relations* (London: Verso, 1994), 35.
246 Fred Halliday, *Rethinking International Relations* (London: Palgrave, 1994), 78.
247 Karl Marx, *Capital: Critique of Political Economy, Vol. I* (London: Penguin, 1990 [1867]), 975–1059. On Marx's concept of 'hybrid subsumption', see Patrick Murray, 'The social and material transformation of production by capital: formal and real subsumption in *Capital, Volume I*', in R. Bellofiore and N. Taylor (eds), *The Constitution of Capital: Essays on Volume I of Marx's* Capital (London: Palgrave, 2004), 243–73.
248 An important point also made by David Blackbourn and Geoff Eley, *The Peculiarities of German History: Bourgeois Society and Politics in Nineteenth-Century Germany* (Oxford: Oxford University Press, 1984). The kind of historical comparison this entails would be compatible with the approach outlined by Philip McMichael, 'Incorporating comparison within a world-historical perspective: an alternative comparative method', *American Sociological Review*, Vol. 55, No. 3 (1990), 385–97.

7 Combined Encounters

1 William Petty, *Political Arithmetic* (Glasgow: Robert and Andrew Foulis, 1751), 26.
2 For an expanded review of these positions see Chapter 1 and Eric Mielants, *The Origins of Capitalism and the 'Rise of the West'* (Philadelphia, Pa.: Temple University Press, 2008); Andre Gunder Frank and Barry K. Gills (eds), *The World System: Five*

Hundred Years Or Five Thousand? (London: Routledge, 1993).

3   Karin Hofmeester, 'Working for diamonds from the sixteenth to the twentieth century', in M. van der Linden and L. Lucassen (eds), *Working on Labor: Essays in Honor of Jan Lucassen* (Leiden, Neths: Brill, 2012), 25–6; see also Ishrat Alam, 'Diamond mining and trade in South India in the seventeenth century', *Medieval History Journal*, Vol. 3, No. 2 (2000), 291–310.

4   Jairus Banaji, *Theory as History: Essays on Modes of Production and Exploitation* (Leiden, Neths: Brill, 2010), 29–30.

5   Maurice Aymard, 'From feudalism to capitalism in Italy: the case that doesn't fit', *Review*, Vol. 6, No. 2 (1982), 121–208, 142–3, 156.

6   For a fuller exploration of this subject, see Cemal Burak Tansel, 'State formation and social change in modern Turkey', PhD thesis, University of Nottingham, 2015.

7   Karl Marx, Capital: *Critique of Political Economy Vol. III* (Harmondsworth: Penguin, 1981 [1894]), 728.

8   Karl Marx, *Capital: Critique of Political Economy, Vol. I* (Harmondsworth: Penguin, 1976 [1867]), 876.

9   Marx, *Capital, III*, 731–2.

10 Marx, *Capital, III*, 444.

11 See Benno Teschke, *The Myth of 1648: Class, Geopolitics, and the Making of Modern International Relations* (London: Verso, 2003), 207; Ellen Meiksins Wood, *The Origin of Capitalism: A Longer View* (London: Verso, 2002), 38.

12 For more on this question see the conclusion of Chapter 5.

13 Marx, *Capital, I*, 873.

14 See section on Political Marxism in Chapter 1.

15 David Harvey, *The New Imperialism* (Oxford: Oxford University Press, 2003), ch. 4.

16 Marx, *Capital, I*, 927. We would like to thank Andres Sáenz de Sicilia for emphasising this point to us.

17 Similarly, Banaji distinguishes between 'forms such as capital which belong to a specific epoch of history' and 'categories which belong to more or less to all epochs, such as e.g. money', thus marking a distinction between the 'capitalist mode of production' and 'historical capitalism', respectively (*Theory as History*, 3, 13). See also Tansel, 'State formation'.

18 Silvia Federici, *Caliban and the Witch: Women, the Body and Primitive Accumulation* (New York: Autonomedia, 2004), 115.

19 For overviews of agrarian relations, the uses of wage-labour, sophisticated commercial instruments and the prevalence of investments in labour-saving techniques in the Northern Italian city-states, see Samuel Kline Cohn Jr, *The Laboring Classes in Renaissance Florence* (New York: Academic Press, 1980); Aymard, 'From feudalism to capitalism'; Franco Franceschi, 'The economy: work and wealth', in J. M. Najemy (ed.), *Italy in the Age of the Renaissance 1330–1500* (Oxford: Oxford University Press, 2004), 124–44; John M. Najemy, *A History of Florence 1200–1575* (Oxford: Blackwell, 2006), chs 4 and 6; Mielants, *Origins of Capitalism*, esp. 24–7, 36–7; Rebecca Jean Emigh, *The Undevelopment of Capitalism: Sectors and Markets in Fifteenth-Century Tuscany* (Philadelphia, Pa.: Temple University Press, 2008), esp. 59–60, 72–4, 211; Giovanni Arrighi, *The Long Twentieth Century: Money, Power, and the Origins of Our Times* (London: Verso, 1994), esp. ch. 2; Henry Heller, *The Birth of Capitalism: A Twenty-First Century Perspective* (London: Pluto, 2011), 54–7.

20 Heller, *Birth of Capitalism*, 60–1; Perry Anderson, *Lineages of the Absolutist State* (London: New Left Books, 1974), 168–70.

21 Such a transformation would have likely required the creation of a unified territorial state and national market, which was highly unlikely given the persistent political divisions among the merchant-dominated city-states and their inability to mobilise their over-exploited peasant subjects to such a project. In this sense, the failure of

Renaissance Italian city-states to complete the transition to capitalism was a (geo) political one. See Aymard, 'From feudalism to capitalism', 185–96; Anderson, *Lineages of the Absolutist State*, 156, 162; Heller, *Birth of Capitalism*, 60–1.

22 Arrighi, *Long Twentieth Century*, 41.

23 Carlo M. Cipolla, 'The Italian "failure"', in F. Krantz and P. M. Hohenberg (eds), *Failed Transitions to Modern Industrial Society: Renaissance Italy and Seventeenth Century Holland* (Montreal, Quebec: Interuniversity Centre for European Studies, 1974), 8–10, 9; Domenico Sella, 'The two faces of the Lombard economy in the seventeenth century', in *Failed Transitions*, 11–15, 14.

24 Sella, 'Lombard economy', 15.

25 Jason Read, 'Primitive accumulation: the aleatory foundation of capitalism', *Rethinking Marxism*, Vol. 14, No. 2 (2002), 24–49, 37. Conceiving of the origins of capitalism in this manner assists with two tasks. First, the very multiplicity of vectors through which capitalism reproduces itself have perhaps been unfortunately understood by different schools of thought in disparate conceptual terms – 'merchant capitalism', 'company capitalism', 'monarchical capitalism', 'finance capitalism', 'industrial capitalism', 'agrarian capitalism' and so on. The seemingly irreconcilable division between Political Marxism and WST rests precisely on this tendency to distinguish between different types of capitalist formations. Reconceptualising capitalism and its origins in the manner outlined above might offer ways of negotiating and reconciling variants of Marxist thought that have typically concerned themselves with identifying and prioritising one of these aspects as theoretically primary and historically most important. In this sense, both Political Marxism and WST converge around a shared identification of capitalism with one aspect or dimension abstracted from its multiple constitutive properties. 'Each approach', Dale W. Tomich writes, 'takes a single feature seen in isolation, the wage form or the market, and treats it as if it were the sole defining characteristic of capitalism'. Consequently, the 'complexities of capitalist development are thereby reduced to a single dimension which comes to define its essence as a historical system. These two theoretical perspectives are therefore opposed to one another within a shared set of assumptions, their respective interpretations are mirror images of one another' (Tomich, *Through the Prism of Slavery: Labor, Capital, and World Economy*, Lanham, Md.: Rowman & Littlefield, 2004, 42, 43). Second, and relatedly, such a view of capitalism outlined here might assist in breaking out of the parochial confines of Europe (or even narrower, England) in order to trace the variegated processes of capitalism's formation as a mode of production.

26 This dialectic between the creation and destruction of labour-power is especially important when attempting to grasp not only the capitalist mode of production, but also its origins. Marx's section on primitive accumulation reads effectively as an extensive description of the manifold processes of simultaneous destruction and creation – violence, coercion and dispossession, on the one hand; freeing and the subsumption of labour-power, on the other. This dialectic between the violent destruction of labour and its creation by freeing indicates an additional dialectic at the heart of the reproduction of the capitalist mode of production – a dialectic between free and unfree labour.

27 Marx, *Capital*, III, 446, emphasis added.

28 Marx, *Capital*, I, 274.

29 Subsumption in general refers to the subordination of the labour process to the logic of capital – specifically its valorisation process. This can happen in different ways. *Formal subsumption* refers to capital taking hold of an already existing labour process, in which the latter is left formally unchanged by capital. Since capital does not transform the labour process, formal subsumption is closely associated with the appropriation of absolute surplus value: that is, an absolute extension of the working day. In contrast, with *real subsumption*, capital reshapes the labour process 'in its own image', specifically, by introducing labour-saving technologies to the production process. This

enables capital to increase the productivity of labour and extract relative surplus value through a relative increase in the surplus part of the working day. *Hybrid subsumption* refers to transitional forms in which the valorisation of capital is achieved without a prior 'freeing' of labour (that is, in the absence of wage-labour), but is not based upon a relationship of direct domination. This is a form which 'combines together capitalist exploitation without a capitalist mode of production', for example when a usurer appropriates labour by making 'the actual producer into his debtor, instead of making him a seller of his labour to the capitalist' (Karl Marx, 'Formal and real subsumption', in *Marx and Engels Collected Works*, Vol. 34, London: Lawrence & Wishart, 1993[1861–63], 118–20).

30 Marx, *Capital, Vol. I*, 873–940.
31 Read, 'Primitive accumulation', 32.
32 Read, 'Primitive accumulation', 32.
33 See Federici, *Caliban and the Witch*. At the heart of capitalism's origins, and at the centre of its continuing reproduction as a mode of production, there is a dialectic between 'creation' and 'destruction': 'accumulation by dispossession'; historical tendencies toward the use of unwaged labour; and, the 'moving contradiction' between living and dead labour.
34 Arrighi, *Long Twentieth Century*, 41.
35 Arrighi, *Long Twentieth Century*, 46.
36 For a useful overview of neo-Gramscian approaches to IR, see Andreas Bieler and Adam David Morton, 'A critical theory route to world order, hegemony and historical change: neo-Gramscian perspectives in international relations', *Capital and Class*, Vol. 28, No. 1 (2004), 85–113.
37 This is yet another instance of the 'penalties of priority' taking hold. As Maurice Aymard puts it, 'Italian "backwardnesses"... were the product of Italy's previous "advance"' ('From feudalism to capitalism', 179).
38 Arrighi, *Long Twentieth Century*, 141.
39 Fernand Braudel, *The Wheels of Commerce: Civilization and Capitalism: 15th–18th Century, Vol. II* (London: Collins, 1982), 418–19.
40 Braudel, *Wheels of Commerce, II*, 395.
41 Paul M. Kennedy, *The Rise and Fall of the Great Powers: Economic Change and Military Conflict from 1500 to 2000* (London: Vintage, 1989), 98–111.
42 Arrighi, *Long Twentieth Century*, 142.
43 Niels Steensgaard, 'The Dutch East India Company as an institutional innovation', in M. Aymard (ed.), *Dutch Capitalism and World Capitalism* (Cambridge: Cambridge University Press, 1982), 235–57, 237.
44 See Arrighi, *Long Twentieth Century*, ch. 5.
45 Arrighi, *Long Twentieth Century*, 143.
46 Arrighi, *Long Twentieth Century*, 12.
47 Much of this tendency is a reflection of the dominance of new institutionalism in economic history, and in particular the influence of Niels Steensgaard in the historiography of company colonialism. See Niels Steensgaard, *The Asian Trade Revolution of the Seventeenth Century: The East India Companies and the Decline of the Caravan Trade* (London: University of Chicago Press, 1974). The influence of new institutionalism can also be found in John M. Hobson's arguments about 'resource portfolios' and even Banaji's emphasis on legal agreements in 10th and 14th-century Islamic and Mediterranean instances of 'historical capitalism'. See John M. Hobson, *The Eastern Origins of Western Civilization* (Cambridge: Cambridge University Press, 2004); Banaji, *Theory as History*, esp. ch. 9.
48 Arrighi, *Long Twentieth Century*, 142, 225.
49 Arrighi, *Long Twentieth Century*, 148.
50 For a critique of this tendency, see Daniel Ankarloo and Giulio Palermo,

'Anti-Williamson: a Marxian critique of new institutional economics', *Cambridge Journal of Economics*, Vol. 28, No. 3 (2004), 413–29.

51 By extension, Arrighi does not really consider feudal or tributary forms of exploitation, but reduces them to the homogenous and asociological category of 'territorialism'.

52 Wood, *Origin of Capitalism*, 90–1.

53 Jan Luiten van Zanden, *The Rise and Decline of Holland's Economy: Merchant Capitalism and the Labour Market* (Manchester: Manchester University Press, 1993), 20.

54 Peter Hoppenbrouwers, 'Mapping an unexplored field: the Brenner debate and the case of Holland', in P. Hoppenbrouwers and J. Luiten van Zanden (eds), *Peasants into Farmers?:The Transformation of Rural Economy and Society in the Low Countries (Middle Ages–19th Century) in Light of the Brenner Debate* (Turnhout, Belgium: Brepols, 2001), 41–66, 41–3.

55 Hoppenbrouwers, 'Mapping', 45.

56 Hoppenbrouwers, 'Mapping', 49.

57 Hoppenbrouwers, 'Mapping', 44.

58 Hoppenbrouwers, 'Mapping',46.

59 Brenner makes the claim that despite being distinctly 'non-feudal' and 'non-peasant' in character, the United Provinces experienced a 'constrictive developmental path' since its economy was dependent on a European economy that, in the 16th and 17th centuries 'remained an essentially feudal circuit of production'. 'The Agrarian roots of capitalism', in T. H. Aston and C. H. E. Philpin (eds), *The Brenner Debate: Agrarian Class Structure and Economic Development in Pre-Industrial Europe* (Cambridge: Cambridge University Press, 1985), 213–328, 325–6.

60 Hoppenbrouwers, 'Mapping', 49.

61 Hoppenbrouwers, 'Mapping', 46–7.

62 Van Zanden, *Holland's Economy*, 41–53.

63 Hoppenbrouwers, 'Mapping', 49; cf. Robert Brenner, 'The Low Countries in the transition to capitalism', *Journal of Agrarian Change*, Vol. 1, No. 2 (2001), 169–241.

64 Hoppenbrouwers, 'Mapping', 49.

65 Van Zanden, *Holland's Economy*, 37.

66 Van Zanden, *Holland's Economy*, 20.

67 Van Zanden, *Holland's Economy*, 40.

68 Cipolla, 'Italian "failure"'; Sella, 'Lombard economy'.

69 Brenner, 'Low Countries', 215–16.

70 This very feature has been at the heart of various denials that the Dutch were capitalist at all. See e.g. Eric J. Hobsbawm, 'The general crisis of the European economy in the 17th century', *Past and Present*, Vol. 5 (1954), 33–53; Charles Post, 'Comments on the Brenner–Wood exchange on the Low Countries', *Journal of Agrarian Change*, Vol. 2, No. 1 (2002), 88–95; Ellen Meiksins Wood, 'The question of market dependence', *Journal of Agrarian Change*, Vol. 2, No. 1 (2002), 50–87. Such claims, however, overlook the myriad ways in which capital accumulation can emerge and expand in conditions where labour is scarce and the introduction of labour-saving technologies is (for whatever reason) absent.

71 Andrew Higginbottom, 'Structure and essence in "Capital I": extra surplus-value and the stages of capitalism', *Journal of Australian Political Economy*, Vol. 70 (2012), 251–70, 264.

72 Marx, *Capital, I*, 752, emphasis ours.

73 Van Zanden, *Holland's Economy*, 41, emphasis ours. A large proportion of this came through migration (Jan Lucassen, 'Mobilization of labour in early modern Europe', in M. Prak (ed.), *Early Modern Capitalism: Economic and Social Change in Europe, 1400–1800,* London: Routledge, 2001, 161–74). However, despite the influx of migrants, Dutch population levels in this period appear to have at best plateaued. On other estimates they declined. The sustainability of migrant labour was itself highly

limited considering the context of the so-called crisis of the 17th century. On a purely numerical level, it seems Europe was experiencing an overall decline in population. Hobsbawm suggests the Netherlands were one of the few exceptions to this rule ('The general crisis', 7). Van Zanden's research, however, provides an important corrective in showing not only a plateau in the population, but one that was heavily supplemented by migration from surrounding areas (*Holland's Economy*).

74 An emphasis on the global subordination of labour to capital, and the variegated forms of exploitation, lay at the centre of WST's conception of the capitalist world-system. As Wallerstein argues, the global division of labour, with different zones utilising different forms of exploitation – slavery, semi-feudalism, wage-labour – was crucial in establishing a 'flow of surplus' from periphery to centre which 'enabled the capitalist system to come into existence' (*The Modern World-System, Vol. I: Capitalist Agriculture and the Origins of the European World Economy in the Sixteenth Century*, London: Academic Press, 1974, 87).

75 Om Prakash, *European Commercial Enterprise in Pre-Colonial India* (Cambridge: Cambridge University Press, 1998), 8.

76 L. Shaffer, 'Southernization', *Journal of World History*, Vol. 5, No. 1 (1994), 1–20; Sanjay Subrahmanyam, 'Aspects of state formation in South India and Southeast Asia, 1500–1650', *Indian Economic and Social History Review*, Vol. 23, No. 4 (1986), 357–77; Subrahmanyam, '"World-economies" and South Asia, 1600–1750: a skeptical note', *Review*, Vol. 12, No. 1 (1989), 141–8.

77 K. N. Chaudhuri, *Asia Before Europe: Economy and Civilisation of the Indian Ocean from the Rise of Islam to 1750* (Cambridge: Cambridge University Press, 1990); Chaudhuri, *Trade and Civilisation in the Indian Ocean: An Economic History from the Rise of Islam to 1750* (Cambridge: Cambridge University Press, 1985); Janet L. Abu-Lughod, *Before European Hegemony: The World System AD 1250–1350* (Oxford: Oxford University Press, 1989).

78 Anthony Reid, 'Introduction: a time and a place', in A. Reid (ed.), *Southeast Asia in the Early Modern Era: Trade, Power, and Belief* (London: Cornell University Press, 1993), 1–20, 3.

79 Additionally, when we arrive at the period of European integration (in particular the Dutch and later the English), we find these interconnections increasingly formalised under the auspices of colonialism. For these reasons, we would argue that South Asia does indeed form a useful unit of analysis but only insofar as we proceed with attentiveness to the sociological unevenness that characterised it.

80 Luis Filipe Ferreira Reis Thomaz, 'The Malay Sultanate of Melaka', in Reid, *Southeast Asia*, 69–90, 77.

81 Thomaz, 'Malay Sultanate', 79

82 Prakash, *European Commercial Enterprise*, 123–4; Ferreira Reis Thomaz, 'Malay Sultanate', 77–9.

83 Jeyamalar Kathirithamby-Wells, 'Restraints on the development of merchant capitalism in Southeast Asia before c. 1800', in Reid, *Southeast Asia*, 123–48, 141.

84 Dhiravat na Pombejra, 'Ayutthaya at the end of the seventeenth century: was there a shift to isolation?' in Reid, *Southeast Asia*, 250–72, 258–60. An Englishman, Samuel White, and a Frenchman, Chevalier de Forbin, also gained considerable favour serving in Narai's court. Another Frenchman, René Charbonneau, became governor of Phuket and another, Beauregard, governor of Megui.

85 Kathirithamby-Wells, 'Merchant capitalism', 146.

86 Kathirithamby-Wells, 'Merchant capitalism', 146, 133.

87 Jean Gelman Taylor, *The Social World of Batavia: European and Eurasian in Dutch Asia* (Madison, Wisc.: University of Wisconsin Press, 1983).

88 Ulbe Bosma and Remco Raben, *Being 'Dutch' in the Indies: A History of Creolisation and Empire, 1500–1920* (Singapore: NUS Press, 2008), 10–11.

89 Na Pombejra, 'Ayutthaya', 259.

90 Ferreira Reis Thomaz, 'Malay Sultanate', 78.

91 Kathirithamby-Wells, 'Merchant capitalism', 135.

92 Kathirithamby-Wells, 'Merchant capitalism', 138. For example, English traders complained bitterly that they were unable to buy the services of Chinese traders in Jambi because the latter would not break with their patrons on whom they depended for commercial licences.

93 Many foreign merchants lived in large communities or villages outside the city walls of Ayutthaya. These were administratively autonomous from local rulers. See Bosma and Raben, *Being 'Dutch'*, 4.

94 Bosma and Raben, *Being 'Dutch'*, 4, 14.

95 Alexander Hamilton, an English interloper, described one such merchant: 'Abdul Ghafur, a Mahomedan that I was acquainted with, drove a trade equal to the English East India Company, for I have known him fit out in a year about twenty sail ships between 300 and 800 tons, and none of them had less stock 10,000 pounds and some of them had 25,000 and after that foreign stock was sent away, he behould to have as much more of an inland for the following year's market' (quoted in Makrand Mehta, *Indian Merchants and Entrepreneurs in Historical Perspective: With Special Reference to Shroffs of Gujarat, 17th to 19th Centuries*, Delhi: Academic Foundation, 1991, 35).

96 For example, the 'Chinese entrepreneurs in seventeenth century west Java ... operated not merely as traders and brokers, but also helped develop agricultural production in the "Bataviaasch Omnelanden" (the hinterland to the interior of Jakarta)', Subrahmanyam, 'State formation', 373; Prakash, *European Commercial Enterprise*, 84–5.

97 For example, Shantidas Zaveri was a merchant of such stature that when his boats were captured by English pirates he could call on the Mughal governor of Ahmedabad to arrest two of the English companies' factors (Mehta, *Indian Merchants and Entrepreneurs*, 24). The Mamale of Cannanore was wealthy and powerful enough to push the Sultan of the Maldives to 'harass the Portuguese militarily' (Michel Morineau, 'Eastern and Western merchants from the sixteenth to the eighteenth centuries', in S. Chaudhuri and M. Morineau (eds), *Merchants, Companies and Trade: Europe and Asia in the Early Modern Era*, Cambridge: Cambridge University Press, 1999, 116–44, 125).

98 Eric Mielants, 'The rise of European hegemony: the political economy of South Asia and Europe compared, AD 1200–1500', in C. Chase-Dunn and E. N. Anderson (eds), *The Historical Evolution of World-Systems* (New York: Palgrave Macmillan, 2005), 126–7.

99 Partha Chatterjee, *The Black Hole of Empire: History of a Global Practice of Power* (Oxford: Princeton University Press, 2012), 51.

100 See Sanjay Subrahmanyam, *The Political Economy of Commerce, Southern India 1500–1650* (Cambridge: Cambridge University Press, 1990), 258–96.

101 Prakash, *European Commercial Enterprise*, 4.

102 André Wink, *Al-Hind the Making of the Indo-Islamic World: The Slave Kings and the Islamic Conquest? 11th–13th Centuries* (Leiden, Neths: Brill, 1997), 62.

103 Abu-Lughod, *Before European Hegemony*, 361.

104 Prakash, *European Commercial Enterprise*, 51–3.

105 Eric Michael Wilson, *The Savage Republic: De Indis of Hugo Grotius, Republicanism and Dutch Hegemony within the Early Modern World-System (c.1600–1619)* (Leiden, Neths: Brill, 2008), 180.

106 Wilson, *Savage Republic* 179–80. *Mare clausum* – or 'closed sea' – is a body of water that is under the jurisdiction of a state and that is not accessible for other states. *Mare liberum* – or 'free sea' – refers to bodies of water that transcend international boundaries.

107 These fortresses established a permanent presence along key strategic coastal areas and ports, and from them the Portuguese exercised and imposed trading licences, tolls and dues, monopolies on local production, and rents or tributes from local populations and rulers.

108 The *foreiro* was the practice of renting land and granting privileges to individuals who assisted in military campaigns. Pius Malekandathil, *Maritime India: Trade, Religion and Polity in the Indian Ocean* (Delhi: Primus, 2010), 73.

109 The spice trade was crucial to the reproduction of the Portuguese crown. By 1518, it had become the single biggest contributor to royal income. Andrew C. Hess, *The Forgotten Frontier: A History of the Sixteenth-Century Ibero-African Frontier* (Chicago, Ill.: University of Chicago Press, 1978), 33.

110 Sanjay Subrahmanyam, *Explorations in Connected History: Mughals and Franks* (New Delhi: Oxford University Press), 28–34; Charles Henry Alexandrowicz, *An Introduction to the History of the Law of Nations in the East Indies (16th, 17th and 18th Centuries)* (Oxford: Clarendon Press, 1967), 50–1; Giancarlo Casale, *The Ottoman Age of Exploration* (Oxford: Oxford University Press, 2009), 76; Halil İnalcık, 'The Ottoman state: economy and society, 1300–1600', in H. İnalcık and D. Quataert (eds), *An Economic and Social History of the Ottoman Empire, 1300–1914* (Cambridge: Cambridge University Press, 1994), 9–410, 325–6.

111 Malekandathil, *Maritime India*, 72–4.

112 M. N. Pearson, 'Indigenous dominance in a colonial economy: the Goa Rendas, 1600–1670', *Mare Luso-Indicum*, No. 2 (1972), 61–73; Sanjay Subrahmanyam, *Improvising Empire: Portuguese Trade and Settlement in the Bay of Bengal, 1500–1700* (Oxford: Oxford University Press, 1990), 67, 74.

113 Wilson, *Savage Republic*, 180; Arrighi, *Long Twentieth Century*, 157–8.

114 Steensgaard, *Asian Trade Revolution*, 86; Subrahmanyam, *Political Economy of Commerce*, 108.

115 Luis Filipe Ferreira Reis Thomaz, 'The Portuguese in the seas of the archipelago during the sixteenth century', in O. Prakash (ed.), *European Commercial Expansion in Early Modern Asia* (Aldershot: Ashgate Publishers, 1997), 25–41, 26. According to Subrahmanyam, by 1550, the Crown was no longer investing capital in the Pulicat–Malacca route, but instead relying entirely on freight charges. See Subrahmanyam, 'The Coromandel Malacca trade in the sixteenth century: a study of its evolving', in Prakash, *European Commercial Expansion*, 55–88, 51. Similarly, the production and supply of spices was left almost entirely up to Javanese and Malay merchants, with the Portuguese unable to disrupt or control already existing networks of trade. See Arun Das Gupta, 'The maritime trade of Indonesia: 1500–1800', in Prakash, *European Commercial Expansion*, 81–116, 103.

116 Ferreira Reis Thomaz, 'The Portuguese', 29.

117 Prakash, *European Commercial Enterprise*, 3.

118 O. Prakash, 'The Portuguese and the Dutch in Asian maritime trade: a comparative analysis', in Chaudhuri and Morineau, *Merchants, Companies and Trade*, 175–88, 183.

119 Prakash, 'The Portuguese and the Dutch', 185.

120 As Arrighi argues, the VOC 'stressed among their main purposes the objective of attacking the power, prestige, and revenues of Spain and Portugal' (*Long Twentieth Century*, 156).

121 Quoted in Wilson, *Savage Republic*, 159–60.

122 Willard Anderson Hanna, *Indonesian Banda: Colonialism and Its Aftermath in the Nutmeg Islands* (Philadelphia, Pa.: Institute for the Study of Human Issues, 1978), 13.

123 Femme S. Gaastra, 'Competition or collaboration? Relations between the Dutch East India Company and Indian merchants', in Chaudhuri and Morineau, *Merchants, Companies and Trade*, 189–201, 192–4. Gaastra argues that the passes system operated by the Portuguese had in fact become relatively ineffective, since other European merchants could offer protection, while Asian merchants were more than capable of circumventing the system. In short, *competition among merchants* in the Indian Ocean provided the impulse to move away from the *cartaz* system, and compelled merchants

and companies such as the VOC to insert themselves into production. A similar argument is made by Banaji, who claims, '*The stronger the competition of commercial capitals, the greater the is the compulsion on individual capitals to seek some measure of control over production*' (*Theory as History*, 271). See further our discussion of colonial merchant activities in the Americas in Chapter 5.

124 Banaji, *Theory as History*, 270; see also Steensgaard, *Asian Trade Revolution*, 406.

125 Steensgaard, *Asian Trade Revolution*, 114.

126 Wilson, *Savage Republic*, 182.

127 Banaji, *Theory as History*, 274.

128 For example, Braudel argues that the VOC were able to 'use their *own vitality* to manoeuvre [South Asian economies] to [their] own advantage ... [because Europeans] formed a series of coherent economies linked together in a fully operational world-economy' (*The Perspective of the World: Civilization and Capitalism 15th–18th, Vol. III*, Berkeley, Calif.: University of California Press, 1992, 496, emphasis ours).

129 Prakash, 'The Portuguese', 183.

130 Ward, *Networks of Empire*, 59.

131 Ward, *Networks of Empire*, 16–19.

132 Ward, *Networks of Empire*, 33.

133 Jurrien van Goor and Foskelien van Goor, *Prelude to Colonialism: The Dutch in Asia* (Hilversum, Neths: Uitgeverij Verloren, 2004), 80; Maarten Prak, *The Dutch Republic in the Seventeenth Century: The Golden Age* (Cambridge: Cambridge University Press, 2005), 119.

134 Ferreira Reis Thomaz, 'Malay Sultanate', 76.

135 Thomaz, 'Malay Sultanate', 77.

136 Reid, 'Introduction', 4–5.

137 Reid, 'Introduction', 3.

138 Van Zanden, *Holland's Economy*, 73.

139 Van Zanden, *Holland's Economy*, 73.

140 Van Zanden, *Holland's Economy*, 74.

141 Van Zanden, *Holland's Economy*, 75.

142 Van Zanden, *Holland's Economy*, 73.

143 However, the practice of destroying clove trees was limited by the need to placate the local elite since they were 'indispensable as a link between the company and the local population'. Van Zanden, *Holland's Economy*, 73–4.

144 Das Gupta, 'Maritime trade', 109.

145 Das Gupta, 'Maritime trade', 79.

146 Van Zanden, *Holland's Economy*, 72.

147 Where tributary relations did exist, they tended to be 'sporadic and largely nominal'. John Villiers, 'Trade and society in the Banda Islands in the sixteenth century', *Modern Asian Studies*, Vol. 15, No. 4 (1981), 723–50, 730.

148 Hanna, *Indonesian Banda*, 23.

149 Hanna, *Indonesian Banda*, 29–39.

150 Hanna, *Indonesian Banda*, 40; cf. Barbara Watson Andaya, 'Cash cropping and upstream–downstream tensions: the case of Jambi in the seventeenth and eighteenth centuries', in Reid, *Southeast Asia*, 91–122, 108.

151 Villiers, 'Trade and society', 727–8; Hanna, *Indonesian Banda*, 52.

152 Hanna, *Indonesian Banda*, 32.

153 Very much confirming the 'combined' character of the region, the Dutch made use of Asian mercenaries, in particular Japanese, in the military campaigns on Banda (Ward, *Networks of Empire*, 75).

154 Van Zanden, *Holland's Economy*, 76–7; see also Hanna, *Indonesian Banda*, 46–60.

155 Anthony Reid, 'Introduction: slavery and bondage in Southeast Asian history', in A. Reid (ed.), *Slavery, Bondage and Dependency in Southeast Asia* (London: University of

Queensland Press, 1983), 1–43, 15. This appears to be part of a more general, global, technique of exploitation conducted by Dutch colonialists in the period. Contemporaneously, Johan Mauritz, a Dutch colonialist considered using free white labour to work sugar mills in Brazil, before concluding, 'It is not possible to effect anything in Brazil without slaves... they cannot be dispensed with upon any occasion whatsoever: if anyone feels that this is wrong, it is a futile scruple' (quoted in Mark Greengrass, *Christendom Destroyed: Europe 1517–1648*, London: Allen Lane, 2014, 168).

156 Van Zanden, *Holland's Economy*, 77.
157 Hanna, *Indonesian Banda*, 60–61.
158 Van Zanden, *Holland's Economy*, 77.
159 Van Zanden, *Holland's Economy*, 77.
160 J. Fox, '"For good and sufficient reasons": an examination of early Dutch East India Company ordinances on slaves and slavery', in Reid, *Slavery, Bondage and Dependency*, 246–63, 248.
161 Van Zanden, *Holland's Economy*, 78.
162 Markus Vink, '"The world's oldest trade": Dutch slavery and slave trade in the Indian Ocean in the seventeenth century', *Journal of World History*, Vol. 14, No. 2 (2003), 131–77, 139.
163 Hanna, *Indonesian Banda*, 62–63; Vink, '"World's oldest trade"', 139–40.
164 Vink, '"World's oldest trade"', 159.
165 Vink, '"World's oldest trade"', 143.
166 Prakash, *European Commercial Enterprise*, 91.
167 Van Zanden, *Holland's Economy*, 85.
168 Prakash, *European Commercial Enterprise*, 91.
169 M. N. Pearson, 'Merchants and states', in J. D. Tracy (ed.), *The Political Economy of Merchant Empires: State Power and World Trade, 1350–1750* (Cambridge: Cambridge University Press, 1991), 41–116, 52.
170 Pearson, 'Merchants and states', 54.
171 For an overview of specific instances, see Subrahmanyam, *Political Economy of Commerce*, 303–39.
172 Pearson, 'Merchants and states', 56, 74. As with the Ottomans, and unlike Europe, the Mughal state was relatively unconcerned with promoting merchant interests. But unlike in the Ottoman case, where this implied some level of control, in the Mughal Empire this translated to indifference, which in many cases meant a large degree of freedom and autonomy for merchants. Much of this was again the result of specific types of geopolitical pressure, in particular that which came from the north as the Delhi Sultanate constantly had to figure with nomadic incursions. Consequently, war and expansion was a crucial part of imperial reproduction (see Wink, *Al-Hind*, 202–11). However, unlike Europe, this war-making was decoupled from merchants. In this respect, prior rounds of uneven and combined development in South Asia prefigured further unevenness between the Mughals, Ottomans and European states.
173 Biplab Dasgupta, *European Trade and Colonial Conquest* (London: Anthem, 2005), 293.
174 Prakash, *European Commercial Enterprise*, 116.
175 Subrahmanyam, *Political Economy of Commerce*, 29.
176 Prakash, *European Commercial Enterprise*, 166.
177 Subrahmanyam, *Political Economy of Commerce*, 35–7, 88.
178 Mehta, *Indian Merchants*, 36.
179 Prakash, for example, demonstrates that VOC raised capital *locally*, on interest, from local money lenders in Surat (*European Commercial Enterprise*, 161). Mehta's study of Surat also demonstrates the extensive influence of local merchants on European companies. English debt to local lenders, which already stood at $60,000 in 1669, rose to £257,000 by 1694 (see Mehta, *Indian Merchants*, 48). One Asian merchant,

Abdul Goffur, loaned extensively to Europeans, at sums reaching 2 million gold pieces (Morineau, 'Eastern and Western merchants', 125).

180 Banaji, *Theory as History*, 271.

181 Subrahmanyam, *Political Economy of Commerce*, 5; Dasgupta, *European Trade*, 294.

182 According to Prakash, bad debts tended to happen when 'the value of the goods supplied to and accepted by a European company from a particular contract-merchant was less than the sum of money given to him in advance' (*European Commercial Enterprise*, 5, 171).

183 Prakash, *European Commercial Enterprise*, 174.

184 Jose Jobson de Andrade Arruda, 'Colonies as mercantile investments: the Luso-Brazilian empire, 1500–1808', in Tracy, *Political Economy of Merchant Empires*, 360–420.

185 It is worth noting that such techniques in the 'global outsourcing of labour' would once again be replicated from the late 20th century onwards when 'the West' again came up against the limits of relative surplus-value extraction. As such, we would argue that such practices are not merely historically contingent but penetrate deep into the logic of capitalism as a mode of production.

186 Wilson, *Savage Republic*, 491.

187 Federici, *Caliban and the Witch*, 104–5.

8 Origins of the Great Divergence over the *Longue Durée*

1 V. I. Lenin, 'Letters from afar, first letter: the first stage of the revolution', in *Collected Works, Vol. 23* (Moscow: Progress, 1981), 297.

2 Herbert Marcuse, *Reason and Revolution: Hegel and the Rise of Social Theory* (London: Routledge, 2000 [1941]), 109, quoting in part Georg Wilhelm Friedrich Hegel, *The Phenomenology of Mind* (London: Macmillan, 1910 [1806]), 136.

3 See, among others, William H. McNeil, *The Rise of the West: A History of the Human Community* (Chicago, Ill.: University of Chicago Press, 1963); Perry Anderson, *Lineages of the Absolutist State* (London: New Left Books, 1974); Daniel Chirot, 'The rise of the West', *American Sociological Review*, Vol. 50, No. 2 (1985), 181–95; John A. Hall, *Powers and Liberties: The Causes and Consequences of the Rise of the West* (Oxford, Blackwell, 1985); Michael Mann, *The Sources of Social Power: A History of Power from the Beginning to AD 1760, Vol. 1* (Cambridge: Cambridge University Press, 1986), chs 12–15; David Landes, *The Wealth and Poverty of Nations: Why Are Some So Rich and Others So Poor?* (New York: W.W. Norton, 1998); Eric Jones, *The European Miracle: Environments, Economies and Geopolitics in the History of Europe and Asia* (Cambridge: Cambridge University Press, 2003 [1981]); Ricardo Duchesne, *The Uniqueness of Western Civilization* (Leiden, Neths: Brill, 2011).

4 Michael Mann, 'European development: approaching a historical explanation', in Jean Baechler, John A. Hall and Michael Mann (eds), *Europe and the Rise of Capitalism* (Oxford: Basil Blackwell, 1989), 6–19, 6.

5 Duchesne, *Uniqueness of Western Civilization*, 236, 237–8. For a similar rehashing of the 'lost' narrative of European exceptionalism, see Niall Ferguson, *Civilization: The West and the Rest* (London: Penguin, 2011).

6 See, among others, J. M. Blaut, *The Colonizer's Model of the World: Geographical Diffusionism and Eurocentric History* (New York: Guilford, 1993); A. G. Frank, *ReOrient: Global Economy in the Asian Age* (Berkeley, Calif.: University of California Press, 1998); Kenneth Pomeranz, *The Great Divergence: China, Europe and the Making of the Modern World Economy* (Princeton, N.J.: Princeton University Press, 2000); Jack A. Goldstone, 'The rise of the West – or not? A revision to socio-economic history', *Sociological Theory*, Vol. 18, No. 2 (2000), 175–94; Goldstone, 'Efflorescences and economic

growth in world history: rethinking the 'rise of the West' and the Industrial Revolution', *Journal of World History*, Vol. 13, No. 2 (2002), 323–89; Kenneth Pomeranz, 'Beyond the East–West binary: resituating development paths in the eighteenth century world', *Journal of Asian Studies*, Vol. 61, No. 2. (2002), 539–90; John M. Hobson, *The Eastern Origins of Western Civilisation* (Cambridge: Cambridge University Press, 2004); Jack Goody, *The Theft of History* (Cambridge: Cambridge University Press, 2006); Jack Goody, *Capitalism and Modernity: The Great Debate* (Cambridge: Polity, 2004); Jack A. Goldstone, *Why Europe? The Rise of the West in World History, 1500–1850* (New York: McGraw-Hill, 2009).

7 Frank, *ReOrient*, 318, 324. See similarly, Hobson, *Eastern Origins*, 192.

8 Frank, *ReOrient*, 277. Other revisionists stressing the importance of colonies in Europe's ascendency include Pomeranz, *Great Divergence*, 186–94 and Hobson, *Eastern Origins*, 161–89.

9 Goldstone, 'Rise of the West?' 191.

10 Goldstone, 'Capitalist origins', 120.

11 Goody, *Capitalism and Modernity*, 102, 60.

12 Pomeranz, *Great Divergence*, 111.

13 For useful correctives, see Robert Brenner and Christopher Isett, 'England's divergence from China's Yangzi delta: property relations, microeconomics, and patterns of development', *Journal of Asian Studies*, Vol. 61, No. 2 (2002), 609–62; Stephen Broadberry and Bishnupriya Gupta, 'The early modern great divergence: wages, prices and economic development in Europe and Asia, 1500–1800', *Economic History Review*, Vol. 59, No. 1 (2006), 2–31; Robert C. Allen, 'India in the great divergence', in T. J. Hatton, K. H. O'Rourke, and A. M. Taylor (eds), *The New Comparative Economic History: Essays in Honor of Jeffrey G. Williamson* (Cambridge, Mass.: MIT Press, 2007), 9–32.

14 Joseph M. Bryant, 'The West and the rest revisited: debating capitalist origins, European colonialism, and the advent of modernity', *Canadian Journal of Sociology*, Vol. 31, No. 4 (2006), 403–44, 418.

15 Bryant, 'The West', 432fn27.

16 This tendency is most dramatically exemplified in the works of Andre Gunder Frank and Barry K. Gills, 'The cumulation of accumulation', in A. G. Frank and B. Gills (eds), *The World System: Five Hundred Years or Five Thousand* (London: Routledge, 1993), 98–105; and Hobson, *Eastern Origins*.

17 Bryant, 'The West', 434.

18 Kamran Matin, *Recasting Iranian Modernity: International Relations and Social Change* (London: Routledge, 2013), 15.

19 Hobson, *Eastern Origins*, 313.

20 Goldstone, 'Rise of the West?', 187.

21 Pomeranz, *Great Divergence*, 13. For a critique, see P. H. H. Vries, 'Are coal and colonies really crucial? Kenneth Pomeranz and the great divergence', *Journal of World History*, Vol. 12, No. 2 (2001), 407–46.

22 Bryant, 'The West', 435.

23 Bryant, 'New sociology', 164–5.

24 Key representatives of this literature include Charles Tilly, 'Reflections on the history of European state-making', in C. Tilly (ed.), *The Formation of National States in Western Europe* (Princeton, N.J.: Princeton University Press, 1975), 3–83; Aristide R. Zolberg, 'Origins of the modern world system: a missing link', *World Politics*, Vol. 33, No. 2 (1981), 253–81; Anthony Giddens, *The Nation-State and Violence: Vol. 2 of a Contemporary Critique of Historical Materialism* (Cambridge: Polity, 1985); Mann, *Sources of Social Power*, I; Michael Mann, *States, War, and Capitalism: Studies in Political Sociology* (New York: Blackwell, 1988); Charles Tilly, Coercion, Capital and European States: AD 990–1992 (Cambridge: Blackwell, 1992); Thomas Ertman, *Birth of the*

Leviathan: Building States and Regimes in Medieval and Early Modern Europe (Cambridge: Cambridge University Press, 1997).

25 Mann, *Sources of Social Power, I*, 490.

26 Mann, *Sources of Social Power, I*, 454; Mann, 'European development'; William H. McNeil, *The Pursuit of Power: Technology, Armed Force, and Society since AD 1000* (Chicago, Ill.: University of Chicago Press, 1982).

27 Benno Teschke, *The Myth of 1648: Class, Geopolitics, and the Making of Modern International Relations* (London: Verso, 2003) 118. See also Teschke, 'Revisiting the 'war-makes-states' thesis: war, taxation and social property relations in early modern Europe', in O. Asbach and P. Schröder (eds), *War, the State and International Law in Seventeenth Century Europe* (Surrey: Ashgate, 2010), 35–62.

28 The following paragraph draws on Jamie C. Allinson and Alexander Anievas, 'The uses and misuses of uneven and combined development: an anatomy of a concept', *Cambridge Review of International Affairs*, Vol. 22, No.1 (2009), 47–67, 63–4.

29 Such transhistorical generalisations regarding the essentially 'timeless' character of inter-societal relations as an inherently anarchically driven war-prone 'state of nature' are common among neo-Weberians. According to Mann, 'warfare has been a normal way of conducting international relations throughout recorded history', and as he states else-where, 'there are some features of relations between states which are repetitive, if not timeless' (*States, War and Capitalism*, 131; Michael Mann and George Lawson, 'The social sources of life, the universe and everything: a conversation with Michael Mann', *Millennium*, Vol. 34, No. 2 (2005), 487–508, 499). Such claims are nearly identical to those found in the works of neorealists: for example, 'the texture of international politics remains highly constant, patterns recur and events repeat themselves endlessly', rela-tions between states 'are marked by a dismaying persistence', and 'the classic history of Thucydides is as meaningful a guide to the behavior of states today as when it was written in the fifth century BC' (Kenneth N. Waltz, *Theory of International Politics*, New York: McGraw Hill, 1979, 66; Robert Gilpin, *War and Change in World Politics*, Cambridge: Cambridge University Press, 1981, 7). Though great powers may rise and fall throughout world history, everything remains more or less the same. As we have sought to demonstrate throughout this book, such reifying ahistorical claims obscure more than they reveal and are profoundly problematic both historically and theoretically. For a critique of Mann's neorealist conception of 'the international', see John M. Hobson, 'Mann, the state, and war', in J. A. Hall and R. Schroeder (eds), *An Anatomy of Power: The Social Theory of Michael Mann* (Cambridge: Cambridge University Press, 2005), 150–66.

30 See Alexander Wendt, 'Anarchy is what states make of it: the social construction of power politics', *International Organization*, Vol. 46, No. 2 (1992), 391–425; Barry Buzan, Ole Waever and Japp de Wilde, *Security: A New Framework for Analysis* (Boulder, Colo.: Lynne Rienner, 1998).

31 Mann actually admitted as much, writing how, in the 1980s, sociologists 'grabbed for the Realist state' ('Review of Justin Rosenberg's *The Empire of Civil Society*', *British Journal of Sociology*, Vol. 46, No. 3, 1995, 554–5). Though admitting the problem, Mann has done little to ameliorate the methodological and theoretical difficulties arising from such 'raiding'. See e.g. Michael Mann, 'Explaining international relations, empires and European miracles: a response', *Millennium*, Vol. 34, No. 2 (2005), 541–50.

32 Teschke, *Myth of 1648*, 123.

33 Tilly, 'European state-making', 15.

34 Waltz, *Theory of International Politics*, 128.

35 Benno Teschke, 'IR theory, historical materialism, and the false promise of interna-tional historical sociology', *Spectrum*, Vol. 6, No. 1 (2014), 1–66.

36 See esp. Tilly, *Coercion, Capital and European States*; Mann, *Social Sources of Power, I*.

37 Justin Rosenberg, 'Why is there no international historical sociology?' *European Journal of International Relations*, Vol. 12, No. 3 (2006), 307–40, 310.
38 Teschke, *Myth of 1648*, 124.
39 Perry Anderson, *Passages from Antiquity to Feudalism* (London: New Left Books, 1974), 128, 18–19.
41 Matin, *Recasting Iranian Modernity*, 32.
42 Hobson, *Eastern Origins*, 112.
43 The 'Eastern' origins of European feudalism are well examined in Hobson, *Eastern Origins*, 99–115. Further regarding the impact of the Ottoman Empire in the formation (and decline) of Christendom in Europe, see Chapter 4.
44 Anderson, *Lineages of the Absolutist State*, 32.
45 To reiterate, as discussed in Chapters 1 and 2, we are not claiming that the feudal mode of production was inherently stagnant or that agents operating under feudal rules of reproduction were incapable of introducing labour-saving technologies and developing the productive forces more generally. Indeed, they often did in significant ways. The point we are making here is rather that despite such technological innovations and the development of the productive forces, feudal rules of reproduction still set clear limits to the nature and extent of such developments, and that these limits compelled lords to find other means of expanding their incomes, particularly through processes of geopolitical accumulation.
46 Robert Brenner, 'The social basis of economic development', in J. Roemer (ed.), *Analytical Marxism* (Cambridge: Cambridge University Press, 1986), 23–53, 31–2.
47 Anderson, *Passages from Antiquity*, 147.
48 Anderson, *Passages from Antiquity*, 148.
49 Teschke, *Myth of 1648*, 43–4.
50 For further details on the 'crisis of feudalism', see Chapter 3.
51 Ronald Findlay, 'The roots of divergence: Western economic history in comparative perspective', *American Economic Review*, Vol. 82, No. 2 (1992), 158–61, 160.
52 Philip T. Hoffman, 'Prices, the military revolution, and Western Europe's comparative advantage in violence', *Economic History Review*, Vol. 64, No. S1 (2011), 39–59, 41.
53 Anderson, *Lineages of the Absolutist State*, 18.
54 See, among others, McNeil, *Pursuit of Power*, 117–43; Neil Davidson, *How Revolutionary were the Bourgeois Revolutions?* (Chicago, Ill.: Haymarket, 2012), 539–42; Pepijn Brandon, 'Masters of war: state, capital, and military enterprise in the Dutch cycle of accumulation (1600–1795)', PhD dissertation, University of Amsterdam, 2013, 139–207, 314–15.
55 Irfan Habib, 'Merchant communities in precolonial India', in J. D. Tracy (ed.), *The Rise of Merchant Empires: Long Distant Trade in the Early Modern World, 1350–1750* (Cambridge: Cambridge University Press, 1990), 371–99, 396.
56 Mielants, *Origins of Capitalism*, 70–1.
57 Chirot, 'Rise of the West'; Mielants, *Origins of Capitalism*, 79; Thomas A. Brady, 'The rise of merchant empires, 1400–1700: a European counterpoint', in J. D. Tracy (ed.), *The Political Economy of Merchant Empires: State Power and World Trade, 1350–1750* (Cambridge: Cambridge University Press, 1991), 117–61, 149–50.
58 Philip D. Curtin, *Cross-Cultural Trade in World History* (Cambridge: Cambridge University Press, 1984), 116, 128.
59 Paul Van Dyke, 'How and why the Dutch East India Company became competitive in the inter-Asian trade in East Asia in the 1630s', *Itinerario*, Vol. 23, No. 3 (1997), 41–56, 42.
60 Quoted in Geoffrey Parker, 'Europe and the wider world, 1500–1750: the military balance', in Tracy, *Political Economy of Merchant Empires*, 161–95, 179–80.
61 Findlay, 'Roots of divergence', 159.
62 McNeil, *Pursuit of Power*, 101–2.

63   Quoted in Joyce Appleby, *The Relentless Revolution: A History of Capitalism* (New York: W.W. Norton, 2010), 39.

64   Hobson writes that 'while China was the leading power for much of the second millennium, its identity led it to choose to forgo imperialism .... Ultimately, China's identity was more a defensive construct that was designed to maintain Chinese cultural autonomy in the face of the potential "barbarians" invaders (e.g. the Mongols) and reproduce its domestic legitimacy in the eyes of its own population. Accordingly, the Chinese chose to eschew imperialism' (*Eastern Origins*, 307–8).

65   Michael Mann, 'The sources of social power revisited: a response to criticism', in *An Anatomy of Power*, 343–96, 382; see similarly, Hoffman, 'Military revolution', 55–6.

66   Davidson, *How Revolutionary*, 545–6.

67   Parker, 'Europe and the wider world', 163. See more generally, Geoffrey Parker, *The Military Revolution: Military Innovation and the Rise of the West, 1500–1800* (Cambridge: Cambridge University Press, 2nd edn, 1996). Concerning Europe's military conquests prior to British industrialisation as indicating very little in regards to explaining the 'rise of the West', Goldstone writes: 'if we were simply to equate military conquest of vast lands and civilizations with greatness, then the Mongols outshone all civilizations and societies prior to the twentieth century; but I know of few European scholars who would want to give the Mongols the prize for "world's greatest and most advanced civilization" simply because of their military conquests' ('Capitalist origins', 188). Yet the key difference between the Mongol and European conquests was the manifold ways in which the latter appropriated and soldiered the material resources (both in the productive sphere and in sheer manpower) of conquered lands (particularly India) in the service of capitalist ends and developments. European conquests not only transformed the social structures of the states they conquered, but used their resources in furthering their own development in a capitalist direction in both internal and external (i.e. further expansionism) ways, as examined below.

68   Hoffman, 'Military revolution', 39. Though generally discounting the role of geopolitical competition and war as causal factors in the 'rise of the West', Pomeranz does concede that '[t]o some extent, of course, the overseas conquests themselves were the result of intense military competition within Europe. That competition led to significant advances in military technology and tactics, which enabled the Europeans to compensate for their very long supply lines and the limited size of their overseas forces' (*Great Divergence*, 199).

69   For a notable exception see Frank, *ReOrient*, 267–71.

70   Giovanni Arrighi, 'Hegemony unravelling – 2', *New Left Review*, Series II, Vol. 33 (2005), 83–116, 103; see also Eric J. Hobsbawn, *Industry and Empire* (London: Weidenfeld & Nicolson, 1968), 146–9.

71   Giovanni Arrighi, *The Long Twentieth Century: Money, Power, and the Origins of Our Times* (London: Verso, 1994), 263.

72   Mike Davis, *Late Victorian Holocausts: El Niño Famines and the Making of the Third World* (London: Verso, 2000), 300, 299.

73   Jeffrey G. Williamson and David Clingingsmith, 'Mughal decline, climate change and Britain's industrial ascent: an integrated perspective on India's 18th and 19th century deindustrialisation', NBER Working Paper, No. 1 1730, Cambridge, Mass., 2005, 24.

74   See Davis, *Late Victorian Holocausts*, 299–301; Williamson and Clingingsmith, 'Mughal decline', 24.

75   Tarak Barkawi, *Globalization and War* (Lanham, Md.: Rowman & Littlefield, 2006), 45 quoting in part Jeremy Black, *War and the World: Military Power and the Fate of Continents* (New Haven, Conn.: Yale University Press, 1998), 178. On the importance of the British Indian army in the British war effort during the Second World War, see Tarak Barkawi, *Soldiers of Empire: Army, Society and Battle in Postcolonial Perspective*, book ms, 2014.

76 David Washbrook, 'South Asia, the world system, and world capitalism', *Journal of Asian Studies*, Vol. 49, No. 3 (1990), 479–508, 481.

77 Washbrook, 'South Asia', 481, emphasis ours.

78 Parker, 'Europe and the wider world', 184–5.

79 For a conception of the Mughal Empire as a tributary mode of production and a review of the debates surrounding its modal characterisation, see Kate Currie, 'Problematic modes and the Mughal social formation', *Critical Sociology*, Vol. 9 (1980), 9–21.

80 Chris Wickham, 'The uniqueness of the East', *Journal of Peasant Studies*, Vol. 12, Nos. 2/3 (1985), 166–96.

81 Irfan Habib, *The Agrarian System of Mughal India, 1556–1707* (Oxford: Oxford University Press, 2nd edn, 1999), 298–9, 364.

82 Whether this revenue actually ended up with the central authorities is debatable. See David Washbrook, 'India in the early modern world economy: modes of production, reproduction and exchange', *Journal of Global History*, Vol. 2, No. 1 (2007), 87–111, 103–4.

83 Wickham, 'Uniqueness of the East', 186–7, 185–6.

84 See Alex Callinicos, *Imperialism and Global Political Economy* (London: Polity, 2009), 117–18.

85 See Habib, *Agrarian System*, 365–6.

86 Callinicos, *Imperialism*, 118.

87 This practice was established by Akbar in 1568: Habib, *Agrarian System*, 301.

88 Habib, *Agrarian System*, 384, 386. See also Jos Gommans, *Mughal Warfare: Indian Frontiers and the High Road to Empire, 1500–1700* (London: Routledge, 2002), 79–80; John F. Richards, 'Warriors and the state in early modern India', *Journal of the Economic and Social History of the Orient*, Vol. 47, No. 3, (2004), 390–400, 392–3.

89 On the socio-economic background of the leaders of the Maratha Revolt, see Satish Chandra, 'Social background to the rise of the Maratha movement during the 17th century in India', *Indian Economic Social History Review*, Vol. 10 (1973), 209–17; H. Fukazawa, 'Maharashtra and the Deccan: a note', in T. Raychaudhuri and I. Habib (eds), *The Cambridge Economic History of India, Vol. I: c. 1200– c. 1750* (Cambridge: Cambridge University Press, 1982), 193–202, 197; Habib, *Agrarian System*, 389, 400–4; Gommans, *Mughal Warfare*, 76–80.

90 Fukazawa, 'Maharashtra and the Deccan', 197.

91 However, this is not to claim that the feudal mode of production in its totality was ever fully established or secured in the Maratha Empire, but rather that its socio-economic system can be characterised as sharing certain commonalities with feudalism while nonetheless remaining overdetermined by the wider dominant tributary context of which it formed a part. It is better to view it as 'feudalistic' rather than properly feudal, strictly speaking. These feudalistic characteristics of the Maratha economy are well brought out in Fukazawa's discussion, where he writes of an entirely 'new type of state structure in Indian history' having emerged with the so-called Maratha confederacy. Though the kings at Satara were the confederacy's nominal heads, the real power was exercised by the Peshwas at Poona who 'ruled over the *svarajya*, and beyond it a number of Maratha feudatory chiefs administered their own territories, with the obligation to pay homage and a certain tribute to the head of the state, and to provide military force for the state in emergency' ('Maharashtra and the Deccan',199).

92 Habib, *Agrarian System*, 400; Gommans, *Mughal Warfare*, 77.

93 John F. Richards, *The Mughal Empire* (Cambridge: Cambridge University Press, 1995), 244–5, 252; Rohan D'Souza, 'Crisis before the fall: some speculations on the decline of the Ottomans, Safavids and Mughals', *Social Scientist*, Vol. 30, No. 9–10 (2002), 3–30, 21; Śekhara Bandyopādhyāya, *From Plassey to Partition: A History of Modern India* (Hyderabad, India: Orient Blackswan, 2004), 4–5; Munis D. Faruqui, *The Princes of the Mughal Empire, 1504–1719* (Cambridge: Cambridge University Press, 2012), 276.

NOTES

94 Williamson and Clingingsmith, 'Mughal decline', 13; C. A. Bayly, *Rulers, Townsmen, and Bazaars: North Indian Society in the Age of British Expansion, 1770–1870* (Cambridge: Cambridge University Press, 1983), 70–71.

95 J. F. Richards, 'Mughal state finance and the premodern world economy', *Comparative Studies in Society and History*, Vol. 23, No. 2 (1981), 285–308, 299–300. In 1702, Aurangzeb attempted to secure interest-free loans to pay for troop arrears in the Deccan. He was however turned down by various indigenous banking firms: Karen Leonard, 'The "great firm" theory of the decline of the Mughal Empire', *Comparative Studies in Society and History*, Vol. 21, No. 2 (1979), 151–67, 160.

96 Habib, *Agrarian System*, 367–8.

97 Shireen Moosvi, 'Scarcities, prices and exploitation: the agrarian crisis, 1658–70', *Studies in History*, Vol. 1, No. 1 (1985), 45–55, 53.

98 Habib, *Agrarian System*, 367.

99 Douglas M. Peers, *India under Colonial Rule 1770–1885* (Harlow: Pearson, 2006), 17. Further regarding the economically dislocating effects of the Deccan Wars marking a decline in agricultural productivity and an increased burden of taxations in the late 17th century, see S. Arasaratnam, 'Indian merchants and the decline of Indian mercantile activity: the Coromandel case', in *Maritime Trade, Society and European Influence in Southern Asia, 1600–1800* (Aldershot: Variorum, 1995), 27–42, 32–4.

100 Richards, *Mughal Empire*, 186.

101 C. A. Bayly, *Indian Society and the Making of the British Empire* (Cambridge: Cambridge University Press, 1988), 47, 51, 57.

102 Tapan Raychaudhuri, 'The mid-eighteenth-century background', in D. Kumar and M. Desai (eds), *The Cambridge Economic History of India, Vol. II* (Cambridge: Cambridge University Press, 1983), 3–35, 17.

103 R. P. Rana, 'Was there an agrarian crisis in Mughal North India during the late-seventeenth and early-eighteenth centuries?' *Social Scientist*, Vol. 34, No. 11/12 (2006), 18–32, 21–2.

104 C. A. Bayly's study of 18th-century northern India, for example, shows how increased urban prosperity nonetheless coexisted with aggregate agrarian decline, noting 'large penumbras of agricultural decline, particularly in the northwest' (*Rulers, Townsmen, and Bazaars*, 76). For similar assessments highlighting the Empire's agricultural decline by the early 18th century, see Raychaudhuri, 'Mid-eighteenth-century background'; Williamson and Clingingsmith, 'Mughal decline', 7–17.

105 Rana, 'Agrarian crisis', 27. Further concerning the agricultural crisis besetting the Mughal Empire in the late 17th and early 18th centuries, see Habib, *Agrarian System*, 364–405; and Moosvi, 'Scarcities, prices and exploitation'.

106 See R. P. Rana, 'Agrarian revolts in Northern India during the late 17th and early 18th century', *Indian Economic Social History Review*, Vol. 18, Nos 3–4 (1981), 287–325; Irfan Habib, 'Forms of class struggle in Mughal India', in *Essays in Indian History: Towards a Marxist Perception* (New Delhi: Tulika, 1995), 233–58.

107 Williamson and Clingingsmith, 'Mughal decline', 14.

108 Satish Chandra, *Medieval India: Society, the Jagirdari Crisis and the Village* (Madras, India: Macmillan, 1992), xiv.

109 Washbrook, 'India', 105–6. See similarly, C. A. Bayly, 'The Middle East and Asia during the age of revolutions, 1760–1830', *Itinerario*, Vol. 10, No. 2 (1986), 69–84, 75.

110 The Maratha admiral Kanhoji Angre famously never lost a battle to Europeans during his 58-year career. See T. R. Raghavan, 'Admiral Kanhoji Angre', in K. K. N. Kurup (ed.), *India's Naval Traditions: The Role of the Kunhali Marakkars* (New Delhi: Northern Book Centre, 1997), 72–8.

111 Ram Krishna Tandon, 'European adventurers and changes in the Indian military system', in H. Hagerdal (ed.), *Responding to the West: Essays on Colonial Domination and Asian Agency* (Amsterdam: Amsterdam University Press, 2009), 29–43, 33.

112 S. N. Sen, *The Military System of the Marathas* (Calcutta, India: Orient Longman, 1958), 85.

113 Tandon, 'European adventurers', 37.

114 V. G. Hatalkar, *Relations Between the French and the Marathas (1668–1815)* (Bombay, India: University of Bombay, 1958).

115 Tandon, 'European adventurers', 41.

116 M. Athar Ali, 'The passing of empire: the Mughal case', *Modern Asian Studies*, Vol. 9, No. 3 (1975), 385–96, 388.

117 K. N. Chaudhuri, *The Trading World of Asia and the English East India Company, 1660–1760* (Cambridge: Cambridge University Press, 1978), 309, 294.

118 Rila Mukherjee, 'The French East India Company's trade in East Bengal from 1750 to 1753: a look at the Chandeernagore letters to Jugdia', *Indian Historical Review*, Vol. 17, Nos 1–2 (1990–1), 122–35, 128, as quoted by A. G. Frank, 'India in the world economy, 1400–1750', *Economic and Political Weekly*, Vol. 31, No. 30 (1996), 50–64, 61.

119 Richards, 'Mughal state finance', 306.

120 A. Dasgupta, 'Indian merchants and the trade in the Indian Ocean', in *Cambridge Economic History of India*, I, 407–33, 433.

121 S. Arasaratnam, *Maritime Trade, Society and European Influence in Southern Asia, 1600–1800* (Aldershot: Variorum, 1995), 28–9.

122 As Arasaratnam further notes:

> right up to the end of the 17th century, the European Company was not an effective competitor to the Indian merchant. The latter successfully undersold the former in every market of open competition. But the position begins to change at the end of the 17th Century .... All these powers [the English, Dutch, and French] were taking advantage of the weakness of the hinterland political authorities to flex their muscles, to back trade with force more consistently, to defend their territorial and fiscal privileges and to attempt to extract more such privileges.
>
> ('Indian merchants', 37)

123 Richards, *Mughal Empire*, 239.

124 For a narrative of the events, see Partha Chatterjee, *The Black Hole of Empire: History of a Global Practice of Power* (Princeton, N.J.: Princeton University Press, 2012), 1–32.

125 A significant point well emphasised by Frank, 'India in the world economy'.

126 See Leonard, '"Great firm" theory', 158–9; Bayly, *Indian Society*, 50–2; Washbrook, 'India', 106–7, 110; Chatterjee, *Black Hole of Empire*, 29–30. Indian merchants, largely drawn from Hindu backgrounds of the 'traditional' commercial castes or Jains, were progressively accumulating both political and economic power over the 18th century, particularly as they became an important lender to rulers and nobles in the midst of war and revolts. As the Mughal treasury buckled under the weight of such pressures, they became a significant force in India's capital markets, 'moving money from one part of the country to another with their credit notes. In this capacity they came into contact with foreign merchants, supplied them with resources, and at the same time benefited from the Europeans' own growing political significance. By the middle of the eighteenth century the indigenous merchant people were a powerful interest in all the major states which had emerged from the decline of the Delhi power' (Bayly, *Indian Society*, 10).

127 Bayly, *Indian Society*, 51.

128 Mann, 'Social power revisited', 383–4.

129 Frank McLynn, *1759: The Year Britain Became Master of the World* (London: Vintage, 2004), 1.

130 McLynn, *1759*, 391.

131 Immanuel Wallerstein, *The Modern World-System, Vol. II: Mercantilism and the Consolidation of the European World-Economy, 1600–1750* (Berkeley, Calif.: University of California Press, 1980), 257.

132 Davidson, *How Revolutionary*, 586.
133 James Joyce, *Ulysses* (Mineola, N.Y.: Dover, 2002 [1922]), 34.
134 Theodore W. Adorno, *Negative Dialectics* (New York: Continuum, 1973), 320.
135 Bret Easton Ellis, *American Psycho* (New York: Vintage, 1991), 399.

Conclusion

1   Karl Marx, 'Letter to Ludwig Kugelmann in Hanover', *Marx-Engels Collected Works, Vol. 43* (London: Lawrence & Wishart, 1988 [1868]), 67.
2   Gilles Deleuze, 'Postscript on the societies of control', *October* (1992), 3–7.
3   Samuel Beckett, *Nohow On: Company, Ill Seen Ill Said, and Worstward Ho* (New York: Grove Press, 1996 [1983]), 89.
4   Leon Trotsky, *History of the Russian Revolution*, 3 vols (London: Pathfinder, 2007 [1930]), 28.
5   Karl Marx, *Grundrisse* (Harmondsworth: Penguin, 1973 [1857–58]), 101.
6   The political implications of uneven and combined development are, however, partly indeterminate. This recalls the argument made in Chapter 2, that general abstractions are question-begging and as such contain very little content of their own, and that theory is therefore best understood as a weapon of critique and less as clearly mapped out guide to action. In this question-begging, essentially critical form, theory can be useful for identifying political problems and challenges that can only be solved and overcome beyond the realms of theory; that is, through concrete struggles. Indeed, issues arise with theory when the question-begging, critical nature of theory is lifted itself out of history, out of concrete struggles, into ossified general – programmatic – guides to action. In this respect, it is worth recalling Marx's famous yet often unheeded adage: 'if constructing the future and settling everything for all times are not our affair, it is all the more clear what we have to accomplish at present: I am referring to the ruthless criticism of all that exists!' ('Letters from the *Deutsch-Französische Jahrbücher*', *Collected Works of Marx and Engels, Vol. 3* (New York: International Publishers, 1974 [1843]), 133–45, 142). In the same spirit: 'Communism is for us not a *state of affairs* which is to be established, an *ideal* to which reality [will] have to adjust itself. We call communism the *real* movement which abolishes the present state of things. The conditions of this movement result from the premises now in existence' (Karl Marx and Friedrich Engels, *The German Ideology* (London: Lawrence & Wishart, 1974 [1848]), 56–7).
7   Arno Mayer, *The Furies: Violence and Terror in the French and Russian Revolutions* (Princeton, N.J.: Princeton University Press, 2000), 533.
8   Vladimir I. Lenin, *Collected Works, Vol. 29* (Moscow: Foreign Languages Publishing, 1960 [1919]), 153.
9   Andrew Linklater, *Beyond Realism and Marxism: Critical Theory and International Relations* (Basingstoke: Macmillan, 1990), 3.
10 One example of how such an approach has been historically problematic is the unbending emphasis on the European experience as an ideal-type of struggle. Here, the priority of wage-labour struggles is understood as the 'highest stage' of political activity, one which simply needs to be extended, replicated and 'grown over' into revolutionary politics. This has led, in the current period, not to revolutionary politics, but to an empty nostalgia for the politics of the post-Second World War settlement between capital and labour. It has also led to the marginalisation of those forms of oppression that have historically sat outside these formal party and union structures, and the struggles they have participated in.
11 Insofar as proletarian is understood to denote not just wage-labourers but other subaltern classes too.

12 This is not to argue for the liberal pursuit of purely legal rights, nor is it a call for identity politics (however conceived). It is rather to decentre any normative or historical privilege assigned to any particular – singular – identity in anticapitalist politics. Insofar as capitalism was built and subsequently reproduced through historical processes that go beyond the exclusive exploitation of a Western industrial working class, this strikes us as an urgent and immediate necessity.

Index

linear developmentalism *see* Eurocentrism
Linebaugh, Peter, 159
Locke, John, 127–8, 160, 324fn63
Long 13th Century, 46, 52, 63, 67, 76, 273
Long 16th Century, 52, 93–4, 140, 143, 193, 259
Long 19th Century, 176
Long Twentieth Century, The (1994), 222
lords (*see also* feudalism), 22–4, 27–9, 78, 80, 82–4, 87–90, 99, 104, 117–19, 136, 185, 192, 197–8, 200, 255–6, 263–7, 291fn103, 309fn128, 310fn133, 311fn162, 313fn40, 342fn69, 363fn45
Low Countries (*see also* Dutch Republic), 19, 75, 81, 86, 108, 114–15, 117, 188, 204, 275, 283fn7, 329fn193; origins of capitalism in, 180–5, 307fn92
Lucassen, Jan, 182
Luther, Martin, 95, 319fn179
Lutherans, 2, 113

M
Machiavelli, Niccolò, 95
Malta, 110–11, 115
Mamluk Empire, 105
Manchu Dynasty, 71
Mann, Michael, 29, 116, 246, 252, 258, 362fn29, 362fn31
mansabdārs (*see also* Mughal Empire), 263
Maratha Empire (*see also* Mughal Empire), 265–9, 365fn89, 365fn91, 366fn110
Marcuse, Herbert, 245
mare clausum ('closed sea'), 232–3, 356fn106
mare liberum ('free sea'), 232–4, 356fn106
Margaret of Parma (Governor of the Netherlands, 1559–67 and 1578–82), 188
market dependence, 8, 23, 148, 160, 166, 184
Marx, Karl, 1, 8, 17, 22, 24–6, 29, 35–9, 51, 55, 97, 102, 143, 146–9, 163, 168, 171, 199, 216–17, 227, 245, 289–90fn76, 294fn151, 295fn183, 295fn186, 295fn198, 296fn199, 331fn193, 336fn315, 368fn6; and abstraction, 36, 58–60, 291fn99; on 'double relationship', 46–7; on primitive accumulation, 25, 122, 141, 217, 219–20, 352fn26; on subsumption, 17, 214, 220, 350fn247, 352–3fn29; on slavery, 30, 163, 333fn245, 334fn262; on transition to capitalism 170–1, 336fn315
Marxism (*see also* Political Marxism, World-System Theory), 1, 31–2, 58, 135, 140, 142, 177, 180, 193, 199, 203, 215, 245, 280, 289fn76, 293fn124, 298fn20, 300fn63, 303fn108, 336fn314, 344fn114, 344fn125, 352fn25; and 'the international', 41–3, 148; and origins of capitalism, 7, 13–4, 22; and

postcolonial theory, 38–9
Matin, Kamran, 40, 50, 204, 348fn193
Matto, Jan Domingos de, 229
Mauritz, Johan, 358fn155
Mayer, Arno, 175
McLynn, Frank, 272
McMichael, Philip, 55
McNeil, William H., 28, 142, 257
McPhee, Peter, 212
means of production, 22, 26–7, 53, 67, 84, 99, 102, 104, 119, 130, 163, 167, 169, 199–200, 202, 208, 212, 215, 220, 225, 227, 241, 255, 292fn121
means of subsistence, 23, 30, 46, 119, 148–50, 181, 198, 215, 217, 226, 238, 292fn121, 309fn129, 331fn193
means of violence, 252, 254, 256, 260, 264, 271, 276
Mediterranean, 19, 86, 91, 93, 103, 109–10, 112, 114–16, 120, 142, 181–2, 188–9, 215, 257, 259, 274–5, 307fn84, 353fn47
Mehmet II (Sultan of Ottoman Empire, 1444–6 and 1451–81), 95
Mehta, Makrand, 359fn179
Meiji Restoration (1868), 214
Melaka, 228–31, 235, 237
Menshevik Party, 39, 54
mercantilism, 35, 105, 195, 257, 337fn319
merchant capitalism, 162, 170–2, 185, 195, 216–17, 226, 240, 249, 257, 270, 336fn310, 336fn314–5, 336fn318–9, 337fn322, 352fn25, 366fn99
merchants (*see also* capital), 2–3, 29, 61, 73–6, 96, 101, 105–6, 109, 115–17, 120, 130, 145, 155, 160–2, 168, 170–3, 181–5, 189, 193–5, 201, 204, 208, 216–17, 223, 226, 229–33, 235, 237, 239–42, 249, 254–7, 259, 270–1, 306fn78, 307fn84, 332fn210, 335–6fn310, 336fn314–5, 336fn318–9, 337fn322, 351fn21, 352fn25, 356fn93, 356fn96–7, 357fn115, 357fn123, 359fn172, 359fn179, 359fn182, 366fn99, 367fn122, 367fn126
Merchants and Revolution (1993), 336–7fn318
methodological internalism *see* Eurocentrism
Metternich, Prince Klemens Wenzel von, 209
Mexico, 130, 145
Mielants, Eric, 18–22, 72, 75, 289fn73, 307fn87
Mies, Maria, 325fn101
Mill, John Stuart, 294fn151
Ming Dynasty, 72
mode of production (*see also* capitalism, feudalism, kinship, lineage, nomadism, slave, tributary), 18, 22, 24, 30–2, 49, 56, 58, 61–3, 78, 92, 97–8, 170, 216–17, 219, 261, 314fn45, 324fn69

Songhay, 156
South Asia, 16, 34, 114, 228, 230–5, 241–2, 244, 355fn79, 358fn128, 359fn172
South China Sea, 228–9
South Pacific, 257
Southeast Asia, 228, 270
sovereignty, 4, 103, 121–2, 129–30, 134–7, 139–40, 188–9, 193, 209, 245, 259, 275, 298fn22, 322fn44
space/spatial relations, 4, 10–11, 28, 38, 41, 45–7, 54, 57, 60, 63, 73, 88, 103, 137, 139, 141, 146, 159, 168, 180, 189, 232, 242, 245, 285fn43, 298fn20, 326fn101
Spain, 2, 25, 86, 106, 110, 111, 114–15, 118, 121, 136–7, 141–3, 146, 151, 182, 184, 186–7, 189, 192–3, 233, 248, 253, 256, 259, 272, 283fn7, 328fn136, 328–9fn138–9, 329fn144–5, 329fn152, 343fn95–6, 357fn120
Stalin, Josef, 49
state(s): capitalist, 28, 30, 45, 53, 199, 214, 250, 259, 271, 343fn100; feudal, 89, 203, 218, 247, 306fn69; intervention of, 29; precapitalist, 177, 214; proto-state, 47, 69; state-building, 27–8, 94, 115, 120, 188, 191–3, 196, 252, 259; and state-derivation debate, 291fn105; state-formation, 24, 47, 65–6, 77, 98, 127, 134, 139, 156–7, 185, 252–3, 255, 325fn97; and state managers, 28, 208–9, 256; tributary, 101–3, 105, 218, 237, 264, 277
'state socialism', 179
Statues of Labourers (1349–51), 80
Steensgaard, Niels, 223, 234, 243, 253fn47
Stone, Bailey, 207–8
Subaltern Studies, 31, 33, 35,
Subrahmanyam, Sanjay, 357fn115
Substitutionism, 44, 49–50, 196, 211, 299fn47
Sudan, 157
Süleyman II (Sultan of the Ottoman Empire, 1687–91), 95
superstructure, 97–8
surplus-value: absolute, 352fn29; relative, 216, 227, 352fn29, 360fn185
Sweden, 223
Sweezy, Paul, 7, 14
Sylvius, Aeneas (Pope Pius II, 1458–64), 96, 107

T
Taiwan, 233
Taki-Onqoy, 132
Tansel, Cemal Burak, 57, 103
Tawney, R. H., 342fn78, 344fn125
taxes/tax system, 23, 25, 28, 69–70, 73, 96–101, 104–5, 118, 141, 155–6, 159, 186,

188, 192, 198, 206–7, 220, 223, 228, 232, 252, 259, 262–4, 268, 349fn207, 361fn27, 366fn99; tax farming, 268, 315fn62, 316fn111
technology, 227, 260, 364fn68; diffusion, 52, 67, 73, 107, 197, 310fn154, 311fn154,
Terlouw, C. P., 18
Ternate, Kingdom of, 235
territorialised states system (see also capitalism), 27–8, 65, 123, 134–5, 137, 139–41, 247, 252, 259, 298fn22
territoriality, 11, 66, 88, 137, 139, 259
Teschke, Benno, 27, 31, 199, 252–3, 291fn105, 292fn107, 293fn127, 298fn22, 303fn108, 344fn112, 347fn175
t'Hart, Marjolein, 341fn55
Thirty Years' War (1618–48), 191–3, 222
Thompson, E. P., 128
Tidore, Kingdom of, 235
Tilly, Charles, 253
Tımar, 99–100, 315fn62, 316fn111
time (see also universalism), 127–8, 137, 141, 180, 323fn53
Tomich, Dale W., 352fn25
trade, 2–3, 7, 306fn69, 307fn84, 356fn109; and Africa 155–8; Asian, 145–6, 229–36, 240, 243, 257–60, 269–70, 355fn92, 356fn95–6, 367fn122; Atlantic, 122, 142–7, 151, 155–7, 161, 163–6, 168–72; and the Dutch, 180–3, 215, 231–6, 240, 243, 329fn147, 340fn41; and England, 193–5, 275; and France, 200–3, 206, 211; and Mongol Empire, 65, 69–70, 73–6, 80; and Ottoman Empire, 94, 105–9, 115–17, 119–20, 319fn201; and transition debate, 12, 14–15, 21–2, 147, 168–72, 307fn92, 330fn171
transition debate, 13–42, 171, 307fn92, 336fn318
Treaty of Nymphaeus (1261), 75
Treaty of Paris (1763), 272
Treaty of Tianjin (1858), 262
Treaty of Tordesillas (1494), 137
Treaty of Westphalia (1648), 137, 189, 222
tributary mode of production (see also modes of production, Mughal Empire, Ottoman Empire), 70, 97, 99, 101–2, 104, 130, 241, 256, 261, 263–4 314fn45, 315fn78 364fn79
Tripoli, siege of (1551), 242–3fn86
Trotsky, Leon, 39, 43, 295fn198, 299fn47, 300fn58, 328fn138, 329fn144, 346fn148; on Russian history and development 39, 314fn45; and uneven and combined development, 7, 39, 44–6, 48–9, 51–7, 176, 285fn30, 298fn20, 300–1fn64, 301fn66
Tuscany, 19, 111

U

Underwood, David, 191
unequal exchange, 16
uneven and combined development (*see also* combined development, uneven development), 43–64; and agents/agency, 49, 50–2, 53, 66, 88; and Eurocentrism, 39–40, 42, 52, 54–7, 63, 93–4, 276, 278, 301fn66; and feudal mode of production, 47, 49, 56, 62,104–6, 186, 204–5, 256, 259, 298fn22, 359fn172; and forces of production, 52–3, 158, 169, 277; and general abstractions, 51, 57, 58–61, 62, 368fn6; and intersocietal relations/'the international', 19, 22, 36, 42, 44, 62, 63, 66, 78, 87, 93–4, 114, 119, 140, 174–6, 179–80, 209, 228, 235, 242–3, 246, 250, 251, 253–4, 261, 276–7, 285fn30, 293fn127, 297fn5, 298fn22, 299fn33, 300–1fn64; as law, 303fn108, 314fn145; and Marxist theory, 31, 58, 61–3; as methodology, 58, 61, 63, 276; and mode of production-centred approach, 49, 57–8, 61–3, 261, 303fn109; and nomadic mode of production, 47, 49, 62, 66, 67–71, 72; and ontology, 47, 58, 61, 63, 276; and permanent revolution, 53–4, 300–1fn64; and political strategy, 53–4, 276, 279–82, 300–1fn64, 368fn6; and revolutions, 53–4, 174–214, 339fn32; and slavery, 152–62; spatiotemporal vectors, 61, 63, 66, 71, 85, 119, 121, 141, 146, 244, 277; and stagism, 39, 49, 54, 66, 87–88; as transmodal, 62, 303fn110; and tributary mode of production, 47, 49, 56, 62, 96–106, 359fn172; and 'triple relationship', 47
uneven development (*see also* uneven and combined development), 34, 93, 128, 205, 258, 259; and class relations, 45, 47, 50–1, 56; and culture, 45, 47; defined, 44–7; and 'double relationship', 46–7; and nature and geography, 11, 46–7; and space/spatial relations, 11, 45, 47, 98, 179, 213, 298fn20; and states system and territorialisation, 11, 27, 45, 298fn20
United Provinces *see* Dutch Republic, Low Countries
United States, 53, 128, 210, 262, 272, 273, 300fn58
universalism, 33, 34–5, 123–6, 141, 321fn6, 335fn53
unwaged labour, (*see also* reproductive sphere, slavery), 37, 39, 221, 222, 365fn33
Urbino, 111
use-value, 59, 60

V

Valladolid Controversy (1550–51), 322fn23
Venezuela, 223
Venice, 75, 76, 92, 106, 108, 109, 111, 112, 115, 116, 184–5, 218–19, 221, 223, 232, 256, 306fn78; Venetian Arsenal, 29, 292fn115
Vink, Markus, 240
violence (*see also* means of violence, war-making), 12, 29, 32, 35, 65, 80, 123, 132, 133, 141, 158, 161, 168, 207, 217, 219, 221, 237, 239, 252, 254, 256, 257, 260, 264, 271, 276, 278–9, 280, 294fn150, 325–6fn101, 352fn56
Vitoria, Francisco de, 124–5, 135–6, 321fn11, 321fn13, 321fn15, 323fn53
VOC *see* Dutch East India Company
Von Braunmühl, Claudia, 291–2fn105

W

wage-labour, 8, 9, 15, 16, 19, 21–2, 23, 24, 29–30, 81, 84, 118–19, 149, 183, 194, 195–6, 200–1, 202, 211, 215–18, 220, 225–7, 289fn71, 351fn19, 352–3fn19, 368fn11; and unfree labour, 9, 30, 121, 158, 160, 163, 169, 218, 220, 221–2, 227, 243, 277, 278, 281–2, 333fn245, 355fn74, 368fn10
Wakefield, E. G., 331fn193
Wallerstein, Immanuel (*see also* World-System Theory), 7, 13, 14–22, 30, 189, 272, 324–5fn84, 340fn41, 343fn95, 343fn96, 346fn156, 355fn74; and class struggle, 17–18, 21–2; and core–periphery, 14, 15, 16–17, 18, 20, 21; definition of capitalism, 15–16; and Eurocentrism, 14, 16–19, 287fn22; and origins of capitalism, 14–15, 17, 18, 21–2, 216, 288fn38; on unequal exchange, 14, 16; and wage-labour, 15, 16, 21, 355fn74; on world division of labour, 15, 16, 18, 355fn74; on world empires, 15, 19
Walt, Stephen, 338fn6
Waltz, Kenneth, 175, 253
War of the Austrian Succession (1740–48), 197–8
War of the Roses (1455–87), 90
war-making, 99, 104, 157, 187, 218; and development of capitalism, 27–9, 135, 223; and markets, 28; Marx on, 29; and merchants,105, 256–7, 359fn172
Washbrook, David, 34, 167, 262–3, 268
Wealth of Nations, The (1776), 16
Weber, Max, 147, 168, 245
Wess, Robert, 59
West Africa *see* Africa